LAST THEATRES

To Max
    to remind him of the good old
    days when he sat with Harley-Lady,
    and Labby and Charlie Dilke
    in the stalls of the dear little
    Strand. Those were the days, indeed!

LAST THEATRES

1904–1910

MAX BEERBOHM

WITH AN INTRODUCTION BY
RUPERT HART-DAVIS

RUPERT HART-DAVIS
London
1970

© Eva Reichmann 1970

First published 1970
Rupert Hart-Davis Ltd
3 Upper James Street
Golden Square London W1

Printed in Great Britain by
Western Printing Services Ltd
Bristol

SBN 0246 63998 9

CONTENTS

6

CONTENTS

8

INTRODUCTION

This volume completes the republication of Max Beerbohm's dramatic criticism, which was begun in *Around Theatres* (1924) and continued in *More Theatres* (1969). Everything here appeared in the *Saturday Review*, on the date given at the end of each article. Once again I have eschewed the footnotes that Max would certainly have disliked. I have included the article on Christabel Pankhurst (p. 392), since it is clearly worth reviving, and, although not dramatic criticism, has theatrical connotations.

By 1904, when this volume starts, Max was fully accustomed to his weekly stint, but he found it increasingly irksome, and when in 1910 he married and went to live in Italy, he resigned his post with immense relief and seldom went to a theatre again.

His long love-hate relationship with Bernard Shaw was exemplified at a dinner given by the Stage Society on 29 April 1904. Shaw proposed the health of the critics and Max (as reported in the *Stage Society News* of 11 May) replied:

My Lord, Ladies and Gentlemen, Mr Shaw has called me his fellow-critic. He says that he, too, is a gentleman of the Press. When he said this I was reminded of the time when I was a small boy at a private school. On the first day of every term the headmaster used to end a little speech by saying 'And remember, my boys, I am one of you.' That was a nice genial thing to say; but the fact remained that he was not one of us. And likewise the fact remains that Mr Shaw is not one of us critics. He has passed from criticism to creative work; and the difference between him and us critics is as great as the difference between master and boys. We critics are the masters and Mr Shaw is a pupil; and I fancy Mr Shaw regards us as every right-minded schoolboy regards his teachers—he simply can't abide us; and most especially he cannot abide me; for I am the one critic of all who has most consistently and most warmly praised him. He is very sensitive about praise. He doesn't mind being attacked at all. You can go up behind him and deal him a severe blow on the skull with a bludgeon, and he goes on quite happily. But if you pat him ever so lightly on the back, then there is the devil to pay. He rounds on you in a storm of agony and indignation; for it appears that one always praises him for just the wrong reasons. Somehow one praises him for qualities he does not possess. I have an awful faculty when I write to get straight on to those very qualities, and my reward comes always by the next post in the form of a long, very brilliant, and quite unanswerable protest from Mr Shaw; so I am glad to reply to him tonight and not he to me. Even so I can only answer for myself; I cannot answer for my colleagues. I have really nothing to say. I am not at all a representative critic. I could not, for instance, stand up here and represent Mr Courtney whom you have heard tonight. I know Mr Courtney in private life, and I hope he does not dislike me. I like him immensely; but I know perfectly well that he utterly repudiates me as a fellow-critic. It is my misfortune to find myself almost always at variance with almost everyone, and it is Mr Courtney's constant pride and distinction to command the acquiescence of nearly everyone. So I cannot answer for Mr Courtney, and I cannot answer for my fellow-critics. I can only vouch for one thing, that they feel flattered and pleased at your drinking their health even at the eleventh hour, and I daresay they are as grateful as I am to the Stage Society for all it has done and is doing to improve the breed of plays.

In 1932 Harley Granville Barker contributed to a symposium called *The Eighteen-Sixties*, edited by John Drinkwater, an essay entitled 'Exit Planché—Enter Gilbert.' He had some copies off-printed and bound in plain paper wrappers; one of them he sent to Max. Barker's inscription and Max's illustration of it form the frontispiece to this volume.

Once again I owe a great debt to Mrs Eva Reichmann, and to my dear dead friends Allan Wade and Sally Kavanagh, who between them transcribed all these articles from the *Saturday Review*.

May 1970   RUPERT HART-DAVIS

LAST THEATRES

A PLAY, AND TWO ENTERTAINMENTS

Nearly always, when a man writes his first play, the mischief is that he does not try to be himself. His technique may be already so sound that he could do the trick quite well. But he does not, in his diffidence, attempt it. Sometimes, of course, our neophyte has no self to be. But now and again our neophyte is one who, in some other art-form, has established his claim to a quite definite and delightful self; and we, looking vainly for it here, rightly grumble. The theatre seems to have the same terrorising power over neophytes as has the House of Commons. A man of European reputation for something or other, deigning to honour St Stephen by his advent, tries to efface himself at the outset. He takes the oath and his seat, and everything else he basely surrenders. His maiden speech will be a faint effort to acquire that dreariest and nullest thing which is called 'the House of Commons manner.' In recent years there has been but one exception. Mr Keir Hardie tried to enter Palace Yard in an open van, bright with bunting and tuneful with trombones. He wanted to be himself. He was right. The means he chose were not the right means; for he has in him (as you will acknowledge, if you have listened to his speeches) a strain of poetry and dreaminess. The van suggested mere blatancy, and so he began by being misunderstood. But if his means had been quite appropriate, he would have been not less keenly resented. The House of Commons demands uniform mediocrity of its neophytes, hating the notion that anything remarkable can be developed elsewhere. Thus its neophytes may plead an excuse for their shrinking behaviour. That excuse, however, cannot be pleaded by the neophytes of the theatre. Theatrical audiences will always welcome the kind of work that is familiar to them, if it be well done. But they have no sacred prejudice against new work. A great portion of them is always agog for new work—for the revelation of a new personality in drama.

Especially were we agog the other night at the Avenue Theatre, for the production of *All Fletcher's Fault*. This was a first play, written by a man of definite and delightful personality. For a long time we have known Mr Mostyn Pigott's verses, known him as an always witty and caustic observer of life, as one with a power for hitting (not the less surely because rollickingly) the right nail on the

13

head. Presumably his play would be in prose. That was a pity. A humorist with a mastery of versification, like Mr Pigott, depends so much on actual metre and rhyme. Translate (for example) a Gilbertian opera into prose, and you will find that, though plenty of fun remains, plenty of fun has vanished. So much consists in the technical twists and flourishes. One wished, therefore, that Mr Pigott had dared tradition by writing a modern comedy in rhyme— why not? In prose, however, he might still be delightfully himself. That keen and fearless eye of his, surveying life and character, with a constant twinkle and an occasional flash . . . surely a new note in comedy was to be struck for us. Alas, we must wait for Mr Pigott's next play. This one, I fancy, will be commercially a success, and will encourage Mr Pigott to write another very soon. The sooner the better; for he will, I am sure, be more daring at a second venture. He will not be indebted to Charles Reade for the foundation of his story, and he will clutch by the way at nothing from *A Message from Mars*. That play, even for a sophisticated audience, was well enough; for Mr Ganthony was so evidently an unsophisticated sentimentalist who really and truly believed in it all; and the sincerity was touching, ingratiating. But we know that Mr Pigott is not such a simple soul as to believe in the similar sentiment of *All Fletcher's Fault*. He, the sane, the acute mocker! And a man with a tear in his eye and a laugh in his sleeve ministers not at all to our enjoyment: we can neither weep with him nor join in the laugh. However, 'we,' sophisticated persons who go to first nights, are not a typical audience. I fancy that from those very unsophisticated others, who form the bulk of the play-going public, the sentiment of Mr Pigott's play will wring any number of salt tears. The Earl of Liss, doing good by stealth in Covent Garden Market, and falsely suspected by Lady Lilian Lexborough, whom he loves, of doing harm, when she finds him in the centre of a dancing ring of old comrades who have just emerged from the Covent Garden ball, and by her reproached harshly and left alone to order a cup of coffee at the coffee-stall and to turn up the collar of his jacket in the approved manner of men stricken on the stage by Fate, is a figure nightly much wept-over at the Avenue, I am sure, and destined to be much wept-over there for many nights to come. I look into the far future, spreading my vision over the provinces and the colonies, and there I see clearly several Lord Lisses, still being much wept-over. I see, too, Mr Mostyn Pigott blushing over the receipts, with the blush of one who, having duly 'found' and revealed himself in the art of play-writing, would rather not be reminded of his past.

It is a pity that Mr Pigott, instead of writing his play round Lord Liss, did not write it round Mr Harold Harringay, a really fresh and delightful invention—a hedonist-dosser, who contrives to win an unbroken 'series of exquisite moments' from the sordid conditions which life has imposed on him. He, having picked up a ticket for the Covent Garden ball, passes through unchallenged by the attendants, and in the course of the evening wins a prize for his wonderfully realistic costume. This prize, consisting of a pair of silver fish-carvers, is ever after his one crumpled rose-leaf. He cannot pawn it, for no pawnbroker will believe that he has not stolen it. Lord Liss, on whom he presses it as a gift, will not hear of accepting it. The whole episode, more elaborately treated, might well have been made the basis of the play. Harringay is certainly Mr Pigott's trump-card. And his impersonator, Mr C. W. Somerset, made the hit of the evening, playing with an admirably fruity and fantastic humour. Mrs Maesmore Morris, as a flower-girl, and Miss Beryl Faber, as the aforesaid Lady Lilian Lexborough, were both too nervous, on the first night, to do themselves justice. Mr James Erskine, as Lord Liss, has never played better. But his method is still that of private life rather than that of the stage. I am all for realism in acting; and perhaps you will say that as Mr Erskine is an Earl in private life, I ought to be perfectly satisfied by him as an Earl on the stage. But the real thing does not necessarily mean realism. Take the case of horses. When real horses come on the stage, they do not seem at all like real horses elsewhere. They have the air of being huge extinct monsters, and their hoofs sound queerly on the wooden boards. There is a similar danger in real Earls. However, Mr Erskine's was a very pleasant performance, and, technically, a marked advance on anything he had done before.

Children would have been as good an analogy as horses. On the stage they create for us no illusion of childhood—none, at least, when they are there to do more than merely romp around in a chorus. There you have my objection to two Christmas entertainments that I have seen—*Alice through the Looking Glass*, at the New Theatre, and Mr Philip Carr's *Snowdrop and the Seven Little*

Men, at the Court Theatre. In both an important part is played by
a little girl, aged seven or so—in the one, Alice herself; in the other,
the Fairy Queen. Poor little things, so over-weighted and self-conscious, gasping and piping, and making so obediently the little
automatic gestures that have been drilled into them! Pretty little
dears, doubtless, both of them, and apparently sources of great
pleasure to the adult audience. Legitimate pleasure? Hardly, I
think. It is the pleasure of pity—the pleasure of being sorry for
creatures set to perform a task that they cannot accomplish, and
cannot even essay painlessly. It is the same pleasure that is derived
from the sight of performing dogs. How any real lover of dogs or of
children can but be repelled by such exhibitions is a problem which
I don't pretend to solve. Quite apart from the moral aspect, it is
aesthetically absurd that a leading part should be taken by a child.
The play loses all its brightness and 'go,' through the child's invariable incompetence. There is no lack of young actresses who can,
at a pinch, impersonate children. They should be requisitioned.
Snowdrop has over *Alice* the advantage that the title-part is of an
adult, played by an adult. It has another advantage: its characters
are not, as are Lewis Carroll's by Tenniel's illustrations, fixed for
us into an ideal convention, from which any departure shocks us.
Moreover, the adaptation of *Alice*, though it is the peg for a cheerful
entertainment, is artistically a crude piece of work; whereas Mr
Philip Carr's *Snowdrop* is prettily and ingeniously wrought from
the original Grimm.

[*2 January 1904*]

'JOSEPH ENTANGLED'

Other of Mr Jones's comedies have been more perfect in form, I
think; but none has been more amusing, more alive. In the art of
writing realistic comedy of manners, he is far pre-eminent over our
other playwrights. Not one of them can match him in that lightness
of solidity which is the essential of the art. Not one of them can so
quicken and vitalise a story. Vitality—that is Mr Jones's chief
point of excellence. Up goes the curtain, and with it our spirits, for
not a moment is lost: we are already in the thick of the interest.

16

Mr Jones never makes us conscious of his technique, and for that reason his technique is better than Mr Pinero's. To Mr Pinero technique seems almost to be an end in itself. He lingers proudly over its perfection. We, too, become absorbed in it. How ingeniously this or that point is prepared, how ingeniously that or this difficulty smoothed over, in how exact co-operation all the wheels go round! You know those faceless clocks that were popular in early Victorian days. Mr Pinero's plays are rather like them. After all, the best reason for a clock is not that it should fascinate us by its labyrinth of wheels and screws and what not, but that it should tell us the time—the right time, never mind how. We get the right time from Mr Jones—the right time, I mean, for the stage, where speed is so essential. Mr Pinero always 'loses' a little. He gives us more the sense of art than of life. Another advantage that Mr Jones has over his rival is in the manner of his dialogue. His characters really talk. They do not merely repeat rigmaroles that would look ugly enough in print and that destroy in an ugly manner all verisimilitude in a realistic play. In Mr Jones's dialogue there is never a line that has not the true oral ring. To sound that note consistently should be the aim of every realistic playwright. Mr Jones succeeds in doing it, and his plays have, therefore, a very real literary quality. They are not literary in that finest sense which I was explaining the other day. Mr Jones does not perform that hard but possible trick of making his characters talk charmingly despite the brevity and brokenness of their speech. Of living playwrights Mrs Craigie alone possesses that inestimable secret. But Mr Jones's characters do express themselves in a live and natural way. And that is, far and away, the most important point in the 'style' of playwriting.

In *Joseph Entangled* Mr Jones adheres to his usual milieu—the milieu of the aristocracy. And I am quite ready to admit for the free play of purely comedic emotion this is the best, the rightest milieu. Where the standard of sexual morality is less strict, and the passion of love is more diffused and, accordingly, less intense, there, surely, is the happiest hunting-ground for the writer of comedies, so long as drama continues to confine itself to affairs of the heart. Comedy has nothing to do with matters of life and death; and rightly, therefore, the middle class is shunned by it. Not only in milieu, but also in theme, *Joseph Entangled* resembles that which is from a strictly technical standpoint the most perfect of Mr Jones's plays, *The Liars*. The greater part of it is spent in the frantic efforts of certain ladies and gentlemen to explain away certain compromising circumstances. Only, here the situation is intrinsically funnier than it was in the previous play. The heroine of *The Liars* was telling lies, which nobody believed. The heroine of *Joseph Entangled* is telling the truth, the whole truth, and nothing but the truth, which everybody believes to be a lie, and which even to herself sounds exactly like a lie—and not a clever lie, at that. The thing comes about in a complicated way; but there is nothing forced or unlikely in the imbroglio. Lady Verona Mayne hurries up to London, one evening in August, to dissuade a younger sister from eloping. She has been staying with her people, in Oxford. Her husband is away in Scotland. Their house is occupied only by a butler and a housekeeper. The butler has gone out. The housekeeper sees her mistress to bed, and herself goes to bed. The butler comes home. Standing at the open window in his shirt-sleeves (one of the play's charms for us is in its grateful illusion of summer), he is hailed from someone from the street. This is Sir Joseph Lacy, an old friend of the Maynes. He is passing through London; but, having lost his luggage, cannot very well go to an hotel. The butler, who was at one time in the Lacy household, naturally assents to his suggestion that Mr Mayne would be delighted to let him have a bed for the night. Next morning, Sir Joseph and Lady Verona meet at breakfast, each amazed at sight of the other. Sir Joseph was in love with Lady Verona, and she with him, before her marriage. She, whenever she wishes to make her husband angry, has the habit of implying that the old sentiment survives in her. In Sir Joseph it actually does survive, more or less—less than more, for he is specifically a Lothario. Across the breakfast-table he makes love to Lady Verona in a light and tentative fashion; but he is not encouraged. As she says, the thing to be considered is how to hush up the *contretemps*. Neither of them must say anything about it; the butler and the housekeeper shall be bound over to silence, and —but the simple plan is frustrated by the entry of two friends, who have come to see Mr Mayne about some matter of business, thinking that he would already have arrived from Scotland. The ensuing scene is delightful—the embarrassment of the friends, who, quite incredulous, protest that 'nothing in the world could be more natural' than the situation as explained with such anxious minuteness by Sir Joseph and by Lady Verona. They agree, however, that perhaps it would be better to say nothing to Mr Mayne. A few weeks pass by. The story leaks inevitably out, and is heard by Mr Mayne. He is desperately anxious to believe that there is nothing in it; but he is not a man to be trifled with. His friends gather round him, trying to soothe him; but his cross-examinations of them, and of his butler, and of his housekeeper, gradually drive him to the determination that he must and will have a divorce. Sir Joseph and Lady Verona both asseverate their innocence: but what *they* say is, of course, 'not evidence.' The infuriated husband dashes out of the room, on the way to his solicitors. The end of the play is approaching. How on earth is the comedic ending to be compassed? There is apparently but one possible way. Will Lady Verona's sister consent to reveal her own escapade? Re-enter Mr Mayne, quite calm, but rather ashamed. He had stopped and listened outside the door. The conversation between his wife and his friend has made it clear that there had been no harm. He apologises profusely to all concerned. This seems to me a very ingenious and a very right ending. Ingenious, because it is so completely a surprise. Right, because it is so completely natural. Some of the critics have been solemnly wondering that so original a playwright as Mr Jones should stoop to the old stage-trick of 'overhearing.' No objection could be more muddle-headed. By no means, at this time of day, let us have a peripety caused by the casual overhearing of something in the nick of time. But, in this case, the overhearing is a deliberate action, and a perfectly natural action. Desperately anxious to get at a truth which could not be got at in conversation, but which might be got at through a keyhole, Mr Mayne would have been a fool indeed if he had not tried that obvious keyhole.

From the purely technical point of view, it would be well if Mr Mayne had been (generally speaking) more of a fool than Mr Jones made him, or more of a brute. As he stands, he is a very decent type of man, whom we all like and respect; and thus the prolonged baffling that he suffers comes very near to evoking a sense of tragedy. We feel for him, in his jealous frenzy, as for a sort of Othello. Nor is he the only figure to queer the comedic pitch. Sir Joseph, whom during the first act we supposed to be wholly Lotharioesque, turns out to have cherished through the years a very real passion for Lady Verona. He really does want to marry her, and is very much disappointed by the abandonment of the divorce. He confesses himself 'hard hit,' and departs, jarred by the many mutual congratulations of the rest. For comedic rightness, he should have heaved a sigh of relief. The inconsistency in his character mars also the consistency of the character of the play. Lady Verona is drawn quite perfectly—a thoroughly consistent and thoroughly comedic person. And there is a round dozen of subordinate characters, not less delightful on a small scale. One of Mr Jones's strongest points is in his power to distinguish brightly and sharply any number of characters, however little they may have to say or do.

I have not space, this week, for *The Duke of Killicrankie* at the Criterion, and *The Question* at the Court. The latter play is preceded by *The Gipsy*, a congestion of sentimental melodrama which typifies the kind of thing that in England is thought worthy to 'raise the curtain.' It is somewhat redeemed by one of the performers—Miss Ethel Van Praagh, who, as the stage-gipsy, infuses a real, un-stagey power of imagination and pathos. I wonder how soon the right principle for a short play will be mastered by our playwrights. The right principle for a short story has for many years been no secret. Why are these things from France filtered so much slowlier for us through drama than through literature?

[23 January 1904]

THOMAS HARDY AS PANORAMATIST

Eight years ago *Jude the Obscure* was published. Since then Mr Hardy has given us two or three volumes of poetry, and now a volume of drama [*The Dynasts: Part First*], but no other novel. One assumes that he has ceased as a novelist. Why has he ceased? The reason is generally said to be that he was disheartened by the many hostile criticisms of *Jude the Obscure*. To accept that explanation were to insult him. A puny engine of art may be derailed by such puny obstacles as the public can set in its way. So strong an engine as Mr Hardy rushes straight on, despite them, never so little jarred by them, and stops not save for lack of inward steam. Mr Hardy writes no more novels because he has no more novels to write.

A fascinating essay could be written on the autumnal works of great writers. Sooner or later, there comes for the great writer a time when he feels that his best work is done—that the fire in him has sunk to a glow. And then, instinctively, he shrinks from the form in which he cast the works of his youth and of his prime, and from the themes he then loved best. But he cannot be idle—the fire still glows. Other forms, other themes, occur to him and are grasped by him. In England, during recent years, great writers in their autumn have had a rather curious tendency: they have tended to write either about Napoleon or about Mrs Meynell. The late Mr Coventry Patmore wrote about Mrs Meynell. Mr Meredith has written both about Mrs Meynell and about Napoleon. Mr Hardy now readjusts the balance, confining himself to Napoleon. So far, his procedure is quite normal: a new theme, through a new form. But I mislead you when I speak of Mr Hardy as 'confining himself to Napoleon.' 'Excluding Mrs Meynell' would be more accurate. He is so very comprehensive. Pitt, Sheridan, Nelson, George III, and, throughout Europe, everyone who played a notable part during the First Empire—here they all are, in company with various spirits, shades and choruses, marshalled into the scope of six acts and thirty-five scenes. Nor has Mr Hardy done with them yet. This book is but a third of his scheme. The trilogy will comprise nineteen acts and one hundred and thirty scenes. Prodigious, is it not? And it marks its schemer as (in the strictest sense of the word) a prodigy. Normally, the great writer, forsaking the form of his greatness, gravitates to littler forms. The theme may be great or little, but he treats it within a little compass. Mr Hardy's vitality would seem to have diminished only for his own special form. At any rate, it is such that he believes it sufficient for an attack on the illimitable and the impossible.

Impossible his task certainly is. To do perfectly what he essays would need a syndicate of much greater poets than ever were born into the world, working in an age of miracles. To show us the whole world, as seen, in a time of stress, by the world that is unseen by us! Whoever so essays must be judged according to the

degree by which his work falls infinitely short of perfection. Mr
Hardy need not fear that test. *The Dynasts* is a noble achievement,
impressive, memorable.

To say that it were easy to ridicule such a work is but a tribute
to the sublimity of Mr Hardy's intent, and to the newness and
strangeness of his means. It is easy to smile at sight of all these
great historic figures reduced to the size of marionettes. I confess
that I, reading here the scene of the death of Nelson, was irresistibly reminded of the same scene as erst beheld by me, at Brighton,
through the eyelet of a peep-show, whose proprietor strove to
make it more realistic for me by saying in a confidential tone
"Ardy, 'Ardy, I am wounded, 'Ardy.—Not mortially, I 'ope, my
lord?—Mortially, I fear, 'Ardy.' The dialogue here is of a different
and much worthier kind; yet the figures seem hardly less tiny and
unreal. How could they be life-sized and alive, wedged into so
small a compass between so remote and diverse scenes? Throughout
this play the only characters who stand to human height, drawing
the breath of life, are the Wessex peasants. 'When,' says Mr Hardy
in his preface, '*The Trumpet Major* was printed, more than twenty
years ago, I found myself in the tantalising position of having
touched the fringe of a vast international tragedy without being
able, through limits of plan, knowledge, and opportunity, to
enter further into its events; a restriction that prevailed for many
years.' Well, that restriction has vanished. But remains the
difference between a writer's power to project the particular thing
which he has known lovingly in youth and his power to project
the general thing which he has studied in maturity. For my own
part, I wish these Wessex peasants had been kept out of *The
Dynasts*. They mar the unity of an effect which is, in the circumstances, partially correct. The general effect of littleness does,
without doubt, help the illusion which Mr Hardy seeks to create.
That miraculous syndicate of which I dreamed anon would have
kept the figures as tiny as here they seem—as tiny, but all alive,
like real men and women beheld from a great distance.

Pushing ingenuity a step further, one might even defend the
likeness of these figures to automata. For Mr Hardy's aim is to show
them, not merely as they appear to certain supernal, elemental
spirits, but also as blindly obedient to an Immanent Will, which

'works unconsciously, as heretofore,
Eternal artistries in Circumstance,
Whose patterns, wrought by rapt aesthetic rote
Seem in themselves Its single listless aim,
And not their consequence.'

From the Overworld the Spirit of the Years watches the eternal
weaving of this pattern. The Spirit Ironic watches too, smiling.
The Spirit Sinister, too, watches laughing. There is a Spirit of the
Pities; but she is young, as Mr Hardy insists, and quite helpless.
Beneath them 'Europe is disclosed as a prone and emaciated
figure, and the branching mountain-chains like ribs, the peninsu-
lar plateau of Spain forming a head. . . . The point of view
then sinks downwards through space, and draws near to the
surface of the perturbed countries, where the peoples, distressed by
events which they did not cause, are seen writhing, crawling,
heaving, and vibrating in their various cities and nationalities. . . .
A new and penetrating light descends, enduing men and things
with a seeming transparency, and exhibiting as one organism
the anatomy of life and movement in all humanity.' The Spirits
draw nearer still to earth. They flit over the English ground, near
the open Channel. A stage-coach passes. 'See, now,' says one of
the passengers to another, 'how the Channel and coast open out like
a chart. . . . One can see half across to France up here.' The irony
of this contrast between their vision and the vision just vouchsafed
to us strikes the keynote of the whole drama. How ridiculous that
historic debate in the House of Commons! Sheridan thundering at
Pitt, and Pitt at Sheridan, and above them in the gallery, in the
guise of human Strangers, those abstract Spirits, sitting till they
are 'spied' by an officious Member! Anon these Spirits are in the
cathedral of Milan. Napoleon, in all his trappings, places the
crown of Lombardy upon his brow. Before him the Cardinal
Archbishop swings a censer. The organ peals an anthem. 'What,'
asks the Spirit of the Pities, 'is the creed that these rich rites
disclose?' And the Spirit of the Years answers

'A local thing called Christianity,
Which the wild dramas of this wheeling sphere
Include, with divers other such, in dim,
Pathetical, and brief parentheses.'

The Imperial procession passes out to the palace. 'The exterior of the Cathedral is seen, and the point of view recedes, the whole fabric smalling into distance and becoming like a rare, delicately carved ornament. The city itself sinks to miniature, the Alps show afar as a white corrugation . . . clouds cover the panorama,' and our next sight is of the dockyard at Gibraltar. Thus we range hither and thither, with the Spirits, listening to their reflections on the infinite littleness and helplessness and unmeaning of all things here below. We see, at last, the toy field of Austerlitz, and the toy death-bed of Pitt. Thereat the book closes, looking strangely like a duodecimo.

The book closes, and (so surely has it cast its spell on us) seems a quite fugitive and negligible little piece of work. We wonder why Mr Hardy wrote it; or rather, one regrets that the Immanent Will put him to the trouble of writing it. 'Wot's the good of any-think? Wy, nothink' was the refrain of a popular coster-song some years ago, and Mr Hardy has set it ringing in our ears again. But presently the mood passes. And, even as in the stage-directions of *The Dynasts* we see specks becoming mountain-tops, so do we begin to realise that we have been reading a really great book. An imperfect book, as I have said—inevitably imperfect. And less perfect than it might quite easily have been. That Mr Hardy is a poet, in the large sense of the word, nobody will dare deny. But his poetry expresses itself much more surely and finely through the medium of prose than through the medium of rhyme and metre. I wish he had done *The Dynasts* in prose, of which he has a mastery, rather than in a form wherein he has to wrestle—sometimes quite successfully—for his effects. No one, again, will deny that Mr Hardy is, in the large sense of the word, a dramatist. But his drama expresses itself better through narration than through dialogue and stage-directions. He writes here not for the stage; and, except an eye to the stage, there is no reason or excuse for using a form which must always (be our dramatic imagination never so vivid) hamper and harass us in the study. But, when every reservation has been made, *The Dynasts* is still a great book. It is absolutely new in that it is the first modern work of dramatic fiction in which free-will is denied to the characters. Free-will is supposed to be a thing necessary to human interest. If it were so indeed, we should get no excitement from Homer. Not that Mr Hardy's negation resembles Homer's. Achilles and the rest were life-sized puppets, whose strings were being pulled, at near hand, by gods scarcely larger than they. Mr Hardy's puppets are infinitesimal—mere 'electrons,' shifted hither and thither, for no reason, by some impalpable agency. Yet they are exciting. Free-will is not necessary to human interest. Belief in it is, however, necessary to human life. Cries Mr Hardy's Spirit of the Pities

> 'This tale of Will
> And Life's impulsion by Incognizance
> I cannot take.'

Nor can I. But I can take and treasure, with all gratitude, the book in which that tale is told so finely.

Having quite shaken off that awful sense of proportion which *The Dynasts* forced on me as I read it, I can turn, with proper enthusiasm, to the events of the moment. *Old Heidelberg* is back at the St James's. The cast is as when first I saw it, except that Kathie is now played, very prettily, by Miss Lilian Braithwaite. From February 10th to 16th the O.U.D.S. will perform *As You Like It*.

[*30 January 1904*]

'WE, THE UNDERSIGNED, ...'

Man is a name-signing animal. Lock him into a room, with nothing but paper and pencil, and he will while away his confinement, quite agreeably, by writing and re-writing his autograph. Leave him there with nothing but a diamond, and on your return you will find the window scored faintly over with the captive's name in various sizes and at various angles. Take away the diamond, and anon with his forefinger-nail will he be graving upon wall or door the artless expression of his egoism. The persons who scatter (with or without stamped envelopes) requests for autographs have often been decried as a nuisance; but the true cause of the bitterness against them is that they are not a public nuisance: they don't write to everybody. Such terms as 'autograph-fiend' are used only by the writer whose autograph has never yet been solicited. I implore the collectors to cast wider their nets. It is awful to think how many men and women whose names are before the public, but do not excite enthusiasm or curiosity, are watching hourly their letter-boxes, and tearing open their letters in the wild faith that the request has come at last. On their writing-tables are stacked pathetically in readiness their graceful compliances: *Dear Sir, I have much pleasure in acceding to your request, and in signing myself, with kind regards, yours truly So-and-So;* and *Dear Madam, My only reason for hesitating to give you that which you so kindly demand is that scarcity is the one thing which could render valuable the signature of yours truly So-and-So;* and many other missives not less neatly to the same effect. Shall the space left in each, for the insertion of the date, be filled up never? Shall that ink fade, and that cream-laid superfine note-paper become yellow—to be splashed, at last, by the tears of groping executors? . . . Ah, let the nets be cast much wider.

It is a strange thing, this passion of men and women for signing their names. Political economists tell us that there is a great deal of 'locked-up capital' in our midst. I do not believe it. There may be a few antique misers, brooding by night in their bedrooms over piles of gold. But, generally speaking, 'locked-up capital' disappeared when cheques were invented. When you sign a cheque, you never grudge the amount, however loth by nature you be to 'part' (even with the smallest sum) in specie. You make the cheque out for such-and-such an amount, but your loss is not real to you. Your imagination is not strong enough to solidify and visualise a thing so remote, so vaguely symbolic, as those cyphers. The one thing that you realise in the cheque is your own signature —your own strongly flowing and flourishing, or delicate and delightful, autograph. I had a friend, a man of extravagant habit and slender means, and quite unblest with that persuasive magnetism which is the secret of the successful adventurer. I once asked him how he contrived to keep his head always above water. He replied that anyone was always willing to back a bill for him. A fact, but not an explanation; *why* was everyone so accommodating? My friend smiled. He said it was quite true that, if he asked a man to promise to back a bill at some future date, or even to accompany him to the place where the bill was lying unbacked, he met with a polite or curt refusal. But this was a mode which he had abandoned long ago. Simultaneously with his appeal, he always produced from his pocket the bill in question and a stylographic pen; and then, somehow inevitably, the trick was done.

Many other startling phenomena can be understood in the light of this human weakness. One of the rights of the free-born Briton is to petition the High Court of Parliament. It is one of the rights he most dearly cherishes. Yet he knows that the High Court of Parliament takes not the slightest notice of the vast and innumerable petitions that are so assiduously thrust on it. True, he does not, for the most part, want any notice to be taken. His signature is no mere means to an end. He will sign, for signing's sake, anything that comes his way. I wager that, if I had the time and the folly, I could get any literate resident in any given district to sign a petition for, and a petition against, any given proposal. And if I had these two petitions printed and published broadcast together, the petition-habit would, I wager, go on flourishing as bravely as ever, rooted, as it is, in the needs of our mystic souls. My experiment's sole result would be that the signatories (they always call themselves the signatories) would preen themselves on seeing their names in print.

In print! The fascination of it! And, as we know, it is a lure not merely for the poor and lowly and simple folk. The rich, the fashionable, and the illustriously intellectual—they, too, dearly love it: custom cannot stale it for them. And they, too, of course, being but human, share the primary lust for writing signatures even without a view to publication. Thus I am not so much cheered as I should like to be by the current number of the *Fortnightly Review*, which reveals in Roman capitals the names of seventy-two ladies and gentlemen purporting to think that 'something must be done' for our drama. Some of these ladies and gentlemen are very rich, some are very fashionable, and some are, in very various degrees, intellectually illustrious. But the fact that their names are thus printed for him who runs to read (with a reverent pause in his wild career) does not suggest to me that they are keen for anything to be done—still less, that they are keen to do anything themselves, or even to bestow the favour of their esteemed patronage on anyone who is trying to do anything. True, there is Mr Frederick Harrison, amplifying his signature with the news that he once whispered in the ear of 'a well-known

27

philanthropist' the temptation to endow a theatre. But this philanthropist appears to have been a deaf one; and Mr Harrison is left
lamenting that the people who go to the pit of a theatre think it
necessary to wear evening-dress. This innovation is, I confess,
since my time. I have not been to a theatre in the past fortnight.
I wonder how often Mr Harrison goes? I should not blame him if
I heard that he went very seldom. The theatre is not, generally
speaking, a fit place for clever men. But one may make reservations.
The Stage Society, for example, has produced several plays of an
intellectual kind. Does Mr Harrison subscribe to the Stage Society,
I wonder? And of those other clever signatories, how many, I
wonder, subscribe, or have any intention of subscribing, to the
Stage Society? And yet that 'something' which, according to
them, 'must be done' could be done better and more easily by
encouraging such an institution than by any other means. A State
Theatre or two would be very nice? The State won't give us them.
Municipal Theatres would be very nice? The Aldermen sit tight.
A millionaire-endowed Theatre would be very nice? The millionaire smiles vacantly. But there is no reason why a theatre should
not be endowed for the Stage Society, or for some new equivalent,
and thus an intellectual drama be fostered, by subscriptions from
the eager rich and the eager fashionable . . . no reason at all,
except that the rich and fashionable are eager only for those
musical comedies which Mr W. L. Courtney deprecates. As for
the intellectuals, who might use their intellects in the art of
wheedling out subscriptions—they, for the most part, find fodder
enough in life and libraries, and care little what becomes of the
drama, so long as they are allowed to sign protests about it.

Stay! I think I see a glimmer of hope. Mr Courtney's seventy-
two stars are not to be left in sole possession of his firmament. He
describes them as a 'First List.' Others will coruscate, presumably,
in March. Let them pay for it. Let no one who is not willing to
pay (say) a guinea for the *Fortnightly*'s Roman capitals be suffered
to join the illustrious protest. And let no one who *is* willing be
excluded. As a student of human nature, I guarantee that within
a few months the Editor would have enough in hand to endow the
theatre of his dreams. My only regret is that the high tone of this
little essay will preclude as signatory Max Beerbohm.

[*6 February 1904*]

'SKETCHES' AND THEATRES

The theatrical manager is incensed by the 'sketches' in the music halls. They incense me, too, when I happen to see them. It seems to me ridiculous that song and dance should be suspended for two or three mimes of the tenth rank to perform a little bit of dramatic twaddle. I do not agree with the theatrical manager that such 'sketches' can keep the public away from the theatres. The music halls themselves are the likeliest sufferers. However, I side with the theatrical manager on the question of principle. The theatre should have a monopoly of drama. Only in the theatre can drama thrive. If—a not unlikely hypothesis—the quality of these 'sketches' were improved; if persons of talent were suborned to write them; and if persons of talent were suborned to play them, then, undoubtedly, the art of drama would be endangered. For the persons of talent, scribes or mimes, could not do their best work under such conditions; and the fact of its being their work would lower the currency all round. Good wishes, then, to the crusade of the theatrical manager against the manager of the music hall. But I do not approve the manner in which Mr Charles Frohman is fighting the common foe of himself and his brethren. It were better not to carry the war into the enemy's country; and that is what Mr Frohman is doing just now, from the Duke of York's Theatre. He 'presents' not merely *Captain Dieppe*, a light comedy by Mr Anthony Hope and Mr Harrison Rhodes: he 'presents' also, half an hour earlier, *The Dandies*. I went early to see (as I expected) it, and was surprised to find 'them.' I was surprised to find on this classic stage two ebullient gentlemen in purple coats, and two ladies in black and silver, singing comic part-songs. They withdrew ere the curtain rose on the light comedy, and were not seen again. But they had the obvious air of being the thin end of the wedge. I foresee that in the immediate future Mr Frohman will 'present' 'turns' in every entr'acte. A little later, there will be 'turns' in the course of the play. The Duke of York's will at length be devoted, like so many of the other theatres, to musical comedy. That would be a score off the music-hall managers. But it would not be a useful score. Leave 'turns' to the music hall, and the music hall will the likelier cease its clutchings at drama.

I confess there were moments in the light comedy when I sighed for a brief interlude by *The Dandies*; so very severe was the strain of following the plot. I am no grudge of mental effort. My usual grievance against plays is that they demand no mental effort of any kind. Still, when a play does make such a demand, one has to consider afterwards what it has given one in return. And *Captain Dieppe* seemed to have given me rather little. Ingenuity in drama is but a means to an end. The point of a dramatic intrigue is not how much is closely knotted and deftly unravelled, but how much we are edified by the process. In other words, we must be interested in the persons of the play: they must appear to us as human beings, or, at least, as brilliant figments. The persons in *Captain Dieppe* do not appear to me in either light. They appear to me as unreal, and as uninteresting, in themselves, as the pieces in a game of chess. In chess the moves are everything; but in drama the quality of the pieces is the principal matter. Take a Shakespearean comedy. Who cares for the silly little ins-and-outs and upside-downs of the plot, however craftily manipulated? What delights us is the vividness of the characters, and the vivid beauty of the words they speak. Mr Anthony Hope and Mr Harrison Rhodes have themselves taken something very like a Shakespearean comedy; and, though they have transferred it into the present time, they have pointed the likeness by giving an Italian setting and mostly Italian names to their (very English) characters. Lucia and Emilia are bosom friends. Emilia is suspected by Andrea, her husband, of loving Paul. The two are not on speaking terms. Both are living in the same castle, but they do not meet. It is important that Emilia should see Paul once again. Lucia agrees to remain in the castle, while Emilia dresses up as Lucia and starts on her journey. Comes a stranger, a wanderer, the hero. He is fascinated by Lucia, whom he supposes to be Emilia. Later he sees Andrea, who likes him very much, and makes him promise to act as intermediary between Emilia and himself. The hero is thus wedged between love and duty. Emilia returns, and the hero sees her in the embrace of Andrea. Imagining Andrea to be a faithless profligate, he feels that there is no opposition between love and duty. Finally, everything is cleared up. There you have baldly the plot. It is just the sort of plot Shakespeare would have stolen; and Shakespeare, doubtless, would have made it delightful. But take away Shakespeare's poetry, and his power of making puppets seem quite like human beings; and substitute some side-issues about modern European politics, and secret police, and stolen bank-notes: substitute, in fact, Sardou; and there you have *Captain Dieppe*, a not exhilarating hybrid. However, Miss Irene Vanbrugh and Miss Miriam Clements, as Lucia and Emilia, keep up an appearance of sprightliness; and Mr H. B. Irving puts a bold front on the part of the hero. Evidently he is glad to be, as are we to see him, once more detached from that modern English milieu which is so incongruous with him. As a foreigner of uncertain date (for he wears a romantic costume, apt to a soldier of fortune in whatever historic or prehistoric period you will), he lets himself go, or rather is able to preserve himself, to very gallant effect.

At the New Theatre is *My Lady of Rosedale*, adapted by Mr Comyns Carr from *La Châtelaine*. It has the especial merit, the very rare merit, of not seeming like an adaptation. I have neither seen nor read the original play, which is said to be an early work, furbished up by the author after the successes of his prime. Certainly, it has not the peculiar sharp qualities by which M. Capus is distinct from other French playwrights. For no adapter, however ingenious, could have altogether eliminated them, had they been there; nor could any adapter, however patriotic, have resisted the temptation to preserve as much of them as possible. But the slightest trace of *le vrai et veritable* Capus would have been quite fatal to the verisimilitude of a play about English people. *My Lady of Rosedale* bears no such trace. Without the evidence of the programme, I should have vowed that Mr Carr had written all of it himself. And that is the greatest possible tribute to his skill. To adapt a play by even the least French of Frenchmen without implicitly betraying its origin is of all theatrical tasks the hardest. I suspect, from internal evidence, that a great deal of *My Lady of Rosedale* is indeed Mr Carr's own undiluted output. For years Mr Carr has been accounted the most accomplished of all after-dinner speakers. How many tables has he kept in a roar, hushing them, at exactly the right moment, by a peroration instinct with true emotion for the subject of his toast! No one else has a touch quite so sure and masterly in this art. And what other art can be quite so gratifying to the adept in it? To a man who can always be counted on for a good after-dinner speech it must be a temptation to make after-dinner speeches even before breakfast—to make them even when he is adapting a

31

play, and to incorporate them in his MS. Rather a dangerous temptation, this; for an after-dinner speech depends as much on the mode of
its delivery as on its matter; and there are on the English stage so
few actors who can be agreeably consecutive. But in writing *My
Lady of Rosedale* Mr Carr was safely able to let himself go. For was
not the play to be produced by Sir Charles Wyndham? And is not
Sir Charles pre-eminent for his power of so modulating a monologue that we can listen delightedly for any number of minutes
at a stretch? A powerful, an irresistible combination—after-dinner
speeches composed by Mr Carr and delivered by Sir Charles. *My
Lady of Rosedale* simply teems with them. Some of them are compressed. Some are almost fragmentary. But others are whole, un-
abridged, verbatim; and it is in this form that they give us the
keenest pleasure. If the whole play were but a sometimes interrupted
monologue, Sir Charles's strong and supple art would carry it
safely through, and we should be resenting only the interruptions.
On the other hand, from the strictly dramatic standpoint, it is well
that the action of a play in which one of the characters has a great
deal to say should be more or less affected by the things which
that character says. *My Lady of Rosedale* does not fulfil this requirement. Mr Ralph Wigram, lover and *raisonneur*, has a great
deal to say, and the other characters listen very attentively to him;
yet, though he professes to be a man who always gets his own way,
he does not seem to make converts. When he does get his own way,
it is through some quite external bit of luck. In the last act, for
example, he delivers a magnificent homily to the villain—a man
who refuses (for motives of spite) to let his wife divorce him. He
launches the most awful threats, he insinuates the most exquisite
cajoleries. Like Sir Macklin, he argues high, he argues low, he also
argues round about him. He leaves the villain without a leg to
stand on. And yet the villain continues calmly to stand. Comes an
opportune telegram, to announce that the husband of the rich lady
who loves the villain has died conveniently; and then, but not till
then, comes the happy ending—tamely, lamely. How tame and
lame it would be if, at a dinner given in aid of some deserving
charity, and after one of Mr Carr's most eloquent appeals, all the
donors proclaimed that their munificence was a mere whim, quite
unconnected with anything that had fallen from Mr Carr's lips!
Perhaps the French prototype of Mr Wigram was a man with no

special gift of eloquence—a mere nonentity, dependent on opportune telegrams. But Mr Wigram himself is irresistible, and, being an irresistible force that sweeps nothing before it, he is rather absurd.

[27 *February 1904*]

AN UNCOMMERCIAL PLAY

A Man of Honour was produced lately at the Avenue (where it is still running). Thanks to the Stage Society! For, certainly, no manager would have dared the play on the merits of the MS. Only the impression made through the previous medium of the Stage Society could have won the benefit of commercial doubt. I hope the thing will pay its way. A little tragedy of modern life, unrelieved by taradiddles or even by titles, is a rather bitter pill for the public maw. No visual splendour of frocks or scenery can be dragged in. The manager of the Avenue does not attempt to gild the pill. He does but add a little jam, nervously. Throughout the entr'actes, the orchestra plays the newest waltzes and selections from the newest musical comedies; and, when the curtain falls on the conclusion of the whole matter, the house is played out to a tune whose words (have you been to the Adelphi?) are 'My heart's in a whirl as I kiss each curl of my cosy-corner girl.' A very fair house it was, on the night of my visit. And the play was very well received—with many hearty laughs in the wrong places. There, you perceive, is the best chance of success for a modern tragedy. The public is so very unsuspicious.

I called Mr Maugham's play 'a little tragedy' with no loose use of the diminutive. For here we have a tragic love-conflict not between naked soul and naked soul, but between upper-middle-class soul and lower-class soul. An average barrister marries an average barmaid, and all that intervenes to make them unhappy is the divergence of their up-bringings. Their tragedy is not the less real, however, because it is superficial, social, little; and Mr Maugham has made of it a more poignant play than any we have had since *Grierson's Way*. Not that the play is perfect, by any means. Basil Kent, the barrister, is not so well drawn as the barmaid, Jenny Bush. Her commonness is real and convincing, his gentility is—

33

genteel, in the later sense of the word. He is, in fact, a snob. In the first act we see him with his friend Halliwell, a brother of the woman with whom he is really in love. Jenny Bush, whom he has promised to marry, arrives with her brother, Harry. Harry swaggers aggressively, and addresses his host's friend as "Alliwell." 'Halliwell,' says the friend. And Kent is like unto him. He offers Harry a cigar. Harry is impressed by the brand. 'How much,' he asks, 'do these run you in for?' 'They were a present to me,' replies corrective Kent; 'I do not know what they cost. . . . Won't you take off the label before you light it?' I do not say that well bred people never behave in an ill-bred way: they very often do. But Kent's misbehaviour is dramatically an irrelevance; and it is a damaging irrelevance, for (dramatically) it stamps him as a snob, and so mars the right balance of the play. In the second act again, after his marriage with Jenny Bush, we find him engaged in lording it over Harry with long-worded sarcasms; and for us Harry becomes the far less insufferable of the two. All our sympathy goes to the wife. Mr Maugham, of course, meant to hold the scales evenly. He meant us to feel no less sympathy for the husband than for the wife. Those are the most interesting, the most moving cases of incompatibility—the cases in which neither person is to blame. Kent's part ought to be revised unsparingly.

The last act has been revised since the first production, but not unsparingly enough. Indeed, I prefer the original version. Jenny, as you may remember, had committed suicide, and there was to be an inquest. Kent gradually confessed to Halliwell his intense relief at finding himself free; and the play ended with the entry of the widow whom he wished to marry. Well, this was too harsh, too indecent, to be real. Kent was a sentimentalist. He would not have confessed to himself—much less to anyone else—the unlovely joy that was in his heart; and he would not have sent for Mrs Murray. Nevertheless, she and he would have come together, after a decent interval, and by that time he would have become callous enough not to conceal the truth about his own sensations. In fact, the ending of the play was right in itself, but wrong in its date: for verisimilitude, that decent interval was needed. In the amended last act, we don't get the decent interval, and we don't get the logical conclusion. Except for a word or two blurted out by Kent just before the curtain falls, we know nothing of his sensations, except that he is shocked by his

34

wife's suicide. As for the future, we are left to presume that the widow will marry a ridiculous person to whom she is engaged. The whole act has to depend for its interest on the success of Halliwell in preventing Harry Bush from making a fuss at the inquest. And who of us cares twopence whether Harry Bush makes a fuss at the inquest or not? That is neither here nor there. Why niggle over this travesty of a happy ending? Such irrelevant manoeuvring is quite unworthy of the play that Mr Maugham has written—unworthy of the simplicity with which he has carried the story forward, and of the insight and sympathy with which he has drawn all the characters—yes, all of them, for the faults in the presentment of Kent, though they are so damaging, are merely superficial. I have read two or three novels by Mr Maugham, and *A Man of Honour* seems to me inferior to any of them. But it is a blessing, and a surprise, to find a novelist trying to do his best in dramatic form and failing to do it only through lack of experience in the new medium, instead of trying to do his worst, for lucre, and doing it. There is no reason to suppose that anon Mr Maugham as playwright will not be the equal of Mr Maugham as novelist. Meanwhile, as a matter of conscience, and for sake of practice, let him re-revise the last act of *A Man of Honour*, and cleanse Kent of that deadly coating of snobbishness. Also (a smaller matter, but not unimportant) let him test the vocal quality of his dialogue, throughout. For the most part his characters talk vocally enough; but now and again they tend to become scriptive. Halliwell, for example: 'Matrimony, like hanging, is rather a desperate remedy.' I have no objection to epigrams: people do occasionally make epigrams in real life. But they don't do it like that; and the sentence I have quoted is an example of how it is not done. 'Matrimony is like hanging. It is rather a desperate remedy'—there you have the speakable form. I am hair-splitting? Well, the difference between what can be written and what can be spoken is a subtle difference, I admit; but it is a difference that matters a good deal, especially in a realistic play. Sometimes, Mr Maugham errs in the opposite way: his characters sometimes talk too naturally. Halliwell, again: 'The smiles of women are the very breath of your nostrils.' Halliwell, in real life, might be guilty of that dreadful phrase—surely the most dreadful phrase ever uttered. But the dramatist must select, must edit. Nothing that does not sound as if it could be spoken by a real person should be put into the lips of a puppet; but, gentle syllogist, not everything that sounds so should be put there.

Mr Maugham's play is performed by clever people. But it is not well performed by them. They are on the wrong tack. This is not surprising. It would be surprising to find a poetic romance acted in the right manner; for poetic romance, though we still have examples of it, is a bygone dramatic form; and always the dramatic form conditions the acting; and, when it dies, the right way to act it dies also. Prosaic realism is the form towards which we are tending; but we have not reached it yet: such plays as *A Man of Honour* are only, as it were, the outposts of the form; and consequently our mimes have not yet acquired the right method of interpreting it. Their style is conditioned by the form of drama which they, and we, know best—a form in which romanticism and realism are commingled. And thus, when the curtain rises on *A Man of Honour* and discovers Mr Ben Webster as Kent and Mr Charles Hallard as Halliwell, we very soon feel that though neither Mr Webster nor Mr Hallard is a swashbuckler talking in iambics, neither the one nor the other of them is (as Mr Maugham means him to be) an ordinary young man of today, sitting in an ordinary room in the Temple, and behaving in an ordinary manner. Both are physically so very radiant, so very gallant in bearing, in manner so very significant. Both talk sometimes slowly, sometimes quickly, but always slowlier or quicklier than is usual; and always their voices either rise higher or sink lower than is usual. Of the two, Mr Ben Webster is the further from our humdrum existence; and this is a pity, for on him falls the greater burden of the play. The best scene is in the second act, when the husband and wife quarrel. It is a wonderfully natural and well-graduated scene—vulgar suspicion from the wife, weary irony from the husband, violent taunts from the wife, long-pent outburst from the husband, and so forth. But there are no gradations in Mr Webster's acting, and no naturalness: from first to last he is the agonised troubadour, desperately facing the audience. And Miss Muriel Wylford, who plays the wife—she, too, is constantly appealing to the audience. She is a clever and sensitive actress, evidently; and she does try, conscientiously, to be quite natural. But the absence of any experience in frank realism, coupled with the presence of Mr Webster, forces her to decorate an admirably conceived performance with stage-tricks. She tries hard, moreover, not to be charming and refined and obviously sympathetic; but only now and then does she succeed. All the other performers, with one exception, are of the stage stagey. Mr George Trollope, as Harry Bush, is a very sharp exception. His performance is interesting as an example of how much a part depends on its interpreter—how creative a power for good or evil the actor can be. When the play was produced by the Stage Society, the part of Harry Bush seemed to be just that bit of threadbare convention, the stage Cockney, the shade of Sam Weller. Later, when I read the play, I found that Harry Bush was quite a possible figure. But, now that he is impersonated by Mr Trollope, he becomes something more than that: one sees in him the incarnation of a whole class—of a whole modern class that is quite new upon the stage. One has seen them, these young men, lounging outside public bars and music-halls—a little lower than the baser sort of bank-clerk, a little higher than the Hooligan; pretentious, without the vitality to rise; malevolent without the vitality for mischief; gloomily dissipated; the most sordid outcome, so far, of our urban civilisation. And here we have, as it were, a synthesis of them all. Mr Trollope is a character-actor of the first water.

[*5 March 1904*]

TWO PLAYS OF ARTIFICE

It seems absurd to mention either of them. The writer of theatrical history finds last week all overshadowed by one tremendous event—all bathed, rather, in the supernal radiancy of one tremendous event. Mr George Edwardes produced *The Cingalee*. I wish this Review had a mirror to reflect for you, and to blind your eyes with this 'heavenly light.' Alas, I am no expert in music, and J.F.R. is no expert in drama. On the staffs of other newspapers, however, are the necessary dualists; and through them you will have been dazzled enough already. It is impossible to doubt the honesty of their opinions. If they were slaves to expediency, they would hasten, whenever a musical comedy were produced, to assure you of its dullness. For their editors are always deploring and reprehending this art-form. Constantly in the editorial columns you are told how shameful it is that the public taste should be debauched by these tawdry inanities and made insensible to the higher kinds of art. And yet Mr George Edwardes may always depend on a favourable notice for whatever he essays; nay, he is always sure to get a dithyrambic rhapsody. Except the King, no man in England is praised so warmly and so humbly for his every action. I learn from one of the best-known newspapers that *The Cingalee* is remarkable for 'admirable vivacity and smoothness' and for 'marvellous smoothness'; that it is 'really beautiful' and was 'smiled on by Royalty in the persons of Her Majesty the Queen and the Princess Victoria'; that it is 'a magnificent production,' and had 'a magnificent reception,' and 'is a triumphant success which marks the top notch in the all-conquering musical play.' The dresses and the scenes are all 'simply exquisite in their beauty.' All the acting is perfect. So is all the music. And (an item which to me, as dramatic critic, is most important of all) the story is told 'with rare skill and magnificent stage-craft by Mr James T. Tanner.' And these things I quote, not because they are peculiar, but because they are, on the contrary, typical of the things said of *The Cingalee*, and of anything else that Mr Edwardes may give us, by nearly all the daily papers. Surely, to be an expert in musical comedy is one of 'the dangerous trades.' The men who follow it cannot live very long, surely. To be in a state of constant bedazzlement, of constant hysteria—'superlativitis,' as the pathologists call it . . . However, I did not set out to write a philanthropic plea. My point is that when these men, chosen for their dual expertness, and sorely tempted to please their editors by decrying every musical comedy that they may see, never can do anything but turn delirious somersaults and yell delirious paeans, we are driven to the conclusion that musical comedy has been brought to such a pitch of perfection that it is sheer madness in us to patronise any of the few theatres not yet developed to musical comedy. Might not the editors, those high-souled deplorants and reprehendents, muzzle these experts, and so confer a real benefit on the drama which they love so well? Of course, Mr Edwardes, controller of many concerns, might fiercely withdraw his advertisements from pages which ceased to praise him. But, equally 'of course,' to the high-souled deplorants and reprehendents no sacrifice for their faith would come amiss.

Every editor, at any rate, might (justifying the means by the end) insist that his critic of drama proper should match paean for paean, and somersault for somersault, with his critic of Mr Edwardes. As it is, the public is often led to suppose that plays which really are worth seeing are quite negligible. I do not say that the critics apply too high a standard. By few of them, indeed, is applied a standard nearly so high as mine. The mischief is that they so often apply the wrong standard, blaming a tragedy because it doesn't amuse them, or a comedy because it doesn't fill them with pity and awe, or a realistic play because it isn't romantic, or a fantasy because it isn't absolutely lifelike. A victim to this instinct for irrelevance is *When a Man Marries*, a play by Mr Murray Carson and Miss Norah Keith, lately tried at a matinée in Wyndham's Theatre. It is not of the kind that I like best; but it is of a kind that has a perfect right to exist, and to be judged by a special standard. It is neither realism nor fantasy, but a deliberate blend of the two things. A Scotch nobleman, in the prime of life, does not know whether he be or be not in love with a lady who was his playmate in childhood. He marries her, at the instigation of two sentimental aunts, and promises her that if ever he find himself in love with someone else he will immediately warn her. He is bored by her, and falls in love with a young ward who comes to stay in his castle. He tries to warn his wife, and, while he is fumbling for words, she anticipates him, and helps him out, and is not at all angry. Her kindness causes in him an instant revulsion. He is bored by the mere notion of the ward, and desperately in love with his wife. Well, of course, in real life, things do not happen quite like that. The kindness of the wife who had bored him would produce in the husband a mood of repentance—lasting repentance, perhaps; but the ending would not be a happy one: kindness never yet made A fall out of love with B and out of boredom by C into boredom by B and into love with C. Only, all that is neither here nor there. Mr Carson and Miss Keith did not (as the critics seem to imagine) sit down to depict the realities of human character. They sat down to compose a pretty little romance—a fairy-story without fairies. Is the figment prettily wrought out? Is it amusing? These are the only proper tests. *When a Man Marries* survives them. The dialogue does not make for roars of laughter, but it is light and humorous; and the sentimental passages are very gracefully written. At Wyndham's the whole thing was performed in just the right key. Neither Mr Carson, as the Scotch nobleman, nor Miss Esmé Beringer, in the wife's part, struck too deep a note: both of them were duly debonair throughout. A dangerous part is that of the ward—a wild minx. Played by the averagely maladroit British ingénue, it would have been quite intolerable. It was delightful as played by Miss Jean Sterling Mackinlay, an ingénue with real quicksilver in her veins.

At the Imperial Theatre is a play which, were it judged by the standard so foolishly applied to *When a Man Marries*, would have to be similarly condemned. But there is no danger of this similar miscarriage of justice. For *A Marriage of Convenience* is Mr Grundy's adaptation of Dumas *père's Mariage sous Louis XV*; and, of course, it would never do to say a word against Dumas père; and so the play is criticised from the standpoint of what its author intended. I have called both plays 'plays of artifice.' But in Dumas the artificiality goes much deeper. The emotions of the characters are purely conventional: no attempt is made even to distort real emotions; and the play's sole point of contact with reality is in its presentment of manners. The manners of the Court of Louis XV were very light, very gay, very elegant, very absurd; and the play depends for its charm on the skill of its interpreters in suggesting to us the semblance of these manners. Well! Compare with the flight of a butterfly in a garden of flowers the flight of an aeronaut guiding a flying machine round the dome of St Paul's. The difference between these two things is precisely the difference between the ideal performance of *A Marriage of Convenience* and the present performance of it. We admire Mr Waller's science and skill, precisely as we admire the science and skill of the aeronaut in mid-air; and when the curtain falls on the last act we heave the very sigh of relief that we heave when the aeronaut brings his machine safely down to earth. A veritable triumph of mechanism! The flight of a butterfly is not nearly so impressive, not nearly so thrilling. Yet that is all we need here; nor will anything else please us. Mr Waller and his admirable company are of too stern a stuff for lepidopteral trifling.

[*12 March 1904*]

BETTER PLAYS AND BETTER ACTING

One of Mr Meredith's earlier novels—*Beauchamp's Career*, I think—opens with a delightful treatise on the uses of panic in British politics. Panic, we are told, has to be periodically fermented by our statesmen, because the public will sanction no expenditure, however needful, till it be frightened right out of its wits. Mr Meredith likens the public to a snoring dame, not easily woken, but once woken, 'all fluttering night-cap and fingers a-grabble for the bell-rope,' and ready for any means of salvation, however venturesome and dreadful. Written soon after the Crimean period, the passage is not less sharply true of our public in relation to artistic matters. Take the art of the theatre. From year's end to year's end, our public is placidly content with its drama, and will not believe that anything could possibly be better than its drama, and is averse from any hint of innovation. But periodically arise certain dramatists and critics who, with one voice, loudly, all over the place, declare that the drama is doomed and deserves to be doomed; insomuch that the public nightcap flutters and the public fingers grabble. There is quite such a flutter and a grabble at this moment. The average newspaper is the voice of—not, as it should be, to—the public; and the average newspaper has suddenly begun to insist on the urgent need for a repertory theatre—anything to raise the tone of the drama. Yes, the public has been thoroughly scared. Only, there is in England this difference between political scares and artistic scares : the latter kind must not be relied on as unbuttoner of pockets. There was just such another artistic scare as now in the early nineties. Then, as now, the arch-alarmist was Mr Henry Arthur Jones; and then, as now, all England collapsed into agreement that there must be a repertory theatre, and that there was not a moment to be lost. Only, every man remembered to make in his panic-stricken breast the reservation that somebody else must pay. Nobody did pay. The panic subsided gradually. But it had done a certain amount of good. *The Second Mrs Tanqueray* was born of it, and for a time there was a general interest in serious drama.

Will the present panic be more definitely fruitful? Will some pocket or pockets unknown be definitely unbuttoned, and a repertory theatre be definitely founded? Mr Walkley, who has a

temperamental aversion from panics, and prefers despair, would
have us believe that there is no use for a repertory theatre—that there
are no unacted plays worth acting, or, at any rate, not so many as
would make a decent repertoire. I do not think he is right. Such plays
are always forthcoming, at a pinch. But for the Playgoers' Club we
should never have known of the existence of *The Finding of
Nancy*. But for the Stage Society, *A Man of Honour* would never
have been seen. That society, by the way, did not invite me this
week to the Court Theatre, and so I did not see *'Op o' me Thumb*,
the new one-act play by Messrs Frederick Fenn and Richard Pryce.
However, I had happened to see the MS, and so have another instance to my hand. Here is a little tragi-comedy, true and touching,
sure in its appeal to tears and laughter, with no taint of amateur-
ishness in technique, and with one magnificent 'acting-part' in it.
Needless to say, the special mime for whom this part was the chance
of a lifetime could not or would not enact it. So *'Op o' me Thumb*
was relegated to the Stage Society. It had—for no apparent reason
but that it was not the usual tawdry twaddle—no chance of being
produced in the commercial way. Another instance occurs to me. It
is but a few days since I read a private copy of a very original and
delightful play, written a year or so ago, by a well-known and
successful dramatist. After I had read it, I asked the author when
and where it was going to be produced. He replied that it had been
'going the rounds' ever since he had finished it, and that no manager
had even 'nibbled'. Here, you see, is no case of an unread MS. The
author's name, and his good commercial record, must have insured
prompt attention from every manager. No case, again, of an original
idea marred by amateurish handling. The play is as sound a piece of
stage-craft as would be expected of so experienced a craftsman.
Originality alone damned the MS. Some day perhaps it will be performed by the Stage Society—or by the phantasmal repertory
theatre. Now, when there is constantly coming into one's ken some
play that ought to be acted, and that cannot at present be acted
except fugitively and more or less in private, one may assume
safely that there are, at least, as many other such plays beyond one's
ken. There is, at least, enough to make a good 'send-off' for a
repertory theatre, even without reckoning the play which Mr Jones
has generously promised to give to it. And, once a repertory theatre
were soundly started, its permanence would be assured. We must

take into consideration not merely what material there is for it, but also the material that there would be. Many men of literary talent, and of possible dramatic talent, refrain from dramaturgy, because there seems to be no middle way between making a huge fortune by conventional twaddle and earning not a halfpenny by honest and original work. Few of them can afford to write for nothing; and so they write books, for therein honest and original work does at least win them a fair wage. But if there were a theatre from which they could earn as much by dramaturgy (or even half as much, for the theatre has an intrinsic fascination for most men), then they would surely take heart of grace, and occasionally write a play. But . . . will such a theatre be founded? Will the plutocrat come forward? It is on him we pin our fluttering faith. There is no hope that the general public will subscribe anything in advance— no hope of a State theatre, or of a municipal theatre; though a privately endowed theatre, devoted to good plays, would attract enough of the general public to prevent its losses from being excessive. But it is always the most obvious things that are not done. And this panic will probably subside, like that other one, leaving no tangible or lasting good behind it. However, it is fun while it lasts. I do not grumble. Happy the expert whose subject excites, if only for a moment, his fellow-men.

The panic is not merely about our plays: it ranges to the condition of our mimes also. For them also, it is urged, something must be done. They are decried as duffers. Their equipment is angrily compared with the equipment of the French mimes who annually invade our shores, and up goes the translated cry 'We are betrayed!' I counsel a little calmness, a little justice. The superiority of French acting to English acting is not a remediable phenomenon, not a thing to be made a fuss about: merely a thing to be regretted. The Latin races are races of born actors, as I have often insisted. To make a right effect in the theatre, they have merely to curb their exuberance and ebullience. This they can do by submission to artistic discipline. We, on the contrary, have to generate exuberance and ebullience in ourselves. This positive process is much harder, of course, than that negative process. It is easier to walk slowly down hill than to walk quickly up hill. It is easier to break in a mettlesome charger than to make a fat cob caracole. It is easier for a Latin than for a Saxon to be a great mime; for the former needs only an artificial

43

change from without, while the latter needs a natural change from within. Thus the general level of French acting is bound to be always far superior to our own. And no academy of dramatic art will redress the balance. The functions of an academy in any art are negative functions: 'you must not do this,' and 'you must not do that.' An academy cannot inspire; it can only correct. And for us, therefore, whose faults are not positive but negative, an academy of dramatic art (in the true sense of the title) is not needed at all. We need no trammelling by tradition. Where we fail is in the power to liberate and express our souls through our bodies. This remark is, of course, general in intent. I do not echo the unmitigated charge of dufferdom against our mimes. Some of them, some of the principals, seem to me admirable indeed—far too good for the kind of parts they usually fill. But it is true, beyond question, that in the rank and file dufferdom reigns supreme. Amateurish, nearly all of them. How few of them can walk or talk naturally in a modern play, or scan decently in a Shakespearean play a single line of blank verse! And yet these are not tricks that can be performed by genius alone. A child could perform them, if the child were taught. Not even a grown-up person, however, could perform them without tuition. And there we have one of the most startling facts about our stage: hitherto, the grown-up persons who have gone upon it have had no tuition at all. At length, there is to be an academy of dramatic art. Haters of academicism need not be alarmed. I take it that this school will not be, like the Conservatoire, an academy in the full sense of the word. It will demand no awful surrender of souls. It will be an academy rather, in the Misses Pinkerton's sense of the word. Voice production, delivery of verse, gesture, deportment, bowing, use of the fan, dancing, fencing—I gather from the prospectus that these, and similar things, are the objectives. It is quite absurd that anyone unversed in these accomplishments should go upon the stage, there to pick them up at haphazard. After all, you pay your money to see a play acted, not to see ladies and gentleman floundering in a state from which only when they emerge can they hope to begin to act. Be glad, therefore, that future neophytes will be able to learn privately, methodically, far from the distracting glare of the footlights. And be glad that they, not you, will be defraying the cost of tuition.

[*19 March 1904*]

A PERIL FOR PLAYS

Man is a sympathetic animal. Even the people who, undriven by duty, attend the first nights of plays, and derive some sort of dark gratification from their habit, are human, and therefore sympathetic. They never come wishing to behold failure. They never do any premeditated 'guying.' They realise the trouble that has been taken, and the hopes that have been built, and the fears that are now quivering in the over-strained wretches, their human brothers and sisters, behind the scenes. Oh yes, they are most well-wishing, most sympathetic. But in virtue of their very sympathy they are dangerous. Even before the curtain has risen, those pent-up nerve currents from behind the scenes are flowing out into the auditorium, crossing and re-crossing one another in waves, from floor to ceiling, and charging with their electricity, to a greater or less degree, every member of the audience. Unconsciously, we are all more or less in a state of suppressed hysteria. We are all screwed up to an abnormal pitch. A first night is very like a funeral. It is the common experience of mourners at a funeral that, unless they frankly express their grief through tears, and thus relax the strain that is set on them, some quite ordinary thing seen or irrelevantly remembered, something that at any ordinary time would not ever so slightly touch their sense of humour, will now make them shake helplessly with inward laughter—with a laughter that gains force by their very shame of it and by the need for its controlling. So it is at a first night. The slightest hitch on the stage, the slightest oddity in a costume or in a phrase, will seem matter for mirth unquenchable. So excessive is the strain set on us by our sympathy. Let but one member of the audience laugh outright, being more highly-strung than the rest, and the infection of his guffaw spreads instantly, irresistibly, over the whole house; and the game is up. The audience is ashamed of itself, but, having once roared outright, it will roar again, and yet again, loudlier still, and for yet slighter reasons.

Such a first night as this was evidently last Saturday's at Wyndham's Theatre, when *The Sword of the King* was produced. I was myself not able to be there. Had I been there, I, doubtless, should have been swept under by the electric waves. Even as it was, when I read on Monday morning Mr L. F. Austin's account of the affair, I laughed loud and long to myself. Even after all those hours, and through that cold medium of printed paper, Mr Austin transmitted strongly to me those currents. Those frantically ridiculous things that had been said and done! How is it, I wondered, that experienced managers cannot foresee facts and stare them in the face? Here was a production foredoomed, so obviously foredoomed, to be wrecked by laughter; and yet . . .

I attended the third performance. I was careful to be there before the rising of the curtain; for I had gathered that some of the most irresistible things came at the very outset. After all, there was a consensus among the critics that the play was poor, and I supposed it was bound to be withdrawn very soon: nothing could save it; and so there would be no harm or unkindness in having a good laugh. The same thing seemed to have occurred to many other people. The stalls presented not at all the aspect usual on a third night—especially the third night of a failure. They were quite full, with no signs even of 'paper.' Everyone there was of the kind that does not usually arrive before the middle of the second act. The aristocracy and plutocracy had, for once, wolfed their food, or dined very early, in their cynical zest to see another 'Worst Woman in London.' That, indeed, is the one hope for a serious-ridiculous piece: the booking for the stalls is sure to be good. The curtain rose. . . . Yes, a lady in a nightgown, and a gentleman outside her window, standing on an imaginary mare, but—but—but no laughter, no impulse to laugh. We knew it was excruciatingly funny: we knew we ought all to be holding our sides; yet the fact remained that we were not in the least amused; and in the midst of our disappointment we were conscious of being dramatically illuded, dramatically interested. We believed in the mare outside: it *was* there: we heard it gallop away. We did not smile when the horseman was hoisted in through the window, for we were holding our breath till we should know whether he had outwitted his pursuers. When the knock came at the door, and the horseman slipped into the bed, and the search-party was satisfied by the lady that the person behind the bed-curtain was her old nurse, we were impressed by the readiness of the ruse, and delighted by its success. And so on, throughout the piece. We soon had lost all regret that we were not laughing. It was an excellent play of its kind. It was an excellent romantic melodrama.

46

Dramatic critics may be divided, according to their breadth of view, into four classes. There is (1) the ideal critic who is equally, and extremely, susceptible to every form and manner of drama. Tragic or comic or melodramatic or farcical romance or realism or fantasy, ancient or modern—he revels in them all, and is illuminating about them all. The only drawback in him is that he does not exist. Like unto him, in the matter of impartiality, is (2) the critic who, revelling in not a single one of these forms and manners, pretends to appreciate them all, and is not less trite and tedious about one than about another. The chief objection to him is that he does exist—that he is indeed the average type of critic. But there is, as antidote to him, (3) the critic who really does revel in one or more of these forms and manners, and, revelling in that or them, can neither understand nor abide the rest. Where he revels, he is illuminating. Where he detests, he is entertaining; for the rigid application of a false standard to anything must always produce a grotesque result; and a grotesque must be always welcome. The third kind of critic is my favourite—much dearer to me than the fourth kind (of which I am one). Critic No. 4; he, too, has his strong predilections; but he has no prejudices. He does not detest everything to which he happens to be indifferent; nor will he apply thereto the standard applicable only to what he happens to love; and thus he does his readers out of a lot of stimulating fun. I don't, for instance, love romantic melodrama. A girl dresses up as a boy, and sallies out with a sword, and strikes a blow for William of Orange, and fights a duel in defence of her brother against her lover, and at her lover's bidding is ready to shoot her brother—aye! her own brother—if so be that he have done the Prince an injury . . . and all that. All that leaves me cold (though, for purpose of convenience, I included myself just now as one of the people who were carried away by the first act of the play). My own private opinion is that all that is silly. But I don't take this opinion as a touchstone. I recognise the right of melodramatic romance to exist for the pleasure of the people whom it pleases. And I can discriminate between bad samples and good. A good, straightforward, gallant, workmanlike, swift, virile, romantic melodrama is *The Sword of the King*. I have to fall back on epithets for this kind of play. I don't profess to be able to be illuminating about it. I can merely be just. And I am glad to do justice (dull thing though justice is) to a play which on its first night received such scant justice from Fate. Fate decreed that the highly-strung audience should laugh, soon after the curtain rose, at a point that was not really laughable; and the rest of the play was dissolved, inevitably, in laughter, so that even the trained critics did not see that it was a very good bit of work, with all the elements of a commercial success. But the first night is not everything, and the press-notices are not everything. I bid the management be of good cheer.

The best piece of acting in the play is done by Mr Charles Fulton, as the Prince. Famous figures in drama are usually a sad incumbrance. There seems to be only one bridge over which they can be brought safely across from the firm ground of history on to the firm ground of theatrical illusion. This is a strong natural bridge which can, however, be variously engineered for the transit of the various august passengers. Across it Julius Caesar has come to us, in all his imperial magnitude; and the Duke of Wellington, romantic for all his rigidity; and many another hero, of whom the latest is William of Orange. But I doubt whether the bridge of Mr Fulton's nose, as augmented by a talent for modelling, would alone be enough to illude us. That nose, in its latest form, and framed in a coiffure of glossy dark curls, recalls not more sharply the pictures of Prince William than the caricatures of the young Disraeli. But the young Disraeli was not a dignified figure. Mr Fulton cuts always nothing if not a dignified figure. His port, his magnificent voice, his eyes, his manner, all breathe augustness, greatness. Sometimes I have seen him impersonating a private character, and have been alarmed by the total disappearance of that character beneath the weight of his authority. But as the high-souled, high-nosed hero of all time, or of any special period, he has no rival, believe me.

[*16 April 1904*]

TWO NEW PLAYS

I was very curious to see the 'irresponsible comedy' at the St James's Theatre. For the authors of it, Mr Frederic Fenn and Mr Richard Pryce, were also the authors of *Liz's Baby* and '*Op o' me*

Thumb—two little plays of a very rare kind, in that each of them had evidently been written with a genuine impulse to express something that had been closely observed and keenly felt. It is very rarely that we feel a play to have been a spontaneous growth from brain and heart. To a play that does give us this feeling we will pardon any number of technical weaknesses. (Not that any such mercy was needed for *'Op o' me Thumb* or *Liz's Baby*, both of which were admirably constructed.) The average play gives us the sense that it was written chiefly because the author wanted to write a play. Observation of life, a feeling for the humour or pathos in this or that phase of life, may have gone to the making of the play; but they seem to be there incidentally, and as a means to an end. They are not, and they should be, the origin and mainspring of the whole matter. In *Saturday to Monday* there is plenty of humour, but the play differs from the authors' other (and perhaps later) work in just this vital respect: it does not seem to be a spontaneous growth. 'Irresponsible' is precisely the wrong word for it. When Mr Fenn and Mr Pryce wrote those other plays they really were behaving irresponsibly: they were responsible only to their own brains and hearts. When they sat down to write *Saturday to Monday* they were labouring under a grave sense of responsibility to quite other and external things—how to write a play that would commend itself to the manager of a successful theatre, and to the audience in that theatre; how, in fact, to have not a mere artistic Stage Societyish success, but a regular, popular, lasting metropolitan success with no nonsense about it. With this purpose in view, they proceeded to draw on their humour and their imagination. Inevitably, their gifts would not shine with the proper lustre. And even their tact in technique was dimmed. Technique is a mysterious thing, not wholly separable from inner impulse. A man is likelier to do skilfully what he really wants to do than what he is merely determined to do.

The play begins as a comedy. Lord Culvert, who has been a sailor, but has just inherited the title and the estate of his family, is spending a week-end at the cottage of Mrs Wendover. He is in love with her, she with him; but he is engaged to be married. He wants to break off the engagement. Mrs Wendover tries to dissuade him. His fiancée and her mother arrive unexpectedly to stay with Mrs Wendover. His secretary comes too. To complete the annoyance, the local curate comes with his sister and another lady, in answer to

Mrs Wendover's forgotten promise that the 'reading club' might hold a meeting in her dining-room. So far, all has been comedic—a quite realistic comedy of manners. But suddenly the key changes. Lord Culvert declares to Mrs Wendover that, since she won't let him break off his engagement and marry her, he will before the end of the evening have become engaged to every woman in the house. He accomplishes his threat. Now, in a pure farce, entitled *Jack-a-Shore*, this kind of behaviour might be well enough. But the keynote of comedy, once struck, cannot be silenced. 'An irresponsible comedy'? But comedy cannot, though farce can, be irresponsible. Mr Oscar Wilde called *The Importance of Being Earnest* (which is the prototype of this play) 'a trivial comedy.' But it was not a comedy at all. It was a fantastic farce, and the key-note of fantastic farce was struck as soon as the curtain rose. Lord Culvert, on the other hand, has been fixed for us as a credible human being, typical of a certain definite class, and we cannot, try as we may, forget to take him seriously. Therefore, behaving as he behaves, he offends us. His behaviour is, in the exact sense of the phrase, beyond a joke; and, as Queen Victoria said on a famous occasion, 'we are not amused.' His behaviour is the less agreeable to us by reason of the personalities of the ladies who become engaged to him. Two of them are plain and elderly spinsters, and the third is a plain and elderly dowager. Now, we live in a civilised age. There was an age in which hearty laughter could be evoked by mere mention of women not pretty and not young. But that was an age of barbarism, long past. What was funny then is painful now. The making of jokes about physical defects in women is a mere survival: laughter has long ceased to accompany it. Modern humanitarianism may not be a healthy thing: it may be merely a symptom of nervous debility; it is, nevertheless, a fact that must be reckoned with. But there is another reason, an even stronger reason, why Lord Culvert ought not to have behaved as he did. His behaviour headed straight for monotony. Making three bogus proposals of marriage to three persons of the same kind, he was bound to produce uniform consequences. In the second act we have these uniform consequences, and Lord Culvert treats them uniformly. He assures the three ladies, one by one, that he had been pleading, not for himself, but for his secretary, and he sends them to a place where they are likely to find his secretary. Then, necessarily, there

are uniform consequences for the secretary. Repetition is sometimes a very effective device on the stage; but it must be cumulative repetition; in other words, what happens again must be an
exaggerated form of what happened before. The same thing recur-
ring in the same way is merely a nuisance. And the same things
do recur in the same way throughout the second and third acts of
Saturday to Monday.

Such a play must depend for its virtue on the amount of humorous
conceit which the authors have worked, by the way, into their
dialogue. Of this there is in *Saturday to Monday* quite enough to
make a good evening's entertainment; and on the strength of it
the play will very likely have a long run. For the players a rather
hard task is set. The best way would be to rattle along, from the
first, in the manner prescribed for ordinary farce. But it is almost
impossible to rattle along in realistic comedy, and Mr Alexander,
perforce, is realistically comedic in the early scenes; and no amount
of subsequent rattling can efface our first impression. Miss Braithwaite has a part that is realistically comedic throughout. In a congruous environment her performance of it would be delightful.

Mr Murray Carson has produced a new play at the Apollo
Theatre. It is called *The Wheat King*, and it stands well out from
the ruck of new plays because its subject is a new one. We have
had many gambling scenes on the stage, and a few scenes of commercial business. But here, for the first time, is a play whose central
figure is an operator in stocks and shares—a play whose whole
interest centres round 'the market' as affecting and affected by a
man with the mania for vast speculation. I cannot say that the
authors—Miss Elliott Page and Mrs Ashton Jonson—have risen to
the goodness of their theme. I have not read *The Pit*, a novel by
the late Frank Norris, of which their play is an adaptation; and so
I have not the discomfort of knowing that a masterpiece has been
mauled. True, the reviewers seemed to be unanimous that *The Pit*
was a very great book. But hearsay is a less safe guide to what one
would think about a book if one had read it than is one's own
acquired opinion of other work by the same author. I did, not long
ago, read *A Deal in Wheat*, a book of Frank Norris's short stories;
and their power seemed to be the power of melodrama, not of life;
none of them, however excellent in its way, seemed to rise above
the level of magazine fiction. A man who can create really good

magazine fiction is not a man who could achieve great or sincere fiction: there were more to be hoped from the bungler. I suspect that *The Pit* has a not utterly unworthy version in *The Wheat King*, whose fault, like that of the stories that I read, is a leaning from life to melodramatic convention. What we want in the play—all that we want in it—is a true and vivid presentment of the gambler's career and the gambler's soul. The gambler's career is well and excitingly suggested. But his soul? I do not object to the introduction of a strong 'love interest.' On the contrary, to show us the man as a devoted husband, gradually becoming indifferent to his devoted wife, is a very good means of illustrating his mania. But assuredly we do not want, and do regard as a stupid waste of time, the introduction of a conventional lover for the wife. Here he comes, with his romantic eye, and his impressive hand-clasp; and here she is writing to him a desperate note, which she snatches away from the servant who was to be the bearer of it; and here she is again, throwing herself into his arms, and then recoiling in horror; and doing a score of other oft-done things which not even so accomplished an actress as Miss Esmé Beringer can make tolerable. Assuredly, too, we don't want a pair of comic young lovers; and here they are. But it is not so much the waste of time that matters. The really serious thing is the levity with which the authors develop their central figure. They actually try to heroicise him into 'sympathy.' Here he is, for example, standing over a villain and forcing him, there and then, to refund the money of which he, in bygone days, basely robbed yonder white-haired old gentleman. Melodrama unashamed! However, there is enough truth in the character, and enough newness, to give Mr Carson a very fine chance in acting; and of this chance Mr Carson makes the utmost. His performance is perfectly graduated from the outset, when we see him merely preoccupied and overstrung, to the end, when he is swaying on the verge of lunacy, having all but lost the power of thought, and even of utterance. Horrible? But with a force never out of restraint: artistically horrible, and therefore not horrible at all.

[*23 April 1904*]

'THE HOUSE OF BURNSIDE'

In the office of Mr Richard Burnside, which is open to your inspection at Terry's Theatre, a prominent piece of furniture is the
umbrella-stand. This is of the twirly pattern so familiar to all
Victorians, with the narrow slab of looking-glass let into the middle
of it. One notices it only because the looking-glass has a rather
peculiar surface, having been scoured over with some sort of chalky
substance, and so reflecting nothing. Most mirrors on the stage are
subject to this rather dismal process. It would never do to have the
auditorium reflected behind the footlights—ladies patting their
hair, and gentlemen preening their neckties, instead of listening
to the play. And yet, old playgoer though I am, I never have become used to these blind mirrors. I cannot take them as a matter of
course, like the three-sided room and the upcast light and all those
other conventions. To me they are always an insistent and disturbing
symbol. The function of art is, as somebody once said, to hold the
mirror up to nature. The chief part of the playwright's duty is to
show us human beings, with human characters and human emotions
—in fact, to reflect *us*. But that is the very last thing he would
dream of doing. He (I mean, of course, the average writer of
plays) is too afraid that we should be angry with him. And he is
wise in his generation. The average auditor would be very angry
indeed; and it is, of course, his favour that the average playwright
is courting. And so the bright mirror is carefully 'prepared' in
such wise that the public, gazing into it, shall not be shocked by
any shadow of its own self. Thick coatings of insincerity and sentimentality defeat the tell-tale surface; and all is well. All is well except for a few poor faddists to whom not even an intentional fantasy
seems good unless actual things are fantasticated in it, and who
are beyond measure bored by a play which aims (as most of our
modern plays aim) at mere realism, and which yet will have no
traffic with any real thing.

The play about Mr Burnside is quite as sham an affair as the
mirror in Mr Burnside's umbrella-stand. Mr Burnside is, indeed,
a type of the stage-figure whose feelings and behaviour are conditioned not by the remotest truth to life, but simply by a theatrical
scheme. Let us briefly examine his case. He is a wealthy shipowner,

53

about sixty years old, a rough but tender-hearted creature, whose affections are centred on his two grandchildren. These, a girl and a boy, live in the same house with him and their mother. Their father, who was a drunken brute, has been dead for some years. Mr Burnside is going to leave a vast private fortune to the girl; he looks to the boy as the future head of the great business that he has founded. His daughter-in-law has a faithful housekeeper, who, one morning, calls at Mr Burnside's office, and incidentally receives from him a letter which has just come for her there from South America. She refuses to open it, says it is not for her, and behaves in a generally suspicious manner. Finally she opens it, but will not read it. She leaves it (being, for theatrical purposes, apparently insane) to be read by Mr Burnside. It turns out to have been written to her mistress, by a man who was formerly in Mr Burnside's employment. The writer, a dying man, mentions 'our child.' One of the two children, then, is not Mr Burnside's grandchild. But which? The letter gives no clue. The daughter-in-law, confronted by Mr Burnside, will give no clue. For it is Mr Burnside's express intention to cut the false grandchild out of his will, and the mother fails to see why the innocent creature should thus be made to suffer. Mr Burnside buffets wildly at the mist that involves him. The situation is rather like that of L'Enigme, by M. Hervieu, wherein two husbands suspect of infidelity two wives, one of whom must be innocent, the other guilty. But there is this salient difference between the two situations. In L'Enigme the doubt was a real one. There was no possible means of clearing it up, unless one of the two wives confessed. There was a precisely even balance of evidence for and against each lady. But if The House of Burnside were an episode in real life, not a mere striving after theatrical effect, there would be no mystery at all. Mr Burnside is not an idiot; he is, on the contrary, a very shrewd person; and it would be a very slight tax on his shrewdness to see that when there are two children born of an unhappy marriage, one of them certainly legitimate, and the other certainly illegitimate, the illegitimate one is assuredly the second-born. Having arrived at this simple conclusion, Mr Burnside would clinch it by not less simple means. He knew his son, and he knew the lover of his daughter-in-law, and he is not blind: he has merely to scrutinise the two children to know which is the child of which father. Of course, the case might be an unusual one.

The two fathers might have been (though we are not told that these two were) peculiarly alike; and thus the physical test would be useless. But in any case it would be superfluous. That other evidence is ample, irrefragable. But if the perspicacity and the worldly wisdom which have enabled Mr Burnside to build up a great business did not suddenly desert him at this juncture, and leave him in a state of helpless half-wittedness, the play would be over before the beginning of the second act. And that would not have pleased M. Georges Mitchell, the proud author of that from which Mr Louis Parker has adapted *The House of Burnside*. And so, for two more whole acts, covering a period of some months, Mr Burnside must dodder on unconscious of what stares him and everyone else in the face.

But the absurdity is even deeper than this. Suppose that the paternity of the two children really were an exasperating mystery. How, in real life, would Mr Burnside then behave? Being a quick-tempered man, he would very likely threaten, as here he threatens, to disinherit the illegitimate child, and would try to wring a confession from the mother. But, being also a good-hearted man, and a man of sense, he would quickly drop that attitude, blushing that he had assumed it. After all, there is no great harm done. Many a man has survived the blow of discovering that he was not the father of his supposed child; and it is not likely that a man who discovers merely that he is not the grandfather of a supposed grandchild will reel for long beneath that mitigated blow. For Mr Burnside, the blow is doubly mitigated by the fact that his son was a blackguard, of whom he strongly disapproved. He cannot find it in his heart to blame his daughter-in-law. Her infidelity does not shock him. But the child, who is even less culpable than the mother, shall be made to suffer. To him, or her, not a penny of his money will he leave, so help him Heaven! And yet, as I have told you, he always has been passionately devoted to both these children; and so he still is. But oblige him by telling him which is the love-child, and he will proceed to hate him, or her, relentlessly and for ever. At any rate, he will behave as though this were the case. Such is the attitude of this dear good fellow after several months of thinking the matter over. An hour or two, in real life, would suffice to bring him to that amenable frame of mind in which we see him at last. From the purely theatrical standpoint the objection to the final scene is precisely the reverse of my objection. The scene comes not too late, but too soon. It should by all canons of theatrical propriety have been postponed to Christmas Eve. The play (for no very evident reason) begins on New Year's morning. Thus Mr Burnside would have had to be obdurate for almost a whole year. And why not? Degrees in absurdity don't matter. Of course, in France the peculiar psychic influences of Christmas Eve are not recognised as they are here. But I do wonder that Mr Louis Parker, who must have heartily despised the poor stuff he was adapting, did not make this appropriate little difference, if only for the sake of an extra laugh in his sleeve.

[*7 May 1904*]

A PRESENTATION

'CHARLES FROHMAN PRESENTS MISS ETHEL BARRY-MORE in' something to which you may, if you care to as an after-thought, attach a certain amount of importance. It is a curious formula, Mr Frohman's; and familiarity has not blunted the fine edge of it. I like it very much, as must any one who very much likes to have everything fair and square and above-board. After all, how very rare is the theatrical production in which not the player but 'the play's the thing'! The fault is not the player's, nor the manager's: it is the fault of the public. To the public the personality of this or that player is the prime attraction; and, if that personality is not kept in the centre of the stage, bankrupt goes the theatre. The public does not go to see *Hamlet*; it goes to see an actor-manager in the part. 'MR SO-AND-SO PRESENTS HIMSELF in *Hamlet, or the Prince of Denmark*, by William Shakespeare.' Why not make the announcement frankly? If the cart *must* be put before the horse, why should the horse be given a nominal precedence? If you *must* 'hitch your waggon to a star,' why not let the 'star' be 'starred' for all he or she is worth? It is always best for us to know just where we are—even when the position is a wrong and degrading one.

56

Mr Frohman's formula seems peculiarly apt in the latest instance of it. For Miss Barrymore evidently depends very much on her personality, and very little on her instinct for the art of acting, and very little on her experience in that art. Judged from a technical standpoint, she is a fluttering amateur. The only question is whether she is a fascinating person on the stage. And the only answer to that question is a prompt, loud, unqualified 'Yes.' Thus there is, superficially, something not quite pleasant in Mr Frohman's formula as here applied. The American ogre presents to the English ogre a fascinating young lady: such is the paraphrase that might be made off-hand by a person of too squeamish taste. It seems almost indelicate to write an appreciation of Miss Barrymore's acting, for any praise must seem so very personal. 'Seems,' however, not 'is'; and 'seem' not 'be.' For a personality, as manifested by some one publicly through the medium of an art, may be, and often is, quite a different thing from the actual personality of the owner in private life. In such arts as the art of writing this difference is exemplified again and again. The fiercest writers are often the gentlest men, and the most brilliant talkers are often the dullest writers, and so on. Indeed, I think that writing is generally not a means whereby a man expresses himself as he appears to those who are privileged or condemned to know him, but a means whereby he expresses from his nature something of which not even he himself would otherwise be conscious. Well, and even in the more personal art of acting, the artist—even he or she who makes no pretence to impersonation —is often a person quite different from what he or she on the stage consistently appears to be. For example, persons of excellent breeding in private life often appear, when they tread the boards, to be the veriest bounders; and vice versa. Often, too, obviously mean people can enact only the noblest parts on the stage, and can enact them quite perfectly; and vice versa, again. In acting, as in all other artistic media for self-expression, there is some alchemy whereby, as often as not, one self is transmuted to another. The self of Miss Barrymore, as likely as not, is something quite distinct from the personality shining through the title-part in *Cynthia* at Wyndham's Theatre. I am quite sure that the latter is the only one that Miss Barrymore could ever manifest on the stage, even though she were cast for Antigone, Lady Macbeth, Lady Sneerwell, and Hedda Gabler, in succession. But it may be quite different from her own personality. So a critic need not hesitate to express delight in it.

The charm is rather hard to analyse. It is not a simple, straight-forward charm. It has no solidity, and seems to vanish delicately at the first attempt to explain it. It cannot be classified among the usual charms of womanhood. Indeed, 'womanly' is the last epithet one would apply to Miss Barrymore. One might liken her to many things. She reminds one, from moment to moment, of many various things—of a bird, a fairy, a child, a terrier, a flower, what-not; but of a woman never. Protean, she yet shirks that one meta-morphosis, content to be something more and something less. Perhaps she can best be summed up as a Pierrot. The term has been hideously vulgarised in modern times; but in its original sense, free of its later associations, take it, and you will have some notion of Miss Barrymore's odd charm. Pierrot's gaiety, and Pierrot's sadness, were inhuman; they had no roots in common life; they were shallow and transient, and did not mean much to him or to us; and yet—or therefore?—Pierrot was irresistible, and we mourn him. In Miss Barrymore, surely, he has come to life again. He is more blithe than of yore, sheds not a single tear; and yet we have all the old sense of sadness from him, for in his gaiety there is all the old un-meaning—the old wistfulness of one who is but playing at life and has no hold on what he turns for us 'to favour and to prettiness.' Yes, here, for the first time on the modern stage, is Pierrot himself. In modern real life he is not at all rare. He is never rare in any much civilised community; and it is usually into the body of a woman that his soul enters. Pierrot women—women whose defect and charm alike are in their detachment from the realities of life—women who sadden and delight us by their incapacity for aught but trifles—are as common now in London and New York as at the Court of Louis Quinze. They are, indeed, a salient type of the age. They differ in many ways, of course, from their forerunners. They are not artificial. (There is little time for artifice in the wear and tear of modern life: the motor-car has swept much before it.) And they have that freedom and frankness of manner that comes of being (as women now are, more or less) taken seriously. No play has yet been written with the modern Pierrot woman as central figure. And, indeed, to draw her well would need a far subtler hand than is possessed by the average dramatist; nay, such a plexus of nuances as she could hardly be drawn well but by Mr Henry James himself. But, whether this great part be ever written or not, there is but one person to play it; and Miss Barrymore is that person.

Cynthia is the work of Mr Henry Hubert Davies. He, bless his heart, is not the man for a plexus of nuances. I suspect he would rather I said 'not the boy.' Whenever an infant musician is sprung on the public, his parents and his agent are always at great pains to make the public realise through the interviewers that this is a real, wholesome, childish child, who loves a good romp with others of his own age, and spends most of his time on a rocking-horse. Now, Mr Davies himself is by way of being an infant dramatist; but he is not such an infant that he needs any one else to keep the public keenly alive to the fact of his infancy: he knows how to work the reminders himself. In case his rare instinct for dramatic craftsmanship, and his flashes of very real and delightful humour, should cause the audience to forget how wonderfully young he is, he takes care that his knowledge of life shall seem to be that of a child on a rocking-horse. The scene of the play must needs be a boudoir, peopled by adults; but nothing there shall happen that could conceivably happen anywhere but upstairs in the nursery. It is conceivable that if Cynthia in real life were seven years old she might behave somewhat as Cynthia in *Cynthia* behaves. Long before her ninth birthday she would, however, have learnt better. It would be tedious to examine in detail the impossibility of Mr Davies's Cynthia—an impossibility which none can know better than Mr Davies himself. I will content myself by imploring this gifted young man to let us take our chance of remembering how very young he is. His cunning over-reaches itself. The infant musician does not bestride a rocking-horse on the platform of the concert-hall.

[*12 May 1904*]

'HIPPOLYTUS' ON THE MODERN STAGE

Thanks to the New Century Theatre, Professor Gilbert Murray's translation of the *Hippolytus* was produced last week at the Lyric.

59

I went to the second of three performances, and went very eagerly, as always to anything that is outside the arid little area of commerce. I was determined to enjoy it. It was my sacred duty to enjoy it. All my colleagues on the daily press had enjoyed it immensely. I felt they were rather proud of themselves for having done so. I would do so, but my pride should be dissembled. Such a mood as this, I recognised, was a rather dangerous mood. It might tempt me to pretence. The fear of pretending to enjoy the thing made me morbidly self-conscious. Even before the end of Aphrodite's initial speech, I caught myself wondering whether I were really and truly falling under the poet's spell, and had a vague suspicion that I wasn't. Soon the vague suspicion became a shrewd one, and later a certainty. Came the son of Theseus with his huntsmen to lay the fresh-gathered garland at the feet of Artemis; and came the chorus of women, singing the secret sorrow of Phaedra; yet came not I under the poet's spell. Poet's? The apostrophe should be after the s. For Professor Murray is no pedant: he is that rare creature, a scholar with a bloom upon his scholarship. As translator of Euripides, he is a poet in the service of a poet. Already I had read his version, and marvelled at the skill and beauty of it. The choice of metre—rhyming pentameters— had seemed to me most felicitous, as rendering the sweetness of Greek iambics more nearly than it could be rendered through English blank verse. And the Choruses, in their various metres, rose in real lyric waves. All the verse, throughout the play, was vivid and (rarer quality) vocal. And yet, in the theatre, I was not happy. I blushed for myself. My friend Mr Grein has recalled the fact that Euripides was born more than two thousand three hundred years ago; and 'the thought is apt,' says he, 'to scorch our cheeks with a flame of shame.' I, too, was wishing, amidst my blushes, that Euripides had been born among us. But my wish was not formed by creditable wrath that we, with all our modern appliances, cannot produce so great a dramatic genius as could those poor benighted Athenians. My wish came of the base conviction that, if Euripides were a living dramatist, I could appreciate him better than I can appreciate him as he was, in the modern theatre. The modern theatre—'voila l'ennemi!' Three years ago I saw at Bradfield College a performance of the Agamemnon. The memory of that day abides with me as the memory of a true aesthetic delight. This month, another Greek play is to be done at Bradfield; and I doubt not that the *Alcestis* will enthral me there as did the *Agamemnon*. For the proper enjoyment of a Greek play, circumstances are everything. One must—I, at least, in my unimaginativeness, must—have that which switches the play out of the present into its own past. Firstly, the play must be acted in the original Greek. As I have said, I cannot imagine a more skilful and beautiful translation of a Greek play than Professor Murray's of the *Hippolytus*. But so remote a thing from me is Greek drama that even the best setting of it in my own language is fatal to my receptivity. Secondly, the play must be acted in some such theatre as that for which it was written, and by which it was conditioned. I am no pillar of the Elizabethan Stage Society. I regard that institution as premature. Elizabethan drama is still near enough to us to dispense with any archaistic mode of presentment. There are, indeed, in Elizabethan drama many things which only through modern presentment can gain the exact value at which the Elizabethan dramatists were aiming. But Greek drama is on quite another plane. Realism is fatal to it. The sharp, minute effects of the modern theatre do but make its sublimity a kind of baldness. It needs the open air. Itself a sacrament, it needs the sacramental sky above it. Itself so simple and so ideal, it needs a simple mechanism that shall keep it from all contact with reality. At Bradfield, thanks to a happy freak of nature wrought on by art and archaeology, there is a real Greek theatre. In our midst there, beneath us, the chorus circles round a little altar; and above them is the royal palace, with its three doors. Nothing is there amiss— nothing to intrude modern thoughts on us. We are Athenians in Athens. In our veins flows the blood of the heroes represented on the stage; and we, with them, are in the power of the gods. It may be that even in the auditorium of the Lyric Theatre some people may have abandoned themselves even thus. Happy people! For me that row of footlights, shining on that excellent scenery, was a fast link to the inappropriate present. Self-detachment, self-abandonment, were impossible. Some of the ladies in the chorus evidently wore corsets beneath their draperies; and that seemed to me a symbol of the whole matter. Artemis came strolling sedately from the prompt side, through the well-painted glade, mounted a step or two of the palace, and stood beneath a dreadful little statue of herself. Aphrodite had stood on the side beneath an equally dreadful little statue of herself. Why these two statues? They may have had in themselves some kind of archaeological justification (though they certainly had none, and no reason of any sort, on the stage). From my distance they looked as if they might be Tanagra figures, enlarged and gaudily painted; but they looked much more like German angels of wax, adapted. In any case, I never saw a more ignoble effect. I suppose their purpose was to distinguish as goddesses the two figures who stood under them. But the effect was ludicrous, as any one could have foreseen. The King and Queen of England, when they particularly wish to impress us with their high estate, do not go and stand beside their effigies at Madame Tussaud's. They drive out in the state coach. Similarly, Aphrodite and Artemis at the Lyric should have appeared on some modified form of the Θεολογεῖον. They could not of course, have appeared, in the old style, on the roof of the palace. The best way would have been for them to appear simply through the royal door. As it was, they were ridiculous. But, after all, could they, in any case, have impressed me rightly? Not in the modern theatre. Olympians won't do there. And if they won't do, how am I to be impressed by the play itself? For on the grandeur and awfulness of these Olympians all the play depends. Take from me the illusion of their grandeur and awfulness—that illusion which is mine in reading the original version to myself, and were mine in seeing a thoroughly archaic performance—and for me, thus shown, what remains? Unless I believe that the persons of the play are but puppets worked by all-jealous powers from above, the play has no meaning for me at all. Judged as a whole, it becomes (despite manifold details of beauty and truth) at once hideous, incoherent, and unreal. Losing the illusion of Olympus, and hampered with the illusion of free will, one judges the story from a modern standpoint. It becomes a modern story. Colonel Smith is ordered to South Africa. He leaves behind him Mrs Smith, and a young man who is his illegitimate son. This young man is of character so consciously blameless that some people think him rather a prig. But . . . you may parallelise the rest for yourself. Having done so, you can imagine the effect that the *Hippolytus* had on me in the modern theatre.

Even in ideal conditions, one would have to confess that the play does not show Euripides at his best. And no one, I fancy, would be quicker to make this confession than Euripides himself. As it stands,

the *Hippolytus* was written to conciliate the Athenian public. There
had been a previous version, traditionally known to us as the *Hippolytus Veiled*. Therein Phaedra told her love to Hippolytus, was rejected by him, and straightway accused him before Theseus; seeing
him dead, she was stricken by remorse, and killed herself. That is
a strong and straightforward story. But the Athenian public flinched
from it, and Euripides proceeded to write the second version. Herein
the great scene between Hippolytus and Phaedra is shirked. Hippolytus hears of Phaedra's love only through the agency of an indiscreet nurse. And even weaker than this alteration is the manner of
Phaedra's death and revenge. To take a living vengeance by making
a false accusation, and to kill oneself for remorse, is a natural tragic
development. But to kill oneself and leave a false accusation against
the living is as unnatural as it is ignoble. However, the Athenians
accepted the revised version of what they had rejected. Like our
own public, evidently they were tolerant of an unpleasant play so
long as there was not in it much truth to nature. I offer this deduction to Mr Grein, in the hope that it may somewhat subdue that
frequent 'flame of shame.'

The performance of the play was wonderfully good, considering
that all the performers, with one exception, had been chosen from
among the younger mimes, and considering how little experience
these younger mimes have had in this kind of work. Miss Olive, as
Phaedra, and Mr Webster as Hippolytus, and Mr Brydone, as
Theseus, all comported themselves with the proper dignity and
restraint, and all spoke the long speeches with admirable clearness
and sense of rhythm. The most salient success was that of Mr
Granville Barker, as the bondsman who brings the news of Hippolytus's death. Beginning in a low key, his voice rose by subtle
gradations to the highest pitch of passion, and then, towards the
end, gradually declined till it sank into silence. A fine achievement
in declamation, and worthy of the speech itself. As the speech was
written so was it spoken, with just that mastery of climax and anti-
climax which makes an artistic whole.

[*4 June 1904*]

A PLAY AND A MIMIC

Not to be bored by a melodrama is a rather strange and pleasant experience, which was mine, a few nights ago, at the Duke of York's Theatre. How came it? Partly because the players themselves looked so strange and pleasant, in the costume of the 'fifties—the ladies with bandeaux and pellerines and mushroom hats, the gentlemen with 'chokers' and 'Palmerston curls.' But more especially because they, in this gracious by-gone guise, were impersonating credible human beings. How came credible human beings into melodrama? Because Miss Margaret Young had pitched her play *The Edge of the Storm* in a milieu where human beings really do behave melodramatically. She wafts us first into the thick of the Magyar surge of '48, and thence into the Indian mutiny. It seems to me quite credible that an Hungarian girl, named Szentes Leta, should release an innocent captive who had been brought to her father's castle, and should hand to him the knife with which she had severed his cords, and that he therewith should stab, unwittingly, her father, who tried to bar his exit. My friend Mr Archer brands this episode as 'picturesque, but wholly unreal.' To me, too, no doubt, it would seem unreal, if the girl were represented as the daughter of an English gentleman, residing at this moment in this or some other calm metropolis. Given Hungaria and '48, it strains my credulity no more than the story of a courtesan who marries and is furious that the neighbours don't leave cards, or the story of a lady who, discovering that her husband does not take her seriously enough, goes out and slams the front-door. In the dim future mankind may grow so utterly calm and well-regulated that Mr Archer will be looked back on as a raving lunatic for having supposed such persons as Paula and Nora to bear some resemblance to real persons. Or perhaps that posterity will be elastic-minded enough to put itself in Mr Archer's place, thus shaming the ashes of him who could not put himself in Leta's. If Leta were an English girl, with two English cousins, who, after her father's death, travelled with her for nine years, seeking to avenge blood with blood, I should shrug my shoulders uniformly with Mr Archer's. But, as the three travellers are scions of an intense and barbaric race, I am quite unable to pooh-pooh them, and I gladly believe in them, and am in-

terested in the things that are to happen so soon as they come up
with the murderer. Nor do merely melodramatic things happen
then. On the contrary, there is quite enough inward emotion to go
on with. The situation is a strong one, and it is worked out by Miss
Young with considerable restraint and skill. To explain it, I must
explain that the murderer, Mr Poulett, has become a man of some
importance in India. He is so faithfully guarded by his servants
that the two cousins are unable to poison him. So they contrive
that Leta shall marry him. She, though she has taken an oath to
avenge the murder does not know that her husband is the murderer,
for the shock of her father's death has deleted all memory of what
just preceded it. Poulett, again, does not know that it was her
father he killed, nor, indeed, that he dealt a fatal blow to any one.
There you have the situation. Very skilfully written is the scene in
which Poulett gradually learns the truth from his wife. I was
especially struck by one point. In the early part of the conversation,
Leta has been laughing because her English husband has so limited
a range of endearments, and can but say 'Leta. My Dear. My wife'
over and over again. At the end of the scene, as he moves away
trying to conceal his agitation, she calls to him, asking what is the
matter; and he, in an access of tenderness, turns to her, and becomes quite eloquent of his love; but she stops him, saying that she
likes best the way she had laughed at; and so he repeats 'Leta. My
dear. My wife.' There you have an example of true dramatic instinct—of that art of preparation whereby a scene may be made to
yield its full measure of effect. Admirable, again, is the scene in
which Leta, knowing now who her husband is, stands torn by
inward conflict—on the one hand her oath and her half-savage
instincts, and on the other her love for her husband. He, characteristically of his type, does not try to influence her unduly; he just puts
the case fairly to her; and she, not listening to the masculine British
arguments, waits for the stronger emotion to come upmost in her,
and presently falls into his arms. And then—bang! Melodrama has
re-asserted its rights. The male cousin, entering unseen, has aimed
a bullet at the husband, but has hit the wife. (By the way, Mr
Forbes Robertson seemed to have swung Miss Gertrude Elliot
neatly round in self-protection. A most un-English effect.) Leta is
carried to a couch; and her husband is just going to be beside
himself with grief, when a servant rushes in with the news that

the mutineers are at the gates. So the husband is sunk in the Englishman, and Poulett heads the household against the common foe, and presently the foe is driven off, and—oh joy!—Leta's wound is not fatal. This description sounds rather flippant, but I vow I did truly rejoice that Leta was not going to die. For Leta had become a real person to me, and so had her husband; and thus her salvation gave me the same thrill as runs through simpler— enviably simpler—souls than mine when all is well with the heroine of an ordinary melodrama that has no connection with reality.

To Leta Miss Gertrude Elliott lent all her charm. It was a per- formance exquisite in prettiness and pathos, but it lacked the strain of semi-savagery which is needed to give full effect to Leta's final submission. Needed, too, for that full effect, is that Poulett should appear to be, as the author drew him, just a plain, decent Briton. Mr Forbes Robertson cannot help appearing to be some- thing more than that—a disability which is, in other impersonations, the secret of his hold on us.

Mimicry is a thing that has always interested me. As is parody to literature, so (at its best) is mimicry to acting—a subsidiary art, but still, authentically, an art. The two things have this further point in common: each of them is, for the most part, a speciality of youth. Read any undergraduate journal, and you will find that it is mainly composed of parody, unconscious and conscious. Only a very precocious undergraduate has original thoughts or feelings. His soul is still vacant, gaping for the contents of other souls. It is still malleable, and may be from moment to moment moulded to any shape. Maturity fills it from within and fixes it. And thenceforth its owner has no power of parody, and no desire of parody. That is the normal course. But sometimes a mature man retains this desire and this power. Mr Kipling is an instance of a mature man with the desire but without the power. Signally precocious in artistic execu- tion, he has always been signally backward in intellectual develop- ment. As a young man he took exactly the same kind of interest in soldiers and sailors and steam-engines as most of us take between the ages of five and ten. Last year I was amused to find that he had just reached the undergraduate stage: he was trying his hand at literary parodies. And here came in the pathos of the situation: these paro- dies, so dull and feeble that no undergraduate editor would have accepted them on their merits, were blazoned forth, day after day, as a special feature of a newspaper that has a huge circulation among quite grown-up persons. Now, the power of mimicry deserts the average man at the same time, and for the same reason, as the power of parody. Before he is twenty the average youth can catch, more or less recognisably, the tone of voice and the tone of mind of his friends. Later, his own mind acquires so distinct a tone, and he becomes so accustomed to the sound of his own voice, that his efforts at mimicry (if he make any) are dire failures. Occasionally, however, a man retains the knack even in his prime, and even though he has a distinct individuality. In him, and in him only, we behold the complete mimic. For mimicry is a form of criticism, and a distinct individuality—a point of view—is as needful in the mimic as in the critic. Mimicry that is a mechanical reproduction of voice and gesture and facial play is a mere waste of time, and trial of patience. Yet that is the kind of mimicry that is nearly always offered to us. A man comes upon the platform, and reproduces verbatim some scene of a recent play exactly as it was enacted by this or that mime. If he were a parrot, the effect would be amusing; for it is odd to hear a bird uttering human inflections. But he happens to be a man; and so we are merely bored. His method being an exactly faithful reproduction of his subject's, we have no inclination to laugh; and the only pleasure we might be expected to gain would be when the subject were one for which we had a profound admiration; but even so we should be more irritated than pleased. We should be wanting the real thing. An exact reproduction of the real thing can never be a satisfactory substitute. And if the average mimic is not a satisfactory substitute, what, in reason's name, is he? The proper function of the mimic is, of course, like that of the parodist in words, or of the caricaturist in line, to exaggerate the salient points of his subject so that we can, whilst we laugh at a grotesque superficial effect, gain sharper insight into the subject's soul, or, more strictly, behold that soul as it appears to the performer himself.

This function is well understood and performed by Mr J. Arthur Bleackley, whose imitations I heard last Monday at the Queen's Gate Hall. True, he is, to a certain extent, still influenced by the phonographic convention. His first imitation was of a well-known scene in *A Pair of Spectacles*, enacted by Mr Hare and Mr Groves. But as soon as that was over, he took the proper tack, riotously exaggerating how his subjects would appear if they were called on to do some quite incongruous thing, and thus showing up clearly to us their peculiarities in the performance of appropriate and familiar things. Even better, as giving yet more scope for his critical instinct, was Mr Bleackley's imaginary rehearsal of an imaginary play in which all the leading mimes were to take part. Mr Bleackley prefaced his entertainment with an earnest assurance that there was no malice in it, and that he had the most profound admiration for all his subjects. Strange that people do not understand that for any one to laugh at what he loves is quite as natural and inevitable in him as to laugh at what he hates, and that the only things which never amuse him are the things to which he is indifferent.

[*11 June 1904*]

LOVE-SCENES ON THE STAGE

Undoubtedly, the passion of love is the best of all themes for drama. But it is not the only theme, and I regret that it is so regarded by our playwrights, and, that, even when some adventurous one dares to take another central motive, such as the passion for gold, always must Eros be dragged in by the curls. However, my present concern is not to deplore this custom, but to note a rather curious fact in connection with it. In all these love-plays there are very few love-scenes, and these few are always very brief and perfunctory. Scenes of doubt and misunderstanding between the lovers are common enough, and elaborate enough. But, when the course of their love is running smoothly—howsoever smoothly—we have but the faintest and most fugitive glimpses of their so important love-making. What reason is there for this anomaly?

The reason is partly in the national character—in that self-consciousness which makes English people so very inarticulate, so very inexpressive of their emotions. English people often can and do, as is proved by the reports of actions for divorce or breach of promise of marriage, write ardent love-letters. Through an indirect medium they can express themselves finely enough (though I suspect that these letters are not so much a spontaneous ebullition as the fruit of a resolve to do what is romantically expected of themselves both by their correspondents, and by themselves, and that a good deal of time and at least one rough copy are needed in the composition of them). Set the two people face to face, and they are practically tongue-tied. They can perform love's pantomime—kisses, clasped hands, and so forth. But love's litany is beyond them. They can deal only in the conventional formulae of one or two syllables, or in the conventional question and answer. Anything like a gush of words or a flight of fancy would put them to the blush. It would sound insincere to them both. In only the tritest kind of talk, quite inadequate to express what they are feeling, will they dare indulge. 'D'you love me?' 'You know I do. D'*you* love *me?*' 'Yes, you know I do.' Of this interchange of question and answer, repeated at short intervals in exactly the same form, and eked out with a small stock of endearing ejaculations, is composed the English love-scene (whatever its duration) in real life. It is, no doubt, a very various and beautiful scene to the two persons by whom it is enacted. But transfer it verbatim to the stage, and even the most indulgent audience would presently be bored by it. Realism, then, won't do. On the other hand, the interlocutors must not be made eloquently expressive. Of course, in a romantic drama, with costumes of a by-gone age, you may have a love-scene of passionate avowals in tirades, with tropes and metaphors, with sun and moon and stars. It is a moot point whether at any time in the world's history, and even in the most meridional countries, have lovers orally expressed themselves in such a fashion. No matter: romance is licensed. But if in the modern realistic or quasi-realistic drama of English life there appeared two lovers capable of expressing orally the depth and heat of their mutual sentiment, the audience would instantly and unanimously be rocking with laughter. Thus the dramatist is beset by two dangers: on the one hand, his love-scenes will be tedious because inexpressive: on the other, they will be ridiculous because expressive. It is, however, possible to effect a compromise, and the dramatist does his best. He tries hard for such a blend of the actual prose and the needful poetry as shall counteract the ill-effects of each. I think I see him at his desk, biting the tip of his pen, gloomily. At length, after a long mental struggle, he sets his pen to paper, and writes

HAROLD. '*Mildred!*'

MILDRED. '

He paces up and down his room for a few minutes, and then, with a shrug of his shoulders, inserts *Harold!*'
More pacing up and down, and presently is added

HAROLD. *'My darling!'*
MILDRED. *'My darling!'*
(*They embrace.*)
HAROLD. '

He nerves himself with a cigarette, and writes boldly, blindly

The very first time I saw you—you remember? it was in the orchard.'—(She presses his hand.) 'The apple-blossoms
He deletes the apple-blossoms, and hurries on to

'Well at the moment of seeing you, I knew—even then—that I loved you.'
MILDRED. '

After some hesitation, the dramatist rises, puts on his hat, and goes out for a long, brisk walk. On his return he is delivered as follows:

And I, too, Harold, knew that I loved you.'
HAROLD. *'Dear one!'*
MILDRED. *'Dearest!'*
(*They embrace.*)

Such is the compromise that our dramatist makes; and really, considering all things, I think his work is as good as it could possibly be. But oh the feeling of utter fatuousness in doing it, and oh the fatigue of doing it, and oh the long refreshing sleep when it is done! I do not wonder that the poor fellow does it as seldom and as succinctly as he can. An Englishman is always embarrassed in writing a love-scene—always feels that he is making an ass of himself. If it be a love-scene in a novel, he can save his face by turning it from the lovers to the landscape. The lovers must say something from time to time; but . . . *All nature seemed to be holding her breath. In a glory of gold and purple the sun sank behind the western hills. A heron came flying across the lake. It tipped the water with a wing of silver. Somewhere in the distance a chaffinch was calling to her mate. Her insistent note* . . . and so forth, *ad infinitum.* Or again, if Nature is out of the environment, *From below there came to them, like the sound of some great distant orchestra, the murmuring hum of the great city.* Here follows the author's apostrophe to London, or to Manchester, or whatever the place happens to be. After that, perhaps, the lovers say something;

70

and then, *Under the window a street organ was playing some waltz. For years after, Harold could never hear that air without living again that hour that he had spent with Mildred.* And then, either we are told that he could always remember clearly what she was wearing (this is described), and every object in the room (these are catalogued), or we have a disquisition on the mnemonic power of sound as compared with that of sight and scent. Thus in novels the love-scenes are comparatively long and elaborate. But the poor dramatist is debarred from the novelist's happy subterfuges. He cannot write around his characters. He must simply find in his heart words for their lips to utter, and kisses for their lips to exchange. Play-writing—I mean, of course, the writing of plays for the theatre: the only defensible kind of play-writing—is always, necessarily, the form of art least satisfying to the practitioner. It is but a series of suggestions thrown out in the hope that other people will, later on, make something of them. The task of play-writing can be tolerated only by a man who either loves the theatre for its own sake or is very keen to make money. For it is not a task lightened, as the task of writing a poem or an essay or a story is lightened, and transformed into a joy, by the sense of an effect that is being accomplished, once and for all, by oneself. Play-writing is so indirect and so incomplete a form of artistic activity that no man, however apt to it, can work himself up through it to any heat of creative passion. The playwright cannot lose himself in his task, for his task depends not on himself alone, and is his but in part. He must work always in cold blood, with an austere eye on the horizon, and with a pious hope for mercy from powers unseen. No wonder that he, working under these conditions, and he an Englishman, with all an Englishman's reticence in matters of sentiment, dreads the task of partially unpacking his heart with words for Mildred and Harold, and writing them solemnly down on foolscap paper in order that they may be hereafter spoken by Mr Dash and Miss Blank at the Theatre Royal Asterisk. The wonder is that he does not shirk altogether a task so hard.

[18 June 1904]

THE 'ALCESTIS' AT BRADFIELD COLLEGE

Two performances have already been given. Today—Saturday—there will be another; others again on Monday and Tuesday. And Bradfield is a very accessible place, and the special arrangements made for visitors preclude any discomfort. So that, really, no one who cares for Greek drama has any excuse for not going to see the *Alcestis*. Every such one must be grateful to Dr Gray, the Warden. For by him is offered to us a unique pleasure—the unique pleasure of seeing a Greek play performed under the only conditions which are appropriate and satisfying. Let us be grateful to the stray enthusiasts who, from time to time, enable us to see a Greek play under makeshift conditions. But gratitude for what is merely better than nothing must be of a somewhat chastened kind. Greek drama performed in a modern theatre is merely, and barely, better than nothing. There is the right and the wrong place for everything, but especially for some things. In a Scotch tabernacle the rites of the Free Kirk of Scotland, as by law established, are finely impressive. In a Gothic cathedral they would leave you cold. You are finely impressed by His Majesty's Levee in St James's Palace. But the ceremonial would seem absurd if it were repeated, however faithfully, at the corner of Fenchurch Street. In like manner, whose sense of fitness is not fatally outraged by Greek drama in a modern theatre, however well ventilated? The open air is essential to such drama. For such broad and grandiose effects there must be a broad and grandiose setting. We must have the sky, with its sunshine or its clouds. At Bradfield we have it. If the day be fine, so much the better. But a downpour of rain would not be really amiss. No mood of the elements could be really amiss. Of course, the open air, though it is essential, is not in itself sufficient to our perfect pleasure. We must be sitting in a Greek theatre. Only so can we appreciate the play, seeing the chorus in its right relation to the play's action, and the actors in their relation to ourselves. There is no marble at Bradfield (why does not some less than usually unimaginative millionaire step forth to play Augustus?); but the benches of the amphitheatre, hewn from what was erst a chalk pit, are as hard as marble, and the little cushions handed to us by the wand-bearers are presumably like those which the Athenian playgoers brought with them. There is nothing to mar the illusion created by the lozenged orchestra, by the faintly burning altar of Dionysus, and by the proscenium, with its columns and its pediment. Above us, fringing the uppermost benches, are trees in full leaf, with birds at song in them; and one spies not the absence of fig and olive. Somewhere beneath the eaves of the proscenium a swallow had built her nest; and she was darting hither and thither, last Tuesday, over the obsequies of Alcestis. It seemed right that the bird that comes from afar should have her habitation in this theatre that has come from afar to us. It seemed peculiarly right that the *avis Attica* should be just here, in this place so redolent of the poets who loved her. Anxious Procne!—does she think that she has found at last, in this dell of Berkshire, Tireus's palace?

The performance of a Greek play at Bradfield is a lesson in the extent to which archaeology may minister to art. Because the conditions are just those under which Greek poets wrote dramas, our receptivity is that of a Greek audience. Because everything is as it was everything is as it should be. Everything? No, there is one exception. I think that when I was writing about the *Agamemnon*, four years ago, I expressed a regret that the mimes were not masked and buskined. They are not yet in that proper state. 'All the essential features of Greek Tragedy,' says the programme, 'will be reproduced, except the masks and the high cothurni, which are considered unsuitable to the conditions of modern art.' I agree that they are utterly unsuitable to the conditions of modern art. Aubrey and Paula Tanqueray, strutting exalted, and mouthing expressionless, would be more than mild surprise. But they, you see, are meant to represent an ordinary lady and gentleman of today, and masks and buskins have not yet come into fashion among us. The Greek dramatist did not seek to represent ordinary ladies and gentlemen. His characters were mythical and conventional figures. He was an idealist. What have 'the conditions of modern art' got to do with the production of a Greek play in a Greek theatre? I admit, of course, that Euripides was not an undiluted idealist like Æschylus or Sophocles. He was feeling his way towards a realistic presentment of human beings. His characters had, now and again, thoughts which could hardly be expressed through masks—thoughts which needed the ordinary play of human features. His characters seemed sometimes to be trying to climb down from their buskins. But it

73

would be absurd to call him a realist. Realism was but an under-current of his art. His characters lose, therefore, much more than they gain by any effort to present them in terms of realism. Any departure from strict archaelogy, in the performance of a Greek play, is a hindrance to aesthetic pleasure. It is tedious to find oneself saying what one vaguely remembers to have said four years ago. But, in doing this, I am sustained by the hope that I shall not have to say it again four years hence. I submit to Dr Gray that his refusal to be correct in these two details leaves a real blemish on an otherwise perfect endeavour. I suspect that, when he speaks of 'the conditions of modern art,' what is really in his mind is a fear that masks and buskins might seem ridiculous to a modern audience. It cannot be a fear of difficulty that restrains him, the overcomer of so many difficulties. Besides, it is obvious that there would be no difficulty. Masks and buskins could be designed and made quite easily, and the boys could quite easily be taught to speak through the masks (which, indeed, were so fashioned as to aid the resonance of the voice), and to walk in the buskins. It must be the fear of a ridiculous effect that causes the deliberate inaccuracy. But why should the effect be ridiculous? An Apollo on whose cheeks the light of day illustrates the rouge, a dead Alcestis on whose cheeks the light of day illustrates the powder—such sights as these, seen by us last Tuesday, really are rather ridiculous. But there is in the sight of a tragic mask or a tragic buskin nothing more ridiculous than in the sight of the columns and pediment of a Greek proscenium. More-over, accuracy in this matter would be a source of real benefit to the mimes. To lose self-consciousness is the first essential to good acting. Boys, even among themselves, and in the ordinary routine of life, are more self-conscious than any other class of human beings. If you dress them up in scanty classical costume, and set them in broad daylight on a stage, in the midst of their pastors and masters, their sisters and their cousins and their aunts, then the burden of their self-consciousness must become almost intolerable. To some extent, no doubt, the Bradfield mimes are helped—taken out of themselves —by the remoteness of the language that they are speaking, and by an enthusiastic wish to do as well as possible the thing through which their school derives so much peculiar honour. But it is quite certain that they would be much happier, and would be able to act much more spontaneously, if they were not face to face with their pastors and masters, their sisters and their cousins and their aunts. For their sake, as well as for ours and archaeology's and art's and Bradfield's, I respectfully conjure Dr Gray to re-consider his prejudice in the ample time that will elapse before the next production.

I understand that these productions are regarded by Dr Gray as primarily educational—as a means to quickening in his pupils an understanding and a love of their Greek studies. I suspect that, when he chose the *Alcestis* for this year, he was in a more than usually scholastic mood. The *Alcestis* is a standing dish at Matriculation, Smalls, Mods. As a play, however, it is surely the least good thing that Euripides did. The theme is not really susceptible of tragic treatment. Admetus, as central figure of a tragedy, won't do at all. You may make all kinds of ingenious excuses for him. You may say that he was very hospitable, and that he was very fond of his wife, and very grateful to her for dying in his stead, and that he would always have been faithful to her memory. But all that is beside the mark. The point is not whether he is a bad man. The point is that he cuts a ridiculous figure. To the Greeks, by whom women were held of less account than by us they are, he did not, of course, cut quite so ridiculous a figure. But even to the Greeks a hero who stood uncomfortably but unresistingly by, while a heroine died to prolong his existence, could not have been acceptable. So it boots not that at Bradfield we can see Admetus through Greek eyes. No sense of pity or awe is raised in us. We can but raise our eyebrows. And the worst of one ridiculous figure in tragedy is that he abides not alone in ridiculousness: inevitably he infects the rest. Poor Alcestis! We cannot take seriously her self-sacrifice for such a figure of fun as is Admetus. Evidently, Euripides himself felt the impossibility of his theme. Heracles in his cups is not a figure which he would have introduced into a tragedy that seemed to him tragic. But it was natural that he should foist in this fragment of satyric drama to redeem from dulness a tragedy by which not he nor anyone else could be tragically impressed; for better no unity of impression than an impression of uniformly wasted tragic poetry. Thus the *Alcestis* survives for us not as a work of art, but as a curiosity.

[*25 June 1904*]

CLEMENT SCOTT'S WORK

There is always something rather ghastly in the thought that every daily newspaper keeps in its pigeon-holes obituary notices of every living man or woman who is at all conspicuous. Rather ghastly, this careful preparation of salutes to follow 'pat' on that which may strike down unawares its actual victim. Even in the case of a man whose death has been long foreseen, sensitive people would prefer that the end should be patiently awaited by journalists, for composition, not less than for publication, of the elegies. I admit that any single daily paper which submitted to this ideal would find itself at a grave disadvantage with its competitors. I suppose, too, it were Utopian to hope that all the proprietors and editors might hold a conference, and feel their way to a general disarmament—a general consent to clear these pigeon-holes of their contents. But it is natural to desire even an impossible remedy for an unseemly system. This particular system is even less pleasing when the subject of the pigeon-holed obituary is a man intimately associated with the newspaper to which the pigeon-hole belongs; and especially worse if the obituary contains a destructive criticism of his services to that newspaper. I wonder if the obituarist of the *Daily Telegraph* has already recorded that Mr Bennet Burleigh was not, in the true significance of the word, a war-correspondent, and that Lord Burnham was not, in the true significance of the word, a Baron. These would be ungracious sayings; but not less ungracious than to say of the late Mr Clement Scott, as was said of him in the *Daily Telegraph* last Monday, that 'he was not, in the true significance of the word, a critic.' Perhaps the ungraciousness may be condoned for the candour: one cannot but admire the candour of a newspaper which states that what it purveyed as criticism for twenty-five years was not really criticism at all. However, I am concerned rather with the validity of the statement than with the propriety of making it; and I think that to deny that Mr Scott was a critic betrays a stupidly and dangerously narrow view of the functions of criticism. 'A brilliant impressionist, and unflinching advocate, a fearless partisan if you will, but,' reiterates the pious obituarist, 'not a critic.' It is evidently implied that a critic is a dry person, who can minutely dissect his subject, and then can separate those parts of it which are respectively, according to certain rules which he has learnt, good and bad, and can then with a steady hand weigh them in a pair of scales and register the balance for our inspection; and it is evidently implied that no other kind of person is a critic. Well, the kind of person here described is indubitably a critic, and indubitably a useful critic, and not so uncommon as one might fear. But it is foolish to pretend that he exhausts the possibilities. It is foolish to pretend that the art of criticism includes nothing which is outside his range. There are many other kinds of authentic critic; and one of them is he who passionately loves the art-form which is his subject, and cannot treat it calmly—must, rather, dance around it in a frenzy of worship, like a Bacchanal around the woodland altar. On such a man we must keep a watchful eye. We must not implicitly trust him. We may dance with him, but warily, ready to retire at any moment and leave him to his own gyrations. Assuredly, such a man is apt to be dangerous. He is full of passionate superstitions. He, for whom his altar is the world's hub, must needs falter in knowledge of the world. His sense for art overrides his sense for life; and, since life is art's theme, his judgments must often be amiss. Moreover, it is likely that he, like other fanatics, will be as narrow as he is intense in his interpretation of the nature of his god. For him his god is this and this, but not that and that. Some sacrifices on the altar are, he thinks, acceptable, but others are abominable. Some methods of art, thinks such a critic, are right, but others are all wrong. The truth is, of course, that in every art all the methods are right, and the only thing that matters is the degree of skill used in the practice of this method or that. But it is likely, and usual, that the very intensity which makes a man whole-hearted in devotion to one art-form will foster in him strong predilections and prejudices concerning the various methods in that art-form. Thus will he be often blind to the merits of a thing well done in a way of which he disapproves, and blind often to the defects of a thing ill done in a way of which he approves. On the other hand, he will be a far keener and more stimulating interpreter of good things within his rubric than ever can be his more expansive—and therefore less intensive—brother in criticism; and a far keener and more stimulating exposer of bad things outside his rubric. His work will teem with injustice; but also he will be capable of a finer justice than can be dealt by gentlemen who lack his limitations. You may prefer the writer who, having no

77

point of view, is never wrong. But it is unfair to withhold the title of critic from the writer who, having a point of view, is either sharply right or sharply wrong. Such a writer, and such a critic, was Mr Clement Scott. I admit that, in his later period—the period in which his writings were known to me—he seemed to be more often sharply wrong than sharply right. He was wont to pour scorn on those critics who had been in their cradles whilst he was fighting the good fight of dramatic progress. I was one of these critics, and it was our misfortune that he, subject to the inexorable law of time, was no longer in the vanguard, lustily and invaluably one of ourselves. We knew him only as a reactionary. Other reactionaries there were, but they did not count. He alone was redoubtable, in virtue of that very intensity which had made him erst a redoubtable progressive, and in virtue of the power to express that intensity through the medium of writing. He alone had, as it were, a voice that carried. Not every intense person has that, though none but the intense person has it. There are emotionally intense persons whose voices don't carry among the many, and intellectually intense persons whose voices don't carry even among the few—persons whose vocal cords don't happen to have the needful formation; in other words, persons born without the talent for writing. It is easy to say that Mr Scott was a bad writer. But a writer, most assuredly, he was. His language lived—lived every moment of that brief life for which it was destined. Born awfully in the small hours amid printers' devils, it came to crow and kick lustily on all our breakfast-tables. A short life, but a merry one—a very real one so far as it went. Never was journalism more hot and strong, more provocative. We might laugh, we often did laugh; but we could not help being rather angry, too. For here was a voice that carried, and instinctively we wanted to interrupt it, to shout it down, to intercept the mischievous message that it carried to the public. It seemed such a pity that this voice had been bestowed on a man insensible to just those things which ought, in the higher interests of the theatre, to have been especially encouraged. To us, anxious coddlers of the drama of ideas, anxious gropers for the drama of beauty, it was painful to watch this doughty man trampling on every idea as on some noxious beetle, and bayoneting poor beauty. Certainly, Mr Scott did harm to British drama during the 'nineties. But he had helped it not less signally throughout the two preceding decades.

When first he began to write, British drama lay at its nadir, woe-begone and contemned. Mr Scott, with his vivid love of the theatre, and his dreams of what a vivid thing drama ought to be, was shocked and appalled. He went about with a banner and a bludgeon, exhorting and menacing; and gradually the listless throng was shamed. New life crept into the drama, and Mr Scott tended it jealously, lovingly. Let us remember him as he was then, in his youth and prime, the keen reformer—the leader on the right side. And let us not forget that throughout his life he did more than any other man to keep the public interested in the theatre. In England the theatre has always been an artificial institution. Playgoing is not in our veins. We must needs be driven to the theatre. And Mr Scott, even when he was standing in the way of dramatic progress, was indirectly doing good, for that he excited interest not less in what he hated than in what he loved. People were tempted to see what he cursed, not less surely than they were tempted to see what he blessed. It is bad to excite animosity against good things. But it is worse to engender indifference to them. That is what the ordinary critic succeeds in doing. Thus Mr Scott, with his perfervidly positive spirit, may have done, even in the 'nineties, more good than harm. But, after all, he is chiefly memorable not as a stimulator of public interest in plays, nor as a reformer of drama in his earlier years, but as a critic of the art of acting. In that department of criticism he was unrivalled. Here, too, he was not always a safe guide. He had his antipathies and his predilections. But, at worst, how entertaining were his diatribes and his paeans! At best—and his best was frequent—how just and penetrating they were! Certainly, our mimes suffered a very real loss when Mr Scott ceased to write about their art—an art for which so few English critics possess any sense at all, and for which Mr Scott's sense was incomparably keen. It seems a pity that he, whose labour was so imbued with love, outlived the capacity for labour—did not die, as he would have wished to die, 'in harness.' But, had he died so, one could not have seen him thus quickly in perspective, appreciating in him the so much that was admirable.

[2 July 1904]

79

A GEORGIAN PLAY

Women are quite comfortable in some fields of artistic labour. No one is surprised to find them doing light and little things very prettily, very perfectly. There is nothing unfeminine in that sort of power. But it is surprising to find a woman tackling large and heavy things. Such a woman labours under two disadvantages. She is regarded as something of a monstrosity. Also, we are incredulous of her power to compete successfully with men in masculine labour. We are apt to smile with more indulgence than is actually needed, perhaps. She, to ward off our cruel chivalry, shields herself behind a masculine pseudonym. The surname is a matter of choice, but 'George' seems to be almost inevitable. Had George Sand happened to be Edouard Sand, George Eliot would undoubtedly have been Edouard Eliot, and all our other literary ladies would be Edwards, too. As it was, 'George' was the obvious choice for the would-be-masculine heart of Miss Mary Anne Evans, and her successors have caught the trick. An irritating trick, I think. Especially must it irritate gentlemen who, having been baptised George, must either shed the name or be ever dimly associated with womanhood by their readers. Initials are a dreary makeshift for a Christian name; and, moreover they seem to rob the surname of all character. A very distinct personality is discernible behind the writings of 'G. S. Street'; but how insignificant of it is the author's name! 'George Street' would be fully significant—would present to us a sharp and accurate image—but for its instant suggestion of femininity. If Mr Meredith were writing *Richard Feverel* today, he would presently burst on the world as 'G. Meredith.' Otherwise, everyone would suppose him to be a lady. Even after we had read the first few pages, and had discovered quite certainly that this new George must be an authentic man, we should always be hampered by a vague, subconscious vision of him as a very remarkable lady.

Two or three pages of a book, two or three scenes of a play, suffice to determine the author's sex. Last Tuesday, at the Duke of York's Theatre, was enacted *The Pharisee's Wife*, a play in three acts, by George Paston. Even supposing that 'George Paston' were not obviously a pseudonym for a lady, the secret would have been Polichinelle's very soon after the rising of the curtain, and the face

of every man in the audience have been wreathed already with those
indulgent smiles which are so dreaded by ambitious ladies. (Come,
little sisters: once and for all, let go an innocent deception by
which no one is ever deceived.) From first to last, very signally,
The Pharisee's Wife is a Georgian play. By this I mean that it is
unfeminine in so far that its author has tackled a large subject in a
serious spirit, and that it is feminine in every other respect. What,
you may ask, are the respects in which a clever woman's play
differs from a clever man's play? The first respect, then, is that in
a play written by even the cleverest woman the male characters are
little better than dummies. Of course, either of the sexes can only
make guesses at the inner workings of the other. But man's guesses
at woman are admitted even by woman herself to be much better
than woman's guesses at man. The reason may be that man has in
himself more of femininity than there is of masculinity in woman.
Anyhow, there the fact is: male novelists and dramatists often portray a woman to the satisfaction of women, while the converse
wonder has never yet been achieved. In books or plays dealing with
an ethical problem as between sex and sex, there is this further difference between the work of women and the work of men. A man
holds the scales evenly. He lets the opposite sex state its own case
freely, squarely. If anything, he is inclined to let women have the
best of the argument. On the other hand, a woman makes never
more than a pretence of fairplay. Everything is so arranged that the
man's arguments shall be turned inside out and kicked aside as
worthless. Perhaps it is not right to imply that she is consciously
and deliberately unfair. Belike, she is unfair through incapacity to see
more than one side of a question. But, in any case, her one-sided-
ness is a grave defect. It is a grave defect in *The Pharisee's Wife*, a
play which hinges on the relative rights of a husband and wife to
be unfaithful to each other. Henry Carrington, the husband, is not
merely a dummy, as opposed to Mrs Carrington, who is composed
strictly of flesh and blood. He starts further handicapped by being a
Pharisee. He has been married for fifteen years, and has always
appeared to be the incarnation of domestic virtue. One of his wife's
friends has been 'talked about', and he has forbidden his wife to
'receive' her. 'Henry,' his wife says of him, 'was always the most
"proper" of his sex.' Then it suddenly comes out that he has been
having an intrigue with a lady of dubious repute, and that he will

have to appear as co-respondent in the Divorce Court. His wife is horrified by the news, and sends for him. He appears, duly attired in a suit of deep mourning. Then he murmurs a request for forgiveness. 'On what plea,' asks his wife, 'do you ask me to forgive you?' Throwing back his head, he cries out, in ringing accents, 'On the oldest plea of of all! "As you, too, hope to be forgiven." ' The man is evidently a fool, as well as a Pharisee; and no wonder that his wife, having got such a splendid opening, launches out into an overwhelming indictment. Now and again, he interrupts her. But he is hopelessly outmatched. His paltry excuses are brushed aside like cobwebs, gently but firmly—gently, because Mrs Carrington must not for a moment forfeit the sympathy of the audience; firmly, because Mr Carrington must not for a moment gain the sympathy of the audience. All that Mrs Carrington says is quite admirable, as a statement of a faithful wife's case against an unfaithful husband. Of course, no woman in real life, finding herself suddenly in Mrs Carrington's position, would be so ably ratiocinative in prosecution. But that persons in a play should find the right arguments in a crisis, and the right expression for them, is a theatrical convention which one willingly accepts. One asks merely that the arguments shall be tinged with human emotion. Most playwrights, lacking the ratiocinative faculty, give us the emotion without the arguments. Mr Shaw is so strongly devoted to ratiocination that his characters argue as though for mere sake of argument. 'George Paston' is to be congratulated on striking a happy mean, so far as Mrs Carrington is concerned. If only she were a man, to have given Mr Carrington the benefit of being able to stand up to Mrs Carrington and state his case as well as she states hers! It was unfair to make Mr Carrington a fool; and it was unfair, moreover, to make him a Pharisee. Both in mental ability and in charm of character, he ought to have been his wife's equal. Then there might have been a really satisfactory presentment of the general problem that the play raises.

My objection to the play is not merely that it has no general significance. I object, also, that the two particular characters selected by 'George Paston' behave not at all as they conceivably might if they were transferred into reality. The question at the end of the first act is whether Mrs Carrington will, for the sake of her children, continue to live with her husband. In real life she would decide according as whether her distaste for him were greater or less than her anxiety for her children. In this play, she decides that she cannot live with her husband, not because he has deceived her, but because he is not charitable to the shortcomings of other people. She leaves him with the hint that she will return to him as soon as he has 'learnt to forgive.' This is a pretty fancy. We all have pretty fancies, now and again. But we don't so far indulge ourselves as to act on them in genuine crises to which they are quite irrelevant. Besides, how is this pretty fancy ever to be realised? Will Mrs Carrington pay periodical visits of inspection to Mr Carrington's chambers and put him through his paces in the art of forgiveness? Will she prefer to have him watched by private detectives, and receive daily reports as to his progress in the art of forgiveness? A year elapses between the first and second acts; and we find that in this interval even she has begun to see the humour of the situation. She makes merry at the thought of Mr Carrington trying to behave picturesquely for her sake and always being prevented by the unpicturesqueness of the age he lives in. He is, we are told, devoting all his spare time to good works among Hooligans. Presumably he incites them to do wrong things and then practises forgiveness on them.

Another year passes. He has become an adept. A defaulting clerk comes to his rooms, and is neatly forgiven. We wonder if Mrs Carrington is going to rush out from behind a screen and restore conjugal rights. Not so. She is going to test her husband with a fault of her own. She allowed a young man to kiss her a year ago. To Mr Carrington she implies that she went further than that. After a struggle, he neatly forgives her. Then she forgives him, and withdraws her previous implication; and down comes the curtain on an unsatisfactory play. Yet, though we are dissatisfied, we must be thankful to a dramatist who has written something different from the charades to which we are accustomed. We must be thankful for a playwright who is in earnest.

As always happens in a play written by a woman, most of the characters are women, and all the well-drawn characters are women. Mrs Carrington herself, and her mother, and another lady who is separated from her husband, and the lady with whom Mr Carrington fell in love, occupy the greater part of the play. Miss Madge McIntosh played the first of these characters with great sensibility; and Miss Darragh, as the last of them, had a triumph well deserved by imaginative subtlety and technical skill. But Mr Graham Browne, as the young man who admires Mrs Carrington, had little to do but look manly in flannels; and Mr Aubrey Smith, as Mr Carrington, did little but look manly in the deep mourning aforesaid.

[16 July 1904]

'THE CHEVALEER'

Peculiarly blessed, at this season, the lot of the born playgoer. How good it is, for him, to be home once more, going the round of the new plays! His cheeks are flushed, his eyes sparkle, his heart beats high. His holiday soon palled on him. He sighed to find the world so formless, life so diffuse and raw. His stomach rebelled for the neatly cooked slices of life to which it is accustomed. He thought wistfully of those dear neat oppositions of character, those dear slick conflicts of will, framed in gilt frames, with curtains to roll quickly down on them at crucial moments—things with positive beginnings and definite endings, with exciting developments sandwiched in between. The sun seemed to him to be shining too violently, and of no set purpose—to be shining alike on the just and on the unjust—quite otherwise than the gentle and discriminating 'lime'. The sea, too, was over-large, over-insistent—out-of-the-picture. As a back-cloth, seen through a window 'up centre,' the sea is well enough. But as 'mother and lover of men the sea' is outstepping the proper limits of its function. The born playgoer is glad to have left it, and all those other chaotic phenomena, behind him, and to set his face once more to the footlights. The orchestra strikes up. Soon the curtain will rise. And, be the play good or bad, our friend will be well-content. A starving man doesn't stickle about the quality of his meal.

I, who am a made, and not a born, playgoer, find myself in very different case. My dearest delight in the prospect of a holiday is that I shall be quit of theatrical art for a while; and during the holiday itself my delight in being thus quit is cumulative. I become more and more enamoured of the-world-at-first-hand, until I positively sicken at the mention of anything connected with the art of the theatre. Not to be a born playgoer is, in some respects, of course, bad for a dramatic critic in the exercise of his craft. Such an one is apt to be unduly harsh, condemning plays for obedience to conventions which are really inevitable. On the other hand, he has this virtue, denied to the critic who is a born playgoer: he is merciless to the false conventions which the born playgoer either imagines to be inevitable, or imagines not to be conventions at all. He has a wholesome influence, in that he strictly applies to plays the test of actual life; and he may be forgiven if he does not always make due allowance for the necessary little differences between life and art. Towards the end of a season he tends to be less harsh in his judgments. He has become, to a certain extent, habituated to the theatre. He may be deceived even by pieces of flagrant falseness. But this force of habit is only temporary. Away from theatres, he is quickly himself again; and at the end of his holiday he is harder to please than ever.

There are some half-dozen new plays at this moment. As yet, feeling myself to be in a dangerous mood, and wishing my claws to do as little harm as possible, I have seen only one of them. I chose the play at the Garrick Theatre—*The Chevaleer*—because it is by Mr Henry Arthur Jones, who has always seemed to me to be of all successful playwrights the most nearly in touch with actual life—a man of the theatre, assuredly, but a man with only one foot planted in it, with only one eye on it: a man who tries to bring life into the theatre, rather than to clap the theatre down on life.

Though he has never faltered in his allegiance to life, Mr Jones, in his recent work, has (needlessly, I think) narrowed his vision of life. Not only has he, a critic, a man of ideas, kept ideas and criticism outside the scheme of his work, devoting himself almost wholly to comedies of manners and comedies of intrigue: he has further confined himself to the portrayal of one particular class of the community, and to the handling of one particular motive. Letting my memory range over his recent plays, I find that the effect is rather like looking at a frieze in which the same figures recur again and again. Always a fashionable lady and gentleman trying to get themselves out of a scrape; and, though the circumstances of the scrape vary, the scrape is always essentially the same; and the lady and gentleman, and their friends, and the atmosphere, and the issue, are always essentially the same. Nobody could write this kind of play so skilfully—with such lightness and verisimilitude—as Mr

Jones; but it does seem a pity that Mr Jones should be for ever lavishing his power on this one kind of play. Soon after the curtain rose on *The Chevaleer*, I began to fear that Mr Jones had set out determined to give us exactly the same kind of pleasure as we have had so often before. The scene is the hall of the Woolpack Hotel at Grandbury; the time, early morning. A lady, dressed for travelling, cautiously emerges from a door in the gallery. From a door on the other side of the gallery emerges a gentleman. At sight of him she shows signs of great alarm. She says they must not be seen together. We learn that on the previous day she had had a quarrel with her husband, Sir John Kellond, and had hurriedly left the house, to stay with a friend. The young man, who was staying in the house, and who is vaguely in love with her, had followed her to Grandbury, knowing that she would have to wait there to catch her train. Circumstances forced them to sleep at the Woolpack Hotel. Their one object, now, is that no one should know. If the affair leaks out, the lady will be compromised beyond redemption. Here we have all the makings of just such a play as Mr Jones has so often given us. We foresee that there will be dim suspicions and frantic subterfuges, angry accusations by a plain straightforward husband, cynical advice from friends, and all the rest of it. But our prevision is falsified. Mr Jones has so arranged that nobody knows anything about the innocent escapade of Lady Anne Killond and the young man. The rest of the plot hinges on their belief that a certain person does know all about it and is trying to blackmail them. This is a new and amusing idea, and it is worked out very ingeniously. A supposed blackmailer, imagining that the favours showered on him are the reward of his own personal charm, is an invention of which Mr Jones has good reason to be proud. But this invention, in itself, would not be enough to distinguish the play from the rest of Mr Jones's recent work: the atmosphere would be still the same. The play is a departure in virtue of the fact that the blackmailer (who is a central figure, to which all the others are subordinate) is a character copied from low life.

'Copied from'? No, assuredly, Mr Jones invented this Chevaleer out of his own head, or synthesised him out of old novels. I dare say that in the day of Tom Jones, or thereabouts, there may have been travelling showmen not unlike the extraordinary creature that Mr Jones trots out for us. In modern times they do not, could not, exist. The modern proprietor of shows is quite an ordinary man of business; and the Chevaleer, with his wild costume and his wild vocabulary, is not even a caricature: he is a figment, and more frankly a figment than is to be found anywhere in Dickens. The point is whether he is an amusing figment. Usually, on the stage, a character who talks in an eccentric and florid manner, soon becomes a bore. Mr Pinero is very fond of giving us such characters. But Mr Jones has a true sense for the verbal grotesque. The Chevaleer, every time he speaks, says something truly grotesque, and therefore delightful. And, as he talks more or less throughout the entire play, the evening passes very pleasantly.

Mr Bourchier has an admirable conception of the part. But, as usual, he mars his performance by his grim determination to be funny at any price, however cheap. If only he were not manager of his own theatre, if only he were under the control of some stern stage-manager, how capital a comedian he might become! As it is, not content with irrelevant antics and grimaces at every juncture, he is actually beginning to write his own parts. When Lady Anne, in the hotel scene, says that she wants a cup of black coffee and a carriage, Mr Bourchier quickly repeats her order to the proprietor— 'A cup of black carriage.' I urge Mr Bourchier not to go in for authorship. But the exhortation might come with more weight from Mr Jones.

[*10 September 1904*]

SUPERIOR MELODRAMA

The Prayer of the Sword was branded as 'dull' by the one newspaper whose judgments do somewhat affect the fate of plays. Herein, I think, we have an example of one of the many evils of unsigned criticism. When a writer says 'we,' he seems to be striking an average of the community. He is regarded not as a fallible fellow-creature, but as an infallible mouthpiece of the majority of his fellow-creatures. Sometimes the anonymous critic really does attain to that ideal (or, rather, sink from criticism to those depths of insincerity). But, more often, he is a creature of prejudices and moods —things wherefrom he might produce an interesting result if he wrote in the first person singular. Writing in the first person plural, he seems to have no prejudices or moods at all. Even people who know all about journalism from within are often thus impressed by him, despite themselves. How much more surely the outer public! Of course, the impression is usually quite false. When the critic of the *Daily Telegraph* pronounces a play 'dull', he may really have tried, and contrived, to define for himself exactly what constitutes dulness for the average man; and the play of which he writes may come within the rubric of that definition. But, far more likely, he is merely saddling his fellow-creatures with an opinion formed irresponsibly by himself. So it is in this case of *The Prayer of the Sword*. Mr Courtney was depressed by the play. To him it really was dull. But that is no proof that it is dull. On the contrary all the evidence that I have goes to prove that the play is, from the public standpoint, the very reverse of dull. I was unable to go to the first performance at the Adelphi. But when I did go, a few nights later, I found the audience enjoying itself immensely. The comic relief (of which I will tell you presently) was received with deep-throated roars. And the hero was cheered to the echo whenever he said or did anything morally effective, while the villain was hissed conversely. These ebullitions of feeling interested me particularly, as showing the intense fidelity of the English people to local traditions. Outwardly, *The Prayer of the Sword* is a very serious artistic endeavour. Had it been produced in any such theatre as the St James's, the audience would have hardly been conscious that there was a melodramatic hero and a melodramatic villain. Certainly, the audience would not have dared to cheer or hiss. And yet, though the days of the old kind of Adelphi melodrama are gone (from the Metropolis) for ever, and though the Adelphi itself is still echoing to the strains of that piece affectionately known to the many as *The Url and the Gurl*, here is the audience falling straight back into the habits of the Adelphi past. Never anywhere was there less dulness in the atmosphere than when I saw *The Prayer of the Sword*. Keenest vivacity of emotion was all around me.

I have been at pains to contradict Mr Courtney's generalisation, for the play is partly, as I have said, a conscientious attempt to do something good. That alone suffices to set it on a plane higher than the usual, and I should be really sorry if the thing did not succeed. I like Mr James Bernard Fagan for having written it, and Mr

Otho Stuart for having produced it. And now I am free to say that I don't like the play. Mr Fagan's very laudable aim was to write a poetic tragedy; but he seems to me to have achieved neither true poetry nor true tragedy. He has evidently a taste for books. He has evidently ranged, with sensitive appreciation, over all that has been written in the way of poetic drama. He is at home with the Elizabethans. He is at home with Mr Stephen Phillips. Or rather, he is not at home with them: he calls on them, and behaves very modestly and nicely, and after a little while takes his hat, bows himself out, and adds another speech or two to his play. You never feel that his impulse to poetry is from within. You never catch the spontaneous note in him—the original note in him. You feel that he is but chopping words into 'undeniably decasyllabic' patterns.

> 'Let him be led
> Without the city walls. There set him free.
> Messere Scorla, upon pain of death
> We banish you from this our city here,
> From all our territories and our lands . . .'

and so on, and so on, throughout the play. It all scans; but it is all how familiar! Never do I feel that something is really happening, something really being expressed. All I receive is a communication of reminiscences. Ilaria (Duchess of Andola) and Fra Andrea, the heroine and hero, have for me a merely reflex significance. Romeo and Juliet spoke words of love to each other in the dawn. So there is an imitation dawn for a pair of phantom lovers who sedulously ape the manner of Mr Phillips:

> 'Thy lips have wrought a wonder to the world!
> Now do I know the mysteries of the stars,
> The message that the winds have told the trees,
> The cry of all the voices of the sea.'

To say that one hears the joints creaking there would be unjust; for the imitation is cleverly and gracefully done. But it would be foolish to pretend that one derives any thrill of poetry. Enough of 'one': I must speak for myself. Doubtless the hearts of the Adelphi audience really beat the faster when such lines are uttered. For certainly, as I have said, they enjoyed the comic relief as though it had been the freshest thing in the world. In his humour Mr Fagan dallies with

no modern model. He is indeflectibly Shakespearean there. Personally, I have always believed that Shakespeare introduced his
'clowns' and 'fools' when he was fatigued by the stress of creation.
They were, I am sure, just the props of a tired brain—the necessary
resting-places for a man working at high pressure. I can tolerate
them as such. But an energetic imitation of what was done in lassitude three centuries ago is too sore a trial for me. Someone in *The
Prayer of the Sword* speaks of some action being 'most delicately
done.' The Fool is ready for him: 'Oh that I might see *thee* most
delicately done, messers—spitted sweetly on a sword's point and
held *punto reverso* to a hot fire as one might roast a lark.' The Fool
is always ready for everyone, and terribly pervades the whole play.
Everyone encourages him. 'Must I,' the Duchess asks him, 'seek
truth in my heart and wisdom in my fool?' The Fool nods. 'And
thy fool's wisdom,' he replies brightly, 'tells thee that thy heart's
truth is love. Now we wise fools be agreed that love is a disease of
the mind. Good! As the diseased body is doctored with drugs, so the
sick mind is physicked with philosophy.' And thus he rambles on.
The imitation from Shakespeare is amazingly close and clever. But
imagine anyone having the will or the patience to do it. Only the
born bookman could do it. And Mr Fagan, in his humour and in
his poetry alike, is the born bookman. In ordinary circumstances, he
would have been content to swell the output of those blank-verse
dramas pretending to no life outside the volumes in which they are
published (and being consequently lifeless even there). But Mr Fagan
is not a playwright in ordinary circumstances. He is an actor. This
saves him from the folly of writing lifeless drama. On the other
hand, it prevents him, despite himself, from writing tragedy, and
insists that he write, despite himself, melodrama. Tragedy is of life;
melodrama is of the theatre. An actor may know and care about life;
but he knows and cares far more about the theatre. If he write for
the theatre, his first and dominant instinct is for effect—'fat' parts,
'sympathy,' 'tableaux,' and all the rest of it. These things are for
him the real objective, and he goes for them straight. You or I,
when we write our five-act tragedies, only happen on these things
by the way. Our concern is with the inward or outward conflict of
certain human souls. That is why we can afford to look down on
Mr Fagan, and warn him off as a melodramatist. When we take
as our central figure a young monk who yearns for action in the

outer world, and goes forth to champion a lady in distress, and falls in love with her, you and I depend entirely on the soul of the young monk—on the laceration of him between his love and his broken vows; and we let the action of the piece develop quite simply from that towards its sombre close. And always, when the play has been produced, the better sort of dramatic critic says that our triumph is a triumph for the dramatic sense over the merely theatric sense. Mr Fagan, on the other hand, makes of his unfrocked monk little but a vehicle for excursions and alarums. We do not feel that the monk has any true vocation for the outer world. We do but hear the voice of Mr Fagan saying 'Come! Quick! I want you. There's a gallant rescue-scene in Act 2. The whole thing will be ruined if you aren't "on." And there's an I-forbid-the-banns scene in Act 4. And the curtain comes down with an I-launch-the-curse-of-Rome scene. The effect is simply terrific, believe me. And then you have to fight a duel, and the lady throws herself between the two of you, and gets a scratch—poisoned dagger, you know. And then you can slip quietly back again to this place, and be seen in a white wig praying over her tomb. So *come* on!' And the monk is hustled out to his deeds of derring-do, and, having been put through them, is allowed back in the convent. But we do not feel that he has any true vocation for the monastic life. We do not feel that he has a true vocation for anything beyond utility in melodrama. 'We'? I mean 'I.'

For a play of this kind I desiderate the old school of mimes—the fruity, the robust, the rapid. Mr Oscar Asche, who plays the villain, is robust and rapid; but not so the other Old Bensonians who constitute the cast; and not even Mr Asche is fruity. Trained in Shakespeare's blank verse these ladies and gentlemen scan admirably Mr Fagan's. But they don't enter into the melodrama heartily enough. Miss Lily Brayton, as the Duchess, tries vainly to conceal under her graces of elocution a lack of impulse for this particular part. A new Old Bensonian, Mr Walter Hampden, plays the hero. He has the advantage of a fine voice and a fine face. But he keeps the face fixed to one expression, and the voice to one note. If an attendant were posted on either side of him, to jog him in the ribs constantly and with violence, he might become a very good actor.

[*1 October 1904*]

MR PINERO'S NEW PLAY

There are many elements of fun in it; but itself seems to me far less funny than its reception. Fifteen years ago Mr Pinero fell under the influence of Ibsen, and began to take life, and his art, and himself, in laudably grim earnest. He grew very keen on intellectual ideas and on moral lessons. What might be the exact nature of the intellectual ideas that he expressed, and of the moral lessons that he inculcated, was ever a fascinating and insoluble problem for his critics, and, doubtless, for himself. For he was not a born thinker: his mental processes were vague. Nor was he a born preacher: he feared to offend his congregation beyond a certain point, which was usually *the* point. However, half a loaf is better than no bread; and I regret that the public ceased to support Mr Pinero's seriously-intended dramaturgy so soon as the thing had ceased to be novelty. In *A Wife without a Smile* Mr Pinero has evidently tried to give the public just the kind of thing which it can enjoy. But—such is the slowness of the human mind—a belief is always apt to survive the subject of it; and so here are all the critics labouring under the firm belief that Mr Pinero is fundamentally as serious as ever. There they are all a-scraping and a-scratching with hen-like anxiety for that moral lesson and that intellectual idea which must surely underlie *A Wife without a Smile*. How ingenious they are, each with his own conjecture! Mr Keble Howard leaps into the *Daily Mail* with a joyous cry of 'I have it!' He tells us that intellectual idea is expressed symbolically through the doll that appears in the play: the public will not tolerate characters of flesh and blood. We hear a faint 'I *think* I have it!' from the depths of a very deep shaft sunk through the play by Mr William Archer. It may be that Mr Pinero was satirising 'latter-day humour-worship as a whole.' Where, I wonder, did Mr Archer discover evidences of this new and curious religion? Who are its priests? In what tabernacle are its awful rites performed? Mr Archer, vouchsafing no answer, continues to ply his pick, and presently strikes a reason for supposing that he has hewn in vain. 'If,' his voice is wafted to us, 'if the thought suggested to my mind had been present to Mr Pinero's, I cannot but think he would have treated it on a larger scale. Yet what other thought it inspired him I fail to divine.' Divine no more, honoured colleague. There is nothing to divine. Cease, fellow-courtiers, to dilate on the rare tissue of the Emperor's new clothes. The Emperor has nothing on. *A Wife without a Smile* is just an unpretentious little farce, with no purpose more recondite than the purpose of causing the public to laugh. If it had been produced anonymously, Mr Archer and the rest of us would have devoted to it a few lines of kindly patronage, prophesying that so soon as the young author had got a firmer grip of the technicalities of his art, he might be expected to write a really admirable farce.

So soon as we are past the first act, with its rather cumbersome exposition, we find that the play is full of fun and ingenuity. True, we are not so much amused as we were by Mr Pinero's earlier farces. But the reason for this change is not any falling off in Mr Pinero's talent. Mr Pinero is as when he wrote *Dandy Dick*—not a whit less mirthful and ingenious. It is the times that have changed, and we with them. Inevitably, what was fresh and delightful to us fifteen years ago is less fresh and delightful now. But fashion, evil witch, is not alone to be blamed in the matter. Mr Pinero's vocabulary comes also to play the deuce. I am sorry to return to a theme on which I have so often said so much. But Mr Pinero's failure to profit by my previous exhortations to him compels me to keep pegging away. So far from improving himself as a writer, he has gone from bad to worse. In *A Wife without a Smile* his deadly passion for long words has implected him more awfully than ever. The central character is meant to be a dull prig, and it is right that he should express himself in a formal manner. But there is all the difference between an actual bore and the artistic suggestion of a bore. We delight in the bore so long as he devastates merely his fellows in the play. But he must not push his campaign beyond the footlights and devastate *us*. That is what Mr Pinero's bore proceeds to do, very soon after the curtain rises, and he gives us no quarter till the curtain falls on the final act. Never—not even in *Letty*—has Mr Pinero contrived such long-winded journalese. Nor is the specific bore the sole utterer of it. Every character, without exception, has to utter it. In a serious play, perhaps, Mr Pinero's style is a more serious matter. For there it offends us as a violation of realism. In farce we do not need that the characters shall seem real. Let them be as fantastic as possible. We welcome any device that leads to laughter. But Mr Pinero's style leads only to yawns—or tears. I implore him, once and for all, to clear his mind of the delusion that a dull thing expressed at great length becomes amusing, and that an amusing thing becomes by the same means more so. As a matter of fact, the present play bristles with delightful points that are utterly blanketed by the awful rigmaroles so dear to Mr Pinero's heart. I dare say that he, with the best will in the world, would not be able to write otherwise than in his present manner. But, at least, realising how fatal that manner is to his matter, he might engage for a trifling fee someone to translate his next MS into passable English. I entertain the apprehension that the process in question would have the regrettable result of causing an excessive curtailment in the duration of the evening's entertainment. In other words—un-Pinero-ish-words—the play might be rather short. But that were a fault on the right side—might, I conceive, be classified in the category of those defects of which it may with confidence be predicated that they are, in a measure, beneficial.

Mr Pinero is reputed a fine teacher of the art of acting. The mimes who act in his plays must not be grudged their gratuitous instruction. They certainly deserve some reward for wrestling with Mr Pinero's prose. Heroically though they wrestle with it, it throws them every time. In *A Wife without a Smile* the only mime who never bores us is Mr Henry Kemble. So good is he that he plays everyone else off the stage. There is nothing remarkable in that. It happens whenever the old school of acting is matched against the new. Do not suppose that the old school excels the new merely in the art of declaiming poetry, and of producing grandiose effects on the stage. Put an old actor into a play of modern life, and his superiority will be just as salient. How easily, and quickly, and quietly, with what blest economy of means, he makes his points! In comparison with him, what duffers those others seem—working so hard, and so obviously, and so incessantly, with so slight a result! Mr Kemble need but raise an eyebrow, or a little finger, to be fully eloquent. In the moments when there is no need for him to do anything on the stage, he does nothing. And yet he is there—a presence—far more surely than any of those indefatigables. Of course, it is not all a question of technique. Mr Kemble has a strong personality—a magnificent face and voice for comedy. But of these assets how little, comparatively, he would make if he had been born thirty years later! It is not, I repeat, remarkable that he plays

94

his juniors off the stage. His remarkable triumph is that he plays
Mr Pinero's prose off the stage. Only when he makes an exit does
that horror become palpable.

The doll, about which there has been so much bewilderment,
suggests to me more remarks on things in general than can be
crowded into the conclusion of an article. I will deal with the doll
next week. Meanwhile, you should go to the Court Theatre where
Mr J. B. Leigh has produced, for a series of matinees, Professor
Gilbert Murray's version of *Hippolytus*. Writing here lately about
this version, I explained why, in my opinion, Greek drama cannot
be conveyed satisfactorily into the modern playhouse. Never mind.
I should not like Mr Leigh to suffer for his enthusiasm in displaying
to us again Professor Murray's work—in itself so very beautiful a
work.

[*22 October 1904*]

MR PINERO'S DOLL

One of those periodical outbursts which amused Macaulay has
abruptly ceased. The shadow of Bellona, vast and dark, has obscured
Mr Pinero's doll. Patriotism has overridden the sense of propriety,
and the ladies and gentlemen who write letters to the more sensational newspapers, signing themselves 'Indignans' or 'Quo Usque
Tandem?' and enclosing their cards, have turned their attention
from Mr Pinero to Admiral Rojdestvensky. We shall not now see
fulfilled Mr W. T. Stead's desire that Mr Pinero's play should be
publicly burned by the common hangman—or was it the doll itself
that was to be hanged? Whichever it was, I doubt whether, in any
case, the ceremony would have been consummated. Mr Stead is a
neophyte, and has scant knowledge of Mr Pinero's record. That
record is familiar to the playgoing public, and consequently the
agitation against Mr Pinero's doll was half-hearted behind its
surface of fury. The public knew that, however much appearances
might be against him, Mr Pinero could not really have been trying
to corrupt them. He has always done his best to edify. He has
always been strong on atonement, nor have his unrighteous ever
flourished like the green bay-tree. The Profligate blew out his

95

brains. Mrs Tanqueray poisoned herself. Iris was driven forth into the night—there to perish miserably, or be reclaimed, like her sister in *The Benefit of the Doubt*, by a clergyman of the Church of England. Always has Mr Pinero been on the side of the angels; and, if he has mixed with the apes, it has been ever as an intrepid member of the angelic secret service. If he has sometimes seemed to be running with the light and frivolous hare, it has ever been as an avant-courier of the highly-moral hounds. True, in *The Gay Lord Quex*, the avenging pack had not overtaken its quarry before the final fall of the curtain; but everyone felt that it must have merely missed the scent. Everyone, I think, in his heart of hearts—everyone except Mr Stead—feels likewise about *A Wife without a Smile*. Its appearances would look black against anyone but Mr Pinero. Anyone but he would stand convicted of impropriety. In his case, it is felt, there must be some unfortunate mistake. And so, indeed, there is. Mr Pinero has received in audience the representative of a daily newspaper, and has spurned the factitious doubts of his rectitude. He does not, he declares, envy the minds of those who have read an indelicate meaning into his doll. This declaration is as final as it is superfluous. It leaves us nothing to say but that we, whose state Mr Pinero does not envy, cannot but envy him his—cannot but envy a man whose mind is so untainted that he never, in repeated rehearsals, foresaw that we might find an indelicate meaning which was bound to be staring all of us in the face.

Please read no irony into the foregoing sentence. My aim was quite simple and straightforward. It was but to extenuate our offence. Mr Pinero is evidently very much shocked by us. Doubtless he means to put us into a play, showing how prurient people must always come to a bad end (unless, by some lucky chance in the last act, a clergyman steps in to reclaim them). I appeal to him for a lenient view of our case. The effect produced by *A Wife without a Smile* does not really convict us of pruriency. It does not convict us of always thinking about certain facts which are not publicly discussed, or of taking delight in searching out things that might be distorted into sly references to these facts. I admit that there is no real impropriety in the play. If what happens in the play had happened in real life, and if these events had subsequently been sifted in a court of law, then it would be found, through collation of evidence as to time and place and so forth, that the antics of the doll were no proof of improper conduct on the part of anyone. But a theatre is not a court of law. A judicial verdict is one thing; a theatrical impression is another. And, the world being what it is, I cannot see how the average adult could, in the course of *A Wife without a Smile*, escape the impression that the doll meant just that which he, were he a judge summing up on a bench, with all the evidence in retrospect, would absolve it from meaning. Even if he grasped the limitation of the doll's actual significance, he would surely, nevertheless, be beset by the doll's glaring suggestiveness. The suggestiveness would have been less glaring if the doll had not been manipulated as, on the night of my visit, it was manipulated at Wyndham's Theatre. Mr Pinero has disclaimed responsibility for that mode of manipulation. Perhaps the mode has since been altered. In no case, however, could the suggestiveness be destroyed. And, anyhow, the alteration had not been made at the time when the protests were raised. And so I conjure Mr Pinero not to be angry. No man should judge others by himself, if he himself be on a pinnacle. Let Mr Pinero be content with his own superiority.

The admirable little 'Mermaid Society' will presently be to the fore again. Congreve, Beaumont and Fletcher, Ford, Vanbrugh and other persons of the past are all to have a turn. There is a scheme by which everyone who subscribes five shillings to the Society will be able to buy seats at half the usual price. Subscriptions will be received by the President, Mr Philip Carr, at 3 Old Palace Chambers, Old Scotland Yard, Whitehall—an address worthy of his aims.

[*29 October 1904*]

'THE FLUTE OF PAN'

I think that the best, because the most feminine, of Mrs Craigie's plays was *The Bishop's Move*. It is a fault in her as in most other women who write, that she is inclined to disdain the peculiar qualities which are hers in virtue of her sex, and to hanker after virile modes. Women excel men in quickness and certainty of insight into the little recesses of human character, and in quickness and certainty of observation of the fine shades on the surface—

observation of manners, in fact. Where women falter is in the construction of frames for large themes, in the handling of broad motives, in profound thinking, and so forth. The slighter a woman's theme, and the smaller the scale on which she treats it, the more satisfying will her work be. She will be doing what Nature and the Muse meant her to do. And she will be doing it better than any man could do it. All that is good in Mrs Craigie's books was done along the line of least resistance—done by Mrs Craigie. All that does not seem to 'come off' was done with the striving towards virility—done by John Oliver Hobbes. In her plays, as in her books, Mrs Craigie can never be trusted to let herself go all the way along that line of least resistance. Hence the anomaly that her most feminine, and therefore best, play was written in collaboration with a man. Mr Murray Carson, having, in virtue of his sex, the knack of profound thinking, perceived that the lighter and slighter the theme of his scenario, the better would be Mrs Craigie's development of it. Alas, though the play was a subsequent success, the majority of the critics denounced it, in accordance with their sacred canon that to write a trifle is to trifle with the public. It may be assumed that Mrs Craigie, being a woman, loves to be praised, and hates to be blamed. And so she set herself to write a play which should not merely please her by its inherent manliness, but which should also delight the critics by its familiarity and by the certainty that it was going to be popular. Firm and confident, she booked her passage to Ruritania, pausing conscientiously at the bookstall to buy for reference all the Ruritanian literature there displayed. Ruritania, she knew, had long been the Mecca of critics and public alike. Ruritania they should have for all it was worth. The Queen in all her loneliness and her distress, and the English gentleman in all his chivalry, and the Counts and the Barons and the Grand Chamberlains and the Masters of the Horse—nothing should be left out. As a salve to her anti-romantic conscience, Mrs Craigie, it seems, took her theme from real life. She has let it be known that the characters in her play really did—or do exist, and that the incidents in her play really did happen. This being so, Ruritania must certainly appear in all future atlases; for whence but from Ruritania could Mrs Craigie have derived her subject-matter? To me, who am not a publisher of atlases, the actuality of this subject-matter makes no difference at all. For me, as a critic, the question is

not whether a play is founded on fact, but whether it gives me in
the theatre the illusion of truth. Figments may give me this illusion,
and facts may give it me not. Mrs Craigie's facts give it me not.
Nor did Mrs Craigie intend that I should have it. She was thinking
of the average playgoer, who cares not a fig for truth, and was trying to give him just what he does want—a full, thick story of coinci-
dences and cross-purposes. The Queen of Siguria needs a consort.
She loves Lord Feldershey, and Lord Feldershey loves her. But,
in offering him her hand, she will not, by reason of a certain
pique, tell him that she cares for him. In real life, of course, no
two human beings who love each other can be together for five
minutes without mutual understanding, even if nothing be revealed
orally, and even if there be a mutual attempt at concealment. But
then, of how many romances would our stage be shorn if this simple
fact were regarded! In the dear old way Lord Feldershey goes
blundering unconsciously along; and, also in the dear old way, his
blunder is corroborated for him by an auxiliary blunder. He believes
that the Queen made an assignation in his rooms with a man
named Baverstock, and that with Baverstock she is in love. For an
ingenious, but impossible, reason of delicacy, he does not ask her
whether this is true. In a later scene, this auxiliary blunder is
itself corroborated by the appearance of Mr Baverstock on the
balcony of the Sigurian palace. And, in case all this should not be
enough to postpone the embrace of the true lovers till the end of the
last act, Lord Feldershey must, in perfect innocence, and for
reasons over which he has no control, kiss a lady-in-waiting at the
very moment when the Queen happens to come in at the door.
Such games of cross-purposes are, as Mrs Craigie knew, very dear
to the heart of the public. But, as Mrs Craigie did not realise, they
are not all-sufficient to the public if played on Ruritanian soil.
Blood and thunder must be there. The Ruritanian soil must be
steeped in blood, and must quake beneath constant peals of
thunder. Alas, these commodities are not in Mrs Craigie's line.
With the best will in the world, she has to shirk them. She keeps
them 'off.' She huddles them into an entr'acte. What does it profit
the public to hear that there is 'a serious rising in the hills' of
Siguria? Show them that rising. What comfort for them is there
in hearing that Lord Feldershey has covered himself with glory
by the skill and bravery with which he has quelled that rising? He

must be seen in the act of covering himself. And seen he would have been if Mrs Craigie had been a man—a man with a straightforward bent to Ruritanian dramaturgy. Being herself—being a woman with a subtle and delicate talent for realistic comedy—she cannot, with the best will in the world, refrain from treating her characters in a realistic and comedic way. But, by force of the initial scheme, her characters are puppets. Manipulate them never so deftly, she cannot put souls into them—cannot make them live. All Mrs Craigie's delicate strokes of intuition and observation glance vainly off the crude material she has chosen. Vain here, too, is her talent for writing natural dialogue. In Ruritania men must shout, and women must shriek. If they converse at a natural pitch, the effect is a sort of whisper. Let Mrs Craigie's first excursion to Ruritania be her last. Let Mayfair be evermore her milieu, and feminity unabashed her method.

Miss Nethersole, as the Queen, and Mr Waring, as Lord Feldershey, were sorely hampered by the quality of their parts. Mr Waring paced restlessly up and down the stage, as though seeking an outlet to those 'hills' on which was 'the serious rising.' A caged lion, condemned to comedic dalliance, when he should have been springing and rending and roaring for us in the approved Ruritanian fashion! Miss Nethersole fared no better. The Queen was supposed to be a wayward and high-spirited coquette. But Miss Nethersole's art is of sterner stuff. Strong and forthright emotion is the line of her excellence. She is not so good at indirect half-tones. Moreover, she cannot produce the illusion of weakness. The Queen was supposed to be weighed down by sovereignty. But Miss Nethersole's head never seemed to rest uneasy for one instant. Try as she would, she could not but seem self-confident and masterful. And yet her bearing was not that of a self-confident and masterful queen, exactly. Accepting a bouquet, or stripping a rope of pearls from her neck, or opening a sheaf of telegrams, or ordering a special train, always she reminded one rather of a great prima donna. She was, in fact, too queenly for a queen. A fault on the right side; but still, a fault.

Last week the Mermaid Society at the Royalty Theatre was performing *The Way of the World*. The play, as a play, is, of course, as dead as a doornail—was never, indeed, alive. But as a gallery of characters how well it survives! Every one of the many characters

stands out full-bodied and modern, even now. And the dialogue—
every speech a sharply-cut jewel—has kept its radiance as surely as
actual old jewels keep theirs. The first care, in a performance of any
play by Congreve, must be for the utterance of the dialogue. If the
speeches be delivered well and clearly, with a sense of their rhythm,
with a sense of their classic precision of phrase, then the battle is
more than half-won. Unfortunately, these graces of elocution are
things which the modern mime has had no chance of acquiring;
and most of the mimes in the Mermaid Society are young. The best
one of these seemed to be Mr Nigel Playfair, who played Witwoud
with a real reverence for the words as words, and also with much
vivacity and humour. Mrs Theodore Wright was perfect as Lady
Wishfort, giving to the part just that quality of breadth which is of
the essence of a right interpretation of Congreve's characters. Just
that quality was lacking in the pretty and clever impersonation of
Mrs Millamant by Miss Ethel Irving. Next week this Society will
be playing *The Broken Heart*.

[*19 November 1904*]

'LADY WINDERMERE' AND 'AGLAVAINE'

A strange conjunction of names, is it not? I wish I had the
ingenuity to write my criticism in the form of a dialogue between
the charming bearers of these two charming names. But, after all,
the contrast between the two plays denoted by them—the two plays
that confront me this week—needs no pointing by artifice. True,
there is a common denominator for them—the sense of beauty. Each
is the work of a poet with a mastery of prose cadences. Each,
moreover, is the work of a man of philosophic temper. But the
wordly wisdom of Oscar Wilde, playing so brilliantly and so surely
over the whole surface of things—how anti-polar that is to the
childish wisdom of Maeterlinck, gazing through darkness, discerning so faintly, sure of nothing. Maeterlinck is a grown-up man now,
Blindness is no longer his point of view. Almost breezily, he
scours the horizon with a telescope, and is beginning to cut quite
a popular figure. For some of us something of the old magic is
lost in the new cheerfulness. We feel that Nature did not mean

Maeterlinck to become cheerful—to become capable. We are less affected by the clean-cut things he describes to us than by the dim things at which he guessed in awe. It is in his early plays that we find his true soul. With all its beauty, we would barter *Monna Vanna*, as we would, with all their beauty, barter his essays, for those early plays, wherein, having to express something that no other man had felt in his way, he brought so wondrous a new element into theatric art.

Whereas Maeterlinck made the theatre the cradle for his marvellous infancy—infancy, as it were, almost in the literal sense of speechlessness—and is now, in his noble but not inimitable prime, receding from the dramatic to the literary form, it was by way of a brilliant afterthought that Oscar Wilde began to be a playwright. Already he had, from time to time, touched, and adorned, all the literary modes—achieving, I think, his finest mastery in the forms of the fairy story and of the philosophic essay in dialogue. He found in the theatre a new diversion. He did not, at first, take the theatre seriously. He was content to express himself through the handiest current form of play. And that form happened to be Sardouesque comedy. It is inevitable, therefore, that *Lady Windermere's Fan* should seem to us, now that we see it again at the St James's Theatre, after the lapse of twelve years, old-fashioned in scheme. But it is old-fashioned only in the sense in which a classic is old-fashioned. Partly by reason of the skill with which the scheme is treated—that perfect technique which comes to other men through innumerable experiments, but came all unearned to Oscar Wilde—and much more by reason of the dialogue itself, which is incomparable in the musical elegance and swiftness of its wit, *Lady Windermere's Fan* is a classic assuredly. As time goes on, those artificialities of incident and characterisation (irritating to us now, because we are in point of time so near to this play that we cannot discount them) will have ceased to matter. Our posterity will merely admire the deftness of the construction. And no lapse of time will dim the lustre of that wit which won for the play so much enthusiasm last Saturday. One may note, by the way, that the critics have doffed the glory with which, twelve years ago, they covered themselves by declaring that the author's wit was not genuine wit, but merely a mechanical trick which anyone could master. Perhaps they have been experimenting in the interval.

It is unlikely that Oscar Wilde, despite his previous rangings from one literary form to another, would have ceased to write plays. A man may cease to write poems, or essays, or stories. But the theatre has a peculiar mastery over the few who master it. Once a playwright, always a playwright. And there is a melancholy fascination in wondering how much the modern drama suffered by the extinction of Oscar Wilde. Already in *A Woman of No Importance* he was emancipating himself from the Sardouesque convention. There are scenes of strong human power in that play. *Salome* is an example of the fine things he might have done in classic tragedy. But I think that neither of these plays is the true gauge of our loss. His mind was essentially a fantastic mind. Into his last play, *The Importance of Being Earnest*, he poured much of this essence, treating the scheme of a commonplace farce in an elaborately fantastic spirit, and thus evolving an unrelated masterpiece which has often, and never passably, been imitated. I fancy that his main line of development would have been from this play. Abandoning the structure of commonplace farce, he would have initiated some entirely new kind of fantastic comedy—comedy in which the aim would have been not to represent men and women, but to invent them, and through them to express philosophic criticisms of the actual world. It was left to Mr Barrie to do something of this kind in *The Admirable Crichton*. That play is perhaps the most delightful achievement of the past few years. Let us imagine it, and a series of plays like it, written by a man whose intellectual power was commensurate with his humour and his sense for the theatre. Then, I conjecture, we shall know, more or less, what we have missed.

The present performance at the St James's is not very good on the lighter side—the more important side. Some of the characters, in coping with the witticisms, subside into tragic earnestness, others into roystering farce. Lord Darlington (Mr Aubrey Smith), saying the 'extravagant silly things' for which Lady Windermere reproves him, says them as though his life and hers depended on them. 'I wish I had known it was your birthday, Lady Windermere. I would have covered the whole street in front of your house with flowers for you to walk on.' Mr Aubrey Smith says this with all the portentousness of an eminent physician examining an invalid. He seems to be saying 'I wish I had been called in earlier, Lady Windermere.

I would have covered the whole street in front of your house with straw.' Mr Sydney Brough, on the other hand, endows Lord Augustus Lorton with a comic walk and a comic delivery, as though he were playing the 'comic major' of tradition. On the light side of the play, Mr Vane-Tempest, as Mr Dumby, is the only actor who speaks his lines appropriately. The serious side of the play fares better. For Miss Braithwaite gives just the right kind of Puritan dignity to Lady Windermere; and Mr Ben Webster bears himself agreeably as Lord Windermere; and Mrs Erlynne is played, as before, by Miss Marion Terry, who has still no rival in what may be called the graciousness of pathos.

Aglavaine and Selysette, of which there have been some performances at the Court Theatre, was written somewhat later than *Pelleas and Melisande*; and one can trace in it the beginnings of its author's present self. Pelleas and Melisande were not people, but leaves in the wind, or 'flames in the doorway.' They had no tincture of free-will. They were mere playthings for Fate. Free-will, throughout the drama, was monopolised by Golaud; and wisdom was monopolised by Arkal, the old king. But Aglavaine and Selysette have each her share of wisdom—Aglavaine quite a large share. And each has her share of free-will, though Aglavaine makes little use of hers, and Selysette uses hers only in the second part of the play. In that qualification is the reason why the later play is less effective in the theatre than the earlier play. You can have drama without free-will, but not unless the will-less beings are constantly subject to pressure of Fate. There must in drama be some kind of movement, active or passive. In *Aglavaine and Selysette* nothing happens, either visually or spiritually, for a very long while. We saw Melisande beside the well, loved and wooed by Golaud. We saw the dawn of her love for Pelleas. We saw her drop her ring into the well, and go to seek it, with Pelleas, in a certain cave, and not dare to enter. We saw them in the glade of poplars, awaiting the wrath of Golaud. In fact, we saw things happening to Pelleas and Melisande—happening progressively. In this later play, Meleander loves Aglavaine better than his wife, Selysette. This is so from the first; and, until the middle, nothing comes of it. The three characters talk round and round the situation, very beautifully. But the situation does not change, and their comments on it become gradually monotonous. At length, since Fate will not awake, Selysette rouses herself to a resolve. And with this spiritual movement the play tardily begins, and we begin to realise the poignancy of the theme. It is that old and inexhaustible theme, a man's preference of the stronger to the weaker woman; and the end is, as ever, the self-sacrifice of the weaker woman. So soon as Selysette determines that she must die, the play becomes powerful and piteous in Maeterlinck's best manner. The agony is piled on, bit by bit, with an eerie skill of which none but Maeterlinck has the secret. Selysette is not afraid to die; she is afraid only that Aglavaine and Meleander will know that she killed herself. On the wall of the old tower a strange bird has built his nest. She tells her little sister Issalyne about this strange bird. They will go hand in hand to the top of the tower, and then Selysette will lean over and catch the bird for Issalyne. But first she must say good-night to the aged Meligrane. Having said good-night, she goes with Issalyne to the tower. On her way, she meets Meleander, and to his questions she gives evasive answers. She climbs the tower. But when she has come to the top, she remembers that she was not tender enough in taking leave of Meligrane. She goes back. There is a second and longer scene of parting, and afterwards a second and longer scene with Meleander. The effect of this repetition, set down here in writing, may not be impressive. But in the theatre, scene by scene, it is curiously impressive—a cumulative effect which only a born dramatist could have conceived. The finest scene of all is the last scene, in which Selysette, delirious and dying, still fights for her poor little pretence, against the fearful questions of Aglavaine and Meleander. Pathos never was more poignant than it is in that wonderfully-written scene.

[*26 November 1904*]

'EAGER HEART'

I have often lamented that in England it is held to be an act of irreverence for an ordinary dramatist to dare to work on a Biblical theme, or on a theme in which there is any 'sacred' element. If the writers of books in prose or poetry, or the painters of pictures, had laboured under this restriction, how much of what is valuable in art would have been lost to us! It is inconceivable that writers or painters, in any land, or in any age, could have been laid under any such restriction. Yet, as even I must confess, it does not seem unnatural or indefensible that the modern British dramatist, working for the modern British theatre, should be forbidden to handle sacred themes. Drama itself is as respectable an art-form as any other. The theatre itself is not essentially ignoble, not essentially unfit for the presentation of the highest themes. But, unfortunately, in modern England the theatre has become a place of dubious repute, with which it is hard to associate aught but what is tawdry and cheap and foolish. Men who have the capacity for thought do not write plays nowadays in England: they write books. If a thinker chances to express himself through the dramatic form, either his play is not acted at all, or it is acted on the sly, and is a quiet failure. Broadly speaking, the modern English theatre is given over to musical comedy, or to plays which have nothing to distinguish them from musical comedy except the absence of music. In these circumstances how could we expect a theatre to be adjudged a fit and proper place for the presentation of anything howsoever remotely connected with religion? Let the modern British drama purge itself, and become a necessary study (instead of continuing to be an unnecessary laughing stock) for intelligent persons. That done, there will be no jarring incongruity in the idea of seeing a sacred theme presented in a theatre. 'That done?' That won't be done, at any rate in our time. And so, whenever a sacred theme happens to be treated through dramatic or quasi-dramatic form, we shall prefer to see the result in some place that is not a theatre. The revival of that fine mystery play, *Everyman*, was extremely impressive to me in the quadrangle of the Charterhouse. At the Coronet Theatre it jarred on me; and would have jarred even if the producers had not gone out of their way to vulgarise it with all manner of tawdry effects. I fancy that Miss A. M. Buckton's mystery play *Eager Heart*, will be presented often, from time to time. It has a deserving vitality. But I hope it will not find its way into a theatre. Such places as the hall of Lincoln's Inn, where it was presented last Wednesday, are its proper venue.

Such places suit such plays as *Eager Heart*, not merely because they have not been degraded in use, but also by reason of their antiquity. Such plays as *Eager Heart* are written, necessarily, with an archaistic impulse. They are attempts to revive a form that is past. No lady or gentleman, in the twentieth century, could sit down and spontaneously write a mystery play, with a prologue to be spoken by a prolocutor attired in the present fashion of evening dress. The whole thing is a throw-back—a wistful effort to transport us back through time, to cast such spells about us that we shall become, for an hour or so, even as we might have been had we lived in this world some six centuries ago. Be the writer never so cunning, and we never so anxious to submit ourselves, the mystery play must be enacted in an antique place. Else can there be no aesthetic thrill for us, nor any sharpness in that spiritual lesson which is of the essence of such plays.

Simplicity—simplicity secured through elaborate art—is the one possible manner in which to write such plays. Miss Buckton has not strayed from this manner. Both in the development of her scheme, and in the actual writing of the verse, she has kept the proper ideal before her. The story is conventional—obvious, if you will. But in a play of this kind it were wrong that the story should be otherwise. The action of the play is based on the idea that always, on Christmas Eve, Mary, with her child, and with Joseph, wanders over the earth, mindful of that night when there was but a manger for cradle. The rich and the poor keep watch, if perchance these sacred things shall pass near to them. They leave their doors open to the night, hoping that Mary will enter in. Bread and wine are ready, and a couch, in every household, however poor. We see Eager Heart in her cottage, listening and wondering.

> 'No jewelled hall
> This quiet stall,
>   But thatched with simple wit:
> No monarch rare
> Has sojourned here,
>   But love has lived in it.'

Eager Heart has fasted, that there may be bread and wine; and the couch is spread. While she muses, her sisters, Eager Fame and Eager Sense, come to visit her. They laugh her poor hope to scorn. Eager Fame bids her come away.

> 'Up to the terrace of the capitol,
> Where famous deeds are done, and tapestries

Blazon the walls with tales of heroes dead.
There Fame, her golden trumpet at her mouth,
Governs the winds that sweep the echoing world';

and thither, this night, will 'the royal Child' be surely brought. Eager Sense mocks at the coarse bread and the unsweetened wine which Eager Heart has set forth. To the orange-groves, yonder, where the splendid banquet is gleaming, will the august visitors presently make their way. Yet, somehow, Eager Heart prefers to wait in her cottage. Presently she hears a faint sound of singing. She comes to her door to listen. There is no sound. But, as she stands at her door, two ragged wayfarers, a man and a woman, come slowly along the road. The woman holds a little baby in her arms. She and the man beg Eager Heart to give them food and a resting-place. Eager Heart tells them that such good things as she has were being kept for the coming of a King. Still the two way-farers beg her not to turn them away. Eager Heart hesitates, relents, throws wide her doors, and lets the wayfarers in. Again she hears the distant sound as of angels singing. If she hasten, she may yet see the King pass by. She hastens forth to the plains. On the plains, the shepherds are talking together of their poverty, and of the cruelty of all the world. One of them, a very old man, sits in silence. They pause suddenly in their talk. An unearthly music surrounds them. They rouse the old man from his lethargy, asking him if he heard the music. The old man answers that he has heard it all through the night. The shepherds will follow whither the music calls them, to hail the King upon His way. 'He has passed already,' murmurs the old man. 'I saw His face, and my soul blessed Him even as He went.' Maybe, the shepherds will yet see him. The night is dark; but Eager Heart has a little lamp, and they will find their way. When they are gone, the music swells loudlier forth, and a host of singing angels is visible through the night. The old shepherd lifts his arms to them, and dies. Three Kings find him lying there. They are wandering in the hope of seeing that King who is mightier than they. The music has died away; but they will guide themselves by that strange star which is moving across the sky. They come at length to the door of Eager Heart's cottage. Outside that closed door Eager Heart herself and the shepherds are standing. They have lost nearly all hope of their quest now. Seeing the three Kings, Eager Heart timidly begs that they will suffer her and the shepherds to follow them in their quest. One of the Kings points upward to the strange star. It has ceased to move across the sky. It rests in the sky now, above the cottage. Hither, to this cottage, the royal Child is come. Eager Heart, scarcely believing, creeps up to the door, and opens it. And there, in that lowly room, are Mary and Joseph and the royal Child. Eager Heart falls to her knees, and hides her face in her hands; and the Kings and the shepherds, one by one, enter in at the door, and do homage . . . There, so soon as the epilogue has been spoken, the play ought to end. The introduction of Eager Sense and Eager Fame, and the public shaming of them, is aesthetically an anti-climax, and is quite superfluous from a moral point of view. Miss Buckton, in her arrangement of scenes, and in the quality of her dialogue, shows so much quiet sense of drama that I wonder very much that she missed the so obviously right moment at which to cease. I hope she will be persuaded to eliminate the final scene. Future performances would gain much by that loss.

As in the writing of a mystery play, so in the mounting of it, and in the acting of it, a cunning simplicity is prime requisite. Eager Heart's cottage is furnished simply, but with a slight lack of cunning in some respects. Her table, and her chair, ought not to be so glaringly such as would be found in the sitting-room of any High Church curate. Nor ought 'the flask and the cup of wine' which she has prepared be a decanter and a tumbler of the most fashionable modern pattern. Also, some means should be taken to prevent the casting of human shadows against the background of starlit sky. In the production of a play of this kind there should be more than ever strict precautions against things likely to stir a sense of humour. In the acting, I am glad to say, there was nothing ridiculous. The performers behaved quite simply, and were therefore quite dignified, even though in few of them was simplicity conjoined with cunning. Eager Heart herself had the requisite conjunction; and on her almost everything depended.

[*10 December 1904*]

DRAMA OF THE SECOND EMPIRE

This week, at the Court Theatre, have been performances of a play called *Margot*, translated from a contemporary adaptation of Daudet's novel, *La Menteuse*. A rather round-about product; yet (taken in the right spirit) highly encouraging and cheering. A critic who wants the drama to be infinitely better than it is can hardly avoid the pitfall of supposing it to be rather worse than it is. Finding that it rises nowhere near to his standards, he imagines that it must be in a state of motionless prostration in the nethermost depths. He does not realise the possibility that it has been creeping up. By such an affair as *Margot* he is reminded that it really has been creeping up; and he infers that it is still creeping and will continue to creep.

I know not in what year this play first saw the footlights. I have assumed that it was in some year of the Second Empire; for the heroine is, as it were, inextricable from a crinoline. Possibly the year was later. The later the better; the nearer we are in point of time to *Margot*, the higher has been our rate of progression. For here is a play which not the most miserable hack-writer would contrive today. Today *The Second Mrs Tanqueray* seems to us old-fashioned—melodramatic and untrue. That lady, once so alive and modern, has fled, faintly '*indignata*', to the shades. Yet, if Orpheus would have charmed her back, and have set her beside *Margot* on the stage of the Court, as how magnificent a master would Mr Pinero have been acclaimed! For Mrs Tanqueray has this infinite advantage over Margot. She is a definitely drawn specimen of her class. Mr Pinero not only initiated us into her history: he made her express her temperament upon the stage. She was a complete and recognisable figure. But of Margot we are told, and can discern, nothing. All we know is that she is 'an adventuress.' Miss Darragh plays the part; but not all the intelligence that she brings to bear on it can make it intelligible to us. If the 'property-master' of the Court had brought forward, and propped on a table in the centre of the stage, a faded *carte-de-visite* photograph of a *lionne* of the Second Empire, and had said 'Ladies and Gentlemen, I regret to have to announce that Miss Darragh is indisposed. I must crave your kind indulgence for this photograph,' our interest in the play could not have been fainter: the central figure could not have signified less to us. Indeed, we might have been better pleased. The faded *carte-de-visite* would have had some archaeological interest. It would have evoked a little mild sentimentality. We might have pleasantly exercised our fancy in speculating what was the history, what the temperament, of that bygone lady. But there is no pleasure in speculating what is the history, what the temperament, of a lady impersonated on the stage by an actress. And archaeology and sentimentality have no chance when the actress is dressed in the fashion of to-day, and treats the part as though it were something quite modern and vital.

Though the play is innocent of psychology, it is seasoned with philosophy. One gasps at the kind of philosophy that was thought good enough for the stage in Daudet's day. One of the characters is a misogynist. He has arrived at misogyny by the usual route: his wife has deceived him. Was there ever, I wonder, an age when men drew these sweeping general conclusions from one little personal experience? If not, who first introduced the convention upon the stage? As was (till quite recent times) the way of the stage-husband who has been deceived, Jacques Sylvestre 'is wandering round the world, trying to drown himself in oblivion.' But he keeps in touch with his old friends. 'All women,' he mentions in one of his letters, 'are liars. Fraud and deceit are as much a part of them as their taper-fingers'—oh, chignon and crinoline! oh, peg-top trousers and waxed 'imperial'! who, nowadays, would speak of a woman's 'taper-fingers'? One might as well say that 'she wore a wreath of roses' at once. But I digress from the play's philosophy. All women, according to Jacques Sylvestre, are hopelessly wicked. But here Daudet steps in, holding up one hand. 'Don't listen to him,' says Daudet earnestly. 'He is overwrought, poor fellow. Listen to me, who am calm—aye! calm though I have made a discovery which will shake the world. You have heard of people called "adventuresses." Hitherto you have always supposed that they, at least, were all hopelessly wicked. Well! *They are not.* And I am going to prove it to you.' This is how he proves his profound paradox. Margot, the adventuress, happens, of course, to be the lady who deceived Jacques Sylvestre. But that is not the only inconvenient point in her marriage to Sylvestre's friend, Georges de Beaumont. Georges is poor. She loves him truly. ('Yes,' says Daudet, seeing us exchange bewildered glances, 'such women sometimes are capable of true affection.') But true love is one thing, household-expenses are another. A previous lover of Margot appears on (or, rather, off) the scene. Margot pretends to Georges that she is giving music-lessons; but really she is paying mercenary visits to the previous lover. While Margot is engaged in making both ends meet, Georges is engaged in putting two and two together. At length, further deception is useless. Margot (who has not yet betrayed a single characteristic, except a habit of telling the audience that she loves her husband) must drink poison. They find her suffering mysteriously on the sofa, put her to bed, and send for the doctor, who, after a glance at her, announces that 'everything points to poison, taken in some liquid or other form.' He writes out a prescription. 'Drink this,' they bid her. She pours the antidote on the carpet, and presently dies. Hardly is she dead when a bearded stranger enters the room. 'Why,' he exclaims, 'this was my wife!' Georges bursts into hysterical laughter, and the curtain falls. To think that not very many years ago in Paris, where the plays were, as now they are, better than the plays in London, the curtain fell between this play and an audience which this play had impressed! Judged even by the standards of an ordinary unintelligent audience in the London of today, the play is merely the scenario for a bad melodrama. The playwright brought to his theme nothing but that of which Mr Pinero imported a little—a little, and yet enough to prevent us now from taking his play seriously. Because Mrs Tanqueray, a real woman, strayed into melodramatic circumstances, Mrs Tanqueray is not good enough for us. Margot, a perfunctory outline of a woman, never for one moment emerging from melodramatic circumstances, was good enough for our betters not long ago. I feel quite cheerful.

It was, as I have hinted, distressing to see Miss Darragh in such a part as Margot. Last summer, in *The Pharisee's Wife*, she made a very great success in the part of 'an adventuress.' But then she was not making bricks without straw. The author had projected a real character. No actress, however gifted, can create a character for which the author has provided no potential existence. Nay, the more gifted an actress be, the less can she please us in a shadow-part. An actress with nothing but personal charm might walk through the part of Margot safely enough. But Miss Darragh, who has also a vibrating intensity and power, and an almost harsh sincerity, needs some kind of substantial material to work on. To see her otherwise is to be made rather uncomfortable—to have one's sense of fitness offended, as when one sees the screw of a steamboat above the water-line, strenuously churning the air. Mr Graham Browne, a less exigent artist than Miss Darragh, did not seriously incommode us as Georges de Beaumont. And Mr Percival Stevens, one of the few young actors who can turn their hands to anything and do it well, gave a sharp touch of character to the conventional part of a military uncle.

[*17 December 1904*]

THE STAGE SOCIETY

Last year the Stage Society opened its season with Maxim Gorki's play, *The Lower Depths*. This year it chose *The Power of Darkness*, Tolstoy's play. Between the two works there is a superficial resemblance. The theme of each is the degradation of the lower classes in Russia; and each is full of hideous and revolting details. So that the critics, for the most part, have been as much shocked by the second production as they were by the first, and have rebuked the Stage Society as frantically now as then. But really the two plays lie on two very different planes. Gorki's play offended me, and the production of it seemed to me a mistake, because it consisted of nothing but its hideous and revolting details. There was no form, no meaning in the thing; and therefore no excuse for it—no effect from it except the effect of purely physical disgust. Tolstoy is different from Gorki in that he is a thinker, and an artist—has something to express, and knows how to express it. To the simple soul of Gorki, and to those simple souls who take an interest in Gorki, a farrago of ugly facts is an end in itself. To Tolstoy this farrago is a means to an end—is but the raw material for a finished product. Gorki snap-shots his wastrels, and, having shuffled the snap-shots together, offers the result as a play. Tolstoy, on the other hand, creates his wastrels, implants souls in them, and sets them moving in the possession of flesh and blood. He sets them, too, in significant relation to one another. They act and react on one another, and are developed from point to point by conflict. That their souls are hardly human, and their progress is mostly in a circle, is necessary for fidelity to the theme. The characters are alive, and they move, moving in accordance to a set scheme; and thus is fulfilled the main requirement of dramatic art. In the end, the whole play is seen to have been the expression of a fine moral idea. Thus, through our ethical sense, as well as through our aesthetic sense, we are compensated for the hideousness of Tolstoy's material. We have no excuse for being disgusted by it. If we were disgusted during the course of the play, our sense for art has been imperfectly developed; for no art could be finer than Tolstoy's in the presentment of human character; and a proper pleasure in art is a thing quite uninfluenced by art's subject matter. If we are not uplifted by the final scene, we have yet to develop the rudiments of a moral sense. The Stage Society need not feel at all ashamed of having produced the play. Not they, but the angry critics, should be blushing.

For a critic disgusted by a play's subject-matter, it seems to me a rather strange proceeding to describe this subject-matter in great detail and let his description be printed in order that the public, too, may sicken. Yet that is how the majority of the critics proceeded after the performance of *The Power of Darkness*. I am in one way less squeamish than they, but more squeamish in another. By the force of its characterisation, and by the rude skill of its construction, and by the fineness of its purpose, *The Power of Darkness* was saved from physically upsetting me. On the other hand, I would rather not set down in black and white a bare account of what the play is about—a bare account of the things that happen in it. That would be indeed a disgusting process for me, and the result would be not less disgusting for you. As it is impossible to show the fineness of the treatment without describing the subject-matter in detail, I fear I must ask you to take the fineness on trust, and to bear with me while I discuss a side-issue. A side-issue, but not an unimportant issue.

The characters in the play are very many, and not one is colourless or indefinite. But the chance that Tolstoy gave to the mimes was sadly minimised in passing through the hands of the translators —Louise and Aylmer Maude. The mischief is done now, so far as *The Power of Darkness* is concerned. But, as the two mischief-makers are, I believe, habitual translators, through whose hands other foreign plays are likely to pass, it may be useful to give them a few hints as to how translation ought to be done, and to wean them from their present mastery of how not to do it. The translator should work ever with this ideal: to use just such words as the original author would have used if he were the translator's compatriot. I do not know the Russian language; but let me assume, for sake of argument, that Tolstoy does (as he is reputed to) make his characters talk naturally, like human beings. The primary aim, then of Tolstoy's translator, should be to preserve in the dialogue this quality of natural and lively speech. How is this to be achieved? The translators of *The Power of Darkness* would say that this aim is to be achieved only by closest verbal fidelity to Tolstoy's text. The theory is specious. But it ignores the simple fact that Russian idiom is a very different thing from English idiom. And in practice the theory cuts a very painful figure—especially in practice on the stage, where the words have to pass through the lips of live persons trying to behave like live persons. For a dead language must ever result from the translator's grim fidelity to the text. Nay! 'dead language' is too dignified a term to apply to such miserable jargon as was wrestled with by the mimes in *The Power of Darkness*. We need not the letter, but the spirit, of the original. Give us the letter, and we can but make faint, convulsive grasps at the fugient spirit. Of course, the two translators have not made a verbatim translation of Tolstoy's words. I do not accuse them of that. They are guilty of a worse thing—guilty of the fatal endeavour to find some racy equivalent for every phrase. Russian peasants talk, of course, a dialect that is full of homely slang. So do our peasants. But all illusion of reality flies away when Russian peasants use the vernacular of the Old Kent Road. And not further than the Old Kent Road have fared the translators of *The Power of Darkness* in their pathetic quest for equivalents. 'S'elp me,' cries a Russian peasant girl, and down on her head descends the shadow of a huge feathered hat. 'My word!' ejaculates a moujik, and is covered with phantom 'pearlies.' 'That's flat!' and kindred phrases are bandied from lip to lip till the very back-cloth takes on the semblance of the Old Kent Road. Perhaps I wronged the translators in saying that they had confined themselves to that thoroughfare. 'It's a cute thing' seems to show that they went so far as the Bowery. Anyhow, they have managed to obliterate every touch of the local colour which they were piously trying to preserve. In future, let them not attempt to reproduce one kind of slang by another kind of slang. Let experience save them, in future, from a mistake from which instinct ought to have saved them at the outset. To suggest the uncouthness of a foreign peasant's speech, a translator must eschew slang, which immediately switches the reader or hearer off to the slang's own locality. This unfortunate reportation is not effected by the use of ordinary, unremarkable English. Of course, there must be no long words, and no literary refinements. Let the Russian peasant speak more or less like an English child, with a plain Saxon vocabulary. Then we shall be able to regard him as a Russian peasant. Our imaginations, in reading the translation, will not be trammelled. In seeing the translation performed on the stage, our imaginations will be helped by the uncouth utterance and bearing of the mimes. In case the present translators are not yet convinced of their folly, I ask them to imagine what would be the effect if the mimes, instead of merely speaking their lines gruffly, were to assume specific Cockney accents. The translators can imagine how fatal that would be—that which is precisely the thing done by themselves.

Not all the performers in *The Power of Darkness* had the right manner for Russian peasants. Miss Dolores Drummond, for example, though she had an admirable conception of her part, and managed her long speeches with a flexibility that would be impossible to an actress of the modern school, was throughout much too graceful in utterance and in gesture. Mr Lyall Swete and Mr O. B. Clarence, both of whom played important parts, had acquired exactly the right uncouthness. So, also, had Miss Italia Conti, on whom the main burden of the play rested, and who played her part without rehearsal, script in hand, yet rose full-high to every dramatic opportunity. A striking achievement, this, and possible only to a born actress.

[*31 December 1904*]

PANTOMIME FOR CHILDREN

This is a fussy age; and I wonder very much that no committee of busybodies has been formed to collect subscriptions for the erection of some kind of monument to the late Dan Leno. Personally, I have no general enthusiasm for monuments. If a man is memorable, there is no need to commemorate him. As for Dan Leno in particular, if you *are* hankering after a monument (and excuse a 'tag') look around you. What more signal monument could he have than London's sudden and panic-stricken awakening to the fact that Drury Lane pantomime is not for children a mirror of all that in life is cleanliest and sweetest? For innumerable years Drury Lane pantomime has had a full mixture of vulgarity and ugliness. Yet no one perceived the admixture. At any rate, no one took exception to it. No one started a panic. Why? Simply because of the glamour of Dan Leno. Himself neither refined nor pretty, himself working on the traditional lines of the British music-hall, he had yet that kind of genius which silences hostility and banishes doubt. So long as he was at Drury Lane, his fellow-pantomimists and the authors of the libretto passed unchallenged, under his iridescent wing. Now that he is gone, behold us with eyes upturned and hands uplifted, terrifically censorious. Already, I believe, the authorities of Drury Lane have somewhat pandered to our sudden craving for refinement. I wager that next year refinement will govern the whole show, with a rod of iron. We adults shall then, presumably, be quite happy. But still it will be an open question whether Drury Lane pantomime be a thing fully appropriate to children.

It is risky for an adult to dogmatise as to what children really enjoy best. He is beset by the temptation to suppose that they have the good taste to enjoy best the kind of entertainment which best pleases himself. The temptation is fortified by the fact that children cannot go alone to theatres. An adult must accompany the over-excited party. Naturally the adult tries to persuade himself that, in choosing the entertainment least likely to bore himself, he is choosing also that which will most enrapture his dear little friends. Last week, from the standpoint of an adult, I wrote here about *Peter Pan*. I tried to make my enthusiasm infectious. Doubtless, many of my readers were infected, and have gone, or are going, to the Duke of York's Theatre, taking children with them. A play about children —a tender, intimate play about children—little girls with sunny curls, little boys with bullet heads—pattering feet—'Nana' (not of the Rougon-Macquart family, but a term of endearment for 'Nurse') —Dad—Mumsy—little white cots in the night-nursery: 'Why,' cries the doting adult, 'this is just the very thing for me to take Maisie and Molly and Robin to!' Nor have I the faintest fear that our doting adult will not pass an ecstatic evening. But I cannot predict so surely about his protégés. True, there are in *Peter Pan* things which, I imagine, no child could fail to enjoy. There are pirates, and Red Indians, and Esquimaux—marvellous apparitions, all of them, as designed by Mr Nicholson, an artist who has managed to keep in maturity that power of sharp and fantastic invention which is the heritage of childhood. But the greater part of the play is devoted by Mr Barrie to the tender portrayal of ordinary children. The children are always on the stage, talking and talking, to reveal the sweetness and quaintness of their souls for the gratification of an audience of elders. Children in actual life are unconscious of being quaint and sweet themselves, and are rather impatient of such qualities in one another. Except when they are at play, and giving rein to their imaginations, they are extremely prosaic about themselves. They take themselves seriously, from a quite matter-of-fact standpoint, and do not like being laughed at. Still less do they like being cried over. Mr Barrie's view of children, with its mingling of smiles and tears, is very dear to us adults. We are exquisitely tickled by the fun he gets out of children, exquisitely touched by the pathos. Who could resist that scene in *Peter Pan* when the children are debating how they shall amuse themselves? One small boy steps forward and says 'Shall I do my imitation of a bear?' The proposal is coldly received. Somewhat discouraged, he offers to do a conjuring trick. He is met with a howl of refusal. After a pause, he falters the suggestion that he could stand on his head. Another howl of refusal. The small boy sighs, and goes back to his place, murmuring, 'I hadn't any hope really.' Who in the audience, I ask, could resist that heart-cry? My answer is 'any child in the audience.' No child would see anything funny or pathetic in this exquisite moment of the play. To move a child's pity, or to move a child's sense of humour, you must proceed on very broad lines. A child will cry, perhaps, at the thought of a carnivorous ogre. A child will laugh, certainly, at sight of a clown hitting a pantaloon over the head with a shutter. But a child is not, like you and me, sensitive to the finer shades of pathos and humour. And its sensibility is most of all evident when the joke is against itself, or when the tear splashes on its own head.

I fear we shall never get from a true child-lover the kind of pantomime that children would really like. For the true child-lover cannot refrain from being sentimental—lingeringly sentimental —over his theme. Twenty years ago it was quite different. The cult for children did not exist then. Children were not regarded as specimens of a race apart—specimens to be carefully preserved, and dotingly dilated on. They were regarded simply as adults in the making. That they had an intrinsic charm was not a theory that anyone propounded—still less a theory that many people would have accepted. Children were subjected to a purely practical and moral test: were they good? likely to become good men and women? The moral standard was very high, insomuch that, in nine cases out of ten, a child was adjudged naughty—likely to become, later, a grave danger to the community. Child-lovers there were as now. But they were few in number, and dared not proclaim their cult. I suppose that no one—not even Mr Barrie himself—ever delighted more heartily in children or studied them more laboriously, than he who wrote *Alice in Wonderland* and *Through the Looking-Glass.* Yet only by reading between the lines of those two master-pieces can you deduce that the author was a child-lover. Alice herself appears as an ordinary, estimable little prig—the 'good' child of the period. There is no psychology, still less any sentimentality, in the presentation of Alice. All the author's power is concentrated on invention of those queer creatures whom Alice encounters on her way. For that reason, the two books are loved, and always will be loved, by children; for children find in them the lively embodiments of their own grotesque fancies. Had Mr Dodgson been born twenty years later, the books written by him would not at all have endeared him to children, so freely would he have revelled in child-love. A man often dares to be quite frankly in private intercourse what he dares not publicly proclaim himself through an artistic medium. Mr Dodgson, among his friends (who, by the way, were mostly beneath the age of twelve), made no secret of his enthusiasm; and his oral stories were as much imbued with this enthusiasm as is *Peter Pan* itself. I met him once—long after I had passed the age at which I might have interested him. Other adults were present; and I, among them, sat and listened, and was, like them, entranced while Mr Dodgson told to the hostess's little daughter, who was perched upon his knee, a succession of little tales about little children.

What insight, what delicate and whimsical sympathy, was in all those little tales! I shall never forget them. Nor shall I ever forget the vacant expression on the face of the perched child, and the cry of joy with which she slid (in the midst of a story) from the perch, and rushed to meet her nurse, a sour-visaged woman, who appeared at the door, silently proclaiming bed-time.

Mrs Taylor, the immortal writer of those *Cautionary Tales in Verse*, was before my time. No child-lover, she; and probably she eschewed, as much as possible, the society of children—never, certainly, invited them to perch upon her lap. But I like to think that sometimes she beckoned a child to stand submissively before her, and recited, in a hollow voice, selections from her works. And I am quite sure that the child was as much entranced by her as was I, adult, by Mr Dodgson. Children love fantasy, and Mrs Taylor never dabbled in that; but she excelled in just that quality which children love in tales about themselves. She excelled in the moral sense. To children, though we, in our outlook on them, have gone over, bag and baggage, from moral to aesthetic ground, 'conduct is three-fourths of life.' Be a child 'good' or 'naughty,' in the old sense, it is still the difference between right and wrong that most interests the child. Children refuse to see themselves as decoration. Kate Greenaway and Walter Crane, and the later imitators of these artists, touch them not. *Struwwelpeter* they love eternally. For *Struwwelpeter* hinges throughout on right and wrong; especially on wrong, and on wrong's horrible results.

Suck-a-Thumb, Cruel Frederick, Johnny Head-in-Air, Foolish Harriet—these, I suggest to Mr Collins, are figures among which he should select for his next pantomime. *Peter Pan* has been used as a stick to beat him with; and it is likely that he might try to buy in the stick—in other words, offer Mr Barrie a commission to write a pantomime. I urge him not to do this. Let him adhere to the tradition of 'horse-play' and spectacle'—two things which are liked by children—and let fantasy, too, be imported, by all means; but let the basis of his pantomime be an appeal to the moral sense. Then he will have a real 'following' among children. My only fear is that he may not find, in this generation, anyone so bold as to imply that all children are not perfect.

[*14 January 1905*]

DRAMATIC TRANSLATION

What happens 'when an irresistible force meets an indestructible body?' I give it up. But I know what happens when an irresistible person makes an unreasonable request. Mr Bernard Shaw, who is always irresistible, addressed to this Review last week a letter in which he urged me to write 'two columns' conveying 'a canon of translation for plays written in slang and dialect.' Well, three weeks ago I gave my canon, and gave it in quite a long-winded way. But since he wants me to repeat myself in a still more long-winded way, I will see what can be done. After all, questions of dramatic translation really are rather important. And perhaps it is better to convince people about a thing than not to bore them about it. So I will try to provide one of those canons two columns long that on the outstretched finger of Time, &c.

Mr Shaw says that though he, like me, would translate the slang and dialect of a Russian peasant into ordinary, unremarkable English, he would thereby be grossly misrepresenting Tolstoy. And he seems to regard the whole situation as desperate. That is what comes of being a confirmed idealist. Translation can never, of course, be a perfect vehicle. Something must always be lost in it. There must always be a compromise. But let us not wring our hands. Rather, let us try how hard a bargain we can drive with the Nature of Things.

Roughly, there are two methods of translating a play—the scientific way, and the aesthetic way. For the student in his library, let the author's text be rendered with all possible fidelity. Let exact equivalents be found for every phrase, so that the student at leisure shall be made privy to the author's every minutest meaning, and shall drink ever so deep at the well of ethnology, and shall be all the while deeply impressed by the piety and the ingenuity of the translator. But in the theatre we do not want to be constantly pulled up sharp by our admiration for the translator. We want to forget the translator's existence. We want even to forget the author's existence. What we want is merely the play: not ethnology, but humanity: human beings generically, not foreigners specifically. We want to be as nearly as possible in the position of such people as are compatriots of the author and saw the play acted in the original version. Now, assuming that Tolstoy's play has been acted in Russia, to the Russian people who saw it there was nothing extraordinary and remarkable in the utterances of the *dramatis personae*. The Russian characters were using just the queer slang and dialect which Russian peasants use in real life, and which is familiar to all Russians. There would be nothing extraordinary and remarkable to us in hearing Russian characters talk ordinary and unremarkable English. The inherent incongruity would pass unnoticed. But, when these characters talk a lingo which we associate only with certain classes in English life, then their utterances take on a tyrannous importance, and, instead of merely grasping the significance of what they say, we are wondering all the while what they will say next. We are so preoccupied by the form that the spirit eludes us utterly. All that we are conscious of is the glaring incongruity of English language on the lips of Russian peasants. Of course, the translator's aim was to preserve local colour as much as possible— to give us a true impression of Russian peasants. But his means necessarily defeat his end. For in seeing the translation acted we do not say to ourselves 'These are real Russian peasants,' but 'These, we must remember, are not English, but Russian, peasants.' When I said just now that we want in the theatre not ethnology, but humanity, I did not, of course, mean that we want to imagine the foreign characters not to be foreigners. I meant that we want to be able to take their foreignness as a matter of course, and so to go straight to our comprehension of them as human beings. The translator who enables us to do that is really the most faithful translator, for he puts us as nearly as possible into the position of a native audience. Of course, his task is the easier when the original language can be faithfully translated into usual English. His real difficulty is when usual English has to be found for original oddities. But, by hook or crook, found that usual English must be.

Remember (I have not forgotten) that I am dogmatising only about translations for the theatre. It is interesting and valuable for the student, to learn that a foreign peasant will, to express a particular meaning, use some form of speech for which there is, in English, a very near equivalent. But the translator for the theatre has to ask himself 'Would an English peasant, to express that particular meaning, use this very near equivalent for that form of speech?' He has to distinguish carefully between practical equivalents and equivalents that are merely verbal. To explain the difference between these two kinds, let me take the case of 'S'elp me,' which has been so much bandied between Mr Maude, Mr Shaw and myself. 'Nan,' says Mr Maude, referring to the child in whose lips the phrase was placed, 'living among people not careful of the truth, helps out nearly every assertion with a little oath by way of assurance that she is not telling a fib.' I have no doubt that little Russian girls do often swear under the slightest provocation. Nor have I any doubt that 'S'elp me' is a near translation of one of their favourite oaths. But little English-speaking girls are not in the habit of swearing; and so the translation, though verbally near, is practically far. 'S'elp me' or any other oath would be uttered by a little English-speaking girl only under extreme provocation. When Nan utters it on the English stage, it sounds ugly and has at once a violent significance, very different from its original significance. I have been challenged to say what she ought to say 'since she must say something.' Nor have I any diffidence in replying. The matter is quite simple. To get my reply, I have merely to ask myself 'What would Nan, being herself, and being placed in those circumstances, have said, to convey that same meaning, if her language had happened to be English instead of Russian?' Of course she would have merely said 'I promise you,' or 'Really and truly.' Either of these phrases would give to an English audience the exact nuance that was given to a Russian audience by the native equivalent for 'S'elp me.' Something would be lost to us, doubtless. An ethnological detail would be lost. But s'elp me, I would barter that gladly for the dramatic truth.

The duty of a translator for the theatre is very much akin to the duty of an oral interpreter. When two men meet, each ignorant of the other's language, it is the interpreter's business to make them understand each other as fellow-men, not to proclaim the exact width of the gulf that separates them as foreigners. The difference between the uses of two languages is not less than the difference between the languages themselves. Therefore interpretation must, if it is to be effectual, be broad and free. I forget whether Mr Shaw speaks Arabic, and I do not know whether he numbers any Arab chiefs among his friends. But let us assume that he does. And let us suppose that one of these Arab chiefs came to stay with him in London, and were brought by him one day to see me. I should say to the stranger 'I am delighted to meet you.' But this, literally translated, would be a grave affront. As I had meant well, Mr Shaw, indicating me with a wave of the hand, would say in Arabic, 'This, thy wretched cast-off slave, trembleth in his inmost fibres that thou shouldst have deigned to irradiate with the almost intolerable lustre of thy presence the grimy hovel in which he draggeth out his degraded existence.' To which the Arab: 'Nay, but assure him that in yonder mirror I behold myself reduced by the dimensions of his palace to something less than the size of a gnat, and that this is, alas! the last sight that ever will be vouchsafed to me, for that the glory of my host's person hath afflicted me with a sudden but incurable blindness.' Whereupon Mr Shaw (chafing a little): 'He says that any friend of MINE is a friend of *his*.' Now, if Mr Shaw had not interpreted his friend at all freely, I should have been firstly embarrassed, secondly distressed. And if Mr Shaw had not interpreted me, too, freely, I should have been run through the body with a scimitar (or whatever it is that an Arab chief carries). And suppose, further, that Mr Shaw (fired by the example of translators who translate one dialect through another dialect) had reproduced for the Arab chief my own peculiarities of speech. I was born in London, and doubtless have an excruciating cockney accent. Suppose Mr Shaw had, therefore, in repeating my words, spoken Arabic with an atrocious Meccan accent. Straightway the chief would have been mentally transported into the alleys of Mecca, and I should have seemed to him as utterly anomalous and unreal as seem to us Russian peasants speaking English dialect. As it was I seemed quite verisimilar to him. And, moreover, thanks to Mr Shaw's admirable freedom in choice of words, each interlocutor was made to understand more or less what the other was driving at; and who knows but that this will be the basis of a life-long friendship?

A friendship under difficulties, of course. Something must be lost through even the best interpretation. Likewise, something must be lost through even the best translation of plays. English playgoers will never, for example, be so closely in touch with Tolstoy as they are, or soon will be, with the comparatively compatriotic Mr Shaw. But we can (if my hints are taken) be brought into fairly close touch even with quite alien playwrights.

[*21 January 1905*]

MR STREET, PLAYWRIGHT

The Stage Society has two ways of ministering to our discontent. Sometimes it shows to us plays which have been commercially successful abroad, but which could not be commercially successful here. Sometimes it shows to us plays which might well have been commercially successful here if any manager had had the sense to produce them. Either function is salutary; and from either the humiliation that comes to us is not keener than the pleasure. It is sad that we have no large public that will appreciate a play for its poetic beauty, or for its intellectual idea, or for its truth to life. But it is pleasant to have such plays imported for our semi-private inspection. Likewise, it is sad that we have no managers who can be relied on to know a good, yet commercially promising, thing when they see it. But it is pleasant to find that there are such things for managers to see. And, since we should not otherwise have a glimpse of such things, we are glad to see them under the inappropriate auspices of the Stage Society.

Certainly, Mr Street's *Great Friends* is one of such things. Why has it not been produced commercially? I deduce, from internal evidence, that it was written at least five years ago. And I do not suppose that Mr Street, having written 'Curtain' at the end of it, thrust it into a pigeon-hole, with the fluttering hope in his heart that one day the committee of the Stage Society might ask to have a look at it. Presumably it has been seen by managers. Why did they look askance at it? It is not poetic. There is no 'unpleasant' theme in it. It presents no moral problem, is founded on no intellectual idea. There is a Duke in it. It is neatly constructed. It gives scope for any number of pretty frocks and any number of powdered footmen. What, from the managerial standpoint, was wrong with it? I think I know. It is what managers call 'slight.' One of the fixed delusions of managers—a delusion not unfixed by the sharp disproofs that have, from time to time, befallen it—is that even in a small theatre a play must, to be successful, be thick and slab. It is supposed that any play with a light and delicate framework must collapse in the theatre, however soundly and adroitly the framework may have been made. The safety of a structure is gauged by its heaviness; and when the crash comes, as it usually does, the theatrical manager is very much surprised. But no number of crashes teaches him that heaviness is not the test. Nor can he master the converse proposition that lightness is not in itself dangerous. That the theatre is no place for delicate effects is a belief not confined to the theatrical managers. Many clever and cultivated outsiders, who ought to know better, will tell you that nothing which does not hit you violently in the eye is '*du théatre.*' Not long ago in the *Daily Mail* there was from Mr Hamilton Fyfe a violent ebullition which interested and pained me very much. The critics were accused of conspiracy in not having fallen down and worshipped the author of a certain melodrama in blank verse, which Mr Fyfe rapturously described as 'good ding-dong stuff,' and compared very favourably with the work of Mr Stephen Phillips, forasmuch as of 'good ding-dong stuff' Mr Phillips was no master. I am sure that when Mr Fyfe discourses of other arts he does not rate 'good ding-dong stuff' as the properest achievement. He does not say 'This nocturne of Whistler's is all very well, no doubt. But it isn't good ding-dong. Take it away. Frith's my man.' He does not say 'Henry James is clever, I suppose. But there is a deplorable lack of the ding-dong element in him. Now Guy Boothby, on the other hand . . .' Why, then, should he rave about Mr Fagan, and against those who don't? Why should the theatre be deemed worthy of nothing but such things as are contemned elsewhere? By all means, let us do homage to broad, strong, forthright work in drama, if it be on a high level. But if it be on a low level—'melodrama if you will,' said Mr Fyfe—let us treat it as we should treat similar work in other arts. And let us not help to perpetuate the delusion that delicacy may not, as strength may, thrive in drama.

Judged by the ding-dong standard, *Great Friends* would be a very signal failure. One cannot imagine Mr Street ding-donging. Too often, a literary man, when he writes for the stage, puts in just the very kind of work that we could not have imagined him doing. Too often, he deliberately cheapens himself. It is to Mr Street's credit that he has treated his audience as respectfully as he would treat the readers of a magazine. In other words, he has not thrown away his self-respect. He has continued to be his own self. That is a very light, dry, calm, classic self. Classic, yes. There is nothing romantic about Mr Street as essayist. He seems to have escaped the hot influences of the past century. He is an eighteenth-century man. His tone and temperament in writing belong as surely to the eighteenth century as if he had been born in the thick—or, rather, the thin—of it. He is never betrayed into an extreme. He is never excited. He never raises his voice, never flushes with enthusiasm or with wrath. He feels nothing deeply, for he sees everything clearly—sees everything clearly, for he feels nothing deeply. Many things annoy him. Few things shock him; and even these are not essentials, but trifles. He never laughs. He never ceases to smile. He is never expansive. He is always amenable. He is always honest. He is always just. He has but one fault: he is impeccable. Yes, I, with my fallen nature, do reckon impeccability a fault. I like the heel of Achilles. It makes me, who am vulnerable at so many points, feel easier than else I could in the company of Achilles. I like an essayist to have some little romantic twist somewhere, some obliquity of vision, some reprehensible prejudice or other, so that now and again I shall catch him in the wrong—excitedly and defiantly wallowing in the wrong. In a playwright, equally, I like to find some little romantic twist—some narrowness that leads to over-emphasis. I confess to a craving for an occasional hint of ding-donginess. But, of course, I do not educe a general law from a personal defect of mine. There is no reason why a playwright should not be impeccable in his attitude to the world. Indeed, it is only through impeccability that a man can write a comedy that shall be artistically, from first to last, on the comedic plane.

Great Friends has this salient and rare virtue. It is a thorough comedy. There is not perhaps what is called 'arresting originality' in it. Why should there be? It would ill consort with Mr Street's classic temper to be arrestingly original. It would be a solecism. And his innocence of this solecism deepens the guilt of the managers who did not produce the play. One can understand them refusing to risk a play the like of which had never been seen before. Again, one can understand them refusing to risk a play with the contrary drawback. But *Great Friends* is as far from being stale as from being startling. It is perfectly fresh. A familiar theme is treated in a not familiar manner. A man engaged to be married to an ingénue, fascinated away for a while by a brilliant woman of the world, but finally marrying the ingénue—this is the scenario of many plays that one has seen before seeing *Great Friends*. But Mr Street has developed it in a new way. Hitherto, the man has always been a fine fellow, torn manfully between sacred and profane love, and at length, with a terrific effort, reconciling happiness with duty. The brilliant woman of the world has been always a villainess, either caring only for the gratification of her passion, or wishing only to wreck the happiness of the ingénue. And the ingénue has always been a quite passive little person. But here, for once, the ingénue is the pivot of the play's action. She it is who sees that she is likelier to make the hero happy than the woman of the world. She refuses to sit still and be plaintive. She determines to win the hero back; and she does win him back. And he, for his part, is not a hero at all, but quite will-less, and rather a prig. And the woman of the world, schemer though she is, seems to be quite a good sort, with no spite against the ingénue, but with an honest conviction that her lover would be much happier in a liaison with herself than in married life with the ingénue. Mr Street develops this new version with very delicate skill. The three characters are well realised—are alive; and all the subsidiary characters are touched in with a sure hand. All of them, from time to time, talk wittily. It is, indeed, the profusion of epigrams that led me to date the play as at least five years old. Mr Street's epigrams are not of the kind that startles an audience into a roar of delight. But none of them falls flat. Each of them wins its rightful simmer of laughter. Nor are they, by any means, the prime virtue in his dialogue. The other day, in an essay about the Irish Literary Theatre, Mr W. B. Yeats quoted me as saying that no modern play could have style. A realistic play, of course, cannot have literary style. The characters must talk apparently as they would in real life. But, as I was careful to suggest, aptness of phrase and beauty of cadence can be smuggled in. Mr Street's dialogue well illustrates this possibility.

A delicate play like this needs very exquisite acting. The Stage Society's performance of it was not, I must confess, very exquisite. Few of the parts had been well cast. I wish some commercial manager would take the play in hand. With a really good cast, in a fashionable theatre, with music in the entr'actes, it would have far less chance of failure than the average play produced under these conditions.

[*4 February 1905*]

128

MR CARTON ON HIGH AND LOW LIFE

A young lady, on the eve of her wedding-day, engaged a maid for her honeymoon. Her aunt, who had arranged the marriage, found the bridegroom evidently trying to kiss the maid. She smiled genially, and said, in perfect good humour, 'I heard that you had objected to the maid on the score of expense. I am glad you have reconsidered your objection.'

If, a few days ago, you had told me this, and had challenged me to guess when and where it had occurred, I should have said, 'Oh, surely in one of Carton's plays—with the aunt's part played by Miss Compton.' In point of fact, it occurs in *Mr Hopkinson,* a play by Mr Carton, produced this week (with Miss Compton as the aunt) at the Avenue Theatre. So, you see, Mr Carton has not abandoned the '*beau monde,*' nor alloyed his mode of depicting it. Let us hope that the pleasurable shock to Peckham (one has to use these symbols) will not have become less sharp by familiarity, or by scepticism. Let us hope that Peckham will long be faithful to Mr Carton as a lasher of the vices of the age, or as a devil of a fellow —I am not sure which is its standpoint. Anyhow, Mr Carton is faithful to himself. The Duke and Duchess of Braceborough, a middle-aged couple, are 'good sorts' of the prescribed pattern, not living together as man and wife: she has her cavalier, he his mistress. They seldom meet, but are on perfectly good terms with each other when they do meet. Lord Gawthorpe is another 'good sort,' several times tested in the Divorce Court. When last he was co-respondent, so he tells us, the Duchess, like the brick she is, went every day to the Court, and sat on the Bench, and talked to the Judge till he didn't know where he was, thus greatly benefiting Lord Gawthorpe when the case was summed up. Moreover, the Duchess gave a large dinner to celebrate his lucky escape. Lord Addleton is a valetudinarian. There can be no scandal about him. But for Peckham's consolation there are frequent references to some very sensational scandal in which he was the central figure twenty years ago. Lady Thyrza Egglesby, his daughter, has not been seduced. The absence of any hint that she has been may be taken as a proof of her innocence. But lest Peckham's comfortable wrath be mitigated by this one bright patch in the prevailing blackness,

Lady Thyrza is made to hoist a dubious standard of conduct for others. When the lady's-maid is being engaged, the Duchess says that Lady Thyrza will probably make no difficulty about 'followers.' 'Followers?' cries Lady Thyrza to the maid. 'Any number of them! Only, as we're going abroad, you'll have to pick them up and drop them as we go along.' And when, next day, she makes a run-away match with Lord Gawthorpe, she looks shyly up into his eyes, saying 'I will try to make you forget that I am only your wife.' Idyllic, isn't it?

Now, I do not, offhand, condemn a work of art because it is not an idyll. That is a form of judgment quite common among British critics; but to me it never has commended itself. I am not squeamish. Such a play as *The Power of Darkness* disgusts me not at all. Such a play as that, disgusting though it is in the details of its subject matter, is purged for me and made beautiful by the spirit that pervades it. Nay, even when I see an unpleasant play in which is no kind of ennobling philosophy, and in which the aim is merely to depict an unpleasant phase of life, I am saved from disgust, if I have the sense that what I see is sober truth to life. Does Mr Carton go in for sober truth to life? He calls his new play 'a farce'—a term that excludes sobriety. Presumably, the play has been written in a gay mood, with gay intent, irresponsibly to truth, responsibly to naught but fun. But let us be careful to avoid all possibility of injustice. It may be that Mr Carton has, despite his description of his play, lapsed into a serious portrayal of life. He may even have had a purpose. He may have said to himself 'The Empire is still cankered at the core. I must perform yet another operation.' But, with the best will in the world, I cannot find evidence of such grimness; nor does the play seem to me a copy from life. I am quite ready to admit that in one section of Society, the section most familiar to the public, there has been a decline in manners. I do not suppose that sexual morality has declined there much: in every age, the average of sexual morality is low amongst people who can afford not to work for their living. But certainly there is a greater frankness now in immorality. Some people might regard this as a moral gain. I do not say that it isn't. But that it marks a decline in manners is undeniable. The question is whether Mr Carton registers this decline accurately. So far as I can gather from hearsay, the actual people even in that aforesaid section of

Society are not all, as Mr Carton suggests, corrupt, and none of them is so blatantly corrupt as Mr Carton might lead us to suppose them all. Of course, it is hard to prove a negative of this kind. For documentary evidence, I can but direct your attention to the occasional reports of divorce-suits between members of the set with which Mr Carton is dealing. In the witness-box, of course, people are always on their best behaviour; but cross-examination is apt to reveal their ways of behaving elsewhere. And among the admissions wrung, the correspondence or diaries read aloud, I have found none indicative of such a tone as is indicated by Mr Carton. Apart from the question of cynical frankness in tone, certainly the expression of the tone is not so vulgar as among Mr Carton's creatures. Slang, doubtless, there is; but not this kind of slang. 'The Duchess has a feed at the Cecil tonight' is not, if we may trust those diaries and letters which come to light, the way in which gilded youth excuses itself from an invitation to dinner. Nor does gilded youth say to its inamorata 'Steady, old gal,' I think. Certainly, we know that no elderly nobleman says to his valet 'I will now retire to my apartment. Kindly lend me your assistance.' And, if Mr Carton fails to reproduce the formal manner of the elder generation, we may assume that his ear is not likelier to catch the informal manner of the younger. And, if he is inaccurate in his portrayal of the surface, we may assume that he is not less likely to err beneath the surface. We cannot, then, accept his play as true to life. But the play is a mere farce? I am breaking a butterfly on a wheel? That is what I intended to do. Ugly butterflies deserve to be broken. If a butterfly is not beautiful, it has no right to exist. If a farce is unpleasantly invented, it has no right to exist.

Possibly in fear that his portrayal of high life might be beginning to pall on Peckham, Mr Carton has introduced a new and extraneous character, and has made this character the pivot of his play. Mr Hopkinson's father was a rate-collector, and by some means Mr Hopkinson has just come in for forty thousand a year. Ten thousand a year was the amount come in for by Mr Tittlebat Titmouse. Otherwise Mr Carton has not attempted to bring Samuel Warren up to date. In modern life we have compulsory education. Nor is there quite the old hard-and-fast division between the classes. The lower-middle class picks up from 'society papers' a good smattering of the details of high life. The son of a latter-day rate-collector is no Hottentot. Yet, when the Duchess tells Mr Hopkinson that he must have a villa at Nice, 'Nice?' he says, 'that's somewhere beyond Ealing, isn't it?' After he has been moving for half a year in the highest circles, he is as uncouth as ever: ''arf a mo',' 'bit o' orl right,' 'ever eat whelks?' 'My Lord,' and so on. Tittlebat Titmouse, if I remember rightly, acquired a veneer. But Mr Carton will have none of such subtleties. Mr Hopkinson starts as a full-blown 'snob' (in the old sense of the word: we are dealing with antiquities), and he continues in full bloom to the end. Of course the antiquity of him does not matter here. But I am uncomfortably sure that if Mr Carton had been writing not a farce but a realistic comedy, the figure of Mr Hopkinson would have been presented in just the same manner, with a touching faith in its fidelity to life. And, indeed, I suspect that any other fashionable playwright would have sinned likewise. Our fashionable playwrights know nothing of the lower-middle class at first hand. But do they never read contemporary books? Have they never dipped into the novels of George Gissing, or Mr H. G. Wells, or Mr Pett Ridge? Is Samuel Warren the final name on their syllabus?

The modern 'bounder' dresses quietly enough. The ancient 'snob' dressed in a very wild manner. Mr James Welch marks his sense of Hopkinson's obsoleteness by appearing in the wildest costumes, as well as comporting himself as wildly as possible. Of course he is admirable. None knows better than he how to make farce rattle. But far finer secrets are locked up in him. Where is the key? Mr H. G. Wells is said to have written a play for him. If this play be a realistic tragi-comedy of lower-middle-class life, Mr Welch's bosom will be unlocked at last.

[*25 February 1905*]

'THE CLOUDS' AT OXFORD

After seven years of fidelity to Shakespeare, the O.U.D.S. has turned again to Aristophanes; and the interlude is very welcome. Shakespeare is always with us; and it seems hardly worth while to visit Oxford for the purpose of seeing him interpreted by amateurs in the wake of professionals. Aristophanes is inaccessible in London; and Oxford is not too far for us to go for a taste of his quality. As a matter of general principle, an academic institution is best employed in offering what is not offered by the outer world. As a matter of particular practice, the O.U.D.S. acquits itself much better in Aristophanes than in Shakespeare. It is unhampered, in Aristophanes, by models which it must, in the nature of things, imitate, and which it cannot, in the nature of things, imitate well. Its self-consciousness is further diminished in proportion as classical Greek is more remote than Elizabethan English from the current vernacular of 'the High.' Above all, romance exists not in the comedies of Aristophanes. An undergraduate, dressed up, will play the buffoon readily enough. But do not expect him to be romantic. In Shakespeare's comedies the central business is romantic, the buffoonery is a side-issue. Consequently the performance of a Shakespearean comedy in Oxford is like a sparse 'mulberry-bush' danced round unlighted sticks. For Aristophanes the bonfire blazes merrily, and all is well. Aristophanes is the best policy for the O.U.D.S.—the line of least resistance. I hope Shakespeare will be less constantly to the fore in future.

In the production of *The Clouds* no attempt has been made to compromise between the modern and the antique theatre. Unity of place goes hang. From Strepsiades's sleeping-room to Socrates's court, and thence to a street, the scene is shifted by scene-shifters, and all possible use is made of modern contrivances. The clouds themselves, for example, appear first dimly through a gauze, and are then irradiated with pink lime-light. I remember how annoyed I was, and how annoyed many people were by my annoyance, when at Cambridge *Agamemnon* was produced as a pretty spectacle. More recently, when Professor Gilbert Murray's version of *Hippolytus* was acted in London, I lamented that an Attic tragedy, however archaeologically treated, was quite impossible in a modern theatre; and I dilated on Bradfield. But Attic comedy is another matter. The effect depends not at all on its original setting. In modern conditions it is just as amusing as Attic tragedy is unimpressive. And let the conditions be as modern as you will. They cannot be more modern than Aristophanes himself.

The prime glory of Aristophanes is his modernness. Our prime delight in him is through the difficulty of believing that his satire was written not yesterday, but twenty-three centuries ago. His every hit glances off from his own time to ours. No wonder that the scholars of our day translate him in the most modern terms—through the phrases and references of the passing moment. To do so is no tax on ingenuity: it is a saving of trouble, so obvious are the equivalents. Of course, I do not pretend that our delight in witnessing one of Aristophanes's comedies is equal to the delight of the Athenians. We are impervious to many a little point that pricked them sharply. Not all the topical allusions 'carry' now. We care not that Cleisthenes was effeminate and Chaerephon pallid. From the Athenian audience, knowing these men well, the sudden gibes against them must have evolved roars of laughter. The Athenian audience, for whom Pericles's 'ἐς τὸ δέον' was a catchword, and for whom the Corinthians, and the reformed calendar, were burning questions, must have thrilled with rapture at Aristophanes's whimsical variations on these themes. We merely note the wit, and smile a dry academic smile. Yet, broadly speaking, the play delights us not less than it delighted the Athenians. Socrates is not in our midst; but he is still an acute reality to our imaginations: we should not be surprised to encounter, any day, his squat figure and embarrassing questions in Trafalgar Square, or to see him stalking Dr Johnson down Fleet Street. And such difference as there is between an actual presence and a presence thus vividly imagined is cancelled by the fact that the tendencies symbolised by Aristophanes in that actual presence are paralleled with fair exactitude in our life today. Aristophanes hated Socrates as a disintegrator of the social system. Everything, in every social system, is absurd when you come to think about it. When a community has become powerful and prosperous, and the citizens have time for thought, someone is likely to crop up and invite them to think. Such a person is undoubtedly a public danger. Socrates was undoubtedly a public danger; and, from a civistic standpoint, the only plausible argument against the final death-sentence on him was that he would be still more dangerous in martyrdom; but even that argument was robbed of its force by the fact that Socrates had become a public nuisance as well as a public danger. We, in England today, have no one thinker so powerful and pervasive as Socrates. But the sum of modern thought is Socratic. And all that was just in Aristophanes's satire applies more pungently to Socrates individually than to our own seers collectively.

Much in that satire was very obviously unjust. The contemporary Sophists indulged in all manner of intellectual hanky-panky, and also fleeced their pupils. But no man was ever less nebulous or less mercenary than Socrates. Commentators have suggested that Aristophanes was so finely crusted in Toryism—had so little patience with any modern development—that he honestly supposed there was no difference between Socrates and the Sophists. This is absurd. You may hate the doctrines of (say) Mr Bernard Shaw. But, be you never so reactionary, you do not imagine that Mr Bernard Shaw will cast your horoscope or gaze into a crystal for you on receipt of a guinea. Even so, be sure that Aristophanes (whose knowledge of his times was never less keen because his sympathy lagged behind) did not honestly confound Socrates with the Sophists. His confusion was a deliberate means of prejudicing the case against Socrates. But he trusted too much, I think, to the stupidity of his audience. In his address through the chorus to the audience (why, by the way, is this delightful address omitted from the acting edition of the O.U.D.S.?) he complains bitterly that the first version of his play gained only third prize at the Dionysia. His way of accounting for his failure is one of the most modern passages in the play: he has given no scope for (κόρδαξ) a can-can; οὐδὲ πρεσβύτης ὁ λέγων τάπη τῇ βακτηρια τύπτει τὸν παρόντα—there is no 'knock-about business'; καγὼ μεν τοιοῦτος ἀνὴρ ὢν ποιητὴς οὐ κομω —I don't get myself up with a view to photographs in the illustrated papers; and so on and so forth. Possibly these lacks had something to do with the play's failure. But the chief reason, I suspect, was that the audience would not award the palm to a satire which both insulted its intelligence and outraged its sense of fairness. Aristophanes had to pay forfeit for not having 'played the game.' He ought to have cheated with more discretion.

Yet I think that had I been at that Dionysia, and even had I been Socrates's most eager disciple, I should have dissented from the verdict of my fellows. For Aristophanes in his unfairness to Socrates was not less copiously and brilliantly funny than when (as in so many passages) his onslaught had reason as ally. Besides, what was not reasonable as against Socrates, and so was harmless, was deadly reasonable against the Sophists. Nor did Aristophanes satirise merely what he hated. He was too great a satirist for that. He made fun of his friends not less surely than of his foes; and the fun is not the less delicious for being made affectionately. He loved the old-fashioned, stolid, uninquiring bourgeoisie; but he laughed at it. He loved stupidity as a wholesome thing; but he also saw that it was a ridiculous thing, and he did not attempt to tone down the ridiculousness of it. You may remember how, in one of the *Bab Ballads*, the sterling citizens of London were puzzled by the sophistries of the bad ogre, who ate good boys 'because he loved them':

'A fallacy in your remarks our intellect descries,
Although we don't pretend to say exactly where it lies.'

Such is the attitude of Strepsiades towards the sophistries of Socrates. And even Δίκαιος λόγος is worsted ignominiously by Ἄδικος: ἡττήμεθα, he cries, πρὸς τῶν θεῶν δέξασθέ μου θοἰμάτιον, ὡς ἐξαυτομολῶ πρὸς ὑμᾶς. I waited with peculiar anxiety for this passage. The Vice-Chancellor, by whose permission, jointly with that of the Mayor, *The Clouds* is now being performed, explains the passage thus (I quote from his annotated edition of the play published in 1899): 'The Δίκαιος λόγος is now fairly beaten. The theatre is all on the side of Ἄδικος. There is nothing left to do, but to toss his cloak to the audience, and spring down as if to join them, and run off at a side-door.' I thought the members of the O.U.D.S. would hardly dare to reject this gloss. I am glad they plucked up sufficient courage. For, surely, Δίκαιος λόγος is addressing, not the audience, but Socrates and his pupils, to whom he surrenders his cloak as a preliminary to initiation. Let Dr Merry turn back to lines 497–498 of the text. Strepsiades is seeking admission to the academy. Socrates bids him take off his cloak, explaining that it is the rule that all students must take their cloaks off before entering. I wonder that Dr Merry missed this clue. I should like to have been the first to supply him with it, as a very slight return for the pleasure which I, through a summer term, derived from his genial and penetrating lectures on Aristophanes.

[*4 March 1905*]

'STILL IN THE GROVES OF ACADEME'

Last week I joined issue with Dr Merry on a point in Aristophanes. Perhaps, had I not done so, Greek would have triumphed last Saturday at Cambridge even more signally than it did. Some of the dons may have been haunted by a dread of being taught, sooner or later, by the grateful recipients of their tuition. Anyhow, I have received many letters of which the general drift is that I have been foolhardy in attempting to refute so sound and rightly eminent a scholar as Dr Merry. 'You wrote in haste,' says one of my correspondents, 'and will now repent at leisure.' It happens to be true, in a sense, that I wrote in haste. Had there been more time at my disposal I should have argued longer. But penitent—that I am not. I never should have dared tackle Dr Merry had I not been sure that I was on the safe side of the argument. And it is with perfect confidence and composure that I now proceed to put my case more fully.

At this point the majority of readers will have skipped to the next article. And, indeed, it does seem rather absurd that a grown man, in the foremost ranks of time, should bother his head over a tiny point in the interpretation of a thing written in the fourth century before Christ. Are there no large and vital issues in the modern world around me? Have I no sense of proportion? I have. But I try not to give way to it. There is nothing more dangerous than a sense of proportion. Not even the large and vital issues of his day seem important to a man whose sense of proportion is uncontrolled. Besides, few men are by Fate appointed to a contact with these issues. Most men are by Fate confined to contact with small side-issues. But it is necessary that the niggling labours of the world, not less than the world's great labours, be done well and faithfully. To be a commentator on the text of a work written in a dead language is one of the niggling labours. It seems extraordinary to me that any man can devote, as many a man does enthusiastically devote, all his days to such a labour as this. Still, it is well that the labour should be performed. I honour its performers. And I myself am willing to take a turn at it, by the way, in passing. To do so, indeed, is a welcome change in my ordinary avocation—an avocation hardly less niggling than that of a textual commentator . . . Down, sense of proportion, down! I never will desert the modern drama.

137

But even the most faithful attendant craves a holiday, now and then. Today is one of my holidays. And, if I bore you on it, be comforted by the thoroughness of my own enjoyment. The holiday mood is always . . . but you begin to suspect me of temporising. Brandishing a copy of *The Clouds*, I hasten to the grapple.

At the end of his dialogue with the Unjust Argument, the Just Argument exclaims 'I am conquered. Take my cloak (δέξασθέ μου θοἰμάτιον); I desert to your side.' Says Dr Merry 'The Δίκαιος λόγος is fairly beaten. The theatre is all on the side of "Αδικος. There is nothing left to do, but to toss his cloak to the audience, and spring down as if to join them, and run off at a side-door.' I contend that it is to Socrates and his disciples, not to the audience, that the Just Argument addresses his speech. Before giving evidence for my own theory, I will give evidence against Dr Merry's.

The Clouds is a play with a purpose. Aristophanes hated Socrates, and hated all that Socrates represented to him. He wanted to make the Athenians share his own contempt and disgust. The first version of *The Clouds* had missed fire. In the second version Aristophanes was at great pains to catch the sympathy of the audience—to put them in a mood receptive of his ideas. Even had he not wished to convert the audience for conscientious reasons; he would have wished to convert them for reasons of vanity; for it must have been obvious to him that they would not award him the first prize unless they were in agreement with the substance of his satire. His address to the audience through the mouth of the Chorus is a piece of very delicate diplomacy. The gist of it is 'You are so clever, I am sure you will like this comedy, which is really the cleverest I have written.' Is it likely that, later in the play, he would have said to them (in so many words) through the mouth of the Just Argument 'You are so purblind that you cannot distinguish between truth and falsehood'? To admit that he had not converted the audience would have been to admit that he had no chance of the first prize—that his satire had again missed fire. Aristophanes was not likely to drag in any such admission. Aristophanes, believe me, was no fool.

One of my correspondents told me that in Dr Merry's text 'a very gross epithet' is omitted, and that this gross epithet 'is evidently addressed to the spectators.' So I looked up the complete text as edited by Mr Blaydes; and there the gross epithet was —

βινούμενοι. But, since Aristophanes had shown himself anxious
to be on good terms with the spectators, and since it was obviously
needful that he should be so, this new piece of evidence does but
strengthen my conviction that the Just Argument was not here
addressing the spectators.

Of course, in the comedies of Aristophanes, it was quite usual
for a character to make a remark straight to the audience. And the
trick must have been very effective. But no character ever announced his intention of jumping down among the audience. That
might have been effective, had the character proceeded to jump.
But it would have been very ineffective if he had merely disappeared
by a side-door. And, since the actor impersonating the Just Argument, after finishing his speech, had to run off and immediately
return in the guise of Socrates, it is the more unlikely that Aristophanes, with his knowledge of the theatre, conceived the idea
which Dr Merry attributes to him.

On my supposition that the Unjust Argument was addressing,
not the audience, but Socrates and the students, there was no
absurdity in the exit. The character's entry into the academy was
the natural illustration of the words just spoken. Similarly, the
term of abuse, βινούμενοι, was quite a likely term to be addressed
here to Socrates and the students. But, before I pass to the construction of my own theory, let me give one more destructive blow
to Dr Merry's. The ἱμάτιον was not a garment that would have
encumbered a man in the act of jumping. It was just a piece of
cloth wound over one shoulder and under the other. To wear it
trailing to the ground was a rare sign of effeminacy; and we may be
sure that the Just Argument, as representative of all the more
sterling qualities of citizenship, did not wear it so. He would no
more have doffed it before taking a jump than a twentieth-century
man, in similar case, would doff a jacket.

Now for my own theory. In the early part of the play, Strepsiades seeks admission to Socrates's school. 'Come,' says Socrates,
'take your cloak off' (κατάθου θοἰμάτιον). Strepsiades asks why.
Socrates replies 'It is customary to enter stripped' (γυμνοὺς εἰσιέναι
νομίζεται). Here, surely, is the key to the words of the Just Argument,
'Take my cloak. I am deserting to your side.' I do not know why
Aristophanes represents Socrates as insisting that his pupils shall
take off their cloaks. Possibly one of the Sophists had some such

139

rule. Possibly, again, Socrates himself, who was famous for his hardiness, never wore the ἱμάτιον—a garment worn primarily for protection against cold; and he may have set this fashion to his young disciples. Possibly, again, Aristophanes uses the sacrifice of the cloak as a symbol of the avarice which he unjustly imputes to Socrates: as who should say 'he leaves you without a cloak to your back.' When, in the final scene, one of the disciples cries out to know who is setting fire to Socrates's house, Strepsiades answers 'He whose cloak ye have stolen' (ἐκεῖνος οὗπεο θοἰμάτιον εἰλήφατε). Indeed, θοἰμάτιον is a kind of *Leitmotif* throughout the play. I can hardly, with Dr Merry, accept Hersmann's conjecture of θυμάτιον for θοἰμάτιον in line 179 of the MSS.; the pun would have been quite in Aristophanes's manner, and would have been quite obvious to an Athenian audience. But such points are immaterial to my case. Enough that throughout the play there are references to the sacrifice of Strepsiades's cloak, and that the words of the Just Argument in reference to his own cloak have so obvious a solution in Socrates's first injunction to Strepsiades.

I trust that I have not seemed to you arrogant in this my meeting with Dr Merry on his own ground. As I said last week, I derived, *in statu pupillari*, much pleasure and profit from Dr Merry's lectures on Aristophanes. And I feel now, not as a man feels when he is bearding a lion in his den, but rather as that fabled mouse must have felt in the privilege of disentangling from a snare the lion that had erst befriended him.

[*11 March 1905*]

AT THE HAYMARKET

Everybody's Secret enraptured the first-nighters, and will doubtless enrapture two-hundredth-nighters. It has none of the qualities that make for failure. Superficial persons might, perhaps, wonder that either Captain Marshall or Mr Louis Parker was not alone deemed by the management capable of lifting *Le Secret de Polichinelle* into English. Certainly, both Captain Marshall and Mr Louis Parker are grown-up men, and clever men into the bargain. But in the very fact of their maturity and cleverness lay the reason for trusting neither of them single-handed. Be it remembered that the British public is, in regard to matters of art, a public of children. To please them really much, a playwright must himself be childish. Naturally, then, our playwrights do their best to make themselves childish. But the task is not easy for all of them. Clever men are apt to behave cleverly without knowing it. With the best will in the world to write a thoroughly foolish play, a clever playwright will, here and there, by oversight, allow cleverness to creep in. Despite every precaution, he will, over some little bit of knowledge of life, or criticism of life, be caught tripping, and be ground under the public's heel. He needs a collaborator. Two clever men, working loyally together, will be able to detect in each other's work the insidious symptoms which might pass unnoticed by them in their own work. I am convinced that neither Mr Parker nor Captain Marshall could alone have compassed so consistently inane a play as *Everybody's Secret*. Each was necessary as a check on the other. As a rule, I disapprove of collaboration. One might suppose, *a priori*, that the process of collaborating would give us the sum of the good qualities possessed by each collaborator. But experience shows that the good qualities in the one man cancel the good qualities in the other. Perhaps, then, *Everybody's Secret* grew quite easily, like a flower. But I like to think it is the result of the reasoned determination of two men to keep watch and ward over each other, and to guide with blue pencils each other's faltering footsteps along the straight and narrow path that leads to a besieged box-office.

I did not see *Le Secret de Polichinelle* acted in Paris, nor have I read it. But, from what I have heard of it, I imagine it to have had some relation to reality. A young Frenchman has for several years been living with a woman inferior to him in station. She has borne him a child. He is devoted to his mistress, and would like to marry her and so legitimise the child. But he knows that his parents, who have strong notions on the subject of social rank, would never give the necessary consent to the marriage. And so he has kept his parents in ignorance of the whole affair. When, at length, they are told of it, they are furious, and forbid their son the door. That is the end of the first act. Now let us turn to the version made of it by Captain Marshall and Mr Parker. The young man and the young woman are married—have been married for several years, for the child is several years old, and is legitimate. The young man has from his parents an allowance of £500 per annum, and on this he contrives to support the ménage and be in the Guards. He applies for a rise of £100 per annum, and, when this is refused, he blurts out the truth. Let us set aside the initial absurdity of supposing that the parents, living in London, could for several years be ignorant that their son had an entanglement round the corner. Nor let us doubt that a young Guardsman could keep a wife, a child, and himself on £500 per annum. Let us merely inquire what it is that has prevented this young Guardsman, during all these years, from telling his parents the secret. His parents have strong notions on the subject of social rank, and his wife was a girl in a florist's shop, and had lived with him for some months before marriage. Apparently that is the sole reason for secrecy. In the French version, as I have shown, there is a valid enough reason. But how ridiculous to ask us to imagine that a young man would prefer to an unpleasant scene or two a life of unending inconvenience and torment! Of course, the parents would have to accept the accomplished fact; and, being really very kind-hearted people, such as Mr Cyril Maude and Miss Carlotta Addison delight to impersonate, and being, moreover, passionately devoted to their only son, they would soon accept the accomplished fact with a very good grace. The fact that the daughter-in-law was not a lady in the strictest sense would count for very little in the long run, whilst . . . Stay! Of course the daughter-in-law *is* a lady, in the very strictest sense. The play was written for the English stage. Not to make the young woman a perfect lady would have been hardly less fatal than it would have been not to marry her to the young man. As necessary as the marriage-lines themselves is the refinement which marriage-lines confer. Who ever saw on the English stage a mesalliance in which the wife gave jarring token that she was not the social equal of the husband? I did. The play was Mr Maugham's *A Man of Honour*. Therein, a man of position had married a barmaid; and everything hinged on the vulgarity that survived in the wife, who was meant to be a sympathetic character. A sympathetic character, and yet not a perfect lady! Impossible! Such a thing had never been heard of. Such a thing was inconceivable. Mr Maugham's play had a short shrift—a dozen nights at most. It stands as a warning. Perhaps Mr Parker alone, or Captain Marshall alone, would have forgotten that warning, awful though it was. Between them, they have produced the requisite heroine, who describes to her mother-in-law how, when first she saw her future husband across the florist's counter, 'our eyes met. It was only for a moment. But in that moment' various exquisite phenomena occurred, and 'the shop became a garden of flowers.' In real life, I think, perfect ladies don't found their conversational style on that of the heroines of the novelettes in *Chirpy Bits*. But to do so is essential to perfect ladyhood on the stage. In making their heroine do so, Mr Parker and Captain Marshall were not trying to be true to the facts of her case. They were but respecting a popular convention. Of course, in turning out their heroine a perfect lady, they sacrificed the last poor remnant of logic in their hero's conduct. But logic—what does logic matter to the public? To me it matters, nevertheless. And, at the risk of being thought a prig, I shall continue to apply logical tests to the plays that come under my notice. I do not subscribe to the doctrine, so sacred to the majority of dramatic critics, that one ought to be silly about silliness.

The special strength of the play's appeal to the public is in the second act. Here is the grandfather, snoring in an armchair, and being awakened by the grandson with a popgun; presenting the grandson with a toy-sword; telling the grandson that there was a little man, and he had a little gun, and his bullets were made of lead, lead, lead; being told by the nurse that the grandson is a little wonder for his food—especially jam; recalling that he himself was considered a little wonder for *his* food; playing peep-bo with the grandson; and so on, and so on, throughout the act. After a little while, these amenities began to pall on me. But I am sure the public would have continued to revel in them if they had been prolonged till midnight. I am sure the public will continue to revel in them throughout the coming spring and summer. Do not suppose that I, too, am not very fond of children. My misfortune is that I myself am grown up; and that I do not, like most people, cease to be grown-up when I cross the threshold of a theatre.

[*18 March 1905*]

MR DE VRIES'S PERFORMANCE

Last week, so long-drawn were my sneers at *Everybody's Secret* that I had to forgo the pleasure of praising Mr De Vries, who, in *A Case of Arson*, somewhat atones for the rest of the programme. Atonement should follow, not precede, sin; and I think it a pity that *A Case of Arson* is done at an hour when so many of the people who have reserved seats are lingering over dinner. Before going to the Haymarket, let these people order dinner to be served at 9.15. So they will lose nothing either gastronomically or aesthetically.

They lose much by not seeing Mr De Vries. They lose a wonderful display of virtuosity in the art of acting. I must say that, judged in relation to dramatic art, the display is reprehensible. *A Case of Arson* is a tragedy. The central figure is a certain John Arend, 'a cigar merchant in a small way,' who has set fire to his shop, in order to get the insurance money. He appears before the examining magistrate, is succeeded by many other witnesses, is recalled; and gradually, despite his readiness and ingenuity in answering the magistrate's questions, his case breaks down, and his guilt is proved. There is nothing essentially tragic in such a situation. It might be treated comedically, even farcically. But the author, Heijermans, whose *Good Hope* is known to us through the Stage Society, has a sombre mind, and has complicated his play with a motive which ties it down to tragedy. In the fire at the cigar-shop a little girl happened to be burnt to death; and this little girl was the only and well-beloved daughter of John Arend. So that in John Arend we behold not merely a scamp trying to throw dust in the eyes of the law, but also a father overwhelmed with remorse. Now, in comedy or in farce it is not always essential that we should have an illusion of reality. In tragedy such illusion is essential always. We must imagine that the characters are actual human beings; we must forget that they are figments impersonated by mimes. Of *A Case of Arson* the prime attraction is that, with two exceptions, all the characters are impersonated by Mr Henri De Vries. The examining magistrate, and his attendant, are impersonated by two actors, in the usual way. But Mr De Vries, in addition to being John Arend, is a policeman, and a grocer, and a house-painter, and an innkeeper, and the father-in-law of John Arend, and John Arend's half-witted brother, who is at first suspected of having committed the crime, and who tries to save the real culprit by incriminating himself. Obviously, no dramatic illusion is possible. If we had not a programme, we might (so truly Protean is Mr De Vries) not realise that the several parts were not being played by several actors. But of course Mr De Vries wants the credit for his feat—a feat which it would be ridiculous to perform otherwise—and his name recurs on the programme seven times. The piece is specifically a 'show-piece' for him. It is intended, first and last, that we shall admire his skill. Who could withhold admiration? But all the time our admiration depends on the fact that we are not being illuded; and there is something unseemly in a tragedy that does not illude—that cannot be taken seriously. It is amusing to see seven live rabbits produced from a top hat. The conjurer, while he performs this feat, indulges in humorous remarks. He knows, with sure tact, that this is not the time or the place for him to harrow us with reflections on death, and disease, and disaster. Similarly, it is amusing to see seven live characters impersonated by one actor. The dramatist, if he had sure tact, would not choose a tragic pivot for those characters to revolve on. I do not imagine that Heijermans could, if he would, have written a farce for the display of Mr De Vries's pluralistic genius. Yet a farce—some such farce as that in which, a few years ago, at the music halls, Signor Fregoli's pluralistic genius was displayed to us —is the only right artistic medium. Incapable of farce, Heyermans ought to have left to some cheaper spirit the task of exploiting Mr De Vries. It is, as I have suggested, necessarily a mood of amusement that is created in us by Mr De Vries's method. And we, being in this mood, are necessarily jarred by the introduction of horrors, which, unless they can move us to pity and awe, ought never to be introduced at all. What should we think of a conjurer who told us, in the course of his patter over the rabbits, that a few days ago his little daughter was burnt to death, and that, though he, loving her with all his heart, did not of course mean that she should be burnt, yet her death was directly caused by him? We should not believe his story. It would touch no responsive chords in our nature. We should but be offended by a solecism. Even so are we offended at the Haymarket. Only by an exceptionally marvellous power of dealing with rabbits could a tragic conjurer retain his hold on us. I cannot pay Mr De Vries a higher compliment than by saying that never for one moment in his performance did I seriously intend to walk out of the theatre.

Even if illusion were possible to the spectators of a play in which many characters are played by one man, such a play ought yet on no account to be tragic in intent. Not even with full illusion could we get from it a sense of tragedy. Not even so could we take it seriously. For no actor, how Protean soever, can successfully impersonate various types of normal humanity. The types have to be abnormal. They have to be exaggerated creatures—grotesques. Otherwise there would be no variety—no escape from the actor's own individuality. In *A Case of Arson* John Arend is (barring the two characters not impersonated by Mr De Vries) the only normal type vouchsafed to us. He is a man with an ordinary face and figure, an ordinary gait, an ordinary voice. There is nothing absurd about him. Presumably, he is, in all respects, very like Mr De Vries. If the policeman, and the grocer, and those others, also appeared as normal men, then would they too be very like Mr De Vries, and very like one another; and there would be no fun at all. Every one of them, therefore, must have a set of sharp eccentricities behind which Mr De Vries may efface himself. One of them has a vast black beard and a deep bass voice, and suffers from asthma. Another has scarcely any voice at all. Another is hugely fat, rolls in his walk, and speaks in the treble. Another wheezes, and suffers from palsy. Another squirms in his walk, speaks through his nose, and carries his head cocked to one side. None of them but is, in one way or another, grotesque. Even in a tragedy, of course, a grotesque is admissible here and there. But what of a tragedy in which we are introduced to a whole gallery of grotesques, one after another, with hardly a moment's surcease? The thing is intolerable. Or, rather, it would be intolerable if Mr De Vries were not, in his every assumption, irresistible.

I wish that, on one occasion, Mr De Vries would forgo his irresistible pluralism, confining himself to the part of John Arend, and letting the other persons in the tragedy be played, as essentially they ought to be played, as normal human beings, by an equal number of actors. The play has enough intrinsic quality to justify this whim. And Mr De Vries's impersonation of John Arend is, in itself, so fine that one would like to see it in a setting worthy of it— a setting in which its fineness could have full effect on us. On reflection, I think I should allow Mr De Vries to double the parts of John Arend and of Ansing Arend, the half-witted brother. For the latter is, in surface, a grotesque part; and, moreover, I think no actor could play it so well, with so fine a pathos, as it is played by Mr De Vries. Not that I withhold from Heijermans himself the first credit for having created this character, which, interpreted even by a duffer, would haunt one's memory. I know few scenes more poignant than the closing scene of the play. John Arend is in an inner room, under arrest. Ansing stands before the magistrate, still mumbling that he himself is the guilty one. The magistrate takes his portfolio briskly from the table, and, before he goes out, speaks kindly to Ansing and congratulates him on being at liberty to go home. Ansing is left alone with the magistrate's attendant, who throws open the door for him. But Ansing stands twisting his cap round in his hands, and staring at the door of the inner room. At length, 'My brother—he in there?' he asks. 'Yes, my man, your brother's in there.' After a long, vacant pause, 'I go in? See him?' 'No, you can't see him.' Another pause, and then Ansing shuffles out obediently, and the curtain falls. In this ending we have, I think, a perfect example of how a tragedy on the stage should end—and ending in a minor key, and fraught with that kind of relevant ir-relevance of which Shakespeare knew so well the value—an in-conclusive ending, and therefore a right ending, in that it leaves our imagination free and so holds our memory when all is over.

[25 March 1905]

ELSINORE AGAIN OVERHAULED

'It is hardly too much to say, in reference to this latest production of what is perhaps the masterpiece of our great national poet, that the ghost of Hamlet's father is the most impressive within our recollection. Heartiest commendation is due to Mr Maskelyne for having contrived in co-operation (as the programme informs us) with the Committee of the Society for Psychical Research, an illusion so abundantly convincing. The vague diaphanous form scarcely palpable to the audience, and the faint twittering sounds emitted through it by Mr Horne, the well-known ventriloquist—sounds in which, most rightly, only a word here and there was distinguishable—combined to make for the first time credible to us the hitherto somewhat disconcerting scene between the youthful prince and his much-wronged parent.' . . . This is a fragment of dramatic criticism in a morning newspaper which has somehow been wafted to me from the year 1924. It is interesting, as a document. I am glad to have this peep into futurity. But I would rather have learned, thus magically, something which I could not have foreseen, in the ordinary way, by deduction from present tendencies. In the past twenty years or so, the tendency in performing *Hamlet* has been, ever more and more, to present a sensible, realistic, modern drama of psychology, and to let the poetry shift for itself. The Ghost, as being a sort of detached figure, is still allowed to drag poetry in, speaking his lines sonorously and with rhythm. But the days of his privilege are surely numbered. Let him make the most of them. He will soon be brought into line with the definitely corporeal persons of the play. He will soon have to be as real, prosaic, modern a ghost as they are real, modern, prosaic ladies and gentlemen. The Player King and the Player Queen, they too when they appear in *The Mousetrap*, are still allowed to be poetic. But from them too the permission will soon be withdrawn. For remember! the audience at Elsinore is a modern audience; and to a modern audience poetry is a quite ridiculous thing; insomuch that King Claudius and Queen Gertrude would not really, if *The Mousetrap* were declaimed for the music of the words, be quaking with fear upon their thrones, but would be rolling upon their thrones with laughter; and this would never do. *The Mousetrap* must, to produce the requisite impression, be acted in precisely the same manner as *Hamlet*. Perhaps the First Player will always be allowed to recite rhythmically and sonorously the turgid lines of 'Aeneas's tale to Dido'—just to show us how foolish a thing poetry is, and what fools the old-time actors were, and how well we are rid of them. And, maybe, one or two benighted souls in the audience will clutch fondly at the one straw not blown away by the tempest of modernity.

This tempest rages more vehemently now at the Adelphi than it has raged yet elsewhere. I cower. A slight shelter is kindly provided for me by Mr Oscar Asche. He, as King Claudius, does remember that Shakespeare wrote the part in blank verse—does speak rhythmically, and with reverence for sound, and does comport himself with a large tragic dignity. But the rest! Really, 'the rest is silence'—for any pleasure afforded by it to the human ear. Miss Maud Milton, as Queen Gertrude, talks in easy conversational style, exactly as though Queen Gertrude were gossiping across a teacup. It is a wonderfully natural performance; but poetry, tragedy, queenliness, are quite out of it. Mr Lyall Swete is wonderfully natural as Polonius. He gives his advice to Laertes exactly as if each axiom occurred to him on the spur of the moment. Throughout the play he is a light and airy old gentleman, such as you might meet any day, without remarking him much, in the smoking-room of any club. Miss Brayton is very pleasant in the sane scenes of Ophelia; but one would hardly be surprised if at any moment she entered springing off a bicycle. In the mad scenes of Ophelia she tries hard not to be so pleasant, and manages to give a realistic representation of lunacy. This seems to me a mistake. Lunacy is a painful thing, and Shakespeare did not mean the mad scenes of Ophelia to be painful: he merely meant them to be beautiful: he turned them, in accordance to his notion of Ophelia's own power, 'to favour and to prettiness.' The only right way for an actress to interpret these mad scenes is through her sense of beauty. They are too irrelevant to be treated tragically. They are dragged in, just for beauty's sake. Even more obviously dragged in for that sake is the Queen's account of Ophelia's death. 'There is,' says lyric Shakespeare, 'a willow grows aslant a brook,' and he proceeds to revel in the landscape, quite forgetting (to our eternal gain) that he speaks through the lips of an agonised lady. What is the agonised lady to do? There is but one thing for her to do. She must forget that she is an agonised lady, and speak the words as beautifully and as simply as she can. Then there will be no absurdity. But what could be more absurd than to hear a lady talking, as Miss Maud Milton talks, about 'crow-flowers, nettles, daisies, and long purples' with tragic gasps and violent gestures of woe, and dwelling with special emphasis on 'long purples' as though they were quite the most harrowing thing of all? Here the passion for naturalness leads to sheer nonsense. Elsewhere, for the most part, its mischief is merely negative. It merely deprives the play of beauty and of tragic dignity. But beauty and tragic dignity seem to me (who am an old-fashioned pedant, if you will) the two first things to be conserved in such a work as *Hamlet*. They are not the only things. But they are the first things. Remembering them I was not able to be enraptured by Mr

H. B. Irving, who, as the Prince, remembered them, like his colleagues, so very vaguely—or, rather, gave them the go-by so very
sternly.

Of course, I admire his performance very much. He has a strong
personality. He has intellect. He has imagination. He has fire. He
has force. He has all sorts of things. Judged from the fashionable
modern standpoint, his performance is splendid. Judged in relation
to what he himself was especially striving for, his success is complete. Hamlet's character is strongly seized at by him, and is interpreted by him with infinite subtlety in detail. He is a life-sized and
a living Hamlet. I do not say that he gives us a wholly consistent
or wholly intelligible picture. He doesn't. But we must not blame
him for that. We must blame Shakespeare. Or, rather, we must
praise Shakespeare. None of us is wholly consistent or wholly intelligible—at any rate to himself, who knows most about the matter.
To his acquaintances a man may seem to be this or that kind of man,
quite definitely. That is only because they know so little about him.
To his intimate friends he is rather a problem. To himself he is an
insoluble problem. Shakespeare, drawing Hamlet, drew him from
within—drew him with a full knowledge of the many conflicting
elements in him—drew not, in the usual way, one of his sets of
qualities, or one of his sets of moods, but drew him in all his complexity and changefulness. We are all of us as changeful and complex as Hamlet was. There is nothing peculiar about Hamlet. The
peculiarity is but in the fulness of his portrayal. Shakespeare made
of a puppet a whole human being. Necessarily, since every human
being is a mystery at close quarters, Hamlet's character cannot be
made clear to anyone—to anyone, I mean, who studies it at all
closely. If anyone said to me about an impersonator of Hamlet 'He
made me understand Hamlet,' I should deduce that either the actor
had omitted nine-tenths of his lines, or that my informant had dozed
during nine-tenths of the performance. We must not ask of any
actor that he shall explain Hamlet to us. The most we can expect
is that he shall give unity to the divergent characteristics and
moods—that all these shall seem to be contained in one person, not
in many different persons. In a circus somewhere, years ago, I saw
a man drive a team of a hundred and fifty horses round the ring. I
thought him wonderful. I admire not less the actor who does not
let Hamlet get 'out of hand.' I admire Mr Irving's grip immensely.

But—but 'never were Shakespeare's words spoken with so entire an absence of pose and mannerism; never was this melancholy hero, with his rarely beautiful smile, depicted so much as a brilliant and romantic young man whom we could meet round the corner of the next street.' No, reader, this is not another fragment from 1924. I cull it from last Wednesday's *Daily Telegraph*. Hating to cavil frankly, I have recourse to this fragment, which, written with gratulatory intent, does yet define so exactly the grounds on which I myself object to Mr Irving's Hamlet. Just because I, like Mr W. L. Courtney, feel that I might at any corner collide with this Hamlet, and just because of that 'absence of pose and mannerism' (alias, that contempt for the conventions of poetic utterance) for which this Hamlet is remarkable, I cannot acclaim this Hamlet as ideal—cannot even accept it as satisfactory. A thoroughly modern Hamlet, a round-the-corner Hamlet; a Prince (if Prince he be) not of Elsinore, but of Bernstoff; a Hamlet who breaks up his sentences into prose, squeezing the words together, or stretching them interminably out, with no reference at all to their rhythm, and often muttering them inaudibly, on the assumption that they are so familiar to us all that they need not be re-communicated; a Hamlet, in fact, without style—this is not the Hamlet for me. I crave, first of all, the beauty which Mr Irving sacrifices to exact realism. Next to that, I crave the tone of tragedy. Hamlet, of course, is not always in tragic vein. He is often comedic, sometimes farcical. But he is a figure in a tragedy; and in all his moods he should be seen through a veil of tragedy. Mr Irving rends away that veil. In the final scene, for instance, he behaves just like any young man in a fencing-club. We cannot believe that he and all those other persons are going to die. Our aesthetic sense of tragedy is banished; and, consequently, the various deaths, when they occur, seem violently out of place—seem absurd. . . . In 1924, perhaps, these deaths will be omitted, and the whole play trimmed into a comedy. Modern audiences shrink from tragedy. One of the reasons for the great popularity of Mr Forbes Robertson's Hamlet was that he so notably brightened the play up. Mr Irving's Hamlet is as much brighter as it is less beautiful than Mr Forbes Robertson's. I am sure than in 1924 the last vestiges of gloom will have been swept out of Elsinore. A fantastic forecast? Well, twenty years ago you could not have conceived that *Hamlet* would ever be enacted as a play in prose.

And from tragedy to comedy it is not a further cry than from poetry
to prose.

[8 April 1905]

MR BARRIE AGAIN

A proof of Mr Barrie's value to the stage is that his plays would
not have the faintest chance of being produced if they were written
by any other man. 'Silly' the middleman would say, and 'too thin.'
And 'What does it mean?' the middleman would ask. And 'There
is one thing an audience will not stand; and that is, being laughed
at' the middleman would declare, bringing his fist down on his
desk, and hurting himself very much. But Mr Barrie is—Barrie,
and is chartered, and 'Charles Frohman presents' him every time,
with no questions asked, and with great profit to himself. So perhaps, in the near future, it may begin to dawn on Mr Frohman,
and on his rivals, that conventionality in drama is not the sole
way to success; and that for a play which is not like any other play
there is at least as good a chance as for one which resembles every
other one.

At the Duke of York's Theatre are now two plays by Mr Barrie
—and not one too many. In the curtain-raiser, *Pantaloon*, Mr
Barrie does much more than raise the curtain on *Alice Sit-by-the-
Fire*: he gives us a fresh and memorable fantasy. The private life of
harlequinaders has been taken as a theme by many writers. It is a
tempting theme, for of all mimes harlequinaders seem to be the most
remote from actual humanity, and the mere fact that they are
human is enough to startle and interest us. The clown with a broken
heart, the columbine modest and hard-working, the pantaloon a
spirited fellow in the prime of life—always thus, for sake of yet
sharper contrast, have they been revealed to us. Effective, no doubt,
as a trick; but bad psychology. Mr Barrie has gone deeper. He
knows that mimes cannot be utterly secerned from their life of
mimicry—knows that the longer and the better they mimic, the
more deeply do they absorb into their private souls their public semblance. To point this moral, he gives a very new twist to the very
old theme. He conducts us to a shabby lodging-house somewhere on

152

the Surrey side, and shows us the room where the Pantaloon lives.
The Pantaloon is out. But his daughter is in, and a young man is
telling her that he loves her. Neither of them is speaking, however.
They merely dance, and execute a few conventional gestures. For, as
we know by their costume, the daughter is Columbine, and the
young man is Harlequin. In hobbles the Pantaloon, crutch and
motley and all, very querulous of his rheumatism and his poverty.
Times are not what they were. Audiences have lost their sense of
art. He recalls the glorious past, and looks proudly round at the
painted portraits of himself that adorn his walls. In one of them
he appears with a forefinger upheld to his cheek, in another he
gazes across an open book that he has been studying. In another,
full length, he wears a frockcoat and trousers of broadcloth. It was
thus that, in younger and happier days, he once went to a fancy-dress
ball. . . . Hard times have hardened his heart. His daughter must
make a marriage of convenience. The Clown, a great artist, loves
her. He is coming to dinner. He presently tumbles into the room,
crowing 'What a lark!' and proceeds to munch a string of sausages
with his friend Joey. Harlequin has sprung away through the
window. Columbine is executing a *pas de désespoir* in the background. Ordered by her father to kiss her bridegroom, she, with a
face of anguish, leaps lightly with one toe upon the back of the
Clown's chair and thence imprints a kiss upon the Clown's fore-
head. There is a sound of wedding-bells. The Clown rises, crows,
claps his knees together, and bustles out with Columbine on his
arm. But at the door, with uplifted wand, stands Harlequin. . . .
Time has passed. The lonely Pantaloon sits by a fireless hearth.
He is starving. On the fearful day of his daughter's flight, the
Clown cast him off for ever—engaged another Pantaloon. There
is nothing for the Clownless old man to do but wait for death.
Unseen by him, the door is furtively pushed open. Columbine and
Harlequin are on the threshold, and with them is a tiny child—a
born clown, just old enough to toddle crowing to its grandfather
and to rub his shins with a property red-hot poker. With a cry of
joy the old man rises, and the curtain falls.

The little play is an exquisite invention, keeping you surprised
and pleased all the time. Yet nothing in the course of it is so pleasing and so surprising as the fact, afterwards realised, that Mr Barrie
brought the child on only at the very last moment. I suspect that

the play, as seen by us, is but the beginning of a quite long play about that child, and about the tender differences between its mother's, father's and grandfather's exclusive devotion to it; and I suspect that the main part was omitted merely because *Alice Sit-by-the-Fire* is itself a long play. But, even so, I wonder at the unadulterated adultness of the beginning. In *Alice*, of course, so soon as the curtain rises, we hear the familiar music of the coral-and-bells. True, the person 'discovered,' Amy Gray, is no longer a child. She is putting up her hair for the first time, in token of her maturity. But Mr Barrie, pained by this hideous crisis, promptly causes a perambulator to be wheeled past by a nurse, in full view of the audience, and in token that the heavens have not altogether fallen in on him and us. And presently we see the solicitous parents, just returned from India. The mother catches up a tiny slipper from the table, and, inserting the end of her handkerchief in it, so that it shall represent a baby in long-clothes, dandles it on her left arm. The nurse, being a nurse of the right kind, is very jealous of her and of the father, and (bless her good heart!) very 'short' in her replies. The mother, in her too great joy, is rather clumsy with the baby—does not hold it at the right angle, and hugs it too closely. The father is more adroit, it seems. And the father makes a doll for the baby, by twisting and knotting his handkerchief in a very ingenious way. And so on, and so forth. It is all very nice, and pretty, and human; and if Mr Barrie in his work gave it us once and away, or even now and then, I should welcome it. But *toujours bébé*! I conjure Mr Barrie, whose chiefest strength is his unexpectedness, to put aside the one thing that we can always confidently expect of him. Let him, if need be, plunge into one thorough, unmitigated, for-ever-satisfying debauch of babydom. Let him write one play whose whole action passes in a crèche. Let it be whatever kind of play occurs to him—a tragedy, hinging on nettle-rash, thrush, teething; or a comedy, hinging on bassinettes, rattles, indiarubber rings; or even a musical comedy, with an orchestra of babies playing no instrument but the coral-and-bells, and with choruses of nothing but crowing and screaming. Mr Frohman (have no fear!) would 'present' the play, readily and lavishly. So would any other manager. The success would be such as Mr Barrie can always now command. And the gain to Mr Barrie's future art would be even greater.

About *Pantaloon* I wrote at some length, partly because it has
not had justice done to it by my colleagues (who are, for the most
part, better judges of quantity than of quality), and partly in
order that I should not have much space in which to write about
Alice. For the delightfulness of *Alice* cannot be communicated
through criticism: the thing depends so little on its framework—
such framework as it has—and so much on its casual little em-
broideries. Mr Barrie has always excelled in making much out of
little; and here he tops his own excellence. To fill the last act,
for example, there is so little left over from the preceding act that
one feels sure that the play will end in a fizzle. In due course, one
finds that the last act is the best of all. Alone among artists, Mr
Barrie is inspired by very lack of material. Like the Prime Minister,
he is at his best, and most engaging, when he has least, under greatest
difficulties, to say. Mr Balfour never wound up a crushing debate
more deftly, and never rallied his side more surely to him, than
Mr Barrie winds this play up and rallies to him an audience which,
under anyone but him, would be disaffected utterly.

It seems appropriate that Miss Ellen Terry should be in a Barrie
play. For her, among actresses, the public has the same sort of
affection as it has for Mr Barrie among dramatists. And her genius,
like his, is ever childish and irresponsible. But, while his genius
is a delicate and modern one, hers is very boisterous, and seems to
belong rather to 'the spacious days' than to ours. The part which
Miss Terry plays here is the part of Mrs Gray, the mother of Amy
and of the baby; and Mrs Gray is an impulsive and exuberant
woman. But Miss Terry is really too exuberant, too impulsive.
The play is not big enough for her. Like Mrs Gray with the baby,
she all but smothers it in the fervour of her embrace. One longs for
Shakespeare, who, alone among dramatists, can stand up to her;
and one wishes the theatre itself were bigger—better-proportioned
to the wildly ample sweep of her method. Miss Irene Vanbrugh is
Amy. Her personality is in no way Barrieish. She looks, indeed,
quite young enough for her part; but her soul is not childish enough.
Miss Hilda Trevelyan, who is in the cast, might have played the
part ideally. Miss Vanbrugh succeeds, through sheer cleverness and
sense of humour, in playing it very well. Mr Aubrey Smith is
Colonel Gray. He, too, is by no means Barrieish. But he might
surely manage to behave rather more like an amiable and quite

ordinary colonel who is glad to be home among his family, and rather less like a distinguished general whose career has just been blasted by failure in a crucial campaign. He might, in fact, play lightlier.

[*15 April 1905*]

A LESSON FROM THE COURT THEATRE

Performances of *The Trojan Women* at the Court Theatre will be given at intervals throughout this month. I cannot help thinking they ought to have begun earlier in Lent, and to cease at Easter. They are very beautiful; but they are also very penitential. I am not one of the queer folk whom Sir Oliver Lodge scorns for their refusal to go where a sense of pity and awe will be stirred in them. I enjoy an aesthetic sorrow not less keenly than an aesthetic joy. I am not one of the people who, say Mr Gilbert Murray, object to *The Trojan Women* on the ground that it is 'too harrowing.' My objection is that the play isn't harrowing enough—isn't harrowing at all. It harrowed the Athenians, no doubt. Me it leaves quite cold. Not that I am insensible to all performances of Greek tragedy. Both *Agamemnon* and *Alcestis* have given me at Bradfield something (I conceive) like the true and original thrill. *Hippolytus*, however, in the modern theatre, with footlights and limelights, and with the English language (even as used by such a poet-scholar as Mr Gilbert Murray), sent that thrill only very faintly through me. What chance, then, of a thrill at all from *The Trojan Women* in similar conditions? For the play is not a play. It is but an interlude of lamentation. For Hecuba, and Andromache, and those others, our hearts may bleed, quite profusely, when the legends of them are shown to us in terms of tragic conflict. An Athenian audience, in the very fibre of whose minds those legends were implicated, and who took as a matter of course all that had befallen and was yet to befall these great persons, was in ready mood to be made miserable by *The Trojan Women*. But to us these great persons are not definite enough for so indefinite a mode of presentation. This or that legend must be enacted, if we are to weep. Vague reminiscences and foreshadowings of the many legends draw no tears to our eyes. An afternoon of wailings that wake no echo in us is a very painful sort of after-noon. It is an afternoon of boredom. In dull modern comedies I often see all the *dramatis personae* shouting with laughter while dead silence reigns in the auditorium. They seem to think that thus they will drown the silence. If they would but, on the con-trary, catch our grave demeanour across the footlights, the whole effect would be much less deadly. Similarly, at the Court Theatre the other day, I could not help wishing that the performers would be less awfully stricken. Feeling the lack of emotion among us, they seemed to be ever piling on the agony, in the hope that at last the structure must topple over on us. The harder they worked, the safer were we, alas!

But, though I grieved to behold so much waste of energy, I re-joiced to find how much talent, and how much good training, was here to be wasted also. Miss Marie Brema as Hecuba, Miss Wynne Matthison as Andromache, Miss Edyth Olive as Cassandra, and Miss Gertrude Kingston as Helen, all played with a right concep-tion of what is needed in a performance of poetic tragedy. All of them were dramatic, expressing the several characters, and the various grades of emotion, of the women impersonated by them. But to be dramatic—to be real—was not their sole aim. Evidently, they held it of equal importance that they should be poetic. They re-membered that they were speaking the lines of a poet translated by a poet. They remembered that *The Trojan Women* is not a modern tragedy in prose, and that to it poetry is co-essential with the effect of truth. None of them—no! not Miss Gertrude Kingston, who thoroughly dissociated herself from her usual self, though the less elastic critics have not recognised the achievement, and have chidden her for their own defect—ever for one moment sacrificed sound and rhythm to every-day naturalness. Beauty of diction, and dignity of port and gesture, were by none brushed aside as impediments. I hope Mr Otho Stuart, of the Adelphi Theatre, will take his whole company, one fine afternoon, in wagonettes, to Sloane Square. Example is better than precept. What I wrote about the performance of *Hamlet* may have had no perceptible effect at the Adelphi. Mimes are coy of lay mentors. But I doubt not they will learn from fellow-mimes, who have, in their turn, had the advantage of being controlled by a fellow-mime stage-manager with a clear knowledge of what's what from the standpoint of art. Not even

Mr Granville Barker's controlling hand has sufficed to make *The Trojan Women* a thing worth seeing. But his labour were not in vain if it could be, in the indirect way which I have suggested, extended to *Hamlet*. Of course, Shakespeare and Euripides are not one, and must not be interpreted by precisely the same means. But each man wrote tragedies in verse. And beauty of utterance, and dignity of demeanour, are needed equally in interpretation of each man's work.

Though you may not have the chance of making many converts, you ought not to cease from preaching what seems to you needful. Though a dramatic critic has, as I have said, little influence on mimes, he ought not to content himself with perfunctory praise of them. I do not (I regret to say) wonder at the praises that have been sung over *Hamlet*. Mostly, the critics do not care about poetry, and a prosaic rendering of it offends them not at all, and leaves them free to scatter the conventional epithets which save them the trouble of trying to realise their impressions (if any) of the performance. Among the critics who undoubtedly do care about poetry, and about poetic drama, Mr William Archer must surely be reckoned. He cannot be reckoned—would be, indeed, the last to reckon himself—among experts in the general art of acting. In criticising the performers in a modern play, he seldom ventures beyond epithets, making a poor pendant to his always interesting examination of the play itself; and I think he has chaffed himself in print for this shortcoming. But on Shakespearean performances he has always spoken as one having authority—the authority of his knowledge and love of Shakespeare's plays. Even so he has been speaking about Mr Irving's Hamlet. And listen! 'I hear it said that his Hamlet is deficient in poetry. What this objection means I do not rightly know.' Mr Archer, who loves Shakespeare's poetry so much, does not know what we mean when we object to a performance on the ground that it is not poetic. He might say 'This performance seems to me quite poetic: I dissent from you who think it isn't.' Then we should not hold up hands of sorrow and amazement. But, having made the strange avowal that I have quoted, he proceeds to guess that the objection to what he likes so much 'has something to do, perhaps, with Mr Irving's lack of smoothness and elegance in the lighter moments of the part,' and to suggest also that the objectors desire 'an amiable and sentimental

Hamlet.' All this is quite unworthy of Mr Archer. In point of fact, Mr Irving's Hamlet is as smooth and elegant a person as need be; but his smoothness and elegance are of a modern kind—the 'round-the-corner' kind which appeals so strongly to that dangerous rival of Mr Archer in love of Elizabethan poetry, Mr W. L. Courtney. As for amiability and sentimentality—these, too, are but red herrings across the trail. We might not object to salience of these qualities in a rendering of Hamlet: Hamlet comprises them among his numberless qualities. But we are not such fools as to blame an actor for making pre-eminent in Hamlet such sterner qualities as may happen to inhere in himself. Psychologically, Hamlet gives scope for an infinite variety of interpretations—'all of them right.' All that we demand of every actor who plays Hamlet is that he shall pay as much attention to the poetry as to the drama. 'Mr Irving's Hamlet is consistently dramatic,' says Mr Archer; 'and that, after all, is the main point.' It is, say we, one of two main points. We want a consistently dramatic and poetic Hamlet. A prosaic Hamlet does not satisfy us, to whom Shakespeare is not less a poet than a dramatist. And by a prosaic Hamlet we mean—assuming Mr Archer not to know that we mean—a Hamlet who speaks his lines without attention to their sound and rhythm. Shakespeare's poetry and drama are so woven into each other that we doubt whether a prosaic Hamlet can be dramatic. Make the play realistic—bring the play down, as Mr Irving brings it, to the plane of common life—and it ceases to move us. But, as generous antagonists, we won't press this point. The point that we do press is that Shakespeare was a poet. And we are surprised at having to press it against the bosom of Mr Archer.

[22 *April 1905*]

A CONVENTIONAL PLAY

A young Prince or Princess is, of course, a good subject for drama. A human being, but a being compelled by circumstances to fight against his or her human instincts—there you have a sharp conflict ready-made. No wonder that so many playwrights, in

England and elsewhere, on the look-out for a theme, have had re-course to the Princess torn between her love of a commoner and her plain duty to marry the Prince selected for her by diplomacy. The Prince in similar plight is a less frequent figure, for some degree of sympathy is felt for the Princess spurned by him. Such sympathy as might be felt for the Prince spurned by the Princess can always be diverted by the simple means of making the Prince a rake. I admit that I am a trifle tired of the Princess torn between duty and love; but I never give way to weariness of a thing which I shall certainly have to see again, and to see frequently. This distracted Princess is a fixture; and I must make the best of her. But I expect our playwrights to make the best of her, too. I expect them to make her real, and to make her a pretty reality. Her latest patron is Mr James Bernard Fagan. I regard Mr Fagan as a born play-wright—a man with an innate sense for the theatre, and for all the theatrical tricks. Also, I credit him with a desire to be no mere trickster, but a purveyor of beauty, and truth, and humour. Only, so far as I have sampled his work, I find that his humour, and his truth, and his beauty, are not of a high order. They seem to me conventional, derivative, undistinguished. *The Prayer of the Sword* was marked throughout by the quality of obviousness; and that quality I took as an earnest of its success. In *Hawthorne, U.S.A.* the same fault prevails. 'Prevailed,' I ought to say. For the last performance of the play will precede the appearance of this article. I am sorry; for a failure is always distressing, even though it be the failure of a thing that one cannot admire. And I am puzzled, too. I should have thought that *Hawthorne, U.S.A.* would triumph in very virtue of its obviousness. As it is a thing of the past, I would say no more about it, but for the fear that then Mr Hamilton Fyfe, doughty champion of *The Prayer of the Sword*, would arise and slay me for having sneered without justification at a noble and delightful work of art.

It was a good idea to make the Princess's lover an American. A real American would have given a certain freshness to the old Ruritanian theme. But Mr Fagan has never, in real life, met an American man. Or his impression of American men has been nullified by his recollection of that ridiculous stock-figure which on the English stage has for so many years done duty for American men. Always blatant, always cool, always resourceful, always ready with dreadful funniments in the manner of Max Adeler, that stock-figure duly creaked its joints under the label of *Hawthorne, U.S.A.* Thirty years ago, before the development of steamship-navigation, it was natural enough that English playwrights should be content with this figure. But nowadays, when London, throughout every summer, is overflowing with real Americans, it certainly does seem strange that our playwrights can give us nothing better than this one old battered simulacrum. So far as I know, the one playwright who has made an attempt to portray an American from actual experience of Americans is Mr Bernard Shaw. Hector Malone, in *Man and Superman*, is an admirable study. Not only has Mr Shaw used his ears, and delicately reproduced typical modern American peculiarities of speech, instead of offering us a jargon which is as remote as starred and striped waistcoats from reality: he has also entered thoroughly into a typical modern American soul. We all know Hector Malone in real life, and take him as a matter of course. But on the stage he is a startling creature indeed, and we welcome him with open arms. *Arms and the Man* was written long enough ago to have had its influence on Mr Fagan. Accordingly, there was a 'chocolate cream soldier' in *Hawthorne, U.S.A.* Would that *Man and Superman* were less recent! If Hawthorne had been an echo of Malone, his relation to the Princess might have been quite fresh and amusing. As it was, how tedious, how stale! When the Princess learned that her hero was not, as she had supposed, her destined Prince, but merely an American citizen, she instantly gave him to understand that they could not meet again; and he instantly gave her to understand that he came from a free country, where social distinctions were not recognised, and all classes were equal. Theatrically, this was inevitable. One saw it coming. But how much more true to life, and how much more amusing it would have been, and anywhere but in the theatre how obvious, if Mr Hawthorne had been instantly overwhelmed by his sense of the distance between the Princess and himself! Cannot you hear the well-chosen terms in which he would have referred to the antiquity of her race—the peculiar limitations of a life which he, though, as an American, he could not approve of them in theory, could—nay, must—respect in practice? And would not the Princess, for her part, have then been a trifle infected by democratic ideals? At any rate, would not she have coquetted with them, and with Mr Hawthorne? And would not Mr Hawthorne have been delighted, yet shocked? And when the shock had passed off, and Mr Hawthorne had given rein to his passion, would not the Princess have been frightened back into her royal dignity, and dismissed Mr Hawthorne from her presence? At any rate, here would have been a scene of fairly fresh comedy, bringing the play to exactly that point to which Mr Fagan had brought it when he finished his trite first act. . . . I feel that if Mr Fagan, at the outset, had asked me to collaborate with him, instead of leaving me to do so of my own accord when it is too late, the play might really have been quite delightful. But I doubt whether Mr Fagan would have been happy. So many reams of rhetoric would have been by my firm pencil struck from his dialogue. And his love of rhetoric is an overmastering, a frenzied, love. Never for one moment did the Princess or Mr Hawthorne begin to be alive, but only when it was the other's turn did either of them cease to orate. Their communion was a spouting match, in which sometimes he, sometimes she, won. He, in the second act, inherited a vast fortune. And here came *his* great chance. He simply overwhelmed her. Not a King, he? He enumerated all the various forces of the civilised world, punctuating his every period with 'of this I am King.' In the third act came *her* great chance. He had been saving her father's kingship by various loans and disbursements. And, as she proceeded to tell him, he had taught her that the world was one great mart, and the scales had fallen from her eyes, and all sorts of dreadful things had happened; and 'For this I thank you' she said between every sentence in her indictment. In the fourth act, when she discovered that he had not been indulging in a mere business transaction, but had done all for her sake, and was truly worthy that she should become Mrs Hawthorne, one got the effect less of a union of two warm hearts than of a treaty between two sets of overworked lungs. Possibly that was why the play did not capture the public.

Miss Millard was very graceful and Ruritanian; but, naturally, she could not vitalise the Princess. Mr Waller, as the American, amply supplied for me that element of comedy which Mr Fagan had omitted; and he showed splendid disregard for convention, which I wish Mr Fagan would imitate. For the most part he spoke as a Briton born, and the effect of the stage-American lingo spoken without the stage-American intonation is really memorable. Now and again, Mr Waller suddenly changed his tone, and allowed his voice, at the end of a sentence, to drift into a minor key. And only after we had wondered vaguely whether he was imitating Sir Charles Wyndham, did we grasp his true intention. But the comedy of Mr Waller's performance lay deeper than in mere intonation. The part, as I have said, was conceived on the usual lines. Hawthorne was always to be cool, except perhaps in his amorous rhetoric. But it is the essence of Mr Waller's power to be always at white heat. Imagine a white-hot cucumber, and you will realise how much you missed in not seeing Mr Waller as Hawthorne. 'I guess they've spoilt those gates' said Hawthorne, when a distant crash of timber and metal warned him that the royal palace was being invaded by the angry mob. Obviously a comedy line, to be drawled in a quiet nasal monotone. So thought Mr Fagan, I am sure. Not so thought—or, rather, felt—Mr Waller. Standing in profile, with a blazing eye fixed on the King, he shouted 'I guess—*they've spoilt*—THOSE GATES'—making of the words three peals of cumulative thunder, awful to hear. And yet he drew from the audience the laugh that Mr Fagan had meant him to draw. It is seldom (alas for authors!) that an audience thus manages to grasp a meaning in the teeth of an interpretation.

[*10 June 1905*]

AT THE ST JAMES'S THEATRE

I know nothing of M. Emanuel Arène, the collaborator of M. Capus in *L'Adversaire*. He may be as delightful an artist as M. Capus. The inferiority of *L'Adversaire* to M. Capus's usual work is no evidence against this possibility. Collaboration is an excellent thing in theory; but it nearly always fails in practice. One would suppose that the admirable qualities possessed both by A and by B would be all the more admirable in conjunction; and that A, strong at just those points where B is weak, would be of great assistance to B; and that B, conversely, would be a treasure for A. But the fact—the mysterious fact—is that the strong points common to both parties have a way of cancelling each other; also, that such weak points as may be in either obtund the strong points in the other. M. Capus has no weak points that would have prevented him from making, single-handed, a wholly delightful play on the theme chosen for *L'Adversaire*. That *L'Adversaire* itself falls far short of his usual level is the fault of M. Arène, no doubt. But it is unfair to assume, as some of my colleagues have been assuming, that M. Arène is a duffer. His work may have been hurt as much by M. Capus, as M. Capus's by his. Indeed, the defects of *L'Adversaire* are in favour of this courteous idea. A clever artist may in collaboration so far over-ride a mere duffer as to produce a work almost on his own level. But parity tolls the knell.

An ambitious woman, devoted to a brilliant but unambitious husband, and met and loved by a man both brilliant and ambitious, is a promising character for the observant dramatist. Much, I am sure, would have been made of her by M. Capus, had he worked alone. He would have shown to us wittily the gradual transference of her affection to the quarter where her ambition found its mate. When Langlade, the rising barrister, declares to Mme Darlay that he has two passions—his passion for her and his passion for success—she, remembering her fond but retiring husband, answers bitterly that one heart cannot hold both love and ambition. There you scent an idea and a psychological situation. But nothing is made of either. When next we see Mme Darlay, she is Langlade's clandestine mistress. Of her transition—the stage that is interesting here—we know nothing. Her transition has been skipped. The three principal characters stand to one another in the rusty relation of bookworm husband, ardent young gentleman, child-wife. Instead of pausing to vitalise them, the authors have hurried on to a conventional scene of the husband awakened, the husband cross-examining. This scene appears to impress the audience. But it is not good enough for me. I am all for cross-examination, if it be well done. I have spent in law-courts some of the most vivid hours of my life, listening to this or that master of the art. In the theatre, too I have derived great pleasure from samples of cross-examination. That was a fine scene in *Mrs Dane's Defence*, for example, when the trained lawyer, little by little, exposed the well-laid imposture of the heroine. Two keen wits pitted against each other, on either side of a quite plausible case, till, at length, by some tiny flaw in the case, or by some tiny error in the conduct of it, the attack corners and destroys the defence—here is a process which (appealing, if you will, to an ignoble side of my nature) certainly does delight me. But a plausible case, with two dull wits pitted against each other across it, breaking down partly because one wit is more egregiously dull than the other, and partly for no reason at all except the dramatist's need, leaves the gladiator in me unsatisfied. And it is but such a process that is vouchsafed in *L'Adversaire* (hereinafter to be called *The Man of the Moment*). There is no evidence at all that Mme Darlay is Langlade's mistress. Darlay does not suspect more than a flirtation. He begins to cross-examine merely that he may know how far the flirtation has gone. His wife is determined to deny even that she has flirted. But her denials are so clumsily expressed that Darlay soon begins to believe the worst. He takes a peremptory tone. She refuses to answer any more, complaining that all along he has been trying to 'entrap' her into 'committing' herself. 'Ah!' shouts Darlay, thoroughly convinced of her guilt by a phrase that is really quite compatible with innocence. Thoroughly convinced that he has by the irresistible force of his own intellect extorted the equivalent of a confession, he tells his wife that he is now going to confront the lover. Mme Darlay, falling to her knees, implores him not to do that, and confesses her guilt. Had she the brain-power of a rabbit, she would have known that the confronted lover would merely tell the husband not to be a fool, and that the husband would presently have to beg her pardon for having been such a fool as to condemn an innocent lady because of a phrase which, spoken in an excited moment, he, in an excited moment, had happened to misinterpret. The whole scene, in fact, is silly. It has a superficial appearance of strength and tensity. But it has no substance. The appearance appeared to impress the audience. Enviable audience!

After the climax there is a marked improvement. An idea emerges, and has free scope in a scene that is natural, and also novel. Darlay is not an easy-going person, and he refuses to act as though he were. He is not violently angry with his wife, but he is shocked, repelled, and knows that he is likely to remain so. His wife implores him to forgive her aberration, and to live with her as before. But he points out to her that this would be uncomfortable for them both. He might forgive, but he could not possibly forget, and his inevitable memory would cast a constant shadow between them: they must see no more of each other. For his part, he may find happiness in his literary work. She, for her part, may find happiness in marrying her lover. He will not be so unkind as to divorce her: she shall divorce him. That favour he will grant readily. But he utterly refuses that they should live together, for together they could not hope for more than a pretence of happiness. Now, all this is much better than the usual scene of violent re-proaches melting into forgiveness—melting on to a clean slate. In real life, no doubt, the majority of men in Darlay's position would play the part familiarised to us by the stage-hero. But Darlay (we have been told, though we have had to take it on trust, in the first three acts) is a man of ideas, a philosophic man. And so it is natural that he should base his conduct on an idea. And so there is nothing to moderate our welcome of this idea, which (on the stage, at any rate) is a new one, and is certainly a good one—one which would in course of time force itself on the subconscious self of the average sentimentalist in Darlay's position, even though it were never intellectually realised. But not merely by reason of this idea, and of its naturalness in the circumstances, is the last act of this play memorable. It contains a very pretty trick of technique. In plays of this kind, the reconciliation is often brought about by some third party—some *raisonneur*. In *The Man of the Moment*, surely enough, appears this *raisonneur*, but, all the while, unconsciously clinching the separation of husband and wife; and we have a scene not less comic than tragic in its irony. While Madame Darlay still pleads with her inflexible husband, her mother comes into the room, asks what is the matter, is horrified to hear that there is to be a separation. Darlay, of course, explains to her that the fault is his. She goes across to her daughter, and begs her not to take too harsh a view of things: it is in the nature of men to err; this man may have been unfaithful to her, but he loves her; let her go to him and forgive him. The daughter, looking very foolish, goes to him. The mother, looking (to us) very foolish, but feeling not at all so—feeling, on the contrary, very proud of her skill in preaching—proceeds to preach a little more. Of course, she says, if a wife deceives a hus-band, the whole case is altered: people sometimes complain that there is one law for men, another for women; but it is perfectly just that this should be so. Darlay echoes her sentiment. She retires, giving her blessing. . . . Really, this last act almost redeems the play. I am convinced that M. Capus conceived and wrote it without help from M. Arène. Or perhaps M. Arène conceived and wrote it without help from M. Capus? By the way, these gentlemen suffer not at all at the hands of Mr Harry Melvill, their translator. The dialogue is natural and vocal English—rare quality in a translation.

The interpolation of Mme Le Bargy in a British cast suggests to me many reflections, for which there is no space now. I will offer them next week.

[*17 June 1905*]

'THE NEW FELICITY'

Peering into the immediate future, I descry there a number of mysterious objects which, on closer inspection, turn out to be plays written in the manner of Mr Bernard Shaw. I heave a sigh. I mutter against Nemesis, that unkind goddess who, whenever she sees an original artist becoming popular, forthwith encompasses him with a dreadful swarm of 'sedulous apes.' It is always quite easy to distinguish the work of the original artist from the work of his imitators. A hero's valet does not look really heroic in the suits that the hero has worn. The imitators of an original artist can but reproduce something of his surface: his substance is far from them, and they cannot cheapen it. But his surface is, appreciably, cheapened. His personal tricks of style and of construction, his personal preferences in subject-matter—these things, which, unimitated, would be still fresh to us, and delightful, become stale to us, begin to annoy us. If only the persons who have the inclination and the energy for producing works of art, without the power of conceiving anything in their own souls, would imitate purely academic models! But they won't. One and all, they fasten their fangs on *le dernier venu*; and he, thus horribly hampered, must fight his way along as best he can. Poor Mr Shaw! Also, poor us! For I think that imitations of Mr Shaw will be more than usually exasperating. He himself sets out not to please, but to exasperate. It is only the pleasure we get from the perfect working of that exquisite machine, his brain, and from the natural ebullience of that crystalline spring, his humour, that prevents us from being exasperated. He would like us to stone him. Instead, we make a pet of him. Were he anyone else, he would have his desire. Were he one of those imitators whom I descry in the near future, I myself should cast the first stone. Depend on it, I shall be a terror to those imitators. So soon as ever. . . . Why! What is this? Already? Yes, an imitator—the first of the imitators—under my eyes, in the immediate present. I stoop to pick up a stone.

Taking aim, I notice with regret that my mark is a woman. I might have known it would be. For not only are women the imitative sex: they are also the quicker sex—quicker to be 'in the movement.' And it is natural that the Shavian movement should appeal especially to them, for Mr Shaw is so saliently their champion. But, woman though my mark is, the stone must be flung. Indeed, her sex is an added reason for the flinging, for it aggravates the offence committed. I mean that a feminine imitation of Mr Shaw is necessarily worse than a masculine one. Mr Shaw's art is not always human, but it is always masculine. That wonderful 'grip' of his, that consistency and straightforwardness, that intellectual conscientiousness and sense of justice, are qualities which no woman could even passably imitate. And then his humour! I do not raise the old parrot-cry that women have no sense of humour. On the contrary, my experience is that women in real life have quite as much sense of humour as men—more of it, if anything. But, somehow, they seem unable to make use of it through any artistic medium. (Hence, perhaps, the fallacy that they have it not.) Women can, when they see the right way about it, do valuable work in art. They have a peculiarly delicate power of observing themselves and one another (their observation of men is vague and faulty), and they excel in sentiment; and when they confine themselves to sentiment, or to introspection and to criticism of one another, they do finer work than could be done, in that genre, by men. But they ought never to imitate men. And Mr Shaw, as having pre-eminently the two qualities that in art they most lack, is the last man whom they ought to imitate. But imitate him they certainly will; and many of them, belike, will do it worse than it has been done by the first lady in the field, Miss Laurence Alma Tadema.

Like *The Philanderer*, and like *Man and Superman*, *The New Felicity* (produced last Sunday by the Stage Society) deals with the male amorist who dares not marry. Mr Shaw's satire was sympathetic, and just, and therefore effective. The amorist was a human being, with average virtues, and (like all Mr Shaw's creatures) of more than average intellect. Miss Tadema, being a woman, will not bother about justice. She cannot imagine two sides to a case. She cannot conceive that a person of whom she disapproves can be aught but a knave and a fool. And therefore her satire falls flat. Like John Tanner, Cyprien de Steyne writes philosophic books. But, whereas Mr Shaw was at pains to write one of John Tanner's books as an appendix to *Man and Superman*, in order to eliminate any chance of our not doing justice to John Tanner's intellectual sincerity, such of Cyprien de Steyne's philosophy as is vouchsafed to us is but a wild burlesque on a silly attitude. Cyprien de Steyne is purposely presented as an impostor, and as a silly impostor. His name in itself is enough to show Miss Alma Tadema's opinion of him. The mischief is that nothing at all like him exists. He is a mere figment. An amorist in real life is often conceited and selfish; and these qualities might well be shown and satirised on the stage. But when, in real life, an amorist is reproached by a lady for not having called on her lately, he does not, I imagine, say 'Poor little thing! I'm afraid I *have* neglected you.' Still less does he say 'I became immersed in my work and forgot you.' Least of all does he say 'You have evidently been guilty of that antiquated and reprehensible custom of falling in love.' Yet this is how Cyprien talks to Miss Evangeline Percival. To explain the bearing of the last speech quoted, I must explain that Cyprien merely desires Miss Percival to give him a measure of intellectual companionship. He does not make love to her, though she is very attractive. In real life, certainly, there are men who never demand of attractive women more than a stimulus to the brain. But Cyprien is not one of these men. Miss Tadema has chosen to make him a sensualist. A girl has been seduced by him, and has borne him a child. By way of explaining to us the discrepancy between his present and his past, this girl, who is now a music-hall artiste, explains to Miss Percival, in the last act, that Cyprien has had enough of vulgar women as women, and now needs only refined women as companions. But, as Cyprien is still quite young, and not an invalid, this explanation is obviously absurd. The only adequate explanation is that Miss Tadema has bungled through too much zeal. It was not enough for her that Cyprien should be a prig: he must be a scamp also. To make him credible on the stage, either he ought to make love to Miss Percival, or the music-hall artiste ought to be eliminated. No man is two

different kinds of men. Cyprien must be one kind or the other. In
fact, Miss Tadema cannot have it both ways. To have it both ways
is exactly what a woman always demands in an argument. That is
the main reason why a woman can never write an effective satire.
Without justice (or, at least, a plausible semblance of justice) no
satire can succeed. And the reason why women are unjust is not
any innate deficiency in sense of fair play—not any unscrupulous
desire to falsify an issue: the reason is merely lack of intellectual
grip. I don't pretend that the vast majority of men have not this
lack: I say merely that every woman has it. And in this lack you
find not only the reason why no good satiric play can be expected of
a woman. You find also the reason why no good play of any kind
can be expected of her. A good little poem may be built up on
sheer sentiment; a good short story on sheer observation. (Both these
qualities appear, from time to time, in *The New Felicity*.) But a
play must have solid brain-work behind it. Otherwise it falls to
pieces. Miss Tadema's play has from the outset no real substance to
suffer discohesion. But let us suppose that it has real substance. Let
us suppose Cyprien to be a real character. At the beginning of the
last act, what has to be solved is the future of Miss Percival. Will
she, or won't she, dismiss Cyprien from her life? She knows that
he has had a child by the music-hall artiste, Miss Carrie Gilmour.
She goes to see Miss Carrie Gilmour. We have learnt, in the
second act, that she despises Cyprien, though she is in love with
him. Miss Gilmour assures her that Cyprien is despicable, and applies
to his conduct the weird explanation which I have already described.
Exit Miss Percival, determined to have done with him, merely
because she has been told one thing that she knew already, and
another thing which no woman (unentangled in the task of dramaturgy) could possibly believe. So much for the last act, as the
termination of a story. As the termination of a satire it is not less
ridiculous. After Miss Percival has gone off, enter Cyprien, offering marriage to Miss Gilmour, who spurns him precisely in the
manner of Magda. He is much relieved at not being taken seriously,
and at being able to sentimentalise without fear of the consequences.
He is also delighted to see his child, whom he pronounces to be
the image of himself. So far, so good. But then he takes the child
on his shoulder, and dances round the room; and on that tableau
the curtain falls. Now, it stands to reason that the ending of a

satire ought to be relevant. It ought, indeed, to suggest sharply the author's summing-up. Are Cyprien's paternal gambols merely irrelevant? Did Miss Tadema finish her play at a chance moment, merely because she was tired of it? Or did she really think that Cyprien, as father, had at last found his proper vocation—the future that Fate had ordained for him? Respectfully raising my hat, I leave Miss Tadema between the horns of this dilemma.

[*1 July 1905*]

A FANTASY MISBEGOTTEN

This week, again, a short play is my theme. It is called *Aylmer's Secret*, was written by Mr Stephen Phillips (at the tender age of nineteen, they tell me), and is now being acted at the Adelphi Theatre, as a prelude to *The Comedy of Errors*. Itself full of errors that appeal to the comedic sense. As they are youthful errors, I do not hold Mr Phillips gravely culpable for them. I expose them merely that other playwrights, meditating similar work, may not fall into them.

Aylmer's Secret purports to be a serious, philosophic fantasy. I welcome any approach to fantasy on the stage. Fantasy in a setting of modern life—such a fantasy, for example, as *The Admirable Crichton*—especially pleases me. But it must not then be serious fantasy. It may have a serious meaning; but that meaning must be illustrated in an expressly comic way. We must be expected to laugh. We are not expected to laugh at *Aylmer's Secret*. The story is one that could never be told to us except in deadly earnest. Aylmer is a scientist. He has fashioned in his laboratory a human form. Fibre for fibre, cell for cell, the organism is perfect. It awaits only that elixir which shall endow it with life. Elixir in hand, Aylmer is torn between two emotions: pride in his achievement, and terror in having usurped God's prerogative. . . . The creature comes to life, and kneels to its creator, who shrinks away in horror. Aylmer has a daughter, whom he loves well; and his revulsion from his

171

unnatural son is intensified by fear that these two creatures, so
different, yet so akin, should come into each other's presence. He
rushes out into the night. His son follows him. . . . Aylmer comes
home, and finds the creature gone. Henceforth he will abjure his
occult experiments. He will lead a happy and natural life, devoting
himself wholly to his daughter. Time passes, and his mind is at
rest. But, one night, he comes and finds, in his daughter's presence,
his son. Spurned by the world that he had wandered into, the
creature has crept back to its creator, and has stirred pity in the
heart of Aylmer's daughter. Aylmer curses the creature, and bids
it begone. The creature, and the girl, plead with him. He is
merciless. The creature falls down dead. Its heart is broken. 'Who
was he?' asks the girl. 'He was my child,' says Aylmer.

Such is the play, in outline. Many people would object that this
kind of story cannot properly be told in dramatic form—is altogether
unsuited to the theatre. 'It would be all very well,' they might
argue, 'in a book. There we could grant the author's premises, and
be duly receptive. Our imaginations would have free play there.
But on the stage, where definite, corporeal images are presented,
keeping us bound to the actual world, such a story is artistically impossible, for we cannot forget that it is actually impossible. We
could accept "the creature" as presented to us through the hazy
medium of black type on white paper. But when we see a young
man, full-grown, walking and talking behind footlights, we can but
shrug our shoulders, and smile.' Well, I am less ill-equipped for
appreciation of fantasy in the theatre. Definite, corporeal images do
not utterly paralyse (though, certainly, they hamper) my imagination
and my receptivity. If Aylmer, on the stage, were presented as a
mediaeval alchemist, with a long white beard, square-shaped
spectacles, and a furred mantle, and if the whole of the play's setting
were in accord to him, I should be susceptible enough of Mr
Phillips's intent. I should be able to believe. Also, I should be able
to control my features. But I defy myself not to be utterly sceptical,
and not to smile, when Aylmer is standing all the while before me
in dark-grey trousers, a brown velveteen coat, and an up-and-down
collar with a neat black cravat. If a playwright casts a (serious)
fantastic idea into contemporary life, he may as well cast it into
the waste-paper basket at once. Even in a book—even where no
definite, corporeal images are presented—a modern setting is

harmful to a tragical-supernatural theme. I have always regretted that Stevenson made of *Dr Jekyll and Mr Hyde* a modern story. Not even his minutely realistic art makes the thing credible. On the other hand, his farcic fantasies are made doubly good by the familiar modernness of their setting. Delicious is the contrast thus achieved. It would be even more delicious if we could definitely *see* that contrast—*see* those solemn characters saying and doing those impossibly romantic things in the costume of today, and in the streets that we know so well. The more definitely we are reminded of the prosaic facts of actual life, the more ludicrous is a romantic variation on these facts. There you have the exact measure of Mr Phillips's blunder. Having tied us firmly down to actuality, he expects us to take his miracles reverently. Wriggle as we may in our bonds, there is no escape for us; and so we cannot rise to reverence. The trousered alchemist tremulously plucks aside a curtain, and gazes at the lifeless youth who is his handiwork. The youth is not naked. But, we object, he surely would be. The notion of dressing him up before he comes to life strikes us as rather genteel. The alchemist has not gone so far as to clothe him in trousers, up-and-down collar, &c. He has draped him in a tasteful toga. Well, in a garret in Soho (Mr Phillips insists on the exact district) this toga may pass muster. But when, at the end of the act, the youth walks out into the night, we cannot help wondering how the French and Italian denizens of Soho will take this new proof of the madness of English people. A similar anxiety seems to have haunted Mr Phillips. For the wanderer, when, at length, he returns from his wanderings, is attired in an inconspicuous suit of reach-me-downs. The name of the shop where he bought it is not vouchsafed to us. We are left to speculate. Isaacson? Moss? Aaronson? Such speculations are, of course, deleterious, deplorable. But we cannot save ourselves from them. I have no patience with persons who, witnessing such fantasies as Maeterlinck used to write, have so little imagination that they can take the incidents only in reference to actual life. Still less patience have I with them if they titter, for lack of the good manners that would make their mistake inoffensive to other persons. I should blame anyone for tittering in the course of *Aylmer's Secret*. But I should marvel at anyone who were not, throughout, sorely tempted to guffaw. The impossible rooted in the actual: that is the formula on which Mr Phillips wrote *Aylmer's Secret*. Strange, that he did not foresee the sure consequence. True, he was only nineteen years old: I cling to the play's date. But sense of humour is not usually so late in development, is it?

Mr Phillips's theme itself is quite a good one, as you will have gathered from my description, in which I carefully detached it from modern life. But the theme, quite apart from its setting, was not well worked out by Mr Phillips. The treatment is unimaginative, inhuman. It is unimaginative that the creature of Aylmer should be an ordinary, decent, intelligent young man—a very fair specimen (as he seems to be) of the produce of our public schools. Some curious defect should have been imagined for him. He ought to have had no sense of right and wrong, or to have been, in some other way, monstrous. This would have given his creator some justification for loathing him, and wishing to murder him—not, indeed, for letting him loose on the world at large. Yet Aylmer, even with a hatred of his strange son, and with all his sense of blasphemy in having created a human life, ought to have had for this strange son a natural love. And in the conflict between these two feelings would have been found a fine motive, and the one right motive, for the play's action. As it is, Aylmer appears merely as a brute and a bully, who feels not the faintest sense of paternity until his son is comfortably dead. And, remembering that there will be an inquest, we rather hope . . . but I had already pressed enough the point of actuality. It is the essential crudeness and childishness of the conception that I. . . . Enough of that, too. One *is* crude and childish at the age of nineteen. My only quarrel with Mr Phillips is that *Aylmer's Secret* is one of the childish things that he should have put away from him—put away under lock and key—put away in a manager-proof safe.

[*15 July 1905*]

OF MUSICAL COMEDY

The aim of art is to please. The trouble of the critic is that he is never, in the true sense, pleased. He is not at liberty to surrender himself. He cannot revel irresponsibly. He has to keep a sharp look-out, poor fellow, with a view to formulating the report that he will presently draw up. Imagine yourself a private detective, told off to 'shadow' a beautiful woman, to take notes of her movements, and afterwards to draw up a report of those movements, and to deliver that minute report to your employer. Thus projecting yourself, you also project yourself, unwittingly, into the soul of the professional critic of an art. As a private detective, you might derive some cursory, incidental pleasure from the beauty of the lady 'shadowed.' But you would not be, in the full sense, an admirer. The stern duty on hand would pre-occupy you. Even so does the professional critic of an art find himself pre-occupied. Art's aim being to give pleasure, art is almost entirely wasted on him. Such pleasure as he gets in contemplation is seldom anything but the comparatively mean and tame pleasure of hitting on the reason why, in happier circumstances, he would be rejoicing. Do not, then, wonder that his work is so little inspiring. Honour him for doing his best. That his best is rather poor is not his fault, but the fault of the system under which he has to work. Really good and inspiring criticism can be done only by an amateur critic—an accidental and not premeditating critic. 'Emotion remembered in tranquillity' is as sound a recipe for criticism as for poetry. The professional critic fails because he has to keep himself tranquil at the very moment when he ought to be swayed by emotion. The amateur critic often succeeds because he writes, of his own accord, for the sheer purpose of expressing himself, about a thing to which, seeing it for his own pleasure, quite irresponsibly, with no *arrière pensée* at all, he was able to surrender himself utterly.

Polyhymnia-Thalia, Muse of musical comedy, is not one of the ladies I have to 'shadow.' The duty of reporting her movements in this Review falls somewhere between Mr Runciman and myself, and so goes unperformed. Nor do I ever go to see a musical comedy of my own accord. I am far past the stage when one can deliberately, in cold blood, choose to enter a theatre, with a view to enjoyment. Now and again, however, I find myself inveigled, and, to my great surprise, find myself having a very pleasant evening indeed. The basis of my pleasure is, I suppose, my irresponsibility. The strange sensation of not having presently to describe my sensations is quite enough to reconcile me to any kind of entertainment, however stupid. But this is not the full explanation, and is, as I have worded it, rather misleading. My pleasure in musical comedy is not in despite of the thing's stupidity. It is, greatly, by very reason of the thing's stupidity. The perfect achievement of an aim is always a pleasing sight. And musical comedy differs from other art-forms in that it aims, directly and frankly, at stupidity. Nor do I consider that aim unworthy. *Dulce est desipere* (repeats the hardened journalist, without a blush) *in loco*. And, the higher the plane and the more intense the pressure of our thought, the more idiotic must we be in our moments of reaction. Were musical comedy other than it is, the highest intellects in the land would be deprived of an incomparable safety-valve. And what would become of those 'forty millions—mostly fools' (hardened journalists again) who find in musical comedy an art-form conducted precisely on the level of their understanding? I have no sympathy at all with the growls so constantly emitted by professional critics of this art-form. Of course, musical comedy might be made a vehicle for keen satire, for delicate humour, for gracious lyricism, and what not. But I prefer that it should remain as it is. Let us continue to cry aloud for a serious drama, by all means; but long live mere silliness in mere entertainments!

Whenever a new musical comedy is produced, the experts, with touching unanimity, condemn it on the charge of formlessness. 'There is no coherent story,' 'the plot is a mere thread on which songs and dances are loosely strung,' 'in the second act the story is lost sight of, and the whole play degenerates into a variety entertainment,' &c. &c. Could criticism be more inept? Are these critics so lost to all sense of the difference of things that they can take a serious interest in the plot of a musical comedy—can seriously want to know the motives of this and that character for this and that action—can seriously crave a lucidly progressive development of events? For my own part, I complain that musical comedies are not formless enough. Especially in those which are produced by Mr George Edwardes, there is not nearly enough of singing and dancing —the two elements which, to any normal creature, are the only two that matter at all. For all the world as though the story mattered to us, we have long scenes between the principal characters, ex- plaining this and explaining that. Such scenes are tedious in them- selves, but they are doubly tedious as interruptions to the business of the evening. The pleasure that is to be derived from the music and dancing is a purely sensuous pleasure. Even if there were any intellectual pleasure to be derived from the plot, it would be nullified by the simple fact that there were also songs and dances. Intellectual pleasure may be a nobler thing than sensuous pleasure. And the human race may, in course of time, be so nobly developed that its brain will take precedence of its senses. But at present, by right of seniority, it is the senses that take precedence. Men cease to be intellectually receptive so soon as there is any appeal to the sensuous side of them. A very obvious example of this rule is to be found at certain 'public dinners.' In the ordinary course of things, the four or five hundred post-prandial gentlemen will listen placidly, attentively, even enthusiastically, while the King, the Royal Family, the guest of the evening, the two Houses of Parliament, the Army and Navy and Reserve Forces, and heaven knows how many other equally unpromising subjects, are, at heaven knows what length, dilated on. But when, as sometimes happens, professional singers are intercalated between the various toasts, as a counterpoise to the orators—ah, then, mark the lamentable falling-off in the behaviour of the audience. The orators may happen to be brief, audible, and not nonentities; and the singers may be beneath contempt; but the orators stand not a chance. Their wisdom falls on deaf ears—is lost in a buzz of post-prandial conversation, and vainly the stentorian toast-master interposes his 'Chair, Gentlemen, Chair.' The senses of the audience have been aroused, and their brains have accordingly been sent to sleep. The audiences of musical comedies are in exactly similar case. And the wonder is that they do not similarly try to drown the voices of the mimes who are talking instead of singing and dancing. . . . That it contains too little music, and too much comedy, is the only fault I have to find with the average musical comedy. With that single reservation, I am enraptured. That the songs are always stupid, and that the singers of them are almost always stupid, and that the 'chorus' behave as though it were an act of supreme condescension on their part to be there at all, may seem very shocking to the expert critic; but all these various stupidities do appreciably contribute to my delight. 'Emotion remembered in tranquillity.' Yes, I have never failed to get emotion from musical comedy. And I am, at this moment, quite tranquil. I ought to be able to re-create in you, reader, my own enthusiasm. This criticism ought to be one of those masterpieces which I mentioned a while ago. My pen ought to be just getting into its stride. Yet it lags. Apparently, the habit of writing about things which he has studied, with the express intention of writing about them, destroys in a man the power of writing worthily about things in which he has delighted.

[*22 July 1905*]

A 'YELLOW' CRITIC

I received, the other day, an American book entitled *Iconoclasts*, and sub-entitled *A Book of Dramatists*, and written by 'James Huneker.' I am told that Mr Huneker is, on the other side of the Atlantic, an admired writer. Otherwise, my knowledge of him is derived only from this book. I hope he is a young man. I hope and trust he is a very young man. He records that he met Mr Bernard Shaw in Bayreuth 'once upon a time,' and that Mr Shaw there talked to him 'in unmeasured terms' about the local habit of drinking beer. This would seem to show that Mr Huneker is not at this moment a stripling. Still, he may be. We must remember that American children are precocious, as a rule, and that so eager a thinker and talker as Mr Shaw might quite possibly, and quite profitably, share his uppermost thoughts with one of them. Opposite the title-page of *Iconoclasts* appears a list of four other books already written by Mr Huneker—one of them '*With portrait.*' This ominous list does not, however, dash my hope of Mr Huneker's youthfulness— of the beardlessness of the face portrayed. For, if the other books resemble this one, they might well have been written within a very brief space of time. They might well have been written, for example, within that space of time which a man spends at Yale or at Harvard. That this latest book has not been dashed off in the heat of youth I refuse (in the absence of direct evidence to the contrary) to suppose. Looking from my window, I refuse to suppose that the colt in yonder meadow, kicking up its hoofs so blissfully, so uncouthly, so ineffectually, is a full-grown horse. It will become one. Its present gambols are a sign of vitality, which will presently be shaped to usefulness, perhaps to beauty. Even so do I regard, across the Atlantic, Mr Huneker. Vitality he has, and ability. He may do very well in the future. I speak not of the immediate future. In the immediate future he will have to shape himself—learning to think, learning to write.

Nor is this the first process for him to undergo. He must begin by *un*shaping himself. And this, I fear, will be no very easy matter. For he is (considering his tender years) an extraordinarily hardened and perfect specimen of the sensational journalist. His writing is like a series of separate headlines which have, through a printer's error, been printed consecutively in small type. He thinks in vast and separate headlines. Or rather, these headlines occur to him anyhow, and the thought is by them informed. So long as he hits his reader a good bang between the eyes, nothing matters. Savages sometimes 'see red.' Mr Huneker, invariably, sees red—no, 'yellow.' He 'writes up' the subject of dramatic literature exactly as his humbler colleagues 'write up' the subject of a fire or a murder. 'Whim,' wrote Emerson over his study-door. 'Vim,' writes Mr Huneker over the door of the cable-car in which (presumably) he does his work. And to this high motto everything is sacrificed. No matter how mild and commonplace the meaning in Mr Huneker's mind, we must be shrieked at. Take, as a sample of his method, the pages in which he discusses the aforesaid Mr Shaw—pages composed of various articles by which, from time to time, the souls of the readers of the *New York Sun* have been uplifted. Mr Huneker has read *Love among the Artists*, and he wishes to say that the story is not a pleasant one. This is how he says it. 'It is all as invigorating as a bath of salt water when the skin is peeled off—it burns; you howl; Shaw grins.' No matter that we *don't* howl over the story. Enough that Mr Huneker *does* howl at us. No matter that we wince from his voice. Enough that the men of Wall Street, devouring Mr Huneker's writing simultaneously with their 'quick lunch,' do 'grin' over his 'snappy' way of putting things. Down go the unmasticated mouthfuls into the stomachs of the quick lunchers; and down into their souls, to rattle there, go the tough morsels of 'intellectuality' that Mr Huneker purveys. It would never do for Mr Huneker to say, simply, that the moral of *Candida* does not become clear before the final act. 'The play,' he must tell us, 'is arrested in its mid-ocean, and the shock throws us almost off our feet.' Of course, the play is not 'arrested in its mid-ocean'; and, if it were, we should not suffer the discomfort which Mr Huneker, so as to give us a shock in reading him, invents for us. Nor, after a while, does Mr Huneker succeed in his efforts to shock. Ever bellowing, he becomes merely tedious. So far from being thrown off my feet, I merely yawn, and wish that the copy of *Iconoclasts* addressed to me from America had itself been 'arrested in its mid-ocean.' 'Every time I read *Candida*,' says Mr Huneker, 'I feel myself on the trail of somebody; it is all in the air.' Heaven forbid that I should read *Iconoclasts* more than once; and also that I should ever express myself in a fashion so slipshod as its. Nevertheless, Mr Huneker has in this crazy sentence expressed my own emotions in reading him. I did 'feel myself on the trail of somebody'—did feel that somewhere was somebody, by name Huneker, with a keen interest in literature, and with ideas in his head. But he, too, was 'all in the air'—bombinating in a vacuum created by his own lack of literary training, or of literary conscience. And I had half a mind to say nothing about him; and should not be saying anything about him now, but for (1) the chance of saving him, and (2) the impression that he were worth saving.

Its violence and vulgarity are hardly the worst faults of this book. A careful and consistent expression of violence and vulgarity might take rank as literature. But here these qualities are expressed so very carelessly. The writing is so bad that you have generally to read between the lines to discover what Mr Huneker means; and when, as often happens, he means nothing, you naturally resent the waste of your time. Of course, the quick-lunch public has nothing to resent. They don't care what Mr Huneker means, or how unmeaning he be, so long as he produces a momentary impression that he has some sensational meaning or other. But there is a difference (and I want to impress on Mr Huneker the difference) between newspaper-articles and a book. Mr Huneker speaks of his newspaper-articles as 'essays'(!) and announces that he has 'completely revised' them. I shudder to think what they must have been like before this process. I shudder to think what these reeling, sluttish sentences must have resembled before Mr Huneker tried to make them clean and sober enough for admission into a book. But Mr Huneker is not merely careless in form: his carelessness in matter is even worse. Self-repetition and self-contradiction don't much matter in 'yellow' journalism. The quick-lunch public has a short memory. But Mr Huneker might surely, in bringing his articles together, have remembered that they would be read together. Even if we forgive him the lack of energy to weld together the various articles on this or that one subject, we cannot have patience with his self-repetitions. It is worse when he contradicts himself. Mr Shaw, according to him, is 'the most serious man on the planet.' And Mr Shaw, according to him elsewhere, 'doesn't mean a word he utters.' Of course, Mr Huneker doesn't believe either statement: he is merely driving, in each case, at a violent effect. But he might, in courtesy to the readers of his book, have made up his mind to drive only at one effect or the other. If the writer of a book has not in his own self a high standard of work, he ought to try to imagine that his readers have it for him. If the doing of good work gives him no pleasure for its own sake, he ought to try to imagine that his readers won't stand bad work. Mr Huneker may love his own good yellow journalism for its own sake, or he may love it merely for the sake of the pleasure it gives to the quick-lunchers. But he certainly has no inward love of doing the sort of criticism that is worthy to be bound in a book. And so, guessing him capable of such criticism, I urge him to bear in mind the book-reading public.

If he is, as I think, a young man, there is hope for him. He may be reformed. But if he is not a young man, and so is beyond reclaim, he will yet be useful as an example to those of his young compatriots who are going in for literature. A drunken helot, even though he drink for drink's sake rather than for duty's, ought nowhere to be discouraged by mankind.

[29 July 1905]

THE THEATRE REVISITED

A friend of mine, an incurable invalid, once told me that he never awoke in the morning without a vague hope that he was about to find himself quite sound and well. Rationally, he was aware that his case was hopeless. But (let us be thankful) our souls are not much swayed by reason; and my friend, to the last, never lost faith that, one night while he lay asleep, the shattered mechanism of his body would somehow right itself. Even so, year by year, when I return from my annual holiday, I am buoyed up by a lively hope that the

181

British drama will have been gloriously transformed in the interval. Reason whispers to me that I am a fool. She is right; but I do not heed her. Why should not there have been a miracle? Looking back on the past theatrical season, I am ever convinced that it cannot be explained on rationalistic principles. Only by a miracle could so much rubbish have been accumulated in so short a time. Why should not we now be in for a golden shower of good plays? It is in this sanguine mood, annually, that I approach the first theatre to which duty calls me. And what a blight awaits me!

This year my first theatre has been the Adelphi. The play there is called *Dr Wake's Patient*. I do not say that it is below the average of our drama. To me it certainly seemed to be so. But this may be merely because bad things are less tolerable after one has had a respite from them. Nor was it so much the relative badness of the play, as its familiarity, that oppressed me. Here was the old familiar stock-pot, still simmering in position, with the same old odds and ends afloat in it, sickening us with the scent of the same old thin and greasy decoction. Here, as ever, was a play that had been written, from beginning to end, without an effort to portray human beings. Stage yokels, stage aristocrats, stage lovers, were all a-growing and a-blowing for our edification. There were only two characters that had a spark of life in them, and they had very little to do. Mr Gayer Mackay and Miss Edith Ostlere, who had written the play, impersonated these two very subordinate characters. But neither the modesty thus evinced by them nor the great merit of their respective performances was enough to soften my heart to them as writers. Mimes ought not to write plays. (Let me explain, by the way, but once and for all, that in my criticisms I use the word 'mimes' with no derogatory intent, and simply because, as a noun of common gender, it saves the time and space which would be wasted by 'actors and actresses.') The reason why mimes cannot write good plays is that a life spent in and around the theatre is bound to sap the instinct for reality. The theatre (for many people, and for all mimes) has a potent charm—a charm far more potent than that of the actual world. Even the playwrights who never have posed behind footlights feel this charm strongly; and most of them yield to it without resistance, and let the actual world go hang. Some of them yield only after a struggle. Others hold out manfully to the end (which for them, in the present condition of public taste, is usually not far off). But, at least, all playwrights who are not mimes have the chance, if they will but grasp it, of doing some sincere work. Mimes are disabled from the outset. To them the theatre can never seem a mere vehicle for the representation of life. Life, from their standpoint, is a thing that must be adjusted to the requirements of the theatre. And to their roseate vision the requirements of the theatre are nothing more nor less than their own requirements. 'Sympathy' and 'situations' are what they require above all things. It is dear to them to be dear to an audience, and to do (or have done to them), perpetually, things which surprise the audience very much. Whether they be like human beings, and whether their goings-on, active or passive, reflect any goings-on in the outer world, they pause not for a moment to investigate. Nor, indeed, are they qualified to conduct any such investigation to a successful issue. Humanity they have put aside, with other childish things. They know and care nothing about the human race, except that fraction of it which constitutes 'the audience.' How to win the maximum of applause, on the cheapest terms, is the problem for them. And, to do them justice, they generally manage to solve it. Certainly, Mr Mackay and Miss Ostlere, between them, have solved it triumphantly. I never heard applause more frequent and more delirious than it was, a few nights ago, at the Adelphi. Let me adumbrate the terms it was won on.

There was a young man, named James Forrester Wake, who was the most fashionable physician in London. He may not have been so very young as Mr Charles Hallard made him, bounding ever and anon so electrically up and down the staircase of old Mr Wake's humble cot, in which he was spending his holiday. But even if he had reached the top of his profession, as Mr Hallard reaches the top of the staircase, in practically one bound, he must have been old enough to cut a less childish figure than is cut by him throughout the play. A young lady is brought to the cot, suffering from a sprained wrist. He attends to her injury, and loves (and is loved by) her at first sight. But he wishes to tidy himself, and bounds to his bedroom, and so long is he in tidying himself that when, at length, he rebounds into the parlour, the young lady (impersonated by Miss Lilian Braithwaite, and by her endowed with a quite extrinsic charm and reality) has left the cottage in company with the two stage aristocrats who are her parents. She has not inquired the name of her benefactor. Nor does she suspect that he is the son of the two stage rustics named Mr and Mrs Wake. After a lapse of time, during which the two lovers pine, each wondering who and where the other is, we see the famous physician raving about his beloved to a perfect stranger who has come to him for medical advice. His beloved is nearer than he supposes. She is even now in the waiting-room. Instead of sending someone to the cottage to inquire the address of her benefactor, she has been pining so intensely that the stage aristocrats have insisted that she shall consult the famous physician. Lo! here she comes. Mutual, but suppressed, joy. Lady Gerania (such is her name) is ordered to a salubrious watering-place; and, a week or so later, while we watch her recuperation, lo! here comes Dr Wake. But there are rocks ahead. She has reason to suppose that he loves another. He, for his part, sees her in another's arms. These necessary misunderstandings having been cleared up, and the marriage arranged, enter the two stage rustics. It never occurs to Dr Wake (whose professional practice, though it must have given him considerable experience of the world, has left him little time for studying the theatre) that stage aristocrats are ever loth to let their daughters wed the sons of stage rustics. In the simplicity of his heart, he imagines that Lord and Lady St Olbyn will see nothing at all amiss in Mr and Mrs Wake, who (she with a Scotch accent, he with a sort of Devonshire one) can talk only about cattle, pigs, and poultry, except when they are talking about their son. And so, when, without a shadow of misgiving, he has brought the two old couples together, the shock caused in him by Lord and Lady St Olbyn's surprise, and by their withdrawal of their consent to the marriage, is so terrific that he goes straight away with his parents, leaving Lady Gerania in the lurch. Next day, she follows him to the cottage. But he will none of her. He loves her, loves her madly, but will not fly in the face of stage aristocrats. One of these, the father, presently arrives in pursuit, and has to cope with old Mr Wake, who is now in great form and announces his intention of selling up his farm and emigrating to Canada, in order to remove the Earl's objection. Not that he is ashamed of himself. On the contrary, he is as proud as ever of his yeoman lineage, and makes free use of the entries in the family Bible, pointing finally with special pride to the entry of 'James Forrester Wake, only son of Andrew and Martha Wake' (an entry paralleled only by the words of the departing hero to the heroine in a melodrama which I once saw, 'Where am I going? I am going forth to the Thirty Years' War.') So affected is Lord St Olbyn by the notion of Mr Wake going forth to Canada that he straightway withdraws his objection to the marriage. And King Edward, tele-pathically, has been so affected by the whole business that he, with his unfailing tact and forethought, has graciously decided to confer on Dr Wake the honour of knighthood. The telegram containing this news arrives just before the fall of the curtain.

Comment on this masterstroke were waste of words. On the play crowned by this master-stroke comment were wasted also. But I may express my disapproval of those critics who, capable of appreciating things that are not cheap twaddle, can yet bring them-selves to apply such epithets as 'pleasant' and 'charming' to such a play. Flattery of this kind debases not merely the currency of words. It debases, also, the currency of plays. So long as educated people profess to be pleased in the theatre by cheap twaddle which they would frankly spurn anywhere else, they are not likely to get the kind of plays which would give them true pleasure. I appeal to them not to dally doatingly over lumber, but to help me in clearing it away.

[*16 September 1905*]

'THE CONQUEROR'

Generally, in modern times, a poetic drama is chiefly pleasant and impressive as a sign of its author's great strength of character. Of his temperament, as apart from his character, it tells us little; and this little is the merely negative information that he is not a poet. If he were evidently a poet, we should have no proof of his boldness and tenacity. There would have been nothing morally grand in his resolve to write a poetic drama, nor in his power of sticking to his task till the task was finished. He would simply have been following his own bent; and we should be well prepared to hear of him as being actually among the weakest and most self-indulgent of mortal creatures. He, the true dramatic poet, is, as I have hinted, rather rare; and rarity is apt to affect our judgment. Perhaps it is for this reason that, when we do come across a true poetic drama, we make more fuss about its author than we make about those ninety and nine just persons who are his rivals. The reason, I do trust, is not that our aesthetic sense is stronger than our moral sense. Surely we are not so fallen as to prefer the butterfly to the ant—the bird to the bee. If either birds and butterflies or bees and ants had to be exterminated from this world, surely it is with our butterfly-nets and our guns that we should instantly set forth. Likewise, if we had definitely to choose between a few poetic dramas by possible weaklings, and a vast number of poetic dramas which testify to the stern stuff that their authors are made of, we should not disgrace ourselves in the eyes of the moral world. Yes, we are sound enough. Our heart's in the right place. But this makes it none the less regrettable that we should appear, as we generally do, grudging in our acknowledgement of—or even blind to—the grand qualities underlying the majority of poetic dramas in modern times. The authors of these may feel no bitterness at our discourtesy. They, in their strength, may be indifferent alike to the obloquy and to the applause of audiences. They certainly do not seem ever to be discouraged. Uninspired by heaven, uncrowned by men, they go on from strength to strength, from dulness to dulness, tramping most sturdily, careless whether their good deeds shine, or briefly and obscurely flicker, in a naughty world. But, as I was just suggesting, the world is less naughty than it appears. And we ought, in fairness to ourselves, to let these authors know, from time to time, how very deeply we do, in our heart of hearts, esteem them. To the latest of them—'Mr R. E. Fyffe,' whose play *The Conqueror* was produced last Saturday evening in the beautiful Scala Theatre—I offer a frankly respectful welcome.

I had intended, as an appropriate compliment, to write the whole of my criticism in blank verse. After I had composed twenty lines or so, I decided to fall back on prose. The blank verse line is not for me the line of least resistance. Yet I do not fancy that it offers a more stubborn resistance to me than to Mr Fyffe. Nor do I fancy that I am below the average in will-power. Thus am I the better enabled to gauge the will-power of Mr Fyffe, who has written four long acts of a play in the very medium which I abandoned at the outset. There was, certainly, no need for me to write in that medium. But neither was there any need for Mr Fyffe to do so. On the contrary, there were two good reasons why he should not do so. British mimes, for the most part, are shy of blank verse; and so (unless it is Shakespeare's, and therefore inevitable) are British audiences. Yet Mr Fyffe was not to be deflected. He was going to be thoroughly decasyllabic, or perish in the attempt. Thoroughly decasyllabic he is. Every line that I heard uttered from the stage of the Scala seemed to scan perfectly. And all the characters talked a more or less Elizabethan rhetoric. There was a profusion of highly respectable metaphors. The years were bridges across which Morven (Lord of Abivard) came to Amoranza; recollection seized him by the throat; the moon's white face hung i' the sky; κ.τ.λ. Everything was correct. There was only one moment when Mr Fyffe was caught tripping—the moment when Amoranza, being asked by a stranger whether the maid who lived in yonder castle were 'fair,' had to reply, with coquettish embarrassment, '*Passing* fair,' as who should say '*fairly* fair.' But for his evident belief that Polonius only loved Ophelia fairly well, Mr Fyffe seems to be quite a good scholar. He has a nice discretion in the use of words. He is never guilty of an obvious bathos. Perhaps he might be, if ever he scaled a height. But that he never does. He is, as it were, duly accoutred as a mountaineer, with ice-axe and alpenstock and smoked glasses and all the rest of it; but in these accoutrements he plods ever along the level and beaten track. He has, in other words, all the paraphernalia of poetry, but does not for a moment begin to be a poet. He has all the tricks of the form, with never a spark of the spirit. In art, form without spirit very soon becomes tedious. The audience on the first night was fairly—though not passing—enthusiastic; but I fancy that the greater part of it acknowledged to itself that it was being considerably bored. In less than three hours, for us, the play was over. How many scores of hours must have been spent in the writing of it? Guess the extent of Mr Fyffe's own previous boredom. And join with me in admiration of his 'grit.'

Shakespeare had the habit of interpolating in his serious plays scenes of comic relief. No poetic drama, therefore, is complete without one or two such scenes. Mr Fyffe, resolutely, has supplied one or two. He himself may, in private life, have a very keen sense of humour. I have known several extremely amusing men who, when they tried to express their humour through the medium of writing, instantly became dull, and were acutely conscious of their own dulness. Whether Mr Fyffe be of this order, or whether he be a man with no natural bent towards humour, it is equally admirable that he should have set himself, and accomplished, the task of writing the scenes of comic relief that appear in *The Conqueror*. But ought anyone's character, however strong, be submitted to such a strain? There are some forms of heroism that it is painful to contemplate. Surely, this is one of them. It is akin to the dangerous trades. If I were in Parliament, I should introduce a short bill to illegalise the introduction of comic relief into poetic dramas. Humanitarianism apart, the present system is wrong aesthetically. Wedges of even good comedy, thrust into (good) poetic drama, are a nuisance, not a 'relief.'

Strictly speaking, dramatists, like poets, must be born, not made. I do not fancy that Mr Fyffe is a born dramatist. He will never, I suspect, create a dramatic masterpiece. But he shows in *The Conqueror* that he has a power for orderly construction; and the last act of the play is theatrically effective. The fault of the first three acts is that they merely lead up, in an orderly fashion, to the last act. They are not effective in themselves. However, orderliness is a virtue in the building of a play. And in time, Mr Fyffe, using the keen intelligence that he evidently possesses, will be able to write thoroughly effective plays. But let him write them in prose. He has proved sufficiently his powers of perseverance. These, henceforth, let him bring to bear on things more susceptible to them than poetry.

When I say that Mr Fyffe is no poet, I do not mean merely that his verse is undistinguished. There are true poets who cannot write well in verse—can only handle well the medium of prose. But Mr Fyffe is prosaic in invention. His hero, Morven, is an impossible hero for poetic drama. That a man should be fascinated by a little girl of ten years old, and should intend to marry her later on, and finally should return for this express purpose after the lapse of eight years, is not at all an impossible idea. But it is an idea which makes the soldier a slightly ridiculous, or perhaps a slightly unpleasant, figure. Not even Mr Forbes Robertson could be expected to make Morven wholly dignified or delightful. He, moreover, was handicapped by the fact that Morven was a soldier—a trampling and blood-thirsty soldier. Mr Forbes Robertson's method does not blend well with even the most modified forms of militarism. He is at his best in the

last act, when Morven shows a more civilian side to his nature, and
renounces his chosen bride because she does not love him. I have
seen Mr Forbes Robertson renouncing his heart's desire in more
last acts than I should care to count. But I never saw him do it
more beautifully than last Saturday evening. Mr Henry Ainley, in
the part of second hero, was as romantically right as ever. And Miss
Gertrude Elliott, though she had the air of being rather bewildered
than impassioned in the last act, where passion was needed, supplied
fully all that was needed in the acts preceding.

[*30 September 1905*]

MR CARTON'S NEW (?) PLAY

It is in a kindly spirit that I insert that note of interrogation. To
suppose that Mr Carton had just written *Public Opinion* would be
to suppose that his work had fallen-off most lamentably. There is
good reason to reject the supposition. By internal evidence, the
play can hardly have been written less than fifteen years ago. True,
it has an 'up-to-date' air. Here is the slangy and unscrupulous lady
of title, who recurs in all Mr Carton's recent work, and who seems
to be his sympathetic version of 'Rita's' unsympathetic version of
the 'smart set.' And she talks about motors, massage ('At first you
feel as if you had come off second best in a glove-fight. But it does
buck you up'), telephones, and other paraphernalia of a world that
has forgotten H. J. Byron. But these 'up-to-date' touches do not
disguise the play's essential antiquity. Mr Carton's method, in his
recent comedies or farces, has been essentially modern. He has
eschewed obvious mechanism in construction. Nor has he relied
much on the charm of horse-play. He has relied, rather, on the
fun that is to be extracted from absurdity of character. I refuse to
believe him capable of un-learning so much as he would have had
to un-teach himself if *Public Opinion* were really fresh from his pen.
The plot of the play has that dismally rigid symmetry of repetition
which, in the dark ages, was regarded as a means to the end of
mirth. A music-hall artiste is suing a young man for breach of
promise; and the office of her solicitor is the scene of the first act.
Under another name, she has made a fool of her solicitor, and holds

compromising letters that he has written to her. To consult this solicitor, comes a young nobleman. The artiste, under yet another name, has made a fool of him, and holds compromising letters that he has written to her. Comes presently the judge who is trying her suit for breach of promise. Under yet another name, she has made a fool of him, and holds compromising letters that he has written to her. Comes presently a fashionable doctor, brother of the judge. Under yet another name, the star has made a fool of him, and holds compromising letters that he has written to her. . . . I am boring you, reader? That is just what I intended to do. I intended to produce on you just that maddening effect which is produced by the iterative method in dramaturgy. There is no accounting for fashion. This iterative method did, doubtless (for a while, in the dark ages), make for mirth, even among the elect. But its knell was tolled long since; and Mr Carton's revival of it at Wyndham's Theatre is, I assure you, as depressing as my description of it, and induces precisely the same quality of depression. So you must blame Mr Carton, not me, for my apparent waste of the valuable space of this Review. I admit that the audience laughed uproariously on the first night. But audiences are composed mainly of dullards who will laugh at anything; whereas every 'reader' of a writer is, traditionally, and beyond doubt, a very bright and intelligent creature. So you must not mistrust my advice, reader: you must not go to Wyndham's Theatre on the chance of enjoying yourself after all. The more surely to withhold you, I am going to describe what happens in the second and third acts. These are not one whit less symmetrical than the first. We are shown the flat in which the artiste lives. Presently, comes the judge, with the felonious intent to steal the letters. Comes also the solicitor, with like intent. Comes also, with like intent, the fashionable doctor. The young nobleman comes also, with like intent. I hope you note the instinct of mercy for you that has led me to contrive a spurious variety by shifting the position of the words in the foregoing sentences. Mr Carton, too, has been merciful in that his characters do not enter in the exact order of precedence established by the first act. But they all do enter. The line of them stretches out till the crack of doom— stretches to the third act, wherein again they all do enter with a view to recovering the letters, which were at the beginning of the first act stolen from the artiste's flat by the lady of title, and by her taken to the flat of an irascible ex-Colonial Governor. This gentleman, and one or two others in the play, have not written letters to the artiste. For him, and for them, one returns heartfelt thanks—so far as thanks can be felt by a heart that is breaking under the strain of so much intolerable monotony. Another cause for gratitude is that Mr Carton has not given a 'catch-word' apiece to the judge, the solicitor, the doctor and the young nobleman. That would have been quite in the spirit of the whole enterprise. The 'catch-word,' as a means to mirth, belongs to exactly the same period as the device of symmetrically repeated action, and springs of course from a cognate superstition—the superstition that a dull thing said becomes funny if it is only said often enough. I suspect that in the MS of the play (which my fancy figures as writ in faded ink on sere, foxed pages) every one of those gentlemen has some special phrase allotted to him. Why, when he was putting in the topical allusions to which I have referred, did Mr Carton cut these phrases out? I am sure they would have ministered, in their humble way, to the happiness of the majority. For though, as I said, the greater part of an audience will laugh at anything, it does not always laugh because it is amused. Slow-witted, and unwilling to betray itself, it laughs, as often as not, on the chance that there is something funny which eludes it. These are not comfortable laughs. But when one thing is said many times, then the audience knows that this thing is meant to be funny; and so it splits its sides quite honestly, with no misgiving, at every repetition. These laughs it really enjoys. And I cannot help wondering that Mr Carton did not give it a chance of laughing as whole-heartedly at the dialogue as at the action.

While he was thus mischievously uprooting old finger-posts, why did he not lay a few stumbling-blocks? Why did he not, in his later manner, rely on the interplay of eccentric character? He might well have furbished up the ragged and tarnished puppets that figure here, when he took them from their long-locked cupboard. These poor, stiff melancholy mementoes of a bygone age! The irascible ex-Colonial Governor, the pompous judge, the pompous doctor, the dashing young man of title, the scatter-brained solicitor, each puppet with its same old soiled label affixed to it—how saddening, to you and me, they are now! But the public opens its arms to them, opens its great heart to them, and rocks with rapture when one of them treads on the toe of the irascible ex-Colonial

Governor, and when the scatter-brained solicitor looks up the chimney and smudges his face with soot, and when the pompous judge collapses through a dressing-table and involves himself in the vallance, and when . . . but the catastrophes are without number or intermission. Had Mr Carton written the comedy within the past decade, he would, I am sure, have got some worthy fun out of it. The main motive is quite good. The breach of promise case brought by the artiste is simply a collusive device for getting enough money on which to marry the defendant (whose money is in the hands of trustees) and live happily ever after. Skilfully handled, this notion would make an admirable farce. Mr Reginald Turner handled it very skilfully, two or three years ago, in his novel *Cynthia's Damages*. I do not for a moment suggest that Mr Carton plagiarised from Mr Turner. The notion on which *Cynthia's Damages* was founded is one which might easily occur to someone who had not read the book. Besides, how could Mr Carton have read fifteen years ago a book that was so recently published? And how, if he had had that wondrous prevision, could we have failed to profit by what he foresaw? Cynthia (who, if I remember rightly was an actress, not a music-hall artiste) and Cynthia's lover joyously succeeded in their scheme; and that was the only way in which the story could have ended rightly. Whether 'Pansy' and her lover, in Mr Carton's play, succeed in their scheme, I am not sure. No stress seems to be laid on the point. Nor need there be, as the two characters are quite unsympathetic. But, obviously, they ought to have been (in a farcical way) sympathetic. And their absurd triumph over authority ought to have been the dénouement. As it is, the dénouement is simply the recovery of the letters by the several writers of them. A more uninteresting, and less artistic, dénouement could scarcely be conceived—could scarcely have been conceived all those years ago by Mr Carton.

[*14 October 1905*]

'LIGHTS OUT'

Having had recourse to Germany for a play with which to inaugurate his presence at the Waldorf Theatre, Mr H. B. Irving strengthens the case against the English dramatist. But he has been careful not to strengthen the case against the actor-manager. The part that he plays is, from the professional standpoint, a very bad one. It strikes no chord of 'sympathy.' It strikes not even a chord of (the next best thing) antipathy. Nor is it a part with which Mr Irving's personality can be well blent. Mr Irving is not, and cannot become, soldierly. One might perhaps imagine him dominating a regiment by the gleam of his intellectual and penetrating regard, and stirring in them a vivid interest in the things of the soul. But one cannot see him strutting up and down the ranks like an automaton, examining buttons, and rapping out words of command. And Lieutenant von Lauffen is, alas, as ordinary a young soldier as could be found in the Kaiser's army. He is all that Mr Irving does not appear to be on the stage. He is very sentimental, for instance, and rather a fool. Mr Irving is better than he used to be at striking the sentimental note; but the sound, even now, is less lyric than philosophic. Ardour there is, but seeming to glow rather from the brain than from the heart. For this reason, Mr Irving does not shine in the part of a foolish, impulsive, puzzled youth. 'I am not good at reasoning things out,' deprecatingly says the lieutenant to the girl he loves, when their love has brought them to a crisis. We simply don't believe him; and we wonder for what dark purpose he dissembles. Nor for one moment does the lieutenant convince us that he is specifically German. And this lack of local colour is shared by his fellow-officers and by the privates of his regiment. They draw their heels together sharply, and salute stiffly, and clank their swords a great deal; yet they produce no illusion that they are not Britons. No doubt it is a difficult task for actors to suggest that they belong to another nation than that of which they are speaking the language (necessarily without a foreign accent). Nevertheless, it is a task which they can, by subtle and unflinching stage-management, be drilled to perform. In such a play as *Lights Out* it is peculiarly essential that the task be performed.

For *Lights Out* is not one of those plays which, being based on some universal passion or idea, do not depend on preservation of the original 'atmosphere.' It is a distinctly local play. The conflict that pervades it is not the conflict of an abstract Fate with certain typical human beings, or the conflict of certain typical human beings with one another, or the conflict of a general duty with a general inclination. The German officers and privates here shown to us are, of course, men of like passions with ourselves; but they are made dramatic here by the conflict of their souls with a thing for which we have no local equivalent. On the one hand, their human instincts; on the other, the German military code. And the odds, every time, are a hundred to one on the German military code. The play was evidently conceived by Herr Beyerlein as a tract against this code's inhumanity. It is human that a young man should need the influence of women. The code sets its face against that influence. Lieutenant von Lauffen has to indulge his heart under strict secrecy. The girl whom he loves is discovered in his room by a man of her own class—a corporal, who is her rejected suitor. The corporal draws his sword; but the code withholds him from striking his lieutenant. The code also withholds the lieutenant from overlooking this act of insubordination. The guard is called in, and the corporal is placed under arrest, though of course the lieutenant sympathises with him. Next day, the court-martial. Here the ordinary human code has a brief innings—the lieutenant and the corporal both denying that there was an extenuating lady in the case, and the lady herself coming forward to confess. Her father, a sergeant, is about to fling himself against the lieutenant; but he remembers the code just in time to stifle his instincts and escape imprisonment. The lieutenant would like to marry the girl; but, of course, that would never do. The father would like to fight a duel with him. That, again, would never do. In default, the father would like to shoot him where he stands. The code does not forbid an officer to be shot thus by a common soldier; and so the lieutenant stands without flinching while the muzzle of the pistol is held to his breast. But the code does forbid a common soldier to shoot an officer; and the sergeant, after a struggle, obeys. His daughter comes in, and declares that she will not abandon her lover. She is the apple of her father's eye; but she is not in the army. The code ignores her existence; and so it is she whom the sergeant shoots. You perceive that, every time, the human instincts have to knuckle under. Thus, unless the characters are portrayed as specifically and unmistakably Germans (to whom this code is a tremendous reality, as inevitable as Fate itself), the human instincts in them must appear to us very weak, and consequently we cannot be much stirred by the dramatic conflict. I must admit that the audience on the first night did seem to be stirred very deeply indeed. And I make this admission quite cheerfully. I am of a nature too philosophic to demand that a theory should work out in practice. A theory stands or falls by itself. And I maintain that the thorough un-Germanness of Mr Irving, Mr Dawson Milward, Mr Charles Fulton, Mr H. V. Esmond, and the rest of the actors here engaged, is a fatal flaw in the performance. Miss Eva Moore is the only actress in the cast; and, if the whole galaxy of males were saturated through and through with the Teutonic spirit, she alone would suffice to spread an English glamour over the whole concern. In itself, without reference to its insularity, her performance is admirable—charged with that true power for emotion (on the smaller scale) which Miss Moore possesses, and which is possessed by so very few of our actresses.

Not the mimes alone are to be blamed for the absence of the right 'atmosphere.' I hoped I had written often enough about the use of slang in translations to deter all future translators from the pitfall. But no! 'He could teach you a thing or two,' 'She has a head on her shoulders,' 'It's devilish interesting,' 'You can't have a spicy case every time'—these and similar flowers of speech are scattered throughout the dialogue of *Lights Out*. Of course, English soldiers do not talk like that. (The ingenious translator always harks back, for some reason, to the slang of bygone decades.) But still less do German soldiers talk like that. Of course, again, foreigners don't converse in the English language. But in the English theatre the convention that they do so can be easily accepted by us, so long as the language is natural and unremarkable English. So soon as queer idioms, of a local and temporary kind, are foisted in, we are brought sharply face to face with the unreality of the whole convention, and our illusion of reality is dispelled. Another fault of whoever has translated *Lights Out* is that the common soldiers and the officers express themselves in exactly the same manner. I admit the difficulty that a translator has in making the needful differentiation between classes without creating the very mischief against which I have warned him. But that differentiation can be made, without hurt, by putting into the mouths of the lower-class characters shorter words and simpler constructions than into the mouths of the rest. Mainly, of course, he must trust to the appropriate deportment and diction of his mimes. In *Lights Out*, alas, it would be impossible, without a programme, to discern which were the officers, which the privates. The privates and the officers comport

themselves with equal distinction, and enunciate with equal refinement. Here again I admit a difficulty. For the privates to use anything like a cockney accent, or a rustic accent, would be obviously a
disaster. But they could, nevertheless, if they were properly taught,
import a little roughness and coarseness into their tones, without
committing themselves to an accent, and thereby mark the difference
which happens to be scarcely marked for them by the German
uniform. As the whole play hinges on this sharp difference, the
effort ought surely to be made.

[28 October 1905]

MR SUTRO, STRATEGIST

It is difficult for a clever man to become a popular playwright. It
is even difficult for him to get his plays produced. To achieve either
of these ends, he must go warily, circuitously, not letting his talent
entrap him. True, there is Mr Bernard Shaw. There he is in Sloane
Square, impregnably entrenched; and he won his way there by a
series of frontal attacks. But he, before he wrote plays, was already
a picturesque public figure, a chartered libertine; and he was, moreover, in command of a little army of admirers, few but fit. He was
thus enabled to go straight ahead, letting his conscience make no
compromise with a wicked world. He is an exception to the rule of
which Mr Alfred Sutro is an example. For years Mr Sutro was
writing plays, and trying to get them produced. Vainly. Had the
managers cared to produce them, the public would not have cared
to listen to them. Mr Sutro had written them in accord to the
dictates of his conscience. So, at length, Mr Sutro gathered himself
together for a great and strange effort. Fixing his eye on the
managers and the public, he concentrated all his ability on the task
of evolving that which would, instantly and inevitably, 'knock
'em.' He wrote *The Walls of Jericho*. It is still running. One of the
results of it was the production of *Mollentrave on Women*. That
delightful little comedy had a very short run indeed. *The Walls of
Jericho* had sufficed to get it produced, but not gain for it the
success it deserved. Mr Sutro, evidently, felt that the time was not

yet ripe for him to indulge in the luxury of an unstained conscience. Not yet was his position strong enough for delivery of a second frontal attack. He made, therefore, a strategic retreat, and planned a second turning movement. He wrote *The Perfect Lover*. The second victory thus won is as complete as was the first. Mr Sutro is secure now, I fancy. Henceforth he will be able to make the public accept that which it shall please him to create.

I admit that Mr Sutro must have had some pleasure in the creation of *The Perfect Lover*. Parts of the play are quite worthy of him. And even in composing the unworthy parts of it he may have been pleased by his ingenuity. But that sardonic pleasure cannot have been commensurate with his shame. Apart from the conflict in Mr Sutro's own breast, the play itself consists of two conflicts between duty and inclination—the conflict in a man who has the chance of becoming rich by dishonest means, and the conflict in a pair of lovers who are separated from each other by what they regard as the moral law. Of these two conflicts (which are intersected, but can be considered apart), the first is sincerely and interestingly worked out, while the second is to me as uninteresting as it is insincere. (I need hardly say that it is to the second that the play owes its triumph over the public.) The hero, Joseph Tremblett, is a journalist. No shadow of doubt is cast on his industry; and thus, as his annual income never exceeds three hundred and fifty pounds, his ability cannot, one fears, be very remarkable. No matter: we are concerned with his honesty. This is put to the test by his brother, who has grown rich by promoting shady companies, and wishes to grow richer by buying an estate that (he has reason to believe) contains coal. This estate belongs to a friend of Joseph— Lord Cardew, who knows nothing about the coal. It is only through Joseph's indirect influence that Lord Cardew could be induced to sell the estate. If the sale is effected, Joseph shall receive from William a cheque for five thousand pounds 'down.' At first, Joseph (who is admirably played by Mr Waller) will none of the transaction. He sends his brother away. His wife, however, shakes his resolution. She, being a woman, has not his meticulous sense of rectitude in matters of money and friendship; and she describes cogently the advantages of five thousand pounds. Their daughter, aged sixteen, has had to begin to typewrite. She is a cheerful child now, but soon, if she is kept at work, she will become anaemic, like other typists. Her father suggests to her the hypothesis that he had become a rich man, and that she could be sent to college. She, taking the fact for granted, claps her hands, dances round the room, expresses her pent-up hatred of the typewriting machine, and rushes out to give the glad news to her mother. Her father stares at the fire, and the curtain falls. This has been an admirable conflict, made poignant by many little human touches. But now for the other conflict. I have said that Joseph's 'indirect influence' is needed. He has to ask his sister-in-law who is very fond of him, to ask Lord Cardew to sell the estate. Lord Cardew is the Perfect Lover, who cherishes an undying (and reciprocated) passion for Mrs William Tremblett, but will not call on her. If she went to him and asked him to do anything for her sake, he would instantly do it. Joseph's distaste for asking her to ask is intensified by the obvious danger of bringing the two lovers together. In fact, this becomes the sole reason of his distaste. He tells his sister-in-law, quite frankly, about the coal. And she, when, at length, she undertakes the errand, is equally frank to Lord Cardew. Financially, all is fair, square, and above-board. There is only the menace to the marriage-tie. Lord Cardew, knowing that Mrs William Tremblett is coming to see him, has made arrangements for her to elope with him. Shall she yield to his entreaties? Here the conflict between duty and inclination is a poor and factitious one. Mr Sutro has been too afraid of the British public's morality to create a genuine and dramatic conflict. Humanly, there is nothing to restrain Mrs William Tremblett from yielding. Her husband is a brute, who bullies her, and delights in bullying her, every day of their lives. She had never loved him, and was only forced to marry him by her avaricious father. She has had a child by him; but the child is dead. She had always loved, and always will love, Lord Cardew. If the child were alive, or if the husband were a decent person, or if she were merely sorry for Lord Cardew, whose life has been wrecked through her, then there would be a good human reason against the elopement. The two scales would be balanced. The mere accident of matrimony is all that Mr Sutro has dared to drop into the anti-elopement scale. Moreover, he has not even dared to let us imagine that the lady might choose justice and happiness at the cost of a formal fidelity. There is no question of infidelity. It is simply a matter of 'What will the world say?' Lord Cardew is going to be accompanied by his maiden aunt, who is also Mrs Tremblett's god-mother; and he 'will speak no word of love till that word can be honestly spoken.' When Mrs Tremblett consents, enter her brother-in-law. He implores them not to 'desecrate' their love. 'There is duty—the law: you cannot set yourselves above the law,' with torrents of rhetoric to the same effect, and with nobody allowed to get a word in edgewise—'Ah, you are silent! You cannot deny the truth of what I am saying!' To this windy gentleman the two lovers entrust the arbitrage of their destinies. They will part for ever, or set sail (with the maiden aunt, who is also Mrs Tremblett's god-mother), as he shall decide. Having exhausted his rhetoric, and sufficiently edified the audience of British matrons, he decides that they shall set sail. A more grotesquely trivial scene I cannot imagine. And in the ensuing entr'acte, the orchestra plays the Pilgrims' March from *Tannhäuser*. Malicious minstrels! Or was it Mr Sutro himself who commanded that commentary? I think it must have been Mr Sutro himself.

The last act is much better. Joseph Tremblett has no more sermons, and plays an ingenious trick by which his brother is forced to offer him twenty (instead of five) thousand pounds. The effect of his final determination to accept nothing at all, and so remain a poor man, is marred, however, by the inadequacy of the motive. If he had really been dishonest, or if he had wrecked by the way a not wholly unhappy home, there would be reason enough for his renouncement. But, in the one case, where would have been the 'sympathy' for the hero? In the other case, where would have been the 'sympathy' for the second hero? Mr Sutro knows his business. He knows, also, his art. I rejoice to think that his use of the former knowledge will have enabled him to indulge and enforce evermore the latter.

[*4 November 1905*]

A PLAY ADRIFT

Among the more obvious injunctions in my Manual for Playwrights is 'If you make a fool your protagonist, you must make your play a comedy.' It is of the essence of a fool that he cannot, except by other fools, be taken seriously; and every playwright must work on the assumption that his audience is composed of wise persons. When the protagonist is a fool, working out his folly, we derive an added pleasure in proportion to the seriousness with which he is taken by the other characters on the stage. But by a demand that we ourselves shall take him in that way we are naturally affronted. It is thus that Mrs Lucette Ryley affronts us, in the play [*Mrs Grundy*] now enacted at the Scala Theatre.

As a comedy, it might have been excellent. A fool with a set of strict principles which he misapplies to the affairs of life, strenuously, and with the best intentions, is an especially promising character. He was used recently, and delightfully, under the name of Mollentrave, by Mr Sutro. Mrs Ryley has now pressed him into her service; and I suspect that, at first, she meant to use him in the right manner. She made him a clergyman, of the muscular Christian type, and transferred him from the regiment whose chaplain he was into a remote English village, there to fail through energy unallied to intelligence. She sketched prettily the type. The Rev. Edward Sotheby tears around the parish on a bicycle, exhorting the parishioners to play bowls and hockey, and promising to give up smoking if they will give up betting. His gardener grumbles at having to sweep away such heaps of leaves. 'Ah,' shouts Sotheby, 'that's what we're here for: to make a clean sweep of things!' No priestly contemplation for *him*! He is of the church militant. 'I have never,' he shouts, 'held with the old saying "Get thee behind me!" What *I* say to his Satanic Majesty, is "Come right up in front, and let's have it out!"' Having conceived him, Mrs Ryley cast around for a situation in which he should come ludicrously to grief and she found a very good one. She conceived a poor relation of some rich parishioners eloping (*pour le bon motif*) with a youth who was engaged to her cousin, but repenting and returning after an unlucky absence of some twenty-four hours. Mrs Ryley conceived that Mr Sotheby should proceed to bully the family for being shocked, and for declining to throw open its arms to this young lady. Mrs Ryley conceived that he (a widower, with a soldier-servant) should promptly instal her in his own home. She conceived that when the parishioners began to 'talk' and ceased to attend the services in the parish church, Mr Sotheby (loving another) should spring an offer of marriage on the young lady (loving the young man with whom she had eloped), and should shout her into acceptance. Mrs Ryley conceived that Mr Sotheby's desire to save, by wrecking his and the young lady's life, a social situation which could easily have been saved by advising the young lady to marry the still eager young man, or by advising her to become a governess (as she finally does) elsewhere, would be an admirable illustration of Mr Sotheby's ineptitude for things in general. Of course, Mrs Ryley was not going to let him achieve his folly. (That would have been too painful for comedy.) He was to be (as he is) saved by the second-thoughts of the young lady, and left (as he is not) gasping at his own folly, and being quietly advised by the other lady to be in all things less strenuous henceforth, since the number of muddles he will make will be proportionate to his activity. Such, I conceive, was Mrs Ryley's conception. Having a sense of humour, she could have realised it very nicely on the comedic plane. But she, also, is a sentimentalist. And she wrote *Mice and Men*. And she remembered how good Mr Forbes Robertson was in it. And so she has treated her muddle-headed clergyman as the romantic hero of a sentimental drama, and has asked us to take him at that valuation. But a fool whom we are asked to take seriously, and to cry over, with never a smile but of doting fondness, is not less exasperating than a fool in the midst of comedy is delightful. Nor does Mr Forbes Robertson, with his constitutional incapacity for playing the fool, prevent us from being exasperated. He seems, as ever, a man not less wise than noble. But the surface of wisdom that he imposes on the part of the clergyman does not obscure for us the clergyman's inanity. Another reason why he should not have played this part (which, indeed, I deem worth no man's while) is that he is incapable of looking, or behaving, like a disciple of Charles Kingsley. All the time that Mr Sotheby is saying bluff things about physical exercise, and about tackling the devil, and about the joys of tobacco, and about distribution of blankets and soup-tickets, we feel that he is thinking of other things—especially of the Early Fathers; and that his soul is truant in the quadrangles of Oriel, or in the lanes round Littlemore. Throughout, Mr Forbes Robertson's performance has this beautiful and mystical dignity, except in one scene—the scene where Mr Sotheby converses with his six-year-old son. Here, for me, the effect was rather ludicrous. The child had a peculiarly fixed smile, and a peculiarly squeaky voice, and, sitting stiffly beside Mr Forbes Robertson, it squeaked a string of precocious questions which were parried in a deep, sonorous baritone. It is a curious thing that whenever I see a ventriloquist perform, in a music-hall or elsewhere, I fall immediately under the spell of illusion. I am not conscious of a doubt that the puppet on the ventriloquist's knee is a real child, asking awkward questions by which its elder is really embarrassed or annoyed. But, in this scene at the Scala Theatre, I suffered the exact converse of that illusion. I could not believe that the child was of flesh and blood, and that Mr Forbes Robertson was not putting the words into its mouth, and pinching it to make its head turn and its jaws open and shut. Squeak, squeak; and then the embarrassed baritone; squeak, squeak—I even fancied that I saw Mr Forbes Robertson's lips moving, ever so slightly. I was quite astonished when, at length, instead of being caught up in the gentleman's arm, and bowed over with a genial smile, before being carried to the wings, the creature walked off all by itself. In a play that could have been taken seriously, the effect of this scene would have seemed deplorable to me. Even in this play it ought to be avoided, I think. Perhaps if Mr Forbes Robertson did not let the little boy sit quite so close to him, one would get the illusion that Mrs Ryley intended.

The lady whom Mr Sotheby really loves is impersonated by Miss Gertrude Elliott with the quaint and elfish prettiness of manner that is hers. The part confirms my theory of Mrs Ryley's first intention. It is a sheerly comedic part. The lady, who is a rich Australian, goes by the name of Mrs Patullo, and often refers, more in sorrow than in anger, to her husband, who is 'in the Bush.' But it turns out that there is really no husband at all. He has been invented to keep fortune-hunters at a distance. When the lady finds herself in love with Mr Sotheby, she 'kills' Mr Patullo, and comes on dressed in deep mourning. The scene is, of course, a reminiscence of the classic scene in *The Importance of Being Earnest*; but, not having been properly led up to, it falls flat. In any case, it would be inappropriate to a sentimental play. Miss Van Buskirk tries hard to make pathetic the part of the eloping young lady who consents to marry the clergyman, and then runs away from him. As the crises in this young lady's life are consistently marked for us by her recitation or consultation of railway time-tables, Miss Van Buskirk's task is not a very grateful one. The other characters are conventional stage daubs. Mr Sydney Brough manages to make one of them live, and live delightfully, by his own humour and naturalness. The other members of the cast try to vivify their parts by violent and chaotic over-acting. They mouth, shout, strut, beetle their brows, continuously, making a desperate fuss about nothing. Let me give an example of their method (if the term 'method' can be applied to a thing so closely resembling madness). One of the unimportant characters, a major, happens to meet in the clergyman's room a still less important character, named Harmony, and, when he makes his exit, he has to say 'Good night, Mr Harmony.' The actor, of whom nothing is here required beyond an ordinary tone and deportment, shouts 'Good night' at the top of his voice, then says 'Mr,' and then, after a pause, letting a rich smile steal over his features, he enunciates 'Harmony.' Then he makes a dash for the door-handle, and flings himself out into the passage. I can imagine how surprised and puzzled would be any French, or German, or American visitor by such exhibitions of British art in acting. I can imagine, too, how easily such exhibitions might be suppressed by a good stage-manager.

[*25 November 1905*]

A VAPID PLAY

I will not pretend to have been gladdened by my visit to the Haymarket. Here is one of the most distinguished theatres in London; and here is Mr Harrison, one of our acutest managers; and here, at Mr Harrison's disposal, is Mr Hawtrey, perhaps our best comedian; and yet, apparently, Mr Harrison can find nothing better to put up, nothing less difficult for me to put up with, than a mediocre adaptation of a third-rate Parisian comedy. This is humiliating. The one ray of light is shed by the very fact of the humiliation. In the 'eighties no one would have blushed. The thing would have been taken as a matter of course. The consciousness of having acquired ideals is some solace for not finding them realised.

In *The Indecision of Mr Kingsbury*, from start to finish, there is not one moment of similitude to life. The characters are purely diagrammatic, and are not even amusing diagrams. Such fun as there may once have been in them has long since been obliterated by constant use of them on the stage. Never for one instant does the adapter give token that either he or the original author has ever for one instant observed anything in the actual world. One of the characters is a young man on the eve of a political career. The adapter knows, of course, that there is such a thing as politics in England. He has seen various plays in which there was a political background. He has seen, may be, the Leader of the Opposition, infatuated by a beauteous foreign adventuress, steal a secret treaty from the escritoire of the Secretary for Foreign Affairs. He has heard, too, on the stage the echoes of questions that were burning ones in the time of Lord John Russell. Let it suffice him to echo such echoes. Why should he trouble to look at a daily newspaper, or to seek oral information from one of those people who are dull enough to be interested in such a dull thing as politics? And so the young politician in this play is by an elder man accused of being 'an odious democrat.' To which he sharply replies by asking whether his interlocutor agrees that the people ought to be governed in such a way as shall be most conducive to the people's good. 'Certainly,' says the interlocutor. The young man then declares that the people must be the best judge of what is good for them. The interlocutor maintains that they are not. The discussion then drops. Of course, I do not contend that a serious discussion of modern politics was necessary to our enjoyment of the play. Only, as politics are introduced, it does seem to me rather a pity that the adapter cannot make his characters say something—something, too, a trifle less elementary—about some such thing as Imperialism, or Socialism, or any other of the many subjects of political discussion in the twentieth century. I am afraid he will call me 'an odious democrat.' He himself, certainly, is a staunch member of what used to be (and, he probably thinks, still is) called 'the stupid party.' He will brook no innovation in dramaturgy. He would keep intact the glorious theatrical heritage of our forefathers. He does not spare us even the comic Frenchman of the loose principles and the broken English. Nay, the better to ensure this survival, he plays the part himself. But where is the flat-brimmed hat, the flowing cravat, the moustache waxed in the manner of Louis Napoleon? Appearing in clothes of the latest English fashion, and made up to look really very like a contemporary Frenchman, Mr Cosmo Gordon Lennox is strangely untrue to his conservative intentions. Egomet, I think he ought even to have insisted that Mr Hawtrey, as Mr Kingsbury, should wear Dundreary whiskers and peg-top trousers. Nor do I conceive that Mr Hawtrey would have been unwilling. That he consented to play the part assigned to him is evidence of an infinite submissiveness.

He knew that he was in the prime of life, and that he could not, by taking thought, change himself into a stripling. He must have known, also, that only by a man of extreme youth could the part of Mr Kingsbury be played appropriately. The whole play depends on the fact that Mr Kingsbury is extremely young. His mother wishes him to marry; but, as he says, he is 'not ripe for marriage.' He wishes to have a fling. Flings, possible on the French stage, are impossible on the British. Mr Kingsbury's wild oats consist, there-fore, of taking a house in Park Lane, and marrying a lady of rather doubtful reputation who has thrown herself at his head, and whom, in virtue of his youth, he has for a long time been afraid to kiss. On the British stage, even retrospective flings are eyed askance; and it turns out that there was no real cause for gossip against this lady. It is undeniable, though, that she has a taste for frivolous enter-tainments. And thus we come to the time-honoured situation of the husband imagining that his wife does not love him, and refusing to show her the tenderness for which she pines. He imagines that she is fascinated by the Frenchman, whose advances she really rejects with scorn. When, as was bound to happen, his elderly aunt and uncle arrive from the country, and are scandalised by the singing of coon songs and the dancing of cake-walks under his roof, and, when, as was also bound to happen, they urge him to separate from his wife, he rather inclines to their view of the matter, and goes to the country to think things over. And indeed, it does seem as if Mrs Kingsbury had eloped in the Frenchman's motor. But she hasn't really. And. . . . I said that the play was vapidly conventional 'from start to finish.' I ought not to have said that. I did not stay for the 'finish.' When the curtain fell on the third act, I blinked, stretched myself, gathered up my coat and hat, and went forth into the night. All invisible the stars; but there were the chimney-pots, and such-like things, which, being real, brought balm to the soul of me.

I do not believe that Mr Harrison, who is so acute, intends to produce any more twaddle of this kind in his theatre. The day for it is past. But why has Mr Harrison not yet gone over to the winning side? He does not imagine that the thousands of people who, at the Court Theatre, have been laughing with all their lung-power at the vital comedies of Mr Shaw, and rejoicing in them whole-heartedly as a revelation of what may be achieved through dramatic form, will not yawn away from such stuff as *The Indecision of Mr Kingsbury*. And these are the people who will soon be in a majority. Of course, there will always be room for twaddle in the theatre. But it must be live and native twaddle. And, even so, Mr Harrison ought to leave it to inferior theatres. Mr Shaw himself may, for aught I know, be bound hand and foot to the Court Theatre. But how about such writers as Mr Street and Mr Hankin, each of whom, within the past year, has had an excellent comedy produced on trial? I don't say that Mr Harrison would make a fresh fortune out of either of these gentlemen. But there is the chance that he might. And he certainly would not lose so much money as he certainly will if he lags behind with lifeless adaptations. I am sure he is not intending to lag.

Not only for hints in choice of plays, but also for hints in their production, ought Mr Harrison to visit the Court Theatre. At the Haymarket, seemingly, every member of the cast is allowed to act according to his or her own sweet will. There is no attempt at harmony. Miss Nina Boucicault, having emotional power, is allowed to treat her part as one of poignant tragedy. Mr Hawtrey, of course, is allowed to be quiet, calm: it would be useless to attempt to make him be otherwise, even if it were well that he should be otherwise. But why should Mr Cosmo Lennox be allowed to make, in contrast, such a terrific noise whenever he appears on the scene, and never for an instant stand still? And why should Mr Holman Clark be allowed to make himself up as a quite impossible monster and behave accordingly? In itself, his performance is ingenious and amusing. But it is quite out of relation to any other performance in the play. And so are the other performances.

[*16 December 1905*]

A LOAD OF WEEDS FROM THE KAILYARD

Some ten years ago, I used to read and hear much about a Presbyterian minister who laboured in literature, under the name of Ian Maclaren. I did even, at length, read one of his books—a book of short stories. Through the gibberish in which it was written I discerned dimly one or two things: either Mr Maclaren's fancy traduced his countrymen, or Scotland was honeycombed with the most insidious forms of maudlin sentimentality, snivelling sanctimoniousness, and cheap funniments. Anxious to settle the matter, I proceeded to consult every Scotchman who came my way. One and all, without shedding one tear, or quoting one text, or cracking one bad joke, they assured me that it was Mr Maclaren who was to blame, and that if I would be so good as to cross the Tweed I should find it a quite tolerable nation. I believed them, and presently dismissed the subject from my mind. Already the people within my ken had begun to talk and write less about Ian Maclaren, and presently I forgot that such a person existed. It was not till last Wednesday evening, at the St James's Theatre, that the awful spectre resurged. 'A dramatised version, in four acts, of Ian Maclaren's work, entitled *Beside the Bonnie Brier Bush*.' How heavily scented with the decaying vegetation of the kailyard this title is! But is it really the title of a work by Ian Maclaren? There was another Presbyterian minister, Samuel Crockett, who wrote books of a very similar kind. Do I err in my vague impression that *Beside the Bonnie Brier Bush* was his? Let some agile antiquary go to Scotland and burrow among the archives of the period. It were impossible to settle the point simply by reference to the undisputed works of Ian Maclaren. One can say 'Shakespeare did not write *Titus Andronicus*. It is the work of some inferior writer.' But where shall one find a writer inferior to Ian Maclaren? And who shall discriminate between the respective twaddle of Ian Maclaren and Samuel Crockett?

Even if the adapters, Messrs Augustus Thomas and James MacArthur, be proved to have strayed in 'attribution,' I shall not retract the compliments I now pay them on their pious and skilful fidelity to the author adapted. The *dramatis personae* affect me exactly as did the characters in—whichever it was of Ian Maclaren's books that I ventured to read. The adapters have performed their task perfectly. It was not, perhaps, quite so hard a task as falls to most adapters. To bring back from a book to the stage a set of characters that had originated on the stage is easier than to coax on to the stage a set of characters that had stepped out of real life through the author's brain. Ian Maclaren, I suppose, had never entered a playhouse; but it was from that hell, by some curious process, that his characters came to him. They did not remain exactly as they had been. Their extreme sanctimoniousness was an added grace. But their dulness and their maudlin unreality had fallen straight from the 'flies.' That was the sharp difference between them and the characters in *A Window in Thrums* or *The Little Minister*. It is true, doubtless, as most Scotchmen assert, that Mr Barrie's characters were not true to Scottish nature. But, at least, they were not stagey. They were inventions from within Mr Barrie's own brain; and very delightful inventions they were, too—presented with a salt humour that saved us from being cloyed by the inherent sentimentality. To transfer safely to the stage these literary creatures of his own brain was an achievement that attested in Mr Barrie the highest theatrical skill. Less skill was needed to make Ian Maclaren's puppets relapse into their original sphere. Nevertheless, skill was needed; and I congratulate the adapters on having made the puppets so instantly and so thoroughly at home behind the footlights, and on having preserved in them a full measure of the sanctimoniousness that they had picked up during their excursion.

For the success of the play, perhaps, it would be well had this same sanctimoniousness been stripped away. I presume that there is a terrific outcry from those critics who raised a terrific outcry at the Biblical quotation uttered by Major Barbara. The fact that Ian Maclaren, unlike Mr Shaw, is a clergyman, can make no difference at all. The point is this: either the theatre is so polluted a place that any reference made therein to Holy Writ must offend all persons of reverent feeling, or it is not so polluted a place. The critics who cried out at Major Barbara's Biblical quotation can have done so only in the belief that the former of these two alternatives is the true one. How much shriller, then, must be their outcry against *Beside the Bonnie Brier Bush*! It is dramatically appropriate that Major Barbara, of the Salvation Army, should quote the text that she does quote. Is it appropriate that a young Scottish nobleman should swear 'by God and under His stars' that he and the heroine of the play shall be man and wife? It certainly is not needful. It certainly is dragged in. Doubtless, it is dragged in not for a cheap theatrical effect, but for the purpose of edifying us. But how fearful a blasphemy it must have seemed to the aforesaid critics; I hope they rose and left the building. If they stayed, they exposed themselves to further shocks. Even I, who do not hold the theatre polluted, was shocked by the frequency with which sacred subjects were bandied in the course of *Beside the Bonnie Brier Bush*. However fine may have been the motive of the adapters in mentioning these subjects so frequently, the fact remains that their play is a wretched bit of tawdry claptrap, in which any use made of these subjects is bound to offend anyone who combines a sense of reverence with an aesthetic sense.

To justify my description of the play, I must, alas, tell you what the play is about. You may have already guessed that it hinges on a Scotch marriage. The bride is the daughter of a sheep-farmer. There are the usual reasons for not letting the marriage be known; and so, while Lord Hay leaves the district, Flora Campbell remains with her father, and flits in and out of the cottage, wearing a sun-bonnet, but seeming not to be her bright natural self. Her father, Lachlan Campbell, suspects that her gloom is connected with Lord Hay. Just as she entrusts to a postman (chief of many low-comedy characters) a letter for her lover, her father intercepts it. He reads it aloud, and asks her what she means by 'our secret.' As she refuses to tell, and as he is a stage-father, he jumps to the conclusion that she is a wanton, and, having shouted himself hoarse, turns her out of the cottage, neck and crop. Then comes, of course, the family Bible. Just as Flora's name is going to be struck out, enter a Laddie, who asks 'Wut's the mitter?' The mitter having been explained to him, he makes a suggestion to the effect that the father should behave less like a stage-father. This suggestion is rejected. Exit the Laddie. Flora is deleted. The father catches sight of Flora's sunbonnet, and into that receptacle he pours the tears on which the curtain was bound to fall. Already, I think, he has had something to say about 'the Laird's will'; but it is (so far as I know) in the next act, when his hair has turned white through grief, and when 'the Laird has laid his naem i' the dust,' that he is at his strongest in Biblical references. He meets two children in a wood, and beckons to them. Rather reluctantly, they come; and he, folding them in his arms, and turning up his eyes, quotes a text which I will leave you to guess: if I wrote it down here, I should feel as uncomfortable as I felt in hearing the actor mouth it. He then proceeds to repeat the story of the ewe-lamb. I have said that it is 'so far as I know' in this act that he is most Biblical. But I dare say he is even more Biblical in the last act, for which, partly because I was bored, and partly because I was disgusted, I did not stay. What becomes of him finally I do not know. I conjecture that he dies in sight of the audience. Ian Maclaren, as I well remember from that book of stories, had a large and varied assortment of death-beds, with moonbeam or sunbeam fittings as required.

[*30 December 1905*]

AT THE SHAFTESBURY THEATRE

If Mr C. M. S. McLellan has not already joined the Y.M.C.A., let him be elected an honorary member. This were a recognition well earned. Nobody in our time has enforced so constantly on such large audiences the lessons which that admirable institution would have us learn. I have seen now three of Mr McLellan's plays. With all their differences, there is one factor common to them all—one thing which their author cannot keep out. And this is, a study in the manifold temptations which beset the path of a young man, and in the disastrous consequences of yielding to them. In *Leah Kleschna* there was the sad case of a young Frenchman, bearer of an ancient and honoured name, endowed with no mean intellect, impersonated by Mr Herbert Waring, but having a fatal weakness of character, in virtue of which he fell into bad company, squandered his substance in riotous living, sank so low as to steal a diamond necklace from the room of a friend, was detected, and 'went under.' You remember, also, the case of Harry Branson in *The Belle of New York*. He had youth, health, a fond and wealthy parent, the opportunity of carving out for himself a useful and honourable career. But metropolitan temptations were too strong for him. When the curtain rose, Mr McLellan, with unflinching hand, showed Harry in the midst of intoxicated boon-companions, and showed him presently making love, on the morning of his wedding-day, to a girl from a confectioner's shop. And this was the son of a man fulfilled with missionary zeal. Mr McLellan underlined the contrast unrelentingly. You remember the arrival of the father, and how Harry, docked of his resources, went forth into the world and became a bar-tender. But, clearly though you remember him and his counterpart in *Leah Kleschna*, Mr McLellan has not done with the type yet—does not yet feel that he has driven his lesson fully home. He gives us, at the Shaftesbury Theatre, yet another tract on the subject of youthful depravity 'and all the woes it brings.' René Delorme is not born rich, but he has great gifts for literature. He goes to perilous Paris, and there, writing for that peril within a peril, the Parisian theatre, he becomes wealthy; and with wealth comes sloth, self-indulgence, conjugal infidelity, love of champagne, followed by preference for brandy. His new play fails deservedly. What does he do? Does he pull himself together—shake off the evil influences of the theatre, and divert his talent into some cleaner channel? No; he sinks lower and lower. He urges starving workmen to attack the offices of David Martine, the industrious apprentice, his awful foil. The attack is repulsed, but he finds a way into the premises, and fires a revolver at David Martine, who, in reward for his own industriousness, bears a charmed life: the bullet kills Madame Delorme, René's long-suffering wife. In danger of arrest, René flies to a dense wood near the cottage in which he lived when he was an innocent child; and here he dies, stricken with remorse and terror.

It is a lesson to us all. And Mr McLellan, so as to make it the sharper and more haunting, has had recourse to a new device. There is no prologue to *The Belle of New York*. Harry Branson is not first shown to us 'dying of his excesses,' and imploring a figure of Death to let him live his life all over again. Nor is this how we first behold the young nobleman in *Leah Kleschna*. René Delorme is, so far, unique. The figure of Death refers his prayer to the Jury of Fate, who consent to let the young man be born again into the next generation, with exactly the same temperament as he had before, but with full memory of his previous existence. René is sure that he will thus redeem his soul, living wisely and nobly in the light of his experience, grasping the opportunities which he had let slip, and shunning the pitfalls into which he had stumbled. But Death prophesies that his new life will, by reason of his weakness, be no better than his old one. And Death, as you know from what I have told you of the subsequent play, prophesies correctly. When the curtain fell on this prologue, I prophesied an interesting evening. Mine, however, was a prophecy that was not fulfilled.

Undoubtedly, the idea that had occurred to Mr McLellan is a a very fine idea indeed. The problem that he had taken is so large and philosophic a problem that I could not conceive him utterly shirking it for cheap and irrelevant issues. Such daring, I thought, must postulate some power. No previous dramatist had dared so greatly. The theme of *Faust* was trivial in comparison with this theme. That an old man should sell his soul to the devil in return for renewed youth, for the simple purpose of having that 'good time' which he deemed more delightful than eternal salvation, may be a great and profound scheme in itself; but it is assuredly small, shallow, and easy to handle, as compared with Mr McLellan's. There is no larger, more philosophic problem than this: how should we acquit ourselves if we were born again, just as we were, but with all the experience that we have gathered in our waywardness? Though no dramatist (so far as I know) has ventured to tackle this problem, it is one which has often occurred to every one of us. It is, in fact, an universal problem. Are we utterly the slaves of our inclinations? Do we merely drift? Old people, looking back on the failure of their lives—and every life seems more or less a failure to the man who has lived it, however satisfactory it may seem to outsiders—will tell you that with a new lease of life, and with the experience that has come to them, they could order themselves with perfect wisdom, achieving all that was in them to achieve. But in these old people the instincts that blinded them and made them stray have lost all strength. Experience reigns in their stead. If all those instincts were renewed in all their vigour, would they always—would they often—would they ever—knuckle under to experience? One thing is certain: there would be between them and experience a constant warfare—a highly exciting warfare. Here, for a dramatist with keen intellectual insight into human nature, is a grand chance indeed. If René Delorme were vividly and intimately shown to us struggling, in his second incarnation, between that which he wishes for morally and intellectually and that to which the impulse of his unconscious nature is driving him, then Mr McLellan would have written a great drama—a drama for all time. But

René Delorme, ushered in with a fanfaronnade that prepares us for an imaginatively created world-type, is but a little wooden puppet, having no pretension to be more than a little wooden puppet, and being utterly irresponsive to the brain-power expended by Mr H. B. Irving. You see, Mr C. M. S. McLellan has been only pretending to be pretentious. He never meant to essay the high task he had set himself. Re-incarnate René, with perfect insouciance, repeats his previous existence. There is never a sign of a struggle in him. He just goes through his hoops, with monotonous agility. At one point in his performance, I had a false hope that Mr McLellan had at any rate remembered his theme so far as to get some fun out of it. This was when René, two years after the failure of his play, was shown to us spouting incendiary politics in a cabaret. I thought of the hectic ne'er-do-well Gambetta—Gambetta as he was before eighteen-seventy. And I foresaw Death coming in due course to claim René, a few years later, and finding a prosperous gentleman with a tricolour across his paunch, and with an unceasing flow of stentorian rhetoric—a national idol, potent in the councils of Europe, and enjoying excellent health. This would have been an amusing conclusion to the play. But I over-rated Mr McLellan's sense of fun. He sent his puppet rolling down the hill of ordinary melodrama, with pink-lit back-cloths to represent burning factories, and with battering-rams and pistol-shots and thunderstorms, and heaven knows what else of extraneous tomfoolery. *The Belle of New York* was a cheerier entertainment than *The Jury of Fate*; but it was not one whit less silly; and I see no reason to suppose that, if the theme of re-incarnation had occurred to Mr McLellan ten years ago, he would not have tacked it on to Harry Branson as readily as he has now tacked it on to René Delorme.

I deem it a pity that there is no means of saving a fine theme from the claws of such dramatists as can but mutilate it and deter from it their betters. I wish there were some sort of Academy, to which every dramatist would have to submit his every scenario, and without whose permission no dramatist would be allowed to develop a scenario. I do not approve of Academies in general. They tend to become corrupt, as well as stupid. But however stupid and corrupt might become the Academy that I have adumbrated, it would, at least, nip in the bud such blossoms as *The Jury of Fate*.

[*6 January 1906*]

THE COURAGE OF ONE'S OPINIONS

I have expressed more than once my admiration for Mr Gilbert Murray's translations of Euripides. His version of the *Electra* is not less fine than—is as vivid and sensitive and graceful as—his versions of *The Trojan Women* and the *Hippolytus*. Last Tuesday afternoon, when it was produced at the Court Theatre, I found myself bored beyond endurance. Partly, this result was due to the extreme darkness of the stage, and to the extreme slowness with which Miss Wynne-Matthison spoke her words. Darkness of environment and slowness of utterance are supposed, nowadays, to be things owed to Melpomene. Darkness is, certainly, appropriate to tragedies in which the note is one of mystery and eerie romance. It is appropriate, for example, to the early tragedies of Maeterlinck. But romantic eeriness was not a part of the Greek spirit. Nebulous twilight is not the atmosphere in which to set the clean, clear, simple structure of Greek tragedy. Likewise, where, as in Maeterlinck's plays, the meaning of the words is vague, and the characters are groping to express through speech thoughts and emotions of which they are but dimly conscious, it is right that they should speak lingeringly, wearily. But the thoughts and emotions of the persons in Greek tragedy are quite forthright and sharp-cut, and so is the verse in which they are expressed; and one does not care to have this verse droned, droned, droned, as it is at the Court Theatre. To speak rhythmically, it is not needful to speak slowly. If only Miss Wynne Matthison could be induced to hurry up, she would do justice to her beautifully-conceived impersonation of Electra. I do not say that she would prevent the afternoon from boring me. I think that a Greek tragedy in a modern theatre, however perfectly it be enacted, is bound to be tedious. An overt theatre, built on the Greek model, seems to me indispensable. Not otherwise than by becoming in spirit somewhat as the Greeks were, can we really enjoy a Greek play; and, without the scenic conditions by which Greek tragedy was shaped, we must fail in the effort to assimilate ourselves to a Greek audience. At Bradfield all is well. But at the Court Theatre the gods and the heroes are far from us. There is no background of legend. The characters of the play seem merely barbarous and foolish. The action of the play seems merely spun-out. The chorus, above all, are mere intruders and interrupters. If Messrs Vedrenne and Barker intend to produce further translations by Mr Gilbert Murray, I suggest that they should buy up Sloane Square, at present a rather dreary and meaningless stretch of ground, which could, by excavation, be made into an admirable Attic theatre. They may tell me that this would be more expense than they could afford, and that I ought, in any circumstances, to be able to *imagine* myself in an Attic theatre. Well, I admit the lack of imagination. But I do not admit that it is peculiar to myself. I doubt whether of the audience last Tuesday one person in twenty had the imagination necessary to enjoyment of the play. I doubt whether one person in twenty was not thoroughly bored. But I doubt whether one person in twenty confessed that he was thoroughly bored. It is my honesty, not my lack of imagination, that is peculiar. So few people have the courage of their opinions.

Not that I am proud of having the courage of mine. Indeed, I do not see where 'courage' comes in. I do not understand why a man should hesitate to say, as best he can, just whatever he thinks and feels. He has nothing to fear, nowadays. No one will suggest the erection of a stake for him to be burned at. No one will be at all angry with him. Euripides, if I remember rightly, had finally to leave Athens, so hotly were his opinions resented. He, then, had been courageous in insisting on these opinions, despite all Athens, throughout his career. But nowadays, especially in England, there is no obstruction to sincerity. Are there not, on the contrary, great inducements to it? So far from being angry, people admire and respect you for your 'courage.' You gain a cheap reputation for a quality to which, as likely as not, you have no real claim. It is as though a soldier in battle were accounted a hero for charging up to the muzzles of guns which he knew to be unloaded. Oddly enough, the quality which enables a soldier to advance in a hail of bullets is far more common than the quality which enables him, in civilian life, to tell the truth. I should think twice before advancing under a hail of bullets. I should be eager in so far as I knew that I should be admired. I should be reluctant in so far as I expected to be dead. You, reader, think that I show moral courage in this very confession of my lack of physical courage. Yet you are not despising me for the lack: you are but honouring me for the confession. So what in the world was there to prevent me from confessing? Clear your mind of this cant of moral courage, I beg you; and, knowing that you have nothing to fear, go in for sincerity on your own account. If I have exploded the fallacy of moral courage, your friends will not, perhaps, proceed to admire your character; but you will find, for the first time in your life, that they listen to you with pleasure. 'That is all very well,' you say; 'but what if my mind happens to be an utterly commonplace mind? What if my emotions and my opinions happen to be precisely those of the man in the street, and of the leader-writer for the morning newspaper?' Do not be afraid. No two men are alike really. If the man in the street would say what he really thinks and feels, instead of what the leader-writer has written, you would find him quite delightful. If the leader-writer would express in writing what he really thinks and feels, instead of what he supposes the man in the street to be thinking and feeling, you would find that not even he is leaden. You, too, believe me, have in you the power to be interesting. I do not say that this article is an enthralling piece of literature. But it is much better than anything else that I have written about the performance of the *Electra* at the Court Theatre. I might have written merely what the critics seem to think they are expected to write: I might have remarked on the 'modernity' of Euripides's thought, and have said that the tragedy 'marched' towards its appointed close 'relentlessly,' and that it held me and a large audience 'spell-bound,' and that it was 'a purgation through pity and awe,' and so forth and so on. How much better to admit that I was bored! Not that there is anything original in having been bored. On the contrary, as I have hinted, my admission must strike responsive chords in the great majority of the audience. But I have made my admission in my own way; and therefore it has a value of its own. Go to any other person who was in the audience, and ask him to tell you in his own way, frankly, just how and why he had been bored. If you prevail on him to do so, the result will be not less valuable. But—such is the force of custom, and so great the fear of not 'doing the right thing'—he will probably tell you that he had enjoyed his afternoon very much.

[*20 January 1906*]

'THE HEROIC STUBBS'

Mr James Welch, at Terry's Theatre, has begun well. I have often deplored that he, a born comedian, with a peculiar power for pathos, had never played a part worthy of his gifts. Year in, year out, he has been condemned to knock-about farces, distressing in themselves, and all the more distressing because so fine an actor was being wasted on them. I know not whether Mr Henry Arthur Jones conceived and dramatised the character of Roland Stubbs without reference to any particular actor, or whether his initial motive was to give Mr Welch a belated chance of glory. Certainly, if the part of Stubbs was not written 'round' Mr Welch, it suits him as well as if it had been.

It gives equal scope for precisely those qualities of pathos and of humour which belong to Mr Welch, and which have but peeped out, hitherto, from his performances. In those moments of emotion which he has sometimes contrived to foist into his farcical impersonations, he has revealed a true power for tragedy. I know no English actor whose voice can sound so surely the tragic note. A voice is usually a good index to a soul; and tragedy, I suspect, is Mr Welch's true métier. I can imagine him a magnificent Hamlet, even a magnificent Prometheus. Such dreams cannot, of course, be realised. Nature, jealous of Art, has enclosed Mr Welch's soul in a tiny body, and has topped this tiny body with a comedian's head. Thus Mr Welch's tragic power will never be able to manifest itself except in minor pathos—the pathos, especially, of a little man whose great soul finds no outlet, and no recognition, because the world judges by appearances. Such a little man is Stubbs. No one, looking at him, would take him for an idealist. Yet he is an idealist of the straitest sect: he has only one ideal. A certain Lady Hermione Candlish has presided over his soul ever since he was a boy. As he is only a bootmaker, she is unaware of her presidency. His sister has no patience with his infatuation. 'What is the whole thing but an illusion?' she asks. Stubbs defends himself on the ground that 'illusions pay.' If he had fallen in love with a girl of his own class, he would have married, and would have lost that imaginative faculty in virtue of which he has thriven. He would have still been an assistant in that obscure shop where first he set

eyes on Lady Hermione. He is master, now, of a shop in Picca-
dilly. And it is by the roundabout way of Lady Hermione that he
has come there. He is a philosopher, you perceive. But, though he
is not embittered, he feels the pathos of his position. Though he
harbours no unreasonable wishes, he would like Lady Hermione to
know something of what she means to him. He tries to tell her,
while he is fitting her with a new pair of shoes; and Mr Jones
has written here a scene of admirable comedy—Stubbs's anxiety
running away with his timidity, and Lady Hermione's sense of
humour running away with her resentment. Throughout the play,
Mr Jones shows a keen observation and understanding of the class
to which Stubbs belongs—the well-educated, vulgar, aspiring,
frightened class of man that Mr H. G. Wells has so often de-
lineated. It is the first time we have seen this class of man on the
stage; and he could not have been more cunningly shown to us 'in
the round.' Lady Hermione herself is a very well-drawn character.
But Mr Jones has often drawn her for us. She is but the latest
addition to Mr Jones's group of married ladies who have, for
curiosity's sake, hovered on the verge of infidelity, and almost
incurred a scandal. Usually they have been rescued by the sort of
man whom Sir Charles Wyndham delights to impersonate. This
time, the rescuer is Stubbs. It is Stubbs's ambition not merely that
his love be told, but that it be proved. Lady Hermione has been
flirting with a 'dangerous' man, Mr Dellow, who wishes to compromise her in the eyes of the world. He invites her to dine on his
yacht, which is lying in port at Yavercliff. His intention is to take
her, unawares, across the Channel. She, after some demur, accepts
the invitation. Stubbs overhears her, scents mischief, determines to
become her knight-errant, and telephones for a special train which
shall reach Yavercliff before the train by which Lady Hermione and
Dellow are to travel. Thus ends the first act, with all the bustle of a
frantic chase. The second act, which passes in the parlour of the
inn at Yavercliff, consists chiefly of a duel of wits between Dellow
and Stubbs—a brisk and amusing duel, in which Dellow gains the
day. Just when Stubbs is triumphing in the belief that the departing
Dellow has surrendered Lady Hermione for ever, he finds that
Lady Hermione has left the inn and joined Dellow on the yacht.
He dashes to the window, sees the yacht steaming out of port,
shouts for the landlord, charters a fishing-boat, and dashes out to

the beach. Thus ends the second act, like the first, with all the bustle of a frantic chase. The third act ends with a midnight escape. Stubbs has rescued Lady Hermione from a watery grave, thus proving himself a hero in her eyes. But, though he has saved her body, her reputation is at the mercy of an enterprising and indelicate journalist who is staying at the inn, and who is anxious to discover her identity, with a view to booming the incident of her rescue. Stubbs decides that she must fly with him; and she flies. So far, the play is well-knit and ingenious, and never for a moment bores us. Mr Jones has always been strong in the art of telling a story on the stage—unrolling a swift succession of cumulative incidents; and the first three acts of *The Heroic Stubbs* are a good example of his excellence. But in more than one of his plays he has tripped up over the fourth act. I think the fourth act of *The Heroic Stubbs* is decidedly an anti-climax. Apart from the character of Stubbs himself, the play appeals to us simply as a play of action. The character of Lady Hermione is, as I said, well drawn; but she is familiar to us, and we do not really care about her, except as one of the wheels in a swiftly-moving machine. When the machine ceases to go round, we are still interested in Stubbs; but we retain no interest in Lady Hermione. Will she confess her escapade to her husband? Will she be forgiven by him? These are not questions that enthral us. Will the journalist discover her identity after all? In so far as that question is not yet decided, the play's machine is still moving; but only with a slow motion. We know that the journalist will be baffled, or 'squared,' or reduced to silence by an appeal to his better feelings. But, even if there were any doubt as to a happy ending, we should not really care. The play (like more than one of Mr Jones's, and like more than one of many another dramatist's) ought assuredly to have ended at the third act. As it stands, it could not end there satisfactorily. But, with a little alteration in the scheme of it, it might easily have been made to end there quite well. A good fourth act would postulate the writing of quite another play.

Mr Jones has often lamented the paucity of competent English mimes. I myself hold that there are many of them. And I should have liked Mr Jones to be cheered and convinced by a wholly admirable performance of his latest play. I am afraid that the actual performance of it will not lighten his gloom. Mr Welch is, as I have hinted, perfect. But not one of the rest of the parts seemed to me played appropriately. The essence of Lady Hermione is an agreeable weakness. The essence of Miss Gertrude Kingston's personality on the stage is an agreeable strength. A cool, direct, unfluttered Lady Hermione, always quite capable of taking care of herself, is not the Lady Hermione to whom Mr Jones gave Stubbs as a guardian angel. She is, however, the Lady Hermione whom Miss Kingston represents. By reason of the definiteness of her personality, there are some parts which Miss Kingston can play better than any other English actress. There are, by the same token, other parts which many a far less accomplished artist would play more satisfactorily than she. Lady Hermione is one of them. Mr Dellow is a rather perfunctory figure; but he is not a mere villain of transpontine melodrama; and it is as such, relentlessly, that Mr Eille Norwood represents him. Lady Hermione's husband is not a character out of whom much could be made. But Mr Dennis Eadie, one of the cleverest and most resourceful of our younger actors, ought surely not to seem turned to stone by him. The landlord of the inn at Yavercliff is an admirably studied character. Mr E. Dagnall's version of him is amusing in itself, but is quite untuned to the key of realistic comedy: it is in the key of uproarious farce. As for Mr Sydney Brough, who appeared in a small part in the last act, I thought that either he must be mad or I be dreaming. A few weeks ago I praised his admirable performance of a soldier-servant in a play at the Scala Theatre. I wish I were vain enough to think I had thereby turned his head. I am afraid that his extraordinary and quite uncalled-for antics and noises in the last act of Mr Jones's play were simply the result of innate high spirits triumphing over art. It did my heart good to see how happy he was. But I could not help sympathising with the horrified stage-manager. Or had Mr Brough really behaved like that during rehearsal?

[*27 January 1906*]

MR PINERO'S NEW PLAY

The plays that one enjoys most are not always the plays that one most praises. Enjoyment—unless it be an archangel's—can never

be a sure touchstone for merit. Nor can boredom be ever a sure
touchstone for the other thing. One has to discount one's own
emotions. What does not, on reflection, commend itself highly to
one's 'best self' may, at the moment, have pleased one's inferior self
very much indeed. And conversely. I was, as I told you the other
day, bored by the *Electra*. But had I not been preoccupied by the
duty of shaming certain other bored critics by an elaborate avowal
of my boredom, I would have raved to the full about Euripides,
and about Mr Gilbert Murray. By *His House in Order*, on the
other hand, I was not bored at all: I enjoyed it immensely. Mr
Pinero is a born playwright. One always does, more or less, enjoy
his plays. That is his strong point. His weak point is that when one
goes home, and thinks over the play that one has just seen, one is
always ashamed, more or less, of one's enjoyment. Most playgoers
are thoughtless. They live in the moment, and do not attempt to
check their impressions. The same thing may be said of most critics.
Most critics declare that *His House in Order* is a masterpiece among
masterpieces. Having enjoyed it so much, I wish it were. But I
cannot pretend that it is. My 'best self' prevents me.

In nearly all Mr Pinero's later plays you will find one common
denominator—a careful study of some woman. This study is
always the central thing in the play; and always the best thing in
the play. The men, for the most part, are negligible—conventional
types, drily and arbitrarily drawn. Mr Pinero is a feminist. He
has a real interest in the feminine soul, and can enter into it
with vivid sympathy. The feminine surface that interests him
most—the manner, as apart from the spirit—is that of a woman
who is best described only by the rather snobbish term 'second-
rate.' Mrs Tanqueray had acquired a veneer of vulgarity. The divor-
cée in *The Benefit of the Doubt* was essentially a vulgarian. So, of
course, was the manicurist in *The Gay Lord Quex*; and so was Letty.
In reproducing the tricks of speech peculiar to women of this kind,
Mr Pinero, who has usually no ear for human speech, displays an
unerring proficiency; and he evidently revels in his power. He has
not been able to restrain this power in his presentment of Nina
Jesson, the heroine of his latest play. For instance, 'I am agreeable,'
says Nina, when her brother-in-law proposes that they should call
each other by their Christian names. Nina, I admit, is in like case
with the other heroines whom I have enumerated, in so far as she

constantly shocks the other characters in the play. But she is well-born and well-educated; and the other characters in this play are shocked only because they are provincial prigs to whom anything like freedom of manner seems an offence. 'I am agreeable' is just the kind of genteel provincialism that could not possibly have fallen from Nina's lips. For the most part, however, Nina's manner of speech suits her tone of mind admirably. She is the one person in the play who talks like a human being. Perhaps this is because she is the one person in the play who *is* a human being. Were the others like her, the play would be a masterpiece indeed. It has the makings of a really fine drama in psychology. Nina is the second wife of Filmer Jesson. Her predecessor, Annabel Mary, was accounted a paragon. She had just the virtues which commended themselves to her husband. She looked very beautiful, gave him no trouble, and saved him no end of trouble. She kept 'his house in order,' and was altogether the ideal wife for a man bent on public life. Soon after her death, he was bewitched by Nina. The spell has not long survived matrimony. Nina knows nothing about housekeeping. Nina is childish and high-spirited. She shocks the relations of Annabel Mary—the Ridgeley family. She shocks Filmer, insomuch that, day by day, he is becoming less and less a husband, and more and more a sorrowing widower. If Mr Pinero's intellectual conscience and courage were worthy of his wonderful sense for the theatre—if, in fact, Mr Pinero were not Mr Pinero—he might have built a lastingly fine play on this basis. He might have so developed his theme as to show Filmer's gradual realisation that it was better to have a warm-hearted woman to wife, however inconvenient she might be to his career, than to have a cold-blooded helpmeet. He might . . . but these speculations are futile. Mr Pinero is Mr Pinero. He prefers the theatre to life. He heads straight forward along the line of least resistance—the line that leads to 'thrills,' with plenty of 'fun' by the way. Above all, he insists on getting the utmost 'sympathy' for his heroine. So here she is in the midst of a crew of quite impossible people. It is not conceivable that any man could be so egregious a poltroon as her husband, who allows the Ridgeleys to persecute and insult her, up hill and down dale, every moment of the day. The Ridgeleys themselves are but a set of caricatures. They are very funny caricatures indeed. There are four of them, all executed in precisely the same manner. In *The Voysey Inheri-*

tance Mr Granville Barker showed what could be done in presentment of a family. Every member of the Voysey family had a
separate identity, such as has every member of a family in real life.
Had Mr Barker chosen to caricature them, they would still have
been individual. The Ridgeleys (barring a few superficial differences
according to their ages) are all exactly alike. All are shaped to one
mould of impossible stupidity and brutality. They are not a family,
but a burlesqued regiment. Evidently Mr Pinero meant to use them
as a lash for middle-class Puritanism. His *raisonneur*, Hilary, the
brother of Filmer, declares that they, and such as they, are 'individually and collectively one of the pests of humanity.' But, since they,
and such as they, have no existence, Hilary is merely lashing the
air. Nor does Hilary himself exist, save in that warm corner which
Mr Pinero keeps in his heart for his ideal of 'a man of the world.'
If it were possible to meet him, I should shun him even more carefully than I should shun the Ridgeleys. His prattle about chefs, and
about Paris and Vienna, and Tokio and Washington, and about
a little museum in which he preserves 'the blood-stained handkerchief of a matador, and a half-smoked cigarette that has been
pressed by the lips of an Empress,' who was 'one of the noblest of
her sex,' exasperates me only a trifle less than the rant and cant that
he reels out for Nina's benefit in the play's crisis. Nina has discovered a packet of letters proving that Annabel Mary had been
unfaithful to her husband, and that her child was another man's.
One of these letters had been written on the morning of the very
day when Annabel Mary was killed by an accident. It seems that,
when she met her death, she must have been in the very act of
eloping. Hilary reminds Nina that her father was a clergyman, and
suggests to her that 'the finger of Providence' is traceable in the
late Mrs Jesson's fate. He suggests that the sudden death was not a
punishment, but an act of grace. Providence, if we are to accept his
theory, had not interfered to prevent Mrs Jesson from sinning privately; but, when she was going to make the neighbours 'talk,'
Providence stepped mercifully in, very much as the Bishop stepped
in to save the face of the lady in *The Benefit of the Doubt*. Mr
Pinero has, of course, a perfect right to his own views in theology.
But I think it unwise of him to express them through the lips of a
character in a serious dramatic crisis. They let the thing down, as
it were. We can believe that Nina might be persuaded to make no

223

use of the compromising letters, and thus forgo her revenge on the Ridgeleys; but we refuse to believe that she would let herself be led to this renunciation by such a catch-penny windbag as Mr Hilary Jesson. At a crisis in her life, she could not have listened patiently to him for one moment. Nor, for that matter, could she, at any time, have put up with the Ridgeleys. Either she or they would have had to leave the house. Thus Nina herself becomes incredible to us. And thus is illustrated the iron law (which I have just invented) that one real character in a play is not enough. If the others be unreal, even the real character will be shorn of its reality.

Remember, it is my 'best self' that is speaking to you. As a critic, retrospective and cerebrative, I cannot ignore the play's fundamental weaknesses. But do not forget that my inferior self enjoyed the play immensely. Figments though the Ridgeleys are, I was really anxious that Nina should put them to rout. I really was touched by her magnanimity in handing the letters to Hilary, and really annoyed by it. I was really delighted when, in the fourth act, Hilary, provoked beyond bounds by the continued insolence of the Ridgeleys, and by his brother's continued acquiescence in it, drew the letters from his breast-pocket and thrust them into his brother's hands. Judged on a low plane, *His House in Order* takes very high rank indeed. And it contains one line which is a real masterpiece of dramatic wit. Filmer Jesson, having read the letters stares blankly into space. His ideal has crumbled away. His soul is in darkness. 'To think,' he says, 'to think that she—so methodical, so orderly—omitted to destroy these letters!' Neatness, which had been outwardly her ruling passion, is inwardly his; and it surges up in him now, taking precedence of all his despair and his wrath and his humiliation. His words are perfectly in keeping with his character. But to have found them for him was a master-stroke of insight; and to have allowed him to speak them, before an audience wrought up to emotion, was a master-stroke of daring; and these two master-strokes together form what I have called a master-stroke of dramatic wit. Mr Pinero must allow me to congratulate him.

He must allow me to congratulate him, also, on the casting and the stage management—in both of which, I take it, he had the main share. Mr Lyall Swete, Miss Bella Pateman, Miss Beryl Faber, and Mr C. M. Lowne, play in exactly the right key for the grotesque Ridgeleys, never for a moment yielding to the temptation

to overdo the grotesqueness. Miss Irene Vanbrugh, as playing the
one real character in the play, wins, of course, the success of the
evening, and would win it even were not the part so well within the
range of her cleverness. Mr Alexander and Mr Waring are hampered
by parts that are neither real nor amusingly grotesque. They are
hampered also by Mr Pinero's ghastly modes of speech. 'Permit
me,' says Mr Alexander, 'to apprise you of an indisputable fact.'
'Permit me,' says Mr Waring, 'to postpone my defence to an
occasion when you are less heated.' That is a fair sample of their
manner throughout the play. I don't object to Mr Pinero's touching belief that it is a 'literary' manner. I merely urge him, once and
for all, to realise that it is a manner deleterious (as he would say) to
drama. How can actors be expected to be at their best when they
are hampered by phrases that no one in real life, except a Lord
Mayor, would dream of uttering? Not even when the characters
are labouring under extreme stress of emotion does Mr Pinero relax
his vocabulary. Hilary Jesson has to be appalled when Nina shows
him the letters. His eyes must dilate. His voice must break; and, in
his broken voice, 'I fear,' he must say, 'that your allegations are
only too well-grounded.' It is a great tribute to Mr Alexander's
emotional force that he does, in spite of all, contrive to create an
emotional effect.

[*10 February 1906*]

BRUTUS AS 'VILLAIN'

I have been reading in the February number of *Harper's Magazine* an essay which stirs in me the embers of an old controversy.
Four or five years ago I wrote here that Brutus was the sympathetic
hero in Shakespeare's *Julius Caesar*. Having imagined this to be an
indisputable platitude, I was surprised and pleased when Mr Harold
Hodge, quite seriously, here disputed it. I made a rejoinder; but
either I did not convert Mr Hodge, or Mr Hodge has meanwhile
back-slidden. For the whole of his 'critical comment on *Julius
Caesar*' is informed by the purpose of showing that Brutus, as presented by Shakespeare, was 'a solemn humbug,' and that any

other assumption is 'an injury to Shakespeare.' He scorns 'the finger-mark of the commentator'; but pleads that 'it is not a desecration to try to wash off handprints obscuring the figure's true proportions.' There I perfectly agree with him; and I admire the ingenuity of his essay not less than I respect its pious intention. But, if his theory of Shakespeare's Brutus be accepted, then Shakespeare, I regret to say, must stand forth as a convicted bungler. And these, obviously, are not the 'true proportions' in which Mr Hodge would have us see that clever dramatist.

Seeking for the play a motive that shall square with his theory of Brutus, he naturally rejects 'the failure of ideals in practical politics.' I am quite willing not to press that theory. But I, in my turn, reject Mr Hodge's theory that the play's motive is 'the march of Nemesis on crime.' Of course, Nemesis comes in. Shakespeare's (like North's Plutarch's) Brutus finds that 'the gods were offended with the murther of Caesar.' But this fact does not, as Mr Hodge suggests, 'exclude the conception of Brutus as a single-minded patriot.' Nor, indeed, does Mr Hodge press his theory of the motive. 'Probably Shakespeare had no subjective aim, no thesis to illustrate at all: he merely wanted to dramatise an intensely im-pressive and obviously dramatic episode in history.' Again I agree. But, though Shakespeare was probably not preaching, we must not assume that he had no clear dramatic standpoint. When Mr Hodge says 'we must exclude Shakespeare's intention, which for one thing we cannot know, as an illegitimate argument,' he really does seem anxious to prove Shakespeare a bungler. If Shakespeare's dramatic notion of Brutus could not be deduced from his dramatic present-ment of Brutus, then would Shakespeare in this instance be proved incapable of the A B C of dramaturgy. Certainly 'we must take the words as they are and see what is in them'; but we must, in polite-ness to Shakespeare's memory, assume that what is in them was knowingly put there by the writer of them, and did not merely stray in from the void. Even so, we must not suppose that, for aught we know, Shakespeare may have intended Iago as a saint on earth. By studying Iago's 'words as they are,' we learn surely what was Shakespeare's dramatic notion of Iago. If we don't, the fault is ours. If the whole 'crowd of commentators' is wrong about Brutus, and Mr Hodge is right, Mr Hodge cannot evade the responsibility of having penetrated the (to him sacred) recesses of Shakespeare's mind. If Brutus really is, on the evidence, 'a solemn humbug,' Shakespeare intended him to appear as such. But, if Shakespeare intended him to appear as such, I submit that Shakespeare went a very odd way about the business.

Mr Hodge, with characteristic honesty, does not hush up the singularity of his notion. 'Brutus of the play has imposed on Shakespeare's readers and on his actors as did Marcus Brutus of history on Caesar and on the Roman public. They have taken him at his own description of himself. A great tribute this to the truthfulness of Shakespeare's portrait.' What an ingenious excuse for Shakespeare! What an ingenious confusion of life with art! As though to be a successful humbug, and to give a successful presentment of a humbug, were ends to be achieved by the same means! As though the touchstone of a dramtist's success in this kind were that the audience should be blinded with the very dust that blinds the persons of the play! The art of dramaturgy, let Mr Hodge believe me, is a thing quite separate from the art of mystification. It is not a dramatist's duty to 'keep us guessing' about his characters. Still less is it his duty to deceive his audiences, his actors, and his commentators, so well that they don't even guess, but take as a matter of course that which is precisely the reverse of the truth. Dramaturgy is an art of demonstration. If a dramatist portrays a humbug, be sure that he wishes his audiences, his actors, and his commentators to 'catch on.' Iago was a humbug. He imposed on Othello. But he has not imposed on the rest of us. Shakespeare did not intend him to do so, and took certain obvious means to prevent him from doing so. Iago confessed his true self in soliloquies. Does Brutus do this? On the contrary, he talks to himself exactly as to his fellows. His character seems to be quite as gentle, and his aims seem to be quite as noble, in private as in public. Speaking to himself about Caesar, 'I know,' says he, 'no personal cause to spurn at him but for the general.' If, as Mr Hodge suggests, his motive for joining the conspiracy had been ignoble vanity and ambition, why did Shakespeare take not one of the many obvious opportunities for giving us the necessary information? Mr Hodge is ready for that question. He explains that Brutus was such a humbug that he deceived even himself. Let us suppose, for sake of argument, that Shakespeare saw eye to eye with Mr Hodge. The fact remains that Shakespeare, as a dramatist, would not have wished to keep that view to himself. As surely as Mr

Hodge has given his view to the readers of *Harper's Magazine*, Shakespeare would have given *his* to the audience of the Blackfriars Theatre (or whatever the place was). He would have had Brutus 'shown up' by one of the persons of the play. Personally, I like the notion of a stage-humbug taking in every one—himself included. But then, I am not a dramatist. Shakespeare was. Shakespeare wouldn't have had anything to do with that ingenious and amusing notion.

Mr Hodge himself has evidently felt that the absence of any 'showing up' would be a weakness in his case against Brutus. Accordingly, he is at pains to show that Brutus, for all his good repute, is held in light esteem by Cassius. Certainly, 'the impression he leaves on strong men who are his intimates' would be admissible and valuable evidence. But the evidence is so little valuable to Mr Hodge's case that Cassius has to be treated as a hostile witness. He has said 'Caesar doth bear me hard; but he loves Brutus: if I were Brutus now, and he were Cassius, he should not humour me.' Mr Hodge suggests to the witness that his meaning was ' "You are not strong enough, Brutus, to stand up to men like me. I have a grudge against Caesar: you have none. If I were in your place now, you should not turn me against Caesar as I have turned you." ' I think I hear the witness explaining that, on the contrary, what he meant was 'Brutus is a noble, disinterested creature. How different from me! *I* want to kill Caesar because I don't like him. If it were just a question of the commonweal, I shouldn't budge. But the common- weal is a sure draw for dear old Brutus.' And I think I hear the judge on the bench saying to the witness that this seems to him the only interpretation which could reasonably be applied to the words. And I think I see the whole jury nodding their solid acquiescence. Still the ingenious advocate persists. It was with base arguments that Cassius urged on Brutus the expediency of killing Caesar; 'and though,' says Mr Hodge, 'it has been pleaded that it is not Cassius's arguments that decide Brutus, there stands the fact that certain arguments have been used to produce a certain result, and that result is produced. In such circumstances denial of cause and effect requires very strict proof.' I should have thought the *onus probandi* rested rather with the novel and singular theorist than with the crowd serried on the side of tradition. Nor does Mr Hodge alto- gether shirk that burden. He offers, in the subsequent words 'since

Cassius first did whet me against Caesar,' a proof that it was
Cassius's arguments that prevailed. These words are perfectly compatible with the theory that Brutus's mind was moving on its own
plane; and (in the absence of any contrary evidence, and having
regard to the direct evidence, in the text of the scene between the
two men) we must suppose that obvious theory to be correct. When
Cassius has finished his jealous ragings against Caesar, Brutus says
'What you would work me to, I have some aim: how I have
thought of this, and of these times, I shall recount hereafter. . . .
Brutus had rather be a villager than to repute himself a son of
Rome under these hard conditions, as this time is like to lay on us.'
Brutus, in fact, had already been pondering on what he took to be
the parlous state of his city. He had dallied philosophically with
the idea of assassination. Cassius, the man of action, gave to Brutus's
thoughts a more practical turn. But, in the light of the aforesaid
soliloquy—'save only for the general'—and in the absence of any
shred of evidence (whether by soliloquy or by comment) that Brutus
had any base motive for Caesar's death, we must suppose that
Brutus's mind converged to the point by a curve quite apart from
Cassius's. As to that 'impression' left by Brutus on his 'intimates,'
I would refer Mr Hodge to the text, and ask him whether Cassius's
attitude be not, throughout, one of hero-worship for the beauty of
Brutus's character. In the scene of the quarrel, Cassius says he is the
better soldier (as doubtless he was). But even that remark he
handsomely withdraws, so soon as he has cooled down. Assuredly, a
very hostile witness for Mr Hodge to handle.

Marcus Antonius is just such another. 'This was the noblest
Roman of them all. All the conspirators, save only he, did that they
did in envy of great Caesar,' &c. &c. Mr Hodge seeks to explain this
judgment by explaining away Marcus Antonius. He asks us to
accept this gentleman on his own valuation: 'a plain blunt man,'
who is 'necessarily imposed on.' Sauce for the goose is evidently
not sauce for the gander. We are not to take Brutus at his own
valuation, even though everything goes to prove that valuation
correct. But we are to accept unreservedly the self-valuation of
Antonius, even though it is an obvious little trick of oratory for the
persuading of the Roman citizens. No, no: we really cannot accept
that subtle orator as a fool. We are not the mob in the forum: we
are the audience, on the other side of the footlights. Shakespeare

took good care that *we* should not be deceived. And, had he regarded Brutus as 'a solemn humbug' he would have taken equally
good care to let us into *that* secret.

But the main value of Antonius's testimony to Brutus, as showing
Shakespeare's own private opinion of his puppet, rests not on the
fact that Antonius was astute, but on the fact that the testimony is
delivered at the close of the play. It was ever Shakespeare's habit,
at the close of a play, to sum up his principal character through the
lips of some subordinate character. Nor was it always a kindly
summing-up. If the principal character was a villain, the audience
was told so. If he was a hero, the audience was told so. If Shakespeare, while he was writing *Julius Caesar*, had been so far below
his usual form that he could not make the audience understand what
he was driving at, be sure that he would have snatched this final
opportunity of making himself clear. But, of course, as it stands, the
epitaph on Brutus is, as usual, a simple clinching of the play's
intention—a simple means of stating expressly what the play has
implied.

Mr Hodge speaks of 'the idealisers of Brutus'; and, though he
means by that term the idealisers of Shakespeare's Brutus, I fancy he
thinks that Shakespeare's Brutus has been idealised by us because
the Brutus of history has been idealised. I hasten to assure him
that I, at any rate, am no worshipper of the historic Brutus, who,
indeed, affects me no more than does Hecuba. To Mr Hodge, however, Roman history is evidently a very vivid and instant thing. He
is as passionately moved by admiration for Julius Caesar as he would
be if Julius Caesar had been alive yesterday. And he is as incensed
against Marcus Brutus as he would be if Caesar had been assassinated
this afternoon. He makes no allowance at all for lapse of time. He
seems to believe (though he cannot really believe) that assassination
was reputed in Pagan Rome as great a crime as it is in Christian
London, and that a Roman assassin was necessarily as vile a man as
would be an assassin in this metropolis. He compares the death of
Caesar with Calvary—'the tragedy of time' and 'the tragedy of
eternity.' I am sure he would bracket Brutus with Judas. Brutus
is to him a villain of the deepest dye, in our very midst. Feeling so
strongly as he does, he cannot imagine how anyone else could feel
less strongly. That is the source of his error. He cannot imagine how
Shakespeare, having had the chance of damning Brutus, could have

resisted that chance. Therefore, he argues, Brutus in the play really is damned. Well! if Shakespeare had wanted to damn Brutus, we may, I repeat, be sure that he would have managed to do so in a manner intelligible to his 'actors,' his 'audience,' and to his 'crowd of commentators' throughout the past three centuries. He would not have so cryptographically damned him that Mr Hodge should be the first man to discern traces of the job.

[*17 February 1906*]

A REJOINDER

Bravo! Bravo! Bravissimo! As when, an unit in the mass of plain citizens who have been gaping upward at the dancer on the awful tight-rope overhead, you become vociferous at the close of the performance, even so do I now shout myself hoarse in Mr Hodge's honour. Or rather (if I may give the metaphor a twist), calm in the confusion of my fellows I step forth to offer first-aid. For the intrepid performer has fallen—fallen badly through the underspread net of dialectic. But let no one be deceived by Mr Hodge's likening of me to a fine surgeon. My skill, even though it be successful, is not comparable with his, even though he has fallen. It is not in *my* power to defy, for however brief a time, the laws of gravity. I am but a plain, blunt member of the terrestrial crowd.

Mr Hodge has twitted me with boasting of that fact. He says that the fact of his 'being in a minority' is no evidence against his case. Far be it from me to deny that a minority is often right. There are cases in which even a minority of one has been subsequently proved right. So, *prima facie*, Mr Hodge need not be ashamed that it is in a minority of one that he is standing. Yet he is at pains to prove that he has backers. He denies not the hostility of the 'commentators,' and the 'actors'; but he modifies his previous assertion that the 'audiences,' too, have always been bamboozled by Brutus. Of those 'very unsophisticated neighbours' in the pit 'many, I think, began to distrust Brutus early.' They 'seemed able to achieve an effort of penetration,' &c. Mr Hodge *thinks*; these people *seemed*. Not exactly the sort of evidence that Mr Hodge would deem very valuable in a court of law. Nor can he deem it very valuable here.

That he did not deign to strengthen it, by elimination of all that *seeming* and *thinking*, is, however, valuable evidence of his sincerity.

But why, if 'the appeal to numbers' is 'extraneous,' does Mr Hodge even faintly claim that the hearts of these neighbours were beating in unison with his? It is because Mr Hodge, somewhere in the depths of his consciousness, knows that my appeal to numbers is not extraneous at all. Granted that fifty years ago Tiberius was by the majority of people regarded as a monster; and that this majority was wrong. How has the error been rectified? By the patient research of scholars, who have gradually found that the actual facts about Tiberius do not square with the verdict of contemporary historians. It is conceivable that research might, conversely, prove the actual Brutus to have been (as Mr Hodge thinks him) a villain. But that would not prove the Brutus of the play a villain. When Mr Hodge compares the case of Tiberius with the case of the dramatic Brutus, he forgets this essential difference: the facts about Tiberius had to be unearthed from various obscure quarters; but the facts about the dramatic Brutus have been, within the play's narrow compass, open to public inspection for three whole centuries. If everyone has, all along, been drawing false deductions from these facts, and if Mr Hodge is the first man to draw the right deductions, what a lamentable world Mr Hodge has been born into! Mr Hodge's optimism and his modesty alike shrink from that logical conclusion. Hence his touching recollections of those 'unsophisticated' pittites who 'seemed' to grasp the truth.

He shrinks not less from that other logical conclusion: that Shakespeare was a bungler. It is, however, a conclusion to which I must, respectfully, pin him. Shakespeare, 'cramming' from his 'crib' of Plutarch, must have formed some sort of an opinion about Brutus. At any rate, he must have made up his mind to regard Brutus, for dramatic purposes, from some sort of standpoint. Let us assume that he meant his Brutus for 'a solemn humbug.' As the art of drama is an art of demonstration, not of mystification, Shakespeare's aim was to let his audience see Brutus as 'a solemn humbug.' Allowing for the possibility that some unsophisticated pittites really *have* grasped the truth, Mr Hodge will not deny that the vast majority of all audiences have agreed with all the critics and commentators (many of whom are not mere sightless bookworms, after all) in regarding the dramatic Brutus as a hero. If this consensus be not a proof of extreme bungling on Shakespeare's part, then nothing is a proof of anything. Why, the veriest duffer in dramaturgy would have found means to enlighten the audience. Mr Hodge calls confession by soliloquy 'a clumsy device.' Perhaps it is (from a modern standpoint). But it is sometimes, even to modern playwrights, a necessary one; and it is one to which Shakespeare constantly resorted even when it was not needed. If he had meant Brutus to be 'a solemn humbug,' either Brutus (unless exposed by another person in the play) would have soliloquised, or Shakespeare must have grossly bungled. A humbug who takes himself in, along with everyone else, is possible in life; but he is not a possible figure for drama.

Mr Hodge cannot escape through his plea that not all the characters in Shakespeare are simple. Of course they aren't. Nor have I ever offered a 'canon that every character must be crystal to the spectator from the first word he speaks.' I merely hold that no character ought to be fog to the spectator after the last word he speaks. It is the dramatist's glory (a glory which Shakespeare often won) to present a complex character simply. I don't say he did this in the case of Brutus. But that is only because he seems to me to have been presenting a perfectly simple character.

Take 'what is written as it stands,' by all means. Even though Mr Hodge be right in deprecating any attempt to deduce therefrom Shakespeare's 'intention'—even though, in fact, Shakespeare may but have used language to conceal his thoughts—it is, obviously, on the actual text that we must rely for our conception of Brutus's character. So far from wishing one line of this text 'blacked out,' I should like to quote it in full. But that were more than my indulgent Editor could allow. Mr Hodge must be satisfied if I confine myself to those points which he has selected as being vulnerable in Brutus. (The other points—presumably invulnerable—my readers must remember for themselves.) (1) Brutus is 'great on his own goodness.' That does not prove him a humbug. Many really good men boast of their goodness. It is an irritating trick in real life. But in Shakespearean drama one is not so easily irritated by it. Whenever, as so often happens there, a bad character talks about his badness, we do not feel necessarily that he is proud of it. Similarly, whenever a good character talks about his goodness, we are not outraged. He may be merely purveying information which is necessary to our understanding. Self-confession is one of the conventions of Shake-spearean drama. However, I am quite ready to admit that Brutus may be taken as actually conscious and proud of his virtue. It is not part of my case to argue that he is an altogether 'sympathetic' hero. In the tent-scene, most of the 'sympathy' goes to Cassius, who was not a hero at all. Heroism is not a thing to be gauged by the pro-portion of 'sympathy' that it inspires in our emotional bosoms. (2) *'A wondrous man of words.'* From what important character in Shakespeare's plays could that title be withheld? (3) *Caesar has done no actual harm; therefore Brutus must have had only a personal reason for deploring his ascendency.* A statesman does not regard only the past and the present: he regards through them the future. According to the text 'as it stands,' Brutus thought that the Roman people were becoming servile, and that their degradation would soon react badly on Caesar's character, and that the State would suffer all round. He may have been wrong. But there is nothing to show that he was not honestly wrong. (4) *Cassius, 'whetting' Brutus against Caesar, flatters him and uses ignoble arguments.* The flattery may not have been insincere. It is in strict accord to Cassius's dog-like admiration throughout the play. Possibly this was only an attitude? If it was not sincere, why was it not abandoned when, later, there was nothing to be gained by it? Certainly, if we are not to believe that Cassius loved and venerated Brutus, we must do a great deal of 'blacking out.' Suppose that Cassius *was* insincere in his flatteries. How are we to know that Brutus was moved by them? Cassius did, of course, use very ignoble arguments. But that does not show that he thought ill of Brutus. In his impulsive way, he raged hotly against Caesar, laying bare his own personal grievance against Caesar. He showed thus his own ignobleness, but not that he knew that Brutus would be swayed by a similar personal grievance. And how are we to accept Mr Hodge's suggestion that Brutus *was* swayed thereby? *Post hoc* isn't *propter hoc*, if I remember rightly. Brutus acknowledges that Cassius did 'whet' him; but that phrase is perfectly compatible with the theory (borne out by the whole text) that Brutus, long hostile to Caesar for the State's sake, and wishing him out of the way, but having a philosophic hatred of violence, had been stirred from inaction by the headlong eagerness of Cassius. Mr Hodge has not, ever so little, shaken that theory. (5) *The 'anonymous scrawls' thrown through Brutus's window.*

Doubtless, a private gentleman in modern life takes no notice of anonymous letters about his private affairs. So much I grant to Mr Hodge's sense of deportment. But a public statesman in modern life does read anonymous leading-articles in newspapers, and (rightly or wrongly) is apt to attach some importance to them. There were no newspapers in Rome. Those 'anonymous scrawls' received by Brutus were a sort of substitute. Brutus was not 'swept away by them headlong.' But they tended to confirm his decision. They were a sign to him that his help was needed urgently. There is nothing to show that they acted on his vanity. We have only Mr Hodge's word for it. (6) *Antony's speech over Brutus's dead body.* I gather that 'what the soldier said is not evidence.' 'The arch-murderers are both dead: the justice of Heaven is satisfied: passion is spent.' Why, then, doesn't the soldier, 'shedding a kindly influence on the close of this tremendous tragedy,' say something nice about Cassius? Why sentimentalise over Brutus exclusively? Why say 'All the conspirators, save only he, did that they did in envy of great Caesar'? Perhaps Antony, being a soldier, cherished a professional jealousy of Cassius—though glad enough to put in a good word for that philosopher fellow, Brutus. I cannot find in the text any evidence for this professional jealousy. But I daresay Mr Hodge could. I think it would not tax Mr Hodge's ingenuity to find evidence of anything anywhere.

[*24 February 1906*]

MR HEWLETT AT THE COURT THEATRE

I had thought Mr Maurice Hewlett's Muse well equipped for entry into the theatre. For in all his books I have felt a something akin to the glare of the footlights. The fascination of his books has always seemed to me rather like the fascination of the theatre— the fascination of a thing which, though it appears so very real, one knows to be not real at all. The characters created by some novelists live in our imagination, are phantom friends to us, or phantom enemies. Though we see them but dimly, we know they are with us: we believe in them. It is not dimly that we see the men and women who ruffle it through the pages of Mr Hewlett. He has a passionate clarity of vision. He sees his characters steadily, brilliantly, from top to toe. Not a turn of the wrist, not a wrinkle nor a buckle, escapes his hawk-like eye. And he makes us partakers of his vision. In the round we see them, these fair ladies and their gallants, these proud virgins and generous wantons, these knights with clanking harness and beetling brows. We visualise them as distinctly as we visualise the people who pass us in the street. They are solid, mobile, life-sized. But is there life inside them? They are often very violent. They express, very picturesquely and delightfully, all the symptoms of love, hatred, despair, political ambition, religious fervour, and what not. They are very eloquent. There is nothing they cannot express. And they flourish their arms, they stride, strut, lurk behind arrases, scale walls, stab themselves, die, exactly as people do in real life—or would do, if they had the chance, and the necessary technique. But somehow, for me at least, they do not seem to be real. When I close the book that has revealed them to me, they do not enter into my spiritual life. I feel about them as about the ladies and gentlemen who, when the curtain falls between them and me, retire to their dressing-rooms, and cleanse themselves of their greasepaint, before driving home to supper. Mr Hewlett, I feel, has not seen into the souls of his characters. They have not been created out of his own soul. Their appearance has been created out of his own vision. But their souls have originated in his fine taste for literature, and in his fine talent for writing.

For sheer artistry in the use of words, Mr Hewlett beats anyone since Robert Louis Stevenson—or Walter Pater: I forget which predeceased the other. His is not so elastic a style as Stevenson's, nor so subtle a style as Pater's. It 'burns with a hard, gem-like flame.' It is rather too steadily dazzling. But, as compared with the guttering and spluttering murkiness of the average novelist's style, it is a flame for which one must be thankful. Such conscious and obvious artistry in the use of words is not, I confess, conducive to illusion in the characters presented, and in the story told, by the novelist. Some such style as Thackeray's seems to me the ideal style in writing novels. One can delight in that perfect manner which was Thackeray's, long after the story is so familiar that it does not impress one at all. But, at first reading, the manner does not intertrude its beauty between the story and oneself. Stevenson's manner, even at first reading, was always thus intertrusive. In the essays—

and Stevenson was an essayist by birth, a tale-teller by accident—one could not have been so foolish as to resent the tyranny of manner. The essayist's business is to express, above all, himself. The more elaborately personal be his manner, the better we know him. But the story-teller's business is to express other people. Stevenson, who wrote novels rather because Sir Walter Scott had written novels than because he had any strong inward impulse for the form, endeavoured, with admirable Scottish tenacity, to carry the business through. But the result? What character in Stevenson's novels lives vividly for us—except Stevenson himself, the all-pervasive? In Mr Hewlett's novels not even Mr Hewlett himself lives vividly for us. We do not see him, do not know him, behind those glittering arrangements. Perhaps we should not thus see and know R.L.S., had we not first read his essays. Mr Hewlett's self may be not less unique and delightful than Stevenson's, and might be as vivid to us, in his fictional work, had he first written essays. He, too, perhaps, is a born essayist. That he is so evidently, like Stevenson, a made novelist, seems to me proof presumptive in favour of this theory. I should like him to write a volume of essays. Thus he might win for his fiction the sort of extraneous vitality that Stevenson's fiction has. Except as an indirect revelation of self, Stevenson's novels live only by the sharp visualising power that was his, and by the beauty of the language. Mr Hewlett's visualising power is yet sharper; and his use of language is but a shade less beautiful. Let him win for his cunningly made puppets the significance that is in Stevenson's.

It was silly of me to suppose that Mr Hewlett's Muse would, in virtue of her theatricalism, well adapt herself to the theatre. To see embodied, in the round, some character that we have beheld but dimly in our imagination, is a valuable experience that the theatre alone can give to us. But Mr Hewlett's characters, just because they have always been thus so distinctly visualised by us, gain nothing by such embodiments. Moreover, their unreality becomes more palpable when they are studied in just that foot-lighted glare which we had seen figuratively cast on them. *The Fool Errant* is the only one of Mr Hewlett's novels that I have not yet read. I can imagine that therein the little scene which he has adapted for the theatre, under the title of *The Youngest of the Angels*, might have passed muster. The dialogue is quick and clean-cut, and full of pretty conceits and mannerisms. The whole scene might, in the book, have seemed rather brilliant. Its utter unrealness and triteness might have been mitigated by the manner of its presentment. But here, in the literal glare of those footlights that shone but figuratively on its inception, oh! away with it! The old husband, a curmudgeon scholar; and the young wife, who pines to be no mere plaything; and the youth whom she innocently inspires with calf-love, and who, at the husband's approach, is hustled into a cupboard, wherefrom he emerges on hearing the old man say in soliloquy that his wife has faults—the youth's gradual conversion of the old man—the assurance of a brighter, better future for the old man's wife: oh! away with the frigid, dusty twaddle of it all! In the course of an eighteenth-century comedy, the scene might pass muster. It would be depressing enough, even so; but its antiquarian interest might save it. I have no words to describe how irretrievably depressing it is as a single scene, written by a contemporary man of letters. Imagine any man— even were he not, like Mr Hewlett, a brilliant man—offering to us, in cold blood, and in the twentieth century, this sort of thing as one of his maiden efforts in drama!

This lack of any genuine impulse is not less awfully exemplified in the comic scenes of *Pan and the Young Shepherd*. Shakespeare's clowns are not, nowadays, very inspiriting, even in their own setting. Only by projecting ourselves into the past can we laugh at them with any semblance of heartiness. Only by an extraordinary over-development of the mimetic literary faculty, and an extraordinary under-development of a sense for what is going on around him, could a man set himself the task of reproducing, with all possible fidelity, those stale humours. Yet this is the task which Mr Hewlett has set himself. Whether he has accomplished it ill or well is neither here nor there. What matters, and appals, is the fact that the task was set. And just this lack of genuine impulse in the comic scenes is reflected in the whole aspect of the play. Shakespeare brought Oberon to Warwickshire, because his fancy impelled him to do so. It is not Mr Hewlett's fancy that impels him to bring Pan to a similar place. It is Shakespeare's fancy, collated with the fancy of other writers. Tasteful, ingenious, brilliant—what you will—is Mr Hewlett's arrangement. But never for an instant is there a spark of original poetry in it. You remember what cruel, yet tenderly cruel, fun was made by Heine in 'The Gods in Exile.' You remember the wistful and haunting fantasy that Pater wrought in 'Apollo in Picardy.' Pater and Heine were touched by the old legend. They really did, as it were, bring the poor Olympians into modern life. It is not, I think, the old legend itself that has touched Mr Hewlett, but rather the old legend as it has been treated by illustrious predecessors in the art to which he is honourably devoted. The result is a clever little exercise in that art; but dry. It presses me, all unwilling, to the conclusion that Pan *is* dead, after all.

[*10 March 1906*]

AT TERRY'S THEATRE

Mr Brandon Thomas's new play, *A Judge's Memory*, was produced by Mr Welch last Tuesday evening. It very evidently delighted the audience; and I imagine it will be a great success. It is not the kind of play to which I can extend my own limited affections. It is the kind of play which, I think, I do not rightly understand. I feel diffident in the attempt to criticise it.

I can appreciate sheer fantasy, such as Mr Barrie sometimes gives us—a set of creatures and incidents quite detached from ordinary life, and bearing to ordinary life a merely symbolical relation. On the other hand, I can appreciate sheer realism, such as Mr Granville Barker has lately given us. Men and things, as they are in the actual world, interest me very much. I delight in a seemingly faithful reproduction of them. Mr Brandon Thomas evidently does not think so highly as I do of the actual world. He finds it lacking in colour, vivacity, variety. He regards it as a thin wine that must be heavily doctored before it can be palatable and exhilarating. He does not, you see, utterly despise the wine. He has not, like Mr Barrie, a vine of his own growing, and a vat for his own treading. He regards the actual world as a very good basis for drama. There are queer folk here and there; and queer things happen now and then. Collect a few of these queer folk, and of these queer things, and make them far more queer than you found them, and stir them well together. Such, I take it, is the recipe which Mr Thomas would offer to nascent playwrights. It is certainly the recipe from which *A Judge's Memory* has been concocted. I use the word 'concocted' in no derogatory sense. Cooking is an art, and all art is a form of cooking. *A Judge's Memory* is, I daresay, a beautifully cooked dish of its kind. But some persons, by reason of some defect in palate or in digestion, have a real aversion from certain dishes, and cannot, therefore, pretend to discriminate whether or not those dishes have been cooked well. Not knowing, I cannot say whether *A Judge's Memory* be good, bad, or indifferent of its kind. The fact that it was liked so much by the audience may be taken, perhaps, as proof presumptive of its goodness. For the rest, I can only describe it.

The central figure, Mr Frazer, has a very picturesque history, which is unrolled, at great length, in the first act. His father, an officer in the army, died, leaving him and an elder brother to be brought up by a costermonger. The two brothers grew up. The younger married and begot a son. The elder became a burglar; and in one of his burglaries the younger was innocently involved. Arrested, the younger refused to betray the real culprit, and was sentenced to five years' penal servitude. His son was looked after by the elder brother, who went to San Francisco and amassed there a fortune by some safer and more lucrative means than burglary. When the younger brother came out of prison, he joined the elder in San Francisco. The elder died, leaving him a rich man, on condition that he did not jeopardise his son's career by revealing his parentage. So that nobody may suspect his identity, he adopts the name of Frazer, takes a castle in Scotland, and pretends to be Scotch. A complex 'part,' you perceive, is here, with plenty of chance for 'character': an English gentleman by birth, a Cockney by accent, and a Scotsman by pretence. 'Character' at any price: that is Mr Thomas's motto. In search of 'character,' he presses all Great Britain into his service. Ireland supplies him with a certain Lady Judith O'Hara, who talks, throughout, with the accent and the idiom of a Tipperary colleen. It matters nothing that in real life a well-born and well-brought-up Irish lady talks with no semblance of that idiom and that accent. Where would 'character' be without those adjuncts? The only wonder is that Lady Judith does not appear with a green shawl, a kilted skirt, bare feet, and a harp. Quite analogous to that are the costumes actually worn by Lord Harrowfield (formerly Mr Justice Hoggett, who sentenced Mr Frazer to penal servitude). He is the fine old English gentleman, one of the olden time, and is dressed more or less according to the period of

the song. Possibly it was Mr Fernandez's, not Mr Thomas's inspiration to deck him out in that manner. It certainly was a happy
inspiration, well in accord to the spirit of the play. Was it Mr
Fernandez's or Mr Thomas's inspiration that Lord Harrowfield
should exhibit symptoms of tipsiness after sharing a decanter of port
with Mr Frazer? I do not think these symptoms quite congruous
with the fine old English gentleman, however appropriate they
might be to the frail and battered Mr Frazer. Also, they tend to
destroy the effect of the sentimental scene into which they are imported. Lord Harrowfield is showing extreme magnanimity. He
proffers his hand to the man whom he had erst frowned on in the
dock. Symptoms of tipsiness surely detract from the grandeur of
this action. However, they give the actor an extra chance for
'character'; and to that end dramatic propriety may as safely be
sacrificed as truth to life.

It is not Lord Harrowfield, but his wife, who first recognises Mr
Frazer. A strong 'character'-part is Lady Harrowfield's. Before her
husband's retirement, it was her habit to sit by him on the bench,
and to take notes of every case tried by him. Fortified with her
notes of the long-forgotten burglary case, she confronts Mr Frazer
and wrings from him an admission of his identity. Shall her daughter
be given in marriage to a young man who derives his fortune from
such a person as Mr Frazer? She, a very proud woman, is adamant.
Her daughter, Mr Frazer, Mr Frazer's son, and everyone else, are
racked with anguish. How can the play end happily? Lady Harrowfield, with quick feminine intuition, sees that there is only one way
out. She must cease to be adamant. And cease she suddenly does,
with a very good grace.

The centre of the play's gravity is, I suppose, the love of Mr
Frazer for the son whom he may not claim. Mr Welch, as I have
often said, has an exquisite gift for tragi-comic pathos. But, as Mr
Frazer, not for one moment does he move me. The reason for my
immobility is that Mr Frazer is so obviously constructed for the
purpose of drawing (1) tears, (2) laughter. He is made as pathetic
as possible on the one hand, and as funny as possible on the other.
The fun and the pathos are not blent. He is a dual puppet; not a
human being. Consequently, the pathos doesn't come off. One can
laugh over a figment; but one can't weep over a figment. Perhaps it
was in the consciousness that Mr Frazer would not be all-sufficient

as a pathetic figure, and with a lively recollection of King Lear, that Mr Thomas introduced a thunderstorm at one point of the play. But Lear was out in the thick of the storm, whose blasts were well attuned to his rage and anguish. Mr Frazer is cosily indoors, talking quietly and quaintly to his son. I see no reason for these peals of incidental thunder. Perhaps Mr Thomas merely wished to give a touch of 'character' to the weather. But then, why should he, who lets himself go so freely in dealing with human beings, have curbed himself in regard to meteorology? Why have stopped short at a thunderstorm? Why not have let the play end with an earthquake? I do not think the engulfing of the various 'character'-parts, after they had served their turn, would strike a really tragic chord in any bosom.

[*17 March 1906*]

'A GREAT DEAR'

Captain Brassbound's Conversion seemed to me, at the Court Theatre last Tuesday, less delightful than when it was launched some years ago by the Stage Society. One reason for my disappoint-ment is that Mr Shaw writes much better plays now than then. When he wrote *Captain Brassbound* he had not yet found his own 'form' in drama. He was still relying on a conventional technique, not consonant with the kind of thing he had to express. He was pouring new wine into old bottles; and, though the old bottles did well enough at first, a good deal of the new wine is wasted from them now: *Captain Brassbound* seems cheap beside *John Bull's Other Island* and *Major Barbara*. But there is another reason for my disappointment. The three main characters of the play—the Captain, the Judge, and Lady Cicely—were less satisfactorily im-personated last Tuesday than in the original production. Mr Kerr is a very admirable actor. But, versatile though he is, he cannot be-come romantic. And the Captain is, of course (like Mr Laurence Irving, who first impersonated him), romantic to the core. Another very admirable actor is Mr Barnes. But he cannot help being genial. And the Judge is, of course, dry essentially. Nature has given to each of these actors a voice and face that prevent him from compassing

242

just that effect which is needful here. The effect that ought to be made by Lady Cicely is an effect of quiet self-confidence. Lady Cicely is more sensible and quicker-witted than any of the men among whom she finds herself. She knows that she can, with easy diplomacy, twist them all round her little finger. She has (except for a few moments, at the end of the play) no hesitations, no misgivings. She is undisputed mistress of herself. Her manner, therefore, must be even and calm in its vivacity, innocent of pauses, of flurry, of over-emphasis. Miss Ellen Terry was duly vivacious last Tuesday. But she was, also, very nervous. She was often at a loss when it was most necessary that she should take her cue instantly. And, in the relief of having remembered her cue, she often spoke with disastrous emphasis. You remember the scene where Lady Cicely is mending the Captain's jacket. The Judge has just been led away under arrest, and the Captain is raging and storming against law and order as represented by the Judge. In the midst of one of his tirades, 'Are you sure,' asks Lady Cicely, 'that this coat doesn't catch you under the sleeve?' Miss Terry put this question in a tone almost as exuberant as the Captain's; and thus the whole point was lost. And there were similar losses in her performance from first to last. Her nervousness not only marred Mr Shaw's conception: it marred the performance of the other parts, and communicated itself, I am sure, to the whole audience. I draw attention to it because I should not like those of the rising generation who saw the performance to imagine that Miss Terry was within measurable distance of her best; and that is an impression which the criticisms of most of my colleagues would be likely to foster.

Two qualities there are in Miss Terry that no amount of nervousness can mar. Nothing can obscure for us her sense of beauty and her buoyant jollity. It is this latter quality that explains the unique hold she has on the affections of the public. Was ever a creature so sunny as she? Did ever anyone radiate such kindness and good humour? To no one, I think, so justly as to her may be applied that expressive phrase in modern slang, 'a great dear.' I have often heard people deny that she is great in the art of acting; but her power of endearing herself across footlights is, in itself, such as to earn for her an indisputable title to greatness. This power of hers would not, I think, be less if she had happened not to be so beautiful and so graceful in her person and in her methods. To painters and other artists, of course, her primary appeal has been through the quality of her face, and through the sense of beauty that is evident in all the inflexions of her voice, and in her every movement, pose, or gesture. Mr Theodore Watts-Dunton, writing the other day in the *Tribune*, recorded his opinion that Miss Terry 'has more of the temperament of the poet than any actress or actor' of this age. And a painter would say, doubtless, that she had more of the temperament of the painter. For my part, I am not sure that in sheer sense of beauty, and in power of creating beautiful effects on the stage, Miss Terry is greater than Mrs Patrick Campbell. I think it would be hard to decide justly between these two. But it is certainly natural and inevitable that in England Miss Terry should be held to be unrivalled. For she is so very essentially English. Or rather, she is just what we imagine to be essentially English. The sunny climate of Italy produces a very happy race of men and women, whilst the English climate produces a very dreary race. And yet the poetic genius of Italy has tended always in the direction of gloom, whilst the poetic genius of England has been, in the main, cheerful. Perhaps art is always, everywhere, in opposition to climate—an unconscious reaction from climate. And thus, since the majority of people do not use their own eyes introspectively, but see themselves always as they are told to see themselves by their national poets, it may be that the majority of men and women all the world over see themselves always exactly as they are not. Anyhow, I have no doubt that to the Italians Signora Duse's sadness seems typically Italian, just as the sadness of Mrs Campbell (who is partly Italian) seems typically un-English to the English, and just as Miss Ellen Terry's sunniness seems to the English not less typically English. Exotic though this sunniness is, there is in the actual art with which Miss Terry conveys it a quality that really is native. Hers is a loose, irregular, instinctive art. It has something of the vagueness of the British Constitution, something of the vagueness of the British genius in all things—political, social, religious, and artistic. It is for this reason that French critics are so astonished when they see Miss Terry act, and so puzzled. To French critics, even now, Shakespeare seems a bit of a barbarian. They cannot understand the disorderliness of the English genius in art, any more than they can understand it in religion, politics, &c. They have not ears attuned to irregular rhythm. And they will hardly be persuaded that Miss Terry has any art at all. But it is just because her art is so spontaneous, so irreducible to formulae, that she has been and is matchless in Shakespeare's comedies. She has just the quality of exuberance that is right for those heroines. Without it, not all her sense of beauty would have helped her to be the perfect Beatrice, the perfect Portia, that she is. In modern comedy that virtue becomes a defect. In *Alice Sit by the Fire* her beautiful boisterousness wrought utter havoc; and so it will in *Captain Brassbound* so soon as she is thoroughly at home in her part. She needs a Shakespeare to stand up to her.

Granting that need, it were futile to deny that she is a great actress. Tragedy, I admit, is the highest form of dramatic art; and tragic acting is accordingly the highest form of histrionic art; and Miss Terry is no tragedian: I remember how loveable—what 'a great dear' —Lady Macbeth became through her; and how unaccountable, and unimpressive, the whole tragedy. But to excel in Shakespearean comedy, as she excels, is to be authentically a great actress. And the public testimonial that is being prepared for her is a tribute not less to the great actress than to the 'great dear.'

[*26 March 1906*]

BETWEEN TWO HALLS

For many years Mr Arthur Symons has insisted rigidly on the distinction between aesthetics and ethics. Though he has never, I think, denied that great works of art, at least in literature, have sometimes happened to be wrought with a merely moral impulse, he is not the sort of man whom I had expected to go into the moralising business on his own account. On my way, therefore, to the Victoria Hall, Archer Street, to see *The Fool of the World: a Morality*, it seemed to me that Mr Symons's soul must have travelled as deviously far as I myself was travelling. The sensation of sitting under a pulpit from which Mr Symons would strive to 'edify' and make me a wiser and a better man was certainly a sensation not to be lost—one of those 'exquisite moments' which Mr Symons's own master, the late Mr Pater, so suavely urged mankind not to let slip. I felt that this was not quite the proper spirit in which to approach the tabernacle. But no matter, thought I: the scoffer was

often the first to succumb to the burning words of the revivalist: in
another hour, belike, I should have exactly the right frame of mind.
Neither my hope of edification nor my hope of amusement was fulfilled. I had set too narrow an interpretation on the term 'morality.'
Mr Symons had not come to preach. He had used the antique form
of the morality for the expression not of a moral but of a purely
intellectual idea. Men, in their perplexity, have looked towards
Death as the solver of life's riddle. In the midst of blind folly,
Death, surely, is a seer and a sage. When Death takes us, she will
guide us on our way, giving us a clear chart of eternity. Mr Symons
shows to us a man standing in a wood, calling to Death, afraid but
eager. Death comes at his call. She is masked. On her head is a fool's
cap, and she holds in her hand a staff that has seven bells. She is
'the Fool of the World,' she says, and leader of 'the fools' dance
home to the dust.' She summons her three ministers, the Spade, the
Coffin, the Worm, and bids them tell the man how little terrible a
thing is the grave. One by one, they tell him. Still he is not satisfied:

> 'O Death, we know not if these know
> The whole long way we have to go.'

Death wonders that the man shrinks from her. She summons certain
of her guests, to speak for her. Youth comes and bitterly reviles her.
Middle Age says that for his part he has 'neither a sorry heart nor
glad.' Old Age praises 'the mercy of good Death.' Still the man's
question is unanswered. 'Are not,' he says,

> 'Are not these voices mortal still
> That utter the unforgotten will
> Of mortal flesh, and not yet have
> Found out the wisdom of the grave?
> Only Death knows, only Death can
> Speak the whole truth of death to man.'

Death, with an angry piteous gesture throws aside her staff and her
cap of bells—'a fool's witless bells' she calls them.

> 'I lead
> The dance of fools, a fool indeed;
> And my hands gather where they find,
> For I am Death, and I am blind.'

She takes off her mask, and kneels, an abject figure, before her questioner.

The play is contrived with just the right kind of cunning simplicity; and not Mr Symons, but the nature of things, is to be blamed for that it is better to read than to see. Symbols are much better imagined than seen. An actor impersonating a Worm, for example, even if he were the most magnificent of actors, and even if the costumier and the man who arranged the lighting of the stage were geniuses of the first water, could not make a really apt impression. In a morality, moreover, clever scenic effects and magnificent acting are themselves undesirable. The whole thing must be done simply, straightforwardly. The Worm must be impersonated by a simple, straightforward lady or gentleman, in a strong and steady light, as he was at the Victoria Hall. He had much better, then, not be impersonated at all. And what is true of the Worm is not less true of other symbols.

With *The Fool of the World* was performed a translation that Mr Symons has made of *La Révolte*. In this little play Villiers de l'Isle Adam said all that Ibsen said later in *A Doll's House*. And, as all that there is to be said about what Ibsen said later has been said long ago, I won't now detain you with Villiers, whose play is interesting only in connexion and comparison with Ibsen's—interesting as an example of the needfulness of form to substance. Miss Louise Salom, as the rebellious lady, acted very intelligently, though at times too slowly. It goes without saying that Mr Symons had made an admirable translation.

Mr Herbert MacIlwaine, the novelist who has often described, with such grim power, the horrors of the Bush, has done more than any other living man to prevent people from going to Australia. But he is evidently not content with mere negative achievement. England is not so dull as Australia; but it is not so bright as it ought to be; and Mr MacIlwaine is determined to brighten it up. He has begun by experimenting on the 'lower strata' of our society; and the result of his experiments was shown at the Queen's Hall one evening last week. A very successful and delightful result it seemed to me. Anyone who has paused in a slum to watch children dancing to the tunes of a street organ must have been struck by the grace and precision, often the rhythmic beauty, with which these children dance. Where do they learn to dance so well? I am told there is no tutelage—simply a tradition. It is *in* them to dance thus. Some of the steps they dance are of great antiquity—older than the Morris itself—and may still by experts be discerned among the various other steps that have in the course of time been evolved. The effect of these dances in the slums is not an effect of gaiety. It has seemed to me always a rather morbid effect, a symbolic expression of the gloom of the conditions under which the dancers live. I, not being an expert, have not been able to discern those little shreds of Merrie England. Maybe, many of the music-hall tunes to which the children dance are lineally descended from old folk-songs. But there again, being inexpert, I catch no echo of a younger and happier time. No breath of morning and hillside is wafted to me. The tunes seem to me only symbolic of squalor—of a dreary, un-imaginative acquiescence in squalor. Some day in the dim future, perhaps, antiquaries will rescue these tunes, and these dances, from the dim past, and will discourse learnedly on them, and will use them as sidelights on the souls of the urban population in England in the early twentieth century. And perhaps some of these anti-quaries, deeming it a pity that the wholesome discipline of gloom has been undermined and abolished by the millennium, will teach people these songs and these dances, on the chance that it is possible to make men and women sad through training them to give a formal expression of sadness. Mr MacIlwaine has been indulging in an analogous endeavour. Why shouldn't work-girls, even at this time and in this city, become happy by dancing and singing the sort of things that were danced and sung by their happy ancestors? This, I take it, is the hope on which the 'Esperance Girls' Club' has been founded. An illusory hope? The cart before the horse? I dare say that Mr Keir Hardie, who was in the audience at the Queen's Hall the other night, may have objected to the manifestation of an hilarity for which there could not as yet be any true inward basis. 'A few Sessions hence,' he may have murmured, 'this sort of dancing will come naturally. No "Hon. Musical Instructor" nor "Hon. Dance Directors" will then be needed. They should have waited for me to give the signal.' Perhaps the very presence of Mr Keir Hardie, as symbolising at least the distant dawn of the millennium, inspired the souls and bodies of the Esperance Girls. Or perhaps the impetuous Mr MacIlwaine had been right in his theory of the reaction of form on feeling. Anyhow, these girls did really seem to be taking to the

Morris and the folk songs like ducks to the water. Aesthetically these songs are enchanting. 'Blow away the Morning Dew,' 'The Blue-eyed Stranger,' 'There come Three Dukes a-riding,' 'Mowing the Barley,' 'Constant Billy,' 'Hares on the Mountains,' 'The Trees they do grow high'—are not the mere names of them enough for enchantment? But a merely aesthetic performance of them would hardly yield you their finest flavour—the flavour of the very soil from which they have grown. It is a far cry from the hedgerows to the slums. But children of the slums have in them more of the quality needed for folk songs than could be instilled into any professional singers. I suppose the Esperance Girls, flushed with our applause, will give their performance again. We must be careful not to spoil them.

[*14 April 1906*]

'A FLORENTINE TRAGEDY' AND 'SALOME'

Last Sunday, at the King's Hall, the Literary Theatre Club performed these two plays of Mr Oscar Wilde. Neither of them is a cheerful play. So neither could have a chance of success in England. For that minority which is capable of taking the drama seriously as an art, and does not object to receiving tragic emotion now and then, these two plays have an extrinsic power of depression. They indicate anew to us how much was lost to dramatic art in the downfall and death of the great artist who composed them.

A Florentine Tragedy (produced for the first time) is akin to *Salome* as being an essay in the art of suspense. In *Salome* the end is foreknown; and the main horror comes of the deliberate slowness with which the action is conducted to that end. Often the dramatic movement is deliberately arrested to make way for merely decorative passages, such as Salome's metaphors about the eyes, the hair, the lips of Iokanaan, or Herod's description of the jewels and the peacocks and the various other things that Salome might take instead of the one thing that she demands. Merely decorative in themselves, these passages are relatively dramatic in that they give us time to realise more intensely the horror of what is in store. In *A Florentine*

Tragedy we know there must be at least one death before the curtain falls; and the elaborate decorations interposed do not make us forget it: they do but give us time to become uncomfortable. Nor are they, as in *Salome*, a mere artistic device of the author. They come from the nature of the chief character devised. Simone, the Florentine merchant, is a man of grim humour; and so, when he surprises his wife in the company of a young nobleman, he does not instantly draw his sword. He is furious; but his fury he will be able to express later. Meanwhile he can have some fun. He can fool the couple to the top of their bent, then suddenly drop a hint that will make them start, then again soothe them into security till he choose to frighten them again. His vengeance will be all the sweeter, all the more terrible, for such dalliance. He plays on his young wife's contempt for him, cringing to the stranger, descanting unctuously on this or that ware that he would sell. His desire is not merely to humiliate her. If she does not love the stranger yet, she shall by force of contrast be made to love him. His death shall be a dagger through her own heart. At length, after he has taken his fill of pretence, he challenges the lover to fight. The lover, worsted, begs for mercy, and is allowed to go on begging before Simone, with more than necessary violence, despatches him. The wife shrinks against the wall. She sees in her husband's eyes that she, too, is doomed. And now comes the ending for sake of which, I take it, the play was written—the germ of psychological paradox from which the story developed itself backwards. The wife falls to her knees, and, with real love in her voice, cries 'Why did you not tell me you were so strong?' The husband pauses, stares at her, lets drop his dagger, saying 'Why did you not tell me you were so beautiful?' There is, of course, no great paradox in the first of these two speeches. (One remembers, for instance, Becky Sharp's sudden admiration for Rawdon Crawley after the ejection of Lord Steyne.) But the second speech is certainly a daring invention. Is the paradox a sound one? I think so. It is not unnatural that the merchant, having won his bride with money, should not have appreciated her at her full human value until he had won her by more primitive, more human means. Her contempt for him, moreover, would have prejudiced him against her. The light of admiration for him in her eyes, besides making her actually more beautiful, would have quickened his perception of her beauty. And then there was the fact that she had inspired a passion in the nobleman. This, too, would have quickened the merchant's perception. My sole objection to the paradox is concerned with the placing of it. No play—no work of art whatsoever—ought to finish on a top note. We ought never to be left gasping, at the fall of the curtain. The paradox that I have examined ought to have been led up to, so that its meaning would have been plain when the curtain fell. It ought to have been a summing-up, not a challenge. Mr Wilde's sure artistic sense here failed him, for once.

Obviously, the part of Simone is a fine part for an actor. I should like to have seen it played by Sir Henry Irving. I know of no one else who could have given fully the sardonic essence of it. Mr George Ingleton, however, who played it the other night, is a very capable actor; and his performance seemed really distinguished in the glare of incapacity shed by the young lady and gentleman who played the two other parts.

When *Salome* was produced last year at the Bijou Theatre, I reflected that only the finest acting and the most tactful stage-management could reconcile us to the physical horror of the play. Reading the play, one has no more than the right tragic thrill. Seeing the play—seeing Salome kiss in triumph the severed head of the prophet —one is thrilled with mere physical disgust, unless the scene be arranged with great compunction, and unless the acting of Salome shall have been on a lofty tragic plane. Neither of these requisites was supplied at the Bijou Theatre. At the King's Hall, Miss Darragh supplied one of them. She is not the ideal Salome; for she looks rather modern, rather occidental. But, besides having a beautiful voice, and speaking the words with a keen sense for their cadence, she is a genuine tragedian, and thus was able to live in the part, and, living there, to purge somewhat our physical disgust through spiritual terror. She was, as nearly as need be, the veritable daughter of Herodias. Miss Florence Farr was not, alas, the veritable mother of Salome. She was very much too pleasant. She seemed to be trying to make Herodias 'sympathetic,' and was quite out of the key of the tragedy. Mr Robert Farquharson re-appeared as Herod; and I was more than ever struck by the fineness of his performance. His delivery of the three long decorative speeches is a marvel in the art of elocution. Other English actors may know how valuable an effect can be got from sometimes talking quickly; but I have never found them taking advantage of their knowledge. Perhaps they have not the necessary skill. Mr Farquharson can, without slurring a syllable, speak English as rapidly as Madame Sarah Bernhardt can speak French; and the effect in his case is even greater than in hers, because none of his compatriots has attempted to compete with him. Apart from its technique, his performance is memorable for the rare imaginative power with which he realises the grotesque and terrible figure of Herod.

As the scenery and the dresses were designed by Mr Charles Ricketts, it need not be said they were beautiful. They were also, however, dramatically appropriate—just enough conventionalised to be in harmony with the peculiar character of the play. The stage-management was faulty only in the final scene; and that, alas, is the scene where perfection is most needed. Not even the quality of Miss Darragh's acting could wholly purge our physical disgust. It is obvious that Salome ought to be in the far background, and in deepest shadow, while she holds in her hands the head of the prophet. This would not merely militate against physical disgust. It would aid illusion. When we distinctly see the head, we are conscious of its unreality, however realistically it be made. And our consciousness of its unreality does not make it one whit the less unpleasant.

[*16 June 1906*]

LANGUISHING THEATRES

The theatrical season is near its end. Only fifteen of the many theatres remain open, and most of these will be closed anon. At six of them are musical comedies; and of the nine legitimate plays that are being acted five are revivals. I wonder, with gentle melancholy, what is the future of our drama. Throughout the past year there has been, indeed, no lack of plays. Play has succeeded play, frantically, stumbling over the prostrate body of its predecessor, quite unheeded by the public. Failure has been piled on failure, and most of the failures have been well-merited. It would be cheering to suppose that the public has been educated above the kind of thing which managers offer to it, and that success awaits any manager who shall offer it something good. The success of Mr Shaw's sequence of plays at the Court Theatre gives some plausibility to this supposition. But, even if there is a large enough intelligent public to support half a dozen theatres devoted to good contemporary drama, the outlook is not, I think, rosy. Where is the good contemporary drama to come from? About a year ago, the sanguine and ingenious Playgoers' Club instituted a competition for hitherto unrevealed dramatists. Complaints had often been made about the indifference of managers to any work not signed by a practised playwright. It had often been suggested that masterpieces were flying around, merely unable to find an inlet to the stage. Having regard to the enormous number of people who do write plays, and do send them to managers, it seemed quite reasonable to suppose that some of these plays might happen to have merit. They might not be technically good. They might, moreover, have no chance of commercial success. But the especial object of the Playgoers' Club was to discover, and hand over to Mr Philip Carr for production, a play that had, at any rate, the savour of life in it. I myself was a member of the reading committee; and, soon enough, huge parcels began to be delivered at my door. I remember the agreeable tremor with which I broached the first one that came, and gazed at the six or seven plays that it contained. Was there a masterpiece among them? It was presently plain that not one of them came nearly up to mediocrity. The other parcels that followed were no more inspiriting. I waded, waded, ever so conscientiously, through them; yet found not one scene, not one character, that was not a weak imitation of this or that current theatrical convention. I thought it rather hard that I should have such bad luck. But subsequently it appeared that I was no exception on that reading committee. Some of the members had, indeed, thought it worth while to pass on to others a few of the plays received, but without hearty commendation, and rather in the spirit of men wishing to be confirmed in their judgment that the thing wasn't good enough. The whole affair, so promising in its inception, ended with the committee's lugubrious announcement that they had nothing to place in Mr Philip Carr's hands.

As there is, apparently, no chance of a crop of interesting plays, it is perhaps superfluous to speculate as to whether the public's taste in plays is improving. Personally, I mistrust the evidence of Mr Shaw's success. It is heart-breaking to hear the whole audience at the Court Theatre laughing from the rise to the fall of the curtain—laughing without any discrimination at all. Mr Shaw has been industriously boomed, by no one more industriously than by myself; and it is pleasant to have helped him to his well-deserved success. But the reality of his success is more than doubtful. He is fashionable; but he is not, so far as I can see, appreciated. The echoes of the boom will die away, the fashion will pass, the cult will dwindle back to its old proportions, and the public will be found wallowing in—what? What *does* the public really want? It evidently wants very little of anything. Perhaps the reason is that too much is offered to it. There are too many theatres. In the old days, before the suburbs had theatres of their own, the few metropolitan theatres throve well enough. But what chance is there for a plethora of metropolitan theatres, pitted against a plethora of suburban theatres? I am told that during the past year even the suburban theatres have not been faring well. But, to explain this fact, no one could venture on the hypothesis that the suburban population has been drifting back to the metropolitan theatres. The record of these theatres during the past year shows that they are, with few exceptions, losing their hold even on the metropolis. I do not think any one will deny that what the playgoing public likes best of all is something akin to the art of the music-hall. Yet I am told on good authority that even musical comedy has been, on the whole, languishing. I believe that the only way to revive public interest in the metropolitan theatres would be to demolish (say) two-thirds of them. The theatrical game, as played at present, is up. It continues only as a survival. Within a few years, quite two-thirds of the theatres will be untenanted. In most cases, there will have been the usual desperate effort to convert them into music-halls. But there are already too many music-halls. (Not even the music-halls have been thriving as of old.) There the deserted theatres will stand, pathetic monuments of misguided enterprise, happy hunting grounds of moths and mice; until the ground-landlords of them shall have the sense to pull them down and build up flats or hotels in their stead.

The only theatres that will survive are those which are directed with some definite policy, some definite artistic ideal. I fancy that among the surviving managers will be found Mr Seymour Hicks. He knows exactly what he wants to do, and he does it, consistently, to the utmost of his power. He occurs to me as an instance because

I happened to see *The Beauty of Bath* a few nights ago. It has been said that the ideal thing to do in hot weather is to sit in the shade and watch people hard at work in the sunlight. A visit to the Aldwych Theatre does just as well. This theatre is well ventilated, the stalls are comfortable; and there in the glare of foot-lights and lime-lights, and in costumes too beautiful not to be very uncomfortable, are innumerable ladies and gentlemen working at terrifically high pressure throughout the evening. Mr Hicks does not spare himself. He sets an heroic example of energy and goodwill, and takes care that everyone shall follow it. In the formula of which critics are so fond, he 'lacks restraint.' But I am not going to blame him, any more than I would blame a bomb, for that lack. It is a bomb's business to be explosive. It is Mr Hicks's, too; and he performs it admirably. Never resting, never flagging, ever gagging, driven this way and that by some internal engine of incalculable horse-power, he is the incarnate spirit of musical comedy, and amply repays to you, in his own person, whatever price you may have paid for your seat. The energies of the rest of the company are by way of a 'bonus.' By what threats or entreaties, or by what sheer force of animal magnetism, does Mr Hicks contrive to make everyone else as energetic as himself? Elsewhere the beauteous ladies of the chorus have an easy time, trailing gracefully about like 'mannequins' at a dressmaker's, and not taking the trouble even to simper. In Mr Hicks's establishment they have to work like galley-slaves, and to pretend to enjoy it all heartily, poor things! I am afraid they will not live long.

[*14 July 1906*]

A PLEA FOR A SHORT ACT OF PARLIAMENT

Not long ago a young actress, famous in musical comedy, decided to go back to school; and there, for the present, she remains. I am surely at liberty to mention this fact, for she herself has mentioned it in a daily paper, where the greater part of a page was devoted to her impressions of school-life. In the centre of the page she was largely depicted in the act of going early to bed, up a stone staircase, candle in hand. This drawing was not signed by her, but the article was;

255

and, considering the fluency and vividness of it, I was moved to
reflect that, however imperfect her education might have been in
other directions, in journalism she had really nothing to learn. Considering, too, the length of it, I wondered how, in the midst of an
arduous curriculum, her hand, however facile, had found time to
write it. Was it originally, perhaps, an essay set by the Head Mistress? And had that admirable woman herself suggested its publication? I shouldn't wonder. To her, as to the majority of the British
race, the idea of an actress ceasing to be advertised would probably
seem very terrible, very unnatural. I believe that if an actress decided
to take the veil, and if she were received into even the strictest of all
conventual institutions, the Mother Superior would not at all dis-
courage her from telling the world 'How It Feels To Be A Postulant.'

I do not suggest that the postulant would herein be actuated by
vanity, or the Mother Superior by a desire to add lustre to her convent. Merely, the two women would feel that this little balm ought
not to be withheld from a nation wounded. Why a nation should be
passionately interested in the private lives of its mimes, I cannot
pretend to guess. I do but note, as a fact, the passionate interest taken
by the British nation. 'Nowhere,' as was lately said by that always
pungent writer, Mr Edward Morton, 'are people so much concerned with actors and actresses, or so little with acting, as they are
in England.' I wonder how many tons of picture postcards are
needed, month by month, to meet England's demand for images
of its 'stars,' big and little? To how many photographers, at how
many angles, in how many frocks, with how many varieties of
brilliant smile, must even a quite obscure actress find herself compelled to sit, in the course of a year? By how many interviewers,
with cameras, must every theatrical 'home' be annually invaded?
And the hoops the poor inmates have to jump through! If Mr
and Mrs — have a garden, they must pretend to be' gardening'; if
they have a baby, Mrs — must pretend to be giving it its bath; if
they have a motor, Mrs — must pretend to be driving it. But these
pictorial visions are not enough. Actresses, 'to keep themselves before the public,' must do so in the most literal sense. They must be
seen constantly in the flesh. To hold stalls at bazaars, or at any rate
to 'assist,' is absolutely indispensable. And there are other things
besides bazaars. The greatest of these is the annual fête at the

Botanical Gardens, in aid of the Actors' Orphanage Fund. 'The attendance on these occasions,' I quote from a weekly paper, 'is always of the most astonishing kind, and it is but the slightest exaggeration to say that the player meets here every London play-goer, and the playgoer every London player.' One would forgive even a grave exaggeration, coming from so sunny a writer. Happy playgoers! Happy players? Mrs — — (I omit the name given by the sunny writer), 'who always works so hard at the theatrical garden parties, was found this year to have abandoned her usual "Aunt Sally" business, and gone in for presiding over a gipsy encampment.' To less sunny natures like mine, there is something tragic here in the epithet 'usual.' Think of a talented tragic actress (as Mrs — — happens to be) organising, year by awful year, an ' "Aunt Sally" business,' till at length even *her* steadfast heart fails her. How many years, I wonder, will she go through with the gipsy encampment? Probably she will be forced to discontinue it because it is not undignified enough. For evidently lack of dignity is the very first thing expected of mimes when they rub shoulders with the public. The most popular feature of the Botanical fête is 'the hat-trimming competition among well-known actors, introduced and directed by jolly Miss — —.' Imagine, self-respecting male reader, what would be your feelings if you found yourself forced to make a fool of yourself by publicly trimming a hat! Even if nobody knew who you were, and nobody would ever see you again, you would suffer, I think. If everyone knew you by sight and name, and had a great admiration for your abilities, and were going to follow your future career with great interest, would you not sink into the ground? That would be, indeed, the best place for you—unless you happen to be an actor. 'Cleverest of all actor-hat-trimmers is Mr — — [one of the three or four most important actors in London]. Sitting coolly and very seriously back from the agitated front row of workers, he fastened his design together entirely with needle and thread. The judges awarded him first prize, as much for the quality of his needlework as for the stylishness of his hat.' Do not run away with the idea that Mr — — is lacking in self-respect. Admire, rather, his self-control. It is not advisable for any actor, however eminent, to refuse to make a fool of himself. And there is something to be gained by doing the job thoroughly. Mr — —'s thoroughness here was but an instance of the general thoroughness by which, more congenially applied, he has won so high and honourable a place in his profession.

Much as we admire him, we may wonder whether his artistic merits would not be even greater than they are if professional ambition had not forced him to spend so much of his time in making speeches, being photographed, showing himself in places of resort, and doing the thousand-and-one other extraneous odd-jobs that the British public expects of him. And we may make that speculation equally in regard to all his colleagues, male and female. The average level of acting is admittedly lower in England than in France, or Germany, or Italy. And may not this inferiority be due, at least in part, to the fuss we make about our mimes as men and women? Elsewhere, mimes are a class apart. No one notes them, outside the theatre. They are thrown back on their art. Nothing interests them but their art. They have no distractions. The fact that English mimes are all the while distracted is surely a plausible excuse for their defects. If I thought that without these distractions they would pine away, my human sympathy might over-rule my aesthetic desire for a radical change. But in point of fact I believe firmly that, if the continental system were introduced, our mimes would (not only act better, but) be happier and live longer. It is quite as much for their sake as for art's sake that a short Act of Parliament ought to be passed, making it a penal offence for anyone to exhibit or take photographs of them; or to publish or indite about them anything not directly appertaining to their performances in theatres; or to solicit their autographs or other personal memento whatsoever; or to stare at them in any park, square, high-road, street or other public place that is not a theatre; or to ask, inveigle or invite them to lunch, dinner, supper, or other meal whatsoever; or . . . but I leave the framing of the bill to Mr Herbert Gladstone.

[*21 July 1906*]

TO BOUCH

In bygone days, the dramatist would frankly name his puppets according to their characters or trades: 'George Downright, a *plain Squire*, Thomas Cash, *a Cashier*, Justice Clement, *an old merry*

Magistrate,' and so forth. Nowadays, we are too subtle for that device in drama. But we object not to a converse device in life. We are glad to have our vocabularies enriched with nouns, adjectives and verbs drawn from the names of actual persons.

Already there is a small proud company of persons, past and present, whose names have been absorbed into the language. Signor Marconi sits blushing between Mr Pullman and Mr Hansom; and not far off (though he was not the author, was but the first subject, of the invention) sits Captain Boycott. And there is a higher dais than theirs; the dais reserved for those who have not hit on a mere discovery, or had a mere discovery hit on them, but have done in a superlative and supereminent manner something which a more or less numerous portion of the human race has essayed without distinction. Other prophets than Jeremiah have deplored the times they were born into; other statesmen than Machiavelli have been sly; but who so sly as Machiavelli, so bitter as Jeremiah? The one gives us an adjective, the other a noun. Others than Dr Bowdler have expurgated the classics; but who so unswervingly? Others than the admirable Warden of New College have transposed, in conversation, the initials of words. But who—according to a tradition in which I don't at all believe—so frequently and so remarkably? Others than Mr Gilbert have been, and others yet will be, Gilbertian; but himself is incomparably so. *Vixere fortes ante* the present Minister for Education, and *vivent post* him; but he has in an especial degree, or had (for recent developments may have marred in him), the knack of enunciating with humour and fancy the views of the average professional man. He is unmatched in the pleasant little knack that we call, therefore, 'Birrelling.' He, I think, is the latest, though hardly a new, accessor to the hierarchy which we are observing. But let him not flatter himself that he is the last. We have power to add to these numbers, indefinitely, at our discretion. I modestly rise, clear my throat, and propose the name of Mr Arthur Bourchier, M.A. Oxon, sole lessee of the Garrick Theatre, Charing Cross Road, W.C.

We live in an age of self-advertisement. Many people, of course, do not care to advertise themselves. But they are fewer than they were in any previous era of the world's history. Nor do the self-advertisers blush as perhaps they did in the golden past. Some of them, indeed, have no obvious need to blush. They have brought their art to a fine point, achieving great results by subtle means, and ever drawing down advertisement on themselves by threads of invisible silk. Others there are of lesser cunning. There are they who, perspiring, haul down advertisement on themselves with ropes and grappling-irons. And there are they who haul so clumsily that the advertisement hits them violently on the head. To advertise oneself with great industry but without discretion, to advertise oneself in such a way as to make people tired of one or sorry for one—what verb have we to describe compendiously this intricate and not uncommon form of activity? It is a great inconvenience that we have no such verb. It is a great convenience that we have in Mr Arthur Bourchier one whose fatiguing industry and pitiable lack of discretion in self-advertisement are so signal as to supply our need henceforth. We shall get along very well with the verb 'to bouch.'

How well I remember the stream of documents that used to flow to me from the Garrick Theatre! How often would the management have been 'obliged if I could find space for the enclosed paragraph'! Other managements were wont to send me paragraphs till they realised, at length, that I was not empowered to purvey news here. But few and far between were their offerings in comparison with the Garrick's! Mr Bourchier had just secured the rights of this or that curtain-raiser, Mr Bourchier had received the following letter, Mr Bourchier had made the following speech, *et patati et patata*. If anything can console me for having, two or three years ago, incurred Mr Bourchier's wrath, and not having yet been forgiven for not thinking him a heaven-sent actor, it is that my letter-box is freed from the strain of those communications. I gather, from the aspect of those newspapers which do purvey theatrical gossip, that the strain is undiminished in other directions. Either just before or just after the burial of Sir Henry Irving in Westminster Abbey, I read in some other paper—it may have been printed in many papers—a portion of a letter from Mr H. B. Irving, inviting Mr Bourchier to act as chief steward. At that time Mr Bourchier was playing in *The Merchant of Venice*; and Mr Irving had written that it seemed appropriate that 'the latest Shylock' should bear a prominent part in the ceremony. That was a quite legitimate and graceful thing to say in a letter that cannot have been written with a view to publication. And then, 'Mr Bourchier has replied in the following terms: "My dear Harry. It will be the proudest day of my life."' If Mr

Bourchier did not sanction the publication of that gem of epistolary tact, who was the thief who purloined it and held it up to a dazzled public? Unaware that Mr Bourchier made any subsequent protest or apology, I assume that he held the gem up to us with his own hand; and I cite this action as a good instance of what I call bouching.

Another good, though less obvious, instance is the exclusion of Mr E. A. Baughan from the first night of Mr Bourchier's version of *Crainquebille*. Possibly, the actor-adapter would have preferred that no comparisons should be drawn between himself and M. Guitry, himself and M. Anatole France, by the talented critic of *The Daily News*; but I do not see in this preference the mainspring of his action. He must have known that he could not prevent Mr Baughan from seeing him some other night, if Mr Baughan were so disposed. He must have known that no one would sympathise with him, and that many people would be angry with him. He had tried a similar trick on Mr Walkley, and, after a lapse of time, had apologised to Mr Walkley, in order that the existence of his theatre might no longer be ignored by *The Times*. When he repeated the trick on Mr Baughan, his prophetic soul must have had an inkling that sooner or later he would be apologising to Mr Baughan. At the same time, he knew that Mr Baughan's exclusion would cause a fuss—would cause the name of Mr Bourchier to appear in various paragraphs. And so, flinging other considerations to the wind, he headed straight for the advertisement. In a word, he bouched.

An even more recent instance of bouching is the particular cause of this general survey. In some of the daily newspapers, one day last week, was printed a letter from Mr Bourchier about myself. Now, inasmuch as he is incensed by the reservations in my respect for him as an actor, it were quite natural that he should rejoice in a chance of attacking me effectively. But what chance did I give him when I wrote here that 'the average level of acting is lower in England than in France, or Germany, or Italy?' No one would dream of disputing this platitude. Doubtless there are in England certain mimes who would stand comparison with any mimes that any foreign nation could muster. But that our 'average level' is lower than that of the three nations mentioned by me is a platitude of which I was so ashamed that I very nearly expunged it when I corrected the proof of my article. Yet this same platitude is, according to Mr Bourchier, 'an impertinent attack,' and I am an 'opponent' of his 'craft,' and I had been craftily waiting to attack the exponents of that craft while they were 'away on their holidays,' and am one of the 'Little Englanders,' and am by Mr Bourchier reminded that 'the famous artist, Mr Whistler,' cared nothing about the criticism of anyone who was not an 'admitted master of his own craft,' and am further reminded that I am not 'master of any branch of the difficult art of acting.' Didn't he whom Mr Bourchier would prob- ably call 'the well-known lexicographer, Dr Johnson,' say some- thing about fat oxen and their drivers, thereby killing with ridicule for ever the old fallacy that Mr Bourchier trots out? But I don't summarise Mr Bourchier's letter for the purpose of arguing with him. He knows, as well as I do, what fustian and balderdash it all is. Even when he wrote it he must have known. But he knew, also, that some of the newspapers to which it was addressed would pub- lish it. And so, again, regardless of other things, he bouched.

Poor dear gentleman! Has he no discreet friends to pluck at his elbow, to whisper in his ear? Is there no one to restrain him from making himself ridiculous? After all, I hope not. He would be so unhappy, perhaps so violent, if he were restrained. Also, the public stock of harmless amusement would be impoverished. (To a certain extent, even, the gaiety of nations might be eclipsed; for who knows but that, since his remarkable adaptation of M. Anatole France, Mr Bourchier's own writings are translated for the pleasure of Paris?) Also, the verb which I have recommended might not pass into the language. 'To bouch' is a young and tender plant. I have planted it. Mr Bourchier must water it. And so I say to Mr Bourchier, as Napoleon said to the nigger, '*Continuez*.' I say earnestly to him 'Go on bouching.'

A brief philological note on the verb's form. Purists might prefer the form 'to bourchier.' But I have always felt that Mr Bourchier's name ought to be spelt phonetically. I have always felt that the authorised spelling of it struck a discord, as being horribly suggestive of Gallic finesse. 'Boucher' has always seemed to me the desir- able mode. Therefrom, corollarily, I have deduced the verb in question.

I look forward to the time when in every dictionary there shall be, between the explanations of 'BOTTONY' and 'BOUCHET,' 'BOUCH, *v. n.* To advertise oneself with great industry, but with- out discretion; to advertise oneself in such a way as to make people

tired of one or sorry for one. *Deriv.* = Bourchier, an English actor.
BOUCHER, *s.* One who bouches.'

Thus, when other and (but no! not being on the stage, I must not
say) better contemporary mimes than he shall have passed into
oblivion, Mr Bourchier will have immortality, of a kind.

[*11 August 1906*]

'TRISTRAM AND ISEULT'

Human speech is a very useful thing, so far as it goes. For the
communication of facts, and even of ideas, one could not have a
better vehicle. But as a vehicle for the expression of deep emotion, or
even of superficial sentiment, it is decidedly a failure. If I want to
tell somebody that it is a fine day, or that any two sides of a triangle
are greater than the third, I am at no loss for the means to do so.
But if I want to express the exact quality of the joy with which fine
weather suffuses me, or of the joy that I have in that discovery
about the triangle, I find myself making great efforts which I know
to be foredoomed to failure. I eke out my carefully-chosen words
with gestures and dramatic pauses, and run up and down the vocal
scale from whispers to cries. But still I cannot communicate my
emotion. It surges up in me, full-blooded, but will not be tapped. I
lamely conclude my verbal rapture by saying 'You know the sort of
feeling I mean,' and my interlocutor nods his head, dubiously.
Nor are my difficulties and my failure by any means peculiar to
myself. Indeed, as an habitual writer, I have more than the average
man's command of words: a larger vocabulary, and more knowledge how to use it. The fault is not in myself, but in my medium
—mine and yours. Here I am assuming that you are not a poet. If
you *are* a poet, and a great one, you can, doubtless, to some extent,
express for us through your verse the emotions that have hold of you.
The music of the verse thrills us, awakens answering chords. The
music of the verse exchanged by Romeo and Juliet, in the balcony
scene, does suggest to us something of the passion of love. Something,
yet how little, can verbal music give us! How little Romeo and Juliet
express in comparison with what is felt by even the most commonplace lady and gentleman in love with each other in actual life!

Some music beyond the music of words is needed to express what Romeo and Juliet are feeling. I do not mean Gounod's music. But if Gounod had been a far greater genius than he was—if he had been as great a composer as was Shakespeare a poet—Shakespeare's play would inevitably have been overshadowed. In thinking of Romeo and Juliet, we should think of them through the music of Gounod, not through the words of Shakespeare. Again, if Shakespeare had happened on Malory, and founded a tragedy on the love story of Tristram and Iseult, Wagner would yet have beaten him out of the field. Wagner's words may be poor stuff. My dislike of the German language being as absolute as my ignorance of it, I will not dispute that they are very poor stuff. Also, I will admit, for sake of argument, that Shakespeare's version of the old legend might have been even more dramatic, technically, than the version which Wagner made. Still, *Tristan und Isolde* would have taken first place in our hearts. The passions of joy, doubt, horror, remorse, despair, which, all of them subordinate to the master-passion of love, are illustrated by the music of Wagner's drama, would seem tame to us, by comparison, through the medium of mere words, even were these words fraught with all the magic of Shakespeare at his highest pitch of poetic achievement.

None knows better than Mr Comyns Carr, whose *Tristram and Iseult* was produced last week at the Adelphi Theatre, that where Shakespeare would have been second no other dramatic poet can hope to be first. A man of wide culture and of a fine taste in all the arts, he knew perfectly well that he could not compete with Wagner's music-drama: not, that is to say, in the hearts of persons who are sensitive to music. On the other hand, he knew that England is an unmusical nation, and that a vast majority of English playgoers have not seen Wagner's music-drama, and that a vast majority of the minority have been bored by it. Why, he asked himself, should not the legend of Tristram and Iseult, in itself so intensely beautiful and dramatic, be cast into a form in which the majority of English people might understand and enjoy it? It is well that he himself stepped into the breach. As a general rule, the competent dramatic craftsman is rather a terror. He lays hands on this or that noble theme with no appreciation of aught in it but the opportunities that it offers for 'effective situations.' He is, as a general rule, quite illiterate. Mr Carr, as I have hinted, is very much the reverse. True, he was not born a poet; but he was born with a goodly share of poetic instinct, which he has well cultivated. The legend of Tristram and Iseult is safe in his hands. He knows, and never for an instant mars, the beauty of it. His verse has not the rapture and rush of great poetry; but it is always felicitous and well-graced, always in touch with the spirit of his theme. And he has admirably accomplished the task of selection of scenes, and of general construction. He has welded parts of Malory and parts of Wagner into a simple and coherent whole, not hesitating to draw on his own invention where there was a chance for it. The introduction of the second Iseult in the guise of a spirit, a watcher over Iseult the mortal, is a bold idea which justifies itself by its effectiveness in the fabric of the play. Altogether, Mr Carr may be congratulated on an addition to his various successes in various spheres.

The scenery is conceived in the vein of simplicity which is right for a legend of this kind. The only fault is that the Cornish rocks in the first act are so extremely simple, so grotesquely ingenuous, that they distract one's attention from what is going on in their midst. The dresses and other accessories, throughout, are admirable, producing an impression of no special period, but of having a general unobtrusive beauty. So far as appearance goes, Miss Lily Brayton, as Iseult, leaves nothing at all to be desired. But her performance suffers through what seems to be a certain deficiency in power of imagination. It is such a very clear-cut little performance. Not one shadow of the mystery of romance hovers over it. Also, its decisiveness never varies in quality. Whomsoever Iseult is addressing, under stress of whatsoever emotion, always she stares at her interlocutor with the same expression, and enunciates her lines with the same level intonation, very slowly, as though she were counting the feet. I think Miss Brayton used to be much quicker, and much more variable, than is this Iseult. Mr Matheson Lang, as Tristram, though he is more variable in mood than Miss Brayton, is equally monotonous in delivery. Mr Oscar Asche seems rather too genial as King Mark, but is welcome for his reasonable speed of utterance.

[15 September 1906]

COMFORT FOR THE ACADEMIC

I wonder that the old-fashioned music-halls, which still exist, are not more frequented by persons of academic temper. For only there does an aesthetic tradition linger. Only there do you find an homogeneous 'school' thriving. Only there is originality not striven after, and is eccentricity, in the strict sense of that word, repressed.

Ten years ago, academic persons could still draw comfort from daily journalism. If they did not exactly know what the morning newspaper would say, they did know exactly how the morning newspaper would say it. There was a tone, a form, a hard-and-fast tradition. These things are gone, and the great aim of all the morning papers is to be as unlike one another, and even as unlike themselves, as they possibly can be. You never know where you are with them. They themselves never know where they are with you. They are certainly more amusing than they used to be; but they are not, I confess, so admirable as works of art. In every age, for every art, the supply of strong original artists, capable of doing fine work independently of their fellows, is smaller far than the supply of duffers who, if they are to produce passable work, must be trained by strict discipline to conformity with some approved pattern. In the daily newspapers of ten years ago, by reason of their fixed monotony, obvious dufferdom did not exist. Nowadays the duffers are rampant and unrestrained, naked and unashamed; and of the strong original talent, which is likewise let loose, there is not a sufficient supply to redress the balance. But hardly would the most academic of my friends care to read at breakfast a ten-year-old newspaper, however soothing it may have been to him at breakfast ten years ago.

Nor could he 'lose himself,' nowadays, in a three-volume novel. He could, at any old book-shop, buy for a few pence a whole stack of three-volume novels by forgotten writers, knowing that wherever he dipped he would find the same solid workmanship in construction and in style, the same situations and characters, the same determination to be unremarkable at all hazards. There were no really bad novels in those days. The duffers were all working meekly under discipline—meekly and well. They were doing very carefully a thing for which there were certain fixed rules. Obeying these rules, they could not go wrong. Yet the academic person does not ferret

266

out their works. He cannot shake off the bonds of the present. It is not enough for him that the past was glorious. He wants the present to be equally so. He studies the publishers' lists, and, through his circulating library, makes timid raids into contemporary novels, hoping to discern in them the gleam of a common denominator— the glimmer of a tradition, of a school, to come; and always he withdraws quickly from that dark tumult of highly original incompetence.

He adventures himself among the art-dealers, and finds that the 'one-man shows' are almost as internally multifarious in ambition as are the shows of this or that society. Nowhere is the lack of any unifying principle more apparent to him than in Burlington House itself. With bowed head, he retreats to Trafalgar Square, and, in the this-ian or that-ese room of the National Gallery, feasts his eyes on the work of masters who submitted with so good a grace to the very bonds in which the duffers worked; and rejoices that the work of the duffers is, by reason of those bonds, so often worthy to hang with the work of the masters. And then the darkness of the present is by contrast the more inspissated for my academic friend, and the antique masterpieces swim before him in a mist of tears.

So he dines well and goes to a theatre. Probably it is some years since he visited a theatre. He remembers the dear old stock-companies—the heavy father, the walking gentleman, the juvenile lead, and the rest, all doing their work so capably, in accord to certain rigid conventions. He remembers the orotund school of Shakespearean acting, in which the most insignificant mime spouted the verse with as regular and forthright an emphasis as did a Hamlet or Othello. He remembers also the agonies he suffered, in more recent years, through the vanishing of that tradition and the consequent gallimaufry of personal styles. Genius, he may go so far as to admit, is all the better for freedom. But, he insists, you don't get more than one or two geniuses in one theatrical company, and discipline is essential to the rest. That is why he, by nature an ardent playgoer, has so long shunned the theatre. But the other day he heard that Mr Tree had founded a dramatic academy for young ladies and gentlemen; and knowing that we live in an age of quick developments, my academic friend thinks that the whole stage may already be over-run by well-disciplined, congruously mannered actors and actresses. So he pays his money and he takes his chance, and presently the footlights are swimming before him in a mist of tears.

But with what 'a hard, gem-like flame,' as of well-tended candles before a shrine, would the footlights of an old-fashioned music-hall be lucent for him. In the modern music-hall he would approve the precision of the acrobats, and of the cinematograph, and the performing dogs. But the cinematograph has no tradition to dignify it; and even the performing dogs and the acrobats are constantly introducing new tricks. Besides, a variety show has, as is implied by its very name, no cohesion. It is a lawless growth, and my friend would dislike it. But there is no lawlessness in the music-halls to which I direct him. Geographically, I admit, they are 'eccentric,' nestling, for the most part, neatly where the four-mile radius impinges the circumference. But spiritually they are very much, as Mr Matthew Arnold would have said, 'of the centre.' I have written about them more than once in this Review, and I am afraid that what I wrote was not of a kind to tempt the academically-minded towards them. For, if my memory serves me, I dwelt rather on the ugliness and the vulgarity of the performance than on any other aspect of it. I cannot, alas, say that the performance is not ugly and vulgar. But I can add, handsomely, and with conviction, that the performance is always good. I do not say that it is perfectly even. Not even the thisian and that-ese room of the National Gallery shows an absolute level of accomplishment. As I have hinted, one can discriminate there the masterpieces from the works of painters who, but for the system under which they worked, would have been duffers. Similarly, there are in the old-fashioned music-halls male and female 'stars' who outshine the others; but, similarly again, there are no duffers. Genius and mediocrity work here within the bounds of the same traditional conventions. Subject-matter, philosophy, manner, make-up, method of voice, everything is inexpugnably established. The tiro finds all his work patterned ready for him. He has only to do, to the best of his ability, what everyone else has been doing, and is doing. There is nothing for him to invent: he has only to reproduce; and, when, with a little patience, he has mastered that simple trick, behold an artist ripe for the stage! If there were no school for him, if he were trying, at the outset, to find his own expression for something in his own soul, he would belike be groping and fumbling helplessly for years, even if he were a genius. And if he *is* a genius, and really has something of his own to express, he will in course of time manage to express that something, well enough, despite the limitations by which in the meantime he will have been saved from ignominy.

This, I take it, is a theory which my academic friend would apply to all the arts. Let him hasten, then, with glad footsteps to the one kind of place where in these days he may see the theory worked out in practice.

[*15 December 1906*]

AT WYNDHAM'S THEATRE

I take a certain mild interest in seeing a play that has been running for a long time. I have observed with regret that not often do the plays which on first nights stir my enthusiasm have long runs. Nor, for the most part, do the plays which leave me cold. Needless to say, my good opinion of a work is not shaken, nor do I feel that my bad opinion is confirmed, by commercial failure. But a play that greatly succeeds must, however bad it be, have quality of some kind—must have a strength in its badness. It becomes, in a manner, impressive. And so, when I receive a ticket for the hundredth night or so of a play which I happen not to have already seen, I sometimes avail myself of it. I happened not to see *Toddles* when it was produced at the Waldorf Theatre; so I went this week to see it after its transference to Wyndham's. I am sure it would not have roused me to enthusiasm on the first night. It is a conventional French farce, adapted into English, and one is conscious of the usual gaps where the main fun of the original has been sacrificed to our notions of what is and is not permissible. On the other hand, I should not have been bored; for the adapter (anonymous) is not the usual kind of hack-writer. Here, for once, is an adaptation made by a man who has something with which to stop the gaps. The characters are not mere French people with the essentials omitted. They are (in a conventional way, of course) English, talking quite English dialogue that is really humorous and light-hearted. And thus, evident though the gaps are, I am compensated. I hope that the adapter, whoever he may be, will use his gift of spontaneous original fun in some play conceived by himself.

A priori, one would suppose that, as time went on, the general effect of the acting in a play would be improved. One would be prepared to find in the individual performances a certain lack of sparkle and conviction. For persons of active brain it must be very difficult to be convinced and sparkling in that one thing which they have been condemned to do night after night for many weeks. To them a long run must be a nightmare indeed; and Sunday's sur-cease is not enough to strengthen them against the horrors of the week to come. On the other hand, one would imagine that the 'ensemble' would be better. One would expect a certain unity. Constantly on the same stage, performing the same scenes, the mimes would, one dares hope, learn to play into one another's hands, insensibly adapting themselves to one another, for the common good. But one is very rash in daring to hope anything of the sort. The theory is turned upside down in practice. The longer a play runs, the more diverse and discrepant are the performances of the people engaged in it—the more sharply illustrative of the great fault of the English stage. A very strict and very talented stage-manager can sometimes win for the initial performances of a play almost that effect of unity which delights us in France. Unfortunately, when a play has once been produced, no further rehearsals are called. I think there ought to be at least one rehearsal (conducted by a very strict and talented stage-manager) in every week of a play's run. This, perhaps, would be more than human flesh could endure. I should be loth to lay any fresh burden on the already excoriated victims of the long-run system. But, given that system, I can see no other way of securing decent performances. Soon after a play has been produced, the good lessons (if any) of the stage-manager begin to fade from the mimes' memories. The team gets out of hand. Every mime becomes more emphatically expressive of his or her own particular method. By over-doing in their own special ways what they are compelled to do, they seek to save themselves from bore-dom, from the sense of utter extinction.

One radical fault there must have been from the outset. The play is essentially a farce. But the only two members of the cast who were capable of farce were Mr Cyril Maude and Miss Lottie Venne. Farce has gone rather out of fashion; and fashionable mimes nowadays are, with few exceptions, comedians pure and simple. To a certain extent, of course, they could be drilled to the farcical manner. But, so unwilling are they to demean themselves by doing anything outside their own (admittedly higher) line, that they would take good care to let the audience see that they were kicking against the pricks. No doubt they would rather like to be called versatile; but they are determined not to *be* versatile. Mr Cyril Maude, owing to the fashion of the day, has appeared mostly in comedy, and is, I imagine, sincerely ambitious to excel in this (admittedly higher) line. I have often seen him doing his very best to act in a comedic spirit, but always the farcical spirit that truly abides in him has seemed to be triumphant over his endeavour. In farce he is masterly. And in farce he would be as happy as a king if only he were allowed to wear red whiskers designed by Mr Frank Richardson and a suit of enormous checks. The spirit of the twentieth century forbids him this kind of make-up. Wrongly, I think. In plays whose action has no relation to life and is designed solely for laughter, the characters ought to be allowed to look as amusing as possible. Mr Maude, however, bows to the prohibition, and in *Toddles*, as ever, appears in the sober guise of himself. Perhaps the contrast between this very sobriety and the ingenious quaintness of his manner and deportment creates as funny an effect as could be got by really farcical costume. But I was glad when, in the second act, without violating the verisimilitude which he is forced to regard with irrelevant respect, Mr Maude got his chance of eccentricity in costume. In the night-time our natural manhood asserts itself: we do not try to look like gentlemen, but clothe ourselves in raiment of any egregious hues that our savage fancy may dictate. Thus, when Mr Maude, as Lord Meadows, steps out of bed, he has his chance of revealing himself in his true farcical colours. He makes the most of it, snatching up and placing on his head the top-hat which his servant has just ironed for him, and regarding the effect in a hand-mirror. The audience rocks with laughter, and Mr Maude proceeds to handle the mirror as a banjo, in order to point his likeness to a nigger-minstrel. This is an ingenious and really amusing piece of 'business,' and throughout the whole play Mr Maude is prolific of similar little inventions. His whole performance, indeed, is a perfect invention, elaborately minute, and yet never for a moment tedious, so lightly is it carried off by the actor's intense gusto. I can well imagine that Miss Lottie Venne's performance was a worthy pendant to it. On the night of my visit, unfortunately, Miss Venne was indisposed, and I saw only her understudy, Miss Emma Chambers, a clever actress, whose sole fault was that she was not the lady whose performance she reproduced with such evident accuracy. Her task was the more difficult because no one, except Mr Maude, played up to her. Mr Bishop, that delightful comedian, steadfastly refused to attune himself to the key of farce. Nor did one of the others condescend for an instant from the key of genteel comedy. Some of them, if the play had been a comedy, would have been acting very well (except, even so, in reference to their fellow-mimes). Others would, in any case, have been evident duffers. I won't name these duffers. A critic cannot blame mimes by name without making them miserable. A good stage-manager, on the other hand, can, without cruelty, teach them their business, to a certain extent.

[*22 December 1906*]

COMMERCIAL AND UNCOMMERCIAL

'Happy is the theatre that has no history,' said a manager, not long ago, in answer to a friend who had been reproaching him for his lack of enterprise. Commercially, who shall deny the truth of the adage? A manager who strikes out a line for himself, or a series of lines, may amass a solid fortune; but the chances are that he will amass nothing of the kind. Whereas a manager who doggedly confines himself to the doing of things that have been done successfully by other people is likely to retire with wealth more or less beyond the dreams of avarice. That is, of course, if he does these things well, and has plenty of capital, and a theatre attractive in itself. It is no use to do stale things on the cheap in a dull or devious theatre, as many men have found to their cost. Unless a manager starts on a solid basis, he might as well go in for artistic experiments at once.

A good deal of theatrical history has been made (and, as it happened, quite lucratively) in the Haymarket Theatre. 'Happy is the theatre that has no history' does not mean that a manager ought to eschew a theatre that is haunted by tradition. On the contrary, such tradition is in itself an asset. All that the adage means is that the manager will be wise to avoid the weaving of a tradition for his successors. And it is just this weaving that Mr Frederick Harrison, sole lessee of the Haymarket Theatre, avoids with extraordinary sureness. When Mr Cyril Maude was in joint management with him, there were, at least, some new and original plays. Not new in the sense of being novel; nor original in the sense of startling us; but plays that had not been produced elsewhere. I suspect that Mr Maude must have pleaded hard to get them produced by Mr Harrison. For since Mr Maude's departure Mr Harrison has not (so far as I remember) stooped to the production of anything that is even technically new and original. What has he produced? I really don't remember. Possibly I am wrong in thinking that all his productions have been either revivals or adaptations. Possibly I have not seen his every production. The point—a point which nobody can deny—is that he has done nothing that matters. The Haymarket has been very, very happy under his wise, negative auspices.

Now that the revival of *The Man from Blankley's* has run its successful course, we have a revival of *Lady Huntworth's Experiment*. I went to see it a few nights ago, and found the audience enjoying it very much. One of the stage-boxes was empty until, just as the curtain rose on the second act, a galaxy of fashion revealed itself there. Had Mr Harrison produced a play that really mattered, these ladies and gentlemen would have felt themselves compelled to dine at some unearthly hour; and even so, perhaps, they would not have had enough to eat. Therefore, the chances are that they would have chosen not the Haymarket, but some other theatre, as the scene of their digestion. I have seen quite fashionable people arrive in the auditorium of the Court Theatre before the opening of this or that play by Mr Shaw. But they all looked very hungry, and altogether unlike their own bright selves. Mr Harrison knows that where the aristocracy goes, there will the middle class go too. And this, doubtless, is one of the good reasons for his avoidance of anything that demands close attention.

I remember that *Lady Huntworth's Experiment* amused me very much when I first saw it. There are things in it that amuse me still. But oh the ravages of Time! I did not know that Time went about his business so quickly. The play is incredibly old-fashioned. 'He's a very good fellow,' says Captain Dorvaston to the wife of the vicar; 'he's a damned good fellow.' The wife of the vicar screams, the captain apologises profusely; and we are supposed to rock with laughter. Speaking of some kind of food, 'It is very good', says the captain, 'for the stom—' and again apologises profusely. 'Ah,' says the vicar's daughter to the curate who is in love with her, 'I was a little girl then—all elbows and knees,' whereat the curate utters an exclamation of pained surprise; and again we are supposed to rock with laughter. Is it possible that this recipe for laughter was really successful a few short years ago? And then there is the scene in which three men are stowed away in three separate cupboards. I had thought that sort of thing ceased in the 'seventies. So quickly does fashion change that one imagines that what one enjoyed quite lately was known to one only as a vague tradition from the unknown past. Well, the melancholy effect on me of such things as the cupboard scene in *Lady Huntworth's Experiment* is mitigated by the revelation that, after all, our playwrights have been making strides. Also, it stirs my imagination, making me wonder in just what way the present modes of dramatic humour will strike us a few years hence. Mr Shaw's humour, for instance, or Mr Barrie's, is bound, in the natural course of things, to seem very old-fashioned: we shall wonder how we managed to laugh so heartily at this and that jest. Shall we even assert that it was a poor jest? Impossible! And yet . . . used we not to roar with laughter at Mr Carton's cupboard scene?

Very much the best thing in the play is the character of Lady Huntworth. This seems not a whit less well-observed and vivid than it did before. Perhaps, if it had failed to reappear in every play that Mr Carton has written since, and if we were thus beholding it after a lapse of years, it too might seem old-fashioned and unreal. Miss Compton plays it as delightfully as ever. Captain Dorvaston is a quite null figure, and gives no chance to Mr Hawtrey's particular genius. The hero of *Lord and Lady Algy* was, if I rightly remember, a much more amusing figure. I think I see Mr Harrison noting down *Lord and Lady Algy* for his next production! Mr Weedon Grossmith plays the drunken husband who used to be played, with minute realism, by Mr Dion Boucicault. Mr Grossmith treats it frankly as a comic part, and is therefore much more in key with the entertainment.

I do *not* see Mr Harrison noting down for production the play which was tried on Friday of last week at the Bijou Theatre: *A Point of View*. And, indeed, I can face with something like equanimity the prospect of never seeing this play again. I discerned dimly in it a 'view,' but no manner of 'point.' In the first act we have the old trite theme that consists of a very young girl married to a pedantic scholar who takes little notice of her. The wife has an older half-sister who is an actress, and who urges her to leave her luxurious home for ever and try her luck on the stage. In the second act we see the two young women in provincial lodgings. The run-away has been a complete failure on the stage. Also the manager of the touring company has disappeared without paying any salaries. Naturally, the run-away regrets that she ran away; and naturally (according to the stage convention) she discovers that she had been in love with her husband all the time. Knocking about the provinces is all very well for her half-sister, who is used to it, and who, being of an independent and Bohemian character, likes it; but for a timid, dependent girl, married to a rich man, the sudden experience of it is rather unpleasant. One would have supposed that the half-sister, who is no fool, would have foreseen that, and, having invited it, would take the blame on herself. But then the author of the play, who has read her Ibsen, would not have the chance of writing, in a would-be Ibsenite manner, a long scene in which it is demonstrated by the elder girl that the younger, though she seems so nice, is a mass of selfishness. In the third act, the two have migrated to lodgings in London. The younger has been dangerously ill, but is now convalescent. Her husband has forgiven her, and is going to take her back. She is delighted, though, of course, she is grateful to the half-sister who has been so kind to her. The half-sister reveals that the expenses of the illness were defrayed at the cost of her own honour. The younger sister is horrified, and this gives the elder sister her cue for a long demonstration in self-defence. It is better, argues the elder, to be strong and helpful and unafraid than to be weak and conventional. But the assertion does not make a play. If the author showed us this young woman wavering, before the event, between her desire for respectability and her desire that her younger sister should have every comfort, then there would be a dramatic theme. Or again, there would be a dramatic theme if the younger girl, before the revelation, had had no desire to leave the elder and return to her husband. Or again—but it is not my business to rewrite plays. It is enough to point out where they fail. This play fails because the author imagined that to draw two different kinds of women was all that need be done. Mere differentiation does not suffice. There must be conflict, either between two persons, or inside one of them.

Miss Frances Wetherall played the elder girl with a power that should serve her well in a real play; and Miss Amy Ravenscroft played the younger very prettily. Mr Hubert Dansey, by nature a very ebullient actor, and knowing it, restrained himself rather too strictly in his performance of a minor part. The rest were amateurs, who will live always in my memory as quite the worst amateurs I ever saw.

[*19 January 1907*]

'THE CASSILIS ENGAGEMENT'

Last week, in admitting that Mr Shaw's plays were often marred by the uncontrolled duality of his nature, I protested that I would not wish him one whit otherwise than he is. Nor do I crave the slightest change in Mr St John Hankin. For such a wish there would be no excuse at all. Mr Hankin has no dangerous duality. To write plays that shall be admirable works of art, he needs but be true to himself. Of course the majority of people will urge him to be somebody else. The majority of people, whenever they come across the work of an interesting man, breezily deplore the fact that it isn't the work of some other interesting but entirely different man. It never occurs to them to take a writer as they find him. It maddens them to think of Mr Shaw wantonly throwing away the chance that he would have of being somebody else if only he would eat beef-steaks and drink beer. They acknowledge the gifts of Mr Arthur Symons as poet and critic; but two or three years' service in the Imperial Yeomanry during the South African war would have, according to them, done him all the good in the world. And Mr Rudyard Kipling: two or three years under the refining influences of an university would have done *him* all the good in the world. I, who do not subscribe to the doctrines of the all-the-good-in-the-world school, merely ask myself whether this or that writer has in this or that work been doing his best. When Mr Hankin wrote *The Cassilis Engagement*, a comedy produced last Sunday by the Stage Society, was he doing his best? If I could answer this question in the affirmative, my interest in Mr Hankin would henceforward be rather slight. But fortunately I can reply 'no' without a moment's hesitation.

From a purely technical standpoint there is little to be said against Mr Hankin's new play. The story is developed very neatly, and the curtain falls always at some quietly effective moment. There is no fumbling, no scamping. Technically, Mr Hankin has done his best in a medium for which he has a true bent. In *The Return of the Prodigal*, produced some time ago at the Court Theatre, we had already recognised that bent, and had rejoiced to find it in the possession of a remarkable person—a man with a keen eye for the comedic aspect of things around him. Usually the people who have a natural bent for the dramatic form are in all other respects so very signally dull, so very signally insensible to actualities. Well! had we not seen *The Return of the Prodigal* we should have deduced from *The Cassilis Engagement* that Mr Hankin himself was very little interested in modern life—in any life but that of the theatre. We should have fancied him saying, with an oath or two, 'What was good enough for Tom Robertson is good enough for me!'

In *Caste* Tom Robertson got a lot of fun out of the juxtaposition of 'high' life and 'low' life. Those were un-democratic days, without board schools; and where Miss Esther Eccles had acquired the exquisite refinement necessary to a heroine is a problem that no commentator has solved. In a twentieth century play Esther would not be such a prodigy. She would have been as well educated as the daughters of the rich and proud. Of course an Esther in real life would not be comfortable in the presence of those daughters. There would be differences between her and them—subtle differences which she would be painfully anxious to overcome— differences of manner, of outlook on life, and so on. Ethel Borridge (whose engagement to Geoffrey Cassilis, a young man of good family, is the pivot of Mr Hankin's play) has been well educated, but remains very vulgar. It is not her vulgarity to which I object on the score of truthfulness, but her perfect contentment in her vulgarity. Her mother's vulgarity is of a still stronger kind; and her mother, too, is perfectly unashamed. Mother and daughter, suddenly finding themselves in the Cassilis's country house, are quite themselves, 'terribly at ease in Zion.' That is just what, in real life, neither of them would be. Nor, indeed, would the mother have been invited. As Mr Hankin draws her, she is 'impossible.' Geoffrey Cassilis shows no sign of noticing her vulgarity; but in real life (for love, so far from being blind, is always peculiarly sensitive to all things closely connected with the object of it) this young man would have kept the mother very carefully in the background. Had he not determined to ignore this fact, Mr Hankin would, of course, have had to sacrifice the greater part of the fun that he was determined to get by juxtaposition of 'high' and 'low.' But is the fun so good as to excuse the unreality? Not even Tom Robertson, who was not shackled by any craving for verisimilitude, introduced Eccles as a guest at the Marquise's country house. He, on the other hand, had a more genial humour that Mr Hankin has: he was unctuous; Mr Hankin is caustic. And thus the fun that he got from his contrast between Eccles and the Marquise is of a much better quality than the fun that Mr Hankin gets out of his contrast between Mrs Borridge and Mrs Cassilis. The fun of such contrast must in any case be snobbish. The snobbishness does not so much matter if the spirit of it is kindly. But when the spirit is a dry, sardonic one, the snobbishness jars, and the fun is spoilt. What Mr Hankin ought to have done is to have eliminated Mrs Borridge altogether (just as she would have been eliminated in real life), and to have drawn the daughter as a girl typical of the average girl in her class, behaving in her new environment just as that sort of girl would behave. Mr Hankin's appreciation of fine shades would have enabled him to perform this task admirably. Not even so would the comedy have been a pleasant one. But cruelty is excusable in a setting of truth.

'Oh yes,' Mr Hankin may retort, 'it's very easy to talk about 'fine shades.' But where am I to find a market for my appreciation of them?' I admit regretfully that I don't know. But I point out to Mr Hankin that his attempt to find a market by dispensing with fine shades is not likely to be crowned with success. Indeed, that is practically what he himself, on Sunday night, pointed out in a little speech to the audience. Most of the managers in London, said he, had rejected *The Cassilis Engagement*. Surely it follows that he had much better not bother about a market. He had much better write his plays exactly in his own way, without any reference to what the public wants. And then, some day, the public may begin to want them. Mr Shaw is (and I hope Mr Hankin will be) a signal instance of success achieved at length by a man's absolute refusal to do anything that cannot be squared with his conscience.

Mr Sam Sothern, the other night, was a signal instance of success achieved by the simple expedient of talking at a normal rate of words to the minute. When he made his exit he was followed by a hurricane of grateful applause from the audience. There was no lack of other clever mimes in the cast; but oh their deadly deliberation! I am told that acting in public is a very delightful sensation. No doubt it is. But I do wish our mimes could be shaken in their common resolve to prolong the ecstasy to the utmost possible limit of time.

[*16 February 1907*]

'HEDDA GABLER'

Did Ibsen write a play more masterly than *Hedda Gabler*? If so, I have forgotten it—and I could not possibly have forgotten it. Here is not, certainly, that strange quality that is exhaled by certain other plays of Ibsen (and by the plays of no other dramatist except Euripides), that strange power of creating in us a sort of ferment that cannot be altogether explained by anything in the play's actual and analysable appeal to the intellect or to the emotions. Here Ibsen evokes in us but a straightforward intellectual delight in his study of a certain type of character—a cold and cruel delight, such as he him-self must have experienced, in the clarity and minuteness of his vision; and an aesthetic delight, later, in the technical perfection with which that vision is presented in terms of drama. Not a character in the play—nay, not a line in the play—but contributes to the revelation of Hedda's character. And yet, how natural and simple the whole progress of the play seems! At no moment, so long as the play lasts, are we conscious of any artistic machinery for our instruction. We grow to understand Hedda as naturally as though she were a woman whom we had known well for years in real life. She does not talk about herself more than an egoistic woman

279

would; nor does she understand herself and realise her place in the universal scheme more than a rather superficial woman would; nor do the other characters in the play talk of her or understand her more than is natural. Mr Shaw would have understood the Hedda type as clearly as did Ibsen; but what a world of difference there would have been in his means of communicating that vision to us! We should have known nothing about Hedda except through her own lips, and more especially through the lips of Eilert Lövborg, the man of genius, who would have turned her character inside out for us with more neatness than despatch. I do not wish Mr Shaw to change his method: I delight in his method (as employed by him), and merely point out the difference between that method and Ibsen's. Mr Shaw (except in certain portions of *Major Barbara*) is frankly an expositor, pointing morals, whilst Ibsen (on the surface) is no more explanatory or moralistic than Nature herself; and it is only by putting two and two together—by correlating this and that seemingly casual speech or action—that we are able to see what he is driving at. Nor ought this process to be a hard one for us: we have only to listen attentively to the play. If we let our wits wander but for an instant, we shall have lost some clue. Everything in *Hedda Gabler*, from first to last, is a clue: nowhere one speck of surplusage. There never was so meticulous an artist as Ibsen.

The main point about Hedda Gabler is that she is a woman under-vitalised and under-sexed; and this is a point which the critics seem generally to have missed (doubtless through having let their attention wander now and again). She is not, as some of them suppose, a definitely bad woman, bent on mischief; nor again, as others suppose, a naturally sensual woman restrained by fear of the conventions. She has, truly, a great respect for the conventions; but that sense is the direct result of her lack of natural impulse. She has no instinct at all towards liberty. Life jars on her. She is too fastidious for any direct personal contact with life. She is inquisitive about life. She likes to know all about it at second-hand, and she likes to build romances on this information. She wants, above all, to create something—to have a tug at the wires by which the puppets are dancing. She approaches life from the standpoint of an artist. Ibsen had a great horror of the artistic nature. His parting shot— *When We Dead Awaken*—was fired thereat; and in *Hedda Gabler* he is even more bitter. Hedda wants to be an influence. But she knows in her heart that she is just the sort of woman who never is a lasting influence, as not being real enough woman for the purpose. Hence her jealousy of Mrs Elvsted, a woman who is much less quick-witted than herself, and much less charming, but who happens to be fully normal, fully vitalised, with a will to take her part in the rough and tumble of life, and with a power, therefore, of permanently influencing men. It irks Hedda to think of the good influence that Mrs Elvsted has on Eilert Lövborg—not because it is a good influence, but because it is an influence. She is determined to destroy it, not because she has a natural bent for destruction, but because only as destroying angel can she cut any sort of a figure. She tempts Lövborg to drink, and rejoices in his downfall. She hands him the pistol, and rejoices in his suicide. She rejoices in burning the MS of his masterpiece. And all these joys are not in doing evil, but in doing, at last, something, and in doing it, of course, on her own detached plane. But her joys are short-lived. Just as her sense of beauty in the idea of Lövborg having 'vine-leaves in his hair' was jarred by the crude fact of his arrest by the police, and just as her expectation that he would shoot himself through the breast was falsified by his shooting himself through the stomach, so now the romance of the destruction of the MS is obliterated by the recovery of the rough notes from which the lost masterpiece can be more or less satisfactorily reconstructed. Even as a destroying angel, she is a failure: there are the real flesh-and-blood people to carry on the business. And I think that her own suicide ought to be caused by her sense of failure, supervening on the awful knowledge that she is going to bear a child—or by that awful knowledge alone —rather than by her horror of the scandal which is threatened by Judge Brack. True, she has an ingrained distaste for anything like a scandal; but that distaste is, as I have suggested, one of the superficial results of an inner lack. And it is straight through that inner lack that the tragedy should have reached its climax. Judge Brack's hold over her is an accidental, external thing, savouring of a mere drama of intrigue; and I am sure that Ibsen, in his later days, would have eliminated it. It is the one flaw in a masterpiece of psychological drama.

The performance at the Court Theatre is admirable, on the whole. I did not see Miss Elizabeth Robins as Hedda, some years ago, and thus I can compare Mrs Patrick Campbell only with Signora Duse, who, in this as in every other part that she plays, behaved like a guardian angel half-asleep at her post over humanity. Her air of listlessness, in this instance, happened to be apt; but otherwise she showed not a shadow of comprehension of her part. Mrs Campbell's only fault is one over which she has no control: she is physically too beautiful: Hedda should be 'mesquine.' But her reading of the character is perfect from first to last. As Mrs Elvsted, the foil, Miss Evelyn Weeden was highly intelligent, and, had she not been acting in juxtaposition to Mrs Campbell, whose naturalistic technique is now more than ever well-developed, the slight staginess of her performance would hardly have been noticed. Mr Trevor Lowe, as Hedda's well-meaning, exasperating husband, gave a performance quite in Mrs Campbell's key. It is to his credit that he never over-did the many ingenious and amusing pieces of 'business' that he had invented. Mr James Hearn was rather too slow, too emphatic, as Judge Brack: he was inclined to make too much of his part. Mr Laurence Irving, too, as Lövborg, had not wholly mastered his lust for emphasis at any price. But the part's chief need from its interpreter is imagination; and that faculty Mr Irving possesses in unusual measure. Nothing could have been better than his handling of the speech in which Lövborg, to save Elvsted the extreme of anguish, describes how he had deliberately torn into fragments and scattered far over the fiord the masterpiece which really he had lost in a drunken bout. That speech is one of the finest and subtlest of Ibsen's inventions; and Mr Irving rose nobly to the level of it.

[9 March 1907]

'JOHN GLAYDE'S HONOUR'

The central figure of Mr Sutro's new play is a great American financier 'en revers.' John Glayde has been married for twelve years, and, ever since the earlier days of his marriage, has taken very little notice of his wife: his days and nights have been monopolised by business. She, being still a young woman, and attractive, is very much bored by her life at home, and is very glad of a holiday. She rejoices to find herself alone in Paris and being painted by a young artist, Trevor Lerode, who conceives a great passion for her.

She reciprocates this passion, and begins to be 'talked about' in the American quarter of Paris. The artist's mother, wishing to withdraw her son from the entanglement, cables to John Glayde: 'Lady Lerode's son painting Mrs Glayde's portrait, strongly advise coming to Paris at once.' Just at this time, John Glayde is involved in a titanic attack on a combination of other American millionaires. So far, so good. Now let us, for a moment, divert our eyes from the actual play, and imagine John Glayde to be a real man, and not a peculiar man, but a normal specimen of his type. How would he feel, and how would he act, on receipt of Lady Lerode's cablegram? He would be very much surprised, and very much incensed, and would cable for further information. Learning that his wife was supposed to be carrying on an intrigue, he would perhaps feel bound to come over to Europe, and to carry on his titanic attack as best he could—by marconigrams. If this sense of conjugal duty prevailed, he would, of course, be all the while chafing furiously at the interruption of his life. Arriving in Paris, he would assert himself in a peremptory way. If his wife showed herself amenable, he would take her back to New York by the next boat. If not, he would take himself back by that boat, after having made preliminary arrangements for a separation or a divorce. He would realise that his wife was not much to be blamed. Her conduct was the natural result of his neglect. There had not been room for her in his life. She had been an ornamental encumbrance. Now he was free. And Wall Street was waiting for him. Oh to be able to buy up the Atlantic, drain it, and proceed to Wall Street by a special train across the bed of the ocean! Such, I take it, would have been John Glayde's sentiments. It is quite certain that the effect of his first journey would not have been to make him realise that he was passionately in love with the lady whom he had consistently neglected in favour of the excitements of finance on a huge scale. Yet, in Mr Sutro's play, that is just the effect produced on John Glayde. His wife confesses to him that she *has* been foolish. He is quite ready to forgive her, and proposes to wind up his affairs in America, become an ordinary private citizen, and live happily ever after in assidious culture of connubial bliss. Finding that his wife has lied to him, he raves and storms, and tears passions to tatters. He wishes to shoot the seducer, but finally relents, and, eliminating himself, allows the two lovers to go away together.

This act of acquiescence is, in itself, as I have suggested, quite natural. But, as Mr Sutro depicts it, it is not natural at all. Wall Street financiers don't deal in heroic renunciations. If John Glayde were a true specimen of his type, he would keep an iron grip on the wife with whom he was desperately in love. But there again: if he were desperately in love with his wife, he would not be a true specimen of his type. Mr Sutro's error is in taking a typical American wife-neglecting financier and then overhauling him and turning him inside out and lavishly re-decorating him in order to enable him to cut a fine figure in a drama of passion. Without untruthfulness to life, there is not in John Glayde any scope for a drama of passion. The play should have been a comedy; a grim comedy, showing John Glayde trying to behave with romantic connubial indignation while his Wall Street conflict was uppermost in his mind, and, in the end, inwardly rejoicing at the definite departure of the two lovers. At one point, indeed, Mr Sutro does seem to have intended to extract comedy from truth. There is a scene in which John Glayde, hearing that his wife has just been seen in Lerode's arms, masters his emotion and continues the dictation of a cablegram to New York. Here we have a glimpse of what the play ought to have been. But only a glimpse. 'He stops' is the stage direction; 'he cannot go on. His head sinks on his chest, his eyes close: he stands motionless. There is silence. The curtain slowly falls.' The romantic hero has not given himself away, after all.

I may seem to have fallen into the very error which I have so often deprecated in other critics. I may seem to be blaming Mr Sutro merely because his play is not another kind of play. But this is not a case in which the artist's standpoint, his way of treating a theme, is a matter of no importance, a choice with which we must not interfere. The theme chosen by Mr Sutro is not one of those themes which can be equally well treated in several fashions. It is one for which, as I have said, truthfulness demands the comedic method. I have a pre-occupying passion for truthfulness in plays, and thus I cannot fling my hat in the air for *John Glayde's Honour*. Nevertheless, I admit the mastery which Mr Sutro shows in the building of his play, and the strength and precision, the knowledge and sympathy, with which he has drawn the characters other than John Glayde. Mrs Glayde is a very vivid person, and the scene in which, to put her husband off the scent, and to be able to escape from him, she pretends to love him is not merely a great chance for an actress, nor merely a device for surprising an audience, but a courageous and truthful representation of the lengths to which in a crisis a usually quite scrupulous woman may be driven by intensity of feeling. The lover, too, is not the dummy of stage traffic, but a quite well-presented character. And there is an admirable study of a raw Americo-Parisian Princess. And, as always in Mr Sutro's plays, the dialogue is of the finest quality— ever natural, and yet ever graceful, in the light passages, and, in the strong passages, eloquent without a suspicion of ranting. For the benefit of budding playwrights, Mr Sutro should publish his plays, as models in the art of writing dialogue.

I think it a pity that Mr George Alexander, as John Glayde, does not venture to assume an American accent. The sort of American accent that English actors usually assume has little resemblance to any accent ever heard in America; but one accepts it as a necessary convention, like the three-walled room in which it is uttered. Mr Alexander's pure English considerably hampers illusion. Nor does he give us an English equivalent, even, for John Glayde. I do not believe in the character as conceived by Mr Sutro; but, if I were called on to act it, I should make more of an effort at impersonation than is made by Mr Alexander. John Glayde ought to be represented as a quite simple, straightforward, masterful man of business—a sharp contrast to all the other persons of the play. Mr Alexander does not point that contrast. He excels in charm, and lately he was doing a great deal of canvassing as candidate for the London County Council. *Too* lately. There is an over-development of charm which has not had time to wear off. It put Mr Alexander at the head of the poll, but plays the very deuce with him as John Glayde. He seems determined to win by sheer charm the vote of every character in the play and of every person in the audience, and gives no hint of that sound business-capacity which we know him to possess, which we think will be of real use in the government of London, and which ought to be obvious in John Glayde. A month or two hence his performance will have become much better. Miss Eva Moore, as Mrs Glayde, leaves no margin for improvement.

[*16 March 1907*]

'HER SON'

This play is being performed on certain afternoons in Mr Cyril
Maude's new theatre [the Playhouse], and will in due course, I
imagine, be performed there every evening. It is just the sort of
puerility that is likely to have a long run.

It is puerile in more than the ordinary loose sense of that word.
There are seven grown-up persons in the cast of it, but these are
really of little account—are mere 'feeders' to a small boy who is
the central figure. Mr Horace Annesley Vachell, author of the play,
has concentrated on this figure all such skill as he has in the portrayal of character. He has gone 'nap' on the modern vogue for
children, and his motive in writing was evidently to supply the
public with a realisation of its ideal of the perfect child—the patent
compendium of all childish graces and quaintnesses and sweet-
nesses, the darling without flaw. This last phrase does not, of course,
imply a child without faults. In the days before they came into
fashion, children with a strain of naughtiness in them were not at
all *bien vus*, and Paul Dombey was the only kind of child whose
death-bed was matter for emotion among adults. But all this is
changed now. The late Paul Dombey is declared to have been a prig.
He is even suspected of having been a middle-aged man masquerad-
ing in knickerbockers. A child without faults is not, for us, a child
at all. At the same time, our ideal child is not composed entirely of
lapses. For all his waywardness, he shall be 'a perfect little gentleman.' He shall be tender even in his tantrums. He shall smile
angelically through his tears, and beg our pardon 'nicely' and of
his own accord. His errors shall arise rather from light-headedness
than from a natural bent to naughtiness. But that he shall be erratic
is a stipulation which we will on no account waive. Mr Vachell
must be warmly complimented, therefore, on the creation of Min.
(The very name is a masterpiece. 'Minnie' would sound rather
effeminate for a boy; but the implication of that soft vocable helps
us–does it not?—fondly to remember what a wee little fellow Min
is.) To form in our minds an ideal of childhood is an easy matter
enough. But to project that ideal for representation on the stage
is surely a dangerous task, needing infinite tact. Mr Vachell has
triumphed over the many obvious difficulties, and in Min the

'perfect little gentleman' merges not ever into the prig, nor the natural child into the savage. He did steal an apple from his nurse's basket on the sands of Bournemouth; but he does not deny the theft. 'Satan,' he says to his nurse, with a sweet frank smile, 'tempted me.' And presently we see Satan tempting him again. Bless his little heart! he is going to steal another apple—but no! a gentleman is watching him—a strange gentleman, with a kind face—and Min, in the expansiveness of his nature, forgets the apple in the excitement of making a friend. The strange gentleman has travelled in Central Africa. Min is a brave boy, and *he* will go to Central Africa. He is afraid of nothing, and of no one, as he remarks in another connexion. But Mr Vachell takes care that he shall not forfeit his claim to our solicitude. Min wants a night-light in his bedroom. But again, when he learns that the strange gentleman does not have night-lights, Min blows his out. Thus Mr Vachell holds the scales evenly balanced. Min refuses to go to bed at bed-time when his nurse fetches him. He is a little petulant for a while. But when his mother asks him to go, he goes like an arrow from the bow. He forgets to say his prayers, but presently he remembers that he forgot. The strange gentleman asks him to say his prayers in the drawing-room; and for a moment we think we are to have the rapture of hearing Min say his prayers. He says he cannot say his prayers in public. Our faces fall; but, a moment later, we see how right Mr Vachell was: Min has risen higher than ever in our esteem. Mr Vachell's only fault is that he has timed Min's bed-time long before the end of the act, and that even when the curtain is about to fall Min does not re-appear to console the unhappy (and wholly uninteresting) lady who is called his mother. At other times, he is great in the matter of consolation. 'Are you feeling lonely?' is the kind of phrase that is never far from the tip of his little tongue. Not only does he arrange sofa-cushions for his supposed mother's head: he even asks to be seated, because she looks so sad, a lady whom, with childish intuition, he had hated at first sight. In fact, from first to last, he is 'immense.' And how Mr Vachell resisted the temptation of 'doing' his death-bed I really cannot imagine. Of course it would have been an unforgiveable thing to make Min really die. But we should have revelled in the pathos of the idea that he was dying. Could not Mr Vachell insert an extra act, in which Min should be pronounced by a doctor to be suffering from a mortal ailment and to have only twenty more minutes to live? Think, Mr Vachell, think of all the exquisitely quaint and touching things that you could make Min say! Think of our heart-strings, and of the joyous reaction in our hearts when, at the end of the act, you brought on another and more eminent doctor to say that Min was quite well!

That Min, though well, should be supposed by his relations to be ill were a device quite congruous with the rest of the drama. It is a drama of misapprehension—or rather of nescience. Almost everything that is done by the *dramatis personae* is done 'in the dark.' Miss Fairfax has accepted Mr Gascoyne's offer of marriage. She does not know that he has recently seduced Miss Wride. Had she known, she would not have accepted his offer. Miss Wride comes to enlighten her. And it appears that had Mr Gascoyne known that Miss Wride was going to bear a child he would not have proposed to Miss Fairfax. His knack of not knowing things is equalled only by Miss Fairfax's own. She does not (eight years having elapsed) know that he is alive in England and not dead in Central Africa; and he does not know that she is not a widow mourning her husband in the company of her child, but a spinster mourning *him* in the company of *his*. Nor does he know that Miss Wride abandoned the child. Had he known this, he would not, as he subsequently says, have married her on his return from Central Africa. Nor does he know that the supposed widow is sunning herself on the sands of Bournemouth. Had he known this, he would presumably have taken his wife to some other salubrious resort, thus bringing the play to an abrupt conclusion. And had he known that his wife was suffering from a complaint which was bound to kill her very soon, he would not have been so agonised when Miss Fairfax explained that the married name under which she was living was only an assumed one, and that she had never harboured a thought of anyone but him. Luckily, his wife is doomed by Mr Vachell, and thus a happy ending is secured. Oh assuredly, *Her Son* will go into the evening bill. But I hope that in future plays Mr Vachell will make *all* his characters children. I can tolerate plays about children written for adults. But plays about adults written for children are apt to bore me.

[*23 March 1907*]

AN AFTERNOON WITH AESCHYLUS

Last Saturday the Literary Theatre Society gave a performance of *The Persians* at Terry's Theatre. The play was originally produced in Athens, some few years after the battle of Salamis. And I doubt not that, had I been alive then, I should have enjoyed it. To say that I enjoyed it last Saturday would be to make a too great demand on the good-will I bear for the Literary Theatre Society.

In writing about the performances of Mr Gilbert Murray's translations, I have more than once explained why, in my opinion, Greek drama is a thing incompatible with the modern theatre—an artform which in the modern theatre is bound to bore even those persons who go determined to rave about it; and I have upheld the Bradfield method as the sole method of making Greek drama truly impressive and delightful. But there are, of course, various degrees in which Greek drama as acted in a modern theatre may bore us. Some of the Greek plays are less remote than others from modern drama. Such a play as the *Electra* is less remote than *The Trojan Women*, and I found the production of it accordingly less tedious. Unfortunately, *The Persians* is as remote as can be. It is simply a sequence of dirges. I am sure the Attic audiences enjoyed immensely these dirges supposed to be uttered by the enemy over whom Athens had so recently triumphed. Nor was their enjoyment merely in the sense of martial superiority. They must have enjoyed the consciousness of their magnanimity in being able to enter into the feelings of the vanquished, and to regard those feelings as a theme worthy of high tragic art. If we, in this our day, had had an Aeschylus to write a tragedy around the humiliation of the Boers, we should not have gone to the trouble of granting a constitution to the Transvaal: the popular success of that tragedy would have fully satisfied our hankering after the '*beau geste.*' But I doubt whether a translation of that tragedy would be a popular success in a foreign land and in the fortieth century or so. In fact I am sure it would bore even the most superior person. For a precisely similar reason *The Persians* bores you and me. Nor does the manner in which it is translated, and acted, and mounted, help to make vivid its revival. The Greek dramatists happened to be poets, and no translation which does not preserve their poetry can be very helpful to us. Mr Gilbert

Murray, a poet, does provide a substitute for the poetry of Euripides, thus somewhat gilding the pill of Greek drama in a modern theatre. In the plays of Aeschylus the poetry is even more essential to us than in the plays of Euripides, because Euripides was more dramatic, and also more modern; and in none of Aeschylus's plays can the poetry be less well dispensed with than in *The Persians*. Mr B. J. Ryan is, I presume, not a poet: else he would not have written his translation in prose. His prose is quite dignified, and is certainly much more welcome than sham poetry would be. But Mr Ryan will not, I am sure, be offended when I hint that his prose, at its best, is a very poor substitute for Aeschylus's poetry. Nor was it improved by the fashion in which the mimes recited it. They were desperately determined to be in the grand manner. And their notion of the grand manner was that peculiarly false notion which haunts all English mimes when they are snatched away from their performances of realistic modern drama. They seem to think that what they have to do is to enunciate every word as though it were their last, giving each syllable as though it were the only syllable, and then pausing so long that the next word comes as a shock to our nerves. If only we could give them a shock to *their* nerves! Their impassiveness is really too exasperating. On they drone, staring vacantly into space, with never a hint that the words spoken by them are words of force and meaning, or even that the characters played by them are supposed to be live men and women. Of course, realism would be a mistake. We want the grand manner. But the grand manner is a thing quite remote from the vacuous and tedious manner which I have been describing, and which we all know so well, but which has never been so awfully exemplified as last Saturday afternoon. Mr Robert Farquharson, as the Messenger, must be excepted from my indictment. He rushed to the opposite extreme of realism. He panted and writhed and gasped as though he really had been running hard for many miles. He was very un-Aeschylean, but he was certainly more Aeschylean than anyone else in the cast, for he spoke his words as though they meant something. Interminably long though his speech was, he never lost his grip of it; and in the whole afternoon it was the one thing that was not monotonous—the one thing that distracted our attention from the scenery and the dresses designed by Mr Ricketts. It goes without saying that these were interesting and beautiful in themselves: Mr

Ricketts could not accomplish anything ugly or uninteresting. But he proves himself beyond all dispute capable of accomplishing things which cannot be brought into relation with the spirit of Greek drama. It is right that the scenery and the dresses should be simple and austere. But the mysterious, romantic simplicity and austerity aimed at by Mr Ricketts, and by him perfectly achieved, is surely quite wrong. A classic clarity and breadth of effect is what is needed to match the spirit of Greek tragedy. Mr Ricketts transports us into a dim little corner of a dreamland. It is an enchanted, en-chanting place, and we are delighted to find ourselves there. But there is one among us who stretches his arms, and stamps his feet, and tries to pull down the beautiful sombre curtains that hem us in on all sides, and shouts for a little light and air and space. Who is this choleric and unmannerly creature? It must be Aeschylus.

With *The Persians* was performed *A Miracle*, a short symbolic play by Mr Granville Barker; and herein Mr Ricketts found material far more appropriate to his method. 'The scene represents the top room in a turret-tower.' Thus an effect of space in the room itself would be obviously wrong; and, though top rooms in turret-towers have usually a certain amount of light and air, the quality of the play itself demands a setting of mysticism. There dwells in the tower a saintly woman whose heart is full of love for the whole world; but she is not beautiful, and no one loves her. There comes to her a very beautiful woman, who, though she is much loved, neither loves anyone nor cares for anything in the whole world, and is going to die by reason of her utter listlessness. It is in vain that the saint tries to infuse love into her, and she presently dies. The saint prays that she herself may die instead, and that her own lov-ing soul may pass into the body of this beautiful woman and re-store her to life. And the prayer is granted. Dramatically, and philo-sophically, this idea is worked out with great skill. But the actual words in which it is written have not the naif magic that is needed. I wish Mr Barker would write it all over again, in much simpler language. Then the little play would be a thing of real beauty. Miss Winifred Fraser played the saint very fervidly and prettily, but ought to have made herself less comely.

[*30 March 1907*]

G. B. S. REPUBLISHED

Some weeks have passed since this book [*Dramatic Opinions and Essays*] was published. But it is not one of those books which, destined to be so soon forgotten, need to be reviewed on the instant of publication. It is most assuredly a permanent book, about which one will never be too late in saying something.

In due time this first edition of it will be valuable. But people who buy books because they want to read them, rather than because they want to brag about them, will prefer subsequent editions. This is a very bad edition. For one thing, the titles of the essays are not printed, as they should be, at the top of the right-side pages. To find this or that favourite essay, you must first search the long 'Contents.' Even if the titles were printed throughout, you would have great difficulty in finding what you wanted. For Mr Shaw's titles are, for the most part, not very indicative: you do not remember the essays by them. Obviously there ought to be an index. But let it not be compiled by Mr James Huneker, an American, to whom has fallen the task of editing these essays. His incapacity for taking a little trouble is proved by the misprints of spelling and punctuation which, sown broadcast throughout the pages (not, of course, by Mr Shaw, but by the American compositors), are a constant source of annoyance to the reader. It is no comfort to be told by Mr Shaw that Mr Huneker has done the task very much better than he himself would have done it. The fact remains that it has been scamped. Scarcely less disfiguring to the book is Mr Huneker's introduction. The writings of Mr Huneker are, I am told, admired in America. One sample of them—a pretentious and loudly muzzy book whose title I don't remember—I gibbeted in these columns a year or two ago. If really Americans are so illiterate as to think well of Mr Huneker, then doubtless Mr Shaw stands in need of an introduction to them. But in England Mr Shaw needs no introduction: he has introduced himself so often and so admirably. And it is absurd that he should be introduced by a gentleman who is almost wholly unknown here and so far as he is known merely excites derision. When I devoted an article to him, I was under the impression that he was a very young man, who might be directed to better courses. But I learned later that he was well on in middle age; and thus it is not surprising that his introduction of Mr Shaw shows no advance in thought or in style. His jocularity is as dismal as ever, and the platitudes howled by him are as incoherent. Only in one passage does he express tolerably a not obvious thing, and that is where he refers to myself as 'a gentle mid-Victorian.' There you have a rather witty half-truth—one solid speck of brightness in a dull deliquium. But it does not justify the deliquium. If Mr Shaw wanted a foil to his own journalism—an illustrious example of 'how not to do it'—he could not have chosen a better one than Mr Huneker. But really such journalism as G. B. S.'s needs nothing to throw its excellence into relief.

'Assuredly a permanent book' of 'journalism' sounds rather like a contradiction in terms? I will not try to resolve that contradiction by saying that Mr Shaw's criticisms, though they happened to be published week by week in this Review, were essentially literature. That would not be true. They were essentially journalism. Of course they were not journalistic in the sense of being written at random by a man without any cohesion of principle, endeavour, or style. No one ever was more inflexibly true to himself than Mr Shaw. No one was ever less mistakable than he for any one else. Through all these reprinted criticisms it is one voice that we hear speaking, one body of co-ordinated doctrines that is being preached at us— preached, too, with all the might and main of the preacher, and with never a moment of carelessness or fatigue. Ruskin spoke with sympathy of the anxious early-Christian preacher who had 'thirty minutes to wake the dead in.' Mr Shaw wrote ever as one who had two thousand words or so of printed matter to wake the dead in. He made every word 'tell' forcibly. He hammered his every phrase home. His style was a perfect thing in itself. But what distinguishes literature from journalism is not vigour and sharpness of expression: it is beauty of expression; and for beauty Mr Shaw cared nothing. Language was for him simply a means to an end. To a man who shall create literature, language must not indeed be an end in itself: it must be a means, but a noble and very dear means. The true artist must love the material in which he works. If he be a painter, he will not be satisfied with a faithful presentment of tones, values, character, and what not: the surface of the paint on the canvas must itself be lovely. If he be a writer, it will not be enough for him to have so expressed as to waken in himself a pious joy in these harmonies of words and cadences which can be found if they are sought for. I think I see Mr Shaw tossing his beard fiercely when he reads this; and I think I hear him mutter 'Bedford Park!' Such things as the art of literature are for him quite inseparable from the idea of Bedford Park; and I would not be such a fool as to attempt to separate them for him. I merely point out that he is not—he would drink hemlock if he suspected himself of being—a literary artist. His essays are journalism. And I hasten to add that they are more delightful and worthier of preservation than all but the very best of literature. The journalism of a man of genius who has also a genius for journalism is of more account than the literature of a hundred and one ordinary men of letters.

Being a man of genius, Mr Shaw never was, in the true sense of the word, a critic. Genius and the true critical faculty are mutually exclusive things. The true critic is he who can understand everything, and enjoy everything that is good, in the art under his survey. You would hardly hail as a genius a man who could do nothing in the art to which he devoted his energies. But a man who can do anything in an art is by so much the less capable of understanding or enjoying the various other kinds of things that may be done in that art. Therefore a true critic must be unable to do anything in art. Therefore a true critic cannot be a man of genius. Therefore Mr Shaw was not a true critic. He was that much more interesting spectacle, the creative artist fighting valiantly in criticism for the one kind of thing that he could do in his own art—the thing by love of which he was prevented from having patience with anything else. When a creative artist speaks of his own work, or of work similar to his own, a light comes into his eyes and irradiates the whole scene. He is more luminous, more worth listening to, than the critic ever is. Even so, he is not wholly to be trusted. He is apt to rate highly the quite feeble efforts of men who share his own ideals and methods—methods and ideals so dear to him that they cover with their glory even the humblest pickers-up of them. Much less is he to be trusted when he speaks of the work of artists whose 'game' is not his. His scorn is splendid; but oh, don't be carried away by it! So brilliantly cogent was G. B. S., and even in his wildest outbursts of wrath so genial, that I think most of his readers (I among them) generally *were* carried away. Nor did the process, in this case, involve any very serious injustice. For the dramatists doing the kind of work distasteful to G. B. S. happened mostly to be inferior fellows, who did not do it well. All the talent that was vital and important was turning in the direction pursued by G. B. S. himself. There was not, certainly, much of this talent, nor was it turning very quickly. But G. B. S., by his criticisms, both increased the amount and accelerated the speed. The effect of his criticisms was not apparent at the time; but it has become apparent since; and a salutary effect it is. Mr Archer has told us how, soon after Mr Shaw began to write dramatic criticisms, he despaired of his old friend, regarded him as a danger to the cause, and ceased to read him. I cherish this vision of Mr Archer not daring to open this Review for fear of the hideous indiscretions of his old friend, and yet (perhaps) *wanting* to open it on the chance that the actual indiscretions were less hideous than his fancy painted them. The goal in Mr Archer's eyes was practically the same as the goal in G. B. S.'s. It was only as to the means of reaching it that the two men differed. G. B. S. was violent, Mr Archer was all for diplomacy. G. B. S. was for burning the rubbish-heaps that cumbered the path. Mr Archer was for making them stepping-stones to higher things. And he still seems to think that his is the more practical method—a belief which adds a touch to the irony of the fact that G. B. S., violent, wrong-headed and (as he now reminds us) with an axe to grind, did in four years accomplish more for the progress of the drama than Mr Archer has accomplished in very many years by that unswerving fairness and sanity of judgment for which he is justly honoured by us all.

However, this book of G. B. S.'s criticisms is perhaps less valuable for the effect that the criticisms have had than for the delight with which one reads them again. American pirates, please note that in the files of the *World*, the *Star*, and other papers, are quantities of G. B. S.'s essays on music and painting, which he will not allow to be re-published unless, as in the case of these dramatic essays, you show signs of activity to be forestalled by him. Come! lay us under further obligations.

[*27 April 1907*]

G. B. S. AGAIN

We do not deserve Mr Shaw. Why was he not born a German? In Germany they have been industriously playing *Man and Superman* from start to finish—the two scenes in the Sierra Nevada, the scene in Hell, and all: a six hours' traffic. At the Court Theatre the scene in Hell is being played as a fragment; and here are many of even the better critics complaining that their endurance is put to a too severe test. Not that they really feel themselves aggrieved. They were not really bored for one moment. Indeed, I do not fancy that a single person in last Tuesday's audience was bored. But in England it is an old and honoured custom to be sulky and grudging in acknowledgment of contemporary genius. People are eager to be assured by critics that what they have been enjoying immensely is really rather tedious. They like to know that what has quickened their brains is something that doesn't bear thinking of for one moment, and that what is good enough for them will certainly not be good enough for anyone a few years hence. 'But do you think he will *"live"*?' is a question which, wherever Mr Shaw is discussed—and that is everywhere—people ask you with such evident anxiety for you to say 'no' that you have scarcely the heart to depress them by explaining that whether or not Mr Shaw will be liked by posterity is no business of ours—*our* business being merely to determine how *we* like him, and to be not afraid of saying how very much we like him, and not to snarl at him for the pleasure he gives us. I have been much amused, just lately, by the many unctuous little references made by the newspapers to the 'slashing attacks' on Mr Shaw in the current numbers of *Blackwood's Magazine* and the *Bookman*. Both these articles I have read; and I found nothing to choose between them in imbecility. I do not know who 'Z' is in *Blackwood's*; and I am similarly handicapped in regard to Mr Alfred Noyes in the *Bookman*. But I am pretty sure that neither of these gentlemen is so foolish as he pretends to be. When one was a schoolboy, and even when one was an undergratuate, the 'slashing attack' used rather to exhilarate one, and even to impress one. I protest I used to revel in the old *Scots' Observer*. But how glumly should I hail now a revival of that publication! When one is grown up, one demands discrimination from a critic, and sincerity; and when a critic indiscriminately slashes, one's doubts of his sincerity are in ratio to his apparent ability. Both 'Z' and Mr Alfred Noyes write rather well; and thus I cannot believe that either of them is really blind to those great qualities which he ignores in Mr Shaw. Like any other man of genius, Mr Shaw is vulnerable at many points. But to treat him as a mere tedious charlatan is absurd on the face of it; and this patent absurdity must have seriously marred the pleasure which these articles have been giving to the British public.

Mr Shaw has never contrived so good an expression of his genius as in *Don Juan in Hell*. In no other work of his is one so struck by the force and agility of his brain, by the spontaneity of his humour, and by the certainty of his wit. The whole conception of the play— Hell as the place where nothing is real, and where beauty and romance and honour and chivalry and all the other things which Mr Shaw will none of are unhampered by any actual purpose in life—is not only witty in itself, but gives Mr Shaw a chance of expounding his philosophy in a peculiarly telling way; and of this chance he has made the most. From first to last the high pressure of thought never lacks perfect expression; the close logical sequence of ideas is never obscured, is only illuminated, by the admirable rhetoric and admirable wit. In point of literary style, this play is very much the best thing that Mr Shaw has done. Since it was published, I have read it many times with unlessened delight. Had I to choose between reading it and seeing it acted on the stage, I should certainly choose to read it. The ideas are too good and too many to be fully appreciated in a theatre by one who has not already lingered over them in his study. But certainly, when you have first got the hang of them, a performance of the play makes them all the more vivid and delightful; and you find yourself hoping that Messrs Vedrenne and Barker will take an early opportunity of producing some of the dialogues of Plato. Nothing could be better than the visual effect designed by Mr Charles Ricketts. In writing of a recent production, I complained that Mr Ricketts had so arranged the stage as to cramp his figures and banish from us the necessary illusion of space. But this time Mr Ricketts has given us not merely space but infinity. Richly dark, Hell stretches impenetrably on and on, so that we really believe ourselves there; and in this rich darkness, sharply outlining the four subtly illuminated figures of the play, in their very beautiful costumes, we have surely the finest and strangest scenic effect that was ever contrived. It will be a shame if this effect is not preserved for us by some worthy painter. (Surely flash-light photographs do not wholly make up to us for the desuetude of the charming art of Zoffany?) As Dona Ana, Miss Lillah McCarthy has not very much to do, except to manage her hoop and her fan gracefully, and to diffuse the requisite radiance of womanhood; and these things she accomplishes perfectly. In point of pictorial style, Mr Robert Loraine, as Don Juan, is quite so good; but it is on Don Juan that the main burden of the dialogue falls; and no one could have spoken the speeches better than Mr Loraine. His excellence is not merely in that variety of pace and intonation necessary in long speeches, and so seldom achieved by actors trained up on a stage where only snippets of speech are fashionable. He seems to be really thinking, really evolving the ideas he has to express, and really rejoicing, too, in his mastery of debate. It is a pity that Mr Michael Sherbrooke, who plays the statue of Don Gonzalo, is not three or four inches taller than Nature made him. It is essential to the fun of the play that the statue should be physically in sharp contrast with its manner and its ideas. Mr Norman McKinnel, on the other hand, is much too tall and imposing as the Devil, and, though his elocution is admirable, he does not really enter into the spirit of the part. Mr Shaw, in his stage directions, described this Devil as 'in spite of an effusion of good nature and friendliness, peevish and sensitive when his advances are not reciprocated . . . clever and plausible, though perceptibly less well bred than the two other men, and enormously less vital than the woman.' All this Mr McKinnel misses. He is Lucifer, Son of the Morning, and the meaning of his part can only be deciphered behind his rendering.

The Man of Destiny, played immediately after *Don Juan in Hell*, comes out rather badly. Never was Mr Shaw so careless of form as when he wrote this little play. Not content with continuing the action long after all that matters is over and done with, he tacked on to it at the last moment a long speech which has nothing whatsoever to do with it or with the character of Napoleon. In itself the speech is amusing and interesting; but used as a device for prolonging a comedy of intrigue it is tedious: we are not attuned to receive it. Miss Irene Vanbrugh plays with much humour the part of the lady who outwits Napoleon. It is an excellent part for testing the capacity of a comedian; and I have no doubt that future actresses will, now and again, wish to exhibit in it their accomplishments. But for that, the play would vanish for ever to the shelves. No really intelligent actor, I conceive, ever wants to play Napoleon: he is too conscious of the impassable gulf between Napoleon and himself—a gulf which his make-up, and his folded arms and widely planted feet, and his trick of pinching people's ears, does but advertise unkindly. Mr Dion Boucicault, who now plays Napoleon, is very intelligent indeed, and thus, though he bears up bravely, soon infects the audience with his own inward embarrassment.

[*8 June 1907*]

TWO PLAYS

Let no one accuse the Stage Society of stinting us. Last Monday afternoon we were not dismissed before half-past six. Mr Charles McEvoy's play, *David Ballard*, was in itself quite long enough for an ordinary matinée; but (besides entr'actes in every one of which you might have smoked a large cigar without haste) Herr Wedekind's play, *Der Kammersänger*, no trifle, was munificently thrown in as a prelude. This play ('translated by a member of the society', whose industry, I suppose, gave out just when he was going to translate the title) might have been a trifle had its author not been a German. Essentially, it is but a scene between an operatic tenor, Signor Gerardo, and one of the innumerable ladies in whom he inspires a wild passion. The German author, at the outset, very thoroughly instructs us about these other ladies; and then, so that we shall have a deeper insight into the career and character of Gerardo, and of tenors in general, he introduces an elderly composer, a true artist, to whose opera the tenor refuses to listen. Then, at length, the play begins. The beautiful lady implores Gerardo to let her accompany him on his imminent journey. He is quite frank with her. He has been, he tells her, loved by hundreds of women, and will be loved by hundreds more. He does not object to gratifying their passion, within reason, but he cannot allow them to interfere with the business of his life. In his contract with his impresario is a clause binding him to travel unaccompanied. As a man of honour, and as a sensible man, he is not going to break his contract.

The more impassioned the lady becomes, the calmer grows Gerardo. It is an amusing situation; and, as Herr Wedekind is not himself a fascinating operatic tenor, naturally Gerardo is made more ridiculous than he would be in real life—more colossally well-pleased with himself. Mr Julian L'Estrange, as Gerardo, rather missed this inherent exaggeration. His performance was too straightforward. He ought to have played more, as the part was written, 'for the laugh.' That he did not do so was probably due to the difficulty of acting in one key while your interlocutor is acting in quite another. Not that Miss Constance Collier was wrong in playing with her fullest sincerity and power. Not otherwise would the lady's suicide at the end of the play be credible. Even as it is, this suicide seems to me a mistake. Tragedy and comedy jostle each other in real life. But this is no excuse for a comic play suddenly becoming tragic. Herr Wedekind himself evidently suspected as much; for he has, I am told, written an alternative ending, in which, after the agitated tenor has hurried away from the prostrate lady, explaining to the manager of the hotel that he must fulfil his contract, the prostrate lady jumps up, furious that her final stratagem has failed. It is a pity that this version was not adopted by the Stage Society. Miss Collier, one of the few versatile actresses, could doubtless have played throughout in the key of conscious comedy as well as she played in the key of sincere realism.

Mr Ambrose McEvoy is famous as an exponent of Early Victorian 'interiors' bathed in mellow light. I am told that Mr Charles McEvoy is a brother of his. I can hardly believe it. Not a ray of sunshine creeps into the Early Edwardian 'interior' which Mr Charles exposes in *David Ballard*. It is a harsh, cold, pitiless grey light that beats on the drawing-room of the Ballards. Do such people as the Ballards really exist? I would fain hope not; but occasional fragments of conversation overheard in the street, overheard from the lips of people who look exactly as the Ballards look on the stage, and occasional revelations in the reports of law-suits, forbid me to hope thus fondly. Even without these side-lights, I should have to submit to the impression that Mr McEvoy was trustworthy; for who for his own pleasure could invent such a hell, and, having invented it, could make it seem so hideously real? No; there must be many households in which the mothers, every afternoon, read aloud to their daughters, in high voices, without

punctuation, the feuilleton in the morning paper—many households which the younger sons cheer by turning on the gramophone
—many households of which the members are nearly always squab-
bling and sulking about nothing. The Ballards belong to a lower
stratum than the Voyseys of Mr Granville Barker; but they remind
me of the Voyseys because every one of them is obviously synthesised
from examples in actual life. Mr McEvoy's skill in presenting a
typical family, with each member sharply differentiated from another despite the family likeness of them all, is as great as Mr
Barker's skill; and I cannot pay him a higher compliment. The first
act of his play is a masterpiece of sardonic observation and presentment. So, indeed, are the other two acts; only they lead to nothing,
and Mr McEvoy's evident intention was that they should lead to
something. I praise the intention. I am not one of those who consider that such a work as Gorki's *Lower Depths* (was not that the
title?) can rank as drama. The dramatist (like any other artist) must
not merely show us life: he must get some meaning out of life:
something must be developed out of the characters. At the end of the
first act of Mr McEvoy's play we have got thus far: David, the
elder son, who is not, like his brother and sister, happy in his
unhappiness, and is an imaginative and sensitive person, with a
taste for writing, determines that he will throw up his clerkship,
say good-bye to his family, and shift for himself. In the possible
consequences of his decision there is plenty of scope for drama.
He might, for instance, manage to make a living for himself, but
presently find that, appalling though his family was, he could not
shake off the ties of natural affection for his father and mother.
Here would be a dramatic conflict. The mere fact that he fails to
make a living for himself, and, starving, has no option but to
return to the bosom of his family, is not dramatic at all, being no
development of character: at the end of the second act the play is
'no forrader' than at the end of the first. You may remember how
in that fine novel *Love and Mr Lewisham* Mr Wells extracted a
great deal of true drama from the hero's inward conflict in the
choice between domesticity and a career. This is just the sort of
conflict that Mr McEvoy might easily have implanted in David
Ballard. But in the third act David is at home again, and again in
solid employment, and still continuing to do literary work in his
leisure moments, and still confident that he will make a name for

himself at last. There is no reason why he should cease to do literary work in his leisure moments. But Mercy Hainton, a cousin who lives with the Ballards, thinks that there is. And so, as he is in love with Mercy, and is going to marry her, he decides to do no more literary work. The end of the play is his departure with Mercy, whom his sister has been insulting with more than her usual vehemence. But the development of the sister's bad manners is not the sort of development for which Mr McEvoy's theme was crying aloud. Now that he has had an experience of the stage, Mr McEvoy will not forget the importance of keeping a play in a state of constant progress. Meanwhile, the Stage Society must regard it as a privilege to have given experience to a man whose gift for observing character and revealing it in dialogue is so remarkable that he ought soon to rank very high among the few considerable dramatists.

Miss Clare Greet and Miss Lilian Revell, Mr Nigel Playfair and Mr Norman Page, entered fearlessly into a portrayal of the Ballard household, all acting well together. Mr Edmund Gurney, as the father (a 'sympathetic' character), was much too slow in his evident determination to extract every drop of 'sympathy'. Also, he did not seem like a real man, but like an actor rejoicing in a 'bit of character.' It was right that Mr Ballard should be in contrast with his family; but wrong that Mr Gurney's method should be in contrast with that of his colleagues. There is a sacred tradition that a 'sympathetic' female character should always speak with exquisite refinement of pronunciation, whatever her up-bringing; but youth gives daring, and I do think that Miss Dorothy Minto, as Mercy, might have ventured to kick over the traces.

[*15 June 1907*]

JOSEPH KNIGHT

Last Tuesday evening many of the people who assembled at the Playhouse, to see the production of *The Earl of Pawtucket*, must have found their thoughts turning to the memory of Joseph Knight. He had been always so very salient a presence in the stalls. Pictorially, the audience had always seemed to 'compose' around him. This was so even in recent months, when old age had caught him up at last, robbing his face of its rich colour, and contracting his huge frame, and keeping him silent and immobile in the entr'actes throughout which he had been wont to waft, with much wagging of his exuberant grey beard, stentorian jokes to friends and acquaintances seated at the utmost distances from himself. Clearly, he was on the wane. One had a sorrowful sense that when he had written his notice or notices of the play in hand he would go to bed—instead of sitting up till unearthly hours at his club, ever listening or discoursing with a convivial gusto that was the envy of a younger and less robust generation. But in his eyes there was still the same old twinkle; and now and again the beard would wag almost as of yore, and a joke be discharged—though seldom further, now, than two rows of stalls. He was still the centre-piece of the auditorium. Time had sapped his vitality, but not his magnetism. Some day, no doubt, science will be able to show in diagrams the various rays of variously magnetic persons, so that posterity will know more or less exactly the kind of effect which these persons produced on their contemporaries. In very large and undulating curves, I think, and with never a sharp angle, would be the record of the Knight rays. It is a pity that no such record could have been made. Some writers who are personally magnetic can translate something of their magnetism into their work—can give to their written words a measure of the peculiar quality which is in their spoken words and in their mere presence. Knight, had he not from the outset of his career been involved in the rough-and-tumble of daily journalism, might have written things that would permanently express him to people who had not the privilege of knowing him. A scholar and a wit, he was (needless to say) very far above the level of the hacks who were told off to do dramatic criticism in the 'sixties. His conversation had always a strong literary flavour; by which I mean not that he was always talking about books, but that he had, as every good talker must have, a strong discrimination in the use of words. Something of this flavour was in his writings, too. But otherwise his work was inexpressive of himself—had none of the boldness and 'body' that distinguished him. Nor as a mere guide to playgoers was it satisfactory. No critic could have had a keener relish than Knight had for what was good in drama; and his taste never fossilised: to the last, he was always quick to appreciate and to praise warmly any new thing that had merit. But how cordially, too, he would write of new things or old things that were quite worthless! He did not, I fancy, do this for diplomatic reasons. Mr Archer is always helping lame dogs over stiles (instead of keeping these stiles clear for dogs who could leap them) because he is convinced that this is the best way to serve the cause of dramatic progress. But I do not think Knight was impelled by any such conviction. I do not think his love of the theatre was deep enough to hinder him from speaking his mind fearlessly. His praise of bad and indifferent plays was simply the result of his excessive geniality: he could not bear not to be kind and pleasant all round. Thus, after all, there was implicit in his writings something of himself. Without that excessive geniality, he would, as a critic, have had an influence commensurate with his gifts. But then he would not have been himself—would not have been 'Joe Knight.' This would have been a heavy loss indeed to all who knew him.

Two or three years ago, I remember, in the midst of a play with a rather complicated plot, he turned to me and begged that I would explain some point to him. I confessed that I was hopelessly at sea. 'Thank you,' he replied, 'thank you for that! I thought perhaps I was past my work.' Last Tuesday evening I wished some younger critic were sitting by me, to reassure me as I had reassured Knight. The preliminary explanations offered by the characters in *The Earl of Pawtucket* were so bewildering that I soon ceased to listen to them, trusting that, as soon as the action of the play began, the mists would drift away. Alas, the further the play was carried, the denser rolled the mists; and the audience's outbursts of laughter had for me the weird, horrific quality of fog-signals. I daresay that a very well-trained lawyer, if he studied the script of the play for several hours in the early morning, might be able to tell you the plot. But I doubt whether even he could make you understand it. I doubt whether he could make even Mr Augustus Thomas, its author, understand it. I associate Mr Thomas with such plays as *Arizona* and *In Missouri*—intelligible plays, full of humour and humanity. I implore him not to write any more farces. His genius for piling complication on complication is such that it cripples all his other faculties. Here and there in *The Earl of Pawtucket* occurs a funny line; but the play as a whole seems to me as mirthless and inhuman as any proposition in the fourth book of Euclid. In America it has been a great success, by reason of Mr Lawrance D'Orsay's performance of the hero, who is the latest (and, I do hope, the last) apparition of the ghost of Lord Dundreary. In America, doubtless, the apparitions of this ghost have not been so constant as here. Possibly, even, the ghost is mistaken for a creature of flesh and blood—for a type that really exists in England. Anyhow, Mr Laurence D'Orsay has been having the time of his life. I dare not hope that Mr Cyril Maude, over here, will have a similar time. One thing I do dare hope; and this is that Mr Maude is not affected (otherwise than to tears) by the praises which the critics have been lavishing on his performance. A funny walk and a funny laugh, maintained with grim conscientiousness throughout the evening, do not, even though their maintainer be a man of pleasant and popular personality, amount to a masterpiece in the art of acting. They do not even amount to a failure in that art. They have nothing to do with that art.

[*29 June 1907*]

ABOUT, AND IN, OXFORD

One day last winter, I was bandying reminiscences of Oxford with a friend who, since his undergraduate days, has much distinguished himself in the sphere of thought; and I asked him whether he ever now revisited Oxford, and, if so, how he got on with the dons. 'I was there,' he said, 'a few days ago. My visit gave me more pain than pleasure. A man who goes back to Oxford after a lapse of years is like a man who, full of tenderness and affection, goes to see his old nurse, *and finds that she is deaf, and blind, and paralysed.* When my mind begins to fail me, I shall once more revisit Oxford (and shall enjoy it, no doubt). But not, oh not, in the meantime.' My friend's metaphor, though witty, does not bear examination. The fact that my friend has progressed does not imply that Oxford has decayed. Nor is there any reason why Oxford should have progressed in my friend's direction, or in any of the various other directions taken by various others of her sons. On the contrary, Oxford's business is to 'sit tight,' unallured from her traditions by the whirling fashions without. Let no rude hands shake the 'adorable dreamer' from her slumbers. Let us listen fondly to her whisperings of the last enchantments of the Middle Ages, and not egg her on to echoings of 'the latest' in this or that up-to-date philosophy. They will soon be old-fashioned, these philosophies— soon be discarded and superseded. But Oxford, if she remain true to herself, will hold her own for ever and ever, and will, in every generation, sway the hearts, even when she ceases to sway the intellects, of all men who were youths in her charge. As I said to my friend the advanced thinker, after I had pointed out the fallacy of his metaphor, 'It would be terrible if a man actually did find his old nurse deaf, and blind, and paralysed. But this would be better than that he should find her dressed up in the very latest fashion, and with her hair dyed and her face painted, and babbling just the ideas that have lately been occurring to *him*.'

This ghastly picture haunted me on my way down—no, I still prefer to say *up*—to Oxford, on the Thursday of last week. I did not like to think of Oxford as a venue for the Greatest Show on Earth; and if the forthcoming Pageant was not going to be the Greatest Show on Earth I had strangely mistaken the purport of the preliminary puffs which Oxford had been vouchsafing to the press. It seemed to me a pity that Oxford should advertise herself so heartily, so insistently. Where, and why, had the adorable dreamer learnt to play the big drum? It would have been all very well to 'go up' to Oxford; but to 'walk up, walk up' rather hurt me. I half expected to find sky-signs on Magdalen Tower. Certainly, Oxford had been 'booming' of late, with a vengeance. It was some comfort that Mr Kipling had not been invited to write a new version of 'The Absent-minded Beggar' for the Oxford appeal; but perhaps he would be called in yet; anyhow, he had just been made a D.C.L. No doubt it was a very popular move to confer an honorary degree on Mr Kipling. But it is not the business of an university such as Oxford to make popular moves. Mr Kipling's gift has its fit reward, I think, in the applause of a crowd which will soon cease to remember him. If Oxford wished to honour a writer of fiction, she should have selected someone working on a less popular, a higher plane of art. The idols of the market-place need no wreaths from an university. But an university may fittingly crown a writer whose mastery does but win him the quiet homage of the finer critics. Mr Meredith is already, I believe, a D.C.L. of Oxford. But no such

honour has yet befallen Mr Henry James, a writer as signally fit
for it as Mr Kipling is unfit. In his own line, Mr Kipling is
masterly. But who shall assert so much in regard to Professor
Herkomer, another of the persons honoured at this year's Encaenia?
He has been honoured for no other reason than that his name may
act as an advertisment for Oxford—genial, hearty, unpriggish, go-as-
you-please Oxford, whose Chancellor is not really, as a certain
rhymer once supposed him, 'a most superior purzon.' I have no
positive objection to the conferring of a degree on Prince Arthur of
Connaught. He has not, as have Professor Herkomer and Mr
Kipling, done anything that an university ought to frown on. What,
indeed, *has* he done? Why should the line have been drawn at
Prince Edward of York? His name would have lent additional
picturesqueness and popularity to a list which, throughout, was so
obviously compiled with a view to popularity and picturesqueness.

When I arrived at Oxford, it seemed as though the sensational
Encaenia had quite killed the Pageant. The always dreary way from
the railway-station to the town was drearier than ever. Hardly a
human being was to be seen. Two or three cabs, driven station-
wards, with luggage on the top and undergraduates inside—
supercilious undergraduates, evidently proud of going 'down' just
before the Pageant—did but intensify the desolation of the scene.
When I reached Carfax, things looked more cheerful; but still there
was no sign of bustle or enthusiasm. I saw several undergraduates
(slouching, shuffling along, in the modern manner) with exercise
books under their arms, as though it were mid-term. It was only
when I neared Queen's that I perceived any unusual signs. The
pavement on either side was lined with spectators. Most of them,
in the absence of anything better to look at, were looking up at the
sky, whose lowering black clouds promised, every moment, to
dissolve in rain. This promise was not fulfilled until, on the stroke of
four, the Pageant began. Poor St Frideswide, bearing up under the
drizzle that synchronised with her appearance, afforded us that
morbid satisfaction which we all take in the ironies of our climate.
Presently, however, the drizzle ceased, and our pleasure in sympathising with everyone concerned in the Pageant gave place to the
more amiable pleasure of observing how good their work was.

I take it as inessential that a Pageant should illude us. Its appeal
is rather to the historic than to the dramatic sense. Yet more than

once, in the course of the Oxford Pageant, I forgot the nature of the performance, and had an illusion of reality, and was living in this or that bygone moment of Oxford's history, quite forgetful of Mr Frank Lascelles's stage-management—or rather meadow-management. Mr Lascelles could not receive a higher compliment. Is he alive to receive it, after drilling three thousand persons for seven months? Some of the credit for my illusion is due, doubtless, to these three thousand persons, who entered so keenly into the spirit of the thing, and disported themselves with so much conviction. And again, credit is due to Mr Dion Clayton Calthrop, who had designed their costumes with not less learning than sense of beauty. And yet again, credit is due to the rain, for having taken away from these costumes that brand-new, stiff, stuffy aspect which betokens the costumier's shop. The men and women looked as natural in the meadow as did the horses and oxen and other four-footed 'supers' who, from time to time, 'walked on' with them. Visually, the whole Pageant was delightful. Aurally, it left much to be desired. To make oneself audible to a large concourse of people in the open air is a feat which can scarcely be achieved but through long practice in the exploiting of exceptional lung-power. Mr John Burns (who, by an oversight, had not been summoned to the comic Encaenia) would have been most valuable as a mouthpiece for the words written by Mr Bridges, Mr Binyon, Mr Laurence Housman and other Oxonian poets. As it was, we had to take the words more or less on trust—excepting those delivered by Mr Henry Neville, whose elocution indoors is so perfect as to enable him to triumph even over the circumambient air of heaven. I think it would have been well to let the Pageant be conducted wholly in dumbshow. The scenes that were without words were by far the most effective.

[6 July 1907]

A BOOK OF SHORT PLAYS

The short play, like the short story, is spurned in England. Sixty thousand words is the least that a novelist, if he wish his books to be read, must devote to his every theme; and three long acts is an irreducible minimum for the playwright who wishes his plays to be seen. And this in an age notorious for its restlessness, its lack of concentration! The daily newspapers have, for the most part, surrendered to the lust of their readers for brevity. And I, personally, do not regret the change. The old-fashioned 'leader' always seemed to me a rather ludicrous institution. I admired the skill with which the writer inflated to the extent of a column and a half such wisdom as would not in its normal bulk have occupied more than half a dozen lines. But I felt, too, that the sage's brain might have been better employed than in wasting the time of the community. So 'leaderettes' seem to me an improvement. How is it that their equivalents in literature and drama are so distasteful to the public? There are, of course, themes which require a large scope in treatment; and there are writers who can fill this large scope without fatigue. Far be it from me to set any limit to the length of books or plays. I merely point out that most of the writers in the present age lack that vitality which was apparent in their predecessors, and which amply justified the lengths to which their predecessors ran. Physically, we may be healthier than our grandfathers; but we are not so strong. And this fact is nowhere more apparent than in our books of fiction. Since Mr Meredith there have been few writers who can compass a long novel without making us regret that it was not (say) half its actual length. Modern novelists do husband their resources in one respect: they no longer deal with a large area of life, with large crowds of characters: they confine themselves to a few characters illustrating some particular phase of life, or some particular idea in the criticism of life. But they (their publishers tell them they must) doggedly force their books up to the sixty-thousand words standard, and as far above it as they possibly can. It refreshes me to find a writer confessing that there is 'no legitimate reason why we should take up twice twenty-four hours of a reader's time with a story that could be told no less effectively in ten minutes.'

These are the words of Mr George Sylvester Viereck, and they occur in the preface to his little book of plays, *A Game of Love* (published by Brentano, New York). He claims to 'have taken the climacteric moments of imaginary novels and embodied them in dramatic sketches.' Whether the sketches are dramatic, in the sense that they would be effective in the theatre, is a point which I will not discuss. 'These plays are unplayable,' says Mr Viereck; and—though I have often found that what has seemed to me (as reader) quite impossible for the stage thrills me (as spectator) through and through—I am willing to take his word for it. What worries me is whether his presentment of life, in this series of 'climacteric moments,' is a generally true or false one. Evidently the author regards himself as an unflinching realist. 'Certain truths, as I have seen them, are here set down,' and he declines 'to be held responsible for anything that the characters may say or do.' I wonder whether Mr Viereck is indeed a dramatist who sees life without any bias whatsoever, and whose characters, and their actions and their sayings, are utterly uncoloured by his own idiosyncrasies. If so, he is indeed a treasure; for no similar treasure has yet been discovered, old though the art of drama is. But against our radiant discovery of Mr Viereck we shall have to set the sombre fact that the human race (at any rate in New York) is in a very bad way. Throughout these plays we are conscious that the various characters, especially the men, are chafing under the burden of existence. The poor dears are under-vitalised to a most alarming degree. And remember, we see them not in their dull routine from day to day, but just in those 'climacteric moments' which might be expected to brace them up a little. Nor does their creator ask us to take them as exceptional specimens. He presents them as quite normally full-blooded types of humanity. 'The expressions, Man-Animal and Woman-Animal,' says he in his preface, 'may jar on sensitive souls, who, rather than confront a problem in erotics, would follow the time-honoured policy of the ostrich; but I know of no combination of words equally decisive and indicative of my meaning.' The timid reader, thus admonished, takes his head out of the sand, and quakingly turns to confront the fierce breed of Man-Animals and Woman-Animals. And lo! were ever beasts so tame? Mr Viereck lustily cracks his whip, but there is hardly a sign of a growl or a jump in the whole sad menagerie.

In the play from which the book takes its name a Man-Animal with 'mystic eyes' has captivated a Woman-Animal. Having captivated her, he goes no further. She wearies of him, and introduces him to another Woman-Animal, whom he proceeds to captivate. He makes for her benefit various poetic speeches which she has already had repeated to her by the first Woman-Animal, and 'his voice intoxicates her like new wine.' 'Something like a magnetic fluid seems to emanate from him.' He straightens himself 'like a beautiful wild animal about to display all its charms before its mate. If he were a cat he would emit sparks at this moment.' 'His head sinks upon her bosom. The air is heavy, athrill with summer, drenched with fragrance. There is triumph in her eyes, weariness in his,' and, as the play ends at this point, we are to suppose that his weariness is the climax, and that the second lady's experience will tally with that of the first. In the next play, *The Mood of a Moment*, a man who 'half approaches the Aesthete, half the Blond Beast of Nietzsche' goes to a party, where he fascinates and is fascinated by a lady on whom falls the light of a red lamp, and on whose lap lies a single rose-leaf. He is torn by 'instincts that have slept a thousand years, primeval, cruel, irresistible.' He bids her go away with him instantly; but she, fearing a scandal, bids him come and call on her next morning. Late at night he sends her a letter. 'I tremble for the morning,' he writes. 'Love shall offer us the full measure of his ecstasies. We shall yield fully with all our being,' &c. He calls punctually at eleven next day, looks at her, tells her she has lost her attraction, and 'draws on one glove.' She, to recapture for him the mood in which he had fallen victim to her charm, orders the curtains to be drawn, and a red lamp to be lit, and presently re-appears in the dress which she had worn the night before, and with a red rose in her hand. He is very sorry, but it is no use. 'The moment a woman begins to love me, she has ceased to interest me.' She calls him brutal, and he retorts by asking whether she would love him if he were not so; and there the play ends. In the third play, *From Death's Own Eyes*, a young poet visits a middle-aged lady, late in the evening. She offers him a cocktail. 'Yes,' says he, 'I'll have one. But put two cherries into it. Then I can imagine them to be two lips reddened with sharp kisses.' She says that she likes to see a cigarette between his 'passionate boyish lips.' He returns the compliment by saying that a cigarette gives her 'a more demoniac air. Little tips of flame seem to quiver about your lips. One wonders then whether it is the reflection of your cigarette or your soul that dances there.' Such conversation as this is not usually compatible with any grosser kind of intercourse; and it is with surprise that we learn that the young poet has been less discreet than the heroes of the two previous plays. Fearing that he will be similarly indiscreet in relation to others, the lady drinks a glass of poisoned wine, and dies. Her niece enters, and the poet explains the situation to the girl, explaining to her also that love 'like a great flame' had visited him and the aunt, making their life 'splendid with immortal bloom.' The bloom, however, is not so immortal as he supposes; for when the curtain falls he has become acutely conscious of the attractions of the niece. He reappears in the fourth play, *A Question of Fidelity*. Years have elapsed. The niece has died, leaving a 'slightly anaemic' daughter, who dislikes young men because they 'never have but one thought—that of possession,' and who tells the poet that she is 'hardly fit to perform the degrading functions of the Mother-Animal.' She insists on marrying the reluctant poet. Subsequently she is unfaithful to him, and is much relieved when her confession moves him to explain that she can be untrue only if her lover represents to her exactly what he himself represents. 'Robert,' he adds, 'is a delightful boy, but he's not I; others will come, but they, too, will not be I.' So there's an end of *that* little fuss. The last play, *The Butterfly*, is described as '*A Morality*'; and here Mr Viereck drops his attitude of stern, unbending realist, and tell us, through a medium of fantasy, that life is (whether we be good or wicked) not worth living.

Well, if the world is actually as it appears to Mr Viereck, I am inclined to back his conclusion. But *is* the world like that, I wonder? Need I have implicit faith in the accuracy of the vision? Mr Viereck himself admits that people in real life do not talk as they do in his plays. He says that his characters use 'the language they *should* have used; and wherever their vocabulary did not suffice, it was the good fortune of the present writer to be able to assist them.' Yet, as you will remember, he had begun by declining to be held responsible for anything that his characters might 'say or do.' And, since he nevertheless accepts the responsibility for their sayings, may we not dare think that their doings, too, were rather evolved from his own brain than copied from real life? If Mr Viereck is an impartial realist, we must despair of New York. On the other hand, if he is a partial and imaginative person, moulding life according to his own ideas of what is amusing, we need not despair even of Mr Viereck. At the end of his volume (despite his express desire to 'muzzle that many-headed monster, the press') is an abundance of press-notices. And I learn from these that he is a very young man indeed. Youth is apt to be morbid; and I doubt not that Mr Viereck will in due course acquire an outlook worthy of his gifts.

[*13 July 1907*]

RE-ENTER MR JONES

The hypocrisy of the English nation is a favourite topic among foreigners. Among Englishmen it is rather an axiom than a topic. They take it for granted, as one of the necessary defects of their qualities, and are rather proud of the good humour with which, shrugging their shoulders, they plead guilty to it. Mr Henry Arthur Jones is exceptional in that he has never got used to the national failing. It haunts and appals and infuriates him yet. Many things swim in and out of the ken of this student of life; but one thing, English hypocrisy, is for ever fixed there in the centre of the foreground. In nearly all the plays he has written—in his comedies as well as in his serious dramas—English hypocrisy has been the objective of his wrath. In some of his comedies, certainly, the wrath has been toned down to seem like mere amusement. But after that strain it has always burst forth with double force. Mr Jones could hardly be so persistent if he were not upheld by a belief that the evil is remediable. And it may be that, some day, shamed beyond endurance, we shall all rush out into the public square and make a bonfire of our pet pretences. Meanwhile, H. A. Savonarola's latest sermon is entitled, with special directness, *The Hypocrites*, and is to be heard at the Hicks Theatre, where, I regret to say, the congregation seems rather delighted than abashed and abased.

Mr Jones's work is always notable for its vitality; and *The Hypocrites*, from the moment when the curtain rises, is as pungently and arrestingly alive as any play that he has written. The characters in it are none of them new as types: generically they are all familiar; but specifically they are vivid and interesting strangers, and we are excited by the prospect of seeing what will become of them. The story, again, is not in itself a new one, but (which is most that matters) it is told in a new way, with plenty of ingenious new twists. Always quick in coming to the point, Mr Jones at the very outset stokes his fire red-hot, and the 'hypocrites' are soon sizzling and spluttering on the grill. Mr Wilmore, lord of Weybury Manor, has been much shocked by the curate's suggestion that a certain farmer should not be compelled to marry a girl of bad reputation who is about to bear a child. Mr Wilmore can admit only one law in such matters; and the farmer must choose between matrimony and his farm. Thus it is embarrassing for Mr Wilmore when he learns that a quite respectable girl, Miss Rachel Neve, is about to bear a child to his son Lennard. Mr Wilmore's estate is heavily mortgaged, and the father of his son's fiancée is in a position to set all that right. The fiancée and her father are not less strict in their views of moral rectitude than is Mr Wilmore himself. Poor Mr Wilmore! There is a great deal of lying for him to do. Not George Washington himself was more in favour of the truth; and Mr Wilmore's lies are doubly painful for the fact that they are so likely to be found out. His one comfort is that he does not lie alone. His wife lies. His son (reluctantly, because he is in love with the girl to whom he is not engaged) lies. And the girl herself (because she does not want to stand in his way) lies. Everybody lies, except the curate. This inconvenient curate, privy to the truth, so loudly and unrelentingly tries to persecute them all into making a clean breast of it, that a general council has to be held in order to allay the suspicions of the fiancée's father. Everybody, for this gentleman's benefit, sticks gallantly to his or her lie. Not one of them (you can imagine how exciting the scene is on the stage) can be tripped up; and it seems as though the curate is destined to look a fool for the rest of his life. Evidently this is his own impression; for, just when, with bowed head, he is about to go forth into the world, he turns round and volleys a final and more than ever bitter jeremiad. Miss Neve utters a cry, and is about to swoon when Lennard Wilmore, stung with remorse, catches her in his arms and implores her forgiveness. Collapse of the other liars, fury of the fiancée's father, deep sigh of relief and tumultuous cheering from the audience. It is indeed a dramatic moment; but the 'thrill' is not so legitimately caused as the similar one in Mrs Dane's Defence. It was inevitable that Mrs Dane should at last break down under cross-examination, and the truth be out. But it is rather a fluke that the curate's parting shot at the Wilmores should cause Miss Neve to swoon; and rather a fluke that Lennard should be unable to take the swoon as all in the day's work which he has been so doggedly achieving. For my part I wish Mr Jones had withheld the thrill, and had baulked the audience of a happy ending. The preacher in him must have known that the play as a sermon against hypocrisy would be by far the deadlier if the truth were shown vanquished by the forces serried against it. There we should have had an ironic climax that would have made the congregation really uncomfortable. Moreover, the very playwright in Mr Jones must have perceived that the end of the third act, as it stands, has the disadvantage of not leaving any real material for a fourth act. Practically, the play is over. It is a matter of course that Lennard will now marry Miss Neve. Mr Jones, to make a fourth act, has to pretend that this conclusion is not foregone. He makes Mrs Wilmore almost persuade Miss Neve to give Lennard up, even now. It was natural enough that Miss Neve, being an unselfish creature, should give the young man up when she thought he was in love with his very lucrative fiancée. But, so soon as she knew that he was really in love with her, and that there was no brilliant alternative to his marrying her, she would inevitably have asserted her natural right to him. She would not have needed any stiffening from the curate. And thus, when the curate bursts again on the scene, and Mrs Wilmore turns on him in an agony of irritation at his perpetual interference, we are scarcely more tolerant of the good man than is Mrs Wilmore herself. 'Now my work in Weybury is done,' he cries as the curtain falls. But his work in Weybury had already been done when the curtain fell on the previous act.

It is owing to this fact, and not to any fault on Mr Leslie Faber's part, that the curate produces on me in retrospect a sense of extreme repletion. Mr Faber, indeed, was excellent, skirting the pitfall of priggishness into which most actors would have stumbled headlong. Mr J. H. Barnes as Mr Wilmore, and Mr Alfred Bishop as a vicar, were admirable, though both of them played rather too much 'for the laugh.' True, both their parts, as written, are tinged with caricature, and must accordingly be played with a measure of exaggeration. But there is no excuse for Mr Bishop accentuating the comedy of an exit by almost bumping his face against a door, nor for Mr Barnes toppling into a 'tableau' after the attempt to imprint a fatherly kiss on the brow of a young lady who has evaded it. Such effects as these cannot have been foreseen, could not be approved, by the playwright; and no laughs that they may win from dullards can drown the sighs heaved by people of average enlightenment. Mr Charles V. France, as the fiancée's father, was less redolent of Weybury than of Wall Street, and served as a pleasant reminder of the play's previous success in America. Miss Doris Keane, whose Americanism is of a less salient order, played Miss Neve with very real pathos. She has a peculiar mannerism of voice—a kind of wheezing peevishness—which might be annoying in other people, but in her is both attractive and effective. Mrs Leslie Faber, as the curate's wife, played naturally and well; and Miss Henrietta Watson, as the wife of a doctor, played an unpleasant part for all it was worth, but with an art that made it pleasant all the while. Miss Viva Birkett, as the fiancée, was so intent on giving a beautiful performance that all naturalness disappeared. She put a world of exquisite meaning into even the most matter-of-fact remarks. When, for example, the fiancée (in order that, for the playwright's convenience, Lennard might be left alone with the curate) said she would walk home alone—'it's only across two fields, and there's moonlight'—Miss Birkett's face and intonation suggested that she was about to float with angels towards the gates of Paradise. In acting, even beauty should not be allowed to trample on sense. That is a lesson which Miss Birkett will perhaps learn in time. I say 'perhaps' because I am conscious that Miss Marion Terry has not yet quite learnt it. Her Mrs Wilmore is harmoniously beautiful from first to last, but is not, like Mr Jones's Mrs Wilmore, a woman fighting grimly, unscrupulously, for an ugly end.

[*7 September 1907*]

'ATTILA'

Poetic drama is a thing fraught for us with dreadful associations. The sound of the words 'a tragedy in blank verse' conjures up a vision of dulness, of inept and stodgy striving after effect. The Victorian era brought forth many poets who had no instinct for the theatre, who had never been inside a theatre, and who yet doggedly wrote plays. These effusions were not (except in one or two unfortunate cases) performed; but they were published; and such people as thought it a duty to read them were thereby taught to regard

316

poetic drama as a thing accursed. There were also many playwrights who, without the slightest instinct for poetry, wrote plays in verse on this and that classic theme. These turgid fellows did even more than the undramatic poets to get poetic drama disliked. And yet, by some hideous irony, every youth who felt within himself the stirring of the literary instinct would inaugurate his career by writing a tragedy in blank verse. That fashion has passed. Ridicule killed it gradually. But the mischief done is not yet undone. We are not yet able to hear without a qualm the news that another poetic drama has been written; and it is with faltering steps that we go to see the thing played. Thus, outside his own breast, there can have been no inducement for Mr Laurence Binyon to write *Attila*; and in the breast of Mr Oscar Asche must have surged many doubts as to the wisdom of producing it. I suppose it was through a genuine delight in the play that Mr Asche derived the necessary courage. And I am glad to find that it was a genuine instinct for drama, not for poetry alone, that had been impelling Mr Binyon. I hope people will not be frightened away from this play by their general impression of its kind. I step forward to assure them that there is no danger.

The besetting sin of the Victorian school of poetic drama, verbosity, does not beset Mr Binyon. Always an austere poet, not letting his love of language run away with him and outstrip the sense to be expressed, Mr Binyon seems to be even more austere when he has the theatre to cope with. Instead of the Victorian poet's contempt for the theatre, he seems to have an almost excessive reverence. Though the language is never lacking in warmth to express the emotion of this or that crisis, one sometimes feels that there is hardly enough of it—that there might well be more lines. Take, for instance, the end of the second act, when Attila is aglow with the prospect of ruling Rome:

> 'Ildico, Ildico,
> Our horses' hoofs shall stamp the sacred street,
> And you shall sit throned on the Capitol;
> For pleasaunce walks, you shall have continents,
> For jewels, subject cities—   (*Trumpet again.*)'

Imagine how sorely the poet must have been tempted to develop this vision! And had he (in moderation) yielded, the dramatic effect would have been the stronger. All the same, I like him for the austerity with which he blows that 'trumpet again' to interrupt his own eloquence. It is a wholesome sign, this mistrust of words, this anxiety for constant action. And, though Mr Binyon lets alarums and excursions come slashing at his poetry, he does not sacrifice to them the development of the characters in his drama. With history he takes just such pardonable liberties as help him to make a dramatic juncture. According to history, Attila, at the time which Mr Binyon has selected, had lost his keenness for conquering Rome, and was no longer in command of an efficient army, and was willing to retire gracefully, and for good, on receipt of the princess Honoria as bride. Mr Binyon presents him as still in his heyday, and as seeing in the existence of Honoria (who loves him without having set eyes on him) the key to the Roman Empire. Rome is a leitmotive throughout the play, and everything hinges on Attila's passion to get there. History tells us that Attila, to pass the time before Honoria's arrival, married *puellam Ildico nomine, decoram valde.'* Of this shadowy young person Mr Binyon makes a high-souled Burgundian princess, torn between her love for her conquered nation and the love inspired in her by the overwhelming Attila. In this conflict it is the personal passion that triumphs. But Attila, though he loves Ildico, does not for a moment shrink from the idea of jettisoning her hereafter in favour of Honoria. Had Mr Binyon made Attila not know his own mind, and be distracted between love and ambition, he would have made his play even more dramatic than it is. He is to be praised for having resisted this temptation, and for having thus given us not the usual romantic version of a great soldier and diplomatist, but something like the actual person. Attila is not sentimental, and he means to throw aside Ildico (so soon as he shall have possessed her for a period) as calmly as he throws aside Kerka, his previous wife. Kerka becomes in Mr Binyon's hands an important figure, and a finely pathetic one. Gibbon speaks of the type of 'faded (Tartaric) matron who prepares, without a murmur, the bed which is destined for her blooming rival,' and Mr Binyon has elaborately dramatised that picture. His Kerka, however, does not submit 'without a murmur.' She not only murmurs: she it is who reveals to Ildico, on the bridal night, the treachery of the bridegroom. The last act of the play is well constructed as preparation for the death of Attila in the moment

of his seeming triumph. Our nerves have been well strained before
Attila and Ildico retire, at length, to the nuptial chamber. Mr
Binyon might have given an extra twist to the rack, might have
got even more dramatic effect than he does get from the climax, if
he had prolonged the interval before Ildico's reappearance. If the
stage had been full of the wedding guests, carousing in Attila's
honour, and if they had presently seen Ildico standing silent in the
door-way, I think the scene would have been still more terrible. The
death of Attila's third and last son, prophesied though it was by
the sooth-sayer, comes at this late moment as an irrelevance—as a
rather obvious device for pouring people on to the stage, there to
discover that Attila himself is dead. Better have left the stage
empty to the last, Ildico cowering and triumphing alone. However,
I hesitate to set up my dramatic imagination against Mr Binyon's—
especially as there is only a column between us! As an instance of
the strength of his dramatic imagination, I quote the first words
uttered by Ildico after the deed, while she is still alone: 'I struck so
hard, the hilt has hurt my hand.' In its simplicity, that is as bold
as it is right. And it shows that for Mr Binyon the deed had actually
been done—that he had seen the woman kill the man, or rather
had been the woman who killed the man. It shows, in fact, that he
is a true dramatist.

Mr Ricketts's scenery, glowing but austere, exactly fits the quality
of Mr Binyon's work. Mr Oscar Asche and Miss Lily Brayton, as
Attila and Ildico, were rapturously applauded by the audience on
the first night; and I have no doubt the critics have been congratu-
lating Mr Binyon on his luck in being interpreted by them. As a
matter of fact, neither of them was up to the mark. In poetic drama,
one essential is that the verse should be spoken rhythmically. Both
Mr Asche and Miss Brayton speak verse rhythmically; and for that
I am duly grateful to them. But the sense of the verse is essential
also, and the characters who speak it must appear to be human.
Mr Asche and Miss Brayton seem to me no more than mouthpieces
worked by some strange and potent mechanism of steel. From first
to last, Mr Asche is exactly the same. Attila was a fierce man, but
he was also subtle, and superstitious, and sensual, and many other
things; and Mr Binyon gives us the gamut of his moods. Mr Asche,
with distended mouth, spouts it all forth as if there were no variation whatsoever in the character. And Miss Brayton, with her

beautiful eyes distended, uses her beautiful voice with an equally disconcerting lack of flexibility. One longs for her voice to 'give' for a moment. One longs to see her blink once. One longs to catch from her a hint of Ildico. She is laudably in earnest; but she is not, in any possible sense of the word, acting.

[*14 September 1907*]

MAYFAIR WHITEWASHED

Raleigh! It is a name to conjure with. Hamilton! It stirs the blood like a bugle-note. In the council chamber, in the court, on the ensanguined field or quarter-deck, the Hamiltons have from time immemorial given a good account of themselves. The name of Raleigh, echoing down the ages, strikes the chords of all that is greatest and most gallant in our national genius. Nor could the continuity of English history be more inspiringly marked for us than by the fact that Raleigh's line has not ended. We rejoice that a Raleigh still ruffles it in our midst, a mettlesome fellow, with the blood of his great ancestor coursing hotly through his veins. He bears, as prefix, another name that is redolent of England's greatness —Cecil. But the massive wisdom of Lord Burleigh does not re-appear in him to chill us. He is essentially a throw-back to Sir Walter. And our hearts beat fast and fondly at sight of him fighting shoulder to shoulder with one of the perennial Hamiltons, and with his back to the wall of Old Drury, fighting like a demon, in defence of the class from which he and Henry his comrade have sprung.

For many a day it has been bitterly and brutally attacked, this class. Innumerable coarse fists have been shaken, coarse epithets hurled, in the blanching face of the aristocracy. The editors of the very newspapers that slavishly chronicle the movements of fashionable persons, describing most rapturously the beauty of the women's faces and costumes and pet-dogs and landaulettes, and proclaiming with greatest fervour the popularity and geniality of the men, are ever quick to open their columns to mordant homilies on the lightness and corruption of the people whom they so profitably exploit. They try to gloss over this discrepancy by hinting always that the 'smart' or hedonistic 'set' is but a coterie, consisting of a few persons who are eyed askance by the true leaders of fashion. But this pretence is too thin to be effective. It is too incongruous with what everyone knows. In attacking 'the smart set,' our editors and their contributors attack the most powerful and the most typical section of the aristocracy; and their lack of frankness saves no bones. Whether or not the bludgeonings be merited, is a question which I have no means of deciding. I have a vague impression that the upper class is not much more wicked than my own middle one. Many quite unfashionable people live beyond their means. This is proved by the reports of cases in the Bankruptcy Court. The reports of cases in the Divorce Court prove that many marriages between quite humble folk end badly. But to amass these proofs you have to keep a sharp look-out. Mr Brown and Mrs Jones are not intrinsically exciting. Their lapses are, therefore, not thrust under your eyes by the purists of Fleet Street. If a fashionable person appear in the Divorce Court or the Bankruptcy Court, the editors make broad their headlines and their phylacteries; and every clergyman who wants to get a cheap reputation for fearlessness dilates unctuously from his pulpit; and we offer up fervent thanks that we do not move in the circles we should like to move in. Yes, I am inclined to think that our conviction of the evil in high places is rather excessive in proportion to the evidence of it. And I am glad that at length from those high places two men have stood forth boldly to gainsay us. They might have carried the war into our own camp, lashing the vices of the middle class. But at present they confine themselves to the chivalrous task of championing beauty in distress. *The Sins of Society* they call their drama, thus sharply challenging that ecclesiastic whose voice has lately been so loud above all others in vituperation. A bold stroke of irony, this, and apt to make a false impression on the literal-minded. Only as the drama progresses do we realise that Mr Raleigh and Mr Hamilton are not traitors to their own order, but are showing how cruelly that order has been wronged.

They take no unfair advantage of the enemy. They do not set out to deny that the awful game of Bridge is played habitually by the élite. On the contrary, Lady Marion Beaumont, the central figure of their drama, is a confirmed player, and has lost so much more than she can pay that she is going to be posted as a defaulter at the Pontifex Club. But we are not allowed to lose sight of the fact that she is a pre-eminently good woman. She has a heart of gold. Could she but coin it, all her debts would be discharged, and a handsome fortune left over. In default of that, what is she to do? There again we must admire the fairness with which the authors present their case. They do not deny that Mr Noel Ferrers, though 'received,' is a bad man. He is, however, the one bad man in their drama; and he it is who tempts Lady Marion to raise the wind by swindling a pawn-broker. She recoils in horror, but, in the desperation of her need, yields. Who are we that we should judge her? Are not the agonies of her conscience an ample punishment? She remains a heroine; and besides, she has every reason to suppose that she will be able to pay the pawnbroker in due season. Even Ferrers has a good side to his nature. Hardened worldling, he is yet no epigrammatist, and delights in the wholesome old fashion of making puns. He tells an overdressed millionaire that 'diamonds are worn only at the opera, and there only by *grandes dames*—not by GRANDEES'; and many similar remarks by him indicate a well of crystal purity springing somewhere in his bosom. Besides, he loves *pour le bon motif* Lady Gwendoline Ashley; and it is mainly his wish to wed her that makes him anxious to get a hold over Lady Marion, her guardian. One of the gravest charges made by outsiders against the aristocracy is that even the débutantes are sophisticated, self-seeking. Lady Gwen-doline—to quote the immortal phrase of Tom Robertson—is 'as fresh as nature, and as artless as moss.' And she loves, to the full capacity of her young heart, Sir Dorian March, an almost penniless guardsman. It does our hearts good to see them together at Long-champs, which he declares to be 'just like Royal Ascot.' Here, too, are Mr Hogg and Lady Goldbury. In the philippics against 'the smart set' the millionaire has ever been damned as the most sinister and corrupting influence of all. In the breast of Mr Hogg, however, love blossoms like the rose, and Lady Goldbury is sun and rain thereof. Is she unworthy? Is she one of those luxurious, irresponsible creatures of whom we have heard so much? No; she revels, as you or I might, in a visit to Paris 'as an escape from the worries and annoy-ances' of domestic life. We have been taught to believe that even very great ladies are eager to know millionaires for the sake of their money. This is another bubble pricked by Mr Raleigh and Mr

Hamilton with a side-thrust of their rapiers. When Lady Goldbury asks Caroline Duchess of Danebury if she may present Mr Hogg, the Duchess says 'no' emphatically, and walks away. Mr Hogg, by the way, is most amusingly played by Mr Albert Chevalier, who, in the give-and-take of a company of mimes, shakes off that deadly deliberation that so mars him as a solo-ist. Miss Fanny Brough, as Lady Goldbury, contrives to make her dry crisp method almost as effective in the vast space of Drury Lane as was the fruity method of Mrs John Wood. As Lady Marion Beaumont, Miss Constance Collier excellently eradiates despair, determination, remorse, and various other emotions that are in the part. Theatrically, as well as morally, it is a fine part; and it could not be played better. Mr Lyn Harding and Mr Julian L'Estrange are respectively admirable as Mr Ferrers and Sir Dorian March. The latter is perhaps the more difficult part. I cannot help thinking that the authors, in writing it, have let their sense of truth be overborne by aristocratic prejudice. Sir Dorian seems to me *too* heroic a baronet. Classical students can, at a stretch, believe that the gods interfered, at this and that crucial moment, to save this or that hero in ancient Greece. But can we nowadays breed heroes of such a mould as to ensure continuance of those divine favours? When, on the moonlit towing-path at Windsor, Lady Marion, flying from the police, thrusts into the hands of Sir Dorian the box that 'contains a woman's honour,' and he bounds into a punt and seizes the punt-pole, would the gods *really* cause the landscape in the foreground to hurry towards the prompt-side of the stage and thus shroud his flight? And again, when Sir Dorian, still flying from justice, leaves Portsmouth on a troop-ship, and a Marconigram arrives from the Home Office, ordering that he shall be put under arrest and landed at the nearest port, would the gods *really* cause the stage to yawn, and all the well-drilled supers in khaki to be lowered gently into the bed of the ocean, and Sir Dorian alone to be saved, and allowed to live happily ever after with Lady Gwendoline? It seems to me unlikely. It seems to me that herein the authors have—without meaning to do so—over-stated their case for the aristocracy.

Nevertheless, the case is a strong one, nobly presented: a deafening counterblast to the myriad mean attacks that have been made. Henceforth the aristocracy will be for us the simple, homely, wholesome men and women that Mr Raleigh and Mr Hamilton have

revealed. I adjure the aristocrats to go and witness their own vindication. Do they need any extraneous inducement? 'The Management
desires to draw attention to the fact that a special feature is being
made of Tea and Cut Bread and Butter (sixpence inclusive) which
can be obtained in the Saloon during the Interval at Matinées.'

[21 September 1907]

AT THE SAVOY THEATRE

One day last week I passed through Sloane Square, and, gazing
at the Court Theatre, was affected somewhat as one is affected by
the sight of a ruined temple. Perhaps this is not quite fair to the
new manager, who has produced *Barry Doyle's Rest Cure*, a play
which I have not yet seen, but which seems likely to be popular.
For 'ruined temple' read 'temple now put to other uses.' I sighed
to think that the rites so fervently celebrated under the high-priest-
hood of Messrs Vedrenne and Barker would be celebrated here no
more. Already those rites have passed into history—literally so, for
Mr Desmond MacCarthy has written, and Mr A. H. Bullen has
just published, *The Court Theatre, 1904–1907*. Reading it, I find
myself for the first time patient of a theatrical record. Hitherto such
records have seemed to me very dull and superfluous, a stirring of
dry bones. But this particular record is all right. Sentiment clothes
and animates for me these particular bones. *1904–1907* is within
my own period; and the names of the various V-B plays re-create in
me the emotions that I had at the first performances. Having been
in the midst of it all, I am in a position to realise that what was
done at the Court Theatre was a really important and vital thing.
And I cannot help thinking that even if I belonged to the generation after next, Mr MacCarthy's book, even if I picked it up from
some old book-stall, would not leave me cold. When Mr MacCarthy
was writing weekly criticisms, I always turned to him as to one by
whom an austere sobriety of judgment was surprisingly expressed in
terms of youthful ardour. In this book he is as ardent as ever, and
as just; and his appreciation of Mr Shaw as dramatist seems to me
both the most suggestive and the soundest that has been done yet. I
am glad that the great doings at the Court Theatre have been

recorded by so admirable a critic; and I doubt not that the doings at the Savoy Theatre, where Messrs Vedrenne and Barker now are, will be not less worthy of enduring fame.

On Tuesday afternoon, as I entered this theatre, I had just the thrill of excitement that I used to have at the Court. The audience, the whole atmosphere, was the same as ever. I settled myself in my seat, rejoicing in the sense that nothing of the old magic had been lost in transit. But, as the afternoon progressed, my sense of well-being was not, I must admit, intensified by the actual play—Mr Galsworthy's *Joy*. We expect much of Mr Galsworthy; and he, in writing *Joy*, seems to have rested content in the knowledge that much would be expected. Anyhow, he gives us little. The fault of his theme? No; his theme is an obviously fertile one, whether for comedy or for tragedy. Mrs Gwyn, a woman of thirty-six or so, living apart from her husband, has fallen deeply in love with Mr Lever, a man of fashion, and a rather shady financier. The main complication of their liaison is Mrs Gwyn's daughter, Joy, aged sixteen or so, and passionately devoted to her mother. While the liaison has been carried on in London, Joy has been staying with her uncle in the country, and clamouring to be with her mother. Thus Mrs Gwyn is confronted with a sharp difficulty: how to avoid sacrificing from her life either the daughter whom she loves or the man whom she loves (and whom the daughter detests). Mrs Gwyn brings Mr Lever down to the uncle's house; and presently Joy discovers her guilty secret. Here again is an interesting crisis. Which feeling will prevail in Joy—her natural love for her mother, or her horror of what her mother is? Joy, of course, assails her mother with reproaches, and is, in her turn, reproached for cruelty—the cruelty of a girl who has had no experience of love. If this crisis in a girl's heart had been treated by Mr Galsworthy with the fulness that it deserves, what a fine play we should have had! As it is, the crisis does not occur till the play is nearly over, and is hustled out of the way in a most absurd fashion. Joy has inspired a passion in a peculiarly idiotic undergraduate, who, after her scene with her mother, philosophises to her in a peculiarly idiotic manner, and, in so doing, wins her heart. We are left to suppose that the well-brought-up Joy, having been kissed in the garden, is ready to take her mother to her arms and say no more about good and evil. Or perhaps Mr Galsworthy would repudiate that conclusion, saying that he had aimed at no conclusion whatsoever. Life is often very inconclusive, no doubt. But art is not life, any more than painting is photography; and an artist must so use his materials that some significance is forthcoming for us: he must, implicitly, interpret as well as portray. As a mere portrait, Joy is admirable; and one is prepared to take an interest in what befalls her. Mrs Gwyn and Mr Lever are not good even as portraits: they are figures so off-handedly adumbrated that we cannot really take an interest in the crisis that besets the former. Mr Galsworthy spends over-much time in portraying the mere 'feeding' parts, such as Colonel Hope, Joy's uncle; and, even when he has had his fill of the sardonic observation in which he excels, he still fights shy of his theme, introducing such expedients for laughter as would seem old-fashioned in a provincial farce. When, to pass the time for us, the parlour-maid waltzed round the garden, clasping a champagne bottle as a partner, I marvelled to think of Mr Galsworthy as heir of all the ages, in the foremost ranks of Vedrenne-Barkerism.

Scarcely less surprising than the parlour-maid is the elderly governess who utters a catch-phrase 'Poor creatures!' at brief intervals throughout the play. Time was, doubtless, when a catch-phrase was a sure means to mirth; but nowadays one does but sit in dread of its every recurrence. Despite her catch-phrase, the governess is evidently meant to be accepted as a lovable and impressive person, full of charity and mellow wisdom—the 'raisonneuse' of the play. 'Life's a funny thing,' says the Colonel. 'No,' says the governess, 'life's not funny, but men and women are.' To my objection that this means nothing Mr Galsworthy might reply that he meant it to be meaningless. But I suspect him of having thought it would impose on a theatrical audience. I am sure it does not impose on Miss Florence Haydon, who enunciates it. She is a very intelligent actress; and I believe that her air of melancholy resignation throughout the play is not assumed for, but is caused by, her part. Mr A. E. George is perfect as the Colonel, a seriously comic part which he never for one moment 'forces'; and Miss Henrietta Watson, as the Colonel's wife, perfectly portrays the 'managing' type. Miss Dorothy Minto, as Joy, distils the poetry of 'the awkward age' delightfully. Mr Lever, as impersonated by Mr Thalberg Corbett, is rather stiff. Stiffness is also a fault of Mrs Gwyn, as impersonated by Miss Wynne Matthison. Mr Galsworthy, I take it, intended Mrs Gwyn to be a woman swayed piteously by emotions. Such an actress as Miss Marion Terry would supply the requisite pathos. In Miss Wynne Matthison's hands Mrs Gwyn is evidently mistress of herself, strong and self-reliant, moving through life with the air of a highly-certificated teacher in a High School. Joy seems less like her daughter than her pupil. 'You overheard, and yet you were not spying?' says Mrs Gwyn to Joy; and we, seeing the compressed lips and astringent regard with which Miss Wynne Matthison awaits an answer to her question, can almost see the maps on the school-room wall. It is a question that exactly fits Miss Wynne Matthison's method. At all other times, her method is amiss. No doubt she feels the pathos of her part. But express it she cannot. Her face and her voice are not vehicles for emotion. She was very good as Everyman, chanting the lines with the rhythmic reverence which was all that was needed to get a touching effect from them. It is a pity that her success in that part should put her in the way of parts for which she has no aptitude.

[*28 September 1907*]

TWO PLAYS

I write of Mr Sutro's play *The Barrier*, and of Mr Anthony Wharton's play *Irene Wycherley*, both of which were produced last week; the one by Mr Frohman at the Comedy, the other by Miss Lena Ashwell at the Kingsway. The two things have a common denominator in their presentment of a lady whose past pitilessly pursues her. In *The Barrier* is Miss Margaret Verral, an actress who is engaged to be married to a younger son of the Duke of St Edmunds. When he learns that she was seduced in girlhood, he is so distressed and alienated that she can but release him from his engagement and sacrifice her prospect of social splendour. In *Irene Wycherley* figures a certain Mrs Summers, who has married after a not at all respectable career. Her husband is a headstrong person who has lived in mining camps; and he puts a bullet through the head of one of her previous lovers, and then another bullet through his own head. Thus do Mr Wharton and Mr Sutro coincide in the moral that for a woman bygones cannot be bygones. For the rest, the two plays have little in common, and I must consider them separately. Their titles are significant of their difference. *Irene Wycherley* is aptly named, as being mainly the study of a character. *Margaret Verral* would have been a misleading title for the other play. Mr Sutro has not set out to analyse his lady very minutely: his aim was to make her the pivot of an exciting comedy. This aim he has well achieved: we are kept interested from first to last—no, not quite to last, as I shall presently suggest. Mr Marrillier, the man who seduced Margaret Verral, has returned to England after a long absence, and has become engaged to be married to Lady Alma, daughter of the Duke of St Edmunds. It is, of course, a painful coincidence for Margaret that her prospective sister-in-law should become the wife of her own seducer. It is not, however, as she is a sensible woman, a 'barrier' to her marriage. She herself, being a kind woman, becomes the 'barrier' to Lady Alma's marriage; for Lady Alma feels an instinctive repulsion from Marrillier, and cannot bear him to come near her. Her engagement has been forced on her by her relations. She confides her abhorrence to Margaret, who determines to rescue her. And thus we have an exciting conflict. Marrillier says that if Margaret tries to prevent his marriage, he will promptly prevent Margaret's. Will Margaret, when it comes to the point, sacrifice herself or Lady Alma? It comes to the point in the third act. The Duke and a great bevy of relations are mustered, and in their presence the battle is fought to an exciting finish. The whole scene is prepared and worked up and carried through with all Mr Sutro's keen sense for drama. Marrillier, having rounded on Margaret, is of course sent to the right about. Margaret is going the same way, when the Duke, a man of common-sense and humanity, declares that all shall be forgiven and forgotten; and on that scene the curtain falls. Of course the play cannot end there. Dramatists of a bygone day, with their hearts set on happy endings at all hazards, might have ended it there, asking us to take it as a matter of course that there would be marriage bells for Margaret. Mr Sutro, of course, will not thus evade the issue. He has presented Lord Ronald as a quite ordinary, unimaginative young man; and it is by no means sure that this young man will be able to take the broad view taken by the Duke; and it is, therefore, on him that the end of the play must depend. The material for the fourth act is a scene between him and Margaret; but this is not material enough for a whole act; and so

Mr Sutro re-introduces at the beginning of the act the Duke and other characters, who are no longer vital to the drama. Thus we have a sense of anti-climax, which lingers to mar our pleasure when the vital scene is at length enacted. It is an admirably conceived scene, one of the best scenes that Mr Sutro has given us. But it ought surely to have been introduced at the end of the third act, there to complete the play. We could well dispense with the final scene of the play as it stands—a scene in which it is foreshadowed that Margaret will some day give her hand to Captain Erquen, a friend who has steadfastly loved her for many years. Margaret is a charming person, but whether her future is to be a charming one or not is no concern of ours. We are concerned with her only down to the moment when she releases Lord Ronald from his engagement.

She is excellently played by Miss Marie Tempest, whom we have come to regard as one of the very few English actresses equipped for emotion. In her passages of comedy she is still rather apt to force the note—to strive after a too sharp effect; but there is no self-consciousness in her pathos; and she moves us as we can be moved only by an actress who is moved herself. Mr A. E. Matthews, as Lord Ronald, is as life-like as ever; and Mr Dawson Milward, as the Duke's eldest son, has a delightful part, well within the scope of his talent, and plays it admirably. Mr Eric Lewis is the Duke; and in the scene where he has to assert a sonorous patriarchal authority, fixing Mr Marrillier with his eye, rebuking him in the name of humanity, and ordering him out of the house, he seems to be somewhat embarrassed by the unwonted duty thrust on him. In all the other scenes, where he has merely to be light and whimsical, genial and charming, his mastery is as perfect as ever, and as delightful. Miss Lillah McCarthy is to be congratulated on her honest effort to be forbidding as the Nonconformist wife of the eldest son. It is not her fault that her success is only partial. On the other hand, it is surely a fault in Mr Allan Aynesworth that he cuts so pre-eminently dashing and graceful a figure as Captain Erquen, the unloved 'big dog,' the Dobbin of the play.

I am told that *Irene Wycherley* is the first play by Mr Wharton that has been produced. But I suspect it is by no means the first play that he has written. If it is indeed a maiden essay, the technical excellence of it is certainly remarkable. Even if it were technically feeble, one would warmly welcome Mr Wharton for sake of his strong sense of character, and would congratulate Miss Lena Ash-well on her courage in inaugurating her management with a play that panders not at all to the public's distaste for grim reality. Irene Wycherley is a woman who has for three or four years been living apart from her husband, on account of his brutality. Meanwhile, a young man named Henry Chesterton has fallen in love with her, and she has formed a decided affection for him, though she does not encourage him to assert himself. She hears that her husband has met with an accident in the shooting-field, and that he will be blinded for life; and she feels it is her duty to return to him. He, quite frankly, hates her; but she manages to remain with him and help to nurse him. When, however, he is mollified towards her by his sensuality, she recoils from him by reason of her physical horror of him. It is then that he invites Mr and Mrs Summers (the people mentioned by me at the beginning of this article) to stay in his house. She, knowing Mrs Summers's antecedents, tells her she must go; and then occurs the aforesaid double tragedy, whereby Irene becomes a free woman, and will presumably marry Mr Chesterton. Personally, I think this dénouement is rather arbitrary—a shirking of the issue. Irene should have been left to fight out the conflict in herself between her affection for Mr Chesterton and her feeling that it is her duty to remain with her blind husband, and to over-come her abhorrence. True, the blind husband is such an unmiti-gated ruffian that the outcome of Irene's inward conflict would have been rather a foregone conclusion. And, for that reason, Mr Wharton ought to have mitigated the man's ruffianism. The story, as it stands, is admirably told; and I do not, of course, suggest that it is an impossible story. I only object that it is not an inevitable story, such as would alone have been worthy of its author's talent for character-drawing. Miss Lena Ashwell, as Irene, has never had a better part, and has never, I think, played so well. In moments of tense emotion she has always been good, sometimes great; but in the intervals between the crises she has often seemed rather absent-minded, rather crude in execution. As Irene, she is unwaveringly good throughout. Mr Norman McKinnel plays the husband, and plays him ruthlessly well; but how he must long to have for once a part in which his natural kindness and gentleness could assert them-selves! Won't some one take a theatre and produce *The Vicar of Wakefield*, with Mr McKinnel in the title part? Mr C. M. Hallard, as Mr Chesterton, gives a very pleasant, sincere performance. I have only one fault to find with it. Doubtless, when a man sits down, even in moments of great emotion, he instinctively parts his coat-tails and pulls up his trousers. But on the stage some concessions have to be made to effect. And I submit that the effect of Mr Hallard's performance in this play is marred by his never remembering to forget to part his coat-tails briskly and briskly pull up his trousers.

[*19 October 1907*]

'THE MOLLUSC'

Mr Hubert Henry Davies always seemed to me a person born to write for the stage; but what he wrote for it fell short of impressing me. I admired his ease in technique; but the ideas and the characters for which that technique was the vehicle seemed to me rather nugatory, and I have but a faint recollection of them. I was always wishing myself a magician, so that I might transfer from Mr Davies his natural skill into one of those good thinkers and observers who ought to be enriching dramatic literature, but have no instinct for the theatre. I see now that this would have been a somewhat unscrupulous thing for me to do. And perhaps the awakening of my conscience is due to the fact that Mr Davies has now proved that he can enrich dramatic literature on his own account. *The Mollusc*, at the Criterion Theatre, is truly delightful. There are but four persons in it; and one of them is an old theatrical friend, and another is not particularly interesting; but the other two are so alive, and so amusingly alive, that we are fascinated from first to last. In them, and in the story that springs from their characters, there is but that touch of exaggeration which is needed to make actuality carry across the footlights. And, though we are smiling or laughing without intermission throughout the play, not once is the fun accidental or irrelevant: it springs always from the inward quality of the characters.

Mrs Baxter, the central figure of the play, is more than a real person: she has the dignity of a human type. We have all met her again and again. Nay, there are traces of her in us all. And the wonder is that no one before Mr Davies has (so far as I know) projected her on to the stage. In the brute creation a mollusc is a shell-fish that firmly adheres to a rock, doing nothing but adhere, while the tide ebbs and flows above it. Thus, in the human race, a mollusc is a person who will not lift a little finger to perform any duty which some one else might be persuaded to perform for her—I may say 'her' for sake of convenience, because, though the human mollusc is often masculine, Mr Davies happens to have portrayed it in the person of Mrs Baxter. It is not merely duties that the mollusc seeks to evade, often expending in the process of evasion far more force and will than would be necessary to the performance of those duties. To any pleasure that needs exertion, and especially to any pleasure that involves the slightest risk and has not already passed the test of constant repetition, the mollusc turns implacably its crustacean back. The mollusc knows the rock, which is smooth of surface, and safe, and quite good enough for the mollusc. A dismal existence? Well, that is 'all according.' Some people are condemned to a life of unpleasant routine; and it is natural that they should imagine routine to be an unpleasant thing in itself. It is natural that they should suppose the secret of existence to be mutability, the fact of never knowing, from day to day, what strange adventure shall befall. Yet even these people, for the most part, would not care to risk, if it were offered to them, the opportunity of gambling with fate instead of submitting to the safe though unpleasant mode of life which fate has proposed to them. Take now the case of a person in the circumstances of Mrs Baxter. These circumstances are decidedly pleasant. She is fond of her husband, with whom she lives in a very pretty house in the country. She is fond of books and flowers, and fond of her little daughter. Living peacefully and happily thus, she has come to have a horror of anything likely to disturb the current of her life. She has got just what she wants, and every day she looks forward to to-morrow as a replica of to-day. A person of restless disposition would, doubtless, be bored, and would be for trying a few experiments. Not so a restful person, such as Mrs Baxter, amenable to the force of habit, and finding that constant repetition intensifies rather than diminishes the charm of simple pleasures. Really, I think there is a good deal to be said for Mrs Baxter's philosophy of life. She does not herself formulate this philosophy for us. She is much too passive for that. It is only through her behaviour that we read her meaning. And it is on her brother's efforts to rouse her that the comedy hinges. Energetic though this brother is, buoyant and 'hustling' after an adventurous life in America, he finds himself generally outmatched by Mrs Baxter's quiet determination not to be deflected. She will *not* do anything for herself that can be done by anyone else; and, above all, she will *not* be a party to cheerful innovations in the routine of the household. There is an idea of a picnic. The brother urges the husband to persuade Mrs Baxter to come. The husband (a beautifully drawn character, sometimes outwardly attracted by the active governess, but always a slave inwardly to the passive tyrant, his wife) mumbles that it would be hopeless to attempt such persuasion. He asks how he could possibly begin. The brother (Sir Charles Wyndham) advises him to rush into the boudoir, throwing up his arms and executing a little dance and crying 'We're going for a picnic—a picnic!' It is beautiful to see Sir Charles suiting the action to the word, subtly acting the man who is not an actor, overdoing the joyous gesture, and vacantly continuing it when its significance has had time to evaporate. And it is a joy to see the phlegmatic husband (Mr Sam Sothern) making an effort, as he passes gloomily upstairs to the boudoir, to reproduce the gesture. Presently is an exquisite scene, in which Mrs Baxter, with resolute sweetness and vagueness, with a will of wax-like iron, evades the proposed picnic. In such scenes the first two acts of the comedy abound. At the end of the second act is an incident that paves the way for a more definite exposition of 'molluscry.' The governess is in distress; and Mr Baxter, much moved, gives her a caress which she accepts as fatherly. Mrs Baxter surprises this caress. When the curtain rises on the third act she has taken to her bed. Poor thing, her routine has been horribly interrupted. Complete prostration is her only possible course. Therefore, of course, she must be nursed. And there is no one who understands how to nurse her so well as the dear governess. Therefore the dear governess must be retained at all hazards. The brother pooh-poohs the husband's conviction that Mrs Baxter is in grave danger. Observe the glad, fixed, fatuous smile of Mr Baxter as he slowly carries his wife downstairs, having persuaded her that a little change of scene might do her good. Her brother stokes the flickering fire of her jealousy, which blazes brightly up when her husband twists his ankle and wishes to be nursed by no one but the governess. Mrs Baxter loses all her lethargy: she, and none other, shall be the nurse. The brother is told that he has wrought a miracle, and we are just beginning to deplore a conventional and untrue ending, when he expresses a doubt as to whether the miracles, in the days of miracles, were always permanent in their effects, and thus brings the comedy to a perfect close.

Often as I have seen and shall see again Sir Charles Wyndham in just such a part as that of Mrs Baxter's brother, I cannot and never shall be able to weary of his perfection. The vitality, as well as the subtlety, of his art makes the thing ever new. Mr Sam Sothern, with his fine humour and restraint, makes Mr Baxter as real and ridiculous a person as Mr Davies conceived for us. Miss Elain Inescort is agreeable as the governess. Unluckily, Miss Mary Moore was out of the bill on the day when I went to the Criterion. Her understudy was by no means a duffer; indeed, she was quite a clever actress; but she was, naturally, nervous; and perfect calm and ease, complete absence of apparent endeavour, are needed for the right rendering of Mrs Baxter.

[*2 November 1907*]

'PETER PAN' REVISITED

It is now as a matter of course that *Peter Pan* is revived for Christmas. One would have thought that by stretching out these tentacles on eternity the play had given proof enough of the esteem it is held in. Mr Frohman, however, is directing its attention to infinity, as well. He has made it spread itself out from the auditorium into the vestibule. The ordinary box-office has been removed, and you now book your seats through a window of Wendy's cottage. Dear sweet little Wendy, for whom we all have such a warm corner in our hearts! How 'awfully fascinating,' as she would say, her cottage looks here! See, it is all complete, with a boot instead of a knocker on the door; and there is smoke coming out through the crownless top-hat that serves as chimney. Real smoke? No, dear, not real smoke. That would make the poor fairies cough. It is steam, dear; the same as you see coming out of the puff-puff when you go to the country to stay with your grandmother. Yes, darling, grandmothers are mothers, too. Crying? Yes, of course I am crying. Didn't you hear me use the word 'mothers'? But see, I am smiling through my tears. I am nothing if not whimsical. There! Slip your little hand into mine while I speak to the nice kind gentleman through Wendy's window . . .

Personally, I cannot help feeling rather sorry for this nice kind gentleman. His new premises must be sadly inducive to self-consciousness. Might he not feel more at home if the management dressed him up as Wendy and had done with it? I daresay this step is already under consideration. Next year, doubtless, the commissionaires will be 'presented' by Mr Frohman as pirates and Redskins; and Mr Frohman himself, attached to a copper wire, will fly hither and thither overhead, in the costume of Peter Pan.

Are such adventitious aids really needed? I should have thought the play was, commercially, quite well able to look after itself. Written ostensibly to amuse children, it was written really to touch and amuse their elders. If children were people of independent means, accustomed to book seats for themselves, and free to pick and choose just whichever entertainments gave them the greatest pleasure, the Duke of York's Theatre would not, I fancy, be quite so well packed as it now is. Or rather, there would be more room for the adults to flock into. If there is one thing which the average child has not, and the average adult has, that thing is sentimentality. Mr Barrie's sentimentality, you will agree, is far more intense than that of the average adult. It is the sentimentality of hundreds of adults rolled into one: the sentimentality, in fact, of a huge crowd. You can make a crowd cry, just as you can make it laugh, at things which would affect not at all any one isolated unit of that crowd. If Mr Barrie led you or me aside to have a good long talk about maternity, I doubt whether either of us, after a while, would be unwilling to change the subject. But neither you nor I constitute a theatrical audience. To you and me a host of other folk must be super-added. When that is done, our receptivity goes up by leaps and bounds, and Mr Barrie cannot dilate too long on maternity to hold our attention, or *too* tenderly to keep us in tears. But the children? Are they, too, rapt and tearful? To a certain extent, I daresay, they are affected by the magnetic currents in the adult crowd around them. But I suspect their thoughts of straying. And is there ever, I wonder, any appreciable moisture in their eyes? I hope not. When children cry, they cry because they are unhappy. Savages, they have not acquired the art of being sentimental. They are not in a position to appreciate the central beauties of *Peter Pan*. The tears and fears of Mrs Darling, the yearning of the pirates for Wendy to mother them, the delight of the poor lost children at having Wendy as mother in the 'Never, Never, Never Land'—all this sort of thing leaves cold their savage breasts. They cannot see themselves as others see them, cannot recognise in Wendy and Peter creatures of like passions with themselves. The curtain that falls in the entr'actes purports to be a vast sampler, worked by Wendy; and among the devices thereon are the following inscriptions: Dear Hans Christian Andersen, Dear Charles Lamb, Dear Robert Louis Stevenson, Dear Lewis Carroll. Wendy, you perceive, is no savage. Her appreciation of *Alice in Wonderland* is no evidence, of course; for that book is not an explicitly sentimental one—far from it. But she has not a word to say for the straightforward Grimm; Hans Andersen, the tender allegorist, is the man for her. And the elaborate naïvetés of the *Child's Garden of Verses* have enchanted her. And she dotes on 'Dream Children.' I am sure 'Dear Charles Lamb' would, as in the case of someone else, have wished to feel her bumps. Her bump of precocity must be the size of an orange; and it is strange that she ever has any leaning towards Redskins and pirates. I wonder, by the way, whether the children of this generation had ever heard of Redskins and pirates until they were taken to see Mr Barrie's play. The innumerable ladies and gentlemen who write books for children are much too preoccupied by the children themselves to take thought of those outlandish and outmoded adults. Of course these books are not read, or are read without pleasure, by children: it is the adults who devour them, while the children satisfy their own romantic cravings with the tit-bits of information purveyed by the popular press, opening wide their eyes and thrilling at the thought that if all the pins that are daily dropped in the streets within the four-mile radius were joined together lengthwise they would reach from London to Milan. What distinguishes Mr Barrie from the hosts of other people writing 'for' children is that he has not utterly forgotten his own childhood, and is able to bolster up the pretence that he is writing 'for' them by introducing now and again such things as really do delight them. All the pirate scenes in *Peter Pan* are of a kind to delight children. Especially the crocodile's slow, unrelenting pursuit of Captain Hook appeals to them, as combining the elements of terror and of moral edification—two elements very dear, believe me, to children. But even in these scenes Mr Barrie slips into indulgence of maturity, as when Hook cries 'Split my infinitives!' and in Hook's dying speech about the vanity of human ambition—'all mortals envy me,' &c. It is for such touches of wayward humour that Mr Barrie's work is beloved by me. In the theatre, of course, I weep with the best of them about darling Mrs Darling's tears and fears and boys and joys. But in the solitude of my study, cut off from the magnetism of the adult crowd, and reviewing the play soberly as a critic, I become even as a little child.

Several differences have been made in the play since I saw it three —or four?—years ago. The Mermaids' Lagoon is new to me, and seems rather dull—perhaps because of the funereal darkness in which it is set before us. A more palpable gain is the disappearance of the squaw whose passion for Peter struck a decidedly false note. Miss Pauline Chase, as Peter, gambols about very prettily and light-heartedly, but of the soul of Peter gives us nothing. Miss Nina Boucicault was eerie and emotional, thus fulfilling the author's intention. Peter is 'the boy who wouldn't grow up,' for the simple reason that he couldn't, being grown up already. Miss Chase is too near her own childhood to realise the part, and plays it as any child would play it, with a wholesome, high-spirited blankness. Miss Hilda Trevelyan must be older than she looks, for she plays Wendy with a sensitiveness of art that utterly belies her air of childhood. Mr A. E. Matthews succeeds Mr Gerald du Maurier as Mr Darling, and the part seems (you can hardly wonder) to make him peevish. He should have been cast for the part of Mr Darling's elder son. The gentleman who plays that part has all the manner and appearance of a rising politician, and thus the scene in which he plays at 'fathers and mothers,' and the scene in which he rebels against having a bath, rather miss the mark. Mr Robb Harwood succeeds Mr du Maurier as Hook, and is even better than Mr du Maurier, who clowned the part admirably, but did not, as does Mr Harwood, make of it a distinguished and haunting grotesque, a grotesque of sombre beauty, worthy of the sombre and beautiful costume that Mr Nicholson designed for it.

[*28 December 1907*]

'A COMEDY OF SENTIMENT'

We were all very much gratified to find, last Wednesday night, at the Royalty Theatre, that Mme Albanesi does not despise the stage. When novelists dip into dramaturgy, almost always they are careful to leave behind them whatsoever good qualities they may possess, for the purpose of not wasting good material. They are convinced that nothing which is not quite obviously foolish has the ghost of a chance of succeeding in a theatre. I do not say they have no reason for this faith. Many twaddling plays have been lucrative, and much money has been lost over good work. But there are degrees of twaddle. And the novelist-playwright sets to work, almost always, too low down in the scale—lower than the point at which the play-going public feels happy and comfortable. And thus, after the first act of *Susannah—and Some Others*, there was an atmosphere of cheerful pride throughout the auditorium. We inflated our chests, nodding and smiling jauntily to one another, as much as to say 'Mme Albanesi does not despise us.' She has given us, indeed, of her best. In her novels she has the knack of projecting characters which are pleasantly natural, ladies and gentlemen (ladies, at any rate) who are very agreeably alive; and she has the knack of writing dialogue which is always light, fresh and felicitous. In her re-creation of Susannah for the foot-lights, she has not husbanded these good knacks. Nor has she (as is the way of novelists) proceeded on the arrogant assumption that every member of the audience will have read and remembered the book dramatised, and that the story need not, therefore, be told with any straining after lucidity. Nor has she refused to sacrifice many features of the book which would not help (and so would mar) the play. Much of her play is, as I shall suggest, not dramatic. But to her credit be it put that she has realised the difference between the narrative form and the dramatic form, without supposing that playgoers are an inferior race as compared with readers of novels. The outcome is a very pleasant piece of work indeed. Not *too* pleasant, as Mme Albanesi's description of it, 'A Comedy of Sentiment,' might incline you to fear. It is not sugary. There is nothing remotely idyllic about its main motive: the sacrifice of a young girl's dignity to the convenience of her married sister. Lady Corneston has been flirting with a young man named Adrian

Thrale, and has compromised herself with him in the eyes of her
husband, Sir Edmund, who threatens her with a judicial separation.
Terrified, she conceives a happy thought to set her husband's mind
at rest. If Adrian were engaged to be married to her younger sister,
Susannah, Sir Edmund could have no more to say, and would look
distinctly foolish into the bargain. It is a pity that Adrian and
Susannah are not in love with each other—have not even met.
Never mind: she will bring them together, and will work on them
separately to induce them to pretend to be engaged until the fuss
shall have blown over. Susannah is devoted to her, and very young:
she won't like it, but she will give in. And Adrian will have to
give in, of course. Lady Corneston is a charming creature in dire
distress, and surely enough, and soon enough, the two young people
are prevailed on to obey her. At first, naturally, they hang back.
The situation is equally unpleasant for them both. But how can
they refuse to accept it? At the end of the first act, we see Lady
Corneston coming down the staircase, with her arm round Susannah's waist, to announce to the party assembled that dear Susannah
and Adrian are engaged to be married. It is an effective scene–the
lamb led to the slaughter, with another lamb thrown in. It is a
situation that has been well led up to; and a situation pregnant with
irony for the immediate future. Adrian's mother is overjoyed.
Adrian has been 'wild' and 'weak,' and marriage with a bright and
innocent young girl is the very thing for him. Besides, Mrs Thrale
has taken a great fancy to Susannah, and regards her as an ideal
daughter-in-law. She is full of plans for the welfare of the two young
people. Altogether, she is a splendid medium for dramatic irony. Or
rather, she would be if we were not so sure that her prognostications,
based on false evidence, were nevertheless perfectly correct. There,
indeed, we touch the flaw that vitiates the whole structure of the
play. We have, from the outset, a foregone conclusion. We know
that the two young people will presently discover an absolute
affinity. Their behaviour, when they first meet, without knowledge
of the use to which they are destined, suggests love at first sight. It
is only the awkwardness of the ensuing situation that obscures their
feelings; and through that veil, very soon, those feelings shine unmistakably forth. Oh yes, of course the engagement will end in
matrimony. Let them be quick and perceive what is so patent to all
of us. But then the play could not fill the evening bill. Evidently

there is to be a misunderstanding. It is duly effected, this mis-understanding, by a jealous woman; and Susannah says she despises Adrian, who thereupon says he will give her reason to despise him, forcibly kisses her, and rushes away. Ten months elapse before the happy ending. Retardation of this kind is not dramatically effective. We are moved at sight of people struggling to overcome obstacles which are inevitably there; but not at sight of people kept waiting until certain obstacles which have been foisted in shall duly have been removed. Mme Albanesi has foisted in an obstacle merely to prolong the play; and, as we know that in due course she is going to remove it, our emotions are not touched: we are only conscious of a demand on our patience. This demand we readily meet, having regard to the goodness of Mme Albanesi's dialogue, and the vivid-ness of her characters—that is, of her female characters.

I have yet to see a woman's play in which the male characters shall seem real and vital. As portrayers of a sex not their own, men have a decided advantage over women. I have seen various plays in which the heroines were as real and vital as though they had been evolved from the brains of women. The heroines, I say advisedly. For heroines are not apt to be either very young girls or old ladies: their time is in the prime of womanhood. On his portrayal of old ladies and very young girls the male dramatist is seldom to be felicitated: these figures come out pale and perfunctory—figures drawn from casual observation, without real interest. And this is where the female dramatist is a little recompensed for her failure to portray a man at any moment of his course between the cradle and the tomb. She has been a girl herself, and will probably become an old lady; and these two personal facts (she is ever personal) are enough to give her an understanding of old ladies and young girls. Susannah, as presented by Mme Albanesi, is not the mere 'ingénue' that a male dramatist would have palmed off on us: she is a live girl; and to this fact is partly due the success which Miss Nina Sevening makes in the part. And Mrs Thrale is an old lady drawn with real insight and sympathy: Miss Florence Haydon, who plays her, does not, as usually she does, have to rely solely on her talent for saying things in an amusing manner. Not less true a character is Lady Corneston herself. She is admirably played by Miss Gertrude Kingston, but is not (unfortunately for Miss Kingston) so good a part as she is a character. Almost throughout the play, it is but in one mood that we see her: the apprehensive, distracted mood, the verge of hysterics. Miss Kingston portrays this one mood with much elasticity and variety, but cannot altogether banish the impression of monotony. Mr Dawson Milward, as Adrian, has very flimsy material to work on, and works very badly on it. The fault is not his, but that of Nature, who has not conferred on him the air of lightness and impulsiveness which is needed to carry off Mme Albanesi's conception of a wayward young man. From the moment when he comes carefully down the staircase, on his way to bathing in the river, with a towel neatly arranged over his shoulder, he is suave, polished, honeyed, exemplary (one would vow) in every relation of life. Mr Fisher White, as Sir Edmund Corneston, has that most 'ungrateful' of all parts—a bore who is meant to appeal to the sympathy of the audience. Mr White does not, of course, dare to be funny; but the more steadfastly earnest and sympathetic he is, the further are we from tolerating poor Sir Edmund.

[25 January 1908]

'HER FATHER'

Human nature is a notoriously inconsistent thing; but, though you cannot often foresee the vagaries of your friends, you can usually account for them after their manifestation. Now and again, however, you happen on a case which utterly baffles you. Such a case came within my ken the other day. In stating it here, to see what you can make of it, I suppress the names of the parties, so as to mitigate my indiscretion. A, then, is a middle-aged man, who married about nineteen years ago. B, his wife, presently bore him a child, who is now a grown-up girl, and whom I must call by that somewhat unromantic name, C. Despite this pledge of their mutual love, the marriage was an unhappy one. A was a man of the 'irresistible' type, and it was not enough for him that B had failed to resist him. He went about testing the resistance of many other women, instead of earning an honest livelihood. He was, in fact, very lazy and selfish, and, despite his charm of manner, his wife presently ceased to regard him as irresistible, so far as she was concerned, and lost all patience with him, and was relieved when he disappeared into the void. Years elapsed, during which she lived modestly but not unhappily in a small flat in Hampstead, under a vague impression that he was dead and would trouble her no more. Picture her dismay when, the other day, she heard that he had just succeeded to a title and to a large fortune, and that he insisted that her beloved C should spend one month in every twelve under the paternal roof. It seemed to her very strange, as well as cruel, that he should make this demand. Had his whole character changed? I happened to know, as a matter of fact, that his character had not changed at all. At the moment when he made the demand, he was living in a particularly rowdy set, and 'going the pace' in a manner which ill befitted his middle age. Thus, at the time, his demand seemed to me even stranger than it seemed to his unhappy wife. I should have been hardly more puzzled if he had demanded restitution of conjugal rights. B herself in perpetuity (thought I, knowing the man and his way of life) were hardly a more inconvenient burden than C for an annual month. An elderly wife may be kept in the background, whereas a marriageable daughter is a salient fact, not to be blinked. An elderly wife, moreover, does not necessarily 'date' her husband, and so diminish his power of general attraction, whereas a marriageable daughter does so inevitably. I rummaged my wits in vain for any plausible explanation of A's amazing desire to harbour the offspring without whom he had existed happily for so long, and whose unwilling advent could but be for him an occasion of acute embarrassment. Had B died, leaving C on his hands, I should have smiled, picturing his despair, hearing his petulant maledictions, and opining that it served him right. But that he should go out of his way to bring the misfortune on himself plunged me into a state of bewilderment in which I beg you to help me, reader, if you can. You say you don't believe a word of my story? You are right: it is a fabrication from beginning to end. Mr Michael Morton, working on material evolved from the fond brains of Messieurs Guinon and Bouchinet, is the fabricator. And I have ventured here to present the thing as a fact of real life in order that the absurdity and impossibility of it may be thrown into relief. However absurd and impossible be the story of a play, people are apt to 'swallow' it because it is told in a theatre. I am not one of that easy-going majority. I do not leave my common-sense in the cloak-rooms of theatres. *Non credo quia theatrale.* And such a story as that which is the basis of *Her Father* I reject as scornfully and quickly when it is told to me in the Haymarket Theatre as I should if any casual liar told it to me outside. If there were more playgoers like me, clever men like Mr Michael Morton would be less apt to waste their cleverness, I think.

It is possible to build finely on rotten foundations. A play with a rotten basis may be an interesting play. *Her Father*, for instance, might have been quite interesting if the authors had chosen to make it so. Irene Forster (the aforesaid C) is quite a promising figure. More than one good novel has been made out of the difficulties besetting a child who lives partly with one and partly with the other of two mutually antagonistic parents. The most natural thing is that the child should be fond of both parents, and the more evenly her affections are divided, the more dramatic the situation is, of course. Despite the bad beginning of *Her Father*, I felt that something good would surely be extracted from Irene's predicament. We should see her gradually realising that her father was not such an ogre as she had been brought up to believe. We should see her beginning to doubt whether her mother were not a trifle 'hard.' We should see her making faint efforts to reconcile these two people whom she knew to be really quite irreconcileable. And in her failure, and in her constant inward distraction from one to the other, she would afford us some good tragic sport. As the evening wore on, it became clear that I had hoped rashly. Miss Marie Löhr showed us to perfection the surface of Irene, and, judging by her evident sensibility, I am sure she could have shown us the soul also, had she had an opportunity. No such opportunity was vouchsafed. Irene duly arrives under her father's roof, duly pining for her mother's. She continues so to pine, until, at length, her father passes his hand over his brow, and says in a voice choked with emotion, but with the air of one who has just had a brilliant flash of inspiration, 'One thing is clear: you want to go away from me.' She cannot deny that this is so. He promises that she shall go next day, on one condition: she must wear to-night the pretty frock that has come for her from Paris, and sit at the head of the dinner table. The pretty frock means much to her. Already she is rather dreading the poverty of her mother's establishment, 'where love is'—but not, by the way, the love that she has recently been inspiring in a certain baronet. Mr Morton cannot, of course, make her forswear her beloved mother in favour of worldly splendour. On the other hand, it would be hardly less outrageous to dash her down from the heights on which she can disport herself in pretty frocks. You scent the solution? Yes, of course, the mother arrives at the house, and, under the angelic influence of Irene, she and the long-lost and (as she had thought) well-lost husband who had for so many years so studiously avoided her are in a jiffy re-united. To point the absurdity of this conclusion, the method of narration used at the beginning of this article would be superfluous. Happy endings such as this do not, I think, send even the most fatuous of playgoers happy away.

Miss Henrietta Watson plays the mother, and the air she always has of being pre-eminently sensible gives the crowning touch of absurdity to her part. Mr Arthur Bourchier plays the part of the father; and this time I have nothing whatsoever to urge against his inveterate habit of clowning: the more he clowned the better I was pleased. When I heard that he was going to appear in a serious comedy at the Haymarket, I rejoiced, thinking that under an alien management he would have to restrain himself, and so would do justice to the very real talent that is in him. But evidently he was given his own way at the rehearsals; and the result, though it may be rather saddening to the manager who took the play seriously enough to produce it, is decidedly a comfort to irresponsible spectators like myself. Mr Marsh Allen plays a shadowy part in the first act, and then (I feel this is no cue for condolence) disappears. The other parts are filled by ladies and gentlemen who cannot have greatly distinguished themselves in the amateur theatricals which (I assume) have been their sphere hitherto. Ten years or so hence, if they are kept hard at work in the provinces, some of them may perhaps be worthy to appear at the Haymarket. And in the course of that period Mr Harrison will perhaps have found a stage-manager, to enhance that worthiness.

[*8 February 1908*]

THE O.U.D.S

Fun, I take it, is the prime object of an amateur dramatic society. Some of the members may happen to have an innate talent for acting, and may be keen to develop this talent, with the idea of going on the stage professionally. Some of them, too, may be imbued with a love of dramatic literature, and a desire to realise through their own persons this and that play which have especially impressed their imaginations. But for most of them the whole thing is merely a frolic. Even a quite ordinary back drawing-room becomes romantic, gathers about itself something of the mysterious charm of a theatre, so soon as a play is rehearsed in it. In every normal young man or woman survives much of the child's love of make-believe, and the child's love of dressing up to intensify the illusion. To learn a long part by heart is rather a bore, certainly; but how very amply you are recompensed when you recite it, with appropriate gestures and grimaces, before a mirror! And then, at rehearsal, the pleasure of seeing what fools the other people are making of themselves, or (if your nature be a genial one) of seeing how infinitely better they are than the celebrated professionals on whose styles they have respectively modelled theirs! All these joys pale for you beside the joy of broaching the parcel from the costumier's, and the parcel from the wig-maker's, and wildly experimenting with grease-paint, for the dress-rehearsal. 'On the night,' until you have spoken your first words, your raptures are probably overcome by your nervousness; but once those first words are out, you have an evening of unalloyed bliss. You do not wonder that professional actors so often get their heads turned and give themselves airs. *Your* head is turned utterly by the applause that the audience lavishes on you; and you are too happy to be sensitive to the fact that a similar result is by similar means produced on every one of your fellow-mimes. Far be it from me, in the ordinary course of things, to hush that applause. I know how to behave myself on these festive occasions. Having been invited in a private capacity to a private entertainment, I feel that my duty is to clap my hands vigorously at brief intervals throughout the performance, like my neighbours, and afterwards to radiate the most lustrous compliments to all concerned. This duty I perform with all my heart.

I am thus calling special attention to my heart, in case you should judge me, by what follows, heartless. When an amateur dramatic company gives a public performance, and invites critics to attend it and write about it, I feel that I ought to curb my humane impulses, and only to applaud and praise as my critical faculty dictates. Of course I do not expect amateurs to act so well as professionals, and would not bitterly decry in them the faults for which in professionals no censure were too harsh. Only I do not feel myself impelled to write rapturously about them when they are bad, ladling out the very epithets that I keep for professionals when they are good. Had I not gone to Oxford last Wednesday to see *A Midsummer Night's Dream* acted by the O.U.D.S., I should have been led (by the *Daily Telegraph*, for example) to believe that every member of the company was by way of being a gifted and finished artist. (I fancy it was not the eye of Mr W. L. Courtney, a steady and ex-proctorial orb, that saw the play for the *Daily Telegraph*.) Doubtless, such criticisms give great pleasure to the performers, and to their relations and friends. But ought one not to feel a little sorry for the people in London, who, fired by such criticisms, hastily pack their portmanteaux and rush off to Oxford so as not to miss a presumably great treat? And ought one not to shed a tear for the performers themselves, who are led to suppose that Fate intended them to shine on the professional stage, that they have really nothing to learn, and that it is a pity they have to stay in Oxford at present and study for non-histrionic 'degrees'? I hereby drop that tear and the remark that I never saw an amateur performance which seemed to me worse, all round, than this performance of *A Midsummer Night's Dream*.

In Oxford, of course, a dramatic society is heavily handicapped by the spirit of the place. 'The Oxford manner,' which all undergraduates catch more or less saliently, is in itself a distinguished and delightful manner, I think. But the calmness of it, the suavity and evenness of it, is the very negation of what goes to make effective acting. Oxford teaches you to seem not to commit yourself, not to unbosom yourself, to be gently aloof. Mr W. R. Foss, this year, as in many previous years, has been imported as 'producer' for the O.U.D.S. He is a clever teacher; but what can he avail against the inveterate spirit of the Benign Mother? The undergraduates who play the lovers in *A Midsummer Night's Dream*, and those who play the comic peasants, doubtless enjoy themselves very much, and doubtless would like to appear to be doing so. But how tame and dull is their effect! How terribly afraid they seem of demeaning themselves! The lady who plays Helena gives a reading of one passage which seems as if it must have been suggested to her by her undergraduate colleagues. 'O, that a lady, of one man refused, should of another therefore be abused', cries Helena, rushing distraught into the shadows of the wood. It had never struck me that the tragedy lay in the fact that the misused Helena was of gentle birth. The actress brings this point out with intense force, raising her voice to a scream, and flinging her arms wildly upwards, at the word 'lady.' O, that a gentleman should so let himself go as to make himself a motley to the view!—this was evidently the unuttered cry of every undergraduate in *A Midsummer Night's Dream*. Stay, I must make an exception. One performer there was in whose enjoyment lurked no canker of misgiving. Mr E. Hain, of New College, must either be a freshman, or a man extraordinarily impervious to 'the spirit of place.' He played Puck in the wildest and merriest way imaginable, and had exactly modelled his appearance and voice on those of Mr George Robey. His physical agility was quite amazing. Every time he ran off or on, one thought he would surely break his neck. But he never did. And this series of feats was our sole consolation for the fact that he had not burdened himself with the slightest conception of the poetry of his part, and that everything was subordinated to the imitation of Mr George Robey. It is a pity that so beautiful a part as Puck should be thus degraded, especially as it cannot be degraded without ruining much of the poetry of the other parts. Thus, when Oberon delivered that exquisite speech whose opening words are 'Thou rememberest since once I sat upon a promontory,' all the enchantment vanished at Puck's interjection 'I remember,' which was mercilessly delivered in Mr Robey's falsetto. Not that there was much enchantment to vanish; for Mr G. C. Colmer, of Christ Church, who played Oberon, had not even a rudimentary sense of the music of verse. Unlike most of his colleagues, he was audible; but his sole recipe for the delivery of poetry was slowness—a limp and lugubrious slowness. Though, for the reason that I have suggested, undergraduates of Oxford can hardly be expected to act well, there is no reason why they should not learn to recite. A good all-round recitation of a Shakespearean play is delightful, and ought to be well within the scope of the O.U.D.S. After all, the poetry itself is the first and most important thing in Shakespeare. Let the O.U.D.S. try for it next year.

[*29 February 1908*]

A PLAY OF FANTASY

I went the other day to the New Royalty Theatre, to see *The Philosopher's Stone* produced by 'The Play Actors'—a corporation whose aims are akin to those of the Stage Society. On the same evening the Stage Society was producing a play on its own account; and thus the extreme fullness of the New Royalty was a pleasant sign of increase in the number of people who care about this sort of thing. Of course a rather wide margin must be left for the people who go merely because they have nothing better to do. One reason for the popularity of these Sunday performances is the sense that you are doing a rather bold thing in attending them—a sense that is rooted ineradicably in the breasts of all who are old enough to remember the Sundays of the mid-Victorian era. I confess, however, that me this memory does not save from a vague sense of gloom. There is that in theatrical art which needs the public, needs the spontaneous flocking-in of the unrelated units of a great public. Without them one is conscious of a void, a void which cannot be filled by 'subscribers,' however numerous. I look forward to the day when the whole vast public will be so enlightened, so eager and curious, as to flock to the experimental dramas which now perforce are condemned to hole-and-corner production. That day will never come; but I insist on looking forward to it.

Distinctly an experiment is *The Philosopher's Stone*, written by Mr Isaac York, whose very name sounds distinctly experimental, and is not, I conceive, more fantastic than its owner or assumer. A desire to mingle the impossible with the actual is the hall-mark of truly fantastic minds. Quite prosaic people may delight in an impossibility carefully insulated from actuality. They will accompany you gladly into fairy-land or cloud-cuckoo land, though the looking-glass or to the other side of nowhere, and will come back pleased and refreshed. But they will be bewildered and vexed if into their own well-ordered area you suddenly introduce a fairy, a god, a monster, or any such phenomenon. And that is just what you cannot resist doing if you really love fantasy. It is not enough for you that there are strange realms afar. Flying visits to them are not enough for you. You insist that the dwellers in those realms shall return your visits. Far more strange and dear they are to you when you

348

see them in sharp contrast with the people who walk this humdrum earth; and by their presence you are reconciled to your surroundings. Shakespeare did not leave Puck, and Pease-blossom, and those others, in fairy-land: he whisked them to 'a wood near Athens'— as near Athens as was compatible with the fact that the wood was in the heart of Warwickshire. Nor did Heine care much about the heyday of Olympus: it was the fallen gods, working at this and that trade in Germany, that struck the chords in his fantastic bosom. 'Once a fairy, light and airy, married with a mortal,' sang Sir W. S. Gilbert, and the idea so haunted him that, years later, he founded on it what is perhaps the most delicious of his operas. Then there was Mr Anstey's *Tinted Venus*; and there was Mr Wells's *Wonderful Visit*, the story of an angel's adventures in England at the close of the nineteenth century. Superficially, Mr Wells is less fantastic now than when he wrote that story. Yet, if you think for a moment, are not all his sociological books about the future founded on the idea that this earth will in due time be populated by a vast majority of angels? He knows subconsciously that the thing will not be. But if it *could* be, where (he subconsciously argues) would be the fun? And so he writes yet another treatise, describing the future in yet greater detail, and with yet more angelic earnestness. He is the most fantastic genius of his time.

Far more modest are the demands of Mr Isaac York. He, like the earlier Wells, is content with one fantastic visitant. Her name is Mimi; and her origin, so far as it can be traced, is that the sea washed her up in a basket upon the shore of Brittany, when she was still a baby. Much of the mystery of the sea clings about her. Shells are her playthings, and the winds are her playfellows, and her mentor is the sea. With the sea she often communes; but she is 'afraid of people,' and at their approach hides herself ever in the cave which is her dwelling-place. The scene in which her way of life is made known to us is very prettily written. But, at the entrance of ordinary 'people,' it becomes clear that Mr York has not listened to ordinary human speech so attentively as he has listened to the speech of fairies. The most important of these people are David Vaughan, a young painter who has genius; Oscar Elisson, a young painter who has not genius, and whom the programme describes as 'the man of pleasure'; and Lady Diana, who, in lieu of surname, is described as 'the woman in love,' and under whose auspices the

others are yachting. It is evidently Vaughan that she loves; and of
him Elisson is rather jealous. 'I wish,' says Elisson, 'she would
turn those aristocratic orbs on my six feet two.' That is an extreme
example of Mr York's indifference to human speech. A fairer
example is Vaughan's declaration that 'the whole of this holiday has
been robbed for me of its pleasure by my physical inability to draw.'
He succeeds, however, in drawing Mimi, for, says Lady Diana, 'this
work shows an inspired pencil.' Such speeches as these go dangerously near to defeating Mr York's primary aim, which is to
accentuate the fantastic against a background of realism. It needs
some exercise of good-will in us to believe in the reality of people
who converse in this amazing mode. Granted this good-will, the
first act is delightful, and an earnest of a happy evening. Mimi's
wild heart has fluttered timidly out to Vaughan, who, in his turn,
is enraptured by her. Lady Diana, a self-sacrificing woman, offers
to take Mimi back with her to Paris. Will Mimi adventure herself
into the world of men and women? She communes with her mentor,
the sea. And the sea bids her 'go and learn.' So far, so good. But,
in a play of this kind, everything depends on whether the fantastic
element and the realistic be interpenetrated throughout, each one
duly mingling with the other, never lost in the other. In the second
and third acts of *The Philosopher's Stone* the fantastic element
seems to me to disappear utterly. Mimi sits constantly as a model for
Vaughan's pictures, and conceives a very ardent passion for him.
It is a fault in Mr York's technique that we are left for some time
under the impression that Vaughan is wildly in love with Mimi.
As a matter of fact, it is Lady Diana that he loves. He persuades
Mimi to live under his roof, merely because he thinks Lady Diana
does not care for him. A year elapses, and Lady Diana (always self-
sacrificing) urges Vaughan to marry Mimi. Mimi overhears him
saying that he loves Lady Diana, and in a passionate scene declares
that she has not the slightest desire to marry Vaughan. She protests
that she wants merely freedom and excitement, and falls back on
'the man of pleasure,' who has all the while been urging her to
come to him. Well, in all this there is nothing at all implausible.
But my objection to it is for that very reason. Why should Mimi
have been a sea-maiden at all? Why should she not be an ordinary
peasant? Nothing in her behaviour, or in what befalls her, is conditioned by her strange origin. And the result is that when, at the

beginning of the last act, we are switched back to the coast of Brittany, and find Mimi dwelling in a cave by the sea, we wonder what on earth she is up to. We have quite forgotten that there ever was anything odd about her. We are out of tune for any fantasy in connexion with her. And when we hear that she has borne a baby which she has 'given to the sea,' we are inclined to make no more allowances than would be made in any ordinary case of infanticide. Nor are we prepared for what happens when 'the man of pleasure' comes to implore her to return. While they are sitting together on a rock, she winds her hair about his neck, strangles him, and 'gives him to the sea.' Some critics would say that a scene of this kind is essentially impossible on the stage. Such a scene, certainly, can more easily be impressive in a book. But if it be discreetly stage-managed, and acted imaginatively, it can be impressive in the theatre, too. Well, the stage-management was good enough, and there was plenty of imaginativeness in Miss Inez Bensusan's acting. Nevertheless, the scene was not impressive. We could not take it as fantasy, having known Mimi for two years or so as a quite normal and un-sea-maidenly young person; and as realism it was, of course, out of the question. I respectfully urge Mr York to do the second and third acts of his play all over again, taking as their pivot the inherent strangeness of Mimi. Then the last act will be as enjoyable as the first; and the whole play (when such phrases as 'inspired pencil' have been struck out with a blue one) will be a good specimen of a kind which is delightful.

[*7 March 1908*]

MR GOSSE'S 'IBSEN'

It is a refreshing book, this. I was, of course, prepared to find lucidity in the exposition of Ibsen's work, and grace in the appreciation of it. What surprised me, as I read the biographical chapters, was a feeling that the chill was being taken off my personal regard for Ibsen, and a pleasant tepidness supervening. In the course of this luxurious process, I quite fancied that I was beginning to glow. That was a passing fancy. Ibsen can by no manner of means be made lovable. He was of too stubborn stuff for that. Every student of his character and career must have felt this resistance in him—

felt it keenly, for are we not all fain to love, if we somehow can, the doers of work which by its greatness wins our homage? Of course, there have been dunces incapable of understanding the greatness of Ibsen's work; and they, of course, have been quick to lay stress on the lack in the man himself. Such criticisms, as coming from such a quarter, I resented as an impertinence. On the other hand, I have been hardly less irritated by the attitude of the reverent—an attitude by which Ibsen was made to appear even more inhuman than he was. Unable, for obvious reasons, to depict his career as that of a thorough good fellow developing into a very dear old gentleman, the reverent said as little directly about him as they could, and, falling back on metaphor, likened him to a glacier in a northern sea, glittering with a cold radiance, slow-moving, moving onward irresistibly, or likened him to the northern star. The most unfavourable thing they could bring themselves to say of him was that he was a Titan. All this depressed me deeply. Why couldn't they treat Ibsen as a human being, and cut their losses? Mr Gosse has done just that. His sense of character is too strong to be hushed down by his natural instinct for hero-worship. Just as he sees Ibsen, so does he display him. And the irrepressible sense of character is enforced by a not less active sense of humour. No one could be more filled than Mr Gosse is with a reverence for Ibsen's genius. His genuflexions are as frequent and profound as the strictest Ibsenite ritual could ordain. But there is in his treatment of Ibsen a lightness and airiness whereby its sincerity becomes the more refreshing. There is in it, unrestrained, a quality peculiar to Mr Gosse among English writers of to-day; a quality too kind to be called malice, too delicate to be called high spirits; a quality for which the word 'naughtiness' seems to be the one apt word in the language. And the effect of it is very much to dulcify our feeling for Ibsen. Strictly, of course, it should make no difference. Nature cast Ibsen in a certain mould, and the fact that Mr Gosse frolics does not make Ibsen the less unbending. But it creates for us an atmosphere of familiarity, wherein the great man appears less oppressive than of yore.

Mr Gosse's possession of this peculiar quality has long been known to his readers. It was evident, for example, in *Critical Kit-Kats*. But it was not nearly so evident, was very much more restrained than in this his latest book. It seems to me that in Mr

Gosse's case we have an exact reversal of the usual evolution of a writer. It is usual for a writer to begin boldly, aggressively, 'on his own hook,' and then, as he grows older, tend to timidity, drift to the beaten track. Mr Gosse exercises to-day those faculties of shrewd and delicate literary appreciation which were recognised in him at the outset of his career. But he does something which he never did then. There used to be in his work a marked shyness of himself, a careful conformity. He eschewed surprises. He took no liberties. He never let himself go. Maturity has gradually emboldened him. And, the development being singular, his boldness is singularly exhilarating. He is doing now, just in his own way, just what he wants to do, and what he by no means set out to do. A lover of books, he has always, I conceive, loved even more the study of human beings. In *Critical Kit-Kats* that greater passion was allowed to assert itself, but not to demonstrate itself as it did, the other day, in *Father and Son*, every page of which is aglow with the very rapture of observation and analysis. And now into the boy-hood of Ibsen he has flung himself almost as fondly as into his own boyhood. The description of Ibsen's adolescence is done with some-thing of the gusto of an eye-witness. But it is in the later chapters, when Ibsen's aloofness is no longer the tragic aloofness of unappreci-ated youth, but the comedic aloofness of very widely appreciated middle age, that the real fun for us begins. It is then that Mr Gosse's 'naughtiness' comes delightfully in. And its coming in is the more welcome because it never slips in unobtrusively, but is always ushered in with a sedulous literary art, so that it shall cut the utmost dash. It is not enough for Mr Gosse to perceive and be amused by this or that point which, in his august theme, would escape the notice of the un-naughty mind, and to hint passingly at his amusement. He invariably takes good care that the naughty mind shall share his enjoyment fully, and that the un-naughty shall be shocked. As an example of this care, take the passage in which he describes the growing influence exercised by Ibsen on that part of the world from which he had exiled himself. 'The poetry, fiction and drama of the three Northern nations had become stagnant with commonplace and conventional matter, lumbered with the recog-nised, inevitable and sacrosanct forms of composition. This was particularly the case in Sweden, where the influence of Ibsen now proved more violent and catastrophic than anywhere else. Ibsen destroyed the attraction of the old banal poetry; his spirit breathed upon it in fire, and in all its faded elegance it withered up and vanished. The next event was that the new generation in the three Northern countries, deprived of its traditional authorities, looked about for a prophet and a father, and they found just what they wanted in the exceedingly uncompromising elderly gentleman who remained so silent in the cafés of Rome and of Munich.' At that point, I trust, you sit back and laugh loudly. And then, if you have, besides your sense of humour, an interest in the technique of writing, you will be glad to trace with me how very much of its heartiness your laughter owes to the skill with which the passage is constructed, and to the discretion with which the words are chosen. You will note how the grand manner of the earlier sentences, their stately cadence befitting the importance and impressiveness of their matter, had stirred in you, appropriately, a sense of awe. 'Sacrosanct' and 'catastrophic,' 'breathed upon it in fire,' 'a prophet and a father,' by such words and phrases you had been carefully exalted to a plane from which, at the words 'just what they wanted,' you felt yourself tottering to the infinite bathos in which the sentence ends. A salutary example, this, for careless writers, of the much that can be done through sheer care in writing. A careless writer might have perceived quite as clearly as Mr Gosse the comedy inherent in Scandinavia's enthusiasm for her exile, and have had as clear a vision of that distant and solitary man. But he could not have made us partake thus of his joy. 'The zeal of the young for this unseen and unsympathetic personage was extraordinary,' adds Mr Gosse, 'and took forms of amazing extravagance. Ibsen's impassivity merely heightened the enthusiasm of his countless admirers, who were found, it should be stated, almost entirely among persons who were born after his exile from Norway.' There, again, I ask you to note the art with which Mr Gosse builds up his effect. 'The zeal of the young,' as being a phrase with a classic quality in it, serves to still the last vibrations of the laughter caused by the previous sentence, and, restoring your gravity, deftly exposes you to the full impact of the final naughtiness. I could quote from this book a score of examples not less pleasing than these to the student of literary art, and to the lover of Mr Gosse's mind. Nothing but a sense of fairness to Mr Gosse's publisher restrains me.

[*14 March 1908*]

TICKLED GROUNDLINGS

A strange thing happened at the Lyceum Theatre some nights ago (and happens, I suppose, nightly). The twilight of dawn had crept into Juliet's bed-chamber, and envious streaks had laced the severing clouds in yonder east, and the nurse had announced the approach of Lady Capulet, and all was as it should be, till Romeo, claiming the one more kiss before his flight, clasped Juliet in his arms and kissed her; whereat the audience howled with laughter for several seconds. Shade of Henry Irving!

I have often heard that in the provinces no audience can be depended on not to laugh at sight of an embrace. More than once have I myself seen a provincial audience thus convulsed. And again and again have I tried to account to myself for the mysterious phenomenon. In a recent essay Mr Chesterton chid me for lack of sympathy with the humour of the multitude. He wished me democratic enough to see the point of jokes about bad cheese, mothers-in-law, and other traditional themes; and he eloquently insisted that in all such jokes there was a grand spiritual significance. I have no doubt there is. But just exactly what, I wonder, is the grand spiritual truth signified when an audience laughs at sight of a kiss? Just exactly where does the joke come in? Of course, a kiss may happen, in this and that special case, to be funny. When Bess Crashaw kisses Sir Harry Trimshanks, for example, it is natural that we should laugh, since the whole comedy is so constructed as to hinge on her vow that she never would kiss him—'no, not though all the ladies in Bath should supplicate for him.' But when two young tragic lovers are clasped in each other's arms to exchange a kiss which may be, for aught they know (and, as we know, is), their last, I ignominiously admit myself baffled by the subtlety of the joke. I should, of course, be able to join in the general merriment if the actor and actress impersonating the lovers did not rise to the solemnity of the occasion. I should laugh if they exchanged a resounding kiss, or if, in excess of energy, they lost their balance and rolled over. I assure Mr Chesterton I am quite democratic enough for that. He blames me for not being keen on 'the joke about a man sitting down in the street.' Certainly, that joke leaves me cold, unless there is some special incongruity between the man and

355

the accident. That accident would be specially incongruous with the farewell of Romeo and Juliet, and so would make me laugh despite myself. But on the night of my visit to the Lyceum there was in the demeanour of the two lovers nothing to make their leave-taking ridiculous—to me. They embraced without more or less than the requisite fervour. And when, a few moments after the roars of laughter had subsided, Romeo climbed over the balustrade and was lost to view, the audience testified with extremely loud cheers its approval of his acting. Juliet, when the curtain fell, had a not less stentorian ovation. It is possible that the audience's enthusiasm was meant, not for the manner in which Shakespeare's genius had been interpreted, but for the pluck of a lady and gentleman who had not flinched from making themselves supremely ridiculous in public. But I am still left wondering why the exchange of a kiss is considered funny. One possible solution I perceive dimly. The English are a reserved race, and, as compared with Southern races, sentimental rather than passionate in the relations of the sexes. It is natural that any strong ebullition of passion should appear to them ridiculous. The great success of the Sicilian players here was mainly due to the fact that to the majority of English people they appeared ridiculous. At the Shaftesbury Theatre, of course, the audiences did not laugh outright. The usual prices were charged for admission, and the audiences were of the typical metropolitan kind. But at the Lyceum the prices have been reduced, with the result that quite another kind of public comes flocking in—a simpler, less self-conscious set of people, who guffaw when so disposed. They would have apoplectically died, I am quite sure, if they had seen the Sicilians. I fancy the shade of Henry Irving is lamenting that they were spared to visit the Lyceum.

From their point of view, this production of *Romeo and Juliet* leaves nothing at all to be desired. It has been done in just the right way to 'knock 'em,' I like the vitality of it, the jolly good will of it, very much indeed. The garishness of it does not so directly appeal to me. I do not ask for half-tones. Vivid colour is right for mediaeval Italy. Some of the out-door scenes are quite satisfactorily presented. But it is a shock to find Capulet's hall so very like a ballroom of the Second Empire. And a similar note of garishness is struck continually in the stage-management. The spirit of chromo-lithography is pervasive. At the end of the balcony scene, Romeo is left posturing in precisely the attitude of an acrobat kissing his hand to an audience. Even worse is the tableau at the end of the scene in Friar Laurence's cell. Apparently the marriage ceremony is about to be performed in the cell itself; and the two lovers approach the priest with measured tread, their hands linked high in air, as though they were dancing a minuet, Juliet staring open-mouthed at Romeo as though she were sure she had met him somewhere but couldn't for the life of her 'place' him. And even worse than that is what happens after Juliet has drunk the potion. Down and up goes the curtain, and enter, with beaming faces, several young ladies attired as bride's-maids, and carrying white flowers. They approach the bed softly. The face of their leader suddenly ceases to beam. Something is wrong. She says nothing—because, I suppose, the managers of the Lyceum, Messrs Smith and Carpenter, have not been able to agree as to just what Shakespeare would have made her say—but it is evident that she thinks the worst. 'O Juliet, Juliet, Juliet, thou are dead' is the language of her eyes. Her companions are deeply, though noiselessly, affected. But in the midst of their grief a brilliant idea occurs to them. The flowers that were to have been for the wedding will come in equally well for the funeral. So, one by one, the young ladies deposit their floral offerings on the bed, and I am quite sure there is not a dry eye among the people who thought the lovers' kiss so awfully funny. Miss Nora Kerin's performance is not such as to accentuate the incongruity of this interpolation. She seems to be rather lacking in poetic imagination. She is an experienced and competent young actress, and knows all the usual recipes for simulating high spirits, the dawn of love, yearning, horror, desperation, and the various other moods that Juliet has to run through. All these moods she simulates with neatness and despatch, pleasantly, effectively enough never to forfeit an ovation when the curtain falls between her and the new Lyceum audience. But there is not one moment in which I have either an illusion of Juliet or a distinct impression of Miss Kerin. Mr Matheson Lang, on the other hand, is a really romantic Romeo. Professional experience weighs lightly on him, and he suggests the youngness of Romeo's spirit better than I have seen it suggested by any other actor. He has evidently thought the part out, and he feels it out; and his lapses, I imagine, are not his own fault, but the fault of the stage-management. As character-drawing, there is nothing in all Shake-

357

speare more exquisite than Mercutio's facing of death. Mercutio is just annoyed, exasperated, by the stupid untimeliness of the fluke. Mr Eric Mayne conveys that with just the gallant lightness that the pathos needs. My regret that I cannot praise any other member of the cast is tempered by the fact that every one of them is wildly applauded by the audience.

[*21 March 1908*]

'JACK STRAW'

One sunny afternoon, when the twentieth century was younger than it is now, a novelist and a dramatic critic might have been observed pacing up and down a lawn, in deep conversation. It was of the drama that they were talking. The novelist had not long ago written a play, which had been produced by some society and so much admired that some manager had presently put it into the evening bill. There the critics had admired it as much as ever, repeating their praises of its truthfulness, its humanity, and all that. The public, however, had not taken the advice to go and see it. It was, indeed, a play foredoomed by the melancholy grimness of its subject. The author had extenuated nothing. There was no gilding of the pill; and the pill, accordingly, was not swallowed. Disappointed, but unbowed, the author was now declaring to the critic his resolution to write more plays. The critic, who had always admired greatly the author's novels, urged him to leave the theatre alone. He pointed out that, good as the play had been, it had not been so good as the novels. Drama, he insisted, was a damnable business, at best. The outlines had to be so arbitrary, the colours so thickly laid on. The most subtle of characters on the stage was far more obvious than the simplest and most straightforward of one's fellow creatures. In writing a novel, one did not have to make these wholesale surrenders. One could be as subtle as life itself, said the critic. And, since the talent of the novelist to whom he was talking 'like a father' was essentially a subtle talent, the less traffic it had with the theatre the better it would thrive. The theatre could gain little by it, whereas, insidiously, the theatre would mar it for its proper use. Commercially, of course, the theatre was a tempting thing. There were pots of money to be made out of the theatre, by some people. 'But,' said the critic, pausing in his walk and tapping the novelist on the breast, rather impressively, 'you, my boy, are not one of those people.' The novelist seemed to acquiesce, not without a certain gloom. And the critic, sorry for him, yet conscious of having done a good afternoon's work, briskly changed the subject.

I will not give the name of either the novelist or the critic. Enough that the scene recurred to me, and made me smile not a little, several times in the course of the performance of *Jack Straw* at the Vaudeville Theatre. It is seldom that the public and the critics are found at unison about a play. *Jack Straw* is one of the rare instances. The public acclaims it as loudly as it has been acclaimed by the public's guides. Personally, I cannot be quite so enthusiastic as my colleagues. *Jack Straw* does not seem to me so good an example of Mr Somerset Maugham's talent as was *Lady Frederick* (which was produced when I was away, and of which it is too late to write now). It is altogether on a lower level—the level of farce; and there is little of sheer invention in the farcical figures and situations. The Parker-Jennings family is one which we have seen—on the stage—more times than we could count. In real life they would, of course, be quite new to us. A humble family, resident in Brixton, suddenly inheriting two millions of money, and thereby launched into the great world, would become the more humble in its new environment. It would certainly not assume blatant airs. It would provide a case for sympathy, not for ridicule. By immemorial tradition of the stage, however, *nouveaux riches* are always blatant, always ridiculous; and Mr Somerset Maugham lays the colours on with a trowel. As Mrs Parker-Jennings, Miss Lottie Venne, in whom are no fine shades, and in whom is an incomparable command of the primary colours of farce, has the best part she has had for years. I need hardly say that Miss Parker-Jennings is very different from the rest of her family. Tradition demands a serious 'love interest' in even the wildest farces; and the public will not take seriously the heart of a maiden who is not wholly refined. In *A Man of Honour* Mr Maugham displayed to the public the golden heart of a barmaid. The public would none of it. Even were people tolerant of tragedy in modern life, *A Man of Honour* would have failed because the heroine was not a lady. Miss Parker-Jennings

359

(like so many other daughters of *nouveaux riches* on the stage) leaves nothing to be desired in the matter of lady-likeness. Otherwise, how could the play be rounded off by her betrothal to the hero? Mr Hawtrey, as that hero, has a part that skilfully gives him all his usual chances, with a few new ones thrown in. The effect of him in an auburn and bifurcated beard is in itself so startling as to ensure the success of the first act. And at the end of the second act, before making a silent exit, he has occasion to turn and wink at the other persons of the play. Some twelve years ago, the United States of America were profoundly stirred by 'the Cissie Fitzgerald wink.' I shall not be surprised if the Hawtrey wink creates an equally deep impression here. In its slowness, its solemnity, its richness, it is as memorable as it is indescribable, and can be likened only to an eclipse of the sun. To deceive is (I need hardly say) the hero's business throughout the play; but the character is differentiated from the regular 'Hawtrey part' by the fact that it is a deception within a deception. Jack Straw, a waiter in the Grand Babylon Hotel, is palmed off by Lady Wanley on the Parker-Jenningses as an Archduke of Pomerania, in order that she may avenge a slight. But an Archduke of Pomerania he actually is. And hereby Mr Maugham avoids what would otherwise be a distinctly jarring note in the farce. It was all very well for Congreve, Molière, and other playwrights of the past, to show a lacquey palmed off as a great gentleman on pretentious persons. That, according to the standards of the time, was a quite legitimate joke; and we, switching ourselves back into that time, are not offended by it. But we should flinch from it in a contemporary play. We are too tender for such barbarities. We should be pitying the victims of the joke, and condemning the player of it. Lady Wanley, indeed, does not know that the waiter is what she pretends him to be; but our own knowledge is enough to soothe us, to keep us in the mood of laughter. Mr Maugham keeps us laughing loudly throughout his play. Such as it is, the thing could not have been better done. But it is far from being the best kind of thing that Mr Maugham can do.

[*4 April 1908*]

'A FEARFUL JOY'

I am deeply, incurably sentimental about the past. Show me any bygone period, and forthwith I become maudlin. Old fashions in dress or in thought, manners obsolete, the very names of persons or buildings that are no more, pluck resonant chords in my fond bosom. There is no miracle I dearlier crave than that I be suddenly retrojected into the thick of some period that I know specially well, to behold the streets exactly as their aspect has been preserved in old prints, and pay my respects in person to this and that poet, princess, statesman, of whom the fame yet lingers in the age I was born into. Nor, I think, is any period so strongly and subtly appealing as the period which one has just missed—the things that were still going on when one was in the cradle. What recked I, in my cradle, of Monsieur Labiche, and of the Paris that he kept in fits of laughter —the Paris that was Parisian, and had a life of its own, different from any other; the Paris of which fifteen years ago I discerned a few remnants, remnants that were soon trampled away by the unresisted march of cosmopolitan vulgarity? Paris is a convenient junction, and one can shut one's eyes during the drive from the Gare du Nord to the Gare St Lazare. To stay in Paris, open-eyed, is—for me, at any rate—out of the question. But I can spend any amount of time in poring over the yellowed files of the *Vie Parisienne* and of similar chronicles of Paris in the time of l'Impératrice or of Monsieur Gambetta. How vividly there the dead times live again, with the grace of pathos that the flying years have shed on them! Sadly, and yet (I protest) with a genuine mirth, I can laugh at the jokes that the drawings illustrate—laugh almost as merrily as if I were reading them in the current number. What effect would these jokes produce in me if I found them, week by week, adapted into English, with up-to-date illustrations by Mr Raven Hill and Mr Townsend, in the current number of *Punch*? In such circumstances, I fancy, they would make me look very grave. I should, in an urgent letter to Mr Owen Seaman, gravely point out that they were all very well in their own time, and in their own place, illustrated by Parisian designs of Parisian ladies with chignons, and Parisian gentlemen with peg-top trousers, but that it was foolish to fake them up as local novelties for London in this year of grace. I should insist that the only way to make them acceptable here and now would be to publish accurate trans-lations of the letter-press, and to reproduce the drawings exactly as they appeared in the *Vie Parisienne*. You think my hypothesis far-fetched? Mr Owen Seaman, you say, is not a fool, and would never give me occasion to point out these obvious truths? Well, neither is Mr Sydney Grundy a fool. He is an exceedingly clever man. And yet here he is, giving me occasion to point out not less obvious truths, exactly analogous truths. I have just been seeing *A Fearful Joy* at the Haymarket, a play 'founded' on Labiche, and acted by mimes in costumes of the latest British fashion. Poor mimes! Poor Labiche! Poor me!

What makes Mr Grundy so regardless of our feelings? I do not think he is a hard-hearted man. I believe him, for instance, to cherish as tender a sentiment for the past as I do. Nay, I believe this sentiment in him to be even more tender, even stronger and more absorbing, than it is in me. He loves the past so well that he cannot bear to treat it otherwise than as the present. He concentrates all his powers on a passionate, but foredoomed, endeavour to force the past into the place that the present has ignobly usurped. If he chose to, he could write, out of his own head, an excellent comedy of contemporary life. He has knowledge of the world, and a keen sense for character, as he has more than once shown in plays in-vented by himself. But to these qualities he gives the go-by. Of what use would they be in the business of bringing Labiche up to date? He has wit, too; and for that he finds some scope in his pious enterprise. But not all his wit, nor all Labiche's, would save *A Fearful Joy* from being spectral. Here we have, in a modern setting, the old mechanical framework. There are four characters, as arbit-rary and unreal as the initials at the four corners of a parallelogram. There is A, the unsuspicious husband. There is B, the nervous wife. There is C, the nervous lover. And there is D, the husband's sister who loves the nervous lover and thus enables the playwright to dispose of him symmetrically when the farce is done. Not one of the characters has any inward existence. They are contrived simply with a view to the making of certain situations. And these situations were, doubtless, delightful in the original version. But, as here set forth, with references to taxi-cabs instead of fiacres, to the Carlton and the Ritz instead of Bignon and the Maison Dorée, how hollow, how lugubriously hollow, do they ring! All the fun shrivels away under the adaptation of it into twentieth-century England. Mr Grundy's skill in the art of adaptation makes no difference, saves nothing. The laws of time and place are inexorable, fatal. To all intents and purposes, Labiche is as remote from us as Aeschylus. We have experienced the emotion of awe in seeing the *Agamemnon* enacted archaeologically at Bradfield. But what would be our feelings if the *Agamemnon* were adapted by Mr Grundy into a modern British setting—with Agamemnon as a British General in the South African war, coming home with a clairvoyante, and being murdered by his wife on the way to the bath-room? There would not be much chance of awe in that. We should rather be inclined to laugh. Conversely, *A Fearful Joy* moves us less to laughter than to awe.

I do not suggest that Mr Grundy should proceed to make a faithful translation of a play by Labiche, and then get it acted in costume. I do not want him to do such violence to his sacred theory that the past should be regarded as the present. Besides, it would be a waste of his time. He is too gifted to be a translator. Let him spend his time in writing plays on his own account; thus will he win our gratitude. But by all means let somebody else translate one of Labiche's plays, and let some manager produce it with the requisite chignons and peg-top trousers. We should all rejoice in that. The play would come out almost as fresh as ever, and our laughter would not be the less hearty by reason of the appeal made to our hearts by the presentment of things that are no more.

[*25 April 1908*]

'THE FOLLIES'

Now that I have seen *The Follies* I am not surprised at their vogue; nor do I think that it will soon pass. Indeed, they seem to have all the makings of a permanent institution. The German Reeds entertainment did not survive the extinction of Corney Grain; but for many years it throve splendidly on the large number of people who thought it wicked to go to regular theatres. Similarly, unless the envious gods snatch Mr Pélissier from us in his prime,

The Follies will continue to thrive splendidly on the large number of people who are bored by musical comedies. There is a superstition among the critics that the public wants in musical comedy 'a coherent story.' That is exactly what the public does not want. It flinches from pedantic interludes of dialogue for the development of some plot about which, in the nature of things, nobody can care a brass farthing. Songs and dances, with intervals as few and brief as possible, are what the public wants, wants rightly. In the outlying, old-fashioned music-halls this need is supplied. But there plenty of vulgarity is provided also. Careful men have to leave their women and children behind them. *The Follies* are studiously 'safe.' And there are no tedious interludes in the business of the evening. Off musical comedy and the music-hall alike they score by the further fact that throughout their entertainment, wildly various though it is, is a certain restful unity. It all comes out of the brain of one man, Mr Pélissier, whose physical presence also pervades the stage, in the midst of a little troupe of comedians selected and drilled by himself. Throughout, the fun has a savour of its own—a savour of high spirits running riot in sheer silliness of invention, with yet an undercurrent of solid and sober satire. Especially strong is this undercurrent in the second half of the programme, in which the typical 'benefit matinée' is wildly, yet rather grimly, burlesqued. Miss Sarah Judkins, the beneficiary, is a forgotten 'star' of the 'sixties, dragged forth into a sudden glare of publicity which illuminates her somewhat less splendidly than it illuminates the many eminent artists who have so generously consented to appear in her behalf. We see her arriving behind the scenes—a small, faded, self-respecting person, unrecognised, ignored, elbowed aside by her munificent young benefactors, all of whom are in a fluster about their own respective 'turns.' When the whole entertainment is over, the curtain rises on a painted throng of eminent performers. In front of them, on a high throne, sits Miss Judkins. Mr Pélissier, as the manager, makes a long and florid oration, at the end of which he has to be prompted to make a reference to the beneficiary. This omission he briskly rectifies, at the same time handing to Miss Judkins 'an antique knuckleduster.' Amidst signs of extreme impatience, Miss Judkins then makes a little quavering speech, mainly composed of the words 'kind,' 'kindly' and kindness,' before she is wafted back into oblivion. Certainly, the satire is rather grim. But what a pleasant surprise, in twentieth-century England, to happen on satire! Let Mr Pélissier persist in this vein. And let him enlarge the scope of it. At present, he uses his talent for satire merely against things connected with the theatre. Why should he not satirise this and that aspect of politics, literature, art, and the various other things that are talked and written about? Let him develop his entertainment into a permanent 'revue.' In England the 'revue' has never become popular. But that, I suspect, is merely because it has never been well done. Mr Pélissier could do it well.

As an actor, not less than as an inventor, Mr Pélissier is the life and soul of *The Follies*. He is a comedian of a really high order. He does not make fun. Fun makes itself in him and bubbles gaily up and forth even when he is not doing anything in particular. His mere presence is enough to create laughter. When I say that he does not make fun, I do not mean that he is a comedian of a quiet re-strained kind. On the contrary, he is of an ebullient vitality, and is, for the most part, indefatigably 'all over the place.' But you are never made conscious that he is working for his effects. That, after all, is the test of the difference between the true and the spurious comedian. Mr Pélissier's second-in-command, Mr Lewis Sydney, is a quite competent funny man. He never fails to raise a laugh. But how distinctly you see him raising it! He has certain useful tricks of face and voice which he plays skilfully, over and over again. This iteration is not tedious; indeed, it makes for laughter; but how dry and mechanical is the effect as compared with Mr Pélissier's! It is the old difference between angles and curves. Mr Pélissier's humour is pre-eminently one of curves; and this spiritual fact is physi-cally illustrated by Mr Pélissier's body. He has the good fortune to be a very large and rotund man. A small, thin man may be an exquisite comedian; but his smallness and thinness are disadvan-tages against which his genius has to work. Largeness and rotundity are an invaluable aid. Even in private life, the man who possesses them has a distinct advantage over his fellows. When he enters a room, he diffuses a sense of comfort and well-being, of kindness and goodness. All eyes are turned to him, with a certain gratitude. He inspires trust. He can impose his will on ours. He may, in the end, turn out to be dull, weak, wicked. But it takes us time to discover that. All the omens were in his favour. Conversely, a small, thin man may turn out to be witty, strong, kind and honest. But he has to prove it in the face of doubt. In the theatre, where time is even more valuable than it is in everyday life, it is plain that a large and rotund comedian has an inestimable advantage over the rest. Very often this advantage is counterbalanced by that inertness of movement which is so apt to accompany great bulk. No such handicap has been imposed on Mr Pélissier. He is very light on his feet, and his whole body is, in its way, as quickly expressive as his face. His face is a mirror in which myriads of expressions, broad or subtle, are reflected in bewildering succession. And his hands are, by some strange gift of nature, as nervous, as eloquent, as they are plump. Altogether, he is perfectly equipped to express his humour. A wild, fantastic humour it is; but well based on careful observation of life, or rather of that part of life which is lived in and around the theatres. I repeat my hope that Mr Pélissier will cast his eye over the whole range of things that are going on.

[*9 May 1908*]

'THE THUNDERBOLT'

As such, indeed, this 'episode in provincial life' seems to have fallen on the provinces. For two years Mr Pinero has been forging the missile. Last Saturday evening he hurled it, and the groans of the injured provinces are wafted to us by the *Daily Mail*. We are asked to believe, in the decency of our metropolitan hearts, that our brothers in the midlands and elsewhere are not the narrow, sordid creatures that Mr Pinero supposes them to be. At the risk of being suspected of lack of ready sympathy, I must say that to me the characters in *The Thunderbolt* seem drawn quite fairly. I believe Birmingham, Leeds, Manchester, Liverpool, and similar towns, to be full of just such families as the Mortimore family evolved by Mr Pinero. But (here is balm) I am not so unscientific as to draw any hard distinction between these towns and the town to which I happen to belong. It is in Singlehampton that Mr Pinero has caused the Mortimore family to be born and to dwell. But (barring a few superficial points) he might just as well have selected London. When a man says that a thing does not annoy him and does not surprise him, but simply amuses him—and this is what Mr George Milner, President of the Manchester Literary Club, has said of *The Thunderbolt*—we may always safely assume that he is writhing under a sense of intolerable insult. I suspect Mr Milner—so restrained is he, so perfect his tone—of believing Singlehampton to be no mere symbol for provincial towns at large, but a presentment of fair Manchester herself as she appears to the blurred and distorted gaze of Mr Pinero. Mr Milner does not 'wish to run down the Londoners. They are, of course, in the centre of art, literature, drama, and the rest of it.' I suppose we are. But precious little difference does this fact make in the development of us. I invite Mr Milner to come down to London and have a look at us. And let him bring with him the committee of the Manchester Literary Club, in order that he may have witnesses to support him hereafter in what will otherwise seem to Manchester a mere bold fancy of his, a traveller's tale. For assuredly he will find us not one whit more civilised, warmly though we nestle in the heart of things, than his fellow-townsmen. A few, a very few, of us he will find chattering about 'art, literature, drama, and the rest of it'; but he will note that our chatter is not one whit more illuminative than that which is conducted on his own premises. And the rest of us he will find talking about money and other more or less gross private concerns of our own, and giving never a thought to aesthetic affairs. So much for the surface of us. Now for the soul. It will not, in the course of his brief visit, be so easy for Mr Milner to penetrate our soul and satisfy himself that we are inwardly, as outwardly, not ahead of Manchester. But, if it can possibly be arranged, I will introduce Mr Milner and his committee into some household beset by a crisis similar to that which besets the Mortimores.

With this aim in view, I hereby advertise as 'wanted' a large family, three married brothers and one married sister, severally resident in London, and severally occupying a good social position which they have barely enough money to maintain. A very rich relative of theirs must be about to die, apparently intestate (and timing his death a day or two before the date fixed by Mr Milner and his committee for their visit to London). It is essential that he shall have been for many years on bad terms with his relatives, and that he shall have an illegitimate daughter to whom he has always behaved with extreme tenderness and devotion, and whose existence has not hitherto been known to the relatives. She must be an art-student in Paris; from which city she will be required to arrive in London a few hours after the arrival of Mr Milner and his commit-tee. These gentlemen, meanwhile, unless I am very much mistaken, will have found the family behaving exactly as the Mortimores behave in the first act of *The Thunderbolt*. The three brothers and their wives, the sister and her husband, will all have been found in a state of jubilation only suppressed by their sense of decorum and by their terror that after all a will may have been deposited somewhere, and may yet turn up. They will have been found in the midst of feverish calculations as to how much, exactly, each of them will inherit when the estate is divided between them. And they will be much relieved when the young lady, to whom morally all the money belongs, blankly refuses to accept even the smallest allowance from them. I rather doubt whether the young lady's first impulse will be to behave in this mighty manner; but I think that when it has been explained to her that Mr Milner and his committee have come on purpose to study the family's behaviour under conditions pre-cisely similar to those which Mr Pinero has created, she will hardly refuse to fall into line with Mr Pinero's heroine. I am sorry to be a nuisance; but I must further insist that the wife of the poorest of the three brothers shall have abstracted the will from a safe, shortly before the death of the testator, and, further, that she shall be conscience-stricken, and make a full confession to her husband. And he (I hope I don't expect too much of him) must instantly dash forth to the place where the rest of the family are closeted with the solicitors, and pretend that he himself is the culprit. He will have a very bad quarter of an hour; and of course the professionally sharp wits of the solicitors will soon enough pierce through the flimsy figment. But he must go through with it; otherwise the gentlemen from Manchester will not have an opportunity of seeing his relatives behave exactly as the Mortimores behave, exactly as wild beasts baulked of a meal behave. To encourage him, I may assure him that his wife will not be prosecuted: there will be a comfortable compromise. The person whom I pity most in the matter is the young lady from Paris; her virtue throughout will have to be rather *too* great to be its own reward. I undertake, therefore, to find a handsome young curate for her to marry in the end. This is not my own idea. It is Mr Pinero's. He, good man, has an inveterate weak-

ness for 'the cloth' as a means to a happy ending; and when the Rev.
George Trist appears in the second act of this play it is not for no
apparent reason—to pinerologists: it is in order that in the fourth
act the heroine may fall back on him.

Barring the customary clerical bathos, I take exception to nothing
in the play. Certainly, the heroine and the husband of the will-
destroyer are very self-sacrificing; but in real life people do sometimes go in for self-sacrifice, without any desire to create poignant
situations; and, having drawn these two characters as he has drawn
them, Mr Pinero is quite justified in making them behave so beautifully. The drawing is merely in outline, I admit. I should like to
know more about the heroine; more about the will-destroyer, too. I
wish Mr Pinero had taken the fully-developed character of one of
these two women as the pivot for his play, and thus written a
significant play, a play that we should remember. One doesn't (as
soon as one's criticism of it has been written) remember such a play
as *The Thunderbolt*. It is just an ingenious, exciting story, full of
clever little character-sketches; and, when it's over, there's an end of
it. Of its kind it could not be better. In seeing a play of Mr Pinero's,
always you have the comfortable sense that he has done his very
best. There is always the solid achievement of an unwearying artist.
Even when the thing is of a kind that could have been done better
by someone else, you can always reflect that it probably wouldn't
have been done so well. *The Thunderbolt* is just the kind of play
that couldn't have been done better by anyone else. So why should
I blame Mr Pinero for not having worked on a higher plane?

You will be glad to hear that his use of the English language is
generally much better in this play than it has yet been. For the
most part, the characters talk like human beings, not like newspapers. I wish I could ascribe this portent to a change in Mr Pinero's
theory of style. Alas, it is the bad and the vulgar characters who talk
passably. The two characters who are at once good and refined—
the heroine and the curate—parade the fearsome old locutions. 'I
refused their help,' says the heroine, 'before I was fully acquainted
with these, to me, uncongenial relations of father's—I don't include Mr Tad in that expression, of course'; and she speaks of an
alternative as being 'the more acceptable to the Almighty.' 'You
were assuming a minute ago, in joke perhaps,' says the curate,
'the possibility of my obtaining a living some day.' Is it 'in joke

perhaps' that Mr Pinero writes these speeches? I fear it is that he thinks them 'literary.'

The many members of the Mortimore family are well played. Mr Calvert gives a perfect creation of the oldest brother, perfect in strength and quietness and sense of type. Mr Norman Forbes gives a very droll and pungent rendering of the second brother. Mr Alexander, as the third brother, a weak and not at all a clever man, long-suffering under poverty and social ignominy, has too elastic a tread, too shrewd a frown simultaneous with too beautiful a smile, to befit the character. It is difficult to see him as a man overborne by the rest of the family; neglect and taunt him as they may, you cannot forget that they are but members of his company—except in the scene of the confession, when Mr Alexander brings the batteries of emotional pathos into play, and scores off his natural disability for the character. As the will-destroyer, Miss Mabel Hackney plays very touchingly and well, and Miss Stella Campbell, as the heroine, gives good measure of hereditary grace and sense of beauty.

[*16 May 1908*]

MADAME BARTET

London, this week, has been much fluttered by the presence of M. Fallières. That ample presence in our midst has overshadowed Mme Bartet, just as it has overshadowed M. Pichon and other distinguished persons attached to the suite. From that suite we cannot, somehow, dissociate Mme Bartet. We cannot help mixing her up in it. She seems to fall in so well with it. There is an aureole of officialdom about her golden head. For some twenty years, unfalteringly, she has trodden the boards of the Théâtre Français. Others have come and gone—gone forth, in the lightness or wildness of their souls, from that august citadel; but Mme Bartet stays on for ever, stability incarnate, a tower of edification, the good girl of the class. She it is, very naturally, who has been singled out by the authorities to receive the riband of the Légion d'Honneur. She alone among eminent actresses could be trusted to wear it with discretion. Divine fire is all very well in its way. A tumultuously heaving bosom is very effective in some plays, but it would ill bear the riband of the

Légion d'Honneur. How derogatory for that riband to be torn
from that bosom, as torn it might be at any moment, in some access
of fury or just for the fun of the thing, and flung fluttering in the
face of the Minister of Fine Arts! See Mme Bartet at the Shaftesbury, and you will feel with me that she will never desecrate her
decoration. She is an eminently 'safe' actress. She is official. I find
it hard, in writing of her, to use the terms that are usually applied
to actresses. I could no more speak of her 'fascination' than I could
of M. Pichon's. She has just an official charm of manner: she
conciliates. I could no more speak of her 'restraint' than I could of
M. Pichon's. But it seems quite natural to speak of her air of official
reserve. I don't quite know what a protocol is; but I associate it
with Mme Bartet, all the time. I picture her carrying her 'part'
in a portfolio, and her grease-paints in a despatch-box. And the
vehicle in which she drives to and from the Shaftesbury Theatre I
picture as one lent to her from our Royal Mews, with coachman
and footman in livery of scarlet.

Next week, I am told, Mme Sarah Bernhardt, the undecorated, will
be in London again. Between her and Mme Bartet there are one
or two points of likeness. Neither of them, at first glance, seems
quite like a human being: each gives one the sense of something
too good—too magnificent—to be true. Each of them has an ease, an
assurance, a way of imposing herself, which, in a room, would put
a serried phalanx of *grandes dames* to the blush. Sarah has this
dignity even when she is playing the most absurd pranks on her art.
It is a dignity reared on the solid foundation of her early training
and of her sense of her own genius. Thanks to the discipline under
which she was trained at the Conservatoire and at the Théâtre
Français, she never, even when she is most the show-woman, quite
loses the classic air; and her queenliness is ever enhanced by her
high opinion—how, after these decades of unexampled homage,
could it be other than a very high opinion?—of herself. Mme Bartet's
dignity, I conceive, rests not at all on consciousness of genius, but
wholly on consciousness of having mastered thoroughly all that in
the art of acting can be taught by the most distinguished school of
acting in the world. Mastery has given her no arrogance. She takes
no liberties. She never breaks a rule, never forgets one of the innumerable lessons that have gone to form her method. Ten years
hence she will be illustrating that method as perfectly as she does

to-day. There will never be a trace of falling off. Sarah began to fall off many years ago. Exactly how much further she will have declined in the course of the next ten years is rather a hard sum to do, by reason of her habit of coming, from time to time, gloriously on again. One thing is certain: to the last she will be recognisably and indisputably a woman of genius. Always, in the midst of her eccentricities, her follies and vulgarities, there will yet be flashes of truth and power—flashes of the true Sarah. What is the true Mme Bartet, I wonder? Behind the perfect mask what sort of face is there? Is any reality left in her? One sees no hint of it. And thus I suspect that during the past twenty years or so Mme Bartet, in her way, has been falling off as surely as Sarah in hers. When, as a girl, she went to study at the Conservatoire, there must have been in her, as in other girls, some traces of natural humanity. In her first recitation, though doubtless she expressed herself feebly, some glimpse of a self must have been discernible. And the great success she presently had at the Vaudeville is proof that this self was not uninteresting. Alas, it cannot have been a very strong self. It had not enough resistance to survive the traditions of the Théâtre Français. Those traditions survive in her, beautifully, but to the exclusion of aught else. The method of expression has crushed whatever there was to be expressed.

Her part in Le Dédale is one that gives plenty of scope for genuine feeling. M. Hervieu is not apt to afford such opportunities. In his brain, the thesis takes precedence of the characters; and the characters have to be such as will fit into 'situations.' It usually happens that between this upper and this nether millstone not very much of reality is left to them. Marianne Le Breuil, however, in herself, is a fully real person. That we find it hard to think of her as such, is not M. Hervieu's fault, but Mme Bartet's. From first to last, it is Mme Bartet's beautiful technique, never Marianne or anyone at all like her, that we are made to realise. Mme Bartet has all the best prescriptions for every effect that an actress may be expected to make; and it is surprising to watch with what dexterity, with what neatness and despatch, she makes these prescriptions up. Connubial tenderness, maternal love, friendly sympathy, physical passion, moral indignation, shame, remorse—all these and many other emotions does Marianne experience, and does Mme Bartet illustrate with impeccable gestures, inflections, attitudes. In point of academic beauty, everything she does is exactly right; and our sense that it is exactly right is all the stronger because we have seen it all done, and approved, so often before. Certainly it is a great pleasure to watch her. Perhaps it is a still greater pleasure to watch a dispensing chemist making prescriptions up, and bottling them and wrapping them and sealing them; but that is only because he does not pretend to be somebody else, torn by strong emotion: he is content to seem what he is—an automaton; whereas Mme Bartet undoubtedly desires to create in us an illusion of Marianne. Or has she, perhaps, no such weak desire? Is she content just to give an exhibition of technique, caring not whether we be satisfied with that or be sighing for any howsoever clumsy novice in whom were some spark of real feeling?

[*30 May 1908*]

'NAN'

Now that he has taken a manful plunge into the swift-flowing stream of Vedrenne-Barkerism, Mr Harrison is, I am sure, vastly refreshed and exhilarated, and wonders how he ever could have stayed floundering about in those brackish backwaters from which I was always trying to retrieve him. Judging by the size and behaviour of the audience at the Haymarket last Tuesday, *Nan* is likely to pay well. Even though it turn out to be a failure commercially, Mr Harrison will yet have had a good deal of pleasure and pride in being mixed up in it. For no play that Messrs Vedrenne and Barker have produced am I more grateful than for *Nan*.

About Mr Masefield's other play, *The Campden Wonder*, I was not able to be enthusiastic. I saw in it very positive signs that much was to be expected of Mr Masefield. The characters were thoroughly alive, all of them; and the action was so ordered that the theme yielded its utmost ounce of horror. Only, there was in that theme nothing but mere horror to be yielded. A madman accused himself and his mother and his brother of a murder which they had not committed; and the three of them came to the gallows. That would make an excellent play for the Grand Guignol. And, indeed, I am told that the Grand Guignol's manager has duly acquired the rights of it. But as a work of art—finely artistic though the workmanship of it was—I could not consider it. The story had no meaning, no relation to the broad realities of life. It was but a hideous single accident, better dismissed from the mind. To most of the critics— even to some of the good ones—*Nan* seems to come within the same category. They solemnly adjure the author not to waste his undoubted talent on the task of depressing us and giving us the shudders. Certainly, the life that is led by Mr Masefield's heroine is a depressing one. So, for that matter, was the life led by Hamlet. And certainly Mr Masefield's play culminates in a violent death. That is a way that tragedies have. The trouble is that the critics don't like tragedy. They think it horrid. So it is, in the strict sense; but that is not all that it is. *Hamlet* does not merely make your hair stand on end. Nor do the critics assert that it does merely that. But their moderation is due rather to cowardice than to the power of drawing distinctions between tragedy and horror. If Shakespeare had chanced to be an Edwardian instead of an Elizabethan, and had lately given us a modern equivalent for the unwritten *Hamlet*, be sure the critics would have solemnly adjured him not to waste his undoubted talent, &c., &c. It is not enough for them that the venue and the date of *Nan* are sweetly remote—'Pargetter's Farm at Broad Oak on Severn, 1810.' What they would have said if Mr Masefield had given us a tragedy of 'Paradise Alley, Hackney Road, 1908,' I tremble to think. The mere fact that a living playwright should dare to suggest that anything unpleasant and violent could have happened even a hundred long years ago, and even in far Gloucestershire, is enough to make them very angry. They honestly think Mr Masefield morbid, and imagine that by blaming his choice of theme they prove how healthy their own minds are. Of course, really, the shoe is on the other foot. It is not a sign of morbidness to be unafraid of handling sad and terrible issues. Such issues exist, they inhere, in life. As material for art they can be used just as finely, as inspiringly, as the things that in life are bright and pleasant. The morbid man is he who is so ill-equipped for this world that he dares face only those bright and pleasant things. The writer of a delightful masque may or may not be a morbid person. The writer of a fine tragedy cannot be a morbid person. I daresay Mr Masefield will write a delightful masque some day. In the meantime, power such as his will not be deflected from its natural way by even the

most querulous of busybodies. I advise the critics that their game is
not to interfere, but to appreciate.

The main impression left on me by Mr Masefield's play is the
impression of sheer beauty. Strong is my sense of its reality and of
its power, but strongest is my sense of its beauty. Mr Masefield
proves himself a keen student of character and a true dramatist; but,
above all, he stands out as poet. Even more to me than what he has
done here is the way in which he has done it; and, for this reason,
I cannot hope to give you any adequate account of the play's fineness. Were I myself a poet I might be able to catch for you something of the magic. If I were a shorthand reporter (with unlimited
'space' at my command), then again I might lay you and Mr
Masefield under an obligation. As it is, my dry précis can avail
little; but, since you seem to expect it of me, I may as well state
that Nan is a young woman whose father has been hanged for
sheep-stealing, and that for this reason she comes to live under the
roof of William Pargetter, her maternal uncle (see how signally I
fail to catch the atmosphere!), and that Mrs Pargetter treats her
cruelly. It had been expected that Jenny Pargetter (it is a wonder
I did not say Miss Pargetter) would win as bridegroom the son of a
neighbouring farmer, a handsome young man named Dick Gurvil.
He, however, has fallen in love with Nan; and she with him. They
have a passionate love-scene, in the course of which she tries, but
fails, to tell him that her father was hanged for sheep-stealing.
Shortly after, Mrs Pargetter tells him this news. She adds that his
father is willing to give him twenty pounds if he will marry Jenny.
Reluctantly he jilts Nan, and courts Jenny. Presently a stranger, an
official of the Government, comes to the cottage. He announces that
it has been proved that Nan's father was innocent, and he hands
over to her the sum of fifty pounds. Thereafter, Dick Gurvil seeks to
renew his courtship of Nan. And she, revolted by his meanness,
stabs him to the heart and goes out to drown herself.

As I said, the critic's business is to appreciate, not to interfere. But
I am afraid that Mr Masefield, after reading this précis, would
prefer my interference to my appreciation. I hasten to assure you,
for him, that my account of the plot, though accurate, is utterly
misleading. I assure you that every one in Pargetter's Farm is
thoroughly and wonderfully alive, and that the story is so evolved
that its tragic climax has the full virtue of inevitability. But the

hundreds of subtle touches that go to make every character so real, and that go to make that climax inevitable—what can I tell you of *them*? To offer a few examples would be useless. They would be but as threads torn out from some closely-woven tapestry. And the all-pervading beauty of the play, as apart from its truth and strength —still vainer were the effort to describe *that*! Mr Masefield's peasants use no finer words than are used by actual peasants. They have a very small vocabulary, and have difficulty in expressing their few ideas. And yet in the love-scene which I have mentioned there is a lyric beauty that holds you enthralled, the little words singing magically one to another. So it is, too, in all the utterances of Gaffer Pearce, an old man, who—but no: I will *not* describe Gaffer Pearce. I won't mar my memory of him. Enough that he is one of Mr Masefield's most beautiful inventions, and that, though superficially he has nothing to do with the action of the play, fundamentally the whole thing depends on him. For further information about the play, see the play itself.

It is acted in the best traditions of Vedrenne-Barkerism. Mr Horace Hodges, as William Pargetter, is especially good, in his absolute naturalness and perfect sense of type. As Nan, Miss Lillah McCarthy is hardly pliant enough for the pathos of the earlier scenes. But, so soon as Nan's soul begins to rise up in its might, to the level of Miss McCarthy's, there is no fault whatsoever to be found.

[*13 June 1908*]

'HOW "DARE" HE'

The Explorer is great fun. Quite apart from its intrinsic quality, the fact that its author is Mr Somerset Maugham is a very strong recommendation indeed. This fact is in itself enough to endear the production to us through what may be called our cumulative sense. If a horse win two important races, we are all anxious that it shall win a third, and a fourth. We want it to win a greater number of important races than any other horse ever won before. When we hear that Mr Pierpont Morgan has acquired Lord So-and-So's priceless collection of this or that, we experience a thrill of delight. We want Mr Morgan to possess *all* that is worth possessing in every kind of artistic product. Statesmen—even the imperialistic ones, nowadays —declare that the British Empire is large enough. Do they think so? Not they. Even the strictest Little Englander would inwardly rejoice if another strip of territory were added to our accumulation. So, for that matter, would the keenest Anglophobe abroad. There is nothing rational, nothing selfish, in the workings of the cumulative sense. It is a sense that defies reason, transcends self. Our colonies are of no use to the foreigner. We do not intrude on Mr Morgan's store-house in Grosvenor Gate. We do not back the sensational colt or filly that we hope will win the record sum in stakes. We may disapprove of the theatre, or be bored by it, and so have no intention of going to see any of the four plays that Mr Maugham has running in the metropolis at this moment. Nevertheless, he is for all of us the hero of the year, even as Signorinetta is like to be the heroine. We rejoice in the news that yet another play of his will be produced in July. Five plays running simultaneously! Stupendous! Even without counting provincial and American rights, he must be 'making at the rate of' whatever vast annual sum it please us to mouth. Colossal! Yet, after all, what are five theatres among so many? Why shouldn't *all* the theatres in London be Maugham-ised? Say that in the past five years he wrote only three plays annually. That would make fifteen rejected plays. Deduct five. That leaves ten plays now accepted for production. Come, let room be found for all of them forthwith! In such dreams do we fondly revel. We are only human.

Other playwrights than Mr Maugham have been, and are, revered by some playgoers. The privilege of being revered by the whole community has been given to him alone. His name is a household word even in households where the theatre is held unclean. They pencil it honourably in the margins of *Smiles on Self-Help*. It is lisped by children in their nurseries, and rolled over the tongue of the aged and infirm. Other playwrights complain that the majority of playgoers is bent not on seeing this or that play, but on seeing this or that mime, and leaves the theatre without having glanced at the author's name on the programme. Presently we shall have Mr Maugham complaining that the majority of playgoers is bent on seeing his plays because they are his, rather than on seeing this or that mime whom he has so exactly fitted with a part. In *Mrs Dot* have not we the quintessence of Miss Marie Tempest, and of Mr Hawtrey in *Jack Straw*? And now, what could be so quintessential of Mr Waller as *The Explorer*? Mr Maugham, sated with our enthusiasm for himself, will coldly bid us give precedence in our hearts to the leading lady or gentleman for whose genius his art is a vehicle. It is, he will remind us, the King that we cheer when he drives past, not the King's coachbuilder.

I doubt whether this rebuke will be really deserved—at any rate in connexion with Mr Waller. How *could* precedence be taken of Mr Waller? The thing's impossible. As I have said, we are only human. And Mr Waller himself, perhaps, is only human. But it needs a stretch of scepticism, greater than we may compass, to imagine him other than divine, when he has a part that properly shows him off. In him we see an amalgam of the sterner deities familiar to our childhood. The voice, I admit, is the voice of Apollo; but the eyes are the eyes of Mars, and the jawbone is exactly the jawbone that Jove had beneath his beard; while the air of grimly concentrated force is Vulcan's own. As the Explorer, Mr Waller has a superb opportunity for the use of these divine assets. 'Alexander Mackenzie,' the hero's name, is hardly a name well-chosen, conjuring up for us, as it does, the mildness of our native and academic music. But the misnomer does not matter after Mr Waller has been on the stage for a few seconds. 'Alexander Mackenzie' is thenceforth a synonym for all that is quietly strong and grim and fearless and overwhelming. All the more terrific is the effect of the Explorer by reason of the milieu in which he appears. If he is like this in a London drawing-room, what, we rapturously wonder, must he be like in the heart of Central Africa? If this is the figure he cuts among the dear homebirds, what *can* he be like when he is facing starvation and suppressing the slave-trade out there? See him standing in the centre of the drawing-room, his heels joined, his shoulders squared, his fists clenched, his lips compressed as by a vice of steel, his eyes flashing luminous shafts as he turns his profile this way or that with the abruptness of a ventriloquist's puppet! See him as he paces the drawing-room carpet, and admit how inadequate is the inevitable simile of the caged lion! In the second act Mr Maugham shows us the lion at large. Night is falling on the plain, the food-supplies are all but exhausted, the native tribes are menacing, hostile

Arabs are in the offing, Alexander is in his element. Vibrating as we are under his personal magnetism, we wonder that his followers, with no footlights between him and them, have not long ago been shaken to death. Some of them have indeed perished; but Alexander, with the modesty of your true hero, ascribes their decease to tribal bullets, climate, &c. Among the survivors is a young man named George Allerton, supposed to be a weakling, but in reality the toughest person in the whole retinue: he can resist Alexander's magnetism. Alexander has warned him not to drink; yet he went and drank deeply. Alexander has warned him not to outrage the sensibilities of the tribes; yet he made advances to a native woman, and finally shot her. Alexander accuses him of the crime; yet he is able to look Alexander in the face and tell a lie; nay! when Alexander bids him submit his revolver to examination, he pulls the trigger on Alexander. Of course, even if he aimed straight, the bullet could have no effect: gods are invulnerable. Nevertheless a thrill of horror passes through the entire audience. And, on the night of my visit, a young lady sitting in the front row of the pit cried out in a hollow voice, 'How *DARE* he?' Her outburst was a concise expression of what we all were feeling.

I suspect Mr Maugham of not being so perfectly satisfied as we are with the part that he has written for Mr Waller. It is evident he conceived Alexander Mackenzie as a type of 'the strong silent man,' and as a man whose whole soul was devoted to the glorious hazards of exploration; one to whom woman could be no more than 'a toy.' Yet Alexander Mackenzie is loquacious, and a lover. Mr Waller, had he only his art to think about, might have accepted a play in which he had not to open his firm lips once in the whole course of the evening. There are chemical experiments in which an ingredient is said to 'act by its presence.' I can imagine Mr Waller acting by his. But there is the public to be considered. The public would be aggrieved if Mr Waller's voice, that noble organ, were not continuously exploited. Also they would be puzzled and made angry by a play in which Mr Waller's actions were not swayed by love. Such heroes as Alexander Mackenzie do not necessarily, in real life, regard woman as a toy. Mostly they do; but there are exceptions— Nelson, for example. He, however, was not so exceptional an exception as Alexander. Suppose Lady Hamilton had had a brother who was wholly unfitted for the navy, it is not likely that Nelson would have accepted him as one of his right-hand men in a naval campaign; nor is it likely that he would thereafter have chosen to alienate Lady Hamilton by letting her suppose that he had lightly sent this young man out on a forlorn hope which he himself was afraid to lead. He would not have said of her, as Alexander says of Lucy Allerton. 'I think she can live better without love than without self-respect.' What Alexander's speech really means is 'I think I am more theatrically effective without a few simple words of explanation than without an idiotic act of self-sacrifice.' And thus . . . but here am I indulging in my tedious old habit of testing a play by reference to reality! I catch the echo of that feminine heart-cry 'How *DARE* he?' and I desist.

[*20 June 1908*]

AT THE PALACE THEATRE

A few nights ago, I saw, for the first time, Miss Maud Allan dancing. Many people, of course, during the past two months, had spoken to me about her performance, rapturously; but no one had offered to take me to see it; and I, so lazy and incurious am I, had not gone of my own accord. I wish I could now atone for this omission by echoing those raptures. I am loth to add boorishness to my other defects. But confess I must that when Miss Maud Allan's performance drew to an end I found myself somehow reminded of the fable of the Emperor's new clothes. You remember how there came to the Emperor's palace a certain weaver, who promised to weave for the Emperor a suit which would be visible only to honest people; and how he set up his loom, and wove and wove, and how none of the courtiers could discern a single thread, yet all were loud in their praises of the fabric; and how, when the time came for the Emperor to sally forth, thus arrayed, through the streets of the capital, the people vied with one another in acclaiming the fabric's beauty, and all went well until one little child innocently exclaimed, 'The Emperor has nothing on.'

Well, it cannot be said of Miss Allan that she has nothing on. She has not, indeed, very much on; and not all of that is opaque; and I daresay that of the many thousands of people who have flocked to the Palace Theatre, a few scores of people have been attracted by a vague notion of impropriety. If so, they must have been disappointed. Propriety and impropriety are not things that can be determined according to quantity or quality of clothing. The gauge is a subtler one than that, depending on physical shape, movement, gesture, and so on. I can imagine cases in which it would be very difficult to decide whether propriety were violated or not. Miss Allan's is, quite obviously, to any normal spectator, no such case; and if the gentleman who travels on behalf of the Manchester Watch Committee was really sincere in his decision that Miss Allan's dancing was unfit for Manchester, he had better go and blow his brains out at once, for his sensibilities must be such as to be shocked by anything under the sky. The question is not of Miss Allan's propriety, but of her genius. Are people really so thrilled as they seem to be? Or are their raptures, like those of the Emperor's subjects, merely a form of timidity? I would no more say figuratively than I would literally that this Empress has nothing on. Having received from nature the gift of grace, she has very evidently studied hard to develop it: she has developed it very charmingly. But to me certainly her equipment seems as 'nothing' when I remember the descriptions of it that have been showered on me. As I was entering the theatre, my eye was arrested by a placard which proclaimed that 'all the noblest arts, the music of the masters, the rhythm of imaginary poems, the triumphs of Greek sculpture and of Botticelli's brush' were summed up in Miss Allan. And these words, excerpted from a newspaper, were but a slightly coloured version of what so many people had been dinning into my ears. Or rather, as I am now inclined to believe, those oral ravings had been but the reflex of a journalistic boom.

On the evening of my visit, Miss Allan did two dances. The first was to the music of the 'Valse Caprice,' and seemed to me very pretty: that and no more. Now and again the dancer ran hither and thither as though trying to escape from some one, and once she fell as in a swoon, but for the rest her movements seemed to me decidedly lacking in caprice, pre-eminently regular, in contrast with the mood of the music. The undulations of the outstretched arms, the wrists wavering to the finger-tips, create a very pretty effect; but they are, of course, just as purely a convention as are the tip-toe pirouettings of the familiar ballerina. They mean nothing;

and, as they go on without intermission, it follows that Miss Allan expresses no more with her arms than does Mlle Genée with her legs. Mlle Genée shines among ballerine by her inalienable power of expressing a thousand quick meanings through her face and her arms. The movements of Miss Allan's legs are prettily rhythmic, but I failed to read any meaning into them; and her face is one which signifies merely youth, sweetness, composure, self-confidence, and other virtues of a static rather than dramatic kind. Her 'interpretation' of Rubinstein's capricious dance seemed to me, in fact, very inadequate; but not so saliently inadequate as her 'interpretation' of 'The Vision of Salomé.' Here the thing to be interpreted is no mere interplay of moods, but a grim and definite tragedy, a terrible character, a terrible deed. It is said of Miss Allan's Salomé by an ardent pamphleteer that 'the desire that flames from her eyes and bursts in hot gusts from her scarlet mouth infects the very air with the madness of passion.' For my own part, I cannot imagine a more lady-like performance. It is true that Miss Allan's lips, like the lips of any other lady appearing on the stage, are painted red; but the rest of the quoted passage is wildly untrue to fact. Miss Allan performs a mild quasi-Oriental dance, the head of John the Baptist appears on the cistern, the dancer takes it squeamishly, sets it in the centre of the stage, performs around it another mild quasi-Oriental dance, overcomes her repugnance, hears some one coming, puts the head behind her, pops it back into the cistern, dances again, and finally repeats the swoon she did in the 'Valse Caprice.' Of course, if the head were shown distinctly to us as a realistic head, not all the prettiness of Miss Allan's dancing could save us a sharp qualm of physical disgust. What is shown to us—and rightly—is a dim convention for a head, whereby, if Miss Allan had an ounce of tragedy in her, we should be illuded and appalled. As it is, we sit quite comfortably, admiring the prettiness of Miss Allan's dancing.

Some six or seven years ago, there arrived in London a certain Miss Isadora Duncan. She danced one evening at the New Gallery, where she made a moderate sensation, but did not succeed in obtaining a public engagement. After that, she had a great success in Paris; and for the past few years has been 'the rage' in Berlin and Munich. It is not, I think, disputed that she was the originator of the method of dancing that is practised by Miss Allan. And such people as have seen her dance seem to be agreed that Miss Allan's dancing is by far the less remarkable. I do not bemoan the case of Miss Duncan, since she has become so great a success elsewhere. Nor do I grudge Miss Allan *her* success, since she certainly deserves to succeed—up to a point. I merely contrast the fates of these two ladies in London, as an amusing instance of the power of mere fluke in human affairs.

P.S.—I have just heard that Miss Duncan is forthwith to re-appear in London, under the auspices of that always paulo-post-enterprising and ridiculous manager, Mr Charles Frohman. Miss Duncan, in fact, has become through Miss Allan a marketable commodity. Irony needed but that.

[*4 July 1908*]

MARINE DRAMA

Alexander shed tears when there were no more lands to conquer. Mr Charles Frohman, a man of tougher fibre, has his eye on the sea. Weep, mermaids, on one another's shoulders. Sound the retreat, Tritons, on your horns. Hand over that trident, Neptune. The sea is to be subjugated. Trust the Trust.

Yes, Mr Frohman has been in communication with the steamship companies. These have 'promised to provide the floating theatre,' and Mr Frohman will do the rest. His idea is not, at present, to provide every steamship with a troop of mimes as permanent members of the crew. That will come, doubtless. Both in England and in America there are multitudes of mimes who cannot get engagements on dry land. The Atlantic will be for them, as for struggling young doctors, a welcome outlet. And maritime discipline will do for their art just what is so signally not done in our theatres. Brisk, handy, unselfish, breezy, trim, they will be attired throughout the day in a neat blue uniform. On their peaked caps they will wear a badge consisting of the masks of comedy and tragedy caught on either tip of an anchor. The leading man will be distinguished from the rest by nothing save a gold stripe or two on the sleeve. All of them will be up at five in the morning for rehearsal—five sharp. They will never be allowed to perform the same piece twice in one week. They will be liable to be put in irons if they miss a cue, or over-act, or under-act. If the ship happens to founder during a performance they will stick to their posts, continuing to speak their lines with spirit and devotion even on their way down to the ocean's bed. This sort of thing will do them no end of good, believe me. But we shall have to wait for it. For the present there is to be no specifically Atlantic school of acting. The performances on the liners are to be given by casual and irresponsible landlubbers. 'I've got,' says Mr Frohman, 'the plays and companies coming and going across the Atlantic all the while,' and it is on them that he relies to charm our transits. How about rough weather? I do not like to think of Romeo staggering for foot-hold in the moon-lit garden, or of Juliet unable to retain her potion. Besides, many though Mr Frohman's companies are, they will not suffice for anything like a regular service on the liners of even one steamship company. They come and go 'all the while' doubtless; but it is rarely that more than two or three of them leave New York on the one hand, and Liverpool or Southampton on the other, in the course of one week. Liners will therefore frequently have to put out to sea with their theatres closed, and their passengers furious. At this moment, of course, there is no sane person who feels the slightest desire for nightly theatrical performances on the Atlantic. But Civilisation never gives us this or that because we want it. What she does is to give us things which we stupidly imagine we can't do without when once we have got them. Personally, I am not very liable to this illusion; and, whenever I go to America, I shall choose an unfrohmanised vessel.

Twelve years or so have elapsed since I was in America. The voyage in those days was a romantic and wonderful experience. For seven whole days one was cut off from the world, and existed, as it were, merely in space, free from the accretion of pleasant or unpleasant little fusses that compose one's everyday life. One sat and watched the sea, in sacramental detachment from all other things. One knew not what was going on elsewhere, and cared not. One rested and was thankful. Well, Signor Marconi has changed all that. At any moment, the purser or some other functionary may appear before you with an urgent Marconigram, reply pre-paid. And every morning you are confronted by the startling head-lines of the local paper—the *Cunard Observer*, let us say, or the

White Star Examiner—whose contents are the food of thought and talk for the rest of the day. Soon, doubtless, there will be wireless telephones in every cabin, and a motor track round the upper deck. Civilisation insists that we shall have these things. She cannot bear to think of us evading for even six short days any of the boons with which she has bedevilled our existence. And it has worried her very much to think of us ever being out of reach of Mr Frohman's Theatrical Syndicate. Nor is she to be satisfied by the prospect of him conquering the Atlantic, 'See,' I hear her whisper in the ear of the great organiser, 'see those little steamboats puffing to and fro between Dover and Calais. Think of the poor passengers on them, with a whole hour of their short lives being wasted.' 'One thing at a time, ma'am,' says Mr Frohman curtly, but jots down on his shirt-cuff 'Channel steamers—one-act plays—why not?'

[*18 July 1908*]

A DEFENCE OF MR BARRIE

Mr Barrie has been for many years a point of agreement among the critics. It is agreed that he is 'irresistible.' Personally, I have often found myself able to resist his pathos quite easily; but his humour, his curious inventiveness, his sure sense for dramatic effect, have always atoned to me for his excesses in the sweetly sad; so that my strictures have been uttered gently, in an undertone that has made no discord in the full-throated chorus. As was proved in the case of Aristides, one epithet constantly applied to one person is apt to pall. I am sure there are many of us who are tired of hearing Mr Barrie called the irresistible; and I have often scanned the horizon for one who would supply the long-felt want of a furious onslaught on Mr Barrie. He has come at last. I am deeply grateful to Mr H. W. Massingham. Always a master of invective, he has made the utmost of his golden opportunity. But I enjoyed *What Every Woman Knows*, even more than I enjoyed his attack on it; and I will not leave Mr Barrie prostrate and unavenged.

There are various recipes for the confection of a slashing attack. One is that you shall single out certain faults in your subject and

severely ignore what is good. Another is that you shall misunder-
stand certain good points and interpret them as faults. Mr Massingham has (unconsciously) used both these recipes; and he has made
excellent use of the best recipe of all, which is to blame your man
for not having set out to do something quite alien from what was
his actual purpose. If you do that, you can't go very far wrong
in your effect; and if you are also a master of invective the result
is bound to be great fun for young and old. Justice be hanged!
What is justice? I will not pretend to define a thing which so many
of the greatest philosophers have striven vainly to define. But
assuredly one of the attributes of justice is that it makes for dulness.
When a critic restrains his natural impulse to knock an artist down
and dance on him, and, instead, says to himself 'What is this artist's
intention? Let me throw myself into that state of receptivity which
he has a right to demand of me, and then try to determine how well
or ill he has accomplished that which' . . . you see how tedious that
sort of thing is. 'What,' asks Mr Massingham, 'is going to happen
to a raw, half-trained Scottish lad, who has got into Parliament on
the strength of his glibness and selfishness, backed by the hints of a
clever, self-effacing woman who loves him?' And, because Mr
Barrie has not worked out that problem in grim earnest, down
with Mr Barrie! away with Mr Barrie! I should echo these ana-
themas, and not be going to bore you at all, if Mr Barrie seemed
to me to have intended, in the play as it stands, to work out the
problem which Mr Massingham magisterially propounds. If the
play pretended to be in the key of sober realistic comedy, I, too,
should be awfully angry about it. Realistic comedy is the form to
which most of the playwrights of our time devote themselves. To the
majority of plays that I criticise the test of actual life is the test that
I apply, therefore; and it is because so few of them do not crumble
under this test that I am so seldom able to give praise. But in *What
Every Woman Knows* the key of fantasy is struck from the outset;
and to that key I attune my ears. The Wylie family has reason to
suspect that a burglar is going to enter the house. So soon as the gas
has been turned out, and the room left empty, we hear the catch
of the window pushed up, and noiselessly the burglar slips in.
Having lit the gas, he goes on tip-toe to the book-case, unlocks it
with a key of his own, takes out certain volumes, arranges them
methodically on the table, and presently is lost in study. The Wylies

creep in and surround him. It turns out that he is John Shand, a young railway porter, and that he comes nightly to feast his mind on the books that are elsewhere beyond his reach. Miss Maggie Wylie is a girl of character, greatly beloved by her father and brothers; but she lacks 'charrm,' and the absence of suitors weighs heavily on the fond breasts of her relations. They are much struck by the force of character implied in John Shand's behaviour, and they offer him an annual income of three hundred pounds for five years on the condition that he will, at the end of that time, marry Miss Wylie—if she be willing. Well, we know that Scotchmen have a passion for learning, and that they will sacrifice much to that. Also, it is very natural that the Wylies should desire nothing so much as that Maggie should be appreciated and wedded. But the chosen means of presentment, the burglary and the subsequent compact, are in the key of sharply fantastic humour; and it is absurd to judge the play otherwise than as fantasy. Do not, however, take me as meaning that fantasy rules out reality. As in the first scenes, so in the rest of the play, Mr Barrie's fantastic method is in far truer relation to life than is the realistic method of the average dramatist. His characters are exaggerated for fun, but in themselves they are real, are types of actual men and women. They are creatures of flesh and blood, winged by Mr Barrie's whim; an immense relief from the sawdust-stuffed figures that the average playwright dresses up in the prosaic clothes of men and women. Of course they won't do if you take them '*au pied de la lettre.*' When John Shand goes into Parliament, Mr Barrie proceeds to caricature politics quite blithely, and—here we strike the root of Mr Massingham's indignation. He took pleasure, as he tells us, in *Peter Pan* and *The Admirable Crichton*. But he is, as we already know, a politician. And he is too earnest and vehement a politician to tolerate any but a perfectly serious treatment of politics. 'It is suggested,' says he, 'that John Shand is an Independent Member of Parliament; certainly he comes from the people, and their trust in him is indicated in a vigorous election scene, with plenty of pantomimic cheering. Here is good, fairly fresh material for almost any kind of play except the type of fitful, farcical comedy which Mr Barrie has actually chosen.' Well, by all means let us have plays dealing seriously with politics, as did *John Bull's Other Island*, for example, and *Waste*. But by what law in ethics or in aesthetics is a dramatist forbidden ever to make fun of anything connected with the House of Commons? Mr Massingham, to whom that place is holy ground, is very angry that John Shand 'has no ideas, no opinions, only an animal zest for pursuing what he calls "ma career."' But surely, surely, a dramatist has the right to select his own characters. The whole pivot of the play is in the fact that Shand has only hard ability and perseverance, with no 'ideas,' no imagination or sense of humour. There *are* such men in real life—even (dare I whisper it, Mr Massingham?) in the House of Commons. Or rather (I hasten to add, in deference to Mr Massingham's sensibilities) there are such men on the Tory benches. Had Mr Barrie made Shand a Tory, I believe Mr Massingham would never have made the onslaught that I have welcomed with such gusto: his sense of realism would not have been offended. I used always to read, in the *Daily News*, his descriptions of the parliamentary debates, with a constant joy in his arbitrary division of sheep from goats. What was 'a cheap sneer' from a Tory was always 'a deadly thrust' from a Liberal. A Liberal's 'high seriousness' was a Tory's 'pomposity,' a Tory's 'gift of the gab' a Liberal's 'flow of closely-reasoned argument,' and so forth through all the manifestations of debate. And the best of it was that Mr Massingham was so transparently honest. In the intensity of his partisanship, any Liberal goose really was a swan to him, and any Tory swan a goose. Any member who, like John Shand, came 'from the people,' and in whom the people had 'indicated their trust in a vigorous election scene,' was to him, *ipso facto*, swan-like. So no wonder he will none of John Shand as presented by Mr Barrie! Or rather, it is wonderful that John Shand, even so, didn't impose on him.

I am convinced that Mr Barrie, by reason of his sacrilege, really does seem to Mr Massingham 'much less witty' than Tom Robertson; and that Mr Massingham, in his piety, was unable to laugh at the jokes which convulsed the rest of us. It is quite true, moreover, that there is nothing amusing in the mere fact of a Scotsman drinking whisky 'neat.' Nevertheless, John Shand's request for 'neat' whisky, at the particular moment when it occurs, is a stroke of true dramatic humour, rightly clinching the scene. Nor does Mr Barrie asks us to suppose that Shand has introduced a bill 'to enable women to grow whiskers.' That is but a phrase used by a lady in the play, as an ironic description of the bill which Shand has introduced to give women a vote in parliamentary elections. Nor is the joke about women being born from a man's funny-bone a fair specimen of Mr Barrie's humour. The whole point of it, from Mr Barrie's point of view, and from ours, is that it is a very elementary joke, which Shand sees. It is Shand's dawning appreciation, and then his slow roar of laughter, that we laugh at; not, as Mr Massingham in his frenzy supposes, the joke itself. However, far be it from me to reason with Mr Massingham. I don't want him to be reasonable. I want him to go on with his invectives. He does them so well. But stay! Why should he not write the serious play that *ought* to have been written by Mr Barrie? He is a born dramatist. His descriptions of parliamentary debates used really to thrill me every morning, with a series of true dramatic thrills, even when I myself happened to have heard, on the preceding evening, the actual thing—the tame, flaccid, fumbled, actual thing. I conjure Mr Massingham to seize the chance that Mr Barrie has let slip. And when I go to criticise his play, I won't attack him for not having written a light fantastic comedy. I promise faithfully.

[*19 September 1908*]

'LADY EPPING'S LAWSUIT'

Mr Hubert Henry Davies has here an admirable theme, and has made of it a play that is likely to succeed, but not nearly so delightful a play as might have been. The hero, Mr Paul Hughes, is a young married man whose first play has just been produced and made a tremendous hit. The heroine is Lady Epping, a pretty '*allumeuse*,' sharp-witted, quite without conscience, and author of several unfinished and very feeble plays. She is a confirmed 'lion-hunter'—a term which, by the way, is rather a foolish one, as applied to ladies of great position, since the lions are always so very ready and even anxious to be caught. Lady Epping catches Mr Hughes before anyone else. His play has hardly been running for a week before he (and his wife) are staying as members of a big party at her house in the country. You see, then, the richness of the possibilities. In more than one of his stories Mr Henry James has touched, with a master hand, the comedy that lies in the situation of an artist in fresh contact with the aristocracy. But he has only touched it; and, so far as I remember, no playwright has ever touched it at all. For a play the theme is as new as it is good; and the special basis which Mr Davies has chosen could not be stronger. I can imagine a lovely structure arising from that basis—Mr Hughes, as an ambitious man, valuing Lady Epping's favour as a more solid mark of his success than any number of favourable press-cuttings; Mr Hughes, as a man of artistic perception, keenly admiring the aspect and manner of the people among whom he has alighted—that so much brighter and more handsome aspect of men and women alike, that so much more frank and free and gracious manner, than he has found among the people of his own sort; Mr Hughes a little shy, but carrying it off quite well, in his inward exhilaration; Mrs Hughes thoroughly uncomfortable, not because she could not (as being a woman) adapt herself more easily and thoroughly than her husband to the new milieu, but because no one there would notice whether she adapted herself or not, all eyes being fixed on the man by connexion with whom she happens to be there. And then, suddenly, let Mr Hughes's delight in his hostess give place (as it does in Mr Davies's play) to a more tumultuous feeling, when it dawns on him that such a feeling would not be discouraged. Let Lady Epping lead him on (as she does) partly because it amuses her, and partly because she would like to use him as collaborator in a play. When she proposes collaboration, let the artist awake in Mr Hughes—the serious and fastidious artist, horrified by the notion of mixing up his own work with anyone else's—especially with that of a shallow and helpless little amateur who couldn't begin to understand what his work meant to him. What would happen then? Would his innate love of his art, and his sense of duty to it—coupled, let us say, with his ingrained fondness for his wife, and his sense of duty to *her*—be overcome by his infatuation for Lady Epping, and his delight in the new world that she has opened to him, his delight in all that she stands for? Which love would triumph in the end—the sacred or the profane? It is an open question; and it is a question well worth an answer; and in the forming of that answer Mr Davies might have written a great little comedy.

But he forms no answer. And, indeed, to the question as posed by him no answer need be formed. It is hard to imagine how having conceived so good a basis for a play about the effect of social excitement on an artist, he could have chosen not to make the artist the principal figure, and have chosen to make the artist no artist at all, but merely a nincompoop. I find a possible explanation in the conjecture that the play was commissioned by Miss Mary Moore, and that Mr Davies therefore concentrated his powers on the part of Lady Epping. He has drawn the character very ingeniously and well. But Mr Hughes, not she, is the character who really matters to us. She is important only in her effect on Mr Hughes. I hazard a further conjecture; which is that Mr Davies, having been served so well in *The Mollusc* by Mr Sam Sothern, thought it would be well to stick to that clever actor for *Lady Epping's Lawsuit*. Mr Sothern excels in the impersonation of gentlemen with neither brains nor character. I have no doubt he would like to play other parts, just as his father must have grown tired of playing Lord Dundreary; and I have no doubt he would play them excellently. But once an actor is identified with any particular kind of part, it is hard for him to escape. And I suggest that Mr Davies made Hughes a fool because he wanted Mr Sothern to have the principal man's part. The result, as Mr Davies might have foreseen, is destructive. We cannot imagine Hughes as capable of a better play than Lady Epping. We cannot imagine him as having achieved anything that could possibly win him fame and launch him into fashion, and we cannot imagine a clever woman like Lady Epping being able to stand a moment's flirtation with him. And even if we could believe in the flirtation as a queer whim on the lady's part, it would not be interesting because it could have no dramatic significance: Hughes, having no possible artistic faculties to cheapen by social pre-occupation, has obviously nothing to lose by it. Perhaps Mr Davies did foresee that by making Hughes a nullity he was destroying all chance of a good comedy. For he strikes from the outset the note of farce. The first character to appear is a lady-journalist whom Hughes has invited to come and interview him in the house to which he has been invited as a stranger. Wholly farcial, too, is the play's turning-point. One of the scenarios evolved by Lady Epping, and revealed to Mr Hughes, is as follows. A married woman has been flirting with an unmarried man. Her husband is jealous. For some reason she visits the unmarried man in his flat. The husband is heard coming upstairs. She hides behind a curtain. So far the scenario. Hearing that these conjunctions occur in Mr Hughes's forthcoming play, she determines to go to law; and the trial of the lawsuit occupies the last act. There is a comic judge, who wears scarlet robes, and is an intimate friend of Lady Epping, with whom he carries on affable conversation from the bench; and the rest of the proceedings are pitched in a similar key of fantasy. This kind of fun does not much amuse me. Upon so definite and familiar a thing as a law-court fantasy cannot be grafted well. Let the law-courts be satirised, through exaggeration, by all means. The trial scene in *Pickwick* is great fun. It is funny because of its solid basis of truth. But satire of a thing imagined by the satirist is never stimulating.

Lately I was defending Mr Barrie against Mr Massingham's anger that he had chosen to write *What Every Woman Knows* as a fantastic comedy, and not as a realistic comedy. And I traced Mr Massingham's anger to his serious interest in the raw material of the play—politics. And I pointed out that there was no reason why politics should not be treated lightly, and that an artist had always a right to choose his own mode of treatment. Yet here am I blaming Mr Davies for writing a fantastic farce, instead of a realistic comedy about an artist. Is this because I am seriously interested in artists, just as Mr Massingham is in politicians? Have I fallen into the very pitfall from which I tried to rescue Mr Massingham? No. Let there be farces about artists, by all means. But it is not the less a pity that Mr Davies did not choose to make a comedy of *Lady Epping's Lawsuit*. A dramatist has the right to choose his own mode; but let him see that it *is* his own mode. Fantastic comedy is the mode most natural to Mr Barrie. To Mr Davies comedy, and not fantastic farce, is the most natural mode. His gift is of quiet, keen, minute, humorous observation—the gift that he used to so very exquisite effect in *The Mollusc*.

[*17 October 1908*]

MISS CHRISTABEL PANKHURST

I was reading lately in the *New Quarterly Review* an essay on the superiority of law-courts to theatres, as places of amusement. And I found a shining instance of this truth last Wednesday morning, in the bleak, very Early-Victorian precincts of the Bow Street police court. There, at the centre, penned but gloriously unhampered in the dock (that dock which is so like a miniature railway-bridge), a very young lady in a white frock sunnily sped the hours in a fashion that no mere actress, no mere playwright, could ever achieve for us.

About the legal aspect of the case against her I must of course say nothing. Nor am I tempted to say anything. I hold no brief for the suffragist ladies: Miss Pankhurst holds the brief too well for competition. Nor do I hold a brief against them. Having consistently for many years ignored the piteous appeals of Liberal and Tory agents alike that I should exercise my undoubted right to have my name inscribed on the register of voters, I feel it is hardly for me to urge that men alone are fit to mould the destinies of the nation. I do but observe the suffragist movement, from without, taking pleasure in it as comedy. The pleasure is keen, for the comedy is good. For fifty years or so, many quiet, thoughtful, irreproachable, elderly ladies wrote and published in the monthly reviews very able and closely-reasoned expositions of the injustice involved in depriving women of the right to vote. And the sole result of all the trouble taken by these quiet, thoughtful, irreproachable, elderly, perfect ladies was that they were called 'the shrieking sisterhood.' Two or three years ago, other ladies, anxious to vote, came forward and have gone around literally shrieking; and the result is that already their desire is treated as a matter of practical politics, and a quite urgent one at that. What a pretty light all this throws—does it not?—on a world governed by the animals which distinguish themselves from the other animals by taking 'reasonable animals' as their label! And yet the light does not seem to have enlightened the brilliantly reasonable animals which write for the press. Invariably, solemnly, at every fresh 'raid' or other escapade of the suffragist ladies, those newspapers which are friendly to the cause itself announce that 'this has put back the clock of female suffrage by at least twenty years.' Bless their hearts! The clock must now, by their computation, have been put back 'at least' twelve centuries. And when a Bill giving the vote to women is passed through Parliament, as will happen in the very near future, it will be hailed as yet another triumph for Reason, mistress of us all.

Invariably, solemnly, after every violent demonstration, such newspapers as are hostile to the cause declare that these ladies are 'actuated solely by motives of self-advertisement.' Doubtless, many of the ladies desire advertisement. But vanity is not, I imagine, a thing peculiar to ladies. Many of the gentlemen who, in the course of the world's history, have done great things for their countries, as statesmen, priests, soldiers, or what not, have not been loth to advertise themselves; nor does their willingness cast any slur on the purity of the other impulses that set them in motion. Mere desire for advertisement may set you in motion, but it certainly will not carry you very far. It will not, for example, carry you so far as the police station. It is nice to be a martyr, no doubt; but it is much nicer not to be one. And when you have your choice of being or not being martyred you will martyr yourself only if you have some sort of a strong faith to sustain you. When, in the midst of an interesting speech by an eminent politician, a lady jumps up and cries shrilly, 'When are you going to give women the vote?' and is promptly hustled out of an infuriated audience, it is absurd to suppose, as people seem to, that she took any personal pleasure in the performance. Most of these women are well-educated, well-brought-up. They don't want to be rude. It is no fun to make everyone dislike you and howl at you. There is no pleasure in being chucked out. Depend on it, the ordeal is one which these women dread, and many of them, after being told off for it, shirk it, and leave the meeting undisturbed. It is only a strong sense of duty to their cause that can enable them to bring their performance off. All such personal vanity as they may have must be a strong deterrent. I admit that, in the case of a suffragist who breaks the law, personal vanity may be an auxiliary incentive. People are all more or less sorry for a woman who goes to prison. But, as I have said, imprisonment is too stiff a price to pay for mere advertisement. Suggest to Mr Hall Caine, on the eve of the publication of his next book, that he should assault a policeman. He would reject the scheme, after hardly more than a moment's hesitation. But if, by assaulting a policeman, he could benefit the Isle of Man, or vindicate Rossetti, or serve any other cause that he has unselfishly at heart, then would the policeman have to be on his guard. Miss Pankhurst may, for all I know, be as vain as most of us. So may Mrs Pankhurst and Mrs Drummond, her dock-mates. Obviously, too, she enjoys the conduct of her case. Indeed, her joyousness is one of the secrets of her charm. But the price she may have presently to pay is not one which she would risk if she were not also very thoroughly and unselfishly in earnest.

And so, when I say she is a most accomplished comedian, do not suspect me of a cheap sneer. That description is but a part of the truth about her. But it is the part with which I, as a dramatic critic, am mainly concerned. She has all the qualities which an actress needs, and of which so few actresses have any. Her voice is charmingly melodious, and the art with which she manages it seems hardly compatible with its still childish ring. And her face, still childish too, is as vivid and as variable as her voice, whose inflexions have always their parallel in her eyes and mouth. And not there merely. Her whole body is alive with her every meaning; and, if you can imagine a very graceful rhythmic dance done by a dancer who moves not her feet, you will have some idea of Miss Pankhurst's method. As she stood there with a rustling sheaf of notes in one hand, her other hand did the work of twenty average hands. But 'work' is a dull term for those lively arabesques with which she adorned the air of the police court, so eagerly and blithely, turning everything to favour and to prettiness. I am told she is great at the mass-meetings in Hyde Park; but I doubt whether her effect can be so delightful there. A setting of trees and grass would strike no contrast to her freshness. But put the wood-nymph in the dock of the police court, and her effect is quite wonderful. . . . No, that is a misleading image. The wood-nymph would be shy, uncomfortable; whereas Miss Pankhurst in her barred pen seemed as comfortable and as self-possessed as Mr Curtis Bennett on the bench. And, as she stood there, with her head inclined merrily to one side, trilling her questions to the Chancellor of the Exchequer, she was like nothing so much as a little singing bird born in captivity.

Mr Lloyd George did not seem at all as though he had been born in a witness-box. His Keltic fire burned very low; and the contrast between the buoyancy of the girl and the depression of the states-man was almost painful. Youth and an ideal, on the one hand; and, on the other, middle age and no illusions left over. Mr Herbert Gladstone's more solid nature has borne up better under the weight of political and official life; and he seemed more capable of coping with Miss Pankhurst. But even for him one would have felt sorry had she been at all aggressive, had she made any unlovely use of her advantage. As it was, her manner was perfect.

To both statesmen she behaved as one admitting the humour of the situation and trying to help them through it with as much speed as might be compatible with duty. 'Now, I want you to concentrate your mind on the hand-bill,' 'I will now suggest to you a definition of the verb "to rush"'—such phrases, as reported, sound rather pompous and priggish. As brought out by Miss Pankhurst, with a keen sense of fun in the contrast between herself and the mature male lawyers whose business it is to use such phrases, they were irresistible. Throughout, indeed, the charm of her youth was made the more manifest by the elderly task she was doing so youngly and so well. And the feminine charm of her was heightened by the fact that it was a masculine task she was doing so well and in so very feminine a way. And . . . no more analysis! Let not my heavy hand rub the bloom off so pretty a recollection.

[24 October 1908]

AT THE EMPIRE

A year or two ago there was a battle raging between the managers of theatres and the managers of music-halls, on the subject of 'sketches.' The managers of theatres protested that their rivals were taking an unfair advantage by purveying these snippets of drama. They protested that it was an illegal advantage, too; and there was some litigation. I suppose the courts decided in favour of the managers of music-halls; for 'sketches' still abound. I am sorry. Not that I believe, as the managers of theatres declared, that people are thus diverted from the theatres. My objection is that I am thus diverted from the music-halls. Singing and dancing, fantasy, absurdity, antic horse-play—these are the things I want in music-halls; and I resent the interpolation of chunks of realism. I was distressed, a few nights ago, at finding that the Empire, which I had always regarded as an impregnable citadel of fantasy, had let the enemy slip in—right into the middle of its programme.

All seemed well in the citadel when I arrived. Two acrobats, called 'Johnny and Charlie', were in possession, and for them I have nothing but praise. In appearance and in method they presented a strange contrast. The one was sheathed, conventionally, in black silk, and was flying round the stage, with the swiftness and lightness of a swallow, turning somersaults in the most classic style. The style of the other man, however, was wholly romantic. He wore a mop of auburn hair and peg-top trousers of some unknown and gigantic tartan. He never ceased to dance, but he exhibited every symptom of intense fatigue. With a weak smile, he doddered this way and that, constantly falling sideways or headlong, but always, as by a miracle, righting himself just before total collapse, and resuming. He had the air of a not very muscular man who had been dancing without cessation since dawn, and was going to dance till the sun rose again, because someone had told him that otherwise the world would come to an end. His mind, evidently, had ceased to work hours ago, and instinct alone was keeping him afoot. Faint but pursuing, with piteous gasps, but always with that weak smile, he would fall on one hand outstretched by the instinct of self-preservation, and then his body would describe thereover a weary arc, and so he would go falling round and round the stage, while the orchestra played over and over again the same few bars of the same cake-walk, until we felt that we too were on the verge of collapse. It was a really wonderful performance—the acrobat's art being carried, by an acrobat greater than the usual, beyond the point of beauty, into grotesque pathos.

Then, after Mr Gordon Cleather had, with his rousing voice, acted as a corrective to the pathos of 'Johnny'—or 'Charlie' as the case may be—came a deadly anticlimax: *After the Opera*. We beheld 'Lady Lulu Devas's Boudoir in Park Lane,' on 'a night in winter,' with a view of falling snow through her window, and a view of her bed through an open door. She and Mr Devas and a young guardsman had just returned from the theatre. Mr Devas had to start on a night journey, and, while he went to change his clothes, Lady Lulu revealed herself as the heartless, deceitful, and wicked woman that she was. Even the guardsman, though he adored her, was revolted. He implored her to 'play the game' and 'do a bolt'; but she, caressing the ropes of pearls which hung about her neck, and which she loved more than aught else, insisted that he should merely return after her husband's departure. And return he did; but, while he and she were parleying, there was a knock at the door, and she, thinking it was her husband come back again, told her lover to climb out over the balcony. But it was not the husband. It was a murderous burglar. And when the husband did come back, after missing the train, Lady Lulu lay dead on the carpet; and the guardsman, who had been observed by the policeman as he dropped over the balcony, was falsely accused of the crime, and would undoubtedly have gone to the gallows, had not the burglar been found hiding in the bedroom. Well, I wonder to whom, at the Empire, this dull sort of rubbish appeals? Doubtless, there is in London a great public for melodrama—for melodrama in its right place, worked out fully, with an edifying moral. Perhaps, too, there is a public that really would welcome a good presentment of the little horrors that we associate with the Grand-Guignol. *After the Opera* is probably derived from the Grand-Guignol. But it is an exceedingly poor specimen of its kind. Even were it a good specimen, what folly to produce it in the Empire! It was proved conclusively, at the Shaftesbury, last spring, that the little horrors of the Grand-Guignol lose all their savour in a big theatre, and become merely tedious. And the Empire is three times as big as the Shaftesbury, so that the style of acting has to be three times as unreal—three times as disastrous to the particular kind of illusion on which the Grand-Guignol business depends. Even in the Grand-Guignol itself there would be no shudders if the horrors were sandwiched in between the turns of a variety entertainment. The manager of the Grand-Guignol is not so foolish as to try that experiment. And I hope the manager of the Empire will have the wit to drop his similar experiment, his far sillier experiment, quickly and for ever.

Perhaps it was partly by force of contrast with the insufferable tediousness of this 'sketch' that the subsequent ballet seemed to me so especially good. But the main credit is certainly due to Colonel Newnham-Davis, who is the author of the ballet, and to Mr Fred Farren, who has produced it. *A Day in Paris* is its title, and my sole objection to it is that one might almost imagine oneself in Paris. Paris itself—I mean, of course, the cispontine part of it—has become so much less like a city than like a stage 'set.' All reality seems to have gone out of it, leaving only a hard artificial glare for the bedazzlement of tourists. Fifteen years ago, there were still in the centre of Paris many remnants of reality, of quietude, of a local and exquisitely civilised life. But these remnants are gone, and I cordially detest the place. If the Empire ballet produced an *absolute* illusion, I should be much oppressed. Luckily, the dancers intervene, and save the situation. The dances are more than usually well invented and well done.

[*31 October 1908*]

'DOLLY REFORMING HERSELF'

It seems quite a long time since Mr Henry Arthur Jones has had a play done in England. I have missed him, and welcome him; and my welcome is the heartier because this new play of his at the Haymarket is surely as good a comedy as he has ever written.

I should say, in evaluating Mr Jones, that his greatest asset is his humour. Mr Shaw has wit—an inexhaustible fund of it; and he has also an inexhaustible fund of rollicking high spirits. In drollery he is as rich as in seriousness. Humour he has not. The essence of humour is a tolerance for men and women as they are—a delight in them as they are; and Mr Shaw, as we know, won't stand us as we are at any price. He is always boisterously angry with us. We respect him for his wrath, and look lovingly up at him while he so splendidly dances on us, and never for an instant do we wish him a humorist. On the other hand, we are grateful that Mr Jones has that comfortable gift which prevents him from dancing on us—that gift of humour whereby he is content to take us just as we are, and to laugh not less with us than at us. Sometimes, indeed, when he was a younger man, he used to put on a heavy frown, and a pair of heavy boots, and proceed to dance on us. He wrote bitter comedies about the hypocrisy of the British middle class, the unloveliness of the Nonconformists, and so forth. But, strenuous though his effect was, I think his heart was not really in the job. As he has grown older, he has found his true vocation, finding it just where every man's true vocation is to be found: along the line of least resistance. He used to think it his duty to be angry. Now he sees that his duty lies in giving rein to the delight that he has in mere observation. No playwright is more joyously observant than Mr Jones; and none observes more accurately, in the milieu that he has chosen. Other

399

playwrights may create more salient and memorable figures. But none of them creates figures so lifelike as Mr Jones's.

Nor is any one of them so fine a craftsman. Mr Pinero is, of course, a marvellous constructor of plays. But he is so much enamoured of his power that he treats construction as though it were an end in itself. He builds up, slowly, before our eyes, a magnificent edifice out of all proportion to what is to be done in it. Mr Jones's craftsmanship is less grandiose. We are not made conscious of it while the play is in progress. From the very outset, we are aware merely of certain ladies and gentlemen behaving with apparent freedom and naturalness. It is only when the play is over that we notice the art of it. The verisimilitude of *Dolly Reforming Herself* is all the more admirable because the play is founded on a philosophic question, and in the whole course of it there is not a scene, not a character (not even the butler's character), that is not strictly and logically relevant to this question. The whole fabric is wrought in a tight, formal pattern, yet the effect of it is as of life itself. The question in point is 'Can we cure ourselves of our bad habits?' and the answer is worked out not through a story, but simply through the behaviour of a few people in a country-house. We see them first on New Year's Day 1907. They have been much impressed by the rousing sermon preached by the vicar—all of them except Professor Sturgess, who has written many books to prove that free-will is an illusion, and that all our actions depend on the quality of the grey matter in our brains. Mr Telfer, the host, has a quick temper, and is resolved to curb it during the year. His wife, Dolly, is very extravagant, and is resolved that she will henceforward not exceed her dress-allowance Captain Wentworth, her cousin, resolves not to flirt any more with young Mrs Sturgess. She resolves to flirt no more with him. Neither of them has anything at all like a grand passion for the other. Mrs Sturgess is vaguely and bookishly romantic, and bored by her husband. Captain Wentworth merely wants to amuse himself. There is a delightful scene in which Mrs Sturgess confides to Dolly that she is unhappy. Dolly is consumed with womanly impatience to hear who is the man, and when she finds that it is her cousin her delight in the romance is amusingly complicated by indignation that such things should go on among the guests under her roof. She is determined that Captain Wentworth shall be got out of the way. He is not an easy person to deal

with, being far too good-natured to resent a snub. Dolly gets her
father, Mr Barron, to use his influence. Mr Barron tries to ride the
high horse, and asks the young man whether he does not consider
it 'a bad habit' to make love to married women. 'Of course in one
sense it is a bad habit,' replies the young man vaguely; 'but it isn't
a bad habit in the sense that other bad habits are bad habits. Look
at all the decent chaps that have been led into it'; and he cross-
questions Mr Barron as to what *he*, when he was young, would
have felt in the matter. 'Well,' Mr Barron is forced to admit, 'I
don't say that at your age I might not have been tempted—and of
course we must all go through a certain amount of experience, or
how should we be able to advise our youngsters?' And presently he
drifts into reminiscence of 'a very remarkable auburn-haired girl,
Madge Seaforth,' and how he raced across Salisbury Plain at night
—'forty-eight miles one glorious May night! I let her beat me!
God bless her! I let her beat me! And just as the sun rose we caught
sight of Salisbury spire.' 'Sounds rather jolly!' says the young man,
sympathetically. 'Jolly?' cries Mr Barron; 'Jolly? It was romance!
It was poetry! Ah, my boy, you may say what you like, there's nothing like it on this side of heaven.' On the verge of further reminiscences, he pulls himself together, and finally awes the young man
into a promise to go back to Aldershot. But this is only a starting-
point for all manner of pretexts for remaining, and, after the young
man has been driven away, he very soon drifts in again. Also, Mrs
Sturgess, who is supposed to be suffering from a bad sick-headache
in her bedroom, is always drifting down again; and so the comedy
of New Year's Day continues. The central scene of the play, however, is the scene between Dolly and her husband. They have
arranged that they will go through her unpaid bills, quietly, in a
business-like way, before bed-time. She is in a state of panic at the
vastness and number of these bills. She faintly suggests one reason
after another for postponing the investigation. Her husband is firm.
The first bill produces a stifled cry from him. She soothes him with
a terrified coquetry, sitting on the arm of his chair, with her arm
round his neck. But, as the investigation advances, and he spells
out the mysterious items and the awful totals, he becomes less
and less susceptible, more and more violent, insomuch that Mr
Barron, whose bedroom is overhead, comes down to implore him
to be quiet. Mr Barron is dragged into the fray—for fray it is,

Dolly being now as angry as her husband, or having rather worked herself up into a rage in order to save the situation. Finally, there is something in the nature of a scuffle, and the scene ends in Dolly's production of a score of other unsuspected bills (which she throws wildly upon the floor) and in her rushing upstairs pursued by her husband, who still insists that they shall go through all the bills together. The whole scene is delightful, worked out with the finest sense of dramatic rhythm: a truly great comic scene, of which Mr Jones may well be proud.

It is New Year's Day 1908 when next we see the persons of the play. And alas, Dolly's bills for the past year are as big as ever; nor has her husband's temper become less hasty. And Captain Wentworth has returned from India, and has a clandestine meeting with Mrs Sturgess. They are all just as they were, including the vicar, who has preached again that rousing sermon.

The acting is worthy of the comedy; and that is as high praise as the cast can wish for. Miss Margaret Halstan plays Mrs Sturgess with an exact sense of the type; and Mr C. M. Lowne, though a trifle too young in appearance and demeanour, plays Mr Barron with his usual distinction and sense of humour. Miss Ethel Irving, as Dolly, and Mr Loraine, as the husband, are exactly suited to each other's method; and the great scene, though it will be played by many comedians in the future, will never, I imagine, be played better.

[*7 November 1908*]

'THE BACCHAE': WITH A NOTE ON SARDOU

At the Court Theatre last Tuesday afternoon Professor Gilbert Murray's beautiful version of *The Bacchae* was performed, and will be performed there again next Tuesday afternoon. Several times, in these columns, I have enumerated the reasons why Greek drama must fail of its effect, and must be more or less tedious, in a theatre constructed on the modern pattern. I have not, however, shaken people's firm belief that they enjoy this drama under these conditions very much indeed. If I doggedly persisted in reiterating my arguments, I might, within a few years, persuade some of these people that what they take to be aesthetic enjoyment is really nothing but moral pleasure in the doing of what they take to be a duty. To me it is always a pleasure to tell the truth. It must be an added pleasure to convince people of the truth. But is the victory worth the struggle? Is the acceptance of a truth reward enough for the awful boredom of having enunciated that same truth ninety and nine times? There is a limit to my capacity for reiteration. Call me selfish, if you will: I cannot trot out again my demonstration of the inherent wrongness of Greek drama in modern theatres. All I can do is to make a few remarks about the particular faults in this production at the Court Theatre—faults that come not of the nature of things, but of the unwisdom of the producer.

As the Court is one of the two smallest theatres in London, it would have been hard to find a place so unsuited to Greek drama. Most of our theatres are, I am convinced, too big for our own drama. Realistic comedy and tragedy (which are the only two forms that at present have any real vitality) stand a far better chance of proper interpretation in a small theatre than in a big one. The players appear life-sized there, and can behave naturally; and such subtlety as they may have is not lost for us. Also, the smallness of the stage helps our illusion of the background. The persons of such modern plays as matter do not dwell in palaces, or wander on plains: their venue is in ordinary drawing-rooms and dining-rooms, which cannot on the average-sized stage be presented illusively. Space, on the other hand, is essential to a right presentment of Greek drama; and pokiness is fatal. The Chorus was no mere accident, was the root, of that drama. Round and round a spacious arena, beneath the sky, circled the Chorus. If the ceiling of the Court were painted sky-blue, and if all the stalls were removed from the floor, to make way for the Chorus, we might get something of the right effect. Again, if the Chorus, drilled by some scholarly ballet-master, appeared on the stage of some very large theatre, against an airy background, there might be a passable substitute for what is needed. On the stage of the Court the Chorus cut a lamentable figure indeed. In the middle of the stage, as set, there was just room for three young ladies to revolve, by dint of taking great care and keeping very close together. And these were the wild maidens of Dionysus's retinue—maidens filled with a mystic ecstasy that causes them to rush headlong down the pine-clad slopes and tear fauns and such-like creatures limb from limb in honour of their inspiring master. And to add to the gloom and discomfort of their effect, the front of the stage was occupied by four other cramped young ladies, immobile in attitudes of the deepest dejection, and looking like nothing so much as drawings by some not at all gifted imitator of Simeon Solomon. These, too, were Maenads, and were singing songs of the wildest lyric passion. Singing? It was not that. I hardly know what it was. Imagine a sound midway between the howling of dogs locked out in a yard by night and the intoning of the Commination Service by curates with very bad colds in the head, and you will have some notion of the noises made by these Maenads. I have said that their songs themselves were of the wildest lyric passion: I possess a book of the words. Few of these words could be distinguished: I was conscious only of the dismal, penitential, intolerable drone. It alone would have been quite enough to wreck *The Bacchae*, to dispel the faintest semblance of the spirit of Greek drama. But, so as to leave nothing to chance, the producer had been careful to elaborate a stage-setting exactly in accord to the maudlin and moping spirit of the Chorus. Space, air, light—that is the effect that is needed, of course. Will you believe that the background was wholly shrouded in curtains of dark purple cloth—sombrous, heavy, ominous curtains that admitted never a chink of Greek daylight, and gave to the little stage the appearance of a *chapelle ardente* without candles? It was with some difficulty that I restrained myself from leaping on to the stage and pulling these curtains down—upon the heads of the Chorus. It would have been a good way of showing my reverence for poor Euripides. Yet I suppose the very dismalness of the production was a sign of the deep and awful reverence that Euripides inspires in the producer. 'Hush! We are in the presence of the Mighty Dead! Let us shut out the light, and pull long faces, and make snuffling noises.' As a memorial performance, nothing could have been in better taste.

Between lugubriousness and tragic dignity there is a vast difference, and lack of tragic dignity did not at all prevent the majority of the principal mimes from being lugubrious. Miss Lillah McCarthy was the only one of them who was tragically dignified. It is a dangerous thing for a woman to impersonate a man, except in Christmas pantomime; but Dionysus, after all, was not a man, but a god, and a 'girl-faced' god. Miss McCarthy, in appearance, answered quite well to our idea of Dionysus. And not in appearance only: her imagination had been at work, and there was a keen sense of the supernatural in her whole rendering of the part. She stood out from the rest not merely in virtue of her elocution, the value she gave to the verse, but also because she was the only one to whom her part was a living thing, and not just a difficult and depressing experiment. The only fault I could find in her performance was that she did not suggest the *humour* of Dionysus in the scene when Pentheus appears dressed as a woman. Of course this scene (when presented to the eye of the spectator) cannot be taken seriously: it is an instance of Euripides's fondness for comic relief in tragedy. I rather regret that fondness; but there it is, and there is no use in representing Dionysus as perfectly grave in the presence of Pentheus. Indeed, it is worse than useless: it makes Dionysus himself ridiculous. Especially is this so if Pentheus assumes, as he does at the Court, a shrill falsetto. I doubt whether Euripedes intended him to do that, and I wonder that the producer at the Court allowed it. However, this effect is not so ludicrous as that of the scene in which Agave enters after slaying her son. As you may remember, this ought to be the most awe-inspiring scene in the play. Agave, full of sacred frenzy, rushes on in triumph, thinking that the severed head she bears in her hands is the head of a lion, slain to the glory of the god. What do we behold? A young lady, apparently quite young enough to be the daughter of the impersonator of Pentheus, and clad in a grass-green dress that strikes the most fearsome discord against the purple curtains, executing a very tame little skirt-dance, and twittering her triumph, while she timidly waggles in the air the head of a white plaster cast from the antique! She makes it rather hard for us to behave with the gravity that befits a memorial performance.

Though Euripides has been dead for twenty-three centuries, and Victorian Sardou for but a few days, Euripides is considerably the nearer man to us. Human characters, and ideas, were his stock-in-trade—just as they are of the few French and English dramatists who interest us to-day. Sardou never had any ideas except for 'situations,' and in the whole course of his vivid and honourable career created not one human character. When he wrote historical plays, the heroes or heroines of history became as lifeless as the creatures of his own fancy—mere wheels for the grinding of 'situations.' Fashion veers. Perhaps before the present century has run its course Sardouism will have as great a vogue as it had in the 'seventies and 'eighties of the century that is past. Meanwhile, peace to the ashes of a brilliant man who had long survived our interest in him.

[*14 November 1908*]

'THE BUILDER OF BRIDGES'

At the beginning of the last act of Mr Sutro's new play there is a passage which is evidently meant to be touching, but which fails to touch me. Mr Peter Holland, a man of fifty or so, whom we have hitherto seen merely as a dry-as-dust engineer, unbosoms himself to his friend and coeval, Edward Thursfield, declaring that 'the only thing in the world that is worth a damn is to hear a girl say that she loves you.' He draws for us a sombre picture of himself as 'dis-inherited'—doomed to lifelong celibacy. Is he too poor to marry? No, he has a very good income. His health, too, seems excellent. The trouble is that he is not handsome. This, according to him, suffices to explain the fact that he hasn't persuaded anyone to marry him, and to debar him from matrimony for ever. Yet we know that there is a great numerical preponderance of women over men, and that not all husbands are beautiful. Mr Peter Holland's heart-cry, uttered by a plain woman, might draw tears. But I refuse to weep over the heart-cry as coming from Mr Peter Holland. If a prosperous and healthy man reaches the age of fifty without having married, the reason is that he hasn't wanted to marry. Similarly, if a man who, like Edward Thursfield, is not only prosperous and healthy, but also handsome, reaches the age of fifty without having had any experience of women, so that he blushes 'like a girl' in their presence, the reason is that he hasn't wanted to have any experience of women, and has been at the utmost pains to avoid them. And from this you must certainly deduce that he will go on in the same way. There is no such thing—in real life—as first love at fifty. Mr Sutro would probably say 'Ah, but you forget: Thursfield is a great engineer.' Sir Henry Killick, the head of the firm in which Thurs-field works, is a tremendous exponent of the theory that no great thing can be achieved by a man who does not resolutely banish women from his mind. That is a theory which I have often heard—

but only across footlights. Among actual engineers, and artists, and statesmen, who have achieved greatness in their respective lines, there have been some into whose lives women entered not at all. There have been others into whose lives women entered excessively much. The majority of them have been in their relations to women just like the majority of other men, we may suppose. This is certain: not one of the great celibate workers has suddenly, after half a century, fallen head over heels in love. Thursfield, in doing so, has no precedents in actual life, but many in the theatre. A sort of precedent for him is to be found even in Mr Sutro's previous play at the St James's. There the hero was an American millionaire, who, after years of immersion in business, during which he took no notice of his wife, became tremendously conjugal when he heard that she was flirting with another man. Of course, this sort of somersault is very effective, in a way. As hero, the strong, cold, detached, elderly man suddenly revealing a boyish heart aflame has a decided advantage (in the eyes of playgoers who have not the inquiring mind) over a young man who has been ardent habitually. Mr Sutro has a keen insight into human character, a keen sense of reality, as he has proved in many passages of his previous plays, and as he proves in many passages of this one. And he will, I am sure, understand my regret that his passion for what is theatrically effective has made Thursfield a not credible hero. Thursfield's heroism is not in itself incredible. A man who is very much in love with a woman would be glad enough to sacrifice a great part of his savings to preserve her brother from disgrace and imprisonment, and would generally comport himself with the delicacy and unselfishness that are to be admired in Thursfield. But Thursfield, as presented by Mr Sutro, wouldn't be in love at all, and would have not the slightest desire to behave heroically. And thus his heroism, like his love, rings false; and he does not illude me as a real man, does but interest me as a stage-figure manipulated brilliantly.

As a result of his unreality, the character of the girl whom he loves, Dorothy Faringay, becomes suspect too. Is she behaving as a girl would, or is she merely being managed in such a way as shall excite the utmost pity for Thursfield and enable him to show off the beauty of his character in the strongest light? I am inclined to think that she is real enough. Granted the circumstances, a girl of her kind might do just what she does. She has a brother, Arnold

Faringay, to whom she is intensely devoted. He is a clerk in the firm to which Thursfield belongs; and he has misappropriated the sum of three thousand pounds in order to win back money that he has lost in speculation. The theft will be detected, probably by Thursfield himself, who is at present having a holiday in St Moritz. Dorothy forms an audacious scheme for saving the situation. She goes off to St Moritz to make Thursfield's acquaintance and to use all her powers to fascinate him and make him propose marriage. One difficulty in her way is that she is already engaged to be married to a young man named Gresham. Her idea is that she will keep Thursfield uninformed of this, and throw him over so soon as he shall have made himself a party to her brother's fraud—in which case, of course, his lips will be sealed. Not a pretty scheme, certainly; but the girl is desperate for her brother, and has never set eyes on Thursfield: he is to her just an instrument for her brother's salvation. Then comes in a further difficulty: in the process of fascinating Thursfield she falls deeply in love with him and detests herself for her cruelty to him. However, having once begun, she must go on, and there is always the chance that she will be able to get quietly out of her engagement to Gresham, and that Thursfield, loving her and knowing that she loves him, will forgive her the stratagem. Unfortunately, Thursfield, soon after he has paid the three thousand pounds out of his own pocket, meets Gresham and hears that he too has been engaged all the time to Dorothy. It is admirably contrived, the scene of this meeting, and the curtain comes down amidst thunders of applause, after Thursfield has riddled Dorothy and her brother through and through with the eloquence of outraged hero. In the entr'acte there is an atmosphere of acute suspense. It is evident that Thursfield is going to forgive. That is an opportunity which Mr Sutro will certainly not deny him. But how is the opportunity to be given? Thus. At St Moritz, Dorothy had given Thursfield a framed photograph of herself, and behind the photograph she had inserted a piece of paper on which she had written words of passionate self-reproach and of passionate love for Thursfield. So, in the last act, when she comes to Thursfield's rooms to tell him that she is not so wholly base as he thinks her, and when he receives her protestations of love with a cold scepticism, the situation is saved by the cryptogram, and the play ends happily. The device is ingenious, of course; but I wish Mr Sutro had secured his happy ending by the more natural means of making Thursfield realise through his own instinct that Dorothy really had been, and was, in love with him.

The character of Arnold Faringay is admirably drawn; but I cannot imagine an actor less suited to it, or less capable of adapting himself to it, than Mr Dawson Milward. It is Arnold's weakness, his irresponsibility, that makes Dorothy's behaviour credible. Herself a person of strong character, she has a maternal sentiment for her brother. He is, as it were, her child; and so she will go to any lengths to shield him. Miss Irene Vanbrugh is a very clever comedian; but I think she could hardly, no matter who were impersonating Arnold, suggest the depth of feeling that is the excuse and the explanation of Dorothy's behaviour. Certainly no actress that I have ever seen could suggest that depth in relation to Arnold as impersonated by Mr Milward. Partly, Mr Milward's badness is due to a physical cause: it is absurd to see a woman wildly shielding a man of six foot three or four. But Mr Milward does not merely kill the play by inches: he kills it by his extraordinary self-possession, and his air of quiet, perfect probity. Arnold is nervous, excitable, and not at all respectable. No man ever was so respectable as Mr Milward seems. Occasionally, Mr Milward contrives, by striking and rigidly preserving an attitude of shame and dejection, to suggest 'The Defaulter' or 'Thou Art The Man!' or some such hypothetical painting by the Hon. John Collier. But there is all the difference between posing as a model and acting; and it is a difference which Mr Milward does not bridge. Luckily, Arnold does not ever in the course of the play appear simultaneously with Sir Henry Killick, the victim of his theft. The method of that very mobile, very fruity and expressive old actor, Mr William Farren, is hardly in key with that of the other members of the company; and I tremble to think what havoc it would make of Mr Milward's. Midway between the old method and the new is that of Mr Alexander, who plays the hero quietly, but with authority and unction.

[*21 November 1908*]

A COMEDY OF THE SUBURBS

Mr Haddon Chambers's new play, *Sir Anthony*, which has been produced at Wyndham's Theatre, is an excellently amusing piece of work. The scheme of it is slight enough. Miss Olive Bruton is one of the belles of Herne Hill, and her heart is divided, in about equal portions, between Clarence Chope and Robert Morrison, both of them clerks in the firm of Bulger and Blount, Pork and Bacon Curers. Morrison is the more dashing and personable of the two; a man noted throughout Herne Hill for his prowess in boxing and other sports. Chope has hitherto cut a rather tame and meagre figure in comparison; but, returning from a visit which he has paid to America in the interest of his firm, he outshines his rival. On board the boat, going to America, he became acquainted with Sir Anthony Mellish, a baronet, whose name he used freely in New York, greatly to the benefit of his errand. By reason of this acquaintance, which he boasts of as an enduring friendship, he is magnified in the eyes of Mr Bulger, who scents further benefits, and of the local Congregational Minister, who scents subscriptions, and of all his family and friends, who would like to meet the baronet. He has written to this baronet 'a cheery little note' recalling their friendship; and the answer is eagerly awaited by everyone. It comes. A sickly pallor creeps over Chope's countenance, and we guess (what we subsequently learn) that the answer is a curt statement, in the 'third person,' that Sir Anthony strongly resents the use that has been made of his name on the strength of a chance acquaintance, and that he requests Mr Chope to desist from troubling him with further communications. Chope has not the courage of his humiliation. He pockets the letter quickly, and, in reply to Mr Bulger's curiosity, says 'Oh, just a cheery little note. He wants me to go and stay—sends his kindest regards to my mother and sister—and so on.' On the strength of this, the family is invited to dine under Mr Bulger's impressive roof in Balham; and it is there that we find them in the second act. To Miss Bruton and Robert Morrison, too, as friends of Chope, invitations have been extended. Morrison is hopelessly in the shade. He has brought his music with him, and sings 'Oh, promise me that some day you and I,' but the song is drowned in conversation. Nemesis, however, is hot on the heels of Chope. Both Mr Bulger and the Congregational Minister have written personal letters to Sir Anthony, on the strength of Chope's connexion. The baronet's answer to Bulger arrives by the last post; and there is a terrible explosion, in which Chope is requested to leave the house, and not return to the office. He stands dazed, alone, staring vacantly, in the conservatory whence all but he have fled. And, as he is impersonated by Mr Weedon Grossmith, you can imagine that we are nearer to tears than to laughter. His sister comes to bring him his overcoat and help him into it. Miss Nina Boucicault plays the sister. She is great, as you know, at suppressed emotion—a sudden catch in the voice, a twitch of the lips, tears welling up but not quite brimming over; and I have never seen her play a part in which there was not at least one chance for this effect, or into which, at any rate, she did not insert the chance on her own responsibility; but I have never seen her create her effect better than at the end of the second act of *Sir Anthony*. In the third act we are back in Herne Hill; and Morrison, of course, is on the crest of the wave. He is impersonated by a young kinsman and surnamesake of mine, whose praises, sung by the other critics, must not be sung by me. I will merely express a hope that Fate will make for my young kinsman an exception in the rule which ordains that a beginner who makes on the London stage a success in a particular kind of part shall not in the course of his life be given a chance of playing any other kind of part. But I digress. In the third act, we are shown how desperation may make a hero out of the most unpromising material. Among the pictures on the wall of the Chopes' drawing-room is a painting (from an enlarged photograph) of the late Mr Chope. The very aggressive expression and posture of this good man fire the son to action. Miss Bruton shall *not* be the spoil of Morrison. And the exact manner of action is suggested by another picture on the wall—a large middle-Victorian engraving of two stags with their antlers laced in deadly combat for the female. Chope has had no experience of fighting, and Morrison is the champion amateur lightweight of the district; but, gradually, Chope, encouraged by his sister, determines that he will risk all on the hazard. He fights Morrison for the favour of Miss Bruton, and, by some extraordinary fluke, beats him. You can imagine Mr Grossmith before and after the combat, can you not? Altogether, he has never had a better part. The excellence of the comedy as a whole cannot be suggested by a mere recital of its story. The great point of it is the extreme fidelity with which Mr Chambers has painted the class of people who are his theme—the exactitude with which he has caught their 'tone' and their manner of speech. Mr Wells and Mr Pett Ridge have, in their books, reproduced the 'lower-middle' and 'middle-middle' classes of Londoners with a serious and delightful accuracy. But Mr Haddon Chambers is the first man who has performed this trick for the stage. There is in his dialogue never a touch of exaggeration, and yet not a line without its queer flavour. The most curious thing in the language of these people is the profusion of proverbs and of quasi-proverbial sayings. They hardly ever say a thing in their own way: almost always they have a cliché to hand, and this they enunciate with a never-fading sense of novelty, and always with startling effect on the interlocutor. Of course, this oddity exists to some extent in all classes; but it flourishes especially in the class which Mr Chambers has depicted. 'My business is my business, and I have pleasure in minding it' says Miss Chope tartly, in reply to an accusation of interference. The dialogue is studded throughout with jewels of just that quality.

In the course of a charity matinée at the Playhouse, last week, was produced a new one-act play, *Love's Toyshop.* Its author, Miss Ella Hepworth Dixon, is known to all of us as a writer with a keen sense of humour, much knowledge of the world, and a manner always incisive. This is the first time, I think, that she has written anything for the stage; but she seems to have been not at all incommoded by her new medium. Her theme is not exactly new. We all know the 'adventuress' who captivates the young man of good family, but is foiled by the polished middle-aged attaché who has met her passing under other names in other capitals of Europe. Miss Hepworth Dixon, however, breathes life and novelty into these familiar figures. The young man, who has a great aesthetic admiration for Rosalie as 'a type of innocent, instinctive, primordial woman,' but is rather bored at the prospect of marrying her against his family's wishes and living quietly in the country with her ever after, is very amusingly drawn. And Rosalie is an 'adventuress' seen from within; a thoroughly convincing human being, in the exposition of whose character there is pathos of a not at all mawkish kind. The play should certainly be produced again.

[*5 December 1908*]

412

'THE LAST OF THE DE MULLINS'

I know it is lamentable of me; but I do prefer the old style of Magdalen to the new. Give me Olivia Primrose and Little Em'ly, and spare me Magda, spare me Janet De Mullin! It is as dramatic critic, not as sociologist, that I utter this cry. And when I say that I, as dramatic critic, like the old Magdalen better than the new, do not accuse me of subscribing to the doctrine that the theatre is no place for ideas. All I mean is that whereas such a person as Olivia was a recognisable (and charming) type of humanity, true to the fashion of her time, such a person as Janet De Mullin never for one moment appears to me as anything but an invention (tedious and jarring) in a good cause.

Had Mr Hankin chosen as the scene for his play the hall of some 'advanced' debating-club, Janet De Mullin might have cut a fairly credible figure. There her inordinate self-complacency and her delight in turning arguments inside out would not have been wholly incongruous with reality. But there is an old tradition, of which modern dramatists have not rid themselves, that the Magdalen must be shown to us in her parental home. So be it. But, in average actual life, how would a Magdalen here behave? She would not, of course, have the drooping head, the quivering lip, the crimson cheek, the footstep faltering on the threshold, which are inseparable from the Magdalen of bygone days. She would not think that she had outraged the laws of God and man, and that she could only hope for redemption by a life of abject self-abasement. Nor would her family take that view. Her family would, however, be shocked and distressed by what she had done. And she (mind you, I am taking the average normal case) would have enough fondness for her family not to resent their feelings, and enough ordinary comprehension to understand their feelings, and good enough manners not to ram sociological theories (however admirable) down their throats. The sort of woman who 'throws her bonnet over the mills' in favour of a man she loves is not likely to be impervious to any other atmosphere of the affections. That sort of woman would have the tact of her humanity. She would feel the awkwardness of the whole situation, and would proceed to pass it off as best she could—*glisserait mais n'appuyerait pas*. But what, then, would become of the sociological cause that Mr Hankin has at heart? The woman *must* sociologise, and be superior and crushing. And so, to reconcile this necessity with her past, Mr Hankin presents her as a woman who has had all her wits about her from the outset, and who overstepped the boundaries of convention not because she fell in love, but because she realised that the mission of women is not to grow old in virginity under their parental roof, but to bear children and carve out careers for themselves elsewhere. In glossing over one improbability, Mr Hankin has surely created another and more glaring one. There have been, doubtless, women who have quite consciously set out to acquire the experience of maternity. George Sand did so, as we know. But the instance of that abnormal woman does but point the abnormality of the proceeding. The maternal instinct is strong both consciously and unconsciously, but no normal woman seeks to fulfil it by the rough-and-ready means of selecting, without reference to any effect that he has on her emotions, the first likely man who comes by. That is what Janet De Mullin did. At the age of twenty-seven, having decided on maternity and freedom from the parental manor house, she marked out, as the father of her child, a young subaltern of twenty, who was staying in the neighbourhood. Having become pregnant, and having had the anticipated scene with her father, she went to London, where, without warning to the negligible subaltern, she bore her child, and, after many bracing vicissitudes, established a bonnet-shop. Apparently, the bonnets were not specially made to be thrown over mills, for she told her customers that she was a widow, whose husband had been drowned at sea. She called him, to satisfy her private sense of humour, Mr Seagrave. Some eight years after the birth of her child, her father fell dangerously ill, and the family telegraphed for her to come to the manor house. The plays opens just before she arrives with her child. Old Mr De Mullin, as acted by Mr H. A. Saintsbury, seems to be at death's door. It is extraordinary that he manages to survive his daughter's visit. He cannot suppose that her pitying smile is for his illness, for she shows so very clearly that it is for his ideas. She patronises him for all she is worth, when she is not trampling on him. She patronises and tramples on her mother, her aunt, and her sister, throughout the play; and most of all does she patronise and trample on the gentleman who happened to be the father of her child. The child himself is the only person to whom she is nice. She seems to cherish him as a cudgel with which

to batter the heads of everyone else. The blows she deals all round
are ever shrewd and resonant. Sociologically, propagandistically, she
is brilliant. But dramatically, humanly—no, she doesn't exist. You
see the dilemma that confronted Mr Hankin? Janet had either to be
a wildly abnormal woman who would vociferate his own admirable
views, or to be a normal woman who wouldn't say anything in
particular. He might, as I have hinted, have dodged this dilemma by
dodging the convention of the Magdalen's return to the parental
roof. Or again (and this, I think, would have been the better way)
he might have let his views be vociferated by one of the other persons in the play—Mr Brown, the curate, for example, or Dr Rolt,
the medical practitioner, to neither of whom does he allow any
quality at all. As she stands, Janet kills the play. But I cannot mourn
very bitterly a play killed by ideas, even though it might have survived them. '*C'est une belle mort*,' and a very rare one.

As you may imagine, no one in the cast, except Miss Lillah
McCarthy, as Janet, has a chance of acting, in the strict sense: to be
passive is all that they can do; and very well they do it—especially
Mr Vernon Steel, as the father of Janet's child. So worsted is he by
Janet in course of the conversation in which he learns of his paternity
that he does not even rise from his seat when the child comes on.
Much of the gleaming and inflexible divinity of manner that made
Miss McCarthy's performance of Dionysus so convincing, a few
weeks ago, re-appears in her performance of Janet, appropriately.

[*12 December 1908*]

MR GRAHAM ROBERTSON AND THE FAIRIES

It is my rule not to write about the doings of my kinsman at His
Majesty's Theatre; and I must not, therefore, appraise his production
of *Pinkie and the Fairies*. But, as I am not related to Mr Heinemann,
I see no reason why I should not now write about *Pinkie and the
Fairies*, by W. Graham Robertson. London: William Heinemann.
1s. net. Indeed, I see a fairly good reason why I *should*. The other
critics, writing about the play from the playgoers' standpoint, have
not, I think, done full justice to the inner charms of Mr Graham
Robertson's work. How should they? Of course, it is right that a

play be judged primarily as a play—as a thing for the theatre. As such, *Pinkie and the Fairies* holds its own. But always, in seeing a play that you have not read, you should leave a margin for un-detected merits in the author's work. The quality of the acting, and of the stage-management, things more or less outside the author's control, are very apt to affect your judgment. The people on the stage are more real to you than is the unseen author, and your sym-pathies go out to them quicklier. If these people delight you, you give them more of the credit than is their due. If they don't delight you, you blame the author for giving them thankless parts. The critics have been delighted not only by the people who act in *Pinkie and the Fairies* but also by the music and the scenery; so that it would have been too much to expect that even the most penetrating of them would do full justice to Mr Robertson's work, by them un-read. For example, when I saw the play, not having read it, I had no notion of the delicate charm of Mr Robertson's lyrics. I was conscious only that certain words were being sung to Mr Norton's charming music. That was not the fault of the singers. It is the fault of music, an art which, whether well or ill exemplified, in-variably takes precedence of any other art which comes into contact with it. Who that had only heard Shakespeare's songs sung on the stage would have any but the vaguest conception of their magic? Or—to take a humbler example—who that had only heard Mr Gilbert's songs sung would be able to revel in the neatness of their wit and their versification? Of course, songs are written to be sung (just as man is born to sorrow), but it is only by reading them that you can appreciate their goodness—or their badness. Without the music, and without the living and moving fairies and frogs and other creatures, and without the moon through the enchanted wood, *Pinkie* would not do on the stage—would not at all fulfil the pur-pose that Mr Robertson had in writing it. But it is exactly when these gracious assets are away that we can judge Mr Robertson's work as in itself it is.

Without appreciation of Mr Robertson's lyrics, throughout the play, we cannot get the full savour of the play's fun. For this fun is based on sharp contrasts between the poetic nature of children and the prosaic nature of grown-up people. Psychologically, of course, this contrast doesn't hold water. There are poetic children, and prosaic grown-up people; and there are not many poetic grown-up people; but neither are there many poetic children. As basis for a fantasy, however, Mr Robertson's proposition will do very well. Aunt Imogen, Aunt Caroline, and Uncle Gregory are sunk in materialism. Their thoughts are ever of the boiler, the kitchen range, the cistern, and the advantages of gravel soil. Their joy is in looking forward to meals, and to the news in the evening paper. Pinkie, the niece, and Tommy, the nephew, despise them deeply, and, seeing in them an awful example, have a horror of growing up, and are determined that, when the awful time comes, they will continue to behave just like children. I need hardly say that actual children— and I won't say it: Mr Robertson's postulates shall not be tampered with. Pinkie and Tommy are both of them in close touch with the fairies, whom the aunts and the uncle cannot see. When, robed in rose colour, the fairies come 'to sing the day to sleep,' Aunt Caroline, 'with condescension,' says 'Quite a remarkable effect of light this evening, Imogen'; and Aunt Imogen, 'with culture,' mentions Turner. 'What's Turner?' whispers Pinkie to Tommy, who replies '*I* don't know. But that's how they always go on when the fairies sing the sunset song.'

> 'Day was born a springing lark,
> Day must die a nightingale.
> Day arose a kindled spark,
> Now he flames on hill and dale.
> Heap the incense higher still
> Till his pyre an altar grows.
> Day was born a daffodil,
>   Day dies a rose.'

Thus sing the fairies, all unheard save by the children. A bell sounds, and the grown-up people spring to their feet, Aunt Caroline singing

> 'Hark! Hark! The Note,
>   The Warning Bell
> From Brazen throat
>   Pours forth its knell.
> Though suns decline,
>   Though night clouds lower,
> We dine! We dine!
>   Within the hour.'

Spiritually midway between the fairies and the aunts is the children's cousin Molly, who has just 'come out.' She is too old to see the fairies clearly, and too young not to see them at all; and, after two nightingales have been singing a lyric to wake the fairies, she says 'there almost seemed to be words.' She is young enough to be invited to the fairies' party in the wood. But when she is 'presented,' the Queen seems a little surprised at her age, and the Herald explains that 'everything is quite regular, Your Majesty. She is in the charge of two very capable babes.' She meets Cinderella at the party—Cinderella more grown-up than herself, and a Princess —but does not recognise her next day in Uncle Gregory's garden. Mr Robertson's treatment of Cinderella—keeping all her story, but carrying it to a logical conclusion, and finally projecting her for a while into everyday life—is one of the best of his flights of whim, and very typical of his whole contrastive method. She arrives late at the fairies' party: she *always* is late: the habit has grown on her. She is inclined to give herself airs: 'balls—banquets—bazaars—foundation-stones—my dear, one can hardly turn round.' But as the clock strikes midnight, her beautiful gown turns to rags. She has got used to that tragedy, and carries it off with a high hand. Also, when her coach is called, and turns out to be the withered half of a huge pumpkin, driven by a rat, she says 'Well, well! Lucky it's a fine night. The open carriage will be rather pleasant.' Some of the critics have scolded Mr Robertson for treating Cinderella, Sleeping Beauty, and other figures of fairy lore in this familiar and realistic way. To them these figures are quite unreal, and can only pass muster in the distance. To Mr Robertson they are real, so that he is able to treat them as such. He is able to treat them familiarly because they are familiars of his. He is a true fantastic. I am grateful for him.

I suppose it is inevitable that one should compare the author of *Pinkie* with that other true fantastic, the author of *Peter Pan*. But, barring their fantasticism, these two authors have really very little in common. Mr Barrie's boy-characters are real in their craving for actual adventure by land and sea, and very unreal (as are also his girl-characters) in their acute sentimentality. Mr Robertson's Tommy and Pinkie are not sentimental at all, and are fond of the fairies because the fairies are more amusing than other people. Mr Robertson shows that he himself is sentimental, but also that he is cynical; and

(though children are no more cynical than they are sentimental) the
balance between the two qualities in him has enabled him to make
his children more real than Mr Barrie's. Nor could two forms of
quaintness in humour be more different than Mr Barrie's and Mr
Robertson's. Mr Barrie is ever sudden, explicit, thoroughly dramatic:
his ideas strike you across the footlights, and convulse you. Mr
Robertson's ideas are of a coyer, slyer kind; and for their full savour
you need the printed page. *Peter Pan*, in its whole structure, is the
work of a born playwright. *Pinkie* is the work of a gifted painter
and poet who set himself the task of putting his fancies into
dramatic form—the work of an altogether gifted man who achieved
that task very well indeed. As a play, *Pinkie* deserves its success.
For the many qualities that do not contribute to that success, *Pinkie*
should be read.

[*2 January 1909*]

A PARENTHESIS

In *The Times* of last Wednesday was printed, in small type, a
letter from Mr Croal Thomson, rebuking certain critics who had
disparaged certain pictures in the McCulloch Collection at Burlington House. One sentence in this letter surely deserved to be printed
in large type, or at any rate in italics; for it is very splendid. 'After
all,' writes Mr Thomson, 'art does not consist of one school of
thought and practice alone, and a writer should be able to rid himself
of his swaddling clothes of criticism and take up a manly attitude of
broad sympathy towards all aspects of art-production.' I suppose I
ought really to have left this gem to be appraised for you by Mr
Binyon. But there is the chance that it did not catch his eye. Let
me, in a neighbourly way, draw his very special attention to it, and
ask him to consider his position. Probably, throughout his life, he
had been supposing that the business of an art-critic was to train
his faculties in such manner that he could distinguish good from
bad, to develop certain general canons which would act as touch-
stones for the works under his survey, and to distribute praise and
blame accordingly, without fear—blame for (let us say) the Leaders
and Stones, the Poynters and Fildeses, and praise for younger,

more sincere and more talented men whose endeavour seemed to him commendable. Criticism, I fancy, had seemed to him a function quite worthy of an adult. It is high time for him to learn from Mr Thomson the essentially infantile nature of the thing. Let him, as 'a writer,' strip off those 'swaddling clothes.' Let him be cured, as soon as may be, of the whooping-cough of discrimination, and the nettle-rash of reasoned judgment. Let him hide that coral-and-bells which his theories of truth and beauty are, and forthwith 'take a manly attitude.' Any baby can embrace what is good in art. The grown-up man proclaims his maturity by embracing also what is bad and indifferent.

Nor is it only Mr Binyon who must pull himself together. Not less urgent are the cases of Mr Filson Young and myself; for Mr Thomson's pronouncement cannot be narrowed to the sphere of pictures: it covers all the other spheres of art. But it is so sudden. I don't know how Mr Filson Young feels, but *I* am too staggered to pull myself together all at once. The old habit of discrimination, of excluding what I adjudge bad, cannot be thrown off in a moment. But Mr Somerset Maugham is a neophyte in the art of dramatic criticism, and presumably more malleable than I in proportion to his freshness. And, as he is very much more exclusive in his judgments than I am in mine, he stands in the greater need of edification. I admit that the plays that give me the most pleasure, and the plays that seem to me (by reason of their present rarity) to deserve the most encouragement, are plays that have 'ideas' in them, and plays that are deliberate attempts to present this or that phase of our various life as it is. These are the plays that I, personally, find the most entertaining. Yet I have never decried a play merely because it did but set out to be entertaining in the usual sense of the word. I have always welcomed the merely frivolous comedies and farces whose frivolity seemed to me of a distinguished kind. I am not hostile to any department of dramatic art. I am hostile merely to such bad work as I find in those several departments. Mr Maugham, on the other hand, is a stern proscriptionist. To him, apparently, the 'serious' drama is a thing very ridiculous, very negligible. He has been telling an interviewer that it is 'most unwise' of dramatists to 'take themselves seriously.' He has no patience with 'great central ideas'; and 'to entertain,' he declares (using the word evidently in the sense of 'causing to laugh'), 'should be the first—perhaps the only—aim of the playwright.' Well, to 'the plain man' this sort of pronouncement by an eminent artist is always comforting and re-assuring. And I am not surprised that the *Referee*, which, in theatrical affairs, represents (always very ably and amusingly) the interests of 'the plain man,' has expressed its joy in Mr Maugham's sound commonsense, and set on record that there is no nonsense about him. But when an artist, in any art, after delivering an opinion in aesthetics, finds himself being patted on the back by 'the plain man,' he may well have misgivings, and examine with some care the opinion that evoked the cordiality. For no artist of any rank, since the world began, has been 'a plain man,' or—in matters relating to his art—on terms of sympathy with 'the plain man.' The qualities that go to make a creative artist, and the qualities that are fostered in him by creation, are very different from those (in their way admirable) qualities of which 'the plain man' is composed. That Mr Maugham had, even in the moment of utterance, some mis-givings as to the propriety of his remarks, I am led to suspect by his insertion of the word 'perhaps' before 'the only.' Of course it is from the commercial standpoint 'most unwise' of dramatists to 'take themselves seriously'; and no doubt Mr Maugham's great com-mercial success was retarded by the managers' suspicion that the author of *A Man of Honour* would never be likely to hit the taste of the public. But it is inconceivable that Mr Maugham, an artist, re-grets his unwisdom in writing that play, and is not proud of that play as a thing that in its own sphere stands on a far higher level than his light comedies stand in theirs. I have no doubt that Mr Maugham has it in him to write a light comedy as fine as that first bitter tragi-comedy. If light comedy is the only form that he cares to practise now, let him devote himself to that, by all means. But it is hardly gracious in him to gibe at other men—fellow-artists—who, conscientiously, but unremuneratively, are treading the path to which his own first ambitions led him. The work that he is doing, and wishes to do, happens to pay. The work that those others are doing, and wish to do, happens not to. But they have as good a right as he has to persist, and more need than he has to be en-couraged. Let Mr Maugham leave to 'the plain man' the task of discouraging them. Artists, however diverse, should uphold one an-other.

Especially ought artists in dramaturgy to do this. Mr Maugham knows as well as I do that the test of a play's value is not in its immediate popularity. He knows that in drama, as in other forms of literature, and as in painting and sculpture, the public hates any-thing to which it is unaccustomed, and can only be bullied and coaxed into acquiescence by the persons—the few persons—who happen to be equipped for appreciating the new thing, whatever it may be. A young painter or sculptor of genius can afford to dis-regard the public. There are always a few enlightened patrons to keep him going. A young poet or novelist of genius can always make a pittance. There is a small enlightened public to keep *him* going. But this small enlightened public cannot keep going a young dramatist of genius, or any other young dramatist whose plays are not of the kind to which the general public is accustomed. No manager, in the ordinary way, can afford to produce such plays. Lately, 'Vedrenne-Barker' produced plays of an unaccustomed kind; and there were signs, after a while, after much bullying and coaxing, that the general public was beginning to be interested, and might presently begin even to appreciate. I never cease to mourn 'Ved-renne-Barker.' Perhaps the new Afternoon Theatre will efface, in due time, the memory of that dear departed. But, however helpful one and another such venture may be, what is really needed for the drama's future is a permanently endowed little Experimental Theatre. A National Theatre, however elastic the intentions of its pious founder, would inevitably, sooner or later—and, I think, sooner—sink into majestic academicism, and be nothing but a great rich paddock for the war-horses of the past. The true re-quisite is a jolly little paddock for the colts to kick up their heels in. Why should not Mr Maugham be the pious founder?

[*9 January 1909*]

A BAFFLING PLAY

Habitually, we take as a matter of course the familiar furniture of our civilisation. That is well for our peace of mind. There do, however, come to all of us moments in which this or that trite and humble object suddenly asserts itself and puts in a claim to be con-sidered complex, mysterious, altogether remarkable, and we find our imagination stirred, and our curiosity piqued, and our heads dizzy with the glimpses we are having into immensity. Such a moment came to me a few evenings ago, on my way to the New Theatre. The hansom in which I was being driven suddenly asserted itself and put in its claim. I found myself dropping a tear over the memory of Mr Hansom, only begetter of these vehicles, and then gasping at the thought of all that had gone to the construction of the one particular hansom that contained me. How many carpenters and joiners had been engaged on it? What woodman had hewed the tree or trees of which it was composed? Who had been the glazier, and who had blown the glass? What assistants of what upholsterer had sewn the buttons on to the leather? Who had tanned the skins? What were the animals whose skins had been tanned? Who had tended these animals when they were alive? How had they met their death? And how—how glad I was when the cab drew up at the portico of the New Theatre! But alas, my mind was not long to be left at rest. It had, as I found soon after the rising of the curtain, only been switched off from one set of these harassing inquiries to another. *Henry of Navarre* soon asserted itself as a product quite as complex as that hansom. On the programme it was said to have been written by 'William Devereux.' Well, I asked myself, who were William Devereux? who were the innumerable journeymen whose identities were veiled under that collective pseudonym? For it was inconceivable that any one man could have sat down with the intention of writing such a play as *Henry of Navarre*. It was as inconceivable as that a man should feel within himself the impulse to turn out a hansom entirely by his own handicraft—framework, cushions, windows, cigar-rests, harness, and all. Suppose a man *did* feel this impulse. The result would not be a hansom in which you would care to be driven. The man could not possibly have mastered the various kinds of skilled labour that were necessary to the fulfillment of his absurd ambition. I admit that an artist, sustained by a great love of his art, often masters this and that craft which is allied to his work. But a hansom is not a work of art. It is just a useful vehicle for you and me. *Henry of Navarre* is not related to art in the remotest degree. It is just a useful vehicle for Mr Fred Terry and Miss Julia Neilson. I can well imagine a man wishing to purvey it, just as I can enter into the feelings of a coach-builder in Long Acre or elsewhere. Where there is a demand it is natural that there should be a supply. The coach-builder wants to make money, so he employs a variety of specialised journeymen who will, between them, turn out good coaches. *Henry of Navarre* is quite good of its kind. And hence the difficulty of imagining 'William Devereux' except as what is called a large employer of skilled labour.

If a play is a work of art, I am never puzzled about its genesis. When I see a play by Mr Jones, Mr Shaw or Mr Barker, by Mr Maugham, Mr Davies or Mr Haddon Chambers, no bewilderment supervenes. The whole affair is quite simple. The author had conceived some idea which he wished to illustrate, or just some story which he wished to tell—and there he was: down he sat, with that impulse, and carried his task through in his own simple fashion. When I admire a play, I always feel that I could have written something of the sort myself—if I happened to have an instinct for playwriting. But I dare not imagine that I could, however keen that instinct were in me, achieve anything at all like *Henry of Navarre*. What possible inducement could there be? The prospect of providing harmless entertainment for thousands of simple souls? That would be all very well if I were a simple soul myself. Is Mr Devereux a simple soul? Not he. A man who could achieve *Henry of Navarre* (and, of course, literally speaking, Mr Devereux is the sole author) must be a very artful soul indeed—very *rusé* and sophisticated. He must first have studied with minute care the methods of Mr Fred Terry and Miss Julia Neilson, and have subtly diagnosed their large, affectionate public. And he must have been a student of French history. 'Henri de Bourbon! Why not?—Marguerite de Valois! Capital!—Massacre of the Huguenots! The very thing!' To have read history is easy enough; but history won't carry our friend far. He must use his own wits—no! not his own: that would be fatal. He must not give his particular public anything it does not know by heart. Marguerite must, when she was just blossoming into girlhood, have leaned out from a balcony and beheld a man whom, knowing him not, she has loved ever since. And he must be none other than young Henry; and his reason for having been in Paris must be that he had fallen in love with her miniature; and he must be even now returning to claim her as his bride. And, when he arrives, he must sit down on the very chair where Marguerite had been sitting, and recount to his rough henchmen the little tender episode that Marguerite had been recounting to her lady-in-waiting.

But before this, since the public demands that Mr Terry shall be a devil of a fellow just at the outset of a play, he must have kissed the lady-in-waiting, strange though this action may be in a man sur-charged with lyric passion for her mistress. And, since Miss Neilson is famous for flouncing and bouncing contemptuously around the stage, tossing her head and covering suitors with raillery, it follows that Marguerite's impression of Henry at close quarters must be an unfavourable one. But how could anyone, without straining the credulity of the audience, form an unfavourable impression of Mr Fred Terry at close quarters? Well, to such masters as Mr Devereux, obstacles are but the stepping-stones to triumphs. Why not drag in Petruchio? Why shouldn't Henry, for no earthly reason, pretend to be a boor? And, as he is a Gascon, a Yorkshire accent would be the very thing. But, of course, by reason of his great love, his assumption must break down from time to time (see *David Garrick*, Act III), and his refined true self shine touchingly through. The play must not, however, end abruptly with Marguerite's discovery that Henry is refined. Another and more serious misunderstanding is needed to carry us along. Let Henry think that Marguerite loves him not, after their wedding—nay! that she seeks to poison him at the behest of infamous Catherine de Medici. And hereby we shall have further opportunities of seeing Mr Terry as a devil of a fellow, dancing the pavane with maids-of-honour to whom he is pretending to make love. The proud set face that masks the breaking heart of beauty neglected is a thing which the public has a right to demand of Miss Neilson for a few minutes every evening. Very well then: here it is. And, in due course of bitterness, Marguerite yields to the importunities of the villain De Guise so far as to permit him to visit her in her chamber, thus securing a strong third act. She repents, of course; but too late: De Guise is here! Whose footstep is that in the corridor? The King's! Heaven help Marguerite! The prayer is answered. A hooded and cloaked stranger, speaking with a German accent, slips in through the window. He has a rope ladder, and he insists gutturally that De Guise shall descend by it. He himself hides in a cupboard; and the King is admitted to the room, noisily de-claring that De Guise is hidden there—there in that cupboard. Out comes—who d'you think?—You will never guess—young Henry of Navarre! Marguerite's honour is saved! And Mr Fred Terry has talked with a German accent! The public is profoundly moved by this double event. And still there is the massacre of the Huguenots in store; and Henry's refusal not to be mixed up in it, despite Marguerite's entreaties; and his triumphant return; and his attempted murder by the bravos of De Guise; and the happy ending. Exigencies of space have compelled me to omit many popular features of the play. Mr Devereux has omitted nothing. There is an astrologer, and there are spiritualistic apparitions, and there is comic relief—everything of every kind that simple souls, however greedy, can desire.

What was it that impelled Mr Devereux to the performance of his awful task, and sustained him through it? Not hope of glory. There is no glory to be got out of this sort of work. The critics do but sneer. And the simple souls talk only of Mr Terry and Miss Neilson. Can it be that Mr Devereux was sustained solely by the desire for gold? If so, I fear he must be exceptionally avaricious.

[*16 January 1909*]

'OLIVE LATIMER'S HUSBAND'

This play, which was produced last Tuesday evening at the Vaudeville Theatre, has made me regret more than ever that there is not, under the present system, any inducement for a dramatist to write plays in less than three acts. Obviously, it is absurd that a man who has a good idea for a one-act play should cast it into the form of a curtain-raiser. Two other courses are open to him. He may cast his idea into the form of a short story, and send it to one of the two or three periodicals not hostile to short stories that have artistic quality. Or (the more lucrative and more exciting way) he may spin his idea out to the length of a play that will fill an evening bill. This is the way that Mr Rudolf Besier has chosen. And the result was that I did not begin to be more than mildly interested in his play before the beginning of the third and last act.

This comparative apathy was not at all due to the fact that Mr Besier's theme was a familiar one, nor to any idea in my head that the theme was not, in itself, one on which a full-length play could rightly be founded. Ibsen handled the theme in *Rosmersholm*; and from the masterpiece one would not wish a word omitted. Mrs

426

W. K. Clifford handled the theme in *The Likeness of the Night*, and I was interested throughout the course of that play. And I am quite prepared to be satisfied by other full-length plays founded on precisely the same basis. All I say is that this theme, in the form in which it presented itself to Mr Besier's mind, ought to have been treated in a play of one act. It is not difficult to strip off the surplusage and see just what Mr Besier's original conception was. He saw three characters on the stage: Mrs Latimer, Sir Charles Weyburn, and Dr Morpeth. Off the stage was a fourth character: Mrs Latimer's husband. The antecedent history was as follows. Mrs Latimer had never been in love with her husband. She had married him when she was a very young girl, simply because her parents wished it. He had known quite well that she did not care about him; but he had thought she might do so in course of time. This hope was not fulfilled. The person she did learn to care about was her husband's old friend, Sir Charles Weyburn. With him she was definitely unfaithful to her husband. Latimer did not perhaps know how far she had gone; but he knew enough to make him forbid Weyburn to come again to the house. Some time elapsed, neither of the lovers seeing each other, and the male one bitterly ashamed of what had passed. Latimer contracted typhoid fever. His life was for many days in danger. If he survived, it would be through the unremitting care of his doctor and nurses. Mrs Latimer felt, and hated herself for feeling, deep down in her heart, the hope that he would not live. And one night, in the very crisis of the illness, when she went into her husband's room and found the nurse fast asleep, and the invalid apparently asleep, she was as tempted to steal softly away without waking the nurse; and to this temptation she did presently yield. All the next day she was haunted not only by her crime, but also by the doubt whether her husband had been actually asleep— whether he might not have seen her. That he had seen her is made hideously certain by what the doctor tells her. Latimer, while his nurse was asleep, had got out of bed (though the doctor had warned him emphatically that the slightest exertion would be fatal) and had written and sealed a letter to Weyburn. Also, he had caused to be dispatched in the morning a telegram bidding Weyburn to come instantly to see him. The letter itself was to be given to Weyburn so soon as he should arrive. Mrs Latimer guesses the contents of the letter: a denunciation of her crime—a dying man's denunciation that shall keep her and Weyburn apart for ever. In vain, she urges the doctor to give the letter into her keeping. When Weyburn arrives, the doctor hands it to him, and goes back to the patient. Weyburn treats Mrs Latimer with coldness, even with aversion. But suddenly, despite himself, his old passion re-awakens, and he kisses her; and then, of course, is overwhelmed by the ghastliness of what he has done. Mrs Latimer persuades him not to read the letter till he has seen her husband. But the doctor comes to tell them that Latimer is now dead. Then Weyburn is going to read the letter. Mrs Latimer puts forth all her ingenuity to persuade him to burn it unread. When she sees that he is inflexible, she claims from him the right to make a confession first. She confesses to him what she has done, and then opens the letter and reads it aloud. Not a word of accusation from the dying man; merely his declaration that he had done wrong in marrying a girl who did not love him; his entire forgiveness of what she and Weyburn had done; and his great hope that they would marry and be always very happy. And when the reading is finished, and Weyburn tries to utter some words of consolation, even of hope, 'No, leave me,' says the heart-broken woman; 'leave me here, with my husband.'

As you perceive, all this falls into the form of a one-act play. The antecedent circumstances can all be gradually and effectively evolved by the dialogue between the three characters. And within the compass of the little play here adumbrated is contained really all that is vital in *Olive Latimer's Husband*. Of the time covered by the action of his play Mr Besier has been sparing, though not so sparing as I have been of the time to be occupied by the performance of this abridged version. 'The action takes place between 6 P.M. and 10.15 P.M. on a Winter's Evening. A minute is supposed to elapse between Acts I and II, two hours between Acts II and III.' But two hours and fourteen minutes of mimic life is too capacious a period to fit just what was essential to Mr Besier's scheme. So there had to be a deal of padding. And the padding is not good of its kind. Colonel and Mrs Mapleson-Finch, the parents of Mrs Latimer, represent, I suppose, an honest attempt on Mr Besier's part to portray types of actual life; but the attempt has failed miserably, and these two personages are very dull caricatures indeed, and would pass muster nowhere except in a Drury Lane melodrama. The younger daughter whom they are offering up on the altar of Mammon is not made real for a moment, nor is the sacrifice of her redeemed of its staleness. And when I say that her middle-aged fiancé has a bald head with black-dyed hair brushed forward over each ear, and that this make-up exactly befits him as created by Mr Besier, you will have an accurate notion of *his* freshness and reality. Such characters as these do not serve to pass the time agreeably; and when, as happens in the last act, they are dragged in at a moment of crucial dramatic interest, simply to spin the evening out, it is a marvel that the play manages to survive them. Its survival is a sure sign of its own essential strength.

The character of Mrs Latimer, a very complicated one, is finely drawn, drawn with insight and with a sense of tragic pity. It is a part worthy to be played by Mrs Campbell. We all rejoice to see again this great actress, whose dramatic power seems to have gone on increasing without hurt to the peculiar magic that is hers.

[*23 January 1909*]

AN ACTOR IN JEOPARDY

If I were about to become an actor, and were given by a good fairy the choice of being either beautiful to the eye and ear or merely passable, I think I should choose to be merely passable. That is, un-less the fairy would 'throw in' such terrific strength of character as would make me adamant to the public's demand for me to be always showing myself off in the most heroic and endearing light that could be arranged for me by the skill of this or that obsequious playwright. Endowed as I am, with no more than average strength of character, I should doubtless yield to the sweet demand of my devout public; and thus (supposing that I had in me the makings of a fine actor) there would be a grave loss to the art of the theatre.

These thoughts occurred to me last Tuesday evening at the Lyric Theatre. I had not within the past two or three years been present at one of Mr Lewis Waller's first nights. I had been present only on subsequent nights, and so had not realised to the full how very tremendous may be the pressure generated by adoration of an actor who is surpassingly beautiful to the eye and ear. The enthusiasm for Mr Waller's self had been, on those subsequent nights, very strong, very remarkable. But only on a first night is its full strength made manifest. I have heard that in one of the suburbs there is—and, for aught I know, there may be in every suburb, and in every district within the four-mile radius—a club called 'The Waller Club,' consisting of some thirty or forty young ladies, who meet once a week to discuss this or that aspect of Mr Waller. On such and such a date (I suppose) 'Miss Eva Robinson will read a paper on "HIS Eyes"' or 'Miss Letty Simpson will open a debate on "What would be the Main Lines of England's Policy at Home and Abroad if HE were Prime Minister?"' or 'Miss Gwendolen Baker will deliver an address entitled "A Critical Estimate of what there is in HIS Little Finger as Compared with what there was in the Whole Bodies of Roscius, Burbage, Garrick and Kemble, Collectively"' or 'Miss Susie Parkes will read a paper on "HIS Profile."' I have heard that it is the custom of this club (or these clubs?) to attend in full force at Mr Waller's first nights, fiftieth nights, hundredth nights and so forth. And, judging by the noise there was when Mr Waller appeared, and at the end of every act, I conceive there was not a single absentee from the first performance of *The Chief of Staff*. But, bless their fluttering hearts and willing lungs, they alone could not have achieved such a shindy as there was to deafen us. Their screams sounded almost faint in the deep-chested masculine roar that rolled and swelled whenever Mr Waller came or went. Their cries were but as the piping of birds in a den of ravenous lions. So I conjecture that every member of a Waller Club makes a point not merely of attending in person at her hero's festivals, but also of taking in tow her father, her brothers, her brothers' boon-companions, and perhaps her 'intended,' under strict orders to shout themselves as hoarse as they can. And I fancy it is always her endeavour to outdo, in the size and resonance of her party, every one of the other girls in *hers*. I can imagine keen jealousies afoot, and bitter comments—'It's all very well for Letty Simpson to bring her seven hulking brothers; but if she thinks she's going to be President next year, she'll find she's *quite* mistaken!' or 'That young fellow that Susie Parkes is engaged to, he never shouted out once, the whole evening. He just sat there muttering to himself. So like Susie to go and *waste* a seat, on HIS first night!' I do not think there can have been many seats wasted in that way last Tuesday. The drums of my ears bore witness to an all but perfect organisation of enthusiasm. I may have heard noises elsewhere, but never so senseless, mechanical and kakophonous a din.

The volume of sound spontaneously emitted by an audience that has been thrilled by fine acting in a fine play is not at all an unmusical sound. Its meaning somehow harmonises it. But heaven stop my ears against the preconcerted howlings of an audience set on out-doing all its previous efforts in honour of Mr Waller's self!

Is Mr Waller's head turned? I dare say he has more strength of character than I gave myself credit for just now, and remains calm in the storm of partly-real, partly-factitious adulation. But it matters not whether he be calm or excited in the storm. What does matter is that he seeks no shelter therefrom, and keeps himself resolutely ex-posed thereto. Himself won't suffer, of course. Years hence, when an equally magnetic but younger and more beautiful man than he shall have come along and cut him out as 'matinée idol,' himself will retire into private life, hale and hearty, with a vast sum of money. But his art, meanwhile, does suffer—through sheer inanition. An actor—however great his gifts—who goes on acting inane parts must presently become mechanical; and that is what Mr Waller is fast becoming. Always there was in his method a certain lack of supple-ness, a certain hardness; and these will ere long be the sole features of his method, unless he takes himself in hand and throws himself into parts that have some sense in them, and some variety. 'If thy right eye offend thee, pluck it out.' I can imagine the ululations that would rise from the Waller Club (or Clubs) if Mr Waller plucked out that lucent orb of his—if, in other words, he gave up the business of playing the reach-me-down heroic parts to which he has accus-tomed us, and bent himself to the task of playing some part worth playing. Nevertheless, I am heartless enough to urge him on. After all, as I have said, some other equally efficacious 'matinée idol' is bound to come along, and then the tears will be dried, and the Club (or Clubs) be renamed accordingly. And it may be that the new man will not happen to have any potentiality for fine acting; in which case we shall not have to grudge him, as we grudge Mr Waller, to his silly public of personal adorers.

Meanwhile, I do not propose to criticise *The Chief of Staff*. It is a rigmarole which shows off Mr Waller personally. This is all one need say of it.

[*6 February 1909*]

A YOUNG OLD PLAY

I suppose that some fourteen years have elapsed since first Mr Alexander tried *The Prisoner of Zenda*. This, for most plays, is a disastrous interval—long enough to have made them old-fashioned, and not long enough to have endowed them with an appeal to our sentiment, to our curiosity. It is touching and amusing to see the plays that pleased our fathers or grandfathers; but we fidget at sight of plays that pleased our own benighted selves. *The Prisoner of Zenda*, however, fails to distress us. Of course, the fashion to which it belongs, or rather the fashion which it set, has gone out utterly. But it was never meant to be taken seriously. It was just a pretty little joke. 'The middle ages,' murmured Mr Anthony Hope, 'are romantic to us, though they were doubtless mere prose to the people who lived in them. Our own period may be destined to thrill posterity; but us it leaves cold. Let us take some pardonable liberties with it. Let us, just for fun, deck it out with whatever mediaeval trappings most delight us, and see what it looks like. Let us have dungeons with kings in them—tourists dressing up as kings—plenty of cold steel, plenty of hot blood,' etc., etc. 'Oh, do let's,' cried the public, clapping its hands; and Ruritania was a huge success for quite a long time. I don't know how many plays were composed on the Ruritanian model. They came thick and fast; but none of their writers, so far as I remember, had Mr Hope's light hand; and a light hand is needed for confectionery. Mr Hope's manner of making his play was not as of a man asking us to believe the story, but as of one inviting us to agree with him how delightful it would be if such things *could* happen. His play was, in the direct sense, a criticism of life. Its great point was in being so frank a fantasy. And therein, too, lies the secret of the freshness it still has for us. If a dramatist sits down to criticise life soberly, through portrayal of men and women as he sees them—if, in fact, he takes the advice that I am always offering him, he will get a very good notice in this Review when his play is produced; but he will get anything but a good notice when his play is revived in 1923 or thereabouts. Essentially, life will be still the same then as it is now; but the superficial tricks of thought and speech will have changed enough to make this unfortunate gentleman's play quite intolerably unlike life. The technique of playwriting will have changed too. Perhaps we shall have grown weary of the tight technique of to-day; or perhaps this technique will seem loose in comparison with what we shall then be accustomed to. What is certain is that the fashion will be quite different, and that, in the light of this change alone, the realism of to-day will carry no illusion of reality. When *The Prisoner of Zenda* was written, the habit of soliloquy was still thriving on the stage. It incommoded no one, even in plays whose aim was the portrayal of actual life. But you know how fatal to us now, in such plays, that innocent convention is. On the other hand, if, in the twentieth (or, to be exact, the nineteenth) century, a tourist happens to resemble the local king so closely that he can successfully impersonate him at a moment's notice, and be crowned thereafter in his stead, and make the lady who is betrothed to the other man think she is beginning to fall in love with the other man, and if, in addition to such feats as these, he can perform in the most approved manner all the fighting and jesting and renouncing prescribed by Dumas *père* and other masters of the historical romance, far be it from me to chide him for occasionally talking aloud to himself in public. Such a man is privileged: not pretending to be real, he is not expected to behave as such; and, as he is a witty figment, he and the play whose hero he is come out just as fresh to-day as they did fourteen years ago. If ever, in the dim future, the world shall revert to the mediaeval way of conducting its affairs, and this play shall accordingly be judged by the standards of realistic art, Rudolf Rassendyll will not, we must fear, pass muster. But meanwhile the play will go on being welcome. Unless Mr Alexander ages more in the next than he has aged in the past fourteen years, he will still be the man for the part. His performance is full of mettle and flourish, and is given with just that outer manner of sincerity which is needed for the full fun of the thing. Mr Frank Cooper, as the Black Elphberg, seems to me to force the note a little—to be a trifle too black. There is no such note of insincerity in Miss Stella Campbell's impersonation of Princess Flavia. Indeed, she seems to be taking the play seriously even in her heart of hearts. Brought up as she has been, in an atmosphere of truly serious art, with only the best of models at hand, she cannot, in the innocence of her young soul, believe that a dramatist would ever draw a not real heroine. To her the Princess *seems* unreal; but surely, she thinks, oh surely this must be a sick fancy; and so she proceeds to represent as best she can the reality that she has vainly looked for. The result is charming, and I hope it makes Mr Anthony Hope blush for his cynicism; nevertheless, I must admit that it is under-acting.

Since *The Prisoner of Zenda* there has been no play that has widely set a fashion. Whatever we may say against the drama of the past few years, we must admit that it has not been monotonous in kind. When Mr Shaw suddenly became popular, I remember, I uttered here my horror in the prevision of a horde of imitators. Except that certain passages in Mr Granville Barker's plays, and in Mr St John Hankin's, show a distinctly Shavian influence, my prevision has not been fulfilled: the foreseen horde has never appeared; or, if it has appeared, its mimicries have been so bad as to escape detection. The fact is that only a very clever man may compass even a passable imitation of Mr Shaw's manner and method. So much the better for us. But, just as any fool was able to write some sort of a play about an imaginary mediaeval kingdom in the heart of modern Europe, and just as most of the managers were willing to produce such plays in virtue of the fashionableness of the theme, so can any fool write some sort of a play around some burning political question of the day, and so are most of the managers now yearning to produce such plays in consequence of the vast success of *An Englishman's Home*. Major du Maurier may, in writing that play, have rendered an admirable service to his country; but against this I set the imminent outburst of imitative ineptitudes. (What a hideously uncouth phrase! But let it stand. If I were a statesman, it would be hailed as a gem of epigram, and would be quoted at least once a week in every newspaper during the next twenty years or more.) I wish I could mistrust my forecast. But, knowing how ovine is the nature we call human, and knowing that playwriting has become, in modern times, almost a natural instinct of the human adult, I know that in nearly every household in Great Britain there is at least one person scribbling feverishly, in his or her leisure moments, to make a fortune out of a play on Major du Maurier's lines. Most of them, I wager, have taken as their theme the peril of islanders unarmed. The less ovine minority is dividing its favours between Old Age Pensions, Education, Aeroplanes, the Licensing of Public Houses, and other burning topics. Some of the writers are perhaps stealing a march on their rivals by combining two or more of these topics in one whole—school children drifting, in Act I, for lack of religious instruction; years elapse, and in Act II we see that the children, having grown up, have all drifted into the public-houses, but are saved in Act III by the discipline of military service (or by the wholesome delight of flying), so that they are in Act IV worthy recipients of pensions of (say) ten shillings, payable at the age of (say) sixty. Of course, of the plays that are being written only a very small proportion will be produced. But think of the hundreds of thousands that are being written! The number of those produced will be ample to make me regret Major du Maurier's existence. My comfort is that the vogue, while it lasts, will be so intense that it cannot last very long. Also, it is well that the theatrical managers will have been taught to discard, once and for all, their passionately-cherished belief that a play's chance of success is in inverse ratio to the closeness of its connexion with the actual world.

[*6 March 1909*]

'NAN PILGRIM'

If Mrs Percy Dearmer had but trusted herself and her theme, *Nan Pilgrim* (twice performed at the Court Theatre this week) would have been an extremely interesting play. I do not say it would have been a technically good play. That is more than a reasonable critic would expect an author's first play to be. My advice to those about to write plays is to dismiss all critics, reasonable or otherwise, from their minds; to think not at all about what is supposed to be necessary in making a play dramatic; to forget the managers; to forget the public; simply to go straight ahead, trusting that their knowledge of life, their sympathy, their imagination, will bring them to the goal. If they will behave thus, at any rate they will produce interesting work—supposing, of course, that they themselves are gifted persons. Such a person is Mrs Dearmer, as her readers well know. But evidently, so soon as she had whispered to herself 'I will write a play,' she was seized with a fit of uncontrollable modesty, and was overwhelmed by a sense of her rashness in venturing towards the frontier of that mystic and perilous land which the sphere of drama is commonly supposed to be. It was no source of confidence to her that she had conceived two characters who were quite alive, and that she had conceived them in a relation that put them both to the test and was psychologically exciting. 'What excites *me* at a writing table,' she gloomily murmured, 'won't excite an audience.' Intimidating apothegms floated up to her from the dramatic criticisms that she had read, and from the talk she had heard about plays. 'The main thing is the story,' 'There must be a progression of incidents,' etc., etc. And so she devoted the best of her energies to the fabrication of a story—the sort of story that seemed to her likely to be understood by the average member of the public—leading up to that 'strong situation in the third act' which she had been taught to believe essential to the art of play-writing. The fear of being dull is the rock she split on.

The two characters of whom I have spoken are a clergyman and his wife, living on an income of rather less than two hundred pounds a year, in a squalid district of London. They have been married for a year or two. Nan Pilgrim had been an art-student, and she still sees the friends she had before her marriage—high-spirited and happy-go-lucky creatures, whose view of life is anti-polar to John Pilgrim's. To him life is a business of self-sacrifice. Joy, beauty, and the rest of it, are gauds which it is one's duty to eschew. Even his love for his wife is suspect to him. He tells her that he loves her more than is good for his soul. She is equally in love with him, but has no misgivings as to the propriety of her sentiment. What troubles her is the unloveliness of their external life—the littleness and sordidness of it, day after day. She does her duty well enough—district-visiting, giving 'work parties,' and so on; but her soul cries out for beauty and gaiety. Thus, for each of these two people is a highly promising inward conflict: in her, the conflict between her love for him and her distaste for the existence into which he has brought her; in him, the conflict between his devotion to her and his devotion to his spiritual ideals. On the one hand, the struggles of a captured Pagan; on the other, the qualms of a celibate astray. In the clash between these two self-conflicting persons are the makings of a finely dramatic play. Suppose, for instance, that in John Pilgrim the celibate instinct overcame the conjugal instinct enough to make Nan's hatred of the circumstances of her life become stronger than her love for her husband. Suppose that her unreciprocated ardour went to make irresistible her longing for the life of freedom and gaiety. Suppose she defied her husband and insisted on having a good time, and perhaps definitely encouraged some man, who did not share her husband's scruples.

And suppose she found that, after all, it was her husband that she loved better than this way of life, and the only question were whether he would forgive her, etc., etc. You see there was plenty of interest to be got out of the material that Mrs Dearmer had chosen. Mrs Dearmer perceived it all, doubtless. But she thought that what was really needed to carry a play through was theatrical intrigue leading to theatrical misunderstanding and to that 'strong scene in the third act.' So she did not trouble to develop any true conflict between the two Pilgrims. Here is what happens. Nan is told by the doctor that John, who is a man of delicate physique, is killing himself by over-work in his parish and by not taking proper nourishment. John must have plenty of succulent food, must drink good port-wine regularly, and so on. How to pay for such luxuries? Nan has, as it is, the greatest difficulty in making both ends meet, and has 'one terrible debt—of five pounds.' Well, her friend Robert Wentworth, the painter, wants her to sit for his 'Alcestis.' He is convinced (in the immemorial manner of painters, on the stage) that this picture will be his '*magnum opus*' if *she* will pose to him; and he would pay her at the rate of ten shillings a sitting. This, as she points out to John, would save the situation. John won't hear of it. It is conceivable that he, being what he is, might prefer that his wife should be a widow rather than she should earn a little money pleasantly. But it is not conceivable that Nan, who is of a character quite as strong as his, would not tell him that she must, since he so fatuously refused permission, take the law into her own hands. She assuredly would not, with the certainty of being found out sooner or later, proceed to sit every morning to Wentworth, while pretending to her husband that she had been visiting this and that sick person in her 'district.' However, that is what Mrs Dearmer (armed with stage precedents) makes her do. And of course (here comes another bundle of stage precedents) the moment the high-souled, simple, trustful, loving husband receives a letter to tell him what his wife is doing, he jumps straight to the conclusion that she is Wentworth's mistress. Otherwise, how should we get the 'strong scene in the third act?' This act passes, I need hardly say, in the studio; and Mr Ben Webster, as Wentworth, in the traditional velveteen jacket, with the traditional mahl-stick, with the traditional pots of azalea, with the traditional bits of brocade hung over the screens, and with the various other appurtenances that are never seen in a studio off the stage, is dabbing at the traditional '*magnum opus*'—of which Mr Ben Webster, by a disastrous oversight, gave the audience on the O.P. side a quite good view enough to leave no doubt that 'Alcestis' was a work by Sir Edward Poynter at his very worst. Mrs Dearmer seems to snatch an awful joy in not omitting from this act a single one of the theatric traditions for life in a studio. Wentworth is induced to make a long and florid oration to explain the 'meaning' that is in his picture. A lady of fashion, with a lorgnette, insults the model. *Rien ne manque*. After these preparations, the model is left alone with the painter, who declares his love, and kisses her by force. She repulses him and shames him, and he says 'Good-bye, my Princess.' Enter anon the furious husband. Vainly does Nan try to persuade him of her innocence. He puts a test question: 'Can you deny that he has kissed you?' She has no reply to this; and judgment goes by default. 'You are no longer my wife. You are his mistress.' Curtain on strong scene in third act.

In the last act, having got that strong scene off her mind, Mrs Dearmer resumes something of the sincerity which marked the early scenes of the play. The scene between the moribund John Pilgrim and his wife is thoroughly well written, with no false note. Its only fault is that it is not, as it might have been, an unwinding: it is merely an ending. Nan declares that she sees now that the things she rated so high are as nothing: all that matters is her love for him. But, as you have seen, she had never ceased for a moment to love him —hadn't known what it was like *not* to love him. Nothing has happened that would enable her to make up her mind really. There has been no development in her. I hope Mrs Dearmer in her next play will let her characters have the benefit of their vitality. Nan and John Pilgrim are fully vital, but in the lumber of theatrical convention there is no room for them to move.

The part of Nan was very well played by Miss Lilian Braithwaite, who presented exactly the type of blitheness and eagerness that was needed. Mr Holmes-Gore, as John, seemed to be in some doubt as to how an ascetic clergyman comports himself when he's at home; but when John was lifted out of the sphere of the particular into that of the general, and became simply a dying man, Mr Holmes-Gore ceased to be uncomfortable, and played very touchingly.

At the Vaudeville Theatre there is a most amusing comedy, *The Head of the Firm*, translated from the Danish by Mr Leslie Faber.

I am sorry I have not space in which to write about it this week. Like Mr Galsworthy's *Strife*, which I have not yet seen, its theme is an industrial 'strike.' I shall deal with the two plays together next week.

[*13 March 1909*]

TWO PLAYS

There are obvious points of likeness in the two plays that I write about this week—*The Head of the Firm* (adapted by Mr Leslie Faber from a play by Hjalmar Bergström) and Mr Galsworthy's *Strife*. The basis of each play is the conflict between capital and labour; and the central figure of each is a great employer of labour, whose men are out on strike, and whose son is out of sympathy with him and in sympathy with the men. But, similar though the material is in these and other respects, nothing could be more different than the two methods of treating it. The Danish playwright has used his economic basis merely as a starting-point from which he proceeds to show up the peculiarities of one particular capitalist, and to build around that person a very amusing and natural little play. *The Head of the Firm* is a good specimen of the usual kind of comedy—the comedy of persons. *Strife* is a comedy of forces; and the chief characters in it, thoroughly and wonderfully life-like though they are, have been so created that they shall be as symbols of those forces—as reverberations of a vast issue in the world at large. *The Head of the Firm* is a good play. *Strife* is a great one.

A play adapted is usually a play spoilt. But either Danish life is curiously like English life, or Mr Leslie Faber has done his job with diabolical cleverness; for, without the announcement on the programme, I should never have suspected that *The Head of the Firm* was not an original play of English life written by an Englishman. There is not a character nor an incident that strikes one as alien to England. Nor is there a turn of phrase to reveal the translator. Often, in the course of the years during which I have written about the theatre, I have had to deplore that our habitual translators have not mastered the rudiments—or not, at any rate, the vital principles—of the art of translation. I congratulate Mr Faber having got so far

away from the exact phraseology of the original version that he has
been able to give us a satisfactory equivalent for it. The central
person of the play, John Lydford, owner of the Lydford iron-works,
is an admirable figure for comedy. He believes in himself as a great
controller of men, a master among masters, generous and just to
those who are wise enough to obey him, but ruthless and terrible to
any one who dares cross his path. Comes an industrial crisis, and his
employees dare to cross his path; and, little by little, it is borne painfully in on him that he is not really a great over-man after all, and
that the person to be really reckoned with is Mr George Heymann,
the able young Jew whom he had some years before appointed
manager of the iron-works. Without Heymann he is helpless; but,
having at the instigation of his family dismissed Heymann from the
managership, he cannot—his dignity forbids him to—allow Heymann to return. Suddenly it is sprung on him that Heymann has
secretly and successfully wooed his daughter Betty. This is an immense relief to him: the situation is saved: what would be cringing
to a dismissed employee is merely magnanimity to a prospective son-
in-law. The part is one that would have delighted the heart of
Coquelin. It evidently delights the heart of Mr James Hearn, who
plays it with a rich sense of fun, keeping this sense well under control, however, so that he never oversteps the bounds of perfect verisimilitude. Miss Ethelwyn Jones, as Lydford's daughter, radiates a
natural vivacity that well suits the part. Mr Harcourt Williams, as
Lydford's son, whose waves of idealism beat with such amusing in-
effectiveness against the facts of the situation, is the vague young
idealist to the life. Miss Sydney Fairbrother and Mr Evelyn Beerbohm, in two extraneous and eccentric parts, revel in grotesque invention, without queering the pitch of the others; and Mr Beveridge, as
an old schoolmaster, who acts as *raisonneur* throughout the play,
and Miss Henrietta Watson, as Lydford's excellent but rather trying
wife, are invaluable, as always.

The cast of *Strife* is an immensely long one, yet here again there
is not a fault to be found. From first to last there was not a false note
in the interpretation. It is evident that we have an abundance of
excellent mimes in England, and that all we lack is a sufficiency of
good stage-managers. Whenever, as in *Strife* and in *The Head of
the Firm*, we have a play 'produced' by a stage-manager who
knows his business, the result is such as to make us quite proud of

our mimes. To say that Mr Granville Barker, the producer of *Strife*, knows his business, is rather an inadequate compliment. Let me rather say that he is a great master of his art. Why should he not lay us under a new obligation to him by opening a school for stage-managers? If he can train actors so well, why should he not train other men to train them equally well? Mr Galsworthy's play rings so true that not even the average stage-manager could have made it ring false, and is so strongly dramatic that not even the average stage-manager could have made it unimpressive. But I shudder to think how much would have been lost had this play been produced under the usual conditions.

Essentially, as I have said, the dramatic conflict of the play is between capital and labour. Mr Galsworthy shows us, as it were, a corner of the battle-field, not for the mere spectacle of that corner, but to give us a dim sense of the whole vast appalling fight. Beyond the clash of these combatants in the foreground, we dimly hear, all the while, the roar of a world-wide war, the unending war between the rich and the poor. John Anthony is more for us than the mere proprietor of the Trenartha Tin Plate Works, and David Roberts is more than the leader of the strike. The one is the rich, and the other the poor. But of course they would not have this symbolic power if they were not projected also as two absolutely real and recognisable persons. We all know that Mr Galsworthy is ardent in socialism. But this ardour does not in the slightest degree affect his sense of dramatic balance. Were it not that this is a play of intense passion, and that a passionate play cannot be written by a passionless man, and that passion is likelier to range itself with the poor than with the rich, there would not be in *Strife* any internal evidence to show on which side Mr Galsworthy ranges himself. Outwardly he is quite impartial, and John Anthony is conceived and presented in as generous a spirit, in as true a light, as is David Roberts. Great figures, both of them, worthy of each other's steel, akin to each other, towering head and shoulders above the little men whose leaders they are. On the one hand, the capitalist, stricken with years and infirmities, but determined to fight, as he has so often fought, and to win, as he has always won. On the other hand, opposed to this heavy old bulk of will, the furious spirit of the strike-leader—the little magnetic man whose soul is aflame with a great class-hatred. His wife is a sick woman, who is dying for lack of food. He is a loving husband, not at all a selfish man. He wraps his overcoat round his wife's knees just before he starts out to the meeting. But he has forbidden her to accept the food and wine which John Anthony (a man of tender personal feelings) has instructed his daughter to take to her. He is an unselfish man, David Roberts, but he would rather that his wife died than they should accept anything from the enemy. It is not for himself that he is fighting, not for the other strikers alone: he is fighting for all labour against all capital, and his eye is not on the local present, but on the world-wide future. It is just in that spirit that John Anthony fights too. The directors of the board whose chairman he is are fighting, as the members of the strike-committee are fighting, just for the well-being of themselves and of their families. On either side now, after the long and embittered struggle, the general desire is for compromise. On either side the men are fighting their leader, but they are worsted. The two leaders can conquer their own men—but not each other. It is the old problem of the irresistible force and the immoveable mass, and one cannot say what would be the solution of the conflict if it depended on these two men alone. Fate at length rouses herself to step in and settle the great matter by one of those trivial devices of which she is so fond. She puts an end to the suffering of Mrs Roberts, the news of whose death, brought to the crucial meeting of the strikers, instantly undoes the effect that Roberts has had in stiffening the men to further resistance. That same news also makes the directors fall away from their obedience to John Anthony. The chairman puts the question to vote, whether the board shall treat with the men on the terms proposed. Hesitatingly, with their eyes on one another, seeking encouragement, they hold up their hands. 'Those who are of contrary opinion,' says the chairman, without a break in his voice, and holds up his hand. The men are summoned to the board room. David Roberts arrives just in time to join them, believing that he will yet save them from surrender. But his ascendency is gone utterly now. And at last, the two protagonists are left alone, face to face. John Anthony raises himself heavily from his arm-chair, and, before going out of the room, bows his head slightly to David Roberts, who (the more emotional creature) bows his head low. That is the end of this intense drama. But there is a colophon appended to it—a little colophon of appalling irony. John Anthony's secretary, with the representative of the

Union, is reading over the terms of agreement between the board
and the men. 'Why!' he exclaims, 'these are precisely the terms that
were offered before the strike began!'

Mr Norman McKinnel is, in both senses of the word, tremendous
as John Anthony; and not less perfect in its breadth of outline and
in its minute fidelity to type is Mr Fisher White's impersonation of
David Roberts. Both performances are great, worthy of the greatness
of the parts.

I observe that some of the critics have been using this play as a
stick to hit Mr Shaw with. Would it not have been seemlier in them
to take the opportunity of acknowledging that, but for Mr Shaw's
own particular genius, which has become popular despite them,
such a play as *Strife* would almost certainly not have been written,
and, if written, would very certainly not have been produced?

[*20 March 1909*]

A COSTUME PLAY

The Noble Spaniard is a play adapted by Mr Somerset Maugham
'from the French of Grenet-Dancourt'—a name which suggests
nothing to me. Grenet-Dancourt may be a quite recent person, or he
may have been thriving at the date which Mr Maugham has chosen
for the play—1850. In the latter case, Mr Maugham is to be commended for his tact; in the former case, he is to be congratulated on
an inspiration. With the costumes and the language of to-day, *The
Noble Spaniard* would be a dreadfully arid affair. 1850 saves it.

I am told that the elder inhabitants of the Shetland Isles can still
listen—not indeed with enthusiasm, but patiently—to farces of
which the fun consists solely of the complications caused by a case
of mistaken identity. Such a farce, evidently, was the original version
of *The Noble Spaniard*; and Mr Maugham's personal knack for
light and witty dialogue would not, in itself, suffice to gild the pill
for us. The pill has four principal ingredients: Marion Nairne, a
young and very pretty widow; a Spanish Duke, of violent nature;
Mr Justice Proudfoot, an elderly man; and his elderly wife. The
Spanish Duke has been for several days following Mrs Nairne
about, and now forces his way into the house where she is staying

with the judge and his wife. He protests his love. Mrs Nairne tells him that she is a married woman, and that her husband is a very jealous man. The Duke believes her. (Ha, ha.) The Duke takes the judge to be the husband. (Ha, ha.) The judge thinks the Duke is in love with Mrs Proudfoot. (Ha, ha.) Mrs Proudfoot thinks so too. (Ha, ha.) The Duke sees the judge kissing Mrs Proudfoot, and believes him to be a faithless husband. (Ha, ha.) The judge presently believes that Mrs Proudfoot is carrying on a guilty intrigue with the Duke. (Ha, ha.) The Duke challenges the judge to a duel. (Ha, ha.) And so on, until the mine has been conscientiously worked to its uttermost recess. These operations are concluded within two acts of the play. So another shaft is sunk, and another mine worked, to fill up the evening. The Duke, finding he was mistaken about the judge, believes Mrs Nairne to be the wife of a certain Frenchman. (Ha, ha.) The Duke challenges the Frenchman. (Ha, ha.) I doubt whether even those of my readers who are elder inhabitants of the Shetland Islands have been able to conjure up a laugh at the points where I have indicated that laughter is expected. But perhaps they are one and all devoted to Mr Hawtrey, and perhaps it was they who occupied the pit and gallery last Saturday evening at the New Royalty Theatre, determined to make the thing 'go' whether they enjoyed it or not. For there certainly were plenty of loud guffaws throughout the evening. I cannot believe that they came from the throats of our own sophisticated metropolitan public. Or was it that this public was guffawing at the idea of Mr Hawtrey, that so very modern comedian, appearing in a play of the kind that did (yes! it really did) please people in the period so delightfully illustrated by the costumes that he and the other members of the cast were wearing?

Certainly, that was the spirit in which I myself took the play. But the interest of the play as a theatrical document was far less for me than its interest as a document of life. Not since *Trelawney of the Wells* have I had the particular kind of pleasure that *The Noble Spaniard* gave me—pleasure in the faithful reconstitution of the manners of a decade so near to us as to make its difference irresistibly touching and amusing. Mr Pinero's feat of reconstruction was really less admirable than Mr Maugham's, for he had lived (though at a very tender age) in 1860, and had authentic memories to help him along; whereas Mr Maugham was born about a quarter of a century after 1850, and has had to rely solely on documents. I wonder what works, principally, he read. I think he ought, in the manner of other historians, to have appended to the programme a list of his authorities. 'Gaskell, Mrs., *Cranford*; *Punch*, *1848–1852*,' and so forth. I daresay the list would be quite a short one. If a man has an innate sense for the subtleties of period, very slight erudition will put him on the right track; and if he hasn't that sense no amount of erudition will help him. In Mr Maugham evidently that sense is strong, and not less evidently he has delighted in his task—delighted in sending English adults out to paddle in the sea at Boulogne, with a sense of their recklessness ('We adore paddling; it is so French!')—delighted in the 'quizzes' and the 'teases' and the 'perfidious creatures' of their day. The soul of 1850 was more romantic than that of 1860, but its manners were far primmer; and this anomaly, throughout the play, Mr Maugham has preserved with a cunning hand. Byron was still in its heart, but its lips were regulated by Mrs Hemans. It is gravely recorded in the programme that 'the words of the song in the Second Act are by Felicia Hemans, and the music by Virginia Blakemore'—a happy little touch, this, as though both ladies were alive in our midst and would insist on having the usual acknowledgments. It is, indeed, the finishing-touch to the picture presented to us on the stage when Miss Lucy Proudfoot stands warbling, intensely earnest and out of tune, with her every ringlet quivering to her every roulade, while young Mrs Nairne tremulously accompanies her at a very pre-Erardian piano, over the back of which leans a whiskered adorer, his soul stirred to its depths. That picture alone would have redeemed the play for me.

The little that Miss Lucy has to do was done very well—done with a real sense of living in the period, and not of having merely dressed up—by Miss Anne Cleaver. Equally good in that respect was Miss Kate Cutler, as Mrs Nairne. And she deserved our gratitude also as being one of the two persons in the cast who did not succumb to that slowness of utterance which is the curse of English acting—a curse specially hard for us to bear when the play is a farce. The other quick utterer was Miss Fanny Brough, who played Mrs Proudfoot, and seemed, moreover, not merely to be living in 1850, but to be the very soul and symbol of that moment in history. In the midst of the profound humour of her performance, there was one point at which she let her tragic power appear, rather disastrously. The fun that is to be made out of an elderly woman's notion that a young man is in love with her is always a dull and jarring kind of fun. In itself the theme is tragic, and thus when a playwright presents it for laughter—as playwrights always do—the only thing for the actress to do is to play as farcically as she can. If her note is anywhere near seriousness, even the coarsest soul in the audience is made to wince. For two or three moments, in the scene where Mrs Proudfoot is alone with the Duke, Miss Brough quietly let herself be tragic, insomuch that the half-hearted titters suddenly died away, and the whole audience was suffused with a blush of horror. Mr Lyall Swete ruined his performance of the judge by intensity of deliberation. He seemed determined to time himself by 'the law's delays.' Mr Hawtrey's deliberation was excusable: he had just recovered from a serious illness, and started in a new management. But I cannot imagine that he will ever be really good as the fire-eating Spanish Duke. It is a part that needs a wild breadth of exuberance, and nothing else. Mr Hawtrey has much else, but he has not that. He is, as I have said, a very modern comedian; and he ought not to spend his great gifts where there is no use for them.

[*27 March 1909*]

A CURTAIN-RAISER, AND 'THE FOUNTAIN'

The Stage Society's next production will be its fiftieth. Let the Society accept my respectful congratulations on its coming jubilee. It has achieved a great deal of excellent work, and has good reason to be proud of itself. But I hope that pride will not be the only emotion when the members meet to banquet themselves. Vague doubts as to perfection, I hope, will creep in. Experience teaches us that a society formed for an artistic purpose—or for any purpose whatsoever—tends in course of time to become narrow-minded. Some one section begins to dominate. Some one line of policy begins to dominate that section—a narrower line of policy than that which the pious founders had conceived. The aim of the Stage Society is to produce the most interesting modern plays that would not have a chance of being produced in the usual manner. The duty of the

committee is to determine which these plays are. I do not doubt
that every member of the committee is guided in his task of selection
solely by his sense of what is in itself the best play available. But I
do suspect that the majority of the committee has fallen into the
habit of believing that any play written with a socialistic bias must
be a masterpiece, or, if not actually a masterpiece, at any rate the
work of a master-mind. Otherwise, how shall I account for the
production of *Unemployed*, a short play that preceded Mr George
Calderon's witty comedy *The Fountain* last Monday afternoon? In
point of intellectual force, and sense of life, *Unemployed* is rather
below the level of the average curtain-raiser in a merely commercial
theatre. And that, I am sure, is the only reason why a merely commercial theatre would none of it. But the mere fact that a play would
be rejected elsewhere ought not to be a passport to the graces of the
committee of the Stage Society. The *best* of the plays that would
be rejected elsewhere is the play to be selected. If the truth is that
the committee had received no short play of finer quality than
Unemployed, then the proper course for them to pursue was to
strew ashes on their heads, and post back *Unemployed* to its author
with all possible speed. I do not, however, for one moment believe
that nothing better, and far better, than this play had been sent in.
And I implore the committee to face bravely the horrid forgotten
fact that a socialistic tendency in a writer doesn't necessarily include genius, or exclude dulness and silliness. I cannot imagine
anything more unilluminating and old-fashioned than the view of
life taken by the author of *Unemployed*: on the one hand the
poor, as hero; on the other, the rich, as villain. The rich are typified
in the persons of a frivolous married woman and a man who is
flirting with her. The poor are typified by a tramp, who comes to
the garden-gate, begging for a day's work, and who, though dying
of starvation, refuses to accept the shilling offered to him by the
rich man. After a long and amazingly crude conversation between
the rich man and the rich woman, in which he explains how well
content he is to batten on the sufferings of the poor, and how well
worth while it is 'that a million *canaille* should labour' to keep a
beautiful and delicate person like herself in luxury, the tramp re-
appears at the garden-gate, and falls down dead. The rich man says
'What a bore!' and runs to fetch a policeman, advising the rich
woman to read a magazine in the meantime. The policeman,

having made some notes, gives the corpse a contemptuous kick, and the plays ends with the departure of the rich man and woman for a walk. The Stage Society must make no more mistakes of this kind.

Mr Calderon's play, *The Fountain*, made me regret once more the cessation of Vedrenne-Barker. Here is a comedy which could not, probably, have a long run, yet a comedy of which two performances do not nearly exhaust the number of people who would delight in it. I think it a great pity that such excellent work should have so fugitive a show. The play is based on an idea—'That which the fountain sends forth returns again to the fountain'; and this idea is worked logically out with a keen sense of fun. There is a certain Mrs Wren, a young woman who is appalled by the thought of the sufferings of the poor, and wants to do something to alleviate them. Her husband agrees with her that it is impossible not to be appalled; but as to the need of doing anything—there he is utterly opposed to her. He is not in the least ashamed of being a mere talker: talkers do help to clarify things, whereas doers invariably make of things a worse muddle than they found. He continues to talk until his wife can stand it no longer; and Mr Calderon begins his play at the moment when she arrives at the rooms of Miss Kerrison, a friend of hers, who lives in the East End of London, devoting her time to settlement work. One of Mrs Wren's troubles is that her income does not leave her any great scope for charity. She begs the trustees of her capital to transfer it in some way that shall bring her in an extra hundred or so a year. She is delighted when they unwillingly consent, and sets to work on queer schemes of charity—one of which is the establishment of an amateur pawnbroker's shop, run on philanthropic lines. Of course the poor people take advantage of her, right and left. She does not mind that. What does horrify her is to find that Mr Palmer, the landlord of the tenement buildings, is putting up these poor people's rents by sixpence a week, having heard of their access of good fortune. Thus, what she gives to them she is giving really to Palmer. So she gives them another bonus. Palmer proceeds to raise the rents by a shilling. Also, he refuses to allow her to use as a hospital or home of rest the house which she has just leased from him. The contract is produced for reference, and, to every one's surprise, it is found that Mrs Wren is not only the lessee, but also the owner of the ground rent. Her solicitors, in order to secure for her the desired addition to her income, had re-invested her money in this very security. She is also owner of the tenement buildings. It was for her emolument, ultimately, that the rents had been raised. What she had been trying to give to the poor, and seeming to give to Palmer, she had been giving to herself, all the time. Her husband, as you may imagine, is delighted at the vindication of his theories. Both he and she are admirably drawn characters, and not the less alive for being slightly caricatured. The majority of the characters are slum types—all of them vivid and amusing. But the prime virtue of the play is not in its characters, nor in the working-out of its idea, but in the quality of its dialogue, which is brilliant throughout, with just that saliency and suddenness that is so much more effective in the theatre than is any other manner of wit. Wren, in one of his discussions with his wife, tells her that the opinion she has just expressed is certainly the opinion of the man in the street. 'And who, pray,' she interjects, '*is* "the man in the street"? 'Women,' replies Wren. Another good instance occurs in the scene when one of the poor women appears in a new bonnet which the clergyman suspects has been bought on the proceeds of a bet on a horse named Mint Sauce. He taxes her with this, and she gives him an evasive answer. 'Do you know,' he asks, 'what happened to Sapphira?' The woman says promptly 'Yes, sir; she didn't start.' Translated thus into the medium of print, such sallies lose immensely; just as literary wit goes for little in a theatre. Mr Calderon has as true a gift for dramatic wit as he showed in *Dwala* for literary wit.

[*3 April 1909*]

AN EXOTIC COMEDIAN

Last Monday, at the Vaudeville Theatre, was produced *The Chorus Lady*, a play by Mr James Forbes. Miss Rose Stahl appeared in it. Or rather, it appeared around Miss Rose Stahl. This lady is well worth seeing. She is quite unlike anything that one has seen, or anything that one would be likely to imagine. In face she strongly resembles the Sarah Bernhardt of the 'eighties; and the likeness is consciously accentuated by the arrangement of her hair. She is very tall and very thin, and her walk is a kind of graceful shuffle. She carries her head thrust forward, her shoulders shrugged up, and her hands on her hips. Her hands are of the type that belong especially to tragic actresses—hands that are mainly fingers. Her face, in repose, seems to be that of one who broods deeply and darkly; and always her eyes seem to gaze right through the other mimes and beyond the 'wings,' or right through the auditorium, into the night. Her voice has the softly plaintive and lingering quality that belongs to the voices of people born and bred in the Southern States of America; but you may hear in it also a ring as of bitter revolt, deep down in the bosom, against something or other—life, perhaps. And the odd thing is that this woman of so tragical mien and aspect is impersonating not Phaedra, nor Clytemnestra, nor any other high figure of antique fable, but just a chorus girl of Broadway; and that the words falling like molten pearls from her lips are not remotely Attic, but of the very latest and wildest fashion in American *argot*. It is in this contrast between manner and matter that lies part of the secret of the spell that Miss Stahl cast over us last Monday. The contrast is irresistibly ludicrous. But it must not prevent us from recognising that Miss Stahl is in herself a comedian of rare and delicate accomplishment. That she seems, as Patricia O'Brien, so exactly like a great tragic actress with a strong sense of humour in private life, is certainly bad for Mr James Forbes's intention—or would be so, if he had had any intention beyond giving her a vehicle for display of her own personal gifts. It is conceivable that Patricia O'Brien might, by miscarriage of fate, be in a musical comedy chorus. But it is quite inconceivable that she should be, as she is, well-content with her career, and thoroughly capable in it. When we first see her, she has just come to stay with her parents in their humble home. Magda, in similar conditions, never seemed more remote, though Patricia is really the soul of good-humour and humdrum commonsense. Her little sister is anxious to go on the stage, but Patricia is opposed to this idea. The little sister is romantic and confiding, and would probably go to the bad. However, in the second act, the little sister has had her way, and we see her in a dressing-room with a dozen other chorus girls, all of whom are emitting torrents of the lingo that Patricia has already made familiar to us—no, not familiar: years of patient study in New York itself would be needed to accustom us to this strange tongue; and, by

the time we had mastered it, it would doubtless have been superseded by some other and yet stranger tongue. Students of Mr George
Ade's writing can imagine something of the manner of the dialogue;
but only something: Mr Forbes has dived deeper in the under-
ocean of human speech, and has brought up more monstrous
trophies to affright us and delight us. The slang of New York has
its origin, of course, in the climate. It is the climate that has produced the terrible doctrine and practice of 'hustle'; and for people
living in a wild chaos of competition, always in a blinding hurry and
in the midst of a deafening din, language has to be pitched up high to
cope with the circumstances. There is no time to pause, nor any place
in which an ordinary quiet phrase would be able to reach your ear.
Language, to produce any effect at all, must be as quick and as
violent as all else. A phrase that has not the properties of dynamite
goes unheeded. An English chorus girl might win a man's sympathy by explaining how difficult it is to keep a fixed smile of enjoyment whilst standing on one foot—to look as if you were doing
quite naturally a delightful thing which you had never done before.
Her American sister would get little sympathy that way. 'It's the
smile that's hard,' she must declare; 'fancy standing with your foot
pointing a quarter-past six, and looking like the cat that's swallowed
the canary!' Then, perhaps, the chivalrous American heart is
wrung. All the chorus girls in Mr Forbes's play talk with an ingenuity and daring of which the sentence just quoted is a fair
example. As uttered by them in the regular New York screech, the
language has not the added quaintness that it takes on for us when
it is given in the velvety Southern tones of Patricia. Nevertheless, it
suffices to make the whole of the second act extremely interesting.

I understand that the play has been evolved from this second act,
which was originally a scene by itself. Quite apart from its language,
the scene shows that Mr Forbes has a keen sense of type; and the
contrast of the various girls' various little minds with the keen and
sober little mind of Patricia gives Miss Rose Stahl an excellent
chance of displaying her peculiar gift for comedy. I wish Mr Forbes
had left it at that. The third act is a slab of sheer nonsense; and not
even Miss Stahl at her best would be able to redeem it; and, in point
of fact, Miss Stahl is nowhere near her best. Apparently, Mr Forbes
was led to believe by Miss Stahl's appearance and voice that she was
a great emotional actress. That was a very natural mistake. I made it

myself. So soon as I saw what sort of things were to happen in the third act, I steeled myself in anticipation of a formidable attack on my nervous system. Stale and artificial though the situation in store evidently was, I imagined that Miss Stahl was going to thrill me. I reckoned without Mr Forbes's capacity for making a foolish situation doubly foolish. The little sister had been lured to the rooms of the seducer, whose servant appeared to be quite unable to prevent any casual person from dropping in for a friendly chat. One of these casual persons was the man to whom Patricia was betrothed. And the little sister was hustled into the bedroom. Later came Patricia herself, suspecting the little sister's whereabouts. Later came again the man to whom she was betrothed; and so she, too, was hustled into the bedroom. When the moment came for the betrothed to insist on searching the bedroom, what could have been simpler than for the sisters O'Brien to step forth smiling and hand in hand? Patricia, however, being an old playgoer, insisted on stepping forth alone, to blast the happiness of her betrothed, and of herself. Not even the greatest of tragic actresses could have covered up the absurdity of this climax. But it had already become clear to me that Miss Stahl was a comedian pure and simple. So soon as she had become dramatically intense, she had become dull. Her tragedy was all on the surface. In her heart, I am sure, she was roaring with laughter —quite right too! I suggest that at future performances the two last acts be omitted, and the first two repeated. Twice would be not too often—nor often enough—to see Miss Stahl in comedy.

[*24 April 1909*]

MR MASON'S PLAY

I found myself rather puzzled on the first night at the St James's. Mr Mason had evolved a thoroughly amusing scheme for his play. There was nothing amateurish in his development of it; and the dialogue, from first to last, was full of grace and humour. Yet I felt unsatisfied. I did not feel that *Colonel Smith* came off. And I was annoyed at not seeing why it didn't come off.

The initial idea is excellent. There are three sisters—daughters of a country-gentleman named Faraday. The second one is already married. The third is engaged to be married. Celia, the eldest, is unmated. Nobody has fallen in love with her; and it is taken vaguely as a matter of course that nobody ever will fall in love with her: she is on the shelf. This position galls her. She knows that she is quite as charming as her sisters, really; and it occurs to her that if any one man happened to perceive her charm the others would follow suit. She therefore invents a fiancé—a Colonel Smith, at present in South Africa. Her world is greatly astonished, and then wonders at its astonishment: Celia is an exceedingly charming girl. She finds herself suddenly a cynosure. Men who had been coldly polite dance attendance on her. She is much amused, and, even more, gratified. An admirable basis, you perceive, for a light comedy. There is in it—granting that measure of exaggeration which is permissible in light comedy—enough of psychological truth to keep it well outside the sphere of farce. One can imagine Celia falling in love with one of her lovers, and confessing to him at length that there was no such person as Colonel Smith. The lover will be considerably *froissé*. Celia will point out to him that he has, after all, many quite tangible rivals; whereat his respect for himself and for her will be restored; and . . . my business is not to write what Mr Mason might have written, but to appreciate his play as it stands. He very soon drops the Cinderella-triumphant motive, and heads straight for such complications as may forthcome from the Smith motive. Some months after Celia's blazoning of her betrothal, she thinks it will be well to dispose of the imaginary colonel, and sends to *The Times* an announcement of his death. Meanwhile, an ardent love-letter which she had written to him and committed to the post (in order to make her story the more indubitable) has been delivered to an actual Colonel Smith. He is a man of humour and curiosity, and, so soon as he returns to England, proceeds to call under an assumed name at the Faradays' house. His intention is to represent himself as a brother-officer of Smith, and the bearer of a message to the unaccountable Miss Faraday. Arriving at the house, he learns that Smith has died; and this news necessitates a change of demeanour. Before Miss Faraday appears, he hastily removes his scarf-pin and wraps it in a piece of paper; then also his watch and chain. These, in due course, he presents to Celia, as trinkets which his friend has entrusted to him before death, to be conveyed to the bereaved-beloved. 'This,' he says in a hushed voice, producing the very massive watch and chain, 'he wished you to wear always on your bosom.' An admirable example, that, of true dramatic humour —the fun of the idea being doubled by ocular demonstration. Quite apart from the watch and chain, Celia's position is acutely embarrassing. The actual Smith enjoys it immensely. He describes in minute detail the last hours of his comrade. And so the game goes on, till it becomes for us, in the absence of any fresh dramatic inventions by Mr Mason himself, rather monotonous. That Smith should gradually fall in love with Celia, and Celia with Smith, is hardly a fresh invention. It is one of those inevitable conventions which one scents from afar, and it does not suffice to keep the play going. Celia, from the moment of Smith's intrusion, ceases to exist vitally as a character: she is merely a peg on which to hang embarrassments. In Smith we have no interest whatsoever, except as the embarrasser. The atmosphere of the play has become wholly farcical. Or rather, it ought to have become so. It remains comedic. That, as I discovered on reflection, is what is the matter with the play. Mr Mason has written a farce in a comical key. He has taken his theme seriously. And, of course, when a frivolous theme is seriously taken, some measure of dulness is sure to supervene. I daresay Mr Mason did not mean to be serious and comedic. Doubtless he tried to abound in the wildest absurdities. But the Muse of buffoonery is a coy creature, and was wooed by Mr Mason in vain. Except at two or three points—such as the incident of the watch and chain—the humour is quiet and sly, instead of being, as it should be, riotously fantastic. In scheme, *Colonel Smith* is as essentially farcical as *The Importance of Being Earnest*; and the two plays are superficially akin in that the pivot of each is a man's impersonation of a man who does not exist and has merely been invented for purposes of convenience by somebody else. Oscar Wilde was adroit, and Mr Mason isn't, in the art of piling up corollary complications. But it is not by reason of such complications that *The Importance of Being Earnest* delights us till the final fall of the curtain. What keeps us delighted is the inexhaustible fantasy of the dialogue. Lady Bracknell's refusal that her daughter shall 'marry into a cloakroom, and form an alliance with a parcel,' and Miss Prism's recognition of the long-lost hand-bag by the mark left on it by 'the upsetting of a Gower Street omnibus in younger and happier days,' are random instances of Oscar Wilde's mastery throughout the play. Robert

Louis Stevenson, in *The Wrong Box*, and *The Dynamiter*, and *The New Arabian Nights*, had shown a similar mastery; and he, if he had had an instinct for playwriting, might have written classic farces. Mr Mason has the instinct for playwriting. But farce is not his form.

In the last act of his play, he gives up his attempt to keep the colonel on a farcical plane; and the gallant soldier emerges as a man brimming over with the invaluable lessons that Mr Mason has learned by contact with the electorate. He has a speech about 'the rows of white faces' at public meetings—a very well-written speech, a speech full of mellow wisdom, which Mr Alexander tries hard to deliver with the impressiveness of a man who wouldn't have dreamt of thrusting himself into a country-house for the purpose of mystifying a defenceless young lady. In the earlier scenes Mr Alexander plays with a light sardonic humour that is exactly right. Miss Irene Vanbrugh does not at all suggest the sometime-Cinderella of Mr Mason's fancy. One cannot imagine that Celia, as played by her, has ever not been mistress of the situation. Miss Vanbrugh is so resourceful and accomplished a comedian that she positively cannot suggest even past pathos.

[*1 May 1909*]

'WHAT THE PUBLIC WANTS'

It was with some trepidation that I went to see this play. Not long ago I read *The Old Wives' Tale*, a novel which deeply impressed me. The adjective 'great,' as applied to novels—or, indeed, to any other literary product—has lost its savour. It has been applied so persistently, and so absurdly, to works not good even in a small way. Nevertheless, I must—there is no way out of it—call *The Old Wives' Tale* a great novel. The actual writing of it has no charm or distinction, has merely the merit of lucidity. But the writer is a true seer and interpreter of life, focussing his vision not on any one little phase, but on the whole range of things. Re-creating for us, with an intense vividness, provincial life in the early 'sixties, and Parisian life at the end of the Second Empire, and provincial life as it is now, he does not give us merely the local and temporal colour, nor merely a large number of recognisable and memorable men and women: he gives us a vision of all existence, and, implicity, a fine philosophic interpretation thereof. Having read the book, with the rare sense of having been quickened, illuminated, and moved, I lost no time in getting hold of other books that Mr Arnold Bennett had written. By these I was keenly disappointed. They were the work, evidently, of a man with a real creative impulse, and a man of humour and imagination and knowledge. But, not less evidently, they were pot-boilers. They were unscrupulous work; and I marvelled that a man who had been for many years demeaning himself in so competent a fashion had had it left in him, at length, to produce a solid masterpiece. So, when I heard that the Stage Society was going to produce a play of his, I trembled. Even writers who preserve a perfect integrity in the writing of books, never doing less than their very best (such as it may be), are apt to lower their standard when they write for the stage. It seemed inevitable that Mr Bennett, who had played so often down to the average reader of magazines, would have played down to the average playgoer—even though, as it happened, his work was to be produced first by the Stage Society. I was glad to find in *What the Public Wants* one of the best comedies of our time.

As its title suggests, the play is widely topical; but essentially it is the kind of play which consists in the minute presentment, from every angle, of one particular character. The character presented by Mr Bennett is a certain Sir Charles Worgan. He is the proprietor of some fifty newspapers—morning, and evening, and weekly papers; serious, comic, sporting, religious papers: papers of every conceivable kind. 'Serious' none of them exactly is. Sir Charles makes no pretension to giving the public anything but just what it wants. Many men have tried to give the public that. The difference between Sir Charles and them is that Sir Charles *knows*, every time, what the public wants; and thus his energy and his power of organisation, which are great, but not singularly so, have made a millionaire of him, a knight, and many other things of which he is pardonably proud. Whence comes it, this knowledge of his? He is not, as his observant younger brother perceives, a man of genius. He is not even, in the ordinary sense of the word, clever. He has just some transcendent and indefineable gift, in virtue of which he *knows*, and, knowing, is able to *do* automatically. None of his clever henchmen but pants and gasps wonderingly in his wake. 'Are We Growing Less Spiritual?'—it seems a good topic for a popular religious paper. Yet the circulation of that paper has fallen recently from 200,000 to 180,000. Sir Charles casts a hurried glance through the current number, and, seeing the main topic, sees instantly what is wrong. After a moment, he is inspired: 'Ought Curates to Receive Presents from their Parishioners?' He is always having inspirations; and these are always right. He is a very happy man. For him there is but one crumpled rose-leaf. It seems to him that the intellectual people don't take him seriously. 'When I go anywhere,' he complains to his younger brother, 'and find people talking about Swinburne, and theosophy, and that sort of thing, they always stop when I come up to them, and begin talking about motor cars.' The brother suggests that he should marry an intellectual woman and found a salon. There is a certain young widow, penniless, undoubtedly intellectual, and very charming, too. She is 'not an actress,' but she is on the stage. She is a member of a very intellectual dramatic society which has been performing plays that are praised by the few and visited by the fewer still. This society is about to cease for lack of funds. Sir Charles is very much impressed by the intellect and the charm of the young widow, Mrs Vernon by name; and he is instantly inspired to put £10,000 into the society, and to use his immense resources for booming it into permanent success. Incidentally, he is reminded of the financial straits of the University of Oxford. He draws for Oxford a cheque of £100,000. One of the most delightful moments of the play is in the last act, when he hears that they want to make him a D.C.L.—'Doctor of Civil Law,' as he discovers on reference to *Whitaker*. But meanwhile his thoughts are concentrated mainly on the dramatic society. And in the second act, when the board of directors meet, there is a great deal of subtle comedy in the clash of ideals between Sir Charles (who wants the society to be as thoroughly intellectual as ever, but wants to make it pay) and the people who mistrust his judgment of what constitutes thorough intellectuality. The founder of the society, Holt St John, is determined to have his own artistic way in everything. One of the things he has decided is that Mrs Vernon shall not remain a member of the company: she is 'not an actress.' Poor Mrs Vernon sobs. This is too much for Sir Charles. Though all his youth has been devoted to newspaper enterprise, and he has never had time for any intimate relations with women, he is a very sentimental man. Seeing Mrs

457

Vernon in tears, he realises that he is boyishly in love with her. He finds very great difficulty in expressing himself. He, who has been always so glib and confident, becomes halting and almost panic-stricken. In a scene of fine comedic gradations, Mrs Vernon accepts him. She is not, we see, in love with him; but she likes him very much, and in a way admires him, and would like to be free of her poverty. Also, it turns out, she thinks she will be able to reform him of his rather gross materialism—to make him a power for public good. It is on this hope of hers that the rest of the play hinges. In the third act Mr Bennett switches his characters off to his beloved Bursley, their birthplace, to the house occupied by Sir Charles's elder brother, who is a doctor. In Bursley Sir Charles is not regarded with the awe that he inspires in the metropolis. Neither his mother nor his brother approves of his newspapers. They strongly disap-prove of a series of 'Crimes of Passion,' a raking-up of unsavoury murder cases, which is now the chief feature of one of Sir Charles's Sunday papers. Especially are they horrified at finding an announce-ment that the next instalment is to deal with a murder committed in the 'sixties by a relative of an old lady, Mrs Downes, who lives under their own roof. The doctor calls Sir Charles's attention to this. He insists that it is an outrage which must at all costs be pre-vented. Sir Charles is rather afraid of his elder brother, but in this matter he will not be dictated to. He regrets that the article has been announced, but, once announced, it must appear. In vain does his brother try to make him understand the enormity of his offence. His fiancée intercedes with him, successfully. 'So you convinced him?' says the doctor. 'No,' she says bitterly, 'I caressed him.' In the last act we are back at the offices of the *Daily Mercury*. Mrs Vernon had thought that the 'Crimes of Passion' series was to be abandoned altogether. But merely another and similar murder has been substituted for the Downes murder, and the horrible series is to go on indefinitely. Mrs Vernon tries to make her lover see that this sort of thing ought not to be done. He simply can't see why not. The public wants it. Let them have it. But, for *her* sake—because *she* asks him—he will stop it with pleasure. (He will, indeed, do anything for her sake. He is just going to start 'a *Mirror* campaign' for the release of certain suffragists who are in goal. Not long ago the *Mirror* had a leading-article entitled 'Ought we to Revive the Ducking-Stool?' But now, just because Mrs Vernon sympathises with the suffragists, he means to force the Home Secretary to re-lease these prisoners.) Vainly does Mrs Vernon try to make him see that she wants him to do not what will please her, but what is right. He has, as his younger brother has pointed out, 'a blind spot.' And it is by reason of this infirmity in him that she finally tells him she cannot be his wife. The poor fellow is dazed by the blow. He offers wildly to give up all his newspapers, and live on the million or so that he has as private capital. What more can a woman want than that a man should do anything, everything, for her sake? For her sake he would see that he was in the wrong—if see he could, but he can't. Her last words to him are 'Supply and demand! And, if the public demanded your wife, I believe you would give her to it!'—a savage thrust; rather too savage, I think, for a comedy such as this. The end, however, is perfect: Sir Charles, still trembling with agitation, sitting down to banish Mrs Vernon for ever from his mind, and dictating into a dictaphone the preliminary steps of the campaign for the release of the suffragists.

Mr James Hearn was admirable in the very complex part of Sir Charles, though he played with a measure of caricature rather less than that with which Mr Bennett had informed his satire; and Mr Hignett and Mr Eadie, as Sir Charles's elder and younger brothers, made much of two thoroughly real characters. The best performance of all was that of Miss Margaret Halstan as Mrs Vernon—a perfor-mance of very fine intelligence and sensibility. In the part of Hen-rietta Blackwood (an actress who had been before the public for twenty-five years), Miss Frances Wetherall played with a keen, and rather cruel, but delicious, sense of type.

[*8 May 1909*]

AT THE HAYMARKET

In September Mr Frederick Harrison will make over to Mr Herbert Trench the right of deciding what plays shall be produced, in what manner, at the Haymarket. Meanwhile, he 'and Charles Frohman present Miss Billie Burke in *Love Watches*, a comedy in four acts, by Robert de Flers and Armand Caillavet, adapted by Gladys Unger.' Perhaps he is a sincere believer in the genius of Miss

Burke. But I think it likelier that his motive is to give lustre to Mr Trench's forthcoming repertory. 'See,' says he, 'see the sort of thing you get when the managerial policy is just to give you what the management thinks you want. You don't want it? Quite so. Come back in September. You'll find the place in possession of a stranger who means to give you what *he* wants, and to give it in the way that *he* deems proper, without any reference at all to your own tastes. Your reception of *Love Watches* is a good omen for him. Remember September.'

Twenty years ago—and it is by what the public's taste then was that the average manager gauges the taste of the present public—*Love Watches* might have been rather liked. I can dimly imagine that *L'Amour Veille* may have had some quality that pleased Parisians not long ago. If so, Miss Unger has carefully extracted it. Her notion of what makes bright fresh dialogue is beyond measure pathetic. Jacqueline, the heroine, squirts some scent over the soutane of an Abbé. 'It is a scandal,' says he. 'No, it isn't,' she replies: 'it's Jockey Club.' A little later, a Marquise, smelling the scent, says 'It is a scandal.' 'No, madame, it isn't,' he replies: 'it's Jockey Club.' And this is a fair sample of the general crudity of the affair. Perhaps in the original version the figure of Ernest Augarde appealed successfully to the sentimentalists. He is a bookworm on whom no woman has ever smiled. He loves Jacqueline, and she knows it; and, believing her husband to be false, she places herself under the protection of the bookworm. He is much delighted. He tries to impress her by boasting of past loves, and produces a boxful of letters and other souvenirs which he pretends to be the spoils of conquests. Later, when he sees that she can't stand him, he confesses to her, in broken accents, and at great length, that all the letters were snubs, and that none of the souvenirs had any romance attached to it. This scene, if the bookworm in the original version was a life-like character, may have had a certain sentimental value —of a cheap enough kind. But it is quite intolerably mawkish when the bookworm has been hitherto presented as a mere figure of fun. Mr Ernest Lawford plays the part amusingly, but he really must (if the play is still going on) not attempt to be touching. Mr Julian L'Estrange, as Jacqueline's husband, puts life into a dummy part. Of Miss Billie Burke, as Jacqueline, what can I say? I have so little to go upon. Mr Harrison presents her. Mr Frohman presents her.

But never for one instant does she present herself. To do so is no part of her scheme. Her theory of acting is quite distinct from mine. Acting, I think, consists in expressing a character through the medium of oneself. Miss Burke (if I interpret her rightly) holds that it consists in obscuring oneself behind a cloud of funny little acquired mannerisms, without reference to any character whatsoever. Neither she nor Jacqueline is allowed to peep out for one moment. And for what we do see, the nearest parallel I can remember is in a performance given in the music-halls by an American gentleman who describes himself as a 'Child Impersonator.' He makes of his voice a sing-song squeak, and all the while wriggles his body and contorts his face in the most surprising way—especially surprising to anyone who has ever seen a real child. It can be but a very few years since Miss Burke was a real child; and thus her likeness to the Child Impersonator is the more curious. Add to that likeness a touch of the good fairy in a pantomime, and a blend of selected mannerisms of Miss Mary Moore, Miss Annie Hughes, Miss Edna May and Miss Lottie Venne, and you will have some dim notion of what Miss Burke's method amounts to. Dimly through this enveloping cloud I could perceive signs of humour and intelligence. Clearly could I perceive plenty of 'go.' Some day, perhaps, Miss Burke will begin to act. But there is no chance of this unless she unlearn all that she has taught herself. I suggest that she should make a 'retreat,' of several months, in some remote convent, spending her days in silent meditation. Then, for several years, let her not go near a theatre, but devote herself to the task of observing minutely the way in which young women comport themselves in real life. At the end of that period, let her apply for a small part in some theatre where the stage-manager is a good one. And at length, after many, many years of hard work, let her go to Mr Frederick Harrison and Mr Charles Frohman, those veterans, and ask them to present her all over again.

In last week's issue of this Review there was an admirable letter from Mr Anthony Scarlett on the subject of Mr Gordon Craig's work. Mr Scarlett was quite right to be surprised at my not having mentioned Mr Craig in my article about the National Theatre scheme. I was not less surprised myself. My excuse for the omission is this. In writing about the National Theatre Scheme and the hopelessness that any good—anything but intense dulness—would come of it if it were established as a reality, and in clamouring for a small endowed repertory theatre, I was thinking of the need for encouraging the young dramatists of the day. It is obvious that the present tendency of all that is vital in dramaturgy is towards comic or tragic realism of contemporary life. Also it is obvious that Mr Craig, arranging the scenery and lighting and costumes of a realistic tragedy or comedy, would either have to forswear his methods, and thus waste his time, or would wreck the play, and thus waste his time and ours. When I wrote the aforesaid article, I did not know that Mr Herbert Trench on the one hand, or Mr Charles Frohman on the other, was about to spring on us an assured scheme for some such repertory theatre as I vaguely clamoured for. Mr Trench's scheme includes the revival of certain Shakespearean plays. I daresay, too, that he will find a modern poetic drama or two, worthy to be produced, and a modern fantasy or two. I strongly recommend him to beckon Mr Craig from the Arno to the Haymarket. Among those monsters in embryo, the directors of the National Theatre (gentlemen to be appointed, as you may remember, by the Crown and the Colonies and the large provincial cities and the academic institutions), Mr Craig, obviously, could not hope to have a look-in. Some sixty pompous and timid mediocrities would shun a man of genius (even if his genius were not working along new lines) as they would shun the plague. It would be useless to recommend Mr Craig to *them*, even if they already existed. Mr Trench exists, fresh and free. I don't ask him to promise that all such poetic or fantastic plays as he may produce shall be according to Mr Craig's methods. Merely let him experiment, and see what happens. It is ludicrous that Mr Craig should be not without honour in all countries but this one. It is also very characteristic of this one.

[*15 May 1909*]

SOME CENSORS

The question of the censor in art has been well to the fore just lately. There have been three separate cases of censorship; one of them in the sphere of painting, another in the sphere of literature, another in the sphere of drama; and each of them implying for us a great deal of courage on the part of the censor—our indignation being the measure of that courage. First of all came Sir Edward Poynter, declaring at a public banquet that it was the function of the Royal Academy to uphold the principles of art, which are eternal, as against the judgments of the crowd, which are transient and erratic. In itself, an admirable platitude, to be applauded. But, in the circumstances, a grand outburst of defiance, sure to raise laughter and wrath. Sir Edward well knew that there is not a single expert of any standing who does not condemn the standard of taste upheld by himself. He had not forgotten that even the official world frowns on him—as was shown by the report of the Commission appointed to inquire into the administration of the Chantrey fund. He knew, moreover, that within a month of his pronouncement would be shown to the world, in the centre of Burlington House, as a lively example of intimacy with the laws of art which are eternal, his full-length portrait of the Duke of Northumberland. This (I think Mr Binyon will not gainsay me) is a portrait so feebly pretentious, so vulgar in conception, so childish in execution, that not even the most 'erratic' unit of the crowd that pays its shillings at the turnstiles of Burlington House could fail to be startled by it and appalled. There is not, I believe, any truth in the rumour that the Duke of Northumberland, fired by the example of the Duke of Norfolk, has disposed of the portrait to Messrs Colnaghi, and that the administrators of the Chantrey fund are going to draw seventy thousand pounds or so out of their capital in order that the masterpiece be saved to these shores. But the comedy is quite comic enough without this added touch. Or rather (since the matter is a serious one) Sir Edward's courage is epic enough in itself. Not only, when he made his pronouncement, had he that ducal portrait up his sleeve: it may be presumed that he knew also that the administrators of the Chantrey fund were going to persist in a favourite pastime by purchasing 'A Favourite Pastime' of a beloved colleague, to the exclusion of aught that there might be (and is) of vital worth outside Burlington House. Fearlessness, in however ignoble a cause it be manifested, is a high virtue. Hats off to Sir Edward!

Cursorily, it might seem that the Dean of Westminster, when he decided not to have the ashes of George Meredith buried in the Abbey, displayed a courage, an indifference to criticism, even more

illustrious than Sir Edward's. I have no wish to belittle the Dean,
but I cannot accept this theory. Sir Edward, being a painter, and
head of an academy of painting, cannot be wholly ignorant of the
trend of modern thought in regard to pictorial art. Even if he
doesn't read the books and the articles that are written, the prices
fetched at Christie's, which are a fair guide to experts' ideas, will
have shown him which way the wind blows. On the other hand,
there is no reason to suppose that the Dean has any theories, or
knows any theories, about modern fiction. He may do so; but it is
not one of his duties; and, as his duties are arduous and many, the
presumption is that in the emergency of Meredith's death he had to
rely solely on the counsel of other people. Doubtless, many illustrious
writers offered to him their counsel that Meredith's ashes should
rest in the Abbey. But it were natural that a priest, holding a sort of
national and official post, should mistrust the counsel of irresponsible
artists, and rely rather on the advice of people as responsible and as
official as himself—the sort of people whose communications to *The
Times*, even when the signatures are not for publication, are
printed in large type. A communication signed 'A Man of Letters'
so appeared in *The Times* a few days ago. It was a defence of the
Dean on the plea that Meredith's place in the history of literature
was not yet fixed. And it ended up with a prophecy that within a
generation or so Meredith might, like Thomas Love Peacock, cease
to be read. Suppose that when (say?) the Poet Laureate dies, the
Dean, jumping to the conclusion that the deceased was a poet, wishes
him to be buried in the Abbey, would any weight be attached by the
reverend gentleman to the objection that thirty years hence the
writings of Alfred Austin might cease to be popular? Surely the
Dean would murmur 'It is no duty of mine to intrude on the book-
market of the next generation—or even of this generation. I have
merely to determine whether a man be in himself great enough to
be interred in the precincts entrusted to me.' The idea of measuring
Meredith by the number of his readers present or future is only less
ludicrous than the coupling of his name with Peacock's. Doubtless,
in the pigmy official mind which concocted this letter there was no
malice in the comparison. Peacock had an odd style of his own, and
so had Meredith; and Meredith, like Peacock, will never be popular
in any full sense of the word. That was enough for the pigmy
official mind. In the eyes of a gnat, it may be conceived, there is no

difference in size between a mole-hill and a mountain. Shrewd and good as many of the appreciations of Meredith have been, I have seen only one that properly stated Meredith's magnitude. The professional critic is always a little afraid of saying anything which might lead to an accusation of 'gush.' After Meredith died, it was reserved for an amateur critic, Sir Ray Lankester, to write the essential thing of him: that he was, with the sole exception of Shakespeare, the greatest man in our literature. This and that of our writers has had this and that gift as signally as Meredith. But only in Shakespeare has there been such a variety of endowment; only in him a range so ample, depths so many. In due course England will realise this. I don't mean that many hundreds of people will in any generation be reading Meredith. Very few hundreds read Shakespeare, though they care to see their favourite actors in such of his plays as contain good parts for those actors. His transcendence is taken on trust. So will Meredith's be. Then England will realise to the full how very foolish she has been made to look by the Dean's decision. No wrong has been done to Meredith himself. No honour we could pay him could be in proportion to his greatness. He loses nothing by not being in the Abbey. A little church-yard in the country, indeed, is a happier resting-place than he could have in a temple packed with the remains of so much that in life was but pompous-small. The loss is all ours.

Whereas the Dean, according to probability, did not know that any one would be indignant, and whereas not even the united indignation of the United Kingdom would be likely to result in the curtailment of his power, Mr Redford, the third of the censors who have been to the fore, very well knew that his refusal to license Mr Shaw's new play would raise a sharp outcry against himself at a rather critical moment in his career. There had recently been introduced into the House of Commons a Bill for the abolition of the post that he holds; and, though of course there was little chance of it being passed this session, there were no signs of opposition to it, and there were many signs of encouragement. Yet this was the moment at which Mr Redford, impelled by his sense of duty, and undeterred by the horrid memory of all the other scrapes which that sense of duty had pushed him into, chose to deprive our legislators of the keenly-anticipated pleasure of seeing a new play by G.B.S. Hats off to Mr Redford! His dangerous victim has promptly done the best possible thing, by publishing to the world that little portion of the play by which Mr Redford was offended. The fact that it is a passage which no newspaper in its senses would refuse to print for us to read shows at once the absurdity of the system by which the play-going public is deprived of Mr Shaw's play [*The Shewing-up of Blanco Posnet*]. Let us all dance on the prostrate body of Mr Redford as violently as we can—but, I repeat, hat in hand.

[*5 June 1909*]

IRISH PLAYERS

They certainly are charming, these Irish players; charming in their remoteness from ourselves and from any other players that we know. They are quite as alien as the Sicilians were, and very much less obvious. What the Sicilians were driving at was clear enough all the time; and they drove at it with a vital energy that in part revolted us and in part made us ashamed of our own insular lassitude. But we have never the sense of discerning surely what these Irish players are driving at. The mist of Col na Grath clings around them, blurs them; and the one thing that seems certain is that we are more vital than they. To see them very often would be, I think, dispiriting. To see them once or twice is to be pleasantly touched. I was pleasantly touched by them last Wednesday evening at the Court Theatre.

Part of their charm is in the naïveté of their method. Some of them, evidently, have a real talent for acting. But none of them, in any strict sense of the word, acts. They are exactly the same on the stage as they are (I conceive) off it: not as they might off the stage be in some moment of pleasant or unpleasant crisis, but just as they would be when nothing in particular were happening. However poignant the scene entrusted to them by the author, they show no sign of being moved: they just talk on in their quick, soft, matter-of-fact undertone, expressing nothing through their faces except a melancholy to which they have long since grown accustomed. At any rate, that is their effect on the Saxon beholder. It may be that to the Keltic beholder, they convey all manner of vibrations. It may be that the genuine Irishman in Ireland does not in any circumstances express emotion in a way that would be palpable to you and me. But

466

I suspect that he does. These players, I take it, are not truly reproducing what would be their manner if the play were a reality: they
are reproducing just their own selves as they are at ordinary times.
Or, rather, they are repeating just those selves. Accurately to reproduce a thing on the stage is a process that involves sacrifice of the
actual truth. It is a process that involves a calculated measure of exaggeration. I am sure that even when Col na Grath (which I have
invented) lies grayest and heaviest in the glens of Tipperary or (I
really am good at local colour) along the sholbeens of Connemara,
these players are more animated than they appear to us across the
footlights of the Court Theatre. But I would not they were otherwise here than we see them. There is a sweet flavour in their lack.
We have plenty of professional players who hit the mean between
too much and too little emphasis. And we have innumerable players,
professional and amateur, who run riot in over-emphasis, and in
tiresome traditional tricks of speech and gait and gesture. Because of
them, these Irish players are an exquisite refreshment. May the
draught be never adulterated!

But, of course, their greatest charm for us is not in their artlessness
but in their Irishness. To me, as to all people reared in a Saxon
environment, a brogue is magical. You may remember that in *John
Bull's Other Island* Larry Doyle describes how, when first he came
to England, he nearly proposed marriage to a barmaid 'because her
cockney accent was so distinguished, so quaintly touching.' It may
be that there is no 'absolute' beauty in the timbre and cadence of a
brogue. But I won't take Mr Shaw's or any other Irishman's word
for it. Mutual disparagement is as natural to the Irish as is mutual
admiration to the Scots. The Scottish accent is just as strange as the
brogue to our ears; yet in none of its varieties does it exercise any
magic on us; indeed, it chills us, hardens our hearts. Perhaps it is
because they know themselves incapable of winning quick sympathy
south of the Tweed, except among such of their compatriots as are
already settled there, that the Scots are always so finely loyal one to
another, so deeply and romantically susceptible to one another's
magic. While I was watching the Irish players the other night, and
watching the rapt affectionate faces of the Saxons in the audience, I
wished Edinburgh had some sort of equivalent for Mr W. B. Yeats
and Lady Gregory—some one who would organise a troupe of native
peasant-players and bring them here to perform plays racy of their

own soil. It would be such fun to study their reception. Of course they would have an uproarious reception nightly from their compatriots, gentle and simple, who would occupy the greater part of the theatre. And of course such Saxons as might gain admittance would be very much interested. But I do not fancy there would be much Saxon applause. Saxon hearts would be hardened by the loud, deliberate, harsh utterance of the players, by the great steady force of character manifested in every inflection, by the length and thoroughness of the disputations, and above all by the 'pawky' humour. I have not forgotten that Mr Harry Lauder is a great success wherever he goes; nor do I suggest that his success depends wholly on his ubiquitous compatriots. But Mr Harry Lauder is no more to be taken as a typical true Scot than is Mr J. M. Barrie. Mr Lauder in his songs, like Mr Barrie in his plays, gives us a romantic personal symbol of Scottishness: it is he, not his material, that we applaud. If you took away from him his imaginative talent and his vocal talent, and put him on the stage as just a Scottish peasant, with others of his kind, to enact plays of Scottish life written by native realists, the London press would not then, I fear, succumb, as it does inevitably to these Irish players. Charm seldom goes with strength. Scotland will not, therefore, take umbrage at my remarks. To be stronger than we is better than to charm us. Besides, Scotland has, as I hinted, the comfort of seeming always charming to herself.

Two of the plays acted on the night of my visit to the Court Theatre were by the late J. M. Synge, that most remarkable of the dramatists who responded to the Irish literary movement. *In the Shadow of the Glen* is, in the bare outline of it, a kind of farce. An elderly farmer pretends to die, in order that he may spy on his young wife. As he lies still on the bed, a tramp comes to the cottage, and has a long rambling talk with the wife. Presently comes a young farmer, with whom she discusses marriage. The husband bounds out of bed, and turns the wife out into the night. The tramp goes with her. The young farmer, as being a spiritless creature, is forgiven; and the two men sit down to drink whisky together. Absurd enough the story sounds, as told thus. But Synge made of it a thing not merely of rich humour, but of deep poetic quality, breathing into it a sense of lonely and humble lives, and (through the persons of the wife and the tramp) a true philosophy. *Riders to the Sea* is an unalloyed tragedy— the tragedy of an old woman whose husband and sons are all, one by one, drowned at sea. As in Heijermans' play *The Good Hope*, the tragedy is made the deeper by the old woman's acquiescence in what fate decrees. Lady Gregory's *Hyacinth Halvey*, of which I wrote here some time ago, came out as freshly humorous as ever. And another capital thing in the programme was *An Imaginary Conversation*, by that very pungent and acute writer, Mr Norreys Connell. The conversation is mainly between Tom Moore and Robert Emmet; and the difference of their characters is drawn most amusingly. The little tragi-comedy is perfect of its kind.

[*12 June 1909*]

A PLAY AND AN ACTRESS

The desire for 'the simple life' is a very good theme for comedy. There is not, of course, anything ridiculous in the desire itself, which is a quite natural and reasonable outcome of twentieth-century existence. To that existence 'the simple life' is a necessary counterpoise. When men and women find their energy undermined by the excessive demands made on it, and their nerves all a-jangle through use of those various artificial stimulants and sedatives that enable them to cope with the exigencies of a world robbed of all its old easy and seemly charm by the various engines of applied science, it is natural that men and women should envy, and right that they should emulate, the beasts of the fields. When penny-stamps and steam-engines were vouchsafed to the world, it was honestly thought that thereby a great deal of time and trouble would be saved for us. When, furthermore, motor-cars and telephones and 'tubes' were shaken out of the cornucopia, you scrambled for them eagerly, not having learned your lesson. You have learned it now. There is not one thinking person among you that would not, for sake of the happiness of the human race, be glad to have these 'tyrannous toys' smashed up and swept away and forgotten. That cannot be, of course. The world is not governed by sense. What you think good for you, what you really want, counts for little. Nobody—except perhaps a fourth-form boy here and there—wants to possess an air-ship. But every nation will have to possess as many of them as it can —until air-ships be superseded by some subtler and swifter vehicle, for use in the very-soon-by-some-inspired-idiot-to-be-discovered fourth dimension of space. In course of time, thanks to science, the human race will collapse and cease. Meanwhile, though the units of it are everywhere collapsing under the burden of life, there is no hope of a collective revolt. The average unit, after a few collapses, ceases. A lucky minority of units has the means to take holidays long enough to restore their vitality; and so, in a state of alternate action and re-action, they can muddle through to the end. To spend many whole days in walking naked through a pine-forest, to eat nuts only, and drink only well-water, to sleep naked on gravel soil *à la belle étoile*— all this is very good for you, is the only way to restore you to the ridiculous life you lead at other times. But it is not, I conceive, very delightful. On the contrary, it must be a great bore. From the out-side, the contrast between it and your usual life is good comedy; and your boredom is good comedy, too.

Mr McEvoy was wise to take the theme; and Miss Horniman, of the repertory theatre in Manchester, was wise to produce his play *When the Devil was Ill*: it is great fun, and has been one of the suc-cesses of Miss Horniman's fortnight at the Coronet Theatre. In the first act we see a famous novelist dictating to his secretary the end of his great new work. His popularity is founded on the breeziness of his style. To urban toilers none brings so buoyantly as he the scent of the bean-fields, the lowing of cattle at sundown, the warbling of dairy-maids as they go forth in the dawn to their simple labours, and so on. He, poor fellow, does it all from within himself, as being essen-tially an urban toiler. His contracts with publishers have kept him hard at work in Clement's Inn for several years. By the strained look in his eyes, by the hysterical sound of his voice, and by other symptoms very cleverly suggested by Mr Iden Payne, you judge him to be on the verge of a break-down. Cigarettes make him dizzy; but to leave off smoking makes him feel worse. His secretary, under protest, doses him with this and that nostrum, holding the glass to his lips. By hook or crook he manages to dictate the last sentence of his novel, and collapses, but rises to a great resolve: he will make a dash for freedom, spend the rest of his days in contact with the soil, never write another line. Even his secretary, a dry and elderly man, is infected by his ardour, and follows him into the wilds. There, after a month, we see them. The secretary has been disillusioned very soon after the outset. The novelist, having retrieved his health, escapes by an adventure from subsequent boredom. The adventure is a young lady who resides in a caravan, and wears the costume and speaks the lingo of a gypsy. The novelist (who is also on the Borrovian tack) sees at a glance that she is a jaded worldling, like himself. She sees not less promptly through him. But each supposes the other to be deceived. The comedy ends, of course, in mutual love, and in mutual agreement that the simple life is rather tedious in itself. The end being so well foreseen, it is a pity that Mr McEvoy did not compress his play into three acts. There is at many points a certain slackness in his handling of it. The theme is developed surely enough, but not quickly enough: there is too much of mere embroidery on it. What Mr McEvoy needs to cultivate is his sense of form. His humour, and his observation, and his inventiveness, will then win him a very high place. All the characters in the play are well drawn—especially the secretary, played with a perfect sense of the character by Mr Charles Bibby. In *Widowers' Houses*, which I saw on the following evening, Mr Bibby was not less pungent as Cokane.

As in the art of life, so in pictorial art, a yearning for the simple life has begun to manifest itself. Mr Sargent, who has excelled in depicting the restlessness of great ladies on priceless sofas, is said to have decided that he can do it no more. There is on view at this moment, as an earnest of his resolve, a portrait by him of a naked hermit in a desert; a hermit at rest (so Mr Sargent would have us think), *planté là* and meaning to stay so, undisturbed even by the urban complexity and velocity of Sargentine technique. Perhaps Mr Sargent will presently shed, just as Mr Augustus John is now shedding, the vanities of twentieth-century technique, and revert to the ways of primitive masters. Not that he will ever manage to produce —except at first glance—a really primitive effect. A man cannot, however great his yearnings, free his soul of its environment. Look (for example) at Mr John's 'Going down to the Sea.' They are ample and simple in outline, these women, and have dignity and buoyancy and repose. Yet, after we have looked awhile, we grow conscious that they are women of our own time. We see it first in their faces. No hillside Etruscans, they! They have just been going through 'the Nature cure.' They have obeyed to the letter the drastic injunctions of the superintendent of the institution. They have eaten nothing but nuts, and have not once been indoors. It has done them a world of good. They have all of them gained two or three stone in weight. They no longer start at a sound. They can concentrate their minds. They can digest their food, and sleep soundly. But we see still in their faces how near they were to a break-down before they were sent here. The stress of modern life has left on their mouths and in their dark eyes traces that no cure, however drastic, can efface. Also, they are bored. They wouldn't admit it. But time, on this the last day of their cure, passes with leaden feet. They are longing for the moment when they can throw off their 'simple life' draperies, and resume their fashionable frocks, and motor back to London.

It is Mr John's good fortune that he, in his yearning for primitive simplicities, and in his failure to achieve them truly, typifies the age in which he lives. He paints, *malgré lui*, the tragedy of the twentieth century. That is the main secret of his hold on us. He has called into visual being the prevalent mood. Already he has many imitators. Anon they will be innumerable. Among the P.R.B. and their imitators, Miss Ellen Terry was idolised, because she in her own face and figure reproduced much of that type which they had evoked on canvas as a symbol of their protest against the circumstances of life in middle-Victorian England. I rather think that the young lady who has been playing the principal parts in the Coronet repertory is destined to be the idol of all the young painters during the next twenty years or so. For Miss Mona Limerick is in three dimensions a synthesis of the figures that Mr John has projected on canvas. She has a barbaric air, and yet an air of being over-civilised. She has an air of belonging to any age but this, and yet she is intensely modern. She might be a Delilah, or a Madonna, or a Cassandra; but always of the twentieth century. Tigresses and monkeys, swans and gazelles, are none of them quite unlike her; yet she is pre-eminently woman. And she might be Persian, or she might be Romany; but her place is in London (though Manchester will be loth to lose her, no doubt). Hers is the most far-fetched personality that you could conceive; and her acting is no anti-climax to her mystical flamboyance: she is a tragedian of great power. Mr McEvoy's gay little comedy somehow managed to exist under the shadow of this power; but it had a very narrow escape. And *Widowers' Houses* was thrown considerably out of gear by the looming up of Blanche Sartorius (that nasty little shrew) as a great and noble incarnation of high-tragic legend. There is no use for Miss Mona Limerick in slight parts; and she could

472

never achieve either prettiness or ugliness. Her tragic beauty and power fit her only for great parts; and these, I hope, will befall her in plenty. Her power is as yet unbridled, verging sometimes to the grotesque. But of its authenticity there can be no doubt.

[*19 June 1909*]

A NOTE ON ST JOHN HANKIN

His death by his own hand was, for his friends, not less a surprise than a grief. He was the sanest and most level-headed of men; and, while the circumstances of his private life were very comfortable and auspicious, he had achieved for himself a high reputation in the art that he practised. Of course he was not a great popular success. He can have made but little money out of his plays. But he was in no need of money, and so astute a seer of things as he must have known well that his plays were not of a kind that could ever be lucrative. He had had no need to court popularity, had been able to do his own work in his own way, and had won the reward of general esteem among artists and critics. He was not, then, a disappointed man. He had no reason to be so, and was the last man to be anything without a very good reason. In the suicide of John Davidson (since suicide it must be: there is no hope now that he is hiding somewhere) there seems nothing strange. Davidson was very poor, and was weighted with heavy responsibilities. Also, he was a man of intense emotional temper, with as much capacity for despair as for joy. Also, he was a man of genius; and he believed—rightly or wrongly, but in every fibre of his being—that he had an indispensable message for mankind. He was determined to be heard; but mankind paid him no attention, except in murmuring how pretty his *Fleet Street Eclogues* had been, and what a pity it was he had lost that agreeable knack. Posterity may—and I hope it will—discover that his was really a great message, and despise us for our obtuseness. Meanwhile, it is not, to anyone who knew Davidson's deep passionate nature, surprising that he killed himself. His act seems to us, in retrospect, an inevitable close to a great spiritual tragedy. Hankin—the fortunate and equable and suave and cynical Hankin—was the last man for

473

whom we should have predicted self-destruction. Nothing in his mind nor in his circumstances was there to impel him that way. It was simply to lack of physical strength that he succumbed. He had not the vitality to go on living. He will be missed by many men as an always amiable and witty companion; especially by Oxford men, who felt their youth renewed by the perfection in which, as the years went by, he preserved the Oxford manner. His comedies had an inalienable flavour—the flavour of Oxford. *The Return of the Prodigal* was certainly the best of them—the lightest and dryest, the most gracefully and lackadaisically acute. It will be his especial monument.

[*26 June 1909*]

'SCHOOL' AND 'THE GROTESQUES'

It must be ten years since Tom Robertson's plays were last revived in London. *School* is now being played at the Coronet Theatre, and is to be followed by *Ours* and *Caste*. Ten years ago it filled me with scorn, which I expressed with all possible vehemence in this Review. In those days one was still fighting. Mr Clement Scott was alive, decrying as a sign of decadence whatever in drama was non-Robertsonian; and there were many other critics hardly less hostile than he to the new movement which a few of us were trying to speed forward. The majority of popular playwrights were still working in the Robertsonian vein: their plays were simply Robertson up-to-date; and, so long as they were there to impede progress, one could not be fair to Robertson: he was the enemy. Well, there is no fighting nowadays. One by one, the old critics have disappeared, and their successors are, one and all, friends of—I was going to say the new movement; but the movement is no longer new: the battle is won, the formula established; realism sits crowned. Presently there will be a revolt, of course. The best among the youngest brains will find that realism, as a method of presenting life in drama, has been exhausted. New banners will appear, with some strange device on them. And we elders will fume and fret and fight, shoulder to shoulder, against these silly striplings who were in swaddling-clothes when we were

474

founding the national drama on a rock which never, never will be shaken! And that rock will crumble, and our grey hairs be brought down in sorrow to the grave, and our posts be filled by persons whose ideas Time has not ossified. Our old age will be as stormy as our youth was. We shall be as fierce in defence as erst we were in attack. For the present we sit successful, unchallenged; amenable, a trifle smug. We can enjoy such plays as *School*. We can give Tom Robertson due credit for the much that there was of charm and talent in him.

Not even in our hot youth did we ever deny his instinct for dramatic form, and for all that appertains to the theatre. The theatre was his very home, and he never looked out of the window; but he was, unlike the playwrights who preceded him, a student: he had actually read the works of Mr Thackeray and Mr Dickens. To the former he owed his notions of the upper class; to the latter his notions of the middle and lower classes. Not one of his characters has the strength that belongs to a faithful copy from life, or to a fantasy founded on fact: all his characters are founded on fiction—the fiction of Mr Dickens and Mr Thackeray respectively. But they have a charm of their own. Robertson had, besides a keen sense of humour, a pretty fancy. His touch was a trifle common, but it was tender. His presentment of the young ladies in Dr Sutcliffe's academy is idyllic in its way. It is in no relation to actual fact, but it is a skilful realisation of a charming man's ideal. I do not wonder that it still enchants the public. And the enchantment would be greater if the play had been produced with the costumes proper to the period. It is disturbing to see these figments of the 'sixties tricked out in the fashion of 1909. David Garrick playing Hamlet in a periwig was all very well; for archaeology was not expected in the theatre; and its absence did not hurt illusion. Nowadays, Hamlet in a top hat would be very deleterious; but no more so than is Robertson's Beau Farintosh as presented in the clothes of a dandy of to-day. This Beau, of course, was already somewhat out of date when the play was written: Robertson had faked him up from Major Pendennis. He might, however, pass muster in peg-top trousers. As it is, the anomaly is too grotesque. 'His language is like Tom Moore's,' says Jack Poyntz, when the Beau has been complimenting the young ladies. Such a remark as this would have a sentimental interest for us, helping us into the heart of the period, if Poyntz and the rest were properly attired. Otherwise, it merely makes us jump. And the matter is even worse when Poyntz tries to match his costume by speaking of the time when he was in Ladysmith—he, the Crimean 'heavy swell!' The most ludicrous moment of all is when Lord Beaufoy, having in a long soliloquy declared Bella to be 'as fresh as nature, and as artless as moss' and 'very different from the young persons that one sees in Paris, and the great tame tigerlilies that one meets in town,' proceeds to cry out 'Oh simplicity, sweet simplicity, how you are neglected in this twentieth century.' Of course this change of date is the logical accompaniment to the change of costumes. The absurdity of it is the measure of the costumes' absurdity. I suppose Mr Robert Arthur does not think it worth while to go to the expense and trouble of procuring appropriate costumes for three plays that are timed to run only a month or so in all, if the public will come and fill his theatre without such inducement. From his own point of view, he is wise. But the shade of poor Tom Robertson will not be appeased, nor I. Nor, I think, will the players at the Coronet. It is impossible for them, in modern clothes, to comport themselves in a manner befitting their utterances. They cannot, being outwardly tethered to their own time, retroject themselves into the Robertsonian spirit. They can only make uncomfortable efforts. These they loyally make.

I saw *The Grotesques* one day this week at the Queen's Hall. Mr Vere Smith, like Mr Pélissier, is a composer and writer of songs, as well as a singer of them; and he has gathered around him a small troupe of comedians, male and female, who unite in a very gay and clever little entertainment, somewhat in the manner of *The Follies*. The troupe is a good one all round; but the outstanding figures are Mr Vere Smith himself, who is a light, genial, and resourceful droll, and Miss Dorothy Doria, an actress to her fingertips, and evident possessor of a keen intelligence and sense of humour. In the second part of the programme, which consists of a burlesque of a village concert, Miss Doria impersonated a very well-brought-up young lady singing a musical-comedy song entitled 'I'm a ripping sort of gal.' The singer's perfect composure and complacency in her well-meant effort to reproduce the right effect, and the completeness of her unconscious failure, were beautifully rendered by Miss Doria, with a sense not less of pathos than of fun. *The Grotesques* are likely to have a vogue. I hope they will not confine themselves to ridicule of

comic and sentimental songs and their singers. Let them ridicule
things in general.

[*3 July 1909*]

ANTINOMIAN DRAMA

Again and again, in the course of the sittings of the Censorship
Commission, 'the young girl' has been trotted out and pondered on
with the customary solicitude. Her twin brother, as usual, has been
passed over. Yet, really, is he not just as important as she? If ignorance of the facts of life be a necessary basis for innocence in her, and
if it be moreover the best means of preparing her for life, let us keep
her blindfold, by all means. But we surely ought, at the same time, to
keep an eye on the twin brother. 'The boy—what will he become?'
A great and good man, let us hope; bating that, a steady, harmless
citizen. His character is not yet formed; it is still elastic, malleable.
Let us not shirk our responsibility. Let us be careful that this boy be,
so far as in us lies, exposed to none but wholesome influences.
We need not, I think, withhold from him the knowledge that evil
exists in the world. We may as well tell him quite frankly that he
has the choice of being wicked or good when he grows up. But, since
it is not in human nature to choose virtue for its own sake, we must
guard him from the suspicion that wrong-doing is not always un-
attractive and unsuccessful and despised, and virtue not always
triumphant and delicious and revered. 'Dear young friend, what is
it that weighs on your mind? Come, out with it! We have told you
always to bring your little troubles to us. You are not sure whether
you want to be a policeman or a burglar when you grow up? Well,
you must choose for yourself. We don't want to bring any irksome
pressure to bear on you. Only remember that whereas the policeman
is the idol of the community, and spends his old age peacefully in
receipt of a huge annual pension, and then goes to heaven, the
burglar invariably comes to a bad and miserable end. Indeed, his
whole life is a series of such ends: he is always being caught by the
policeman, and cast into prison, amidst the hoots of an outraged
populace eager to tear him limb from limb, poor fellow! We merely
mention these facts in passing. Far be it from us to dictate to you in

the choice of a career. What is that you say? Will we give you half-a-crown so that you may go to a theatre to-night? Certainly, dear child, certainly. What play do you want to see? *Arsène Lupin*? H'm. From the French, we suppose. Still, there can be no harm in it; otherwise it would never have been licensed. Go, dear child, and have a pleasant evening.

If there were no licenser of plays, the public (it is argued) would straightway develop a sense of responsibility, and would vocally condemn as assaults on morality many plays of a kind which now they accept as harmless on the strength of Mr Redford's imprimatur. *Arsène Lupin*, let us hope, would be banned promptly. Its power for mischief is incalculable. The hero (save the mark!) is a man who started life with all the advantages of health, strength, genius. To what use has he applied them? To burglary. For ten years he has been cracking cribs with the utmost neatness and despatch, and so cunningly that he has never come within the arm of the law. Nor, alas, is he in the least ashamed. On the contrary, he is very well pleased with himself. And one notes with distress that the authors, MM. Francis de Croisset and Maurice Leblanc, seem to be very well pleased with him. They present him not as a man whose character has been ruined by sin, but as an instance of the powerlessness of sin to make the sinner less admirable than he was at the outset of his black career. What a man does, apparently, matters not at all, and has no relation to what he is. Arsène Lupin is, so we are assured by one of the characters who know him most intimately, 'a man with a heart of gold.' And all that he needs for redemption after ten years of iniquity is 'a wife, a home, and (this in a voice husky with emotion) a child.' The most disquieting part of the matter is that the audience seems to endorse this theory without a moment's demur. You might imagine there would be some measure of sympathy for a humble detective who, in the exercise of his duty, is flung violently to the floor by Lupin, and then has his arm almost wrenched out of its socket, while one of Lupin's confederates robs him of some papers which he had secured in the interests of justice. As a matter of fact, the audience roars with laughter and delight. And when, at the very end of the play, Lupin makes good his escape (quite impenitent, but with every prospect of getting 'a home, a wife, and a child' presently), and the principal detective, mistaken for him, is flung violently to the floor by one of the lesser detectives, the unanimous verdict seems to be that justice has been done; and the evening ends sweetly in tears and laughter.

If the audience were composed entirely of members of the criminal classes, its behaviour would seem natural enough. But I have no reason to suppose that the audiences at the Duke of York's are below the average level of respectability that one finds in other theatres. It is a strange thing, this lack of *esprit de corps* among the virtuous. There is honour among thieves, and a loyal spirit of comradeship. The enemies of society rejoice in one another's triumphs, are touched by one another's failures. But among the decent people on whom they prey there is no corresponding emotion. Every one of these decent people is angry if he happen to be singled out as victim; but he cannot count on the sympathy of any one of his peers. 'Law and order'—one would think, off-hand, that this would be an inspiring and a sacred ideal, for which orderly and law-abiding people would be glad, at a pinch, to lay down their lives. But the fact is that the human biped, though physically gregarious, is incurably individualistic in spirit. In law and order he sees merely a trouble-saving device. He is delighted at any infraction of it which does not directly incommode himself. Such an infraction appeals to his romantic sense, and its perpetrator is thereby endeared to him. If it were possible to make him see the romance of the common good, there might, by the way, be some hope of a practical future for socialism. But, to make him see this romance, you would have to construct him all over again, on a quite different principle; which you might find rather difficult. Meanwhile, he will certainly continue to sympathise with every malefactor whose misdeeds are not of a timid or humdrum order, as against the officers of the general convenience, and will rejoice in every score off these officers, and will mourn whenever a sensational scamp is laid by the heels. All England's heart went out to 'D. S. Windell'; and all Europe's to Köpenick; and I am very sure that our frank delight in these prototypes of Arsène Lupin—our sympathy with them, so well worked up by and so loudly echoed in the press—must have had an evil influence on the minds of the rising generation. We have no official censor of the press, or of human nature. But we have Mr Redford, whose duty it was either to prohibit *Arsène Lupin* altogether, or to insist that the central figure should not be so gifted, so brave, so successful, and so good.

However, the mischief is done, and we may congratulate Mr Gerald du Maurier on a part in which there is excellent scope for his peculiar dexterity and grace of style, and for his inventive humour. The one other part which counts is that of Guerchard, a Gallicised version of Sherlock Holmes, made very real by Mr Dennis Eadie, that Protean actor. Miss Filippi and Mr Eric Lewis do next to nothing admirably.

[*4 September 1909*]

'MID-CHANNEL'

Noblesse oblige; and Sir Arthur Wing Pinero ought to abandon his cult for low life above stairs. Time was when he gave us glimpses of beauteous Princesses and cynical Dukes. They were not altogether convincing. One seemed to have had something like them in the pages of Ouida and other far less gifted novelists. Perhaps they did not convince even Sir Arthur (then Mr) Pinero. For in recent years he has concentrated himself more and more closely on a study of the least pleasing elements in the various strata of the middleclass. Uneducated young women aping the manners of their superiors, and educated young women with a lurid streak of commonness in them, have had a particular fascination for him; and very cleverly he has depicted them. But, as an artist, he ought not to allow any one phase of life to master him; and I was hoping that now that he had received the royal accolade, and passed into the pages of Debrett, he would treat himself to other and wider ranges of vision.

Accordingly, *Mid-Channel* is somewhat a disappointment to me. Zoe Blundell, the central person of the play, is yet another sample of that betwixt-and-between type in which Sir Arthur has specialised; and she is much nearer to the class beneath her than to the class above her. She is, indeed, crudely and monotonously vulgar in thought and in speech. I cannot divine in her circumstances any reason why she should be so. She is the daughter of a successful doctor. As such, presumably, she had the advantages of a good nurse and a good governess when she was a child, and of decent, though possibly dull, society when she 'came out.' In this society, however, moved a very vulgar young man, whose wife she became. She loved him entirely for himself and the good that was in him; for his vulgarity was not counterbalanced by wealth. They were very poor, he and she—so poor that they had to live in that dark and squalid alley, Fitzjohn's Avenue. But in after years, when, through the husband's industry on the Stock Exchange, they had been able to migrate to splendid and salubrious Lancaster Gate, they always looked back on those days of their pathetic early struggles as the happiest days of their lives. As it had been their specific aim to rise in the social scale, one would suppose that whenever the husband was at home it would have been his wife's aim to refine him. But Sir Arthur's belief in the inevitable vulgarity of stockbrokers is as firm as his belief in the benightedness of Fitzjohn's Avenue. So far from refining her husband, poor Zoe became vulgar herself. Indeed, by the time she is thirty-seven years old, she has outdone him in vulgarity; and he rebukes her for 'damned slang'; whereat she rounds on him with the explanation that it was by contact with the friends whom he used to bring to the house that she lost her natural delicacy of speech. Thus does Sir Arthur show us the irony of life, the canker that may be at the heart of even the fairest rose. A hovel where love is—what more idyllic? But peep within, and you may see there the flash gang of which we know the Stock Exchange to be composed, poisoning with their vile locutions the shell-like ears of Angelina, wife of Edwin. One of these brutes, just arrived, says to her 'Let's have a squint at you.' Another, being thirsty, asks her to give him 'a drop of water.' Another, being hungry, suggests 'a snack.' Others are loudly talking of money as 'coin,' of children as 'kiddies,' and so forth and so on. And all these horrid equivalents will, by the time the hostess is verging on middle age, have become ineradicable from her vocabulary. Her only consolation will be that but for them she might not be deemed by Sir Arthur Pinero worthy to be the central figure in one of his plays—nay! might not even be able to smuggle herself in as a subordinate. In *Mid-Channel* there is but one person who is not saliently vulgar; and this is an elderly woman who has little to do with the play, and whose daughter describes herself as 'a straight, clean girl.' Peter Mottram, the *raisonneur* of the play, is not vulgar only when he is *en train de raisonner*. At such times he

becomes quite portentously refined, and evolves the simplest platitudes in terms of most laborious metaphor. He has discovered that
not all husbands and wives are as happy together as they appear.
But, important though it is that the world should receive this tremendous revelation with as little delay as may be, he involves himself in a long, long disquisition on two flawed vases of Chinese
enamel. Another discovery of his is that people, as they grow older,
are apt to lose the impulses and illusions of youth; and for him this
matter is inextricably interwoven with the aspect of the pewter cups
and other trophies of athleticism which he has seen ranged on the
sideboards of his friends; and he develops the analogy with a
patience that appals. But the greatest of all his discoveries is that on
which Sir Arthur bases his play: to wit, that husbands and wives
sometimes get on each other's nerves after the passions of youth
are spent, and before the acquiescence of eld supervenes. In the bed
of the sea, half-way between Folkestone and Boulogne, is a ridge,
which has the effect of making the water choppy, and—if you want
the analogy worked solemnly out in all its ramifications, you must
go to the St James's; I admire Peter Mottram's patience, but can't
copy it.

On the aforesaid basis Sir Arthur might have written a good
light comedy. The first act (granted the needless vulgarity of the
characters) promises well. Zoe Blundell and her husband agree to
bicker no more, and then, by easy gradations, they proceed to bicker
worse than ever. No matter that Sheridan did this business perfectly: Sir Arthur does it very well indeed. The trouble is that he (a
light-hearted man of the theatre) feels he owes it to his opinion of
himself as a thinker, and to his reputation for merciless study of
life, to build up a tragedy. Mr Blundell leaves his wife in Lancaster
Gate, and takes a flat, and starts a liaison with a woman who once
occupied a good social position, but has been divorced and has since
then been associated with various men. As presented by Sir Arthur,
she shows no trace of her past advantages, and has all the manners
of the least reputable type of chorus girl. In fact, there is no
dramatic contrast whatsoever between her and Zoe. This difference
she has: she is not Blundell's wife; and so, following a sacred
tradition of the stage, Blundell takes to the bottle. That a middle-
aged man of sober habit must suddenly become a drunkard when he
separates from his wife and takes a mistress, is a proposition which

one's experience of actual life does not support. However, Blundell takes the stage-traditional course. Zoe, meanwhile, visits Italy, and from Siena (a city on which we should like to hear her comments) she wires to a young man who has flirted with her, suggesting that he should come and cheer her up. She becomes his mistress, but, soon after their return to England, learning that he has played with the young affections of the 'straight, clean girl,' and learning more-over that her husband, for whom she cares far more than for him, is tired of his separation from her, she proceeds to give the young man what he calls 'the boot,' and goes straight to her husband's flat. Meanwhile, Sir Arthur has been reading *Tess*; and so, after Zoe has forgiven the penitent Blundell his infidelity, she proceeds to confess her own infidelity, under the impression that he will cry quits. Needless to say, Zoe, in real life, would have no such de-lusion; nor, being the shallow little vulgarian she is, would she feel any need to ease her soul by gratuitously telling the truth. Sir Arthur, however, is out for poignancy. Zoe, cast forth by Blundell, proceeds to the flat of the young man, to see whether he will eventually marry her. She finds that he is now engaged to the 'straight, clean girl,' and, rather than discommode him, she throws herself out of a window 'off.' Of course we are thrilled. But the thrill is not a legitimate artistic one. Zoe would no more kill her-self than she would have confessed to her husband. Her suicide is a mere device for effect—an effect of physical horror. So why stick at trifles? Why not let the audience actually see Zoe climb on to the window-sill and disappear head over heels?

[*11 September 1909*]

LEAR AT THE HAYMARKET

Mr Trench has shown excellent high courage in using *King Lear* to inaugurate his tenancy of the Haymarket. Tragedy is not popular; and the most horribly tragic of all Shakespeare's plays has been, in recent times, the least popular. In the lusty Tudor days, before 'nerves' had been heard of, men were able to revel in the gloomiest exhibitions. They were not afraid of the dark. We are. They liked to have their blood curdled. We have no blood to spare for that process, thank you. Thunder and lightning, barren heaths cowering under starless skies, exile and despair, the breaking heart, the tottering reason, treachery most foul, death sudden or lingering, seemed to the Elizabethans very jolly indeed. With music of flutes and scent of roses, and plenty of sweetmeats and amber wine, and not a cloud in the sky, we can just support the cruel burden of existence. In a word, we are civilised. 'We don't want to be harrowed' is our constant cry. It was impossible to harrow the Elizabethans. *King Lear* ran through three editions in the first year of publication, and was no doubt advertised as 'endless fun for young and old.' Shakespeare himself was in many respects a highly-civilised man; very far in advance of his time. He would never have been able to conceive the story of *King Lear* on his own account; and, had he been as superior as Mr Trench to the lust for lucre, he would never have taken *The True Chronicle History of King Leir and His Three Daughters* as a basis for work. In their original forms the stories of Macbeth and Hamlet were as barbarous as that of Lear. But Shakespeare breathed into them much of the spirit of his own premature civilisation; so that twentieth-century audiences can just manage to put up with them. The story of Lear he left barbaric. Whereas Hamlet and Macbeth are both of them modern and 'sympathetic' persons, in *King Lear* all the characters except Cordelia, the good and the bad alike, are savages; and their story is one of almost unrelieved horror. 'That's but a trifle here' says Albany when the news of Edmund's death is brought; and, oppressed by the steady accumulation of agonies 'here,' we smile a sickly smile at the aptness of the remark. If Shakespeare had invented his own plots, his genius would not seem greater to us than it does to-day. But it is useless to deny that his work would have been more satisfactory. And *King Lear* is especially one of the plays that are cumbered by their origin. There is too much in it that is merely silly or merely brutal—too much that Shakespeare did not transmute in the crucible of his brain. Mr Trench, in his admirably written note on the play, says: 'What insight, what imagination, to build on that first scene—a mere display of pettish temper on the part of a wilful old man—the mighty structure of the tragedy! . . . His tragically profound sense of humour perceived that the scene supplied a scope for irony which great imaginations have always found in human affairs.' This is a handsome and ingenious excuse.

484

But I suspect the truth is not that Shakespeare 'perceived' any-thing of the kind, but that he just went straight ahead without taking the trouble to make sense of nonsense. Suppose Mr Trench wanted a house built for himself, and the builder said 'I don't mean to bother about the foundations,' would that builder be compli-mented on his 'great imagination?' Would not his sense of humour strike his client as rather *too* 'tragically profound?' However, it is right that one poet should stick up for another. And Shakespeare's great imagination certainly did begin to work at high pressure so soon as he got Lear out upon the storm-swept heath with the clown, and in the hovel where Poor Tom gibbered. Shakespeare never did anything more tremendous than the crescendo of those scenes, nor anything more exquisite than the diminuendo of the scenes in which Lear's life totters to its end.

If the theatrical presentment of such scenes is not to fall ludicrously short of one's vague mental conception of them, there must be an artist with high imagination, and with great power of design, to create the background for them. Mr Charles Ricketts has risen to the level of his great opportunity. His scenery has a large and simple dignity of line and colour. It is a fit setting to tragic issues. It looms ominous in infinity. Darkling forests, sheer scarped cliffs, rude structures of stone—all are admirably right. I cannot praise his storm-swept heath, because I did not see it. Lear raved in inky darkness, which the streaks of lightning strove vainly to illumine. This was a pity. One needed to see Lear as well as to hear him. In real life, on so very stormy a night, one would not be able to see anyone, even at close quarters. But neither would one be able to hear him. The stage-manager at the Haymarket does not carry realism so far as to make Lear inaudible. That would be manifestly absurd. But hardly less absurd is it to make Lear in-visible. Lear's face and figure are needed to illustrate his words. We should be surprised to see footlights and limelights on a stormy night out-of-doors. In the storm-scene of *King Lear*, if they were used rightly, we should not notice them. Obscurantism, on the other hand, is noticeable, and a nuisance. Away with it!

I have never seen a better Lear than Mr Norman McKinnel's; but then, I have never seen another one. Salvini's was before my time; and Irving's I missed. I imagine that the beauty and dignity of Irving's presence must to some extent have atoned for his lack of lung-power, and his inability to declaim blank verse. Mr McKinnel's lungs are magnificent, and he has a true ear for the rhythm of verse. But his voice lacks variety, and is not in itself of a beautiful quality. And his presence, though impressive, is not regal. Lear was a barbarian, but he was a king. And much of the pathos of his tragedy is lost through our difficulty in believing that he, as presented by Mr McKinnel, has ever been anything more than a solid and trustworthy liege. Still more of the pathos is lost through the impassiveness of Mr McKinnel's face. It is a face that has only one expression: a sort of glum astonishment. Wrath, sorrow, fear, remorse, cannot be mirrored there. When he speaks of 'these hot tears, which break from me perforce,' the words ring strange, as coming from one whose lachrymal glands are under such perfect control. All that can be done by accomplishment and keen intelligence Mr McKinnel does. What he leaves undone is the fault only of his physical and temperamental limitations. It is when Lear's spirit has burnt itself out, when his fury has spent itself and him, that Mr McKinnel, who has given us all the forcefulness of Lear, but nothing of the fire, really rises to the level of the part. In that marvellously conceived speech which begins with the words 'Pray do not mock me. I am a very foolish fond old man,' Mr McKinnel achieves a fine and memorable effect of pathos.

Miss Ellen O'Malley, looking curiously like the early portraits of Miss Ellen Terry, is charming and touching as Cordelia. As Goneril and Regan, Miss Ada Ferrar and Miss Marie Polini have an air of wishing to show how charming and touching they too could be if they hadn't been cast for such unpleasant parts. In pantomime the two Proud Sisters of Cinderella are always played by men. In the case of Goneril and Regan, who are uniform with them, this tradition might well be followed. Mr Fisher White, as Cornwall, is as barbaric as one could wish. Mr Hignett puts plenty of fantasy into his impersonation of the clown; but, for the right effect of the clown's juxtaposition to Lear, it is a pity that Mr Hignett is not a smaller and more agile man. Mr Quartermaine is excellently weird as Poor Tom. It is a pity that Mr Hearn makes Gloucester so decrepit from the outset. There is hardly any contrast between Gloucester before his sufferings and Gloucester after them. It is also a pity that Edmund was not meant by Shakespeare to be a quiet, blameless, rising young Civil Servant of the twentieth cen-

tury. For then Mr Dawson Milward's rendering of the part would
leave nothing at all to be desired.

[*18 September 1909*]

'THE MAKING OF A GENTLEMAN'

Mr Sutro is a highly successful dramatist. But against the ease with
which he pleases the public must be set the difficulty he finds in
pleasing the critics. When he writes dramas with strong scenes in
them, the critics accuse him of sacrificing truth to effect, and mani-
pulating his characters so as to secure those strong scenes; and I
myself usually chime in. When he writes mere comedies, the critics
complain bitterly of the absence of thrills. In that chorus I do not
join. Mr Bourchier, timorous man, does not invite me to the
Garrick Theatre; but on leaving that temple a few nights ago I
did not ask the keeper of the box-office to return me my money or
the ground that I was not palpitating and haggard and forworn
with emotion. Let us concede to Mr Sutro the right to do what he
sets out to do, and judge him according to the way in which he
does it. *The Making of a Gentleman* is possibly not a classic. I daresay posterity will be able to get on quite well without it. But I take it
to be, for us, in the autumn of 1909, a very good piece of work. The
persons of the play are not essentially fresh. The homely but
wealthy manufacturer with the heart of gold; the good-for-nothing
son who lives on his bounty; the unscrupulous nobleman who also
lives on his bounty; the daughter of his old clerk, who loves him
for himself alone; the lady with a foreign title and an evil past,
who yet has scruples and a capacity for disinterested devotion to the
son—they don't sound startlingly new, as catalogued drily here. But
Mr Sutro has taken them and breathed plenty of life into them, and
has given them freshness in detail. Though evidently his prime aim
is to please the public, his play is far more convincing, gives us a
far better illusion of reality, than Sir Arthur Pinero's laborious and
wholly successful attempt to make us feel ill. Unflinching realism,
merciless integrity, slices of life, the scalpel—such are the catch-
words which doubtless were revolving in Sir Arthur's brain when
he composed *Mid-Gutter*. But never for a moment does that play

487

impress us as true to human life. The photographer has grouped together, in the harshest light, certain specially ill-favoured persons,
and before removing the cap from the lens of the camera, has said
'Look unpleasant, ladies and gentlemen, please!—Now!' The result
is a meaningless and unrelated ugliness. Fools are they who think
ugly themes are to be eschewed by artists. But it is right to condemn
ugliness to which the artist has given no moral or philosophic
significance; and there is none in *Mid-Gutter*. The fact that Zoe
and her husband agreed when they married 'to have no brats of
children' has no bearing on what they have become. It is dragged
in, for a moment, merely to give simple folk the idea that Sir
Arthur is a profound critic of the age he lives in. To Zoe and her
husband, children would have been but an added *casus belli
Billingsgatiani*. And as if even they, when they were bride and
bridegroom, would have made their compact in the words suggested
by Sir Arthur! One of the several reasons why Sir Arthur fails as a
photographer is that he seems to have so little notion of what people
say, and of how they say it. One of Mr Sutro's chief assets is the
keenness of his ear for human speech. Of course, characters in a
play must not talk exactly as we do in real life. If they did, the play
would be interminable, and we should have but the vaguest idea of
its drift. Human speech, for dramatic purposes, must be abridged
and sharpened, all the time; and yet we must be kept unaware of
the process. In the art of writing seemingly natural and actually
telling dialogue Mr Sutro is, with Mr Henry Arthur Jones, foremost among our playwrights. Mr Shaw has an ear for the rhythm
of human speech; his characters never talk like books; but there is
always something noticeably metallic about the concision of their
utterance. Except when Mr Shaw determines to show us that he
can achieve beauty with the best of 'em—as in the long speech made
by the mystic priest at the close of *John Bull's Other Island*—there
is no charm of rhythm in his dialogue. Mr Sutro never sets out to
display beauty of word and cadence. But he is a constant purveyor
of it. From first to last, his characters talk as charmingly as con-
cisely. The charm is no more protruded on us than the concision.
But it is there, an added grace, and subconsciously we enjoy it. It
is a pity that Mr Sutro, the most literary of our playwrights, does
not publish his plays.

Apart from the quality of the dialogue, *The Making of a Gentle-*

man would not perhaps be deeply impressive in the study. I do not think we should lay the book down with a sense that our experience of life had been extended, and our insight quickened. Segregating ourselves from the magnetic public which Mr Sutro set out to please, we might become more conscious than we are, in the theatre, of the inherent oldness of the story, and less conscious of the freshness with which Mr Sutro has decked it out. The central figure of the play is Archibald Carey, the son of the successful but homely manufacturer aforesaid. The father's ambition has ever been that his son shall be a gentleman. Nowadays the habit of doing nothing is not deemed essential to gentility. Indeed, it is regarded as rather bad form. All the fashionable youths of to-day do definitely something—are in the army, or in business, or in politics. Loafing is outmoded. And one would suppose that even the homely Sam Carey would have known this, and would have wished his son to do something. However, let us accept Mr Sutro's premises. Archibald Carey has plenty of intelligence, and any number of good impulses, but, unluckily, no character; and from his lack of character Mr Sutro distils some admirable scenes of comedy. Sam Carey arrives at the flat in South Audley Street, and confesses to his son that he has been speculating with his capital and is ruined. He has just enough left to enable him to go back to Canada and re-inaugurate there— on a small scale—his business in pickles. Archibald does not reproach him. He is, on the contrary, deeply touched. Also, his manhood responds joyously to the notion of accompanying his father and leading a hard new life in a hard new world. The father becomes very husky, and the curtain falls. The next act takes place in the house of Archibald's sister, Rosie, who has married the son of Lord Parkhurst. Rosie has reason to believe that a certain Baroness von Ritzen would like to marry her brother. This lady has the disadvantage of not having been respectable, and the advantage of being a widow with twenty thousand pounds a year. Rosie and Lord Parkhurst take Archibald in hand. Rosie dilates on the charm and beauty of the Baroness, and Archibald cannot help feeling flattered by her predilection for him. Lord Parkhurst applauds his manly and filial determination to go to Canada. He describes the climate, the lack of civilised society, the long day's unremitting toil with no apparent reward, 'but it's life, my boy—life!' And very soon Archibald is 'off' Canada, and proceeds to the boudoir of the Baroness. She has heard of Sam Carey's losses, and instantly divines the object of the visit, and does her best to make the young man uncomfortable. He manages, however, to express his proposal, and in the agony of the effort he realises that he really is rather in love with the lady. The scene is extremely amusing and well-invented, graduated with great skill. But one cannot believe that the Baroness, being really anxious to marry him, and having had her pride salved by his belated sincerity, and being a spirited woman of the world, accustomed to take what she wants, would refuse to marry him without the consent of his papa (whom she has never seen). See him of course she presently does—rough old Sam, in his homespun clothes, much embarrassed by his intrusion into the luxurious boudoir, but with all the strength of his sound puritan stock opposed invincibly to his son's betrothal. It is an old situation; but here again Mr Sutro's tact and insight save it from being tedious. The end of the play consists in old Sam's gradual yielding to the force of the argument that his son, having been brought up to do nothing, and encouraged to do nothing, is good for nothing, and had better attach himself to a Baroness with a past than to a country with a future.

Old Sam is played by Mr Bourchier with that restraint which he has gradually acquired, and which was all that was needed to make a fine actor of him. Mr Kenneth Douglas well presents the humour of Archibald. The Baroness is a rather difficult part, in that she is a complicated character, who remains mostly in the background. There is little time for an actress to make the audience understand her. Miss Ethel Irving succeeds where an actress of less well-developed method would certainly fail. Mr Edmund Maurice is amusing as Lord Parkhurst; and Mr A. E. Benedict, as Lord Parkhurst's son—a golf enthusiast, whose conversation is described by his father as 'nauseous and asphyxiating'—plays with a keen sense of character and fun.

[*25 September 1909*]

MR H. B. IRVING IN 'THE BELLS'

A wave of filial piety is passing over the land. It is pleasant to have a wave restoring old landmarks to us, instead of washing them away. On all sides we find that the surviving sons of men who were eminent in their day are determined to perpetuate the fame of their fathers by doing as exactly as possible what their fathers did before them. Mr Herbert Gladstone (so I learn from one of the permanent officials at the Home Office) spends the greater part of the day in transcribing his father's pamphlets on the Armenian atrocities of 1876, and will proceed to Midlothian, so soon as Parliament is dissolved, in order to stir the electors to a full sense of the iniquity of Lord Beaconsfield's foreign policy. No one who was in the House of Commons during the recent debate on the land-taxes will ever forget the profound impression made when Mr Winston Churchill rose from the Treasury Bench and declaimed his father's speech on the question whether Mr Bradlaugh should be allowed to sit in the House. Mr Lewis Harcourt is reading hard for the Parliamentary Bar, where he will presently recite a selection of his father's most trenchant orations. Lord Hugh Cecil has very kindly offered to contribute to this Review a series of the articles which his father wrote for it in the distant past. At the Queen's Theatre, Mr H. B. Irving is playing Matthias in *The Bells*; and it will be remembered that he appeared recently in *The Lyons Mail* and in *Charles the First*. On the outer door of Sir Philip Burne-Jones's studio is a card bearing the legend 'No models required.' This is because Sir Philip is making a copy of 'Love among the Ruins,' and will presently make copies of 'King Cophetua and the Beggar Maid,' 'The Legend of the Briar Rose,' and other favourite works of his father. M. Schutzheimer, the universally-respected millionaire, whose splendid hospitality in Park Lane was one of the most notable features of the past London season, has decided to return to Hamburg and do business there in a small way for the rest of his life. 'Dat vot vos goot enough for my fahder, dat is goot enough for me' he replied to an illustrious personage who was trying quietly to dissuade him from his intention. Thoroughly popular throughout the length and breadth of the Empire is the announcement that King Edward has decided to re-open the great exhibition of 1851 in Hyde Park, wearing a costume modelled precisely on that of the Prince Consort. There is indeed something very human, very touching, in all these manifestations of filial piety. The world is the sweeter for them. But, much as I hate to strike a jarring note, I cannot help asking whether the world is also the stronger for them.

French writers have often accused the English people of a comparative lack of reverence for parents. It is well that we have not ignored the rebuke. But let us not, in our anxiety to deserve it no longer, rush to an extreme. Reverence is one thing, slavish reproduction another. A thing that is admirable at the moment of its doing is not necessarily admirable ever after. Times change, and it is our duty to change with them. Let us try to keep ourselves elastic, malleable, fresh. Human progress may be all a delusion; but, for sake of our self-respect, let's keep the delusion up as long as we can. My heart goes out to all these men who are so active in the filial-piety crusade. But I am convinced that they might be employing their time to better purpose. Not by imitating their grandfathers did their fathers achieve greatness, but by striking out lines for themselves—lines appropriate to themselves and to the age in which they lived. All the pietists whom I have instanced are men of high ability; and some of them have genius. I think the greatest service and honour they could do to their fathers' memory would be to use their own powers in their own fashion, freely.

Take, for example, the case of Mr H. B. Irving. Here is an actor with truly fine gifts, with truly great potentialities. His face, his voice, his hands, are admirably expressive, and have the advantage of not resembling those of anyone else—except, in some measure, those of the late Sir Henry Irving. A personality as distinct as it is powerful is his. By years of hard work he has acquired the means of expressing artistically the force that was in him from the first. Gone are all the crudities that once marred his work. He has entered his prime. Nor is he an actor who depends merely on personal force and on beauty of method: he is a thinker. What his performances lack in emotional warmth is counterbalanced always by their strong intellectual quality—whenever, at least, the part he is playing is one which is strong enough to bear intellectual pressure. Decidedly, here is an actor whom the drama needs. I hope the drama may get him. Filial piety is all very well, up to a point. *The Bells* was all very well in the year of grace 1871. Crude stuff though it must have seemed even then, it gave Mr Irving's father his first chance of frightening an audience by the imagination and uncanny magnetism that were his. Mr Irving's father was right to believe in the play, and to fight Colonel Bateman into producing it for him. We respect him for the daring and the initiative that he showed. Would that his son,

entering into possession of the Queen's Theatre, had imitated those
fine qualities! The line of least resistance was for his son to imitate
his performance of Matthias, for the benefit of sentimentally-
minded old playgoers and archaeologically-minded young ones. In
point of finance, the immediate result is very good, I have no doubt.
But how about prestige? Is Mr Irving content merely to show that
he can rival Miss Cissie Loftus? Not that he shows even that. The
filial-piety crusade has not yet spread among daughters, and Miss
Cissie Loftus does not merely give imitations of Miss Marie Loftus,
the mother whom she prettily resembles. Mr Irving's natural resemblance to his father is strong enough to rob him of any great credit
for cleverness in *The Bells*. I commend to him the impiety of being
henceforward himself. Not even Hamlet, sadly lacking though he
was in initiative, spent *all* the time in following his father's ghost.

[*2 October 1909*]

'DON'

Mr Besier's new play, produced by Mr Trench at the Haymarket,
has distinct quality. It is quite apart from the ruck of clever comedies
that might have been written by any clever man with a knack for
play-writing. It conforms with no current pattern of manner or
method. Here and there, in the discussions between the characters,
are traces of Mr Shaw's influence. But it would be impossible for a
young dramatist to escape this influence altogether. The important
thing is that Mr Besier is evidently a man who can see and think for
himself, and that he can construct as setting for the result of that
activity a form of his own. The construction of *Don* is as daring as it
is original. The play begins almost in the key of farce; and only when
it has progressed some way do we realise that the effect of farce
comes not from the treatment, but from the nature of the theme;
and only in the middle of the last act are we aware that the play has
drifted out of comedy into strong drama, narrowly evading tragedy,
and coming to a happy ending which, though one could hardly
have foreseen it, is justified by the nature of the situation. It is always, in play-writing, dangerous to have more than one manner—
dangerous to demand of the audience more than one mood. To

change your manner without incoherence, and to make your audience change its mood without confusion, is a very delicate job. Mr Besier is to be congratulated on having done it.

Conceive a young man bringing to the house of his parents, and into the presence of the girl to whom he is engaged to be married, a woman whom he has taken away from her husband, and with whom he has spent the night; and conceive him offering at first no explanation, and being merely impatient at their unreadiness to receive the woman with open arms. Assuredly this is a situation of farce? But, if we attach due weight to the character of the young man as depicted for us, his behaviour presently resolves itself into comedy. His parents, Canon and Mrs Bonington, are quite ordinary people, uninspired, practical, discreet. But he, Stephen, is a thinker and a poet, whose writings have already got for him a European reputation, and—though, as Mrs Bonington tells us, 'he takes a great interest in strikes, and reads the *Daily News* every day'— he has not had time to learn the knack of behaving like other people, or even to notice how they behave. He is a dreamer, and accustomed to put his dreams into practice as well as into words. He is always going gloriously off at tangents, sped by a sublime logic of his own, and going, in the opinion of his friends, rather too far. It was all very well for him to befriend a waitress in distress, named Fanny; but when she, seeing that he did not reciprocate, and was indeed quite unconscious of, the passion he had inspired in her, became the wife of a Plymouth Brother of the lower orders, there the matter should have ended, with a good riddance. Having become engaged to General Sinclair's charming daughter Ann, and being wildly in love with her, Stephen ought to have taken no notice of the letter in which Fanny told him that her husband was a brute and a bully. He might have known that his conduct would be misconstrued; yet off he went to Fanny's home, and, finding her in a state of collapse, insisted on taking her away with him, and spent the night with her in an hotel, nursing her, and in the morning took her forth on the way to his father's house, with the best intentions, and quite as a matter of course. Meanwhile the Canon and Mrs Bonington, and General, Mrs and Miss Sinclair, had been apprised of the elopement by a letter from the infuriated Plymouth Brother, Albert Thompsett. In the middle of the first act, Stephen breathlessly appears in their midst, with Fanny drooping on his arm, and with no idea that there will be any doubt as to the propriety of his action. Where should he bring the poor girl, if not to the house of his mother? General Sinclair, as a plain soldier, is indignant. The Canon, as a plain clergyman, is appalled. His wife is also appalled, but fluttering and eager to forgive. Mrs Sinclair's fury is tempered only by her sense of the ludicrous. It never occurs to anyone, except to Miss Ann Sinclair, that Stephen may but have been acting according to his own rather too dazzling lights. She alone suspends judgment. The others fume in their several manners; and when Stephen, having insisted that Fanny shall be accommodated with a bed and a meal of eggs beaten up in beef-tea, has leisure to explain to them just what he has done, and why he has done it, still they are incredulous: his unworldliness is too much for them, and he appears in their eyes a heartless and tasteless libertine. To Ann, whom alone he convinces, he confides his intention of appearing as co-respondent, so as to free poor Fanny. 'Then,' says Ann, 'you will have to marry her.' He says he would assuredly not commit the crime of marrying a woman whom he does not love; and he cannot for the life of him see why Ann, knowing him to be innocent, should care whether he is co-respondent or not. The war between idealism and convention, between what matters to Stephen and what matters to everyone else, is waged briskly. The great thing is to prevent a meeting between Stephen and Thompsett. This Thompsett—a man of great physical strength, and of great ferocity and determination—is travelling from his robbed home to the Bonington's house, having received from Stephen news of his wife's presence there. Throughout the second act the audience is held in suspense for his arrival. And it is when we at last see him that the play slips into drama. Thompsett is an admirably drawn figure—the brutish, slow-witted man who has 'got religion,' and who 'got' Fanny with the same dull fanaticism. The Canon, frightfully embarrassed by fibbing, tries to assure him that Mrs Thompsett had come straight from her home to the rectory; but he is interrupted by the entry of Stephen, who promptly tells the truth, adding to it a lie as to his relations with Fanny. There is a long, tense, very effective scene between the two men; and finally the knot is cut by Fanny's confession, through which Thompsett 'gets' the belief that Stephen has done no wrong, and promises to be a kinder husband henceforth. Usually, these conversions are a mere device to secure a happy ending. Thompsett's conversion, however, is quite in character, and brings a very clever play to a worthy conclusion.

Mr McKinnel plays Thompsett magnificently. In parts which demand an effect of uncouth strength and emotion, held stolidly in reserve, Mr McKinnel has no rival; and Thompsett is his reward for having had to play King Lear. Mr Quartermaine, as Stephen, is rather too neat and acute in manner, too dapper, to suggest the poetry of Stephen's innocent and tumultuous soul. Miss O'Malley, as Ann, shows great sensibility and prettiness of method. And the other parts are well and amusingly played.

Don is preceded by *Gentlemen of the Road*, a little play by Mr Charles McEvoy—a very early little play by Mr Charles McEvoy, I suspect.

[*16 October 1909*]

STAGE CROWDS

Mr Chesterton once chid me, in a brilliant essay, for not cherishing in my heart the ideal of democracy. It is quite true that I don't believe at all firmly in (what has always been to Mr Chesterton a dark and mystical reality) the wisdom of the people. I would not stake sixpence on the people's capacity for governing itself, and not a penny on its capacity for governing me. Democracy, wherever it has been tried, has failed as a means of increasing the sum of human happiness. Autocracy, aristocracy, bureaucracy, and all the other modes of government have similarly failed. In theory they are all of them admirable, but they won't work out in practice. They would, doubtless, if man were a rational and an unselfish animal. But man is not built that way, and cannot be trusted either to wield power wisely or to obey wise ordinances. He means well; but original sin and muddle-headedness, between them, make havoc of his good intentions. Political history is the term by which we dignify the record of his ludicrous flounderings. And the political history of the future will be just as amusing or depressing, you may be sure. And let us smile rather than be indignant, since we cannot hope to remedy the nature of things, and since, after all, there will be, as there has ever been, a general impression that life is worth living. The vitality of man will always rise superior to the circumstances of existence. In sounding this note of optimism I hope to conciliate Mr Chesterton. Let him observe also that there is nothing invidious in my mistrust of his darling democracy, since the various other forms of tyranny seem to me not one whit more worshipful.

Furthermore, for his benefit I admit that in estimating the political capacity of the people, he has, and I have not, intimate first-hand knowledge as a basis. He has gone plentifully among them, making speeches to them, delivering lectures to them, canvassing them, and so forth. His impression of their magnificent sanity and sagacity has come through direct contact. He has been forced by the evidence of his eyes and ears to the conclusion that the historians whom he read at school—most of them, indeed, persons with a bias towards oligarchy—had been doing their little best to mislead him. I, all this while, have been deriving my knowledge of the people solely from the theatre. Neither by the popular demonstrations in the gallery nor by the dramatists' occasional presentments of popular demonstrations on the stage am I helped to reject the verdict of history. Wafted down to me from the gallery are shouts of laughter at the wrong moment; uproarious cheers for the cheapest and falsest sentiments; howls and groans, sometimes, for an author who has done fine work; salvoes for the charlatan. Speaking with the authority of an intelligent person somewhat expert in the art of the theatre, I say that the gallery is almost always wrong. Of course, the political and the aesthetic instincts are two different things. Misjudgment in the theatre does not preclude wisdom in the agora. But alas, the dramatists, one and all, when they deal with politics, present the people in the most despicable light. Innumerable are the mobs that I have seen on the stage; and I can recall not one that seemed to possess collectively one ounce of sense. The mode of presentment varies but little. You hear a confused and horrific hubbub before the curtain rises, and presently you behold the sovereign people—tanners, cobblers, blacksmiths, in the costume of the period, all with wild eyes and unshawn lantern jaws—hanging on the lips of some popular hero who is orating to them. At the close of his every sentence they roar themselves hoarse with rapture, those who are in the foreground turning to one another and repeating with hideous grimaces and hideous gestures of approval the last three or four words that have fallen from the orator's lips. We fear there is

497

no doubt that they will tear limb from limb anyone who might dare to oppose the policy of their idol. And when, in due course, such a person bobs up in their midst, pale but determined, his life seems not worth a moment's purchase. There is a noise as of apes and tigers, with the most appalling convulsions all round—cudgels brandished, fists shaken, curses hurtling, eyes starting out of heads, lantern jaws strained to their utmost capacity. Somehow, above the din, the voice of the new orator is heard. His first sentence is punctuated by an ugly rush. But he bears a charmed life; he stands his ground, and proceeds to the next sentence. In a moment or two the din subsides, the lantern jaws slacken, the cudgels are given a rest, and the sovereign people are gazing into one another's eyes with every manifestation of dubiety. This condition of theirs passes not less rapidly into evident approval of the orator's point of view, thence into enthusiasm, thence into an ecstasy of rapture; and, so soon as the peroration of the brief and (as it seems to us) not very remarkable speech has been uttered, the sovereign people, with one accord, seize torches and rush off roaring, with the express purpose of slaying orator number one. The chances are, however, that they will promptly fall under his spell and return to make an end of orator number two.

I think that even Mr Chesterton, if he were a seasoned dramatic critic, would find his faith in democracy somewhat shaken. In me, certainly, the theatre has destroyed utterly such belief as I may once have had in the political wisdom of the people. But I do vaguely suspect that the people are not quite such asses as our dramatists would teach us to suppose. The method of presenting them on the stage is traditional from Shakespeare, who very frankly hated and despised them and doubtless revelled in the opportunity of gibbeting them in the forum scene of *Julius Caesar*. He, however, did have the grace to make Mark Antony's speech a subtle and an eloquent appeal. Whereas the average dramatist thinks that any perfunctory bit of fustian is good enough to make the people change its mind instantly. Without pretending to authority, I doubt whether—in England, at any rate, and in modern times—an orator ever has any practical effect. People who agree with him (so far as they think at all) go to hear and cheer their own opinions expressed by him. A few people who disagree with him go to interrupt. It is quite good fun all round, but I should be surprised to hear of any

498

practical effects. I presume that most of the people in Trafalgar Square last Sunday were there because they were indignant against the Spanish Government, and wanted to hear Mr Cunninghame Graham express their indignation. If there were present any people who approved the execution of Ferrer, could even Mr Cunninghame Graham have moved them to join in the subsequent procession to the embassy? Suppose the whole multitude had been composed of men rejoicing in Ferrer's death—would a few words from the plinth of Nelson's column have turned their joy to horror, and have sent them headlong in the direction of Grosvenor Gardens? Suppose that on their way they had encountered, and wished to slay, the ambassador—would a few words from *him* have inclined them to tear Mr Cunninghame Graham limb from limb? On the stage, yes, certainly.

[*23 October 1909*]

A MATTER OF SEX

Last week, writing about the Gaiety, I permitted myself to laugh a little at the traditional languor of the ladies of the chorus. But for their air of ennui, I could have taken them quite seriously. There seems nothing at all absurd in the idea of pretty young women, dressed in the very latest fashion, singing and dancing in unison certain songs and dances in which they have been trained with a view to showing themselves off to the best advantage. What more natural, asks man, than that woman should wish to please? What more natural than that she should exercise fascination in public, at large, six or seven times a week? He would not care to do it himself. He would deem it beneath his dignity. He reserves his charms for private life. He doesn't mind showing off in a room; but in any public place he hates to draw attention—favourable or unfavourable—to himself. Observe any average man and woman entering a restaurant together. The difference in their costumes is a perfect symbol of the difference in their comportment. Whereas the woman has a garb of bright colours, and, belike, of some fantastic shape decreed by the mode of the moment, the man wears what is the nearest equivalent that our magic-bereft age can find for a cloak

499

of invisibility. In the face and gait of the woman you can see that she is accustomed to be visible, and that she likes being looked at, while the poor man sulkily scowls and shuffles through the ordeal, or tries to carry it off with a high hand, failing utterly. I conceive that the average woman sees nothing ludicrous in the chorus at the Gaiety: the choristers are but doing for a salary, and in a trained manner, what she does casually for nothing. But 'the chorus' is an arbitrary term. There are two choruses at the Gaiety. And I am certain that to the average man the male choristers seem to occupy a very absurd and lamentable position.

This difference of effect is the more interesting because, strictly, the one chorus is an exact pendant to the other. The men, like the women, have been selected for their good looks, and have been dressed in the latest fashion, and sing the same sort of songs in the same sort of way. They have been drilled to wave their walking-sticks at one moment, and at another to draw their handkerchiefs out of their cuffs and flick imaginary dust off their uniform boots, and perform simultaneously other bits of 'business' equivalent to what the women have been drilled to perform. The only differences are that the men do not appear so frequently, and that they do not display that languor which seemed to me the one ridiculous thing about the performance of the women. They work with a will. I suppose it is the courage of despair that upholds them. They feel that since there is no escape they may as well put a brave face on the matter. But, heroes though they are, they excite only amusement and contempt among the audience. . . . Stay! I recall a conversation I had not long ago with a clever woman who writes books. We discussed, or rather I left her to expound, the question of what women most admire in a man—the qualities that especially attract them. I had said, perfunctorily, deeming it a truism, that beauty in the opposite sex meant much more to men than to women; whereupon, with the steadfast and minatory composure of a cross-examining counsel leading a witness on to dangerous ground, she asked me what, then, did I suppose woman most admired in man; and I, with a vague gesture, said 'Oh, I'd always heard it was strength of character, and so on; a square chin, and all that.' The swoop of her eagle glance made me wish I had a beard; but her mind is pre-eminently a generalising one, and swept me forthwith into the vast world-crowd of men who regard woman as a toy. I was but

as an unit of the crowd she addressed. The reason, I heard, why
men imagine strength of character to be a prime bait is that they
imagine themselves the stronger sex. And stronger they are, doubtless, in point of muscle; and more concentrated in purpose; and in
intellect more capacious. But (the lady continued) these advantages
are accidental, not essential. They spring not from the nature of
man, but from the defective training of woman. A very muscular,
very purposeful, very intellectual woman—a woman trained in
advance of the age we live in—is not very attractive to men, because
men sub-consciously feel that she is a foe threatening their sup-
remacy. And so she is. But when the battle shall have been won,
and the principle of equality established, she will be just as attractive
as any other kind of woman. Indeed (I gathered) there won't be any
other kind of woman. They will all be what we, for the moment,
call manly. And they will be attractive to the other sex in ratio to
the amount of physical beauty that they possess. And it is exactly
in that ratio that men, even now, are attractive to women. Strength
of character: what does any woman, in her heart, care about that?
She has been educated, on a man-made system, to think that she by
nature needs a protector—some one to think for her and act for her;
and the lesson has its superficial effect on her. She meekly repeats
with her lips what she has been taught, and often chooses a mate
on the principles laid down for her. But her inward soul is true to
itself. Centuries of oppression and misdirection have not availed
to change it. First and last, it is physical beauty that women admire
and desire in man. They are afraid to say so. They have been taught
that it is immodest to say so. Some of them may not even be aware
that it is so. But so it is (said my informant).

Perhaps, then, I have wasted my pity on the male choristers of
the Gaiety. Perhaps to the women in the audience their aspect is
giving just the same sort of pleasure that the men derive from the
aspect of the female choristers. It may be that they are apt to receive
bouquets and billet-doux from adoring ladies, and are all the while
laughing in their sleeves at the men who sit despising their
gambols. Maybe, it is not the courage of despair, but the consciousness of victory, that makes them seem so cheerful. Still, even so,
their female counterparts on the stage, as not being despised by the
women in the audience, and as being openly admired by the men,
have the happier existence. In the future—I am not quite clear

whether it is a remote or an imminent future—when woman's equality with man shall be established once and for all, here and there you will find a man rejoicing, and him you will know to be a chorister of the Gaiety, no longer overshadowed by his female rivals, no longer serving in a 'man-made' theatre. Nightly the women in the audience will display frankly their delight in him. Week after week, the illustrated papers will reproduce full-page photographs of him, from this and that angle. He will be seen supping nightly in splendid restaurants, under chaperonage of his father or uncle, with splendid young Guardswomen. If he is careful, he may marry into the Peerage—who knows?

[*6 November 1909*]

ADVICE TO MR CARTON

'So,' exclaims the young dramatist to the middle-aged one who is the central figure of Mr Carton's new play at the St James's— 'so you think literary quality a negligible quantity in the art of playwriting?' I do wish Mr Carton thought it so. His determination to write well is positively harrowing. If he placed himself in the hands of a teacher of the art of writing, he would be a centenarian before he had unlearned all the wrong principles that he has so industriously taught himself. Even then, there would be the fact—proved for the connoisseur by the sentence quoted above— that he was born without a sense for the value and the sound of words. That sense must be innate, cannot be implanted, can only be developed. But any man, by keeping his ears open, can acquire a good rough working notion of the manner in which his fellow-creatures converse. Any playwright can, if he will be so kind and unpretentious, write dialogue that is not unlike human speech. To get away as far as possible from human speech, and as near as possible to the crude pomposity that I have so often deplored in the writing of Sir Arthur Pinero, is evidently the ideal of poor misguided Mr Carton. I wish he would be guided by me. Let him imagine for a moment that he himself is Lorrimer Sabiston, the middle-aged dramatist. Let him imagine that he has become a very rich man by writing the sort of plays that the public likes—plays

at which he, however, laughs in his sleeve. Let him imagine himself wishing to write, just once, a true and fine play, but not wishing
it to be produced under his own name, and persuading a needy
young dramatist to take the responsibility for it. Would he, would
he really, before dictating a letter which will save him from any
attempt to fasten the play on to him hereafter, say to the young man
'I hope you will find that pen to your liking'? Would he not say 'I
hope the pen is all right for you'—or something to that less would-
be-lovely effect? And would he presently say 'if you will allow me
to encroach a little further on your leisure'? And does he ever really
say 'the former' and 'the latter,' as do his puppets? Those are
locutions which a writer for print sometimes finds hard to avoid.
Every good writer does manage to avoid them. Conceive a writer
putting them deliberately into spoken dialogue! 'You have been a
pinchbeck Diogenes since first you began spoiling foolscap, with not
a shilling nor a moral to your name'—is it thus that Mr Carton
would chaff a *confrère*? Surely, when he speaks of London, he says
just 'London,' not 'this little world that we call London.' And
surely, to a lady who has liked one of his plays, but not the others,
he would not say 'It left a passing footprint on the sands of even
your approval.' He would say 'Even you liked it.' In writing for
print, a metaphor here and there is all very well; nay, it is delightful, if it be a fresh one and an exact one, and if it be worked out
ingeniously. But how carefully would we avoid the company of
people who could say nothing simply and directly—people who
could not open their lips without emitting a metaphor (usually
trite)! Such are the people whom Mr Carton thrusts on us. The
bedraggled shuttle-cock of oft-used imagery is bandied unceasingly
between the resounding battledores of their respective intellects—
as they would say. They simply can't stop. However agitated or
depressed they may be, they must go on metaphorising. It is a sort
of disease—of which *we*, not *they*, perish, hang it all! The younger
dramatist in the play is embittered by unsuccess and by poverty, is
at his wits' end. 'The Thames Conservancy,' says he, 'has shown
no sign of taking out a fire insurance policy against me.' Lady
Cheynley, whom Sabiston loves, is on the eve of eloping from a
cruel husband with the younger dramatist (whom she loves because
she believes him to be the author of Sabiston's masterpiece), and she
remarks that 'when one is going to take a plunge into unknown

waters, Paris is the most appropriate springboard.' Sabiston wants
her to live with him an untrammelled life in Italy; but, she tells
him, 'Romanticism is dead. The niggers have monopolised the
moon. The banjo has ousted the guitar.' Generally speaking, I
cannot imagine a better way of cooling a lover's ardour than a smart-
journalese utterance such as this. The ardour of Sabiston is, of course,
only intensified by it. He would not wish the woman he loves to talk
otherwise than he. But I put it to Mr Carton that if he were in
Sabiston's place, and were talked to in that style, he would get the
lady off the premises as quickly as might be. I implore him to let his
characters talk like human beings—even when, as in this play, he
won't let them act as such.

The theme of the play is, in its quiddity, a good one. An eminent
artist of middle-age, confronted by a radical change in the taste of
the critics and (in some degree) of the public, is a theme on which
Mr Carton, if he had taken it seriously, might have based a fine
comedy. Some years ago, somewhere, I read a short story in which
the theme was treated well by a writer who had evidently steeped
himself in the method of Mr Henry James. The artist, in this instance, was a painter, a Royal Academician, fifty-five years or so in
age, and full of vigour. For many years of his life he had been one of
the idols of the critics and of the public. But in course of time, very
gradually, the tone of the critics had changed; patrons had become
less eager; old pictures of his that came into the market were sold for
much-diminished prices. To him, as a very sensitive man, whom
fame had always coddled graciously, these tokens were most bitter.
He began to doubt—he who had never doubted yet—his own power.
He had never truckled: his work had always been sincere; but, he
was always asking himself, had he ever possessed the genius with
which he had been credited? Also, had he been, all the time, on a
false tack in his art? These new men, whom he was wont to regard
as charlatans—what if, after all, they were as sincere as they were
brilliant? What if his imperception was merely fogey-dom? He
could paint still as well as ever, in the way to which he had been
trained. Aye, and he was sure he could beat these fellows on their
own ground, if he choose to. One night, from the window of his
studio, he 'knocked off' a nocturne in the manner of the impres-
sionists, and was immensely cheered to find how well he could do it.
But next morning he began to have his doubts of it. No! the thing

didn't pass muster. Overnight, he had thought what fun it would be to exhibit it in the enemy's camp, under an assumed name, and be hailed as a new-risen star. He saw now that there would be no such hailing for him. He must do his own work in his own way, less and less admired as the years went by. In the end, I remember, he committed suicide. This seemed to me a false conclusion. Elderly Academicians 'don't do such things.' But, for the rest, the tale was a fine study of what I take to be a typical case.

A far cry to Mr Carton's treatment of the case! Lorrimer Sabiston, dramatist, is, as I have already indicated, a man who has no belief in the merit of his work, and has for years deliberately prostituted his natural and acquired gifts. In real life such a dramatist would not have enriched himself. He would not have been able to please the mass of playgoers. As Mr Arnold Bennett in a recent comedy pointed out, the man from whom the public gets what it wants is always the man who wants what is wanted by the public. If we assume that a dramatist might manage to go on for years doing bad work for which he had no impulse, even then the story of Sabiston is not plausible. It is quite certain that such a man would not be able to sit down and produce a masterpiece, one fine day, for a lark. He would find his better self atrophied. He would find . . . but I am afraid Mr Carton will think me awfully pedantic, and will wonder why I should prate about real life when his purpose was merely to turn out an exciting comedy of intrigue. So I will retire gracefully, admitting that the intrigue might be exciting enough, to the public at large, if it were not overlaid and bedevilled by Mr Carton's disastrous dialogue. In that tropical forest of metaphors, Mr Alexander, Miss Beryl Faber, Mr James Carew, Mr C. M. Lowne, and the rest of the company, vainly endeavour to hew with the hatchets of their histrionic skill a pathway through the exuberant vegetation of the author's fancy, to the sunlight of success; but the miasmal exhalations of . . . I desist for lack of skill in Cartonism.

[*13 November 1909*]

THE CENSORSHIP REPORT

I cannot say I was disappointed by the Report of the Censorship Committee. Some knowledge of the English character, and of the official mind, had sufficed to save me from hoping for anything better. I should have liked the artists to wrench a victory. By temperament and habit, I am all on their side. If a man of genius wrote a play whose production might tend to lower the moral tone of the community, I should not wish that play suppressed. I make a present of that admission to the people who argue that a Court official is needed to stand between artists who are anxious to corrupt and a public eager to be corrupted. But the argument won't really be useful. Whether or not there is such a public, there are no such artists. And it is very natural that our artists should chafe under the control of an official appointed to keep his eye on them. The European Powers could afford to laugh when they heard that the eye of the *Skibbereen Eagle* was on them. But how if that obscure fowl had been appointed actual dictator of Europe? They would have rebelled then. Even so do dramatic genius and talent rebel against the licenser of plays. Not merely to depict life as it is, but to point therefrom some moral, is the aim of all the dramatic authors who count for anything at all to-day. Very often their moral fervour, their wish to do good, gets in the way of their artistic achievement. Their anxiety to be helpful to mankind does very often make their work clumsy. Propagandism in drama is a passing fashion, I daresay, and the playwrights of the near future will be as little anxious to do good as they will be to do harm. Meanwhile, being even more definitely moralists than artists, our playwrights have especial reason for resenting an official whose effect is so often to prevent them, not merely from depicting life, but from exerting a moral influence.

I do not agree with Mr Walkley that the outcry against the Censorship has been a fuss about next to nothing. His suggestion that the Committee should settle the whole matter by the toss of a coin was not less shocking than witty. Of course, it is well to preserve a sense of proportion. But that is an arbitrary term. Everything depends on the standard one selects. The fuss that is made about the British Empire would offend anyone who chose to take a wide enough survey. There have been many empires, and this particular one will doubtless come to grief in due time, and be forgotten. This planet will still go on revolving in its old orbit, at its old speed. And why—to carry our sense of proportion a step further—should we care if this planet itself came to grief? Our solar system would not be deranged. And, for the matter of that, why—in the face of infinity—bother about our solar system? Well, really, we don't—unless we happen to be astronomers. And even astronomers, I am told, are not wholly indifferent to the things that go on around them in their own homes. They like to see their puny domestic and local affairs being carried on for the best, and are worried when anything goes wrong. If I were a Briton, I should doubtless be very proud of the British Empire. As it is, I can quite enter into the feelings of men who are willing to devote their energies to the task of keeping it together. I should be sorry if no one raised a finger to help it. It may have done, and be going to do, more harm than good; but the world would be a dull place indeed if men did not love, and fight for, the things that most nearly concern them. It is right and natural that the welfare of the British drama should be a matter of passionate interest to British dramatists. It is right and natural that they should make a fuss about the Censor. Not merely through his refusal to license this and that strong and highly moral play, but by the fact that his office discourages from writing such plays many men who would write them if there were a fair chance of production, the Censor has been a strong impediment to the drama's progress, and, in some degree therefore, to the national good. Certainly, he should be sent packing. But, when a Parliamentary Committee was appointed to inquire into the matter, and some enthusiastic friends of mine seemed to think there was a possible chance that the Censor would be abolished, or that his power would be much modified, and way would be made for the dawn of a new era, I smiled.

Ten gentlemen in frock-coats, five lords and five commons, at a long green table—not by them ever are dawns of new eras ushered in. Their business is to find with dignity a common denominator in the opinions severally held by them. Two or three of the members of the Censorship Committee were, as one knows, appointed as disapprovers of the Censor, others as approvers, others because of their open minds. It was, as always, the duty of the first two kinds to examine witnesses from their respective points of view, and of the third kind to examine witnesses from no point of view. And I presume that in the secret conclave of the whole lot the two kinds talked from their respective points of view until, having no more to say, they held silence while the third kind shuffled together all the words that had been uttered, shuffling them long and vigorously till all the meaning was shuffled safely out of them, and then boiling them down to a scale on which they could conveniently be laid as an humble offering upon the altar of the god Compromise. How not to offend one another, how not to offend either of the opposing parties that had come before them—this, I take it, was the aim of the Censorship Committee, as of all such bodies. And very creditably the work has been done. In the whole kingdom there is only one person whom I can imagine being definitely perturbed by the Report, and that is Lord Althorp, who, while we have all been hurling hideous menaces in the face of Mr Redford, has been elegantly aloof and immune. In future, the Report recommends, we ought to curse the Lord Chamberlain. Meanwhile, as a salve to him, he is recommended to go on with his idea of a small committee of appeal, 'consisting of a distinguished lawyer, two gentlemen who are or have been actors and theatre proprietors, a playwright, and the Comptroller of the Lord Chamberlain's Department ex officio.' Cannot one see them— especially the distinguished lawyer—at work? And can anybody for a moment suppose that this five-headed monster will be one whit less mischievous than a single Censor from whom there is no appeal? It will not, however, be more mischievous. Things will be in *statu quo*—a consummation which is, of course, the aim of the report in all its ramifications. To please the artists, there is talk of the duty of encouraging 'writers of intellect who desire to present through the agency of the stage sincere and serious dramas, critical of existing conventions,' and so forth; and it is recommended that a manager should be allowed to produce any play without applying for a license. But, suppose there be legislation to this effect, what difference will be made? Where is the manager who is going to risk those enormous penalties which will overtake him if the Public Prosecutor happen to hale him into court, there to be dealt with by a common jury? Nor do I see that the chance of being haled before a committee of the Privy Council, sitting in camera, is likely to lure our managers on. I repeat, however, that I am not disappointed.

[*20 November '1909*]

A CLASSIC FARCE

The Importance of Being Earnest has been revived by Mr Alexander at the St James's Theatre, and is as fresh and as irresistible as ever. It is vain to speculate what kind of work Oscar Wilde would have done had the impulse for play-writing survived in him. It is certain that a man of such variegated genius, and a man so inquisitive of art-forms, would not, as some critics seem to think he would, have continued to turn out plays in the manner of *The Importance of Being Earnest*. This, his last play, is not the goal at which he would have rested. But, of the plays that he wrote specifically for production in London theatres, it is the finest, the most inalienably his own. In *Lady Windermere's Fan* and *A Woman of No Importance* and *An Ideal Husband*, you are aware of the mechanism—aware of Sardou. In all of them there is, of course, plenty of humanity, and of intellectual force, as well as of wit and humour; and these qualities are the more apparent for the very reason that they are never fused with the dramatic scheme, which was a thing alien and ready-made. The Sardou manner is out-of-date; and so those three plays do, in a degree, date. It is certain that Oscar Wilde would later have found for serious comedy a form of his own, and would have written serious comedies as perdurable as his one great farce.

In *The Importance of Being Earnest* there is a perfect fusion of manner and form. It would be truer to say that the form is swallowed up in the manner. For you must note that not even in this play had Oscar Wilde invented a form of his own. On the contrary, the bare scenario is of the tritest fashion in the farce-writing of the period. Jack pretends to his niece, as an excuse for going to London, that he has a wicked brother whom he has to look after. Algernon, as an excuse for seeing the niece, impersonates the wicked brother. Jack, as he is going to marry and has no further need of a brother, arrives with the news of the brother's death; and so forth. Just this sort of thing had served as the staple for innumerable farces in the 'sixties and 'seventies and 'eighties—and would still be serving so if farce had not now been practically snuffed out by musical comedy. This very ordinary clod the magician picked up, turning it over in his hands—and presto! a dazzling prism for us.

How was the trick done? It is the tedious duty of the critic to ask such questions, and to mar what has been mere delight by trying to answer them. Part of the play's fun, doubtless, is in the unerring sense of beauty that informs the actual writing of it. The absurdity of the situation is made doubly absurd by the contrasted grace and dignity of everyone's utterance. The play abounds, too, in perfectly chiselled apothegms—witticisms unrelated to action or character, but so good in themselves as to have the quality of dramatic surprise. There are perhaps, in the course of the play, a dozen of those merely verbal inversions which Oscar Wilde invented, and which in his day the critics solemnly believed—or at any rate solemnly declared—to be his only claim to the title of wit. And of these inversions perhaps half-a-dozen have not much point. But, for the rest, the wit is of the finest order. 'What between the duties expected of one during one's lifetime, and the duties exacted after one's death, land has ceased to be either a profit or a pleasure. It gives one a position, and prevents one from keeping it up. That's all that can be said about land.' One cannot help wishing it were all that 'the Dukes' had had to say recently. It is a perfect presentation of the case which they have presented so lengthily and so maladroitly. And it is only a random sample of the wit that is scattered throughout *The Importance of Being Earnest*. But, of course, what keeps the play so amazingly fresh is not the inlaid wit, but the humour, the ever-fanciful and inventive humour, irradiating every scene. Out of a really funny situation Oscar Wilde would get dramatically the last drop of fun, and then would get as much fun again out of the correlative notions aroused in him by that situation. When he had to deal with a situation which, dealt with by any ordinary dramatist, would be merely diagrammatic, with no real fun at all in it, always his extraneous humour and power of fantastic improvisation came triumphantly to the rescue. Imagine the final scenes of this play treated by an ordinary dramatist! How tedious, what a signal for our departure from the theatre, would be the clearing-up of the mystery of Jack Worthing's parentage, of the baby in the handbag, the manuscript in the perambulator! But the humour of the writing saves the situation, makes it glorious. Lady Bracknell's recital of the facts to the trembling Miss Prism—'Through the elaborate investigations of the Metropolitan police, the perambulator was discovered at midnight, standing by itself in a remote corner of Bayswater. It contained the manuscript of a three-volume novel of more than usually revolting sentimentality'—and Miss Prism's subsequent recognition of the hand-bag by 'the injury it received through the upsetting of a Gower Street omnibus in younger and happier days' and by 'the stain on the lining caused by the explosion of a temperance beverage, an incident that occurred at Leamington'—these and a score of other extraneous touches keep us laughing whole-heartedly until the actual fall of the curtain.

Or again, imagine an ordinary dramatist's treatment of the great scene in the second act—the scene when Jack Worthing, attired in deepest mourning, comes to announce the death of the imaginary brother who is at this moment being impersonated on the premises by Algernon. I call this a 'great' scene, for, though it is (as I have hinted) essentially stale, it is so contrived as to be quite fresh. It is, indeed, and will always be cited as, a masterpiece of dramatic technique. If the audience knew at the beginning of the act that Jack was presently to arrive in deep mourning, the fun would be well enough. On the other hand, if, when he arrived, it had to be explained to them why he was in deep mourning, and what was his mission, there would be no fun at all. But the audience is in neither of these states. In the first act, Jack has casually mentioned, once or twice, that he means to 'kill off' his imaginary brother. But he doesn't say when or how he is going to do it. As the second act opens and proceeds, the audience has forgotten all about his intention. They are preoccupied by Algernon. And so, when the sable figure of Jack at length appears, they are for a moment bewildered, and then they vaguely remember, and there is a ripple of laughter, and this ripple swells gradually to a storm of laughter, as the audience gradually realises the situation in its full richness. None but a man with innate instinct for the theatre could have contrived this effect. But the point is that only Oscar Wilde, having contrived the effect, could have made the subsequent scene a worthy pendant to it. Miss Prism's comment on hearing that the cause of the brother's death was a chill, 'As a man sows, so shall he reap'; Dr Chasuble's offer to conduct the funeral service, and Jack's hasty explanation that his brother seems 'to have expressed a desire to be buried in Paris,' and Dr Chasuble's 'I fear that hardly points to any very serious state of mind at the last' —these are of the things that have kept the play young, and have won for it, in dramatic literature, a place apart.

It is a solemn thought that Mr Alexander and Mr Allan Aynesworth were playing their present parts fifteen years ago. They both, however, seem to have worn as well as the play itself. Miss Stella Patrick Campbell and Miss Rosalie Toller are charming in the parts of Gwendolen and Cecily.

[*11 December 1909*]

'THE BLUE BIRD'

A few weeks ago, writing here about silly Signor Marinetti, I developed a theory that the thinkers who acquire in their own day a European reputation are never, in the strict sense of the word, sages. A 'carrying' voice implies shouting. Shouting implies cock-sureness —contentment with one definite point of view, one set of convictions. Wisdom, of which the essence is spiritual surrender and elasticity— wisdom, that immensely complicated thing, cannot be shouted. It can only be doled out in murmurs. Murmurs don't 'carry.' There- fore—but, just as I was completing my syllogism, I had the horrid experience which always does overtake the maker of any hard-and- fast generalisation: I remembered an exception which made nonsense of my rule. It was Maeterlinck that I remembered. And, as I was rather pleased with my generalisation, and, moreover, didn't want to have the trouble of writing my article all over again, I disingenuously suppressed that honoured name. It, however, must have occurred to many of my readers. Twenty years ago, Maeterlinck began whisper- ing; and the whisper penetrated Europe, perfectly audible amidst the guffaws which it at first evoked. He has never, in the meantime, raised his voice; and always he has compelled the attention of us all —I mean, all of us who are not fools.

For proper appreciation of Maeterlinck, you must have, besides a sense of beauty, a taste for wisdom. Maeterlinck is not less a sage than a poet. Of all living thinkers whose names are known to me, he has the firmest and widest grasp of the truth. He more clearly than any other thinker is conscious of the absurdity of attempting to fashion out the vast and impenetrable mysteries of life any adequate little explanation—any philosophy. He sees further than any other into the darkness, has a keener insight into his own ignor- ance, a deeper modesty, a higher wisdom. In his youth, the mystery of life obsessed him. He beheld our planet reeling in infinity, having on its surface certain infinitesimal creatures all astray at the mercy of unknown laws. And he shuddered. And he wrote certain plays which, as mere expressions of the pathos of man's lot, and the awful- ness of the mystery of life, will not be surpassed. Little by little, the shudders in him abated. The more a man thinks about infinity, the better does he realise that what he can grasp of infinity is but a speck, signifying nothing; and, accordingly, the more important will become to him the visible and tangible creatures and things around him. Maeterlinck began to look around him, to 'take notice' with babyish pleasure, with the fresh vision of a true seer. The world seemed to him a very-well-worth-while place. Who was he to say that we had no free-will? How could he possibly know that, or anything else? If we are but the puppets of destiny, and if destiny is, on the whole, rather unkind, still there seems to be quite enough of joy and beauty for us to go on with.

Such is the point to which Maeterlinck, in the course of years, has won; and such is the meaning he has put into *The Blue Bird*, this masterpiece of his later years. An Optimist? No; he is too conscious of the sadness of things to be that. A Meliorist? He has too much sense of history, and too much sense of proportion, to imagine that the world, if seven specially selected maids with seven specially designed mops 'swept it for half-a-year' or for a thousand years, would be appreciably tidier. So far as any one crude label can be affixed to him, he is just a Bonist. . . . Off go the two children, Tyltyl and Mytyl, in their dreams, to quest the blue bird, and they do find blue birds, and do catch them. True, these birds die when they are caught, or else lose their colour, or else flutter mockingly away. And, when the children awake in their beds next morning, the bird-cage contains only their own ordinary dove. But see! he *has* turned a *sort* of blue! And bright blue he becomes when the children send him as a present to the little girl who is ill. And she, at sight of him, is made well. True, again, he flies right away out of her hands, and is lost. 'Never mind,' Tyltyl tells her. 'Don't cry . . . I will catch him again.' And again he will lose him. No matter. The quest, even if it were a vain one, were good enough. Sometimes in the wanderings of Mytyl and Tyltyl, as when the hour comes for them to set forth through the forest to the Palace of Night, there is the old Maeterlinck note of terror. 'Give me your hand, little brother,' says Mytyl, 'I feel so frightened and cold,' and as the curtain falls, we experience that strange cold thrill of awe and pity which the dramatist so often, so cunningly, prepared for us in his earlier plays. But, for the most part, the thrills in *The Blue Bird* are of a quiet joy. Mytyl and Tyltyl are crouching in the grave-yard, to wait for the arising of the dead people at midnight. They talk together in whispers. The hour is at hand. The mounds quake, the graves open, a pale mist rises. Little by little, this mist gathers into masses of white, and the place is but a garden of tall white lilies. 'Where are the dead?' asks Mytyl. And Tyltyl answers 'There are no dead!' and the curtain falls. It always was in his contrivance of the ends of acts that Maeterlinck revealed the essentially dramatic quality of his genius. What of mystery and beauty these plays must necessarily lose by visual performance is always counteracted by what they gain—the special power that a true dramatist's work can never have for us except in the theatre.

Even if you happen to have an exceptionally keen theatrical imagination (which I haven't), you cannot, in reading a play, be thrilled by it so much as you may be in an actual theatre; for this reason: that there is not an audience of fellow-creatures around you, thrilled in company with you and unconsciously transmitting through you something of their own electricity. Only a theatrical performance of which you were the sole spectator, or else only a very bad performance indeed, could fail to be more impressive than a mere silent reading. (That is, if the play has, like *The Blue Bird*, true dramatic quality.) The corporeal presentment of symbols and fancies is, as I have just suggested, a dangerous job. Such presentment, at best, cannot vie with the mind's images. And the perfect venue for a production of *The Blue Bird* would be some impossible combination of an actual theatre and one's own cranium.

In that actual theatre, the Haymarket, Mr Herbert Trench has contrived a production which is, I imagine, as good as can be. The scenery is duly various according to the many moods of the play. Mr Cayley Robinson and Mr Sime (welcome!) and Mr Harker have produced scenery that is always imaginative and beautiful—sometimes mystical, sometimes noble, sometimes frightening, sometimes funny, in just accord to the doings for which it is a background. And all the dresses have been designed in a not less eclectic and proper spirit. But the most remarkable thing in the production is certainly Miss Olive Walter as Tyltyl. Some time ago, when first I read the play, it seemed to me that Tyltyl would be an insuperable obstacle to anyone who might wish to put the play on the stage. For Tyltyl is hardly for a moment out of sight and hearing. On his shoulders rests the play's main burden. And it is essential that Tyltyl should be, or seem to be, a little boy, and not a day more than eight years of age. To seem on the stage like a little boy of eight is beyond the powers of any actual little boy of eight: he appears as an awful little automaton of eighty. And five minutes of him appears as an eternity. Imagine a whole evening of him! On the other hand, imagine somebody old enough to act, and to act throughout an evening, attempting to produce the illusion that he—or she— is only eight years old! That alternative 'she' seemed to me, as I mused on the chances of *The Blue Bird*, especially sure to be disastrous. And yet, here is Miss Olive Walter, Tyltyl to the life, and perfect from first to last. She may be no longer in her 'teens for aught I know; but, as she appears on the stage, she is not, in voice or gait or manner, a day more than eight; and is a boy, at that; as absolutely a boy as Mytyl is a girl. Who would have believed it?

[*18 December 1909*]

MR HENRY ARTHUR JONES'S 'SKETCH'

In England the short play has thriven as little as the short story. There has been, of course, a steady demand for 'curtain raisers,' and a steady supply of them. But these, with rare exceptions, are of no more account than the short stories in the popular magazines. It were absurd to suppose that we have hardly any writers capable of writing good short plays. Ardent devotees of the '*conte*' have sometimes proclaimed it a more difficult art-form than the full-sized novel. That is nonsense. One might as well say it was more difficult to build an arbour than to build a house. To present an episode, or a phase, in a few pages, is obviously much easier than to present in combination, and on a large scale, a series of episodes and phases. Every work of art must be a unity. And the difficulty of achieving the effect of unity is proportionate to the number and variety of things to be welded. There are among us a dozen or so of clever men who have more or less mastered the art of writing full-sized plays. Any one of these could with great ease write short plays of good quality. It is not less certain that many of the clever people who try to write full-sized plays, and fail by lack of the requisite instinct and the requisite doggedness, would through the medium of the short play be able to express themselves quite well. The reason why the short play has been left to the devices of the dolts is that there has been practically no chance for a good short play to be produced worthily. 'Curtain-raising' is not a fine enough prospect to allure a self-respecting writer. Mr Shaw has written two or three short plays, knowing that they would have special and adequate production by this or that society. But the other playwrights who count (or who might count), not having that stimulating prospect, have confined themselves to the writing of plays sufficient in length to command a worthy mode of production. From time to time there have been rumours of a theatre in which only short plays were to be produced. But such a theatre, by reason of the conservativism of the public, would, for a long time, have to be run at a loss, and will, I imagine, remain in the clouds. Meanwhile, there seems to be cast a ray of hope from the music halls.

In the past two or three years, actors and actresses of repute, attracted by vast 'offers,' have recited in this and that music-hall. They were at first rather ashamed of finding themselves there, and of smelling so strongly of smoke when they came away. But the leaps and bounds of their bank-balances presently restored their self-respect; and, characteristically enough, they have now almost persuaded themselves that what they thought was smoke is really incense; and they are inclined to savour more of it. Thus, when the insinuating manager of the music-hall says to them 'Why confine yourselves to reciting—exquisite though your reciting is? Why not deign to dangle before the eyes of my humble but honest clients the whole range of your beautiful art?' they don't proceed to wither him with a look. The actresses merely give a little scream. The actors merely say 'H'm.' And forthwith they cast around them for plays short enough to be legally performed on the music-hall stage. It stands to reason that the crude little 'sketches' already current will not suffice as vehicles for highly-trained artists. Gifted playwrights must be requisitioned to write 'sketches' worthy of the occasion. This is a development which I welcome on all scores. It is good for the music-hall audiences; good for the actors and actresses; and (which matters most) good for the future of the short play.

Off-hand, it would seem that the playwright would have to work in a very light vein indeed. A play that stops the way for a comic conjuror or troupe of eccentric acrobats stands no chance, I would have said, unless its aim be sheer laughter. *The Knife* is the title of the play with which Mr Henry Arthur Jones makes his début at the

Palace Theatre; and the play's appeal throughout is to the sense of horror. It bids for no laugh save from the lips of a lady in hysterics. And yet, from the very outset, on the evening of my visit, it held the audience engrossed, and it ended in such a torrent of applause as would have gratified the most comic of conjurers or the most eccentric of acrobats. Much of this applause, no doubt, was for the admirable acting of Mr Arthur Bourchier and Miss Violet Vanbrugh; but the rest of it was for the playwright. In the making of a 'sketch' Mr Jones has an advantage in his inveterate habit of coming quickly to the point. A full-sized play may well begin with scenes of leisurely exposition. Most playwrights strain this dispensation overmuch. Mr Jones's way has always been to dispense with the dispensation altogether, and to plunge us straight into the midst of some kind of action. And thus, in *The Knife*, he performs quite naturally the needful trick of gripping the audience's attention instantly. The scene of the play is a nursing-home in London. The action passes in the 'black week' of the Boer War. The central figure of the play is a distinguished surgeon, Sir Mark Ridgway, who is about to perform an operation on a friend, a young man named Kingsford. The operation is a very drastic and delicate one; and of a kind that no other surgeon could carry through with such fair prospect of success. It is not an operation that can be avoided: unless it be performed forthwith, the patient must die. The conflict of the play is brought about by the surgeon's discovery, just before the operation, that his patient is his wife's lover, and by her beloved. He reels under this blow. How can he go now into the operating-room to save the life of the man who has betrayed him and ruined his happiness? If his hand slipped by the tiniest fraction of an inch, the man must die. His hand is trembling? Can he be sure that he will be able to control it? Does he wish to? He could have his vengeance. His wife sees what is passing in his mind. She tells him that if his patient dies she will denounce him as a murderer. He passes into the operating-room, and she collapses at the door, to listen and wait. Then the curtain falls; and when it has risen the door opens, the surgeon comes back, the operation is over, and the news is that the patient will recover. Then Lady Ridgway has a revulsion of feeling towards her husband; and he forgives her. This second scene is, indeed, rather a foregone conclusion. It seems to me a let-down after the fine dramatic tensity of the first. Of course, Mr Jones could not have finished the play without a second scene. But surely the only way to keep the full dramatic pressure would have been to let the patient die under the operation. Re-enter Ridgway, very pale, and stands with bent head. His wife guesses the news, wildly upbraids him—'murderer,' etc. He answers nothing. The audience knows well that the fine fellow has done his best, and that his silence is due merely to proper pride. But, presently, his pride is overcome by pity for his wife and for himself. 'RIDGWAY (*looking up for first time*): "Look into my eyes . . . Are they the eyes of a murderer?"' LADY RIDGWAY: *comes slowly across stage, takes a long look.* LADY RIDGWAY: "Forgive me, forgive me!" *She falls to her knees.*' Wouldn't that have been the better scenario? But—what are dramatic critics coming to? I really must learn to keep my place.

[*1 January 1910*]

'FOR THE SOUL OF THE KING'

Last week I wrote of the disadvantage suffered by short plays in being produced as 'curtain-raisers.' A few nights later I found at the Queen's Theatre a sharp confirmation of my lament. *For the Soul of the King* is an adaptation from a story by Balzac, and is produced 'by arrangement with Mr Frank Richardson,' whom I like to think of as controlling in our midst the whole of the *Comédie Humaine* and doling it out to us bit by bit in the course of the next fifty years or so. For Balzac I have an intense cult. My veneration for his Titanic genius is not this side idolatry. I believe him to be by far the greatest of the many great men that France has given to the world. I deem him, next to Shakespeare, the greatest creative genius that the world has known. The mere sound of his name, or sight of it written, stirs my heart, as being a symbol of vast things nobly achieved by concentration of genius against awful odds. Any little carping criticism of him, such as one often hears from people who lack sense of proportion and capacity for reverence, irritates me unspeakably. To any rhapsody in his honour my whole soul thrills. No ecstasy of praise ever has seemed to me more than his due. Several times, even, I have tried to read one or another of his books. But I have never been able to wade further than the second chapter. It would not be true to say that I am one of the mere lip-worshippers of Balzac. My whole being, as I have protested, bows down before him. Only, I can't read him. Corollarily, I can't say whether the result of Mr H. B. Irving's 'arrangement' with Mr Frank Richardson is worthy of the original work. I can but say that it is in itself an excellent play; far too good to be a 'curtain-raiser'; deserving a better fate than to be seen amid the interruptions of ladies and gentlemen arriving late and apologising for treading on one's toes and fumbling for sixpences with which to purchase programmes. My objection to the curtain-raising system is not merely that it exposes us to these interruptions. It tends to slackness in the stage-managing and the acting. Compare the production of *The Knife* at the Palace with the production of *For the Soul of the King* at the Queen's! On the one hand, tensity, quickness, naturalness, an exact adaptation of the manner of the acting to the matter of the play; on the other hand, slowness, artificiality, a welter of tedious and old-fashioned devices, making a disastrous setting to Mr Irving's performance of the chief part—a performance which is in itself full of true romantic power and force. I do not know whether Mr Irving produced the play himself. If he did not, let him discharge the stage-manager instantly, with such compliments and good wishes as will salve the feelings of that doubtless well-meaning but hopelessly misguided and misguiding man. The effect that the play aims at is one of suspense. The scene is an attic in the Faubourg St Martin. Here, during the Terror, are lurking two ladies, Mlles de Langeais and Michalet, who were nuns of one of the now-disbanded convents. With them, in constant danger of arrest and perhaps of death, lurks the aged Abbé de Mayral. Mlle Michalet has ventured out of the house on some errand. She is late in returning. Her friends' fear that she has fallen into the hands of the mob is all the more acute because they had seen watching the house a man of sinister and revolutionary aspect, who followed her when she passed down the street. At length, however, comes a footfall on the stair. Mlle Michalet is safe and sound. Through the window they see that the stranger has again taken up his post in the shadow of the house opposite. They feel it is the Abbé that he has marked down as his prey. Presently they see him cross the street. There is a footfall on the stair, an imperious knock at the door. They bid the Abbé hide himself in the bed-room. He does so. But here let me pause to ask you in what manner, to secure the right effect, the scenes which I

have described should be enacted. How, in moments of acute suspense, do people behave? They talk quickly in low tones, and
without affectation of manner. But the impersonators of the two
ladies and the Abbé seem to think that the way to make dramatically
the most of the suspense is to prolong it by such slowness of utterance
as nobody in real life, with however calm a mind and however much
time to spare, would dare inflict on us. 'He-is-still-there,' chants
Mlle de Langeais melodiously, after a horror-stricken glance through
the window. And her manner is not more remote from verisimilitude
than is the manner of her colleagues. How, I ask you, would an
Abbé behave when a supposed assassin batters at the door? He might
conceivably refuse to hide himself. But, if he has no objection to
doing so, he surely would not stand with a beautifully vague and
benign expression while the battering continues, and then, with the
step of one walking in a procession, pass to the bedroom door, and
there, with his hand on the door-knob, pause and turn and dawdle
before we are finally rid of him. Such slowness on the stage has its
origin in the player's notion that we cannot have too much of him,
and that the longer he is with us the better we are pleased. It is the
stage-manager's duty to cure him of this fallacy, or at any rate to
prevent him from acting on it. Such slowness is always tedious.
In such a play as this one it is also destructive of illusion. As if to
banish any illusion that may be left over, the orchestra at the Queen's
has been instructed to play assiduously when any member of the cast
is about to make an entrance. 'I hear a footfall on the stair,' chants
Mlle de Langeais. 'Are you sure, my daughter?' chants the Abbé.
'Yes,' we expect her to answer, 'don't you hear the orchestra?'
When Mr Irving at length appears, to an accompaniment of fiddles,
he has hard work to restore our belief in what is going on. In itself,
the juncture is thoroughly dramatic; and so is the development of it.
The stranger asks for the Abbé. He will not believe the denials of
the two women. He asks them to trust him: he means the Abbé no
harm. They dare not trust him. The Abbé reveals himself. Little by
little, it appears that King Louis has been beheaded this morning,
and that the stranger is the headsman himself, driven hither by remorse, and asking only that the priest shall celebrate a Requiem Mass.
Mr Irving gave a weird and pathetic reality to all this—reality which,
so soon as the orchestra gave the cue for the priest to bring in the
sacrament, tottered, and, so soon as we saw a 'transparency' meant

THE SOUL OF THE KING'

to represent the execution of King Louis, utterly collapsed. Yes, actually, in a would-be realistic play produced in 1910, a transparency! If the impersonator of the remorseful headsman were a duffer, unable to make the audience imagine for itself the scene that is supposed to haunt him, a transparency would be worse than useless. It is lamentable that so gifted an actor as Mr Irving should submit to this ludicrous device. His father submitted to it in *The Bells.* That was a great pity. But in the 'seventies a dramatic absurdity did not seem so absurd as it does now. I refuse to believe that any stage-manager with a method formed since the 'seventies would solemnly now go out of his way to introduce a 'transparency.' Mr Irving's stage-manager must, accordingly, be well-stricken in years. I withdraw my demand for his summary dismissal. Let him be quietly pensioned off.

I am glad to see no trace of his hand in the production of the main play at the Queen's, *The House Opposite.* I was away when this play was produced, and must not write of it so long after the event. I will say merely that it augurs well for Mr Perceval Landon's future in play-writing. The basis of it—a clandestine meeting between a man and a married woman, whereby the man holds the clue to a murder of which an innocent person is accused—is not unfamiliar. But the structure of it is fresh; and the characters are thoroughly well-drawn and vital.

[*8 January 1910*]

ACTOR AND CRITIC

Last week, in New York, Mr Laurence Irving made a great mistake. It cannot be rectified, and I would say nothing about it if I did not think it might serve as a useful warning to other actors. It is very natural that an actor should wish to avenge himself on a critic whom he believes to have attacked him unfairly. In such a case, let awful vengeance be done, somehow. But let not the actor suppose it can be done by a public denunciation of the critic. That is where Mr Laurence Irving, like many actors before him, went astray. True, he did not, in the traditional manner, rush into print. He gave

the enemy a bigger advertisement than that. He stalked to the footlights, and denounced the enemy in a set speech—a speech (to judge
by the cabled fragments) of great eloquence. This was received with
loud applause by the audience; and I doubt not that Mr Irving, as
he bowed himself off the stage, felt he had dealt the enemy a deadly
blow. I wish he had. For that enemy I have no regard whatsoever,
and will not by naming him add my quota to the fine advertisement
he has received from Mr Irving. His gibes at Mr Irving and at
Mrs Irving were vulgar and unjust. Again I judge by cabled fragments; but these are in exact accord to the manner which I have
sometimes, with gloomy curiosity, sampled at full length in the
newspaper which it adorns. I can construct from them the quality of
the whole article. The writer is a man not unendowed with humour
and cleverness. But he has made his reputation by using these gifts
mainly in the cause of crude insolence, and by the elaborate process
of going out of his way to give such offence as right-hearted critics
try to refrain from giving even when they are bound to blame.
The matter of what he says is sometimes right enough; more often it
is shaped to fit the manner; and always the manner is deplorable.

Criticism of acting differs from criticism of other arts, in that it is
necessarily far more personal. You can condemn or ridicule a book,
or a painting, or a piece of music, in terms which, while they would
be brutal and indecent as applied to the work of an actor, leave
personally unscathed the writer, or painter, or composer. Art and
honesty demand that the actor shall not be judged more leniently
than other artists. The actor himself, in common self-respect, demands this (though always, of course, he would rather it were denied
him). Humanitarianism, on the other hand, demands that our
judgment of the actor shall be so worded as not to wound him.
It is very difficult and delicate, this task of telling the truth innocu-
ously. It is not impossible, but it takes a lot of time and tact. I don't
say that the critics of the London daily papers are tactless. I merely
say that they haven't time. When they would blame, they have to
choose between the evils of cruelty and insincerity. All honour to
them for choosing the lesser of these two evils! I am as sick as any
one of their sweet catch-words—'memorable,' 'convincing,' 'invaluable,' 'sound,' 'imagination and power,' 'considerable grace and
charm,' 'considerable charm and skill,' and the like. But I do
homage to the persistent unselfishness of the purveyors. Truth-

telling is in itself a pleasant function. Not so the telling of stereotyped fibs. I do homage to men who mortify themselves rather than mortify a few fellow-creatures. Base indeed do I deem a dramatic critic who makes it his business to attack actors and actresses, be they bad or good, in such language as shall cause them the greatest possible amount of pain. Such a critic is he who has been denounced by Mr Irving. Yet is he alone culpable? How about the public which fosters him? In England no newspaper would employ him. There are doubtless in our midst men who would be willing to write as he does, if they could thereby earn the money and reputation that he has earned. But the British public would not for a moment tolerate them. I have often heard Americans deplore the existence of the critic whom Mr Irving denounced. And I have no doubt that the applause which greeted that denunciation was quite sincere. But it is so easy to sympathise with an actor who is giving vent to righteous indignation on behalf of himself and of his wife. And I daresay that many of the loudest applauders were among the most devoted readers of the offending critic. But suppose that in the whole audience there was not one man who did not hold that critic in contempt. Even so was the responsibility of the audience less awful?

Mr Irving should have stood surveying the house, and then, very slowly, have said, 'I have spoken strongly about this man. But I do not hate him. Rather do I pity him. He delights to bark and bite. It is his nature to. One does not hate a mad dog. But, if I came to a city where mad dogs were allowed to be at large, it would be not enough for me that the citizens should say "Yes, aren't these dogs a nuisance?" I should blame these citizens for their incivism. The critic whom I have named tonight is an extreme case, no doubt. But the fact remains that a great part of American journalism is unseemly, a peril and pest, unworthy of a civilised nation. Why do you stand it? Do you wish me to be forced to the conclusion that you are not yet civilised? You deplore the corruption of your politics, just as you deplore the vulgarity of your 'yellow press.' Why don't you stop it? You could. No one has ever accused you of lethargy. You are a very vital and vigorous people. I have an immense admiration for your immense potentialities. If we in England had such politics as yours, or such a 'yellow press' as yours, I should feel desperate indeed. For we in England are growing old: our organism might not be able to cast off such maladies. But you, the young and buoyant, the aquiline and star-spangled, very surely *you* have the power to set your house in order. Apparently you have not the will. I pray you, be calm. Resume your seats. There is no use in your attempting to storm the footlights. I need but raise my hand and there would appear from the wings a strong force of armed police whom the Mayor has very kindly placed at my disposal for this evening, with orders to shoot if you show the slightest disposition to tear me limb from limb. I ask you to ponder well what I have said to you. Ladies and gentlemen, I wish you a very good night.' If Mr Irving had said something of this sort . . . but no, Mr Irving would have been best advised to say nothing at all. The sequel to the speech that he did make was a public announcement by the managers of the theatre that had they known his intention they would have forbidden it, and that they were, as they had ever been, in favour of the liberty of the press. Thus is Mr Irving snubbed in a strange land, and his enemy crowned with laurel. Mr Irving could not have foreseen this. But he certainly might have foreseen that his outburst would be a good advertisement for the objective of it. If a journalist, criticising an artist, mis-states a fact, it may perhaps be well for the artist to make a correction. But it is never worth his while to denounce a journalist for the statement of an opinion, however vulgar or unjust that opinion may be. By so doing he both forfeits his dignity and improves the position of the journalist.

[*15 January 1910*]

'CHANTECLER'

Yes, I have seen it. And I am going to tell you all about it. I rush forward as Our Special Correspondent, breathlessly to pour into your pricked-up ears the whole story, the whole manner and aspect of the thing. But—I see your ears drooping, and horror in your eyes. You know well, from last Tuesday's newspapers, *Chantecler* scene by scene; and you implore me to assume this. And so, more than a trifle crestfallen, I agree to offer you merely some little impressions and opinions.

Many times, in the course of the evening at the Porte-Saint-Martin, my thoughts turned to the shade of Constant Coquelin.

It was right that one should not now forget him whose last years had been spent in such a glow of enthusiasm for *Chantecler*, and in such an agony of impatience for it—him who, just when the play was at length finished, was finished also. And, as a matter of fact, it was not possible to forget him: wherever the cock strutted, there hovered the shade of him. Guitry, I grant, is magnificent. From first to last, his success is not in question. But it is not the triumph that Coquelin would have won. When Coquelin died, I thought that perhaps, after all, the gods had been good to him, sparing him a tremendous failure. I doubted whether it would be possible for an audience not to be bored, after half an hour or so, by a play interpreted (in so far as it could be interpreted) without human faces and human gestures. Well, as it turns out, there *are* human faces. The original intention was that the mimes should show nothing but their mouths. It was thus that Coquelin was prepared to play Chantecler. But Guitry has not been so accommodating. He and the rest of the persons of the play have their valuable faces to help them. I have no doubt that Coquelin, when the play came to actual rehearsal, would have insisted that he could not, after all, do without his face. I am sure it is by M. Rostand's concession in this matter of masks that the scale of the play's fate has been turned. It would have been pedantic in him to refuse. If poultry have human voices, why not human faces? At the Porte-Saint-Martin they have only human full-faces: their side-faces are veiled by their feathers. And thus, as they strut about the stage (dwarfed, all of them, by the Brobdingnagian 'properties'), there is in our eyes a constant oscillation between the illusion of actual poultry and the perception of actual human beings. And this is just as it should be. If we saw the poultry merely as symbols, and never as poultry, the play would lose much of its charm. If we had not frequent sight of the human faces, not only would the symbolism be blurred, but the speeches and the action would very soon be wearisome.

I have said that Guitry is magnificent. He is, indeed, too magnificent. Not for a moment do we wonder at the awe he inspires in the hens: we share it. Whenever he turns his full-face to us—that face wrought in iron, or hewn out of rock, that face fashioned for heroic villainy or villainous heroism (we know not which), with its glittering eyes and minatory nose, and all-compressing, all-compelling lips, that face more than ever grim now in the shadow of the great beak above it—we quail as in the presence of some great Viking revisiting the earth and behaving in his old fashion. Yes, it is as such that Guitry behaves throughout the play. He has humour, but always it is grim, never comedic; and never is there a touch of the grotesque. And thus, while he personally succeeds by sheer force and splendour, the play itself loses much of its quality. For Chantecler is a dual part. As drawn by Rostand, the cock is at once a great figure and a figure of fun. On the one hand, he is symbolic of all that is best in the French nation. He is full of faith, of conscience, of courage. He is honest, stable, laborious, unselfish. He will work his talons to the quick, if need be, in performance of his mission. Rostand admires him, and would have us admire him, immensely, and has given to him as foil the Blackbird, symbol of all that on the boulevards is frivolous and clever and silly and useless, and has given as further foils the owls and bats and other night-birds who hate him and scheme for his undoing—the Anti-Nationalists, Socialists, Anarchists. As a philosopher, Rostand sees the fineness of him, and as a French-man loves him. But as a philosopher he sees, too, the absurdity of him, and as a Frenchman makes constant fun of him. Chantecler is narrow-minded, unenlightened, and a megalomaniac. Without these defects how could he have the qualities in virtue of which he excels? He thinks his farmyard is the whole world. The Hen-Pheasant, of whom he sets himself to make a conquest when she seeks refuge in his domain, is a symbol partly of the modern woman impatient of traditional burdens and limitations, partly of the world at large, and of freedom and beauty. In both capacities she is meant to make Chantecler seem ludicrous—all the more ludicrous by reason of his condescension to her, and his incapacity for believing that she can conceive anything higher than himself. He imagines that it is he who causes the sun to rise, and that if the sun do not shine brightly throughout the day it is because he has not sung his best, and that if he sang not at all the sun would stay sulking beneath the horizon. I remember hearing Oscar Wilde tell a story which he intended to write, and which he called, I think, 'St Timothy of the Desert.' It was about a hermit-saint who, every night, knelt and prayed God that the sun should rise. When the sun had risen, he always praised God for His goodness in having granted the prayer and vouchsafed the miracle. But one night, the saint, exhausted by some exceptional penance that he had laid on himself in the day, slept a long sleep, insomuch that when he awoke the sun was shining into his eyes. For a while, he was greatly perplexed and agitated. Strange doubts laid hold on him. But presently his face cleared, and he knelt down on the sand, and praised God for that He had had pity and had vouchsafed the miracle that day of His own will. . . . '*Les beaux esprits se rencontrent,*' and Rostand's Chantecler is very like to Wilde's St Timothy. The Hen-Pheasant, partly for love of mischief, partly because she is jealous for herself of her lord's devotion to duty, so manoeuvres that Chantecler is too late to sing for the sun's resurgence. But Chantecler, though troubled, is undismayed. The sun, he reassures himself, has risen in answer to the still-resounding echoes of some previous day's song. There is grandeur in this thought, as in all the thoughts of Chantecler; but the grandeur of Chantecler is the measure of his grotesqueness, and it is because never for one moment does Guitry make fun that one sighs for Coquelin—Coquelin, that natural master of fun, who would have been so broadly comical all the time, without abating one jot of the serious dignity and force essential to the part. In Cyrano, which was a triple part, heroic, comic, and romantic, Coquelin was great by reason of his mastery of heroic comedy and comic heroism: we waived the romance that was not in him. Had he lived to play Chantecler, we need have waived nothing: the performance would have been not only stupendous, but flawless. Guitry is splendid in the forthright passages of the part, the outbursts, as when he denounces and shames the Blackbird, and as when he reveals to the Hen-Pheasant the secret of his power over the sun—the gathering-in through his talons of all the forces that lie deep down in the good earth—'*Et si de tous les chants mon chant est le plus fier, C'est que je chante clair afin qu'il fasse clair.*' But in the specifically amusing passages, as when he courts the Hen-Pheasant, or as when he playfully addresses as '*cher maître*' a newly-hatched chicken, my heart cries out for the unctuous Coquelin. It is in such passages that the need for Coquelin is most salient. But the need for him is strong throughout the play. Guitry presents one element, instead of two elements fused. That he scores even so a great personal success, is proof of his tremendous endowments for—well, not for comedy.

Just where he excels, in potency of presence, and in the grand manner, and in a sense for the rhythm of verse, Mme Simone fails. She is a charming comedian, but, as the Hen-Pheasant, neither is

she like a bird, nor does she suggest either the magic or the meaning
of the character. She is not of the woodland, nor is she modern
woman in the abstract, nor is she incarnate freedom. She is just
Mme Simone skipping about in feathers, very pleasant to look at,
and, when she has to speak more than one alexandrine at a time,
not so very pleasant to listen to. On artistic not less than on sentimental grounds, it is well that M. Jean Coquelin is in the play.
No one could have given a better rendering of the faithful farmyard dog—this dog in whose veins flows the blood of a hundred-
and-one breeds, and who stands as a symbol of the honest bourgeoisie. As the Blackbird, M. Galipaux is perfect—perfect in physical
realism not less than in symbolical suggestion. Hail to thee, blithe
spirit, half devil and half bird! I have no space for mention of the
other persons of the play: they are innumerable. As is his way,
M. Rostand has rioted in material; and, as is also his way, he has
left not a particle untouched by his ingenuity. There is not among
all the birds and other creatures that are crowded into his ark one
that is not amusing and vivid in its own fashion. Other poets,
having conceived this fable of Chantecler, would have been content
to work it out simply: the theme is rich enough in itself. But for
M. Rostand it is a vehicle for all manner of side issues; and the
wonder is not that he took such a long time over the play, but that
he ever finished it at all. Probably he does not regard it as finished.
A host of new ideas for it must have surged in his breast; and what
we now see is but an outline, may be, of what the play will presently
become. Meanwhile, besides the various minor motives and meanings which I have adumbrated, there is in the presentment of
Chantecler a study of the artist, ever straining after perfection, and
haunted by dread of inspiration failing—'*trouverai-je dans mon
coeur le chanson?*' And there is, in the scene of the Guinea-Fowl's
'Five o'Clock,' a fusillade of satire against the literary fashions of
the day. It is well for a satirist to have a point of view; and the
point of view from which he can most powerfully direct his shafts
is always that of a man whose soul is rotted in the classical tradition. I have often doubted whether Aristophanes really cared a rap
for Aeschylus. I am certain that Byron didn't care a rap for Pope. I
wonder whether M. Rostand cares a rap for Racine. No matter: the
effect of his fusillade is terrific. Who shall count the wounded?

There will be reprisals, of course. M. Rostand has never been beloved, has always been belittled, by the superior persons. And with good reason. Such invariable and pre-eminent success as his is not loveable; and there is so much of him to belittle. I myself, as a superior person, have often joined in the game of detraction, finding it good fun. This time, however, I prefer to round on my comrades, stricken though they are. I grant them M. Rostand is not a poet in the strict sense of the word (alas, the sense which fashion, at the present moment, attaches to the word). He is not a shy, pensive, simple, very sincere, very wistful man, brooding on life's mysteries. I like and respect such men very much indeed. But, taking them on the average, I would willingly exchange a round dozen of them for one Rostand. In his exuberant rhetoric and wit and inventive power and knowledge of human nature, Rostand seems to me quite twelve times more treasurable than one of these little ones. Of course, for a really great poet I would barter Rostand. If I had to choose between him and Maeterlinck, for example, I should not hesitate for a moment. But as the choice is not forced on me, I am free to delight in both. A curious conjunction, these two names! Maeterlinck, the massive, the eupeptic, with his motor-bicycle and his bulldog—Maeterlinck, the child-like in heart, the sweet and profound seer, the sage etherial; and Rostand, the delicate of frame, the dandy, the dilettante, yet in his work all gusto and virility and expansiveness. Maeterlinck, the man of imagination; and Rostand, the man of a million-and-one fancies. Rostand, all crowned with the pride and pomps of life, saluting Nature, adoring her, 'au mieux' with her; Maeterlinck knowing her soul from within. I have often thought that the universality of Maeterlinck's mind is his because he has, in virtue of being a Belgian, no nationality to speak of. If Rostand had not been born a Frenchman—but no, the hypothesis is inconceivable. We cannot imagine Rostand as other than French to his finger-tips. He could never have been universal. Yet is it the very strength of nationality in him that speeds his genius across frontiers and seas.

[*12 February 1910*]

CONFESSIONAL

When I went to the Stage Society's production last Monday, I was fresh from Paris; and soon after the curtain rose I was assailed by a suspicion, which presently took on the horrid form of a conviction, that Lady Bell was not so good a dramatist as M. Rostand. This spoilt my afternoon. Vainly I told myself that there was no need to draw comparisons. Patriotism, chivalry, and also my whole theory of criticism, told me that these comparisons were odious. Yet I had to go on drawing them. You wonder at me, frown at me? Go forth, then, next Monday, and take up your position in the crowd to see the King pass by on his way to Westminster. Steep your ears in the music of trumpets and kettle-drums, and your eyes in the lustre of gold and scarlet—steeds caracoling and plumes nodding and cuirasses gleaming ever so vivaciously in the long and well-ordered pageant whose culminating point is the presentment, in an incredibly ornate setting, of the symbol of Great Britain and Ireland and the Dominions beyond the Seas. A little later in the day, before you shall have lost the glow of all this pride and pomp and gaiety and power, go to that corner of Hyde Park which is sacred to the holders-forth on this or that theme from this or that standpoint. Take up your position in one of the little crowds, and listen. The holder-forth is very much in earnest. His theme, peradventure, is (like Lady Bell's in *The Way the Money Goes*) the evils of betting. In grim earnest he is talking very good sense. Are you addicted to betting? Then surely, artless and humble though the speaker is, his words burn themselves into your soul? You move uneasily away from him, you hasten out of earshot. Ah, then you *are* touched! No? You are but drawing comparisons between the pleasure to be derived from that preacher and the pleasure you had derived from that sumptuous procession? But, my dear sir, this is too absurd! The preacher doesn't pretend to compete with the procession. 'No doubt,' you retort, 'but I had just been seeing the procession.' I am at a loss for a repartee to that. Nay, inasmuch as when I saw *The Way the Money Goes* I had just been seeing *Chantecler*, I can quite well enter into your feelings. And now, I think, you can quite well enter into mine.

It is all very sad. In all the years that I have been criticising plays,

530

to one main doctrine I have stood true. I have had my caprices, my somersaults, prejudices of which I have purged myself, fidelities that have lapsed. But one thing said by me at the outset has been throughout my writing a refrain so constant that it might, but for the driving power of earnest conviction behind it, sometimes have made you (as it so often has made me) yawn. It is that what our dramatists need is contact with real life; that mere technical talent for the construction of plays, and for the production of 'theatrical effect,' is a thing of little account in comparison with a sense of actual life; that a dramatist who, without technical power, has that sense for life is far more valuable than the technician who hasn't it; that we go to the theatre to be instructed, and to think, not merely to be amused; that we are willing to barter any number of 'effects' for a few facts and ideas. Well, Lady Bell in her play provides these facts and ideas. Her characters (another demand that I have re-peatedly made) are drawn from the classes of the poor; and it is evident that she has studied with great care the life of the poor in the north of England. She has sympathy and insight. All her characters are alive, and not merely so as individuals: in what they say and do, and in what befalls them, they have the value of types. John Holroyd convinces one as a true study of the better sort of north-country working-man, absolutely honest and conscientious, a good father, a decent husband, thrifty, sober, laborious. It is in virtue of his very virtues that he is tragic. With one spark of imagination, he would, leading the miserable life that is his, be miserable. The tragedy, at root, is that he is quite happy, and expects that his wife shall be quite happy too. She, however, is not such an unit of the industrial system as all that. She has fluttering aspirations. Not all the husbands in the street where she exists are quite so good as hers. Some of them are so improvident as to give their wives a treat, now and again, with the money which it is their duty to put by. Comes the day when she has an irresistible impulse to give a treat to herself. She is still young. The sun is shining. A perambulating tally-man has among his wares a looking-glass, bound in red cloth, with ferns pasted on it. Mrs Holroyd looks in it, sees herself, is swept away by thought of the rapture it would be to see herself thus every day. She possesses the sum of one shilling. This is all that the tally-man needs as first instalment. The looking-glass changes hands. But the owner's joy is brief. When John

Holroyd comes home, it is obvious that he would be enraged if he knew what his wife had done. Also, how to pay the eighteen weekly instalments of one shilling? The looking-glass is pawned. Next door to the Holroyds live the Tarltons, a light-hearted pair, who have recently won five pounds on a race. In their parlour Mrs Holroyd meets a bookmaker's tout. (A policeman approaches; whereat the tout hides himself, and everyone is in breathless suspense. 'It's quite a nice change to be frightened like that!' says Mrs Holroyd afterwards.) The Tarltons are going to pawn all their furniture, for sake of the 'favourite' in the Grand Yorkshire. Mrs Holroyd backs their fancy to the extent of the money she got by pawning the looking-glass. But the horse doesn't—what horse ever did?—win. Mrs Holroyd borrows, so as to retrieve; and her finances become more and more involved. She lives in abject dread. One day, when her husband comes home—offering, in a fit of recklessness, to take her out for 'a drive on tramline'—he finds a blue envelope awaiting him. It is a County Court summons for twenty-eight pounds, ten shillings. This, when it is explained, means to him not merely that he has married a wicked woman, but also that he will not be able to take up the better position that had been offered him in the Works. The manager offers to advance him the sum. But Holroyd has never borrowed money before, and refuses to do so now. That is Holroyd all over. He would rather be disappointed in fate than in himself. Finally, he goes through a form of forgiving his wife. 'Finally' so far as the play is concerned. The forgiveness is assuredly the prelude to years of sulking and upbraiding.

There! ought I not to have spent a happy afternoon? Here was just the sort of play that I am always reviling people for not writing, or managers for not producing, or critics for not praising. Here was a sincere presentment of actual life, with plenty of food for reflection—special reflection on the evil of the tally system, the betting system, the money-lending system; general reflection on the wrongness of the whole social system by which such lives as we see here are possible, and on the unlikelihood that we shall ever, with the best intentions, evolve a preferable substitute. And yet, and yet, all the while, I was but longing to be amused, excited, uplifted; longing for the workman's cottage to be suddenly transformed into a palace, with ornamental and delightful people doing the most preposterous 'theatrical' things in it; longing for fantasy and joy; wondering whether, after all, the theatre *is* a place in which . . . ah, I won't set forth in shameless print the doubts which, even in my breast, I tried to stifle.

[*19 February 1910*]

MORE OF THE REPERTORY

Mr Frohman must be felicitated. Not merely has he stepped in (uninvited, and eyed somewhat askance) to do what Englishmen, in national conclave, have for so many years, so solemnly, been urging one another to do: he is doing it very well indeed. And even if, to a patriot's soul, there is anything ugly in the thought that this astute foreigner seems likely to make a 'corner' in all our most vital dramatists, no one will be so sulky as not to thank him, meanwhile, for having evoked to his theatre the great and gracious shade of George Meredith. A 'shade,' in more senses than one. In the theatre, at best, we could never have more than an adumbration of the true full Meredith of the books. Of dialogue he was an incomparable master; but dialogue was only one of the many instruments he wielded. It was but the fitful side-light cast by him on the characters which he created and made known to us mainly through descriptive narration and through discursive soliloquy. *The Senti-mentalists* is an early and unfinished comedy of his; but even had it been written in the fulness of his prime, and finished, it could be no more than a suggestion of his genius, and not even a suggestion to those who are unversed in his work. So deeply personal a genius as Meredith's, and a genius so exuberant that even the large form in which he wrought seemed always in danger of bursting through pressure of what was packed into it, is not, oh decidedly it is not, for the theatre. Just as a suggestion, *The Sentimentalists* is a treasure for us. It is, oddly enough, quite in the latest fashion of drama, being essentially 'a debate.' But it is a lyrical debate, of course. The characters think and talk in a rarefied air, with that strange blend of delicacy and buoyancy which was ever the constitution of the Comic Muse in Meredith. So ethereal are they, we hardly realise that much of their tonic quality is due to their being also very

533

deeply and richly of the earth; and—but I am writing of them not as they truly are on the stage, but as I conceive them in the light of those illustrious characters in the books. The cadence of Meredith's style: this is what we actually do get in *The Sentimentalists* without having to draw on our own knowledge of the books. And it will be strange if that magic of swiftness and lightness and strength, wafted across the footlights of the Duke of York's Theatre, does not cause to read Meredith many people who never have essayed him: me, certainly, it has launched on a fresh bout of him. And this impulse to take down one of the old volumes as soon as I returned from seeing *The Sentimentalists* was all the stronger, perhaps, because in the theatre, though the cadence thrives there, so much of the significance is lost. Lost, at any rate, by me. My mind is of average agility, I think; but it needs be shod with seven-league boots to keep up with Meredith in the theatre—to leap those crags of metaphor and those chasms of ellipse which everywhere dot the landscape. Here a labyrinth, there a labyrinth; and I am expected to dash through them at a sprint! I have often inveighed against the slow utterance of English actors; but at the Duke of York's, the other night, I constantly wished to hold up my hand and say 'A trifle slower, please!' and 'Be so good as to pause till I have got the hang of that . . . Thank you, yes, now you may proceed.' I do not find Meredith hard to follow when I read him; for then it is I who set the pace; and I do not grudge the time that is needed for the full savour of him. I often cry halt for meditation, I often hark back. I have no patience with the people who complain that Meredith is rather a task than a delight. He must be a fearsome task indeed for anyone who wishes to while away an hour in a railway-carriage with him. Such an attempt condemns the maker of it; and the impossibility of reading Meredith casually is not, as the fatuous reader supposes, a fault in Meredith: quite the reverse. And the other night I was ashamed at finding myself in the throes of that fatigue of which these fatuous people have so often complained to me. Yet, of course, I was not to blame. Is *your* mind shod with seven-league boots? And would Meredith himself, if he had neither written this play nor read it, have been able to appreciate it properly at one hearing across footlights? I think not.

Strain though it is on the mind, visually (not less than aurally) it is a delight. The production is a perfect presentment of the typical

Meredithian 'atmosphere.' The spacious lawns and paths of the great house, and the high hedges of clipped box, and the undulating English landscape beyond—all these are the very setting one conceives for Meredithian romance. And Mr William Rothenstein has designed the costumes. When he undertook to do this, he must at first have had great difficulty in not endowing Professor Spiral and Mr Homeware with long beards and with 'praying-cloths.' But he has succeeded in defying the impulse of his later manner in painting, and has reverted to that earlier manner in which the Early-Victorian period was one of his specialities. All the persons of the play stand out as noble and ingenious embodiments of our vague conception of what Meredithian ladies and gentlemen really looked like. And two, at least, of the performers are as true to spirit as to surface. Mr Dennis Eadie, as Homeware, is a precisely realised type of those brilliant and dynamic 'codgers' whom Meredith loved to create. And Miss Fay Davis, as Astraea, is not less perfect a synopsis of the heroines—of the lesser heroines, that is; the roguish and not overwhelming ones.

The rest of the programme consists of two plays by Mr Barrie. He, like Meredith, has created a world of his own, but a world less obviously based in the rich realities of the world we live in. So long as he sets out to please and amuse, not to harrow and instruct, this detachment from realities is rather a quality than a defect. But in the first of these two plays, *Old Friends*, it is as harrowing instructor that he steps forth; and the result is that we find ourselves failing, with the best will in the world, to be harrowed, and yearning, despite our modesty, to instruct Mr Barrie. I take it that the play was written many years ago, when Ibsen on Heredity was a work over whose pages every young dramatist was tremulously poring. Well, Ibsen was a student of things. Mr Barrie is just a delightful goer-off-at-tangents; and, having read *Ghosts*, he lit his pipe, and, in the fumes, wove a little theory of heredity on his own account. Roughly stated, this theory is that the daughter of a drunkard will herself be drunk. As an argument in favour of teetotalism, it has this drawback: it does not hold water. Medical scientists are agreed that the child of a drunkard, though its health is in many ways affected by its father's habit, will not, when it grows up, have any special cravings for alcohol. Of course, a child brought up to share its father's habit would be likely enough to acquire that habit. But Miss Carrie Brand, daughter of the drunkard in Mr Barrie's play, has been admirably brought up. Her father was reclaimed years ago. Else where would be the thrill for us when, at dead of night, he sees her stealing down from her bedroom to the whiskey-decanter? The scene, as it stands, is very unpleasant; but, as it is only an unpleasant invention, it does not actually thrill us. Nor, when the wife of the reclaimed drunkard rounds on him and, with Ibsenesque 'remorselessness,' tells him that what he had supposed to be his conquest of his habit was merely a passive state of distaste produced by exhaustion, are we so impressed as not to wonder why he does not burst out laughing at her ignorance of the most rudimentary facts about alcoholism. If Mr Barrie has up his sleeve any other tragedies about reclaimed drunkards, there let him keep them. About unreclaimed fairies he can tell us so much that is true and valuable.

He is delightful, too, when, instead of pure fantasy, he gives us a pleasant caricature of reality. *The Twelve Pound Look*, the second of his plays at the Duke of York's, is a farce delightfully conceived and wrought, abounding in the quaintness that makes him dear to us.

[*12 March 1910*]

THREE EXOTICS

The Stage Society goes on thriving, in despite of difficulties—difficulties which are in themselves a token of good work achieved. But for the preliminary labours of the Stage Society, whereby was created gradually a public for better plays than were in vogue, the Vedrenne-Barker management could not have come into being; nor would Mr Trench be at the Haymarket; and Mr Frohman at the Duke of York's would be just what Mr Frohman is in a hundred-and-one other places. It is natural that playwrights whose hopes of production were once centred on the Stage Society should now betake themselves to managers who can grant them a gratification more obvious than is to be found in having a play produced just twice and away. But the Stage Society has not lost good reason for existence. There is no lack of plays which, written by foreign authors about foreign life, would have no chance of even a modest 'run' in

London, and yet are interesting and delightful to connoisseurs, and
may well be produced on the twice-and-away system.

Of such are the three short plays which I saw last Monday—*Count
Festenberg, Life's Importance*, and *The Return*, all of them by
Felix Salten, a Viennese writer, of whom I had never, in my most
attentive moments, heard. The usual objection to a triple bill is that
it distracts: so soon as we have been coaxed comfortably into one
mood, the time has come for another; and in the end we go away
bemused. There can be no such objection where the three plays are
by one man, with unity of motive. Herr Salten's manner is not,
certainly, one manner throughout the triad. Though the plays are
light comedies, in the second the comedy is developed into a scene of
horror, and in the third there is an admixture of farce. But in all of
them the main feature is Herr Salten's peculiar sardonic humour—
a very real and abounding humour, though now and again its effects
are laboured with a somewhat Teutonic thoroughness. And, throughout, the basis of the fun is in the differences—some of them fundamental, some of them merely conventional—between the upper and
middle classes of Viennese society. Herr Salten holds no brief for
either class. He is equally happy in making either class ridiculous in
contact and in contrast with the other. In the first of his plays, it is
the Nobility that he covers with confusion; in the second, the Bourgeoisie; in the third, both alike. He is lucky in being Austrian—in
being born where class-barriers do solidly exist, and where the class
on either side of them is quite unlike the class on the other. If he
were English, he would find it very up-hill and thankless work to
get any comedy out of the motive of class. For here, where nowadays
the classes merge insidiously into one another, the writer who would
make fun of their differences is bound to exaggerate—harking back
fifty years or so for his types. Nor is he merely reproved by us for
being old-fashioned: we call him a snob. Where nobody is sure that
he isn't a little higher or lower in the social scale than he seems to
be, where everybody at heart is in hope of rising and in fear of
sinking, it is deemed brutal, and in bad taste, to talk openly about
distinctions of class. Oh, hush! It is all very well to be frank in
Vienna; for there you are placed definitely, and for ever, beyond
reach of hope or fear, according to lineage or lack of it; and
according to your place your very soul, to say nothing of your
surface, is of an especial and particular kind. It is all very well to

be frank in New York, where you are placed, not less definitely because temporarily, according to your wealth or lack of it, and where there is no apparent difference either of soul or surface between the elect and the mob. But here in England, where neither money nor birth can place you absolutely, and where poverty and humble origin are but a drag, and where there *are* certain differences of soul and aspect to be discerned at this and that indeterminate point of the social scale—oh, where all the ground is so delicate, and the light so dim, take care! beware! tread gingerly!

The first of Herr Salten's exercises in that frankness which we watch with timid envy from afar has for its hero a waiter who has been passing himself off as a count and has married into an aristocratic family. He is no mere vulgar adventurer. He had always been sure that there must be noble blood in his veins, and, though he was not ashamed of being a waiter in a New York restaurant, and was indeed a very good waiter, he felt that the life he was leading was unworthy of him. So he appropriated the title of a certain Count Max Festenberg, who, having been expelled from the Austrian Army, had died obscurely in New York. With the help of this title, and of the money he had made, he won the hand of the beautiful daughter of Count Ludwig Laurentin, from whom he refused to accept any money, proudly preferring to support his wife by the exertions of his own very great ability. He was a devoted and altogether admirable husband. But, not long after the curtain rises, his secret is laid bare by a cousin of his wife, who had been an unsuccessful suitor for her hand. His wife and his father-in-law cannot deny the cogency of his explanations; they acknowledge that he is in himself just as fine a fellow as ever he had seemed to them. His wife's love for him, and his father-in-law's liking for him, are unshaken. But really—no, not even if the scandal be hushed up— they cannot have anything more to do with him: he is not one of *them*. He then tells them that there is nothing to prevent him from getting himself adopted by an elderly member of the Festenberg family who owes him some money. The father-in-law wavers; so does the wife. But at this moment the cousin returns with a policeman, and the hero is taken off in custody. 'You cur!' hisses the Countess to the cousin; and the curtain falls. This conclusion is quite irrelevant. Herr Salten has no business to make us feel sorry for the adventurer, or angry with the cousin. The play, being a light satire, ought to have ended in the family's consent to take the adventurer back to its bosom so soon as he had got himself made a Festenberg.

Life's Importance is a contrast between a young nobleman, named Hugo, who has never done anything, and has no wish to do anything, and Doctor Konrad Hopfner, his brother-in-law, a self-made man. Hopfner, though immensely proud of the 'grit' by which he has worked his way up, nurses a constant envy of people who haven't needed to work their way up. He secretly hates Hugo, who is secretly amused by him and his self-esteem. Hugo has not been feeling very well, and asks his brother-in-law to make a medical examination of him. The result is that Hopfner tells him abruptly that he has not more than six months to live. Hugo collapses, Hopfner preaches unctuously about courage and self-control. Hopfner, it seems, could look death in the face, as he always has looked life in the face, without flinching. Hugo, knowing well that the doctor has thoroughly enjoyed the whole scene, gives him a chance of displaying his fortitude. He 'covers' the doctor with a pistol, tells him that in exactly fifteen minutes he will be shot dead, and asks to be taught how a man should die. At first the doctor laughs, but presently he becomes dismayed, and then abject and piteous. Hugo is obdurate, and, as the clock begins to strike the hour of doom, he pulls the trigger. The doctor falls over in a dead faint, Hugo, throwing away the unloaded pistol, goes out into the garden, very much amused. His brother-in-law, when he 'comes to,' will preach no more sermons. The long-drawn scene of suspense was admirably played by Mr Charles Quartermaine, as Hugo, and by Mr Clifton Alderson, who, as the doctor, worked up to such a climax of suppressed hysteria as I have not seen on the stage since the death of Charles Warner.

The Return presents the farcical tragedy of a man who finds that what he supposed to be his death-bed is but an ordinary sick-bed. Having been assured by the doctors that his last hour was at hand, Konstantin Trubner sent for the shop-girl who had borne him a child ten years ago; and was married to her. He presently became convalescent. We see him now embarrassed, but not altogether displeased, by the fact that he is now a family man. But his wife and child are altogether displeased by the situation. The child is devoted to the piano-tuner with whom her mother has for many years been living. The mother is devoted to him, too. He is devoted to them both. But he is, in his way, a precisian, and he refuses to consort with another man's wife. He is furious at the survival of Trubner. In the end, poor, harassed Trubner decides that the one comfortable thing for him to do is to become as one dead—to let the greater part of his money be distributed according to the will he had made, and to take up his residence in some other city than Vienna. The idea of the play is worked out with a great deal of humour; and all the characters, especially the piano-tuner, have a solid actuality in the midst of the absurdities.

[*26 March 1910*]

INDEX